TEACH

Is teaching for me? Who will I teach? How can I make a difference?

Teach is a vibrant and engaging **Introduction to Education** textbook, organized around **real questions** students ask themselves and their professors as they consider a career in teaching. Using **vivid and contemporary examples**, veteran teacher educator James W. Fraser continually encourages readers to reflect on their experiences and engage in a dialogue about the most **current issues** in education. The thoroughly updated second edition includes fully rewritten chapters, including one discussing the **Common Core State Standards** and another on **today's newest technologies**. Newly selected **primary source readings** integrate the intellectual foundations of education throughout each chapter, offering scholarly and current content in a student-friendly format.

Features and updates include:

- **Up-to-date coverage of new legislation and standards** that influence curricula, with particular emphasis on the debates surrounding and **impact of the Common Core State Standards**.
- A completely rewritten Chapter 8 offers an up-to-the-minute overview of how **technology** can help improve teaching.
- Features such as **"What About Me?"** and **"Teachable Moment"** encourage readers—through a variety of prompts and exercises—to reflect on their own educational experiences and goals, and challenge prospective teachers to imagine themselves in similar situations.
- Rather than relying on additional readers, each chapter of *Teach* is complemented by a selection of **primary readings** exposing students first-hand to writers such as **Howard Gardner, Sonia Nieto, bell hooks,** and **John Dewey,** as well as to point and counterpoint debates on controversial topics.
- **"Notes from the Field"** features **offer insights and advice from real, practicing teachers** in order to provide readers an authentic sense of both the challenges and possibilities of the field.
- Short chapters and digestible sections provide an approach and format to reach students without compromising on high-quality content.
- The concluding chapter explores the question, "Where do I go from here?" to help prospective teachers **develop a plan for their career and design a personal philosophy to guide them**.
- A **comprehensive companion website** includes additional interactive features, prompts for writing and reflection exercises, video suggestions, and more.

Teach presents an overview of the field in a way sure to keep students reading and gives those with questions about teaching the tools and information they need to continue a rich dialogue about their possible career.

James W. Fraser is Professor of History and Education at the Steinhardt School of Culture, Education, and Human Development at New York University.

Welcome!

Welcome to the companion website for the second edition of *Teach: A Question of Teaching*, by veteran teacher educator James W. Fraser. *Teach* is a vibrant and engaging Introduction to Education textbook, organized around real questions students ask themselves and their professors as they consider a career in teaching. It employs vivid and contemporary examples to encourage reflection and dialogue, includes insight and advice from real, practicing teachers, and offers guidance to prospective teachers on designing a career plan and professional philosophy. It also includes primary source readings and foundational texts. This companion website is designed to supplement the wealth of information found in the book with even more materials for both students and instructors.

On this website, you will find the following resources:

Student Materials:
-primary source reading questions
-"portrait of an educator", a feature introducing important members of the field
-videos

Instructor Materials:
-instructor manuals for each chapter
-test banks
-suggested assignments and essay prompts

Other Materials:
-glossary
-detailed table of contents
-additional links

🛒	Paperback
🛒	Hardback
🛒	eBook
📋	Complimentary Exam Copy

Be sure to visit the companion website for the second edition of *Teach: A Question of Teaching* at www.routledge.com/cw/fraser. There you will find a wealth of resources designed to supplement the new edition, including additional information on important figures in the field, links to useful videos, and suggested essay assignments and test questions. Addressing each and every chapter, the corresponding materials are extremely useful for both instructors and students.

The website materials include each of the following:

Student Materials

- primary source reading questions
- "portrait of an educator," a feature introducing important members of the field
- videos

Instructor Materials

- instructor manuals for each chapter
- test banks
- suggested assignments and essay prompts

Other Materials

- glossary
- detailed table of contents
- additional links

TEACH

A QUESTION OF TEACHING

SECOND EDITION

JAMES W. FRASER

Routledge
Taylor & Francis Group

NEW YORK AND LONDON

Second edition published 2016
by Routledge
711 Third Avenue, New York, NY 10017

and by Routledge
2 Park Square, Milton Park, Abingdon, Oxon, OX14 4RN

Routledge is an imprint of the Taylor & Francis Group, an informa business

First edition published by McGraw-Hill 2010

Library of Congress Cataloging-in-Publication Data
Fraser, James W., 1944–
    Teach : a question of teaching / by James W. Fraser.—2nd edition.
        pages cm
    "First edition published by McGraw-Hill 2010"—T.p. verso.
Includes bibliographical references and index.
    1. Education—Study and teaching.   I. Title.
    LB1707.F737 2015
    370.71—dc23
    2015003036

ISBN: 978-1-138-88707-7 (hbk)
ISBN: 978-1-138-88829-6 (pbk)

Typeset in Berkeley
by Apex CoVantage, LLC

Contents

Acknowledgements

Writing a book can be a very solitary exercise. At the same time, developing the ideas that go into a book and then publishing it involves many people with many different types of expertise. In the production of *Teach: A Question of Teaching* a great many people have played their part.

I owe a special debt to my extraordinary editor at Routledge, Catherine Bernard, who has taken the lead in making this second edition of *Teach* a reality on an impossibly tight schedule and with a very special level of care and attention. I am most grateful to Catherine for her friendship and her commitment to this project.

Vicki Malinee of Van Brien & Associates served as the developmental editor for this second edition as she did for the first. Vicki has reviewed every page of this book, argued with me about many of them, and in the end has made it a much better and clearer product.

Trevor Gori, Dan Schwartz, and Marlena Sullivan, editorial assistants at Routledge, have done incredible research on short notice and have worked hard—and fast—to move this from a manuscript to a finished product. At NYU, Noah Kippley-Ogman, a graduate student in the History of Education, took on a major role in revising Chapter 8 on technology.

I also owe a huge debt of gratitude to my colleagues at New York University especially Beth McDonald who co-directs the Inquiries Into Teaching and Learning course with me. Inquiries is NYU's version of the Introduction to Education and leading it with Beth for the last seven years has given me a chance to learn so much from her, from the many instructors— NYU faculty and New York City Public School teachers—who lead sections of the course, and from the hundreds of students who have taught us as well as learned with us.

My wife Katherine Hanson and our dog Pebble have been most patient as the many revisions of this second edition took shape. Our hope is that it is a contribution to some of the teachers with whom our six grandchildren learn every day.

Jim Fraser
January, 2015

Permissions

Letter to the Reader

Dear Prospective Teacher,

The fact that you are holding this book and reading this letter probably means you are a student in an Introduction to Education or Foundations of Education class. And so I am taking the liberty of calling you a prospective teacher whether or not you are quite ready to consider yourself one. Some students take their first education course because they are 100% sure they want to be teachers, others take the class because they want to explore teaching as a possible career option and have lots of questions, and yet others take it because they are simply interested in the topic but really do not plan to teach. In any case, I am delighted that you want to learn more.

You've probably noticed there are a lot of questions in this book. There's a good reason for this. The purpose of this text is not simply to spew forth what professors or publishers think you need to know but rather to address the real questions first-year education students—like you—are asking:

"How will I control my class?"
"Are schools sometimes unfair to students?"
"How can I be sure that I'm reaching all my students?"
"Why do some people stay and some people leave teaching?"

As we tackle these important questions, we hope you will engage in a three-way dialogue involving (1) your own educational autobiography (looking at what you have learned—and where and how you may have learned it—during your years as a student), (2) what can be learned by carefully observing schools and the lives of students and teachers in these schools, and (3) the most current research literature about how students learn, how schools succeed and fail, and the changing demographic and political realities that form the background for education in the United States today.

Teach will offer a lot of material for this dialogue. There are articles from many different perspectives that include some of the most recent research about teaching and learning, and how schools work in modern society. I have done my best to organize this material in response to questions—specific questions that I have been asked over the years in my own teaching of an Introduction to Education course and my work with aspiring teachers. I have also tried hard to present both sides of many of today's debates. For example, there is material that supports and material that critiques the Common Core State Standards, multicultural education, or tracking and ability grouping of students. Your job is to read this material and these debates and enter in to the dialogue as best you can. You will also find that you do this best if you take time to reflect on your own education—which teachers were more effective in your life and which were not—but also to look at schools as they actually operate today in the community where you are studying. If you combine your own observations and a thoughtful look at the research you will have the best chance of coming to careful and thoughtful responses to the many questions presented in this book and in the life of a teacher.

The teaching profession has changed dramatically during the past generation, and it's crystal clear that today's teacher needs to be *more informed* about effective instructional practices and educational expectations, *more prepared* to manage and motivate a diverse group of students, and *more active* in developing professional opportunities that benefit everyone involved in the education process.

So come join the dialogue!

Jim Fraser

Teaching
Is It for Me?

1

> Those who can, teach and they do it every day. I am lucky enough to be one of those who "can."

MELINDA PELLERIN-DUCK

QUESTIONS TO COME

"Why do I want to do this?" Almost everyone who begins any professional program—certainly a program leading to a career in teaching—asks that basic question. "Why would I consider teaching?" is a critical first question in the list of questions and issues we explore in this book.

Although anyone who enters teaching does so for his or her own personal reasons, there are key similarities among people in any particular profession. It is important to understand why other people like teaching—or don't. This chapter is designed to help you hear the voices of current teachers and teachers from generations past as they talk about why they became teachers, what they liked about the work once in it, and why they stayed in the profession (if they did indeed stay). In the process, you will think about how to answer the same question for yourself: *Why do I want to be a teacher?*

For insights into why others have chosen to teach—and have stayed with it—the **Readings** section of this chapter offers a starting point. Ranging from the reflections of successful teachers like William Ayers and Melinda Pellerin-Duck to the latest research on why people stay in teaching or leave it, the **Readings** will show you real teachers' motivations, joys, satisfactions, and also frustrations. Hopefully, they will prod you to ask yourself new questions as you consider this career that can change so many lives.

Why Do People Become Teachers Today?

By signing up for this class, you've already determined that a career in teaching is something that sparks your interest. Why is that? What is it about teaching—or at least about what you think you know about teaching—that sounds appealing? Is it the opportunity to open young minds or "mold young minds," as one of the **Readings** says? Is it the comfort of being part of a professional community more than 5 million active members strong? Is it an avenue for you to share your passion for (you fill in the blank) with the rest of the world?

In 2006, the National Education Association (NEA) asked current public school teachers to identify the main reasons they had originally decided to become teachers (each person could list up to three reasons). Several clear themes emerged, including:

- a desire to work with young people, 71%
- the value or significance of education in society, 42%
- Interest in subject-matter field, 39%
- Influence of a teacher in elementary or secondary school, 31%[1]

 DID YOU KNOW?

There are 3 million public school teachers in the United States. Approximately 1 out of every 60 people in the United States is a teacher.

These reasons have changed over the last 40 years, but not very much. In every survey since the first conducted in 1971, about 70% of teachers have ranked "a desire to work with young people" as a primary reason for deciding to teach. Similarly, between 34% and 42% of teachers have listed the value or significance of a teacher's work in society as a reason they became a teacher, and similar numbers have listed interest in their subject-matter field. Interestingly, the greatest change has been in the impact of a former teacher, which has grown from only 18% in 1971 to 31% in 2006.

Table 1.1 Reasons Why People Become Teachers

	1976	1986	1996	2006
Desire to work with young people	71%	66%	68%	71%
Value or significance of education in society	34%	37%	42%	42%
Interest in subject-matter field	38%	37%	37%	39%
Influence of teacher in elementary or secondary school	21%	25%	31%	31%
Never really considered anything else	17%	21%	19%	14%
Influence of family	18%	23%	19%	19%
Long summer vacation	19%	21%	20%	19%
Job security	17%	19%	18%	17%
Opportunity for a lifetime of self-growth	17%	10%	11%	8%

Source: "Status of the American Public School Teacher 2005–2006," National Education Association.

It is also interesting to note the other reasons listed. Over the years, approximately one-fifth of all teachers have said that they never really considered any career except teaching although that number has dropped to 14% and a somewhat similar number list the influence of their family. Only slightly smaller numbers list a long summer vacation and job security in their responses. Clearly, people decide to become teachers for many reasons.

The Joys of Working with Young People

When teachers talk about their desire to work with children or adolescents, they usually are talking about much more than simply "feeling good" at the end of the day. Most people who become teachers have a deep commitment to young people and their future and find acting on that commitment rewarding. Ayla Gavins, who has taught for a dozen years in several different small elementary schools in the Boston area, says she teaches in part because "I love to laugh." Teaching allows her to interact with kids who are "naturally humorous in the ways they discover and make sense of the world." But she also teaches because "Every day that I teach, I learn something new about myself. I am slightly changed every time I get to know a student. As a teacher I exude my values and what is important to me."[2]

What About Me?

Why Do *I* Want to Teach?

Matters to Me	Reason for Teaching	Really Doesn't Matter to Me
_____	Teaching and supporting our young people is the best way I can contribute to society.	_____
_____	Working with young people will keep *me* young.	_____
_____	The skills and experience will easily transfer to other professions.	_____
_____	I had a great teacher that I want to emulate.	_____
_____	My family thinks this is a good fit for me.	_____
_____	I love learning, and a teaching environment will give me learning opportunities.	_____
_____	There will always be a need for teachers, so there's job security.	_____
_____	I'd like to move eventually into an administrative position in education, such as a principal or superintendent.	_____
_____	I want to have my summers available for other interests.	_____
_____	I like to be in charge of a group.	_____
_____	I'm really excited about a specific subject area and want to share that with others.	_____
_____	I've just always wanted to be a teacher.	_____
_____	Teaching gives me the flexibility to live anywhere I want to.	_____
_____	I want to make a difference in someone's life.	_____
_____	Other:	
_____	Other:	
_____	Other:	

Now go back and rank the reasons that do matter to you. What are your top three reasons for considering a career in teaching?

Notes from the Field

What are the benefits of teaching?

"I can't think of a more rewarding profession. Working with children can be quite challenging, but watching them learn and interact with others is awesome."

—Kathy Cushman, fourth-grade teacher

William Ayers, who has taught in the Chicago area for many years, reflects a similar understanding of teaching when he writes in the first **Reading** of this chapter from his book *To Teach: The Journey of a Teacher:*

People are called to teaching because they love children and youth, or because they love being with them, watching them open up and grow and become more able, more competent, more powerful in the world. They may love what happens to themselves when they are with children, the ways in which they become better, more human, more generous.[3]

Anyone who has spent time teaching or just being with children has experienced a few—if not many—of those magic moments.

Parker Palmer, another longtime teacher, describes the satisfaction that leads many to teaching and keeps them there throughout their careers. In his best-selling book *The Courage to Teach*, he helps us understand what many teachers may have had in mind when they reported in their NEA interviews being motivated by the satisfaction that comes from a career focused on young people and their education. He writes: "I am a teacher at heart, and there are moments in the classroom when I can hardly hold the joy. When my students and I discover uncharted territory to explore, when the pathway out of a thicket opens up before us, when our experience is illuminated by the lighting-life of the mind—then teaching is the finest work I know."[4]

For most of us who teach, this discovery of uncharted territory alongside our students is also one of the great joys that keeps bringing us back again and again over the course of a long career. The moment when student and teacher connect—the moment when, often after considerable struggle, a student "gets it," whether the "it" is how to read a difficult word, understand an abstract concept in mathematics, or make the sometimes dry words of educational theory come alive—is truly one of life's most satisfying. However, Palmer is honest enough to admit that not all moments are like that. There are times when "the classroom is so lifeless or painful or confused—and I am so powerless to do anything about it—that my claim to be a teacher seems a transparent sham." Every honest teacher can describe such moments. But for most of us, on balance, the moments of engagement far outweigh the moments of pain, and the satisfaction is substantial.

The Value of Teaching for Society

I teach in the hope of making the world a better place.

—William Ayers[5]

In interview after interview, many teachers indicate that while they clearly enjoy teaching, they have reasons for being a teacher that go beyond personal satisfaction. Jennifer Welborn, a middle-school science teacher, says: "I teach because it gives me a purpose. Teaching gives me a really good reason to get up and try my best every day. I may be naïve, but I believe that what I do day in and day out does make a difference. Teachers do change lives forever."[6]

Teacher Melinda Pellerin-Duck, whose essay is included in the **Readings**, says: "I teach because I see extraordinary possibilities in my students. . . . As a teacher, I have the most fortunate experience of nurturing our future." Many teachers share that idealism, and it certainly is one important part of the satisfaction of teaching. Talk with fellow students entering teacher education programs in colleges and universities across the country and you will find many young people—and more than a few middle-age career changers—who are entering teaching because they want to "nurture our future" and hope to make the world a better place. They see teaching, much more than some other, more lucrative professions, as a way to do this. At almost any school in the United States, you will find teachers who reflect all the joys that Welborn, Gavins, and Ayers describe, who love watching young lives develop, who like what happens to themselves personally as they interact with the fast-changing people called *students,* and who see these interactions as a way to make the world a better place in which to live.

Herbert Kohl, who has taught children for over forty years, talks about the significance of education to society in his book, *The Discipline of Hope: Learning from a Lifetime of Teaching*, writing, "These are not easy times in which to keep hope alive in poor or even middle-class communities." But Kohl continues, "And yet I have hope" based on the many examples of teachers, parents, and others working together to create educational environments that reflect their aspirations for what children can and should be able to do.[7] Schools of this sort are built by the teachers who enter—and stay in— teaching because they believe that their work has significant value in society as well as in the lives of individual children.

Another longtime teacher and educational researcher, Jean Anyon, argued that if one truly cares about building a better society, teaching is an excellent place to start. She asked, "Why should we put education—and concerned educators—at the center of efforts to build a unified movement for **social justice**?" Her answer to this question rests on her compelling sense that schools are places where many of the most pressing issues of society—and the people who care about them—come together. She also notes that putting education at the center of efforts for social change makes good sense because so many teachers already care about building a better society. "I, like many others, entered teaching 'to change the world.'" There are teachers in every city today who teach a critical, thought-provoking **curriculum**, and who utilize the classroom to discuss issues their students face. And these teachers have access to other teachers, to parents, and to community leaders. Teachers, Anyon believed, can indeed succeed in doing work of significance to society.[8]

> **social justice education**
> Education programs and models focused on the development of a more fair and equitable society for all citizens, with freedom, more equal income distribution, and equal opportunity.
>
> **curriculum**
> The lessons, skills, and evaluations which fulfill the objectives of a particular subject.

Interest in Subject-Matter Field

It should not be surprising that while about one-third of all teachers listed their interest in their academic subject as a reason to teach, there is a major difference between high school teachers and elementary teachers. In the NEA survey cited earlier, 62% of high school teachers said that their interest in subject matter was a prime reason to enter teaching, while only 22% of elementary teachers gave this reason. Middle school teachers were—perhaps as expected—in the middle, with 48% saying they became teachers because of their interest in a specific academic subject. Given the structure of schooling, these differences make perfect sense. High school teachers, and to some extent middle school teachers, usually teach only one or two subjects. On one hand, a high school teacher may teach chemistry and physics, or social studies, history, or English literature. But it would be highly unlikely for any high school teacher to teach all of these subjects. Elementary teachers, on the other hand, nearly always teach all of these and other subjects to the same group of students, even if they occasionally have experts in the arts or mathematics join them for an hour or two a week. For a person who loves a specific field of academic study, secondary school teaching—middle or high school—is one of the best places to indulge that passion—be it for history, mathematics, biology, or the Spanish or French language—and share it with a large audience.

Teacher Jennifer Welborn says:

> I like teaching science. It's hands-on and interesting for many kids. But I want my students to do more than just have fun in science. I want them to come away with some big ideas they can apply later on in real-life situations. I feel it's important for kids to know that science is one way of knowing—a way of gaining knowledge about the material world.[9]

Other teachers like teaching English, social studies, or elementary-level reading. But all good teachers like teaching their subjects and feel that it is important for their students to know what they have to offer. Without a passion for their subjects, teachers would quickly find their profession drudgery.

Educational researcher and longtime teacher Rob Fried describes many different ways teachers can be passionate about their work. One of these ways is having a passion for their subject matter:

> You can be passionate about your field of knowledge: in love with the poetry of Emily Dickinson or the prose of Marcus Garvey; dazzled by the spiral of DNA or the swirl of van Gogh's cypresses; intrigued by the origins of the

Milky Way or the demise of the Soviet empire; delighted by the sound of Mozart or the sonority of French vowels; a manic for health and fitness or wild about algebraic word problems.[10]

A passion for knowledge and for sharing that knowledge with young people has taken many teachers far in their work.

Other Influences

Some people discover an interest in teaching in the middle of their active careers, others in the middle of college, and others almost from birth. Some people are inspired to teach by a teacher they have had, are encouraged by a family member, or simply feel "I've always wanted to be a teacher." In her **Reading** essay, Melinda Pellerin-Duck says, "I could not see myself doing anything else but teaching; it is my vocation. It is part of my life, my soul, and my heart." She also sees herself as coming from a long line of teachers, even if many of them were not formal, paid teachers:

I am descended from a slave who withstood tremendous odds, lived and raised her family, and gave her family heirlooms not of material wealth but of the wealth of words, stories, prayers, and love. This woman, my great-great-grandmother, who had no formal education, was my first teacher, one who helped me understand the power of love, sacrifice, and vocation that teaching truly is.

Other teachers might not use quite the same language, but Judy Logan, in *Teaching Stories*, describes herself as a born teacher. She writes:

Since second grade, when I fell in love with the kindness of my instructor, Miss Miles, I had wanted to be a teacher. In the 1950s, this was the best career I could imagine for myself. Teaching was a traditional woman's profession at that time, but in my family it was still traditional for a woman to be a homemaker.

Notes from the Field

Why did you want to be a teacher?

"I have never had a moment when I wanted to become a teacher; I have simply always been one. Even as a child I helped friends with school work or shared my notes from class. In fact, it is a family joke that I give more information than anyone wants to hear, correct more children than my own, and encourage strangers as though they were cherished friends. Teaching is a natural bent of my personality and pursuing a career in education was only a selfish indulgence."

—Laura Morris, middle school math teacher

Many of us can remember a teacher or two who first inspired us to want to do the same work ourselves. Many can also remember a family member who encouraged us to consider teaching, as well as relatives who thought we were crazy to even think about teaching. But for Logan, and for many of us, it was also an early opportunity to actually teach—in a community group, a tutoring program for younger people, or another informal setting—that made us think teaching was what we were meant to do. The experience of student teaching confirmed what Logan had felt since second grade. As a graduate student, she was assigned a student-teaching placement: "While I always knew I wanted to be a teacher, it wasn't until I taught that I realized how right this was for me. I can't explain this. I was a potter who had discovered clay, a swimmer in water, a gardener with her hands in the dirt." With her initial interest confirmed in this way, Logan began what turned out to be a 24-year tenure as a high school teacher in San Francisco. She is far from alone in telling this sort of story.[11]

Jennifer Welborn, however, like many other teachers, tried several careers before settling on teaching. Some, like Welborn, tried hard not to be teachers. She writes, "I've taken many a twist and turn in my career path to becoming a middle school science teacher, including two stints in private schools and a job with a college textbook publisher." She even cried when a career counselor told her she should be a teacher. But in the end, having tried other lines of work, Welborn came back to teaching with a clear conviction that it was right for her. She says, "At this point in my life, I cannot think of anything I would rather do. Teaching is a compelling profession. I've come back to classroom teaching three times in my life. I'm here now for the long haul."[12]

Why Do Some People Leave Teaching?

Teaching is not for everyone. While thousands of teachers would agree with Ayers, Pellerin-Duck, and the other teachers mentioned, there are others who would not. Sometimes the issue is a matter of individual preference—teaching is simply not as satisfying to some people as it is to others. Certainly not everyone has Judy Logan's experience of immediately feeling at home in the classroom; for some of us it takes a year or two, or even longer, to feel at home as a teacher. Some people plan to teach for a year or two and then move on to something else. However, the current reality is that too many people leave teaching, especially in the early years of their careers, and many of those who leave had planned to stay. Between 40% and 50% of all new teachers leave within the first five years. This is a serious problem not only for our society, which needs more qualified teachers, but also for those individuals who may have spent several years in college or graduate school preparing to teach. That is why it is important to ask early in a teacher preparation program, "Is this for me?" and "What kind of school will be most supportive of my work?"

Perhaps the most thorough research on teacher attrition (as the teacher drop-out rate is called) has been done by Richard M. Ingersoll. In the article that is included in the **Readings** at the end of this chapter, Ingersoll and his coauthor, Thomas M. Smith, summarize their surveys of those who leave teaching.[13] They report four primary reasons why new teachers leave the profession:

- personal reasons, such as health or family matters
- school staffing actions, including the elimination of a position or firing
- other job opportunities
- dissatisfaction (a general term that encompasses a multitude of things but that accounted for almost one-third of all those who left teaching)

While it is clear from this research that some people leave teaching for reasons that are hard to change, such as deciding to stay at home with their own young children or aging parents, other reasons such as frustrations about the structure of schools or the way people feel they are being treated as a teacher impact some and could well be remedied by changes in school policies.

In the Ingersoll and Smith study, those who said they left teaching because of dissatisfaction were asked to list up to three reasons for their decision. More than three-quarters said they were unhappy with the poor salaries they were receiving. Slightly over one-third listed problems with student discipline, while over one-quarter mentioned a lack of support from the school's administration, such as having a principal who was too rigid or critical or a principal who could never be found when help was needed. (People could give multiple answers, so the percentages sum to far more than 100%.) Concerns about student motivation were listed by 17% of the dissatisfied. Other issues, such as class size or the lack of opportunity for advancement or time for preparation, received very low numbers. We will explore some of these issues in more detail here.

> **CONNECTIONS** ➜←
>
> In Chapter 7, we'll discuss why establishing clear expectations for students is critical to maintaining discipline.

Salaries

Am I going to be happy with a teacher's salary? While teachers' salaries have risen dramatically over the last decades and the benefits, including health insurance and **pensions**, are better than for most other kinds of work, teachers are not

> **pension**
> Regular income provided to retired employees by a previous employer or a government or private pension system.

likely to ever make as much money as lawyers, doctors, or people in the business world. There is, of course, extraordinary satisfaction to be found in teaching that many of us believe is "priceless" and cannot be found anywhere else. That satisfaction is a major reason why every year many individuals leave higher-paying but less meaningful jobs to enter teaching. It's important to be realistic as you think about the sources of satisfaction—both financial and nonfinancial—that matter to you.

 DID YOU KNOW?

The average teacher's salary in the United States for 2012–2013 was $56,103. Average salaries by state ranged from $75,279 in New York and $72,334 in Massachusetts at the high end to South Dakota ($30,018), Mississippi ($41,814), and Oklahoma ($41,814) at the low end.

CONNECTIONS →←

In Chapter 9, we'll see how teachers' salaries compare across states and to other major professions.

Support

Am I going to be able to find the kind of support that will help me stay in teaching and be successful at it? This question is harder for you to answer at this point, but it is worth thinking about now. Traditionally, teacher induction—that first year on the job after all the courses and supervised student teaching are over—has been "sink or swim." For many, the first year is when you show up at the school you have been assigned to, get the keys to your classroom, and then are on your own. Teaching has not had the equivalent of a doctor's years of hospital residency or a lawyer's work as a highly supervised junior partner.

But that is changing. More and more school districts are creating mentoring programs, in which a new teacher is paired with a senior teacher who can spend time in the classroom, advise how to handle a difficult lesson or a difficult student, and counsel how to succeed in the work. Many schools also offer induction programs in which new teachers can support each other, learn from experts, and discuss their initial difficulties. Ellen Moir, executive director of the New Teacher Center at the University of California at Santa Cruz, describes five essential stages of a comprehensive system of professional development:

1. *recruitment*—when someone first considers becoming a teacher
2. *pre-service preparation*—when someone participates in an undergraduate, graduate, or alternative program to receive an initial license to teach
3. *induction*—being hired and getting through the critical first year
4. *professional development*—continued mentoring and support
5. *instructional leadership*—as one grows in skill and confidence to be a leader among peers

Right now, you are most likely at the second stage in this list. At every level, it is important that teachers receive support from thoughtful mentors so that they will neither leave teaching nor stagnate in one position.[14] When looking at a first job, asking some hard questions of the school and district is absolutely critical. Remember, in any job interview, you are not only selling yourself to the school or district, the school or district is selling itself to you and mentoring is part of what the best districts have to offer. You want to find the position that will support you and encourage you to succeed and continue to grow so that you can take charge of your professional life.

There are no easy answers to the questions regarding salary and support. Educator Barbara McEwan reflects on what happens to teachers when they run into serious difficulty for the first time: "Some throw in the towel at this point and leave the profession. . . . Some do the minimum amount of work necessary to get by. . . . Others roll up their sleeves, work hard, continually find new challenges, and love what they do almost every minute of their professional lives."[15] No

Teachable Moment
REQUIRED READING

A valuable resource for any aspiring or new teacher is Jonathan Kozol's *Letters to a Young Teacher*. Addressing Francesca, who represents several novice teachers whose rooms Kozol has visited and with whom he has talked, this longtime veteran critic of the public schools offers wise, warm, and thoughtful advice on everything from coping with young students who have "decided in advance that we are someone they won't like and who probably should not be trusted" to wondering "whether anyone I know who's setting education policy these days ever speaks about the sense of fun the children have, or ought to have, in public school or the excitement that they take when they examine interesting creatures such as beetle-bugs and ladybugs and other oddities of nature that they come upon—or even merely whether they are happy children and enjoy the hours that they spend with us in school." In the end Kozol concludes his advice by saying:

> Resist the deadwood of predictability. Embrace the unexpected. Revel in the run-on sentences. Celebrate silliness. Dig deep into the world of whim. Sprinkle your children's lives, no matter how difficult many of those lives may be, with hundreds of brightly colored seeds of jubilation. Enjoy the wild flowers!

These are words of wisdom and encouragement that every first-year teacher, as well as every 20- or 40-year veteran, needs to hear.

Questions

- Why does a teacher need to be prepared for students who have "decided in advance that we are someone they won't like and who probably should not be trusted"? What is a teacher's responsibility in this situation?
- Kozol tells us to "celebrate silliness." Do you agree with this advice?

Source: Jonathan Kozol. *Letters to a Young Teacher*. New York: Three Rivers Press, 2008.

one wants to prepare for a career and then, early on, simply "throw in the towel." Even worse, no one wants to "do the minimum amount of work" and wait to retire. Yet it takes hard work and careful planning to make teaching a career in which it is possible to "love every minute"—or at least most minutes. For most teachers, the hard work is well worth it.

Historically Speaking: What Has Motivated People to Teach at Different Times in the Past?

Unfortunately, there was no NEA survey or other similar study of the reasons people entered or left teaching in the 18th, 19th, or early 20th centuries. Many people undoubtedly became teachers for many different reasons at different times in the past. While we will never know all their stories, we are fortunate that the stories of many teachers have been recorded. From these stories, we can learn a great deal about why teachers taught earlier in times.

The Nation's First Teachers

Two hundred fifty years ago, before the United States became a nation, teaching was often something young women did at home and young men did between the end of college and the beginning of what they saw as their real career, often as a lawyer or minister. Few paid teachers in the colonial era stayed in the profession for more than one or two years before moving on. Teaching allowed young men who had recently graduated from college to earn the money needed to continue their education or to keep themselves gainfully employed while waiting for better opportunities. As many as 40% of the graduates of Harvard College in the 140 years between its founding in 1636 and the American Revolution in 1776 taught at some point in their lives. None of them had any formal preparation for teaching. It was assumed that because they had been students themselves, they could figure out what needed to be done as a schoolteacher. For example, John Adams, who would go on to a career as a lawyer, revolutionary politician, and second president of the United States, spent three years teaching school in Worcester, Massachusetts, following his graduation from Harvard College. In March 1756, Adams wrote in his diary: "Is it not then the highest Pleasure my Friend to preside in this little World." For all the pleasure he received from teaching, however, Adams moved on quickly. He had brought to teaching neither the preparation nor the commitment that an expanded school system would need in later generations.[16]

Teaching Becomes a Women's Profession

In the 19th century, teaching was transformed from a primarily male to a primarily female profession. In 1830, the vast majority of teachers in the United States were men. By 1850 approximately 60% of teachers were women, and by 1900 more than 75% of the nation's teachers were women. One woman who played a key role in the gender change of the profession was Catharine Beecher. Beginning in the 1830s, Beecher set out to create opportunities for middle-class, single women like herself, who were expected to either marry or stay in the home of relatives as the maiden aunt—a pretty narrow set of options. Though she accepted, or pretended to accept, the cultural expectations of the time, based on the belief that women's nature was dramatically different from that of men, Beecher wanted to create a new professional independence within the social norms. In 1835, she wrote: "Woman, whatever are her relations in life, is necessarily the guardian of the nursery, the companion of childhood, and the constant model of imitation. It is her hand that first stamps impressions on the immortal spirit, that must remain forever." Thus, she argued, school boards should hire women to be teachers. Beecher also reminded the ever-cash-strapped school boards that women would work for much less money than men would. Beecher struck a bargain that gave women far greater opportunities than they had had in the United States before 1830, but it also relegated teaching to a lower-salaried profession. Unfortunately, the results are still with us today.

The shift in teaching from a male to a female profession began in the Northeast but quickly included the whole nation. According to a Massachusetts state census taken in 1865, at the end of the Civil War, teaching was the third most popular

An African American teacher instructs her students in 1866.

job (and the most popular "white collar" job) for all women who worked outside the home, a considerable proportion in such a highly industrialized state. As historian Michael Katz has observed, the "middle-class girl who wanted to work at something respectable had little choice; teaching it almost had to be." And what was true in Massachusetts became true for the country. In the 19th century, over a fairly short period of time, teaching became what another historian, Nancy Hoffman, has called "Woman's 'True' Profession," and women came to make up the vast majority of teachers.

In the early years of the 19th century, women—like the men who had gone before them—underwent relatively little preparation for their jobs. In time, educational reformers such as Catharine Beecher, Emma Willard, Horace Mann, and Mary Lyon began to organize some of the first teacher-preparation programs in the United States, the earliest forerunners of today's schools, colleges or departments of education. The first women teachers were hired through a very informal system. Usually someone with political connections in the rural district, town, or city would put out the word that a teacher was needed. Especially in cities, political connections were essential to getting the job. The young women were strictly supervised, and most left after only a few years on the job. Until the early to middle of the 20th century, many school districts expected a woman to leave teaching if she got married.

The First "Peace Corps"—Teachers for the Midwest and South

As the United States expanded and changed in the 1830s and 1840s, young women became teachers at schools in their hometowns, but they also sought meaningful work, freedom, and adventure as teachers in new places. Communities in the new territories and states—Ohio, Indiana, Illinois, Michigan, Wisconsin, and Minnesota were such territories in the 1830s—needed to establish schools to teach children to read, write, and share in the relatively new American democracy. How could these schools find teachers? No one was willing to pay high salaries to attract them, and no one pretended that working conditions would be comfortable.

Once again, Catharine Beecher—along with William Slade, a former governor of Vermont—came to the rescue. In 1848, they created the Board of National Popular Education. It was designed as a kind of early "Peace Corps" to recruit young women as teachers and send them west to "civilize" the frontier. Young women could escape the intense supervision of their families and home communities and at the same time serve the nation. Many young women believed that they were making the world a better place by sharing learning and American cultural assumptions with young people who might not otherwise learn. It was a powerful combination, and many responded to the call.

In 1849, one of the National Board's teachers wrote home from her assignment in the then frontier town of St. Paul, Minnesota: "My labors have been abundantly blessed during the past season. . . . This is a great country to make one grow. All the faculties are brought into action." For this woman, the challenge and responsibility of teaching gave her life a meaning and purpose that she never would have found staying safely in New England, even though many also wrote home about the terrible loneliness of being separated from family and friends. The sense that teaching challenges a person to the extent that "all faculties are brought into action" is perhaps an earlier version of Parker Palmer's reasons for saying that "teaching is the finest work I know." It remains to this day one of the key attractions of the profession.

During and after the Civil War, a similar campaign was launched to send teachers to the states of the former Confederacy to teach the newly freed slaves. Early in the war—as soon as the Northern troops freed the first slaves, in 1862—the leaders of the Union army found a thirst for literacy among those who had so recently been held in slavery. Those few slaves who had learned to read and write were teaching other slaves as the Northern troops arrived, and they never stopped teaching. The first teachers in the new South were newly freed blacks, not Northern whites. African American teachers had a special answer to the question "Why teach?" For them, teaching and learning were keys to freedom. When the call went out early in the war for more teachers, thousands of Northern women responded quickly, including Charlotte Forten Grimké, who had been born a free Black in Philadelphia and was a teacher in Massachusetts. On Thanksgiving Day in 1862, she wrote from her school in war-torn South Carolina:

This morning a large number—Superintendents, teachers, and freed people assembled in the little Baptist church. It was a sight that I shall not soon forget—that crowd of eager, happy faces from which the shadow of slavery had passed. "Forever free!" "Forever free!"

The literacy that people like Grimké taught was seen as the guarantee of that freedom.

As the Civil War was coming to a close, Mrs. E. Garrison Jackson, an African American from Rhode Island, applied for a job teaching in the South, saying, "I think it is our duty as a people to spend our lives in trying to elevate our own race." Fanny Jackson Coppin, an African American woman who educated generations of teachers as principal of the Institute for Colored Youth in Philadelphia from 1865 to 1902, reminded her students: "You can do much to alleviate the condition of our people. Do not be discouraged." The civil rights movement of the 1950s and 1960s grew in part out of this earlier dedication to teaching, fostering yet another generation of teachers committed to "elevate our own race." The belief that teaching can be of value in society has long been a reason for doing it.

Immigration Transforms Teaching

After the Civil War, many thousands of **immigrants** came to the United States from across the Pacific—from China and Japan—to work in the gold fields, on the railroads, and in the emerging industries of the West Coast. In the 1880s and 1890s, the United States was further transformed by the arrival of even more thousands of immigrants from across the Atlantic, primarily from southern and eastern Europe. Catholics from Italy, Orthodox Christians from Greece, Jews from Poland and Russia, and others from countries small and large were fleeing persecution and the terrible poverty that plagued the majority of people in countries still governed for the benefit of a small ruling elite.

immigration
Moving from the country of one's birth to a new country of permanent residence.

assimilation
Minority groups forced or voluntarily blending into the dominant society by adopting social practices and beliefs.

Many different groups of immigrants came to the United States, and their labor was needed in the factories and shops that were transforming the American economy. At the same time, established residents of the United States were worried about the changes. Could the nation incorporate so many new immigrants, with their different cultures, and still remain "American" as the older residents defined it? Others thought they had already found a solution to "Americanizing" the immigrants. Early in the 1800s, at the time of the great Irish immigration, political leaders had devised a solution to **assimilating** immigrants from non-English parts of Europe into a nation still dominated by English culture. Boston's Mayor Josiah Quincy announced that "all children must be taught to

In a Boston classroom, immigrant students attentively follow their teacher.

respect and revere law and order," while Edward Everett Hale told the school committee that it was their responsibility to "save society not with the cannon and the rifle, but with the spelling book, the grammar, and the Bible." Immigrant students must be required to attend school if this solution was to work.

As the number of schools grew to accommodate the children of these new immigrants, the opportunities for careers in teaching also expanded. In 1870 there were 126,822 teachers in the United States, while by 1900 the number had more than tripled to 450,000. Teaching continued to offer the combination of personal freedom and the excitement of fostering learning that has long drawn people to the profession. One Boston teacher reflected on her first day in the classroom in 1889:

> The odd thing about the first class is that while other classes may fade more or less from the memory, that first group given to the young green girl in a September of long ago, emerges strong and clear. . . . There was positively not a thing to worry about except to acquit oneself with credit in a happily chosen profession. Of course the pay was small or so it seems today. But at that time it seemed to me ridiculously large: thirty-eight dollars a month was the handsome beginning. . . . When I reached the master's office and told him it was hard to wait for the school term to begin, he shook with ill-suppressed laughter. That puzzled me. What was funny? Did he not feel that way too?

Across a century and a half, in both rural and urban locations, teaching has been blessed with those who join it each year finding it "hard to wait for the school term to begin."

Progressive Education and the Emergence of the High School

During the first decades of the 20th century, two important developments changed the nature of teaching and thereby impacted the reasons for becoming a teacher. The first was the progressive education movement, a multifaceted campaign to improve the quality of schools and the present and future lives of students. The second was the emergence of the high school as an important part of education in the United States.

Progressive Education Progressive education meant many different things. In essence, it was part of a larger effort to improve the quality of American life—especially urban life, which swept the United States around 1900. There was growing concern among teachers that the immigrant children should not simply be "Americanized" but should be shown respect for the culture they brought to this country. There was also an interest in more innovative styles of teaching to help students be happier and more successful in school. In 1899, John Dewey, perhaps the best-known voice of progressive education, described his goal for a progressive school when he wrote of the need to reorganize schools as "an embryonic community life, active with types of occupations that reflect the life of the larger society and are permeated throughout with the spirit of art, history, science." Suddenly, teaching was an attractive profession for people who wanted to make a difference by creating such communities.

Some progressive educators also wanted to make teaching a more inviting profession for those entering it. Ella Flagg Young, progressive superintendent of the Chicago Public Schools, wrote in 1901 that teachers needed to be given more professional respect and freedom, with "close supervision" (a form of school administration that attempted to regulate every aspect of teachers' lives) replaced by a structure in which the teacher corps was "unfettered in its activity in striving to realize those things which will evolve themselves in a free play of thought." Margaret Haley, the leader of the Chicago teachers' union, argued for a union as the key to teachers gaining power and respect in their work lives. In 1910, New York City teacher Grace Strachan campaigned successfully for "equal pay for equal work" and an end to paying women teachers lower wages than men for the same job. By the end of the progressive era in the 1920s, teaching had become a much more appealing profession for many.

High Schools While the first institutions known as high schools emerged in the United States as early as the 1830s, it was only after 1900 that high schools became widespread across the country. It is hard for us today to comprehend, but only in the 1930s did the majority of Americans begin attending high school at all, and only in the 1950s did the majority graduate from high school. As high schools—and later junior high schools or middle schools—became more common, some teachers were given important new opportunities. High school teachers, especially in cities, usually taught only one or two subjects, so teachers who had a love of a particular subject—be it history or mathematics or the sciences—could specialize in a way that no elementary teacher could. In addition, in the early years, high school teachers were paid more than elementary teachers, sometimes substantially more. This has not been true for a long time, but was an important division a hundred years ago.

One reason for the higher pay was the more advanced education expected of high school teachers; another was the higher prestige awarded to high school teaching. One example is Fern Persons, who spent the first years of her teaching career, between 1914 and 1926, as an elementary teacher in four different schools. In 1926, after further study at Western Michigan College and Olivet College, she became a high school math teacher at Olivet (Michigan) High School, where she subsequently became principal and later district superintendent. Even if they did not become principals or superintendents, many other teachers, women and men alike, followed the same basic career path, beginning in an often rural elementary school and moving in time to cities and to high schools where they were paid more and treated with more respect.

While the salaries of elementary and high school teachers were equalized later in the 20th century, the work continued to be quite different in the two institutions and remains so today. Happily, as the salary and prestige differences have all but disappeared, a prospective teacher can decide whether to prepare for a career in elementary, middle school, or high school teaching based on personal preference for the type of teaching involved—preferences related to subject matter and to spending time engaging young people of particular age and developmental stages.

Movements of the 1960s

Many aspects of life in the United States were transformed, some quite dramatically, in the 1960s. Yet few observers focus on the substantial changes in the teaching profession resulting from several intersecting developments in those years. Like many movements in the 1960s, those that impacted teaching had roots that went far back.

The Peace Corps In the 19th century, many young teachers—mostly women but also some men—found opportunities for service and adventure by going to teach in schools of the new territories of the Midwest and later the post–Civil War South. In the 20th century, teachers and aspiring teachers found equally adventurous opportunities traveling abroad. While the Peace Corps, founded in the 1960s, was perhaps the most far-reaching effort to send Americans overseas to bring American culture and styles of education to different countries, it was far from the first such effort. Beginning in the 1890s, Protestant missionaries, with strong federal support, traveled to the Philippine Islands (newly acquired from Spain as a result of war in 1898), bringing a new style of education to the islands. Throughout the 20th century, similar efforts to export U.S.-style education, culture, and democracy were spearheaded by cadres of teachers. Since it was established by President Kennedy in 1961, the Peace Corps has offered important opportunities for adventure and service to many Americans who have taught in developing countries around the world. It has also brought former volunteers back to the United States with a much more sophisticated sense of the values of other nations and cultures, and often a humbler sense regarding U.S. efforts to transform others who may not be as interested in being transformed.

Increasing Educational Requirements Ever since the first specialized school to prepare teachers opened in the 1830s with a 1-year curriculum, the standards for entry into teaching had been slowly rising. But it was during the 1950s that state after state finally began requiring every new teacher to complete a college degree prior to starting teaching. It is hard to imagine people entering teaching without a college degree, but that was the norm until the middle of the 20th century. As late as the 1930s, most new teachers had completed only 2 years of college, and a quarter of the nation's teachers—especially those teaching in rural areas—did not have even that much education. Then suddenly, after World War II, every state changed the rules, and every new teacher needed a college degree. The results became apparent in schools throughout the following decades. Today the nation's teachers are better prepared than ever before.

The Women's Movement Perhaps the largest impact on teaching of the 1950s and 1960s was on the gender of teachers. In the 1830s and 1840s, when Catharine Beecher proposed to school boards around the country that they should hire women instead of men as teachers, she was seeking to open a profession to women who previously had been excluded from most forms of work outside the home and farm. In the 1950s and 1960s, the women's movement transformed the professional opportunities for women more than at any earlier time. While some jobs had opened to at least a few fortunate women in the many decades between 1830 and 1960, most newspapers still ran separate "men's jobs" and "women's jobs" sections in the want ads, and the realm of acceptable women's work was substantially limited in the 1960s. Today, women make up the majority of those studying in medical and law schools and serve in a wide range of professional and governmental positions, from university presidents to hospital administrators to U.S. Supreme Court justices.

As a result of the changes brought about by the women's movement, women who decide to teach do so because they want to, not because, as women, it is their only option. And men have the freedom to become teachers—including elementary and early childhood teachers—that their fathers and grandfathers never enjoyed. However, women still are not as widely represented in the most prestigious and highly paid professions, and teachers still are underpaid in part because teaching is seen as "women's work" by too many. Men receive quizzical looks when they say they are teachers, especially if they are elementary teachers. Nevertheless, the professional freedom—for teachers and nonteachers, women and men—is greater than in 1960 or at any previous time in the nation's history. And this new freedom has had a positive impact on both individual teaching careers and the diversity of the staff of many schools.

The Civil Rights Movement After the 1954 U.S. Supreme Court ruling in *Oliver Brown et al. v. Board of Education of Topeka, Kansas,* deliberate racial segregation in the schools became illegal in the United States. After years of resistance, states across the South, where the majority of legally segregated schools existed, began to integrate the schools. However, there were unintended consequences of the movement to end racial segregation in the schools. All too often, the new integration resulted in sending Black students to White schools and closing Black schools. In many cases, closing the Black schools also meant firing the Black teachers. Sometimes the teaching staff was integrated along with the student body; however, the Black teachers often were relegated to second-class status, and the Black principal became the assistant principal to the White school leader. In the decade following the *Brown* decision, 31,584 African American teachers lost their jobs in southern and border states. The problem of teaching being far too often a White profession, in spite of the growing ethnic diversity of the nation's students, persists to the present day.[17]

It is also important to note here that the larger civil rights movement had an impact on the job description of teachers that is not always recognized. As we discuss in Chapters 3 and 4, before the 1960s many students were excluded from school informally or formally. Students who arrived in the United States not speaking English, students with a disability, and students who did not find the culture of the school a comfortable place were allowed to simply drop out, with few questions asked. Teachers were expected to teach those for whom school worked well and not worry about the others. Today, teachers are expected to teach every child, to "leave no child behind." This change in the job description of teachers is yet to be fully recognized.

CONNECTIONS ➤◄

In Chapter 3, we'll discuss the people behind the *Brown v. Board of Education* case. In Chapter 11, we'll see how *Brown* reflects the extraordinary role that politics and government—at all levels—play in shaping schools in the United States.

For the last two centuries, women and men have entered the teaching profession because they enjoy being with young people, because teaching provides an opportunity to share in the excitement of learning, because it offers a level of freedom not otherwise available to them, and because, through teaching, they might "make the world a better place," especially for the growing numbers of young people who are attending school longer. Today, the new and higher standards teachers are expected to meet—standards being enforced within a growing shortage of qualified teachers—stand to transform teaching and the reasons for teaching, yet again.

Should I Be a Teacher?

No one expects you to have the final answer to this question yet. However, as you think about the reasons other people have given for choosing, staying in, or leaving teaching, it is important that you ask yourself these questions: "Why am I considering teaching?" "How will I find out if it is right for me?" The reality is that as much as you think about these questions, you may never find the answers until you try teaching. There is no substitute for standing in front of a group of children or youth and seeing what it is like, testing whether your experience is as positive as Judy Logan's or as fulfilling as Parker Palmer's. Today more and more teacher preparation programs are offering the first experience of actually

Notes from the Field

When did you decide you wanted to be a teacher?

"I didn't know for sure that I wanted to teach until I got into the classroom during my student teaching practicum; I had done all the education course-work and still wasn't sure of my career choice until that semester. I found that I loved working with teenagers—I appreciate their idealism, their intelligence, their silliness. It was empowering to have a place in their lives."

—*Dawn Striker, science and math teacher*

being with young people—of actually teaching—earlier and earlier in the program. It is important to ask when your program will give you this opportunity.

It is of great value to be able to observe real teachers and students in actual school settings, and it is even more valuable to become a participant in the teaching–learning process. Tutoring one student, assisting a teacher with a lesson, working with a small group of students during or after school—any one of these can give you the chance to experience that wonderful moment when a child or adolescent "gets it" for the first time. Whenever you first have the opportunity to stand in front of a class, it is your job to prepare for the experience so that it will be as successful as possible, so that you allow yourself, as Parker Palmer says, to know teaching as the finest work there is even if there are also moments (as Palmer also recognizes) of pure agony. Only when you are informed by a personal sense of the range of experiences and of the feelings teaching creates in you, as well as by stories of what has worked and not worked for other teachers, can you make a wise and informed decision about your own future in this fascinating field.

In the end, however, the main reason for you to consider teaching as a career is the one the best teachers have always given. At the core of this work lie the joy and satisfaction that come from seeing a child's excitement at truly mastering something new. This will remain the ultimate reward of teaching. Perhaps Herb Kohl said it best: "There's no end to the delights and joys of teaching, no limit to the challenges we will continue to face in order to serve children well, and no limit to the creativity and love adults can and should bring to helping children grow through teaching, which is at its heart the discipline of hope." It is a rare privilege to pursue a career that offers so much.[18]

 **CHAPTER REVIEW**

- Why do people become teachers today?

Over the years, people have become teachers for many different reasons. Nevertheless, certain basic reasons seem to remain true across time and in different locations. People are drawn to teaching because it seems to be "the work they were always cut out for," because "they enjoy being with young people and watching them learn and grow," or because "they want to change the world." These reasons are not very different from one another. Few people enter teaching in order to become rich or famous. Yet many of us are drawn to the wonderfully engaging work of supporting young people in their learning and, through that support, making the world a better place, one child at a time.

- Why do some people leave teaching?

Sadly, it is also true that too many of those who enter teaching find that they cannot stay and make a career of it. Sometimes the lack of administrative support, low salaries, or poor working conditions wear teachers out. Increasingly, however, school districts are seeking to address these issues by paying teachers better salaries, improving the conditions of teachers' work lives, and offering the kinds of strong continuing induction and mentoring programs that help novice teachers succeed in the early years of their work so that they can stay and prosper in the profession. And teachers have often played a major role in changing the schools and the teaching profession for the better.

- Historically speaking: What has motivated people to teach at different times in the past?

Over the decades many different people have become teachers for different reasons. In the early years of the United States many men became teachers for a year or two until a better job became available. Women became teachers because it was virtually the only job available to them, and over time women made up the majority of teachers. After the Civil War, teachers saw the opportunity to use schools as a means to expand the meaning of freedom, especially for newly freed slaves. Some people became teachers because they felt a call to help new immigrants or because they wanted to make schools more humane places for often bored students. In the 1960s, the civil rights movement expanded the diversity of the student body and the responsibilities of teachers, and a new generation embraced the challenge. Increasingly teaching has come to be a profession with high entrance requirements in which people stay for a lifetime. Throughout history, however, teaching has always been a place where people have derived great satisfaction from helping individual students grow and learn new things and from helping to expand the meaning of freedom and justice for communities.

- Should I be a teacher?

It is important for you, as a prospective teacher, to think realistically about how you will respond to complaints that have been voiced by other teachers. Are teacher salaries realistic for you? How do you think you will respond to a difficult student or a difficult principal? Is there a way to pick a first teaching job—to find the right school or the right district—where support for new teachers is available? The material offered throughout this book will help you in the important process of answering these difficult questions.

Readings

Why Do People Become Teachers Today?

From *TO TEACH : THE JOURNEY OF A TEACHER*

AUTHOR: WILLIAM AYERS

Bill Ayers was a teacher in Chicago. He has taught at every level from preschool to university, and it is clear that he loves teaching and thoughtfully reflects on his chosen profession. During the 2008 presidential campaign, Ayers's name became a household word because of his long-ago leadership in the radical antiwar politics of the 1960s. Many years later he served on a rather large educational board with Barack Obama, and the presidential candidate was criticized because of his association with this "radical." A lifelong educator, Ayers has written compellingly about the importance of his profession. The selection that follows, from his book To Teach: The Journey of a Teacher, *describes his own decision to become a teacher and his commitment to stay with the profession.*

Teachers are asked hundreds, perhaps thousands, of times why they chose teaching. The question often means: "Why teach, when you could do something more profitable?" "Why teach, since teaching is beneath your skill and intelligence?" The question can be filled with contempt and cynicism or it can be simply a request for understanding and knowledge: "What is there in teaching to attract and keep you?" Either way, it is a question worth pursuing, for there are good reasons to teach and equally good reasons not to teach. Teaching is, after all, different in character from any other profession or job or occupation, and teaching, like anything else, is not for everyone.

There are many reasons not to teach, and they cannot be easily dismissed, especially by those of us who love teaching. Teachers are badly paid, so badly that it is a national disgrace. We earn on average a quarter of what lawyers are paid, half of what accountants make, less than truck drivers and shipyard workers. Romantic appeals aside, wages and salaries are one reflection of relative social value; a collective, community assessment of worth.

Teachers also suffer low status in many communities, in part as a legacy of sexism: Teaching is largely women's work, and it is constantly being deskilled, made into something to be performed mechanically, without much thought or care, covered over with layers of supervision and accountability and bureaucracy, and held in low esteem.

Teachers often work in difficult situations, under impossible conditions. We sometimes work in schools that are large, impersonal, and factory-like; sometimes in schools that resemble war zones.

The complexity of teaching can be excruciating, and for some that may be sufficient reason not to teach (for others, it is one of teaching's most compelling allures).

These are some of the reasons not to teach, and, for me at least, they add up to a compelling case. So, why teach? My own pathway to teaching began long ago in a large, uniquely nurturing family, a place where I experienced the ecstasy of intimacy and the irritation of being known, the power of will and the boundary of freedom, both the safety and the constraints of family living. I was the middle child of five children, and I had opportunities to learn as well as opportunities to teach. In my family, I learned to balance self-respect with respect for others, assertiveness with compromise, individual choice with group consciousness.

I began teaching in an alternative school in Ann Arbor, Michigan, called the Children's Community. It was a small school with large purposes; a school that, we hoped, would change the world. One of our goals was to provide an outstanding, experience-based education for the young people we taught. Another was to develop a potent model of freedom and racial integration, a model that would have wide impact on other schools and on all of society. We thought of ourselves as an insurgent, experimental counterinstitution; one part of a larger movement for social change.

The year was 1965, and I was twenty years old. For many young people, teaching was not only respectable, it was one of the meaningful, relevant things a person could do. Many schools then, as now, were inhumane, lifeless places. But we were crusading teachers. We felt that we could save the schools, create life spaces and islands of compassion for children and, through our work, help create a new social order. We were intent on living lives that did not make a mockery of our values, and teaching seemed a way to live that kind of life. We were hopeful and altruistic and we were on a mission of change.

Today, teaching may not seem so attractive, nor so compelling in quite the same way. Not only are the schools in even worse shape than before, and the problems seemingly more intractable, but there is a narrow, selfish spirit loose in the land. Idealists are "suckers" in the currency of the day, and the notion that schools should be decent, accessible, and responsive places for all children is just more pie in-the-sky. With a combative social Darwinism setting the pace in our society, and a cynical sense that morality has no place in our public lives, teaching today can seem a fool's errand.

But it is not. Teaching is still a powerful calling for many people, and powerful for the same reasons that it has always been so. There are still young people who need a thoughtful, caring adult in their lives; someone who can nurture and challenge them, who can coach and guide, understand and care about them. There are still injustices and deficiencies in society, in even more desperate need of repair. There are still worlds to change—including specific, individual worlds, one by one—and classrooms can be places of possibility and transformation for youngsters, certainly, but also for teachers. Teaching can still be world-changing work. Crusading teachers are still needed—in fact we are needed now more than ever.

And this, I believe, is finally the reason to teach. People are called to teaching because they love children and youth, or because they love being with them, watching them open up and grow and become more able, more competent, more powerful in the world. They may love what happens to themselves when they are with children, the ways in which they become better, more human, more generous. Or they become teachers because they love the world, or some piece of the world enough that they want to show that love to others. In either case, people teach as an act of construction and reconstruction, and as a gift of oneself to others. I teach in the hope of making the world a better place.

Source: William Ayers, *To Teach: The Journey of a Teacher*, first edition. New York: Teachers College Press, 2001, pp. 5–8.

From "THE COLORS AND STRANDS OF TEACHING"

AUTHOR: MELINDA PELLERIN-DUCK

Melinda Pellerin-Duck has remained far from the national spotlight. A teacher in the High School of Commerce in Springfield, Massachusetts, she was named the Massachusetts Teacher of the Year for 2003–04. She sees her commitment to teaching as rooted in stories from her family dating back to the time when her great-great-grandmother was a slave in Louisiana and in her experience as a student of the Sisters of St. Joseph at Holy Name Elementary School in Springfield. In this article, her sense of calling and her creative approach to curriculum come through loud and clear.

I was meant to be a teacher. It has not been one experience, but many that have taught me this. Life's lessons have made me the person I am, and continue to transform me into the teacher I am becoming. Lessons from students, family, and friends have taught me that patience is a virtue to be embraced in my classroom every day. I've learned perseverance, even when the struggle seems insurmountable. I've learned love, and I've had this love reinforced by the gifts each child brings to my classroom experiences. I've learned about hope, and I know not to judge a person by outside distractions because it is inner beauty that counts. As a teacher, I continue to search for it in each student. These are the lessons I try to instill in each miracle that walks across the threshold of my classroom.

I have always believed that classrooms must transcend traditional convention. Students should participate actively in their own learning; they cannot just sit passively while knowledge is being poured into them. Instruction must be well planned, relevant, interesting, and exciting. To be an outstanding teacher, you must see your students as fellow travelers and learners. In my classroom, we are all "in this together."

A successful teacher understands there is always room for improvement. I am never satisfied with the notion that the longer I teach, the more expert I become. I am not an expert, but I am striving to learn more and to become experienced. I live in the "learning-mode." I am motivated to learn more because I am a teacher reaching for higher standards for myself and for my students. There is nothing more rewarding than helping transform students who thought they could never create anything meaningful into confident and excited historians. A lesson in world history on the art of Michelangelo finds me jumping on a desk, lying face up, showing students how Michelangelo created his masterpiece. Students are engaged, excited, answering difficult questions about art, style, and form. The students add their own crucial analysis to the work and I, as their teacher, am in awe of them. This is a gift, a miracle.

The rewards of teaching are many. Watching our school's mock trial team, a team that was never supposed to win or achieve, compete against suburban school systems with many more advantages and economic resources makes my heart skip a beat. I have watched the team transform into a confident, well-prepared legal team. It has become a formidable adversary. As the team members advance to the final round of statewide competition, I am inspired by their dedication, their spirit, and their performance. I am like a proud parent watching them soar. In 1995, the team placed second for the Commonwealth of Massachusetts.

Some may question why I continue teaching. My answer is that I teach because I see extraordinary possibilities in my students. I could not see myself doing anything else but teaching; it is my vocation. It is part of my life, my soul, and my heart. It is challenging, at times difficult, but the rewards are overwhelming. As a teacher, I have the most fortunate experience of nurturing our future. If we do it well, combining unforgettable and meaningful instruction with a sense of community, our students will become not only stewards of their destiny, but productive citizens of our nation and the world.

Too often, I hear that old quotation, "Those who can't, teach." It has been used in popular film and culture to poke fun at and criticize our profession. Yet ours is a vocation, a vocation of love; true teachers know this. Those who instruct, who nurture, who hope patiently and lovingly each and every day understand the quotation is really, "Those who *can*, teach." Those who can, find joy in walking into a room with open minds. They teach. Those who can, take students from "I can't" to "I can." They teach. Those who can, counsel and dispense positive discipline, while staying well after school hours with students. They teach. Those who can, struggle with self-doubt but endure. Those who can, worry about their lesson plans and whether a particular student will have enough clothing to wear, or whether there will be heat in that student's home. Those who can, teach and they do it everyday. I am lucky enough to be one of those who "can."

Questions

1. Look at the reason William Ayers gives for not teaching. How do you react to those concerns?
2. What are your thoughts about Ayers's assertion that, in spite of all the reasons not to teach, teaching is worth doing?
3. What do you think when you read Pellerin-Duck's comment "I was meant to be a teacher." Does that ring true for you, or is teaching a more recent interest?

Source: Melinda Pellerin-Duck, "The Colors and Strands of Teaching." In *Why We Teach*, edited by Sonia Nieto, 127–33. New York: Teachers College Press, 2005.

Why Do Some People Leave Teaching?

From "THE WRONG SOLUTION TO THE TEACHER SHORTAGE"

AUTHORS: RICHARD M. INGERSOLL AND THOMAS M. SMITH

Richard Ingersoll, a professor at the University of Pennsylvania, has written a number of books and articles on the problem of teacher turnover and the way this turnover creates a shortage that would not otherwise exist. In this article and in his book Who Controls Teachers' Work? Power and Accountability in America's Schools, *he and his coauthor not only analyze why teachers leave but also give very clear advice to school leaders and districts as to what they could do to change the situation.*

In recent years, researchers and policymakers have told us again and again that severe teacher shortages confront schools. . . . They point to a dramatic increase in the demand for new teachers resulting from two converging demographic trends: increasing student enrollments and increasing numbers of teachers reaching retirement age. Shortfalls of teachers, they say, are forcing many school systems to lower their standards for teacher quality (National Commission on Teaching and America's Future, 1997).

A closer look at the best data available suggests that the conventional wisdom on teacher shortages, although partly correct, also errs in important ways. The demand for teachers has indeed grown. Since 1984, both student enrollments and teacher retirements have increased (Snyder, Hoffman, & Geddes, 1997). Substantial numbers of schools with teaching openings have experienced difficulties finding qualified candidates to fill their positions (Ingersoll, 1999). But the data also show that increases in student enrollment and teacher retirements are not the primary causes of the high demand for new teachers and subsequent staffing difficulties. A larger part of the problem is teacher attrition (leaving the profession)—which is particularly high among teachers in their first few years of service.

Understanding Employee Turnover

The teaching occupation suffers from chronic and relatively high annual turnover compared with many other occupations. Total teacher turnover is fairly evenly split between two components: *attrition* (those who leave teaching altogether); and *migration* (those who move to teaching jobs in other schools). Teaching is also a relatively large occupation: It represents 4 percent of the entire civilian work force. There are, for example, more than twice as many K–12 teachers as registered nurses and five times as many teachers as either lawyers or professors (U.S. Bureau of the Census, 1998). The sheer size of the teaching force, combined with the relatively high annual turnover rate within the teaching occupation, means that large numbers of employees flow into, between, and out of schools each year. . . .

Attrition Among Beginning Teachers

The turnover problem, although high for the entire teaching occupation, affects beginning teachers more than others. Teaching has always lost many of its newly trained members early in their careers, long before the retirement years (Johnson & Birkeland, in press; Lortie, 1975; Murnane, Singer, Willett, Kemple, & Olsen, 1991).

We used the SASS/TFS [Schools and Staffing Survey/Teacher Follow-up Survey] data to provide a rough estimate of the cumulative attrition of beginning teachers in their first several years of teaching. The data suggest that after just five years, between 40 and 50 percent of all beginning teachers have left the profession. Why do beginning teachers leave at such high rates?

Perhaps the best way to discover why employees depart from jobs is to ask them. Many organizations do this through exit interviews. Similarly, the Teacher Follow-up Survey administered a questionnaire to a national sample of U.S. teachers who had left their teaching jobs the year before. Among other questions, it asked teachers to list the main reasons (up to three) for their departure. For this analysis, we focused on new teachers who left teaching after their first year.

About 19 percent of these beginners who left teaching said that they did so as a result of a school staffing action, such as a cutback, layoff, termination, school reorganization, or school closing. Another 42 percent cited personal reasons, including pregnancy, child rearing, health problems, and family moves.

Around 39 percent said that they left to pursue a better job or another career, and about 29 percent said that dissatisfaction with teaching as a career or with their specific job was a main reason. These final two reasons—pursuit of another job and dissatisfaction—together play a major role in about two-thirds of all beginning teacher attrition.

The survey asked the 29 percent who listed job dissatisfaction as a major reason for leaving about the source of their dissatisfaction, again giving them the option of listing up to three reasons. More than three-fourths linked their quitting to low salaries. But even more of them indicated that one of four different school working conditions was behind their decision to quit: student discipline problems; lack of support from the school administration; poor student motivation; and lack of teacher influence over school wide and classroom decision making.

These findings on dissatisfaction-related attrition are important because they point to "policy-amenable" issues. The conventional wisdom places the roots of the teacher shortage outside schools, within larger demographic trends. By contrast, these data suggest that the roots of the teacher shortage largely reside in the working conditions within schools and districts. These two explanations for the teacher shortage point to different prescriptions for fixing the problem.

What Can Schools Do?

The data on new teacher attrition suggest that efforts to recruit more teachers—which have been the focus of much policy—will not, by themselves, solve the staffing problems plaguing schools. The solution must also include teacher retention. In short, recruiting more teachers will not solve the teacher crisis if 40–50 percent of these teachers leave in a few short years. The image that comes to mind is that of a bucket rapidly losing water because of holes in the bottom. Pouring more water into the bucket will not do any good if we do not patch the holes first.

Although the data confirm that raising teacher salaries offers one effective way to plug these holes, this strategy would be expensive, especially given the sheer size of the teacher population. The working conditions identified by new teachers as factors in their decision to leave teaching—lack of administrative support, poor student discipline and student motivation, and lack of participation in decision making—may offer a more effective focus for improvement efforts (Ingersoll, 2003).

Increasing support from school administrators for new teachers, for example, might range from providing enough classroom supplies to providing mentors. Mentors are especially crucial. Life for beginning teachers has traditionally been described as a sink-or-swim proposition. Indeed, data from SASS/TFS show that mentoring does make a difference.

Plugging holes through these kinds of changes will not be easy. But the good news, from the perspective of this analysis, is that schools are not simply the victims of inexorable demographic trends. The management and organization of schools play a significant role in the genesis of school staffing problems but can also play a significant role in their solution. Improving teachers' working conditions would contribute to lower rates of new teacher turnover, thereby diminishing school staffing problems and improving the performance of schools.

Questions

1. How do you respond to the problems described by Ingersoll and Smith?
2. Are there ways to find a school district that offers the kind of supportive programs Ingersoll and Smith describe? How important do you think these programs will be to you?
3. Do you know someone who taught for a year or two and then stopped? Are that person's reasons for leaving similar to or different from those described in this article?
4. Ingersoll and Smith say that many of the reasons teachers leave could be fixed by schools and districts. As a future teacher, are there things you can do to improve the situation this article describes?

Source: Richard M. Ingersoll and Thomas M. Smith, "The Wrong Solution to the Teacher Shortage." *Educational Leadership* 60, no. 8 (May 2003): 30–33.

Good Teaching
What Is Its Impact?

2

> Yet as I look into hundreds of classrooms, watch teachers working with all kinds of students, when I ask myself what makes the greatest difference in the quality of student learning—it is a teacher's passion that leaps out.

ROBERT FRIED

QUESTIONS TO COME

There is a saying among teachers that people enter the profession for one of two reasons: Either they remember a teacher who changed their lives and want to be like that person, or they remember a terrible teacher and want to be sure that no child is subjected to the misery they experienced. Many of us who teach have fond memories of a special teacher who made a difference in our lives, even if some of us also remember some who were not so good. Indeed, much has been written that romanticizes teachers and their influence.

However, some have argued that teachers and schools cannot make much of a difference. They claim that larger social and economic forces, such as poverty, are too powerful for schools to counteract, that teachers are not able to offer what students need, or that the key to reform is a "teacher proof curriculum." Do teachers really make a difference in the lives of their students? New research reveals more clearly than ever before that teaching—when it is done well—definitely does matter and that teachers can make an extraordinary difference in the lives of their students, in spite of poverty or other social forces; perhaps more of a difference than any other single factor.

The **Readings** included in this chapter address each of these questions. The Education Trust, based in Washington, D.C., and led by Kati Haycock, is but one of many centers whose research has led to an almost unanimous conclusion that teachers make much more of a difference than many observers and scholars in previous generations realized. According to Haycock, "Good teaching matters . . . a lot." Of course, concluding that good teachers do make a substantial difference only gives rise to another, far more complex, question: What do good teachers do that makes them so good? We'll begin answering that question in this chapter and pursue it further in subsequent chapters.

Offering students the best education possible is the fundamental ethical responsibility of every teacher. Included in the **Readings** for this chapter is the Code of Ethics for Educators adopted by the state of New York, which outlines six main principles regarding a teacher's ethical responsibility.

As we look at the research regarding the impact of good teaching and discuss what constitutes good teaching, we must remember that no one teaches in a vacuum. While it is no longer acceptable for a teacher to say, "I can't make a difference because there are too many external factors in a child's life that get in the way of learning," teachers who do not look carefully at the context within which

they will teach—such as the family and community in which the children in their classroom spend the majority of their time, the support that may or may not be there for learning, and the opportunities to build on the work of other important people in students' lives—are missing the opportunity to offer students the best education possible. The research clearly shows that teachers and schools that find ways to involve parents in their children's education and in the way the school operates make a huge impact on the educational success of students. Examples of schools that have found ways to foster an appropriate place for parents in the education of their children and to engage parents in the schools allow us to explore further the complex web of relationships surrounding good teachers and good schools. At the same time, a look at William Jeynes's article in the **Readings** section is a reminder that students of different ages need very different kinds of parental involvement and while a young child may be delighted to have a parent present at school, an adolescent may simply be embarrassed. As Jeynes describes, the adolescent also needs parents or other caregivers but in different, much more subtle ways.

What Does the Evidence Say About the Difference a Good Teacher Can Make?

Sonia Nieto, a longtime scholar, activist, and teacher of teachers, tells the story of Beatriz Campuzano, a high school senior whose father came to the United States from Mexico with less than a third-grade education. Early in her own schooling, Campuzano ran into the low expectations and barriers that too often are part of the educational experience of all students, but especially students who are immigrants, who are poor, or whose first language is not English. But in Campuzano's life, there was that one teacher who made the difference:

> In the sixth grade, my English teacher, Mr. Wilke, helped me to understand that I was capable of achieving anything. I began to believe in myself. My self-esteem grew as Mr. Wilke told me day after day that I was a "gift to the world." I loved education because it made me feel smart. Knowing that I had knowledge made me feel invincible.[1]

Many of us have been fortunate to have a Mr. Wilke in our life. But, in the end, we always ask ourselves, do the Mr. (and Mrs. and Ms.) Wilkes really make a difference? Would the outcome be the same for the student no matter how motivating or qualified the teacher? What does the research say about how important the Mr. Wilkes of this world really are—and have been over time—to the majority of students? The answer today is unmistakable—as Haycock says, "good teaching matters . . . a lot." In this chapter we will look further at why.

Historically Speaking: The "Good Old Days"

More than a century and a half ago, Horace Mann told school boards that they needed to view themselves as "sentinels stationed at the door of every schoolhouse in the State, to see that no teacher ever crosses its threshold, who is not clothed, from the crown of his head to the sole of his foot, in garments of virtue." Mann also offered more practical advice. He wisely insisted that teachers should know the subjects they were going to teach, that they "should be able to teach *subjects*, not manuals merely." He also insisted that teachers needed to know how to teach: "Aptness to teach involves the power of perceiving how far a scholar understands the subject-matter to be learned, and what, in the natural order, is the next step he is to take."[2]

Throughout much of the century after Mann wrote schools and the job of teachers changed drastically. One-room schoolhouses in which a single teacher taught all the grades were replaced with graded schools (like those most of us attended) in which teachers became specialists in the first or second or third grade. As urban school systems grew, they were organized in ways that would lead to the conclusion that individual teachers—and their proficiency in any one subject—did not make much difference at all. Every teacher in the same grade level was expected to teach exactly the same lesson, at the same time, in the same way. And growing school systems added more and more supervisors—principals, superintendents, assistant superintendents (nearly all of whom were male)—who were expected to closely supervise the female classroom teachers and keep them in line.

What About Me?

My Learning Autobiography

As you begin to think about the type of teacher you will become—and want to become—you first need to reflect on your own educational experiences when you were on the other side of the desk, as a student.

Start by asking yourself questions about the key learning moments in your life:

- What are some of the most important things that I have learned thus far?
- Who helped me learn them?
- Where were these lessons learned? In school? In other organizations? With my family? Alone?
- What are my educational experiences that I would consider "positive"? Why? What was a teacher's involvement?
- What are my educational experiences that I would consider "negative"? Why? What was a teacher's involvement?

Begin to record these various experiences, lessons, and influences. Be creative in how you approach this ongoing exercise—create lists, journal, make a visual time line, or find other ways to make the refection meaningful.

Discuss your experiences with fellow classmates, either in a class discussion, a study group, or casual conversation. Use this opportunity to get to know one another, to build support systems, to share insights regarding the best (and sometimes the worst) learning experiences, and to begin developing a personal philosophy about education and teaching that will change and evolve to guide you throughout your career.

Many objected to this de-skilling of teachers. In 1904, Margaret Haley, the feisty and tough-minded founder of the Chicago Federation of Teachers, complained about policies that made "the teacher an automaton, a mere factory hand, whose duty it is to carryout mechanically and unquestioningly the ideas and orders of those clothed with the authority of position." Until the situation changed, Haley and many other progressive educators insisted, the schools would not be democratic and would not be using one of their greatest resources: the ability of teachers to make a difference for their students.[3]

"Teacher-Proof Curriculum"

Sadly, this limited view of teachers and their potential to impact student learning did not disappear at the turn of the 20th century. From the 1950s to the 1970s, many argued for what they called a "teacher-proof curriculum" so that students could be protected from supposedly poorly prepared or uncreative teachers. Some still do. Glenn Seaborg, who won a Nobel Prize for his research in chemistry and served as the chair of the U.S. Atomic Energy Commission, complained that "there was and is a feeling that it's not so important that the teacher understand the subject matter, as long as they're good at conveying it." Alan Friedman of the New York Hall of Science, remembering the same effort to "teacher-proof"

Teachable Moment
SELLING THE SUBJECT

A salesperson can sell anything as long as he or she has the skills and flashy marketing. It isn't necessary to understand how the product works or what the customers' needs are.

In essence, that's the philosophy behind a "teacher-proof" curriculum. A teacher who knows how to teach and has "product support"—such as a video, beautifully illustrated textbooks, or detailed lesson plans—doesn't really need to have a firm grasp of the actual "product" (such as science or history) or the "customer" (the students).

But is it really true that all a successful salesperson needs are good communication skills and the right "props"? That may suffice for the short term, but what happens when the customer has questions about how the product works? Or when it breaks down? Or when the user's manual is so poorly designed that the client needs one-on-one help? Or when customers conclude that they don't have any need for the product—and never did? In fact, the most successful salespeople—whether they are selling cars or the wonders of the solar system—use their product knowledge to determine what will solve their clients' needs and to educate their clients as to why the solution will work.

And besides, teachers can't forward their "customers" to a "help desk" or "tech support."

Questions

- Although the thought of a "teacher-proof curriculum" might seem offensive, would a teacher feel a sense of comfort from not being expected to have mastered a subject prior to teaching it?
- What qualities do a successful salesperson and a successful teacher share?

the curriculum, lamented that "the idea was that if you had an activity, a filmstrip, and a book, that was sufficient, and even if the teacher was afraid of science, they could do a good job."[4]

Teachers, Schools, and the War on Poverty

In 1964, President Lyndon B. Johnson declared a national war on poverty, a massive federal program inspired by the **civil rights movement** and designed to dramatically reduce social and economic inequality in the nation. Johnson, who had been a schoolteacher long before he became a politician, believed that one of the keys to ending poverty was improving education and that, given the right resources, schools and teachers could better the educational attainment and future lives of students. In 1965, with one of his own schoolteachers standing by his side, Johnson signed the Elementary and Secondary Education Act, the first major federal financial support for schools. He said, "As President of the United States, I believe deeply no law I have signed or will ever sign means more to the future of America."[5] Here was faith in the power of schools and teachers to make a difference.

However, more was involved in the federal war on poverty than faith in education. As part of the funding of Johnson's programs, the U.S. Congress also

> **civil rights movement**
> A movement in the United States, beginning in the 1930s, growing rapidly in the 1950s and 1960s, and continuing through the 1980s, that meant to secure civil and human rights for all people beginning with the Black Freedom struggle but expanding to the rights of all people regardless of race or gender.

authorized a massive study of the impact of education on reducing poverty. The result of this congressional mandate for research was one of the best-financed and most thorough studies of American education. The result was James S. Coleman's *Equality of Educational Opportunity*, published in 1966. Surprising and disappointing to Coleman, as well as to many in the Johnson administration and to educators across the country, Coleman's study essentially concluded that there was very little, if any, link between educational inputs such as facilities and numbers of teachers—the benefits of expanded funding that could be measured most easily—and educational outputs as measured by student achievement.

While many debated the conclusions of the Coleman Report, the Carnegie Corporation of New York funded a group of researchers, led by Harvard's Christopher Jencks, to duplicate, test, and expand on Coleman's research. Jencks's 1972 book, *Inequality: A Reassessment of the Effects of Family and Schooling in America*, was even more depressing to educators than the original Coleman Report. Jencks concluded that while it was certainly true that educational opportunity was unequally distributed across the nation, it was also the case that "inequality in educational opportunity is not responsible for most of the inequality in educational results that we see all around us" and that "equalizing educational opportunity will not do much to equalize the results in economic competition." Essentially, Jencks said, schools can't "fix" an unequal society, especially in regard to economic inequality. Jencks himself argued that only fundamental changes in the American economy, including income redistribution, would improve the life chances of poor and marginalized people in the United States. Many others, however, simply concluded that Coleman and Jencks had virtually proved that schools and the teachers who taught in them made no meaningful difference in the lives of students.

Ronald Edmonds, who later conducted research on the characteristics of those schools that did, in spite of everything, make a difference for poor students—and there were many schools like that—complained that whatever the motivation behind Jencks's work, it had the potential to let schools "off the hook" for any responsibility for effective teaching—especially in poor and non-White communities—and as such represented a tremendous disservice. Given how vital schooling was to all young people, especially to those born into poverty, Edmonds believed it was essential that educators be held accountable for what their students learned and failed to learn.[6] It would be a long time before the views of Edmonds and others who agreed with him came to be dominant, but slowly some of the conclusions reached by Coleman and Jencks began to be challenged. Coleman and Jencks had looked at some of the easier data to study, such as the total funds expended on education and the impact on all poor children and children of color in the country or in a school district. However, if we look more carefully at the differences from classroom to classroom and teacher to teacher, a very different picture emerges.

> ## CONNECTIONS →←
>
> In Chapter 4, we'll explore what other groups besides racial minorities benefited from the 1960s legislation.

 ## DID YOU KNOW?

President John F. Kennedy originally developed the legislation that eventually became the Elementary and Secondary Education Act. The goal was twofold: (1) to provide every child with a good education, regardless of religious, racial, or class background; and (2) to ensure that American students were competitive with those in other countries, as a response to the Soviets' launch of the world's first spacecraft, Sputnik, in 1957.

New Research, Different Conclusions

The view of what teachers can and cannot accomplish has only recently begun to change. New research indicates that Coleman and Jencks were simply wrong. By looking at whole districts or schools, they failed to study what happened in the classroom—where all teaching and learning takes place. Teachers *do* make a substantial difference in the learning of their students, no matter what external factors might get in the way. The difference—one that Coleman and Jencks did not examine—involves the very significant question of "*Which* teachers?" Coleman and Jencks looked at whole school districts. When more recent researchers looked at individual teachers, they found significant differences, even within the same school.

In a 2010 report, Eric Hanushek, who has probably done as much as any scholar to put a spotlight on the difference a good teacher can make, wrote "The Economic Value of Higher Teacher Quality," in which he said:

> Some teachers year after year produce bigger gains in student learning than other teachers. The magnitude of the differences is truly large, with some teachers producing 1½ years of gain in achievement in an academic year while others with equivalent students produce only ½ year of gain. In other words, two students starting at the same level of achievement can know vastly different amounts at the end of a single academic year due solely to the teacher to which they are assigned. If a bad year is compounded by other bad years, it may not be possible for the student to recover. No other attribute of schools comes close to having this much influence on student achievement.[7]

That is a very significant statement for any aspiring teacher to consider. Teachers, it seems, do make a very real difference for good or for ill.

Kati Haycock of the Education Trust summarized much of the research about the role of good teachers in the lives of their students: "For decades, educators, educators-in-training and the public more broadly have been relentlessly fed the same message about achievement among poor and minority students. . . . Nothing schools do makes a very big difference." But it depends on how the question is asked. Haycock continues: "Recently, however, a number of large-scale studies provide convincing proof that what we do in education does matter. Schools—and especially teachers, it turns out—really DO make a difference. Earlier educational researchers just didn't have very good ways of measuring the variables." The end-of-chapter **Reading** describes the many studies that have convinced Haycock of the error of earlier approaches. She voices her frustration that for too long too many educators have clung to "dog-eared copies of the Coleman Report" and insisted that schools could not make a difference for poor children when in fact they can.[8]

What has changed is the kind of research that Haycock and her colleagues have conducted and the questions they have asked. Other researchers—notably William L. Sanders, Ronald F. Ferguson, and Linda Darling-Hammond—have reached similar conclusions as Hanushek and Haycock by looking at statewide or national data that provide much more information about individual teachers than was previously available. Instead of generalizing as Coleman and Jencks did about all poor students who attended a school or a district, these researchers have gotten much more specific. They have looked at differences in student performance in different classrooms in the same school, as well as at entire schools and school districts where special efforts have been made to ensure that many students have especially well qualified teachers. The differences have proved to be pretty amazing. A teacher just down the hall from another can have a significantly different impact on her or his students, regardless of the economic background or race of the students. Summarizing research that has been conducted by several different researchers working independently in different parts of the country, Haycock concludes:

> If we but took the simple step of assuring that poor and minority children had teachers of the same quality as other children, about half of the achievement gap would disappear. If we went further and assigned our best teachers to the students who most need them (a step, by the way, that makes sense to most people outside of education), there's persuasive evidence to suggest that we could entirely close the gap.[9]

The conclusion of this research is unambiguous. On one hand, those who entered teaching a decade ago (people who may have studied Coleman and Jencks as part of their preparation) inevitably faced the nagging question of whether anything they could ever do would make a difference in the lives of the students they would teach. The research at that time seemed to say no. On the other hand, for those who are teachers today or who are considering teaching, the research points in a very different direction. Do teachers make a difference? The answer is clear: "Good ones do . . . and they make a very big difference." This conclusion also puts a heavy burden on every teacher. If teaching makes a powerful difference when it is done expertly and well, then the responsibility is on us—quite dramatically on us—to be the best possible teachers, well prepared and ready to do whatever is needed to help our students succeed. The outcome, it turns out, is in our hands.

In the end, the debate between those who are most convinced by the research of Coleman and Jencks and those who find the research of Hanushek, Haycock, Sanders, Ferguson, and others more careful and compelling will probably continue for a long time. One study of teachers' attitudes conducted by the Public Agenda Foundation found that teachers were divided in their views. Indeed, they split almost evenly when asked, "Is student achievement mostly determined by such things as parental involvement and socioeconomic factors, or is teacher quality just as important?" Forty-two percent of practicing teachers said that external factors were most important, while 54% answered that teacher quality is just as important.[10] Part of the difference is in the way the question is asked. It is quite a different matter to ask "Do all teachers make a difference?" than to ask "Do teachers with certain skills and abilities and commitments make a difference?" It is also true that this is probably not an either-or debate. To say that teachers can make a meaningful difference for students is not the same thing as saying that teachers can or should make all of the difference in what students learn. Likewise, to say that poverty or prosperity or other external variables make a huge difference in learning is not to say that teachers cannot make a major difference—for good or for ill—in spite of such variables.

Sonia Nieto, who has spent many years teaching teachers and observing teachers in schools, says that early in her career as a teacher educator she began to doubt that teachers could make much of a difference for young people. However, as she continued to teach and work with teachers, she changed her mind. While her ideas are tempered by a realistic sense of the limitations to what teachers can do—limitations that Haycock may underestimate—teachers still can make an extraordinary difference. Nieto says: "I believe more strongly than ever in the power of teachers. This is because I have seen breathtaking teachers in action, and I have witnessed firsthand what they can achieve."[11]

Perhaps the right way to answer the question "Do teachers make a difference?" is with a qualified yes. A tempered optimism and an understanding that the larger society makes a difference *and* that teachers make a difference is probably the most realistic way to proceed. To assume that teachers make all the difference for students is to set ourselves up for constant failure and frustration. But to enter teaching—or stay in teaching—believing that teachers cannot make a difference is to engage in a meaningless activity. This leads us to the most important and difficult questions, which have to do with when and how teachers make a difference—indeed, to the very nature of what constitutes good teaching.

What Is a "Good Teacher"?

If it is true that good teaching matters—a lot—then the obvious question is, what constitutes good teaching? Or, according to current policy language, what is a "highly qualified teacher"? Though different researchers differ on the details, there is surprising consensus about what a good teacher should know and be able to do.

Teachers Need to Know Their Subject

Looking at teachers in Texas and Alabama whose students were most successful on the state examinations, researcher Ronald Ferguson found that these teachers themselves had scored well on their own tests. This could be interpreted to mean that people who are good test takers have a greater ability to teach their students how to take tests. However, there is probably much more to it than that. Teachers who have strong verbal and mathematics skills and know their subject matter very well seem to be much more effective than teachers who are less prepared and/or less confident.

Notes from the Field

What are the real rewards of teaching?

"Having been valedictorian of my high school class of 500 and voted Most Likely to Succeed, I feel as if society feels that successful people may teach for a while, but they do not stay in the classroom. To do so reflects a lack of ambition. This is reinforced by the pay structure. The only way to advance (except for salary step increases or taking college classes) is to go into administration. Those of us who love to teach and excel in the classroom will never realize the financial rewards of excellence in teaching. However, as we teachers know, we did not go into teaching for the money, and if that were our primary goal, we would have chosen another field. We may not make lots of money, but we do make a difference in the lives of each of our students. This is my reward."

—*Phyllis Hoyt, middle school mathematics teacher*

Other researchers have found a correlation not only between a teacher's test-taking success and that of his or her students but also between other measures of teacher content knowledge and student success. In a 2004 study of teachers in North Carolina done for the Urban Institute, Dan Goldhaber and Emily Anthony found that certification of teachers by the National Board for Professional Teaching standards had a high level of correlation with elementary student achievement. While the research also raised questions about the specific factors involved, it was clear from this large sample that individuals identified by the National Board as excellent teachers were having more success with students than their peers. In some fields, such as mathematics and the sciences, the research is clear that teachers who know more have more success with their students. Dan D. Goldhaber and Dominic J. Brewer's detailed examination of the National Educational Longitudinal Study of 1988 (discussed by Kati Haycock in the **Readings**) led them to see a clear link between what teachers had studied and how well their students learned. They concluded, "In mathematics and science, it is the teacher's subject-specific knowledge that is the important factor in determining tenth-grade achievement." Another study (also reported by Haycock) traced the achievement of elementary school students in Dallas, Texas. One group of third graders who averaged around the 55th percentile in mathematics was taught for the next 3 years by teachers who had a high level of mathematical knowledge and were viewed as highly effective teachers. At the end of fifth grade, these students scored, on

> **percentile**
> A ranking system commonly used for testing purposes that expresses an individual's position by the number of people at or below that position.

average, in the 76th **percentile**. Another group of students who started at about the same point—the 57th percentile in mathematics—were taught for the same amount of time by teachers who were viewed as the least effective mathematics teachers. At the end of fifth grade, this latter group scored at only the 27th percentile. Those who have been arguing for some time that high school teachers should have a college major in the subject they teach and that elementary school teachers also need broad content knowledge in the range of elementary school subjects were shown to be correct.[12]

Another scholar, Linda Darling-Hammond, also focuses on the need for teachers who know their subject and know it well. She writes that "as long as over 50,000 people a year who lack training for their positions have entered teaching on emergency or substandard licenses, as is now the case, we will never have the corps of teachers that our young people need." In the United States today, 25% of all high school teachers do not have at least a minor in the field they are teaching, and the percentage is 30% for mathematics, a subject for which research shows subject matter knowledge to be especially important. Fifty-six percent of high school students taking physical science are taught by "out of field" teachers. Darling-Hammond also notes that the teachers who know the least about their subject are concentrated in schools with the highest enrollments of students of color. In these schools, students have a less than 50% chance of having a science or mathematics teacher who holds a license and degree in the field in which he or she teaches. It's not surprising, then, that students in these schools do not seem to do as well in school as students in districts that can afford to hire true experts.[13]

Teachers Need to Understand How to Teach

Knowledge of subject matter, while essential to good teaching, is not sufficient. Teachers also need to know how to teach, how to connect with young people. In the introduction to *How People Learn*, which is included in the **Readings** for Chapter 5, John D. Bransford and his colleagues write that they believe many young people who have had difficulty in school might have done much better if their teachers had known more about effective instructional practices. Even students who have done well in school might have developed much more if their teachers had known the latest research on how people learn and the best ways to teach them.[14]

Knowing how to teach (i.e., having a mastery of pedagogy as well as content) is essential to effective teaching. Another scholar, Lee Shulman, coined the term *pedagogical content knowledge* for the essential ability to not only know a subject but also know how to communicate it to others. Knowing something is not the same as knowing how to ensure that others learn it. Knowing a subject is essential, but knowing how to communicate that subject to sometimes fidgety young children or bored adolescents is also essential. The latter skill is acquired only through a mix of academic study and guided clinical practice in school settings—watching good teachers teach, trying to teach while being observed and critiqued, and trying again. The combination of knowledge and teaching skill is essential to effective, sustained student learning.[15]

Regarding these issues, the differences among the researchers are small compared to the similarities. While not everyone would agree with Haycock when she says that the right teacher can offset virtually *any* impact of poverty or discrimination that students have experienced in their lives, few today would argue against the proposition that having a teacher who knows the subject matter very well, knows how to teach it very well, and is deeply committed to successful teaching is *the most* important guarantee of student success. Does teaching matter? The answer clearly is yes.

Teachers Need to be Passionate About What they Do

As important as knowledge of subject matter, and pedagogical skill may be, they are simply elements of good teaching. Another stream of research focuses on the less tangible, but just as important, aspect of a teacher's commitment—what Robert Fried calls "a teacher's passion." As he says in his book, *The Passionate Teacher*:

> ## Notes from the Field
>
> ### Was there a teacher who had a memorable impact on you?
>
> "One teacher who made an early and lasting impact on my understanding of art, creativity, and indeed pedagogy, was a woman named Helen. My mother enrolled me in her pottery class when I was about 13 that took place at a local college.
>
> "One day, we were told to make animals. I went about sculpting the expected prototype: a four legged thing, kind of a standing dog, frozen awkwardly. Helen approached, issued a rather annoyed look, and pinched its neck, stretching the clay upward and around with her thumb. Then she walked away. Within a second, she'd given the thing life—even at that age, I could recognize the transformation of something soulless into strong, daring expression. Its neck twisted dramatically. The creature was suddenly endowed with a kind of violent confusion. I didn't touch it. It went straight to the kiln, and when I brought it home, my mother, a modern dance choreographer, marveled at it, and praised my expressiveness. I never revealed the effect of Helen's touch.
>
> "In retrospect, I'm grateful to Helen for taking such a role in my 'authorship,' for invading my space, for giving me a dose of her raw artistic integrity. It was a moment of mindful apprenticeship—it's no small thing to feel connected to creativity, even when someone else provides you with this degree of momentum. Indeed, the next time around, my work showed far more of my own courage.
>
> "Occasionally, when I see a student struggling with her writing, I take the pen, craft a new sentence for her, then walk away. I'm aware that this sort of behavior flies in the face of progressive workshop instruction, but it feels right, and I can tell my kids appreciate the intensity of my help. I'm a writer, no? I'm a writer, and it's my job to share the tools of my craft, and, as often as possible, to give students the sensation of writing well. That's the Helen in me."
>
> —*Avi Kline, high school writing and English teacher*

Yet as I look into hundreds of classrooms, watch teachers working with all kinds of students, when I ask myself what makes the greatest difference in the quality of student learning—it is a teacher's passion that leaps out. More than knowledge of subject matter. More than variety of teaching techniques. More than being well-organized, or friendly, or funny, or fair. Passion.[16]

> ## CONNECTIONS ➔←
>
> In Chapter 5, we'll review a number of theories about how students learn.

Some researchers may question whether passion counts for *more than* knowledge of subject matter or specific pedagogical skills, but few would challenge the essential mix of passion, skill, and knowledge in the definition of good teaching.

Teachable Moment
THE LESSON YOU NEVER FORGET

Marta Cruz-Janzen, a professor in the Department of Teacher Education at Florida Atlantic University, tells of her experiences with the negative messages she received in school in Puerto Rico as a young Latina girl whose first language was Spanish and whose family was poor. Everything seemed to reinforce low expectations. Success in school—and certainly aiming for college—was not for her, it seemed.

Then one teacher made a difference. Cruz-Janzen says, "I never forget my fourth grade teacher. She told me, 'I want you to start looking at universities in the United States,' and she brought me catalogs about all the universities on the mainland. She told me that if I was going to do that, I needed to learn English and she started teaching me English at a very young age, but it stayed with me."

Cruz-Janzen transferred to a high school in New York City. After graduation, she attended Cornell University, received her master's degree at Columbia University, and earned her Ph.D. at the University of Denver. She was a teacher and a principal and now teaches other aspiring teachers. Her career was possible, at least in part, because one fourth-grade teacher knew she could make a difference.

Katherine Hanson, coauthor of the book that describes Cruz-Janzen's story, responds to the question "What can a teacher do?" by proposing three actions:

1. Learn more about your own expectations or stereotypes of students or groups.
2. Test your assumptions about who is likely to do well, making sure not to favor one group of students over another.
3. Learn what resources are available to students who may need extra or a different kind of help or support so you can refer students to them.

As this example shows, teachers can make an extraordinary difference—even if it's only one child at a time.

Questions

- Can you think of a time when you felt the way Marta Cruz-Janzen did as a young child; that school or academic success just did not seem to be for you? What made a difference for you? Can you think of a teacher who intervened in your life the way Cruz-Janzen's teacher did and who pointed you in a different direction or revealed new options to you?
- How can you incorporate Hanson's recommendations into your daily routine as a teacher as well as into your overall philosophy on education?

Sources: Katherine Hanson, Vivian Guilfoy, & Sarita Nair-Pillai. *More Than Title IX: How Equity in Education Has Shaped the Nation.* Lanham, MD: Rowman & Littlefield, 2009; interview with Katherine Hanson, June 24, 2009.

Any discussion of good teaching quickly leads us to ask, "Who were my *best* teachers?" and "What made them different?" While there are many answers to these questions, certain themes are repeated over and over when we start thinking about outstanding teachers—our own or ones we have observed teaching others.

Teachers Need an Ethical Commitment to Their Work

In addition to a teacher's knowledge of subject matter, understanding of pedagogy, and passion for teaching, a fourth element of good teaching must not be ignored. Teachers need to be deeply ethical professionals who reflect their ethical commitment to their students in the way they do their work.

DID YOU KNOW?

The nation's largest teacher union, the National Education Association, has a Code of Ethics for the Education Profession that says

"The educator, believing in the worth and dignity of each human being, recognizes the supreme importance of the pursuit of truth, devotion to excellence, and the nurture of the democratic principles. Essential to these goals is the protection of freedom to learn and to teach and the guarantee of equal educational opportunity for all. The educator accepts the responsibility to adhere to the highest ethical standards."

Source: National Education Association, Code of Ethics, 1975.

In 2011, the New York State Board of Regents revised the Code of **Ethics** for Educators (see the **Readings** for this chapter). It reveals just how much the view of teachers has changed since the days when Horace Mann called for every teacher to be clothed "in garments of virtue." In the New York code, virtue is not enough. If teaching really does matter and if teachers really do make a difference—or at least have the potential to make a difference—then they must embrace the opportunity to make a difference for all students, not merely as models of distant virtue but as active, engaging participants in the teaching and learning process.

To that end, the New York code begins with a call for every educator to nurture the intellectual, physical, emotional, social, and civic potential of each student. It goes on to insist that to do so educators must "commit to their own learning in order to develop their practice." Ethical educators who follow this code are expected to collaborate with colleagues, other professionals, and parents and community members in fostering a vibrant intellectual and ethical foundation for learning.

> **ethics**
> Addresses what constitutes right or wrong behavior in both a professional or personal environment.

If teachers are merely models of virtue, as Mann seemed to assume, then this vibrant intellectual and ethical commitment is far too much to ask of them. If teachers are merely cogs in a well-oiled machine administered by others, or if teachers are so insignificant that they need "teacher-proof curricula" to protect their students, then a code like this is simply irrelevant. Indeed, if teachers are limited by external factors—by the class and race of their students—as Coleman and Jencks seemed to assume, then this code makes outrageous and unacceptable demands on them. If, however, researchers and philosophers like Kati Haycock and Robert Fried are right, if teachers can make the most important difference in the learning of their students, then this code of ethical conduct is right on target.

> **CONNECTIONS** ➔◀
> In Chapter 10, we will explore a teacher's professional ethics as related to both legal ramifications and issues of fairness.

When things go wrong around us and, for whatever reason, our students fail to learn, we would love to be able to say, "It's not my fault." Of course, at times circumstances beyond our control affect things in the classroom, in spite of our best efforts, and learning does not take place. However, the clear conclusion of the current research is that those moments are much rarer than many like to acknowledge. An awesome responsibility goes with teaching. It is a sobering fact, but it is also encouraging. In the end, who wants to be part of a profession that really does not make much of a difference? If "good teaching matters . . . a lot," then teaching can be some of the most meaningful, ethical, and powerful work there is to do.

How Does a Good Teacher Involve Parents and the Community?

A Web of Relationships

Educator and author Jacqueline Jordan Irvine adds another significant element to the definition of good teaching: The best teachers understand that they are part—an important part, but only one part—of a web of significant relationships in a young person's life. In her book *In Search of Wholeness*, Irvine writes about what she calls "other mothering," a sense of personal attachment and kinship that many African American teachers felt toward African American children in segregated classrooms. As Irvine describes it:

> These African American teachers were attached both to the individual child as well as the race. Their willingness to "adopt" was not solely because of their desire to help a child but also to advance the entire race. These "other mothers" had strong beliefs about their students' ability to achieve despite widely publicized data, such as the black-white achievement gap, that could have convinced them otherwise.[17]

As Irvine has also noted, not all effective teachers—African American or otherwise—choose to see themselves as second mothers to their students. But all teachers can learn something from the concept of "other mothering." When a teacher has high expectations and sees a student as connected to a web of social relationships within a family and community, the teacher can draw on resources unavailable to a teacher who focuses his or her instruction on each student as an isolated individual.

Teachers who make connections among the subjects being taught, the individual needs of their students, and the community context in which their students are living are going to be the most successful. On another occasion, Irvine wrote that "effective teachers love and care about the student whom they teach, and they also love and are excited about the subject that they teach." The two attributes cannot be divided if high level learning is to be achieved.

If Irvine is right—and there is ample evidence that she is—then teachers need to know the subjects they teach very well and need to know their students in the context of their families and communities equally well. Only when all aspects of a student's life are connected—the material the student needs to master and the context in which the student decides that the learning matters—can successful teaching really take place.

Parents and Other Caregivers

The first and most important network in every child's life is the family, whether it is a traditional nuclear family, some other form of kinship group, or a web of caregiving friends. Yet families and schools do not automatically work easily or well together. In communities in which both caregivers and teachers share a similar socioeconomic background and cultural experience, common purpose can be based on common assumptions. For all their very real problems, the segregated African American schools of the pre–*Brown* decision South often reflected this strength because of the existence of a unified African American community.

Many middle-class suburbs in the United States today, perhaps especially those that are primarily all-White communities, also have this attribute. However, in too many other cases, parents and teachers have different backgrounds, seem to speak a different language, and cannot be expected to automatically trust each other.

Child psychiatrist James P. Comer—who has become one of the leading advocates for parental involvement in schools based on his many years of working with community groups and schools in New Haven, Connecticut—describes what can happen when people begin to try to build stronger bridges between home and school. As he notes, "In the most severely dysfunctional schools, parents, teachers, and administrators don't like, trust, or respect one another." This distrust leads to a culture in which students do not learn very much and in which everyone blames everyone else for the problem. This sense of powerlessness in turn leads to ever more anger and less progress.[18]

It was in a school with just these problems that Comer and his colleagues succeeded in building bridges between parents and school teachers and administrators. Their "Comer model" and the program based on it are now a national framework for how such connections can be built. However, as Comer reminds us, the work is not easy.

A generation ago, many aspiring teachers were taught how to "deal with parents," as if parents were some sort of problem or irritant in the otherwise smooth functioning of the schools. As Comer and others found, this approach was not effective. Parents, especially poor and marginalized parents, were hardly mollified by the efforts of school leaders and teachers to "deal with" them. More fundamentally, there was a profound flaw in the idea that parents were a problem to be managed rather than the most natural and important ally a teacher could have. To assume that every parent will view teachers as allies would certainly be naive. In cases when the school is dominated by educators who have low expectations for their students, parents should not trust school officials. When parents are overly intrusive teachers need to resist. However, researchers and activists like Comer have shown that, with patience, a powerful alliance can be built between school and home, teacher and parent. When that happens, the child is the beneficiary.

Many parents, especially parents who themselves have not had particularly positive experiences in school, can be resentful of schools and the professionals who work in them. If parents were not treated with respect when they were students or if their school was a place that had low expectations for them or related to them as failures, they certainly will approach schools and teachers with wariness as adults. After he got over his initial shock at how deep the divide was between parents and schools, Comer discovered that if a program to include parents were to succeed it needed to be based on respect—real and deep respect, not merely the illusion of respect. Parents and staff needed to be brought together in schools in ways that made the schools a community. Power needed to be shared.

Recently, a group of researchers focused on the ways many Chinese American parents view their involvement in schools. For many Asian Americans, the notion of attending meetings at school or participating in school governance is antithetical to powerful cultural traditions, and they much prefer a "backstage/behind-the-scene" approach. And it is not only Asian parents who feel that way. Studies of groups of Mexican and Haitian immigrant families have found that they too are cautious about becoming active at their children's school, wanting instead to respect what they see as the quite separate spheres of home and school. While some parents may come to feel very comfortable participating actively in the life of their children's school, other parents will see their role as supporting the school's message at home by helping with homework and ensuring that it is done, setting high standards for their children, and promoting discipline and respect, for example. It is essential that teachers not confuse a parent's reluctance to take part in what any one school considers parent involvement activities with lack of interest or concern for their children.[19] As Comer says in another article, "While we strongly support the practice of direct parental involvement in the work of schools, there is evidence that children from families . . . that facilitate academic learning at home often do well in school without direct parental involvement."[20]

Recent research has also shown that young people need different kinds of parental involvement at different stages of their lives. In an article included in the **Readings** for this chapter, William H. Jeynes argues that "parent involvement that works" is adapted to the age level of the students involved. While there is clear evidence that things like attending a student play, talking with teachers about a child's work, or setting clear times for homework make a significant difference in the lives of elementary-level students, something different is needed with adolescents. As students get older, the same person who once welcomed parents to school may be embarrassed by their presence in high school. Children who felt secure when parents checked their homework may rebel if it is done when they are in their teens. Nevertheless, Jeynes argues, there is evidence that adolescents also need parental involvement, just of a different kind. If a parent is wise enough to shift gears, then, Jeynes insists, the "subtle aspects of that involvement are actually larger for secondary school students."

While teachers need to find as many ways as possible to build bridges to parents—to welcome them into the life of schools on the parents' terms, not merely on the school's terms—teachers as professionals also need to respect a wide range of parental involvement. Even as teachers welcome and encourage parental involvement, the lack of such **activism** on the part of parents who for whatever reason simply cannot or will not be involved can never be an excuse for failure. However, parent involvement, when it does happen, can dramatically improve the atmosphere for learning.

> **activism**
> Using action to achieve a goal or result.

A Community Network

In 2000, a book appeared that quickly became a best seller in large part because it spoke so well to a generalized and lingering uneasiness that many people in the United States had come to feel. The book was *Bowling Alone,* by Harvard professor Robert D. Putnam. Putnam wrote:

> Television, two-career families, suburban sprawl, generational changes in values—these and other changes in American society have meant that fewer and fewer of us find that the League of Women Voters, or the United Way, or the Shriners, or the monthly bridge club, or even a Sunday picnic with friends fits the way we have come to live.

Our growing social-capital deficit threatens educational performance, safe neighborhoods, equitable tax collection, democratic responsiveness, everyday honesty, and even our health and happiness.[21]

While Putnam consistently pleaded that his book shouldn't be read as a nostalgic paean to a romantic past when community bonds were stronger and people spent more time in small communities, from bowling leagues to churches, almost every reviewer took it just that way. Many Americans, it seemed, longed for the days when more time was spent in small face-to-face communities around shared common interests. Putnam's ideas are terribly important for anyone who wants to see teachers and schools make a difference for young people. Our educational future is indeed at risk if we do not take time to talk to our neighbors.

Teachable Moment
IT TAKES A COMMUNITY

In her study of African American schooling in the segregated South prior to the implementation of the *Brown v. Board of Education* decision, researcher Vanessa Siddle Walker paints a portrait of a powerful kind of community involvement. Few have any nostalgia for the South of the pre-civil rights era, when schools, churches, and communities were segregated by race and when "separate and equal" really meant rigidly separate and very unequal in terms of resources, access to opportunity, and the "pursuit of happiness." Yet, she notes, it was partly as a result of the terrible discrimination of segregation and the need to unite in the face of that assault that the African American community came together in support of its schools.

Walker describes the case of Caswell County, North Carolina, where often desperately poor parents came together to raise the funds needed to ensure that the school their children attended was first-rate, even if this fundraising was a kind of "double taxation" because they paid taxes that mostly supported the White schools. The school's teachers and administrators also made connections to parents and families at multiple levels. One parent remembered the longtime principal of the school, Nicholas Longworth Dillard: "He visited my home a lot of times. He would get around. Then another thing he would do—if his children's [relatives] or somebody passed, he would try to make it to the churches to the funerals. He had a closeness to people."

Looking back at this example of a time when the community, parents, and teachers were united in support of their school's young people, Walker concludes:

Longtime residents of this Caswell County community who participated in the CCTS [Caswell Country Training School] culture remember the interaction between school and community as a collaborative relationship, a kind of mutual ownership in which the community and the school looked out for each other's needs—the parents depended on the school's expertise, guidance, and academic vision, and the school depended on the parents' financial contributions, advocacy, and home-front support. They were united in a common mission to provide a quality education for their children.

Caswell County was far from unique. Across the segregated South, in many African American communities, the sense of a common mission gave focus to all their efforts.

Questions

- What would it take to build similar community support—a similar sense of "common ownership"—for schools in the more prosperous, sometimes much less closely connected communities in which most North Americans live in the 21st century?
- What is a teacher's role in fostering such communities?

Source: Emilie V. Siddle Walker. "Caswell County Training School, 1933–1969: Relationships between community and school." *Harvard Educational Review* 63, no. 2 (Summer 1993): 161–182, citations pp. 174, 175.

At the end of *Bowling Alone*, Putnam calls on everyone to play a role in building a more engaged community, which could include a community of support for schools. He wrote: "So our challenge is to restore American community for the twenty-first century through both collective and individual initiative."

One critical group in any effort to build stronger community ties in any location must certainly be teachers. As the professionals closest to the schools and the young people who inhabit them, teachers cannot wait passively for such community support to develop. They must be among those who take primary responsibility for fostering community engagement. A teacher who is active in the life of the community where he or she teaches will find that many parents and community residents respond with appreciation and that, in the end, there is much more community support for the teacher and the school as a result.

Notes from the Field

"Why Do You Walk to Work?"

"It happens every year. Usually around the first month or so of school, a student will come into class and ask: 'Ms. Cuffman, do you *walk* to school?' Invariably, they ask with an incredulous look, having seen me on the sidewalk. They can't quite believe that a real live adult, presumably in possession of a drivers' license, would willingly walk anywhere.

My first commitment to the community where my students live is living there myself. Many of my colleagues say they couldn't handle living amongst their students, and I agree it's probably not for everyone. But the benefits are so worth it. When I tell a student on Monday how nice it was to say hi to them at the movies on Friday, I am showing that I like them and that they are seen. I am also showing that their community knows them and might notice if they began making bad choices. When I see how excited and surprised my students are to spot me at their football game, I know that they are experiencing the support and safety that comes from knowing adults care about them. When I bring my husband to a fundraising dinner orchestrated by some of my undocumented students, I show them that people are interested in what they are doing and that I am proud of their hard work."

—Lydia Cuffman, Redwood City, California

✔ CHAPTER REVIEW

- What does the evidence say about the difference a good teacher can make?

Over the years, educators and researchers have had different opinions as to whether teachers—and education—have any impact on a student's success in life, especially for students living in poverty. A century and a half ago Horace Mann contended that teachers should be able to teach subjects they had mastered themselves, but in many places teachers were expected to simply teach uniformly, with some administrators later supporting a "teacher-proof curriculum" that required little mastery of the material by the teacher. With the war on poverty in the 1960s, the Johnson administration focused on education as a key means of ending poverty, but in the 1970s, the Coleman and Jencks reports seemed to say that teachers had little or no impact on a student's lot in life. Years later, research by Eric Hanushek, Kati Haycock, and others concluded that contrary to Coleman and Jencks, good teaching matters—a lot.

- What is a "good teacher"?

While it is hard to define specifically what we mean by a good teacher, we do know that a good teacher has a command of the subject matter he or she is teaching, not simply the ability to "stay one chapter ahead of the students" but rather to be able to travel with students on those adventures on which their active imaginations may lead them. A good teacher also knows the pedagogical methods that will work with a specific age group and possesses a strong passion for his or her work, so that young people will experience an invigorating interest in the subject and understand that the teacher has an equally determined interest in their success. Teachers also need to be deeply ethical professionals whose commitment to their students is reflected in the way they do their work.

- How does a good teacher involve parents and the community?

An effective teacher has an understanding of and respect for the parents, the community, and the surrounding world that shape each of his or her students and with which the teacher must connect in order to be successful.

Readings

What Does the Evidence Say About the Difference a Good Teacher Can Make?

From "GOOD TEACHING MATTERS"

AUTHOR: KATI HAYCOCK

As the following article makes clear, Kati Haycock's research points to a powerful answer to the question of what difference good teaching makes. Haycock and her colleagues at the Education Trust, a national center for educational research and advocacy, have concluded that good teaching makes a greater difference than anything else—greater than the impact of poverty, race, or any other factor. While articles like this call for national policies that will ensure a first-rate teacher in every classroom, they also call to all current and future teachers to take their work more seriously than ever before.

For decades, educators, educators-in-training and the public more broadly have been relentlessly fed the same message about achievement among poor and minority students: "Because of poverty and other neighborhood conditions, these students enter school behind other students. As they progress through the grades, the deficits accumulate, leaving them further and further behind other students." Their conclusion? Nothing schools do makes a very big difference.

As an organization, we have questioned the prevailing explanation for some time. "If poverty always overwhelms everything else," we ask, "what explains the 89% pass rate on the Texas state assessment by the Loma Terrace School in El Paso where almost 90% of the children are poor? Or what about the 95% fourth grade pass rate on the same exam by the entire Mission Independent School District with a 94% poverty rate? And why, if schools really don't make a difference, are the low-income students in Community School District #2 in New York City performing so much higher now than were their counterparts a decade ago?"

Always, the response is the same. "It's that superstar principal/superintendent (choose one). We can't expect those kinds of feats from the mere mortals who lead most of our schools."

But what if that answer is wrong? What if these schools are succeeding not on the force of someone's personality, but simply by teaching students what they need to know to perform at high levels? What if, in other words, poor and minority students are performing below other students not because something is wrong with them or their families, but because most schools don't bother to teach them what they need to know?

By now, those of you who are familiar with our work know that we are absolutely convinced—by both research and extensive experience in classrooms all over the country—that poor and minority youngsters will achieve at the same high levels as other students if they are taught at those levels. In our groundbreaking report, *Education Watch: The Education Trust National and State Data Book,* we document the clear relationship between low standards, low-level curriculum, undereducated teachers, and poor results. We argue, further, that if states and school districts work hard on these three issues, they can close the achievement gap.

Most of the time, we have felt as Ron Edmonds undoubtedly felt: surrounded by researchers clinging to dog-eared copies of the *Coleman Report* and arguing that nothing works.

Recently, however, a number of large-scale studies provide convincing proof that what we do in education does matter. Schools—and especially teachers, it turns out—really *do* make a difference. Earlier educational researchers just didn't have very good ways of measuring the variables.

We have chosen to focus this issue of *Thinking K–16* on what all of the studies conclude is the most significant factor in student achievement: the teacher. We focus here not because we think improvements in teachers' capabilities or changes in teacher assignment patterns are, by themselves, a silver bullet, but because such changes are clearly more important to increasing student achievement—especially among poor and minority students—than any other.

We focus on teacher qualifications here also because this is an issue within our power to change. If we but took the simple step of assuring that poor and minority children had teachers of the same quality as other children, about half of the achievement gap would disappear. If we went further and assigned our best teachers to the students who most need them (a step, by the way, that makes sense to most people outside of education), there's persuasive evidence to suggest that we could entirely close the gap.

Thought provoking, yes? Read on.

Good Teaching Matters . . . a Lot

Parents have always known that it matters a lot which teachers their children get. That is why those with the time and skills to do so work very hard to assure that, by hook or by crook, their children are assigned to the best teachers. (That is also at least part of the reason why the children of less skilled parents are often left with the worst teachers, but more on that later.)

Professional educators typically reject these notions. When parents ask for their children to be assigned to a particular teacher, or to be moved out of the classroom of another, most principals counsel them not to worry. "Your child will learn what he or she needs to from any of our teachers."

Recent research from Tennessee, Texas, Massachusetts, and Alabama proves that parents have been right all along. They may not always know which teachers really are the best, but they are absolutely right in believing that their children will learn a lot from some teachers and only a little from others—even though the two teachers may be in adjacent classrooms. "The difference between a good and a bad teacher can be a full level of achievement in a single school year," says Eric Hanushek, the University of Rochester economist notorious for macroanalyses suggesting that virtually nothing seems to make a difference.

Teacher Effects: Tennessee

Tennessee is one of the few states with data systems that make it possible to tie teachers to achievement in their classrooms. Moreover, the state's value-added approach for assessing student achievement allows observers to look at the gains students make during a particular school year. William L. Sanders, director of the Value-Added Research and Assessment Center at the University of Tennessee, Knoxville, has studied these data extensively. By grouping teachers into quintiles based on their effectiveness in producing student learning gains, his work allows us to examine the impact of teacher effectiveness on the learning of different types of students, from low- to high-achievers.

The chart shows the effect teachers from different quintile levels have on low-achieving students. On average, the least effective teachers (Q1) produce gains of about 14 percentile points during the school year. By contrast, the most effective teachers (Q5) posted gains among low-achieving students that averaged 53 percentile points.

The Tennessee data show dramatic differences for middle- and high-achieving groups of students, too. For example, high-achieving students gain an average of only 2 points under the direction of Q1 (least effective) teachers but an average of 25 points under the guidance of Q5 (most effective) teachers. Middle achievers gain a mere 10 points with Q1 teachers but in the mid-30s with Q5 teachers.

There is also considerable evidence that, at least in Tennessee, the effects of teachers are long-lived, whether they advance student achievement or squash it. Indeed, even two years after the fact, the performance of fifth-grade students is still affected

Table 2.1

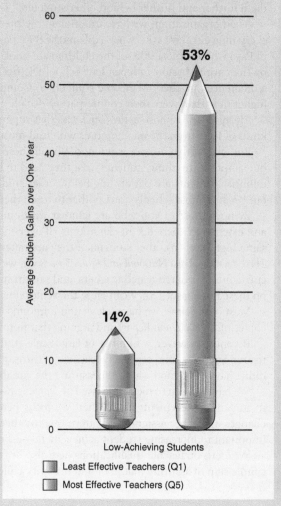

The Effect of Different Teachers on Low-Achieving Students
Tennessee

Average Student Gains over One Year

53%

14%

Low-Achieving Students

☐ Least Effective Teachers (Q1)
☐ Most Effective Teachers (Q5)

by the quality of their third-grade teacher. The chart shows the examples of different patterns of teacher effectiveness for one metropolitan system.

As Sanders points out, students whose initial achievement levels are comparable have "vastly different academic outcomes as a result of the sequence of teachers to which they are assigned." Differences of this magnitude—50 percentile points—are stunning. As all of us know only too well, they can represent the difference between a "remedial" label and placement in the "accelerated" or even "gifted" track. And the difference between entry into a selective college and a lifetime at McDonald's.

Teacher Effects: Dallas

A variety of recent studies in Texas show similar differences in achievement between students taught by teachers of differing quality. Borrowing from some of Sanders's techniques, researchers in the Dallas Independent School District recently completed their first-ever study of teacher effects on the ability of students to perform on assessments. In sharing their findings, Robert Mendro, the district's executive director of institutional research, said, "what surprised us the most was the size of the effect."

For example, the average reading scores of a group of Dallas fourth graders who were assigned to three highly effective teachers in a row rose from the 59th percentile in fourth grade to the 76th percentile by the conclusion of sixth grade. A fairly similar (but slightly higher achieving) group of students was assigned three consecutive ineffective teachers and fell from the 60th percentile in fourth grade to the 42nd percentile by the end of sixth grade. A gap of this magnitude—more than 35 percentile points—for students who started off roughly the same is hugely significant.

Table 2.2

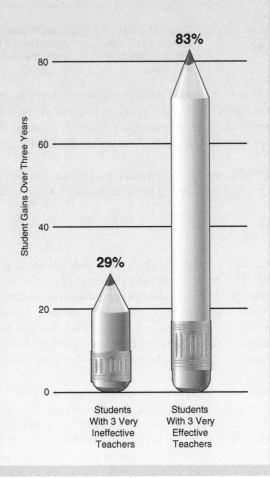

Cumulative Effects of Teacher Sequence on Fifth Grade Math Scores
Tennessee

Table 2.3

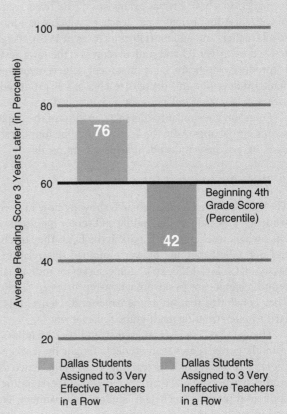

Effects on Students' Reading Scores in Dallas (Grades 4–6)

The impact of teacher effectiveness is also clear in mathematics. For example, a group of beginning third graders in Dallas who averaged around the 55th percentile in mathematics scored around the 76th percentile at the end of fifth grade after being assigned to three highly effective teachers in a row. By contrast, a slightly higher achieving group of third graders—averaging around the 57th percentile—were consecutively taught by three of the least effective teachers. By the conclusion of fifth grade, the second group's percentile ranking had fallen to 27th. This time the youngsters, who had scored nearly the same as beginning third graders, were separated by a full 50 percentile points just three years later.

What Makes for Teacher Effectiveness?

None of these studies has yet advanced to the obvious next step: identifying the qualities that make for an effective teacher. But other researchers have used Texas's extensive database on both teachers and students to examine the impact of specific teacher characteristics on student achievement. Together with work from Alabama and North Carolina, this research helps us to get underneath the matter of teacher effectiveness.

1. Strong Verbal and Math Skills

The first thing that is clear when you look across the various studies is the critical importance of strong verbal and math skills. Harvard's Ronald F. Ferguson, for example, has looked closely at the relationship between student achievement and teacher performance on a basic literacy examination (the Texas Examination of Current Administrators and Teachers, which was administered to all teachers and administrators in Texas in 1986). Ferguson found a significant positive relationship between teacher test scores on TECAT and student scores on the Iowa Test of Basic Skills (ITBS), with higher scoring teachers more likely to produce significant gains in student achievement than their lower scoring counterparts. Indeed, a change of one standard deviation in a district's teacher scores produced a corresponding change of .17 standard deviation in student scores, when other differences were controlled.

Ferguson got similar results in an analysis of the impact of teacher and classroom qualities on student achievement scores in Alabama. As in the Texas studies, he found a strong positive relationship between teacher test scores (in this case, ACT scores) and student achievement results.

2. Deep Content Knowledge

There is also considerable research showing how important teachers' content knowledge is to their effectiveness with students, especially at the middle and senior high school levels. The data are especially clear in mathematics and science where teachers with majors in the fields they teach routinely get higher student performance than teachers who did not. Goldhaber and Brewer examined this relationship using data from the National Educational Longitudinal Study of 1988 (NELS), an ongoing survey of individuals who were in eighth grade in 1988. Goldhaber and Brewer found a significant positive relationship between teachers' degrees and students' achievement in technical subjects. They concluded that "in mathematics and science, it is the teacher subject-specific knowledge that is the important factor in determining tenth-grade achievement."

The data are less clear in English and social studies; in these subjects students taught by majors don't show consistently better scores than students taught by teachers who majored in something else. However, other evidence suggests that content is no less important in these two disciplines. For example, a recent study in Hawaii asked social studies teachers to rate their own level of understanding about various historical periods and teaching methods, then compared teacher expertise to student achievement. Not surprisingly, there was an almost perfect match: students performed best in the domains where teachers indicated the most expertise.

Table 2.4

Effects on Students' Math Scores in Dallas (Grades 3–5)

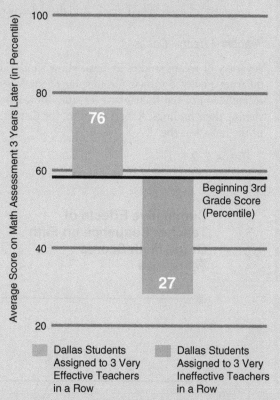

Dallas Students Assigned to 3 Very Effective Teachers in a Row

Dallas Students Assigned to 3 Very Ineffective Teachers in a Row

3. Teaching Skill?

All of this seems to beg the question: what about teaching knowledge and skills? Is content knowledge really sufficient for effective teaching? Clearly not. One only has to spend a few semesters in higher education to see that the deep content knowledge inherent in the Ph.D. doesn't necessarily lead to effective teaching.

That said, the large-scale studies we have reviewed are not particularly helpful in identifying ways to quantify teaching expertise. Neither education courses completed, advanced education degrees, scores on professional knowledge sections of licensure exams nor, interestingly, years of experience seem to have a clear relationship to student achievement. Perhaps the work going on at the National Board for Professional Teaching Standards or Lee Shulman's work on "pedagogical content knowledge" at the Carnegie Foundation for the Advancement of Teaching will advance our understanding of—and options for developing and measuring—teaching knowledge and skill.

In the meantime, we suggest that educational leaders not get sidetracked: there is more than sufficient evidence about the importance of deep content knowledge and strong verbal skills to serve as a foundation for immediate action. At the very least, we know enough to call the question with faculty in the arts and sciences, who, after all, are responsible for developing both content knowledge and verbal skills among intending teachers. It is also enough to justify a second look at hiring and assignment criteria. If good teachers matter, we need to be sure that we are getting the best we can.

Inequities in Distribution

Our emerging understanding of the critical importance of good teachers has especially profound implications for poor and minority youngsters. For no matter how quality is defined, these youngsters come up on the short end. While the teaching force in high-poverty and high-minority communities certainly includes some of the most dedicated and talented teachers in the country, the truth is that these teachers are vastly outnumbered by under- and, indeed, unqualified colleagues.

These patterns are clear in national data tabulations on out-of-field teaching specially prepared for the Education Trust earlier this year by Richard Ingersoll, a professor at the University of Georgia. As is evident in the table, minority and poor youngsters—the very youngsters who are most dependent on their teachers for content knowledge—are systematically taught by teachers with the least content knowledge.

Similar inequities show up at all grade levels in the state-level studies described above, and many more. For example, in Tennessee, black students are almost twice as likely to be taught by ineffective "Q1" teachers as are white children, and are considerably less likely to be taught by the most effective teachers.

The patterns look quite similar in Texas, where, according to researchers John Kain and Kraig Singleton, African American and Latino children are far more likely to be taught by teachers who scored poorly on the TECAT examination. Indeed, as the percentage of non-white children in the school increases, the average teacher score declines. Finding the same patterns in his analysis, Ferguson wrote that "[i]n Texas, and certainly in other places too, attracting and retaining talented people with strong skills to teach in the districts where black students are heavily represented is part of the unfinished business of equalizing educational opportunity."

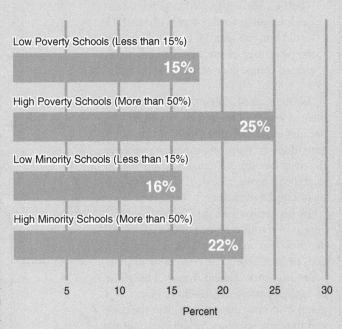

Table 2.5

Percentage of Classes Taught by Teachers Lacking a Major in Field, 1993–1994

Low Poverty Schools (Less than 15%) — 15%
High Poverty Schools (More than 50%) — 25%
Low Minority Schools (Less than 15%) — 16%
High Minority Schools (More than 50%) — 22%

Percent

Race More Than Class?

Contrary to the assumptions that many people may make, inequities in the distribution of teacher expertise are not driven wholly by finances. If they were, we would expect that poor minority children would have teachers of about the same quality as poor white children. But such is not always the case.

In their analysis of Texas data, Kain and Singleton found disturbing differences. Poor white children, it turns out, appear to have a higher likelihood of having well qualified teachers than poor black children.

Similar patterns are evident in teacher quality data from other states. For example, it is clear that students who attend predominantly minority secondary schools in Virginia are more likely to be taught by underqualified teachers than students who attend high-poverty secondary schools. The same is true in Pennsylvania and Oklahoma: students in high-minority secondary schools are more likely to be taught by teachers without a college major in the subject they are teaching.

The problems in central cities are particularly acute, according to a 1995 report from the National Governors Association: "Emergency hiring, assignment of teachers outside their fields of preparation, and high turnover in underfunded schools conspire to produce a situation in which many poor and minority students are taught throughout their entire school careers by a steady stream of the least qualified and experienced teachers."

A More Equitable Distribution of Teacher Expertise

What would happen if minority and poor children had teachers of the same quality as other children? A large part of the gap would simply disappear. The estimates vary somewhat depending upon the statistical model used, but in no case is the effect minor.

- Ferguson's modeling for several metropolitan Alabama districts suggests that an increase of 1 standard deviation in the test scores of teachers who teach black children would produce a decline of about two-thirds in the black/white test score gap in that state.
- Strauss's study of student achievement in North Carolina suggested that a 1% relative increase in teacher scores on the NTE would bring about a 5% relative decline in the percentage of students who fail standardized competency exams.

In other words, much of what we have blamed on children and their families for decades is actually the result of things we have done to them. As a nation, we have deprived our neediest students of the very ingredient most important to learning: a highly qualified teacher.

In his analyses of the Texas data base, Ferguson found a small number of school districts that are exceptions to the general pattern (see chart). A look at how their youngsters benefit from a steady diet of higher performing teachers gives us a glimpse of how the national data for poor and minority students *could* look . . . if we had the will.

Questions

1. Have you ever heard the argument "Teachers and schools cannot make a difference if kids grow up in poverty"?
2. What do you think of Haycock's response to that argument?

Table 2.6

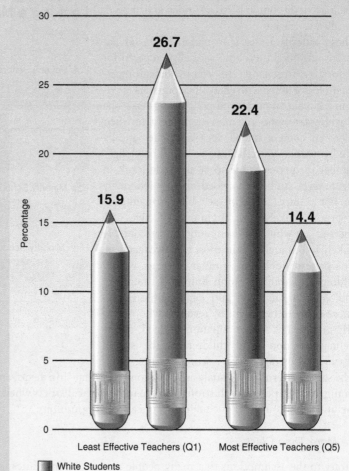

African American Students Are More Likely to Have Underqualified Teachers
Tennessee

Least Effective Teachers (Q1): 15.9, 26.7
Most Effective Teachers (Q5): 22.4, 14.4

White Students
African American Students

3. Is the United States—or are most local communities—ready to make the kind of commitment Haycock calls for?
4. Are Hancock's proposals realistic?

Source: Kati Haycock. "Good Teaching Matters: How Well-Qualified Teachers Can Close the Gap." *Thinking K-16* 3, no. 2 (1998): 1–14. Washington, DC: The Education Trust.

What Is a "Good Teacher"?
From NEW YORK STATE CODE OF ETHICS FOR EDUCATORS

In 2011, the Board of Regents of the State of New York reviewed the Code of Ethics for Teachers. The code was based on several years of discussion that the staff and members of the State Professional Standards and Practices Board of Teaching began in 1998, in consultation with colleagues across the state. The process included public comment so that as many educators as possible had a voice in the development of the code, which was first issued in 2002. Its goal was to provide an agreed-on ethical underpinning for the work of classroom teachers throughout New York.

Statement of Purpose

The Code of Ethics is a public statement by educators that sets clear expectations and principles to guide practice and inspire professional excellence. Educators believe a commonly held set of principles can assist in the individual exercise of professional judgment. This Code speaks to the core values of the profession. "Educator" as used throughout means all educators serving New York schools in positions requiring a certificate, including classroom teachers, school leaders and pupil personnel service providers.

Principle 1: Educators nurture the intellectual, physical, emotional, social, and civic potential of each student.

Educators promote growth in all students through the integration of intellectual, physical, emotional, social and civic learning. They respect the inherent dignity and worth of each individual. Educators help students to value their own identity, learn more about their cultural heritage, and practice social and civic responsibilities. They help students to reflect on their own learning and connect it to their life experience. They engage students in activities that encourage diverse approaches and solutions to issues, while providing a range of ways for students to demonstrate their abilities and learning. They foster the development of students who can analyze, synthesize, evaluate and communicate information effectively.

Principle 2: Educators create, support, and maintain challenging learning environments for all.

Educators apply their professional knowledge to promote student learning. They know the curriculum and utilize a range of strategies and assessments to address differences. Educators develop and implement programs based upon a strong understanding of human development and learning theory. They support a challenging learning environment. They advocate for necessary resources to teach to higher levels of learning. They establish and maintain clear standards of behavior and civility. Educators are role models, displaying the habits of mind and work necessary to develop and apply knowledge while simultaneously displaying a curiosity and enthusiasm for learning. They invite students to become active, inquisitive, and discerning individuals who reflect upon and monitor their own learning.

Principle 3: Educators commit to their own learning in order to develop their practice.

Educators recognize that professional knowledge and development are the foundations of their practice. They know their subject matter, and they understand how students learn. Educators respect the reciprocal nature of learning between educators and students. They engage in a variety of individual and collaborative learning experiences essential to develop professionally and to promote student learning. They draw on and contribute to various forms of educational research to improve their own practice.

Principle 4: Educators collaborate with colleagues and other professionals in the interest of student learning.

Educators encourage and support their colleagues to build and maintain high standards. They participate in decisions regarding curriculum, instruction and assessment designs, and they share responsibility for the governance of schools. They cooperate with community agencies in using resources and building comprehensive services in support of students. Educators respect fellow professionals and believe that all have the right to teach and learn in a professional and supportive environment. They participate in the preparation and induction of new educators and in professional development for all staff.

Principle 5: Educators collaborate with parents and community, building trust and respecting confidentiality.

Educators partner with parents and other members of the community to enhance school programs and to promote student learning. They also recognize how cultural and linguistic heritage, gender, family and community shape experience and learning. Educators respect the private nature of the special knowledge they have about students and their families and use that knowledge only in the students' best interests. They advocate for fair opportunity for all children.

Principle 6: Educators advance the intellectual and ethical foundation of the learning community.

Educators recognize the obligations of the trust placed in them. They share the responsibility for understanding what is known, pursuing further knowledge, contributing to the generation of knowledge, and translating knowledge into comprehensible forms. They help students understand that knowledge is often complex and sometimes paradoxical. Educators are confidantes, mentors and advocates for their students' growth and development. As models for youth and the public, they embody intellectual honesty, diplomacy, tact and fairness.

Questions

1. Is it reasonable to ask a teacher to do everything that the New York Code seems to expect?
2. Are clear expectations like this helpful, or do people already know what's expected?
3. Why do you think leaders in New York State saw a need for such a code?
4. Are there any principles you would like to add to (or subtract from) the code?

Source: New York State Professional Standards and Practices Board for Teaching, *New York State Code of Ethics for Educators.* New York: The University of the State of New York and The State Education Department, 2011. Available from http://www.highered. nysed.gov/tcert/pdf/codeofethics.pdf.

How Does a Good Teacher Involve Parents and the Community?

From "PARENTAL INVOLVEMENT THAT WORKS . . . BECAUSE IT'S AGE-APPROPRIATE"
AUTHOR: WILLIAM H. JEYNES

William H. Jeynes teaches at California State University–Long Beach. While he argues for the importance of parent involvement at every point of a child and adolescent's education, he also argues that unless the kind of involvement changes over the years, particular approaches that worked well for young children will fail miserably as the same child gets older.

One of the greatest lessons I've learned about parenting is that just because you're a good parent with a 6-year-old does not mean that you will be a good parent with a 16-year-old. Good parenting practices are not static, but change to some degree depending on the age of the child.

This declaration was made by the parent of one of my students, and research supports its validity. Over the last three decades, a substantial body of research has accrued indicating that parental involvement has a considerable degree of impact at both the elementary and secondary school levels (Green, Walker, Hoover-Dempsey, & Sandler, 2007). Those studies have identified the components of parental involvement that have the highest degree of influence (Christian, Morrison, & Bryant, 1998). However, recent meta-analyses have been instrumental in suggesting another trend that is difficult to discern via other modes of analysis. A meta-analysis statistically combines all the relevant existing studies on a given subject to determine the aggregated results of that research.

According to these meta-analyses, the overall body of research suggests that the most effective parental involvement components are not the same for those with young children as they are for those with adolescents (Jeynes, 2005, 2007b). Specifically, overt expressions of parental involvement are associated with higher academic outcomes among elementary school students, but are no longer associated with these better results when students reach high school (Jeynes, 2005, 2007b). By the time students are in secondary school, virtually all the aspects of parental involvement that yield higher academic outcomes are subtle in nature (Jeynes, 2005, 2007b).

What the Data Show

The results just described have rather dramatic implications for the advice teachers should give caregivers regarding parental engagement, because the right kind of involvement can have significant ramifications for student academic achievement. These findings appear to support the notion that the most efficacious type of parenting during a student's elementary school years is often not the most suitable for the adolescent years (Hulbert, 2003; Steinberg, 2004). Specifically, family activities such as checking homework, establishing household rules for when it is time for work and leisure, and attending school functions are associated with higher scholastic outcomes to a statistically significant degree among elementary school students, but have little or no relationship to these outcomes at the secondary school level (Jeynes, 2005, 2007b).

Consistent with other research, these results show that the most effective parents are the ones who adapt to the changing dynamics in their children's lives (Berzonsky, 2004). To be sure, this is not a new insight. Many teachers, parents, and children can share anecdotal examples that support this conclusion. For example, younger children often become demonstratively excited when their parents come to see them in a school play (Cherlin, 2008). In contrast, adolescents may respond in a variety of ways. Some will be enthusiastic about the visit; others will show muted appreciation; a certain number will not be thankful; and still others will actually be embarrassed by their parents' presence (Townsend, 2006).

Similar differential reactions by age are also common for parental initiatives such as checking homework and maintaining household rules (Shumow, Schmidt, & Kackar, 2008). Young children often have a sense of increased security and classroom confidence when they know their parents have looked over their homework (Glasgow & Whitney, 2009). They also are more likely to cooperate with and be responsive to homework checking and household rules (Glasgow & Whitney, 2009). In contrast, adolescents, almost by nature, have an aversion to obeying rules and being subject to having their homework checked (Caissey, 1994; Fuller, 2009). When a parent asks whether the homework is completed, the teen often responds, "Yes, I know, I know" or "Yes, I did it already." Research has shown that such answers are typical whether or not the student has actually completed the homework (Shumow et al., 2008). Adolescents are more resistant to rules than they were at a younger age, and myriad teens regard their age bracket as their opportunity to question the majority of rules practiced by humanity (Caissey, 1994; Fuller, 2009). . . .

The Good News

The meta-analyses conducted on parental involvement demonstrate a salient truism that will encourage most parents and teachers. That is, although the effect sizes for parental involvement overall were somewhat smaller for secondary students—(.53) versus elementary students (.75)—the outcomes of parental engagement at the secondary school level are still substantial and statistically significant. These results are especially uplifting when one considers that meta-analyses provide the most complete insight possible into parental involvement. What this means is that many parents who believe they have a dearth of sway once their children turn 13 actually still have remarkable influence. The misconception is perpetuated because adolescents frequently do not want to let their parents know the degree to which they are indeed listening and internalizing many of the truths their parents are passing on to them.

Frequently, the extent of the parents' influence does not become ostensible until the youth has "graduated" from adolescence into adulthood (Townsend, 2006). In fact, the results of these meta-analyses confirm that efficacious and conscientious parenting does have an impact at this age, even though teens may commonly do their best to make this evidence seem intangible and nominal (Jeynes, 2005, 2007b).

According to the meta-analyses, although the effect sizes for overall parental involvement are smaller at the secondary school level than at the elementary school level by nearly 30%, subtle aspects of that involvement are actually larger for secondary school students. For example, the influence of healthy communication between parents and their children is about 33% greater at the secondary school level than it is at the elementary school level. Similarly, for parental style, which reflects raising children with a balanced approach of emphasizing love and disciplined structure in the home, the effect sizes were 12%–14% larger for secondary school students than for elementary. The effect sizes for parental expectations, although about 20% smaller than they were for elementary school students, were nevertheless quite substantial for secondary students. It is true that the impact of parents attending school functions and establishing household rules for this age group is negligible and apparently less of a factor than it is at the elementary school level. Rather, to be an efficacious parent of teens, focusing on the more subtle aspects of parental involvement, in particular, fosters greater benefits. Whatever adolescents might want their parents to believe, research shows that parental engagement does have a noteworthy and probably, in some respects, even a prodigious relationship with academic outcomes (Jeynes, 2003, 2005, 2007a). At the same time, most social scientists, parents, and teachers are not cognizant of this relationship, and current educational policy does not reflect this reality (Henderson & Mapp, 2002). Instead, most educational policy is based on antiquated conceptions that focus on overt manifestations of parental involvement which tend to be more effective in a child's elementary school years rather than on the subtler aspects of involvement that become more salient at the secondary school level. . . .

Closing Thoughts

The results of meta-analytic research indicate that the most effective modes of parental involvement are different for youth in elementary and secondary school. These findings should give guidance and hope to all, but especially to parents of secondary school students.

Questions

1. Were your own parents involved in your schooling? Did it help? Did it ever embarrass you as the author says it might for some adolescents?
2. Do you think a teacher would welcome the kind of involvement this article suggests? As a teacher, would you?
3. Is it possible for parents to be too involved in the life of a school?

Source: William H. Jeynes. "Parental Involvement That Works . . . Because It's Age-Appropriate." *Kappa Delta Pi Record* 50, no. 2 (2014): 85–8.

Student Diversity

Who Will I Teach?

3

> We conclude that, in the field of public education, the doctrine of "separate but equal" has no place. Separate educational facilities are inherently unequal.

BROWN V. BOARD OF EDUCATION, 1954

QUESTIONS TO COME

The simplest answer to the question "Who will I teach?" is "a diverse group of young people." But diversity is a complex issue. Diversity can mean different things, depending on the classroom and the school. Many schools are segregated in ways that reduce or mask diversity. Some cities, states, and regions are extraordinarily diverse; others are more homogeneous. Schools in Maine and Vermont reflect those states' communities, which are predominantly White. In Washington, D.C., the majority of the population is African American, and the school population is only 5% White. Some forms of diversity, such as racial and gender diversity, can be obvious. Other forms of diversity, such as sexual orientation, religion, or diversity of social class

and cultural assumptions, are often far less obvious. Some disabilities may be obvious while others may take time for a teacher or a school to acknowledge. The best teacher is one who knows how to embrace and honor diversity and how to engage a diverse group of young people and create in a classroom a small model of the larger, diverse democracy that schools are expected to foster.

Scholars, political leaders, parents, and teachers often debate the nature of diversity and the ways in which diversity should be recognized, or ignored, in schools. Among the **Readings**, William H. Frey's *Diversity Explosion: How New Racial Demographics Are Remaking America* helps us understand the extraordinary changes happening in the

U.S. population, especially among young people who attend school today. The next pair of articles pull us into one of the major debates about diversity today: How best to support students who arrive in school without a full command of the English language. In the next **Reading**, Orhan Agirdag argues for welcoming all languages, especially a student's home language, while also teaching English in school; while in the following **Reading**, Kevin Clark argues for structured English immersion as the school's key responsibility to students who are still English language learners. This debate is one that no new teacher can avoid.

In the final **Reading**, "The Silenced Dialogue," scholar Lisa Delpit discusses some of the ways White and Black teachers look at race and the best ways to teach in a racially diverse classroom. While this chapter looks at diversities based on race and ethnicity, country of origin, and home language, the following chapter will look more closely at diversities based on gender, sexual orientation special needs, and the sometimes hidden diversities such as religion or cultural assumptions. Anyone preparing to teach should recognize that he or she will have students at many different places along a spectrum of all of these diversities.

Will My Classroom Be Like the Ones I Attended?

Many of us have a vivid memory of our favorite class when we were in school. It may have been in first or second grade, when we were learning to read; or it may have been in middle school, when we started to feel "grown up" and independent; or perhaps it was in high school, when we came to love a specific subject. Most aspiring teachers have at least one memory of school—and usually of a specific teacher—that gives them positive inspiration for the work they want to do in the future.

You may see yourself standing at the front of that very room, filled with students who look and act a lot like you and the students you went to school with. You may have attended a school that was relatively diverse in terms of students' race or socioeconomic background. Or you may have spent your days with classmates very much like yourself.

Whatever your experience, remember that schools and their students are constantly changing. As we see in this chapter, classrooms have become extraordinarily diverse in a way that no one could have predicted a generation ago. High levels of immigration to the United States from Central and South America as well as from Asia have fundamentally changed the ethnic makeup of the nation's student body, if not the mix in every school. The 2014–15 school year was the first in which White students were a minority in the nation's student body. According to data collected by the National Center for Education Statistics, 50.3% of students in K-12 schools in the United States are what were once called "minority students"—students of African American, Latino, Asian American, or American Indian origin. Before long, the United States will be a "majority minority nation" as some call it, and schools are already there. Part of this demographic change is due to differential birth rates, especially the growth of Latino families and the shrinking size of European American families, and part to immigration, especially from Latin America and Asia. A careful look at the first **Reading**, a selection from William H. Frey's book *Diversity Explosion: How New Racial Demographics Are Remaking America*, shows that since 2011, more babies of color have been born each year in the U.S. than White children. While it will take decades for the nation to shift, classrooms across the country are feeling this huge demographic change now.[1] At the same time, schools in some places are becoming more homogeneous as efforts of past decades to end racial segregation slip away due primarily to increasingly segregated housing patterns in many areas.

Given these changes, you need to understand that most of the classrooms of today and tomorrow are going to be very different from those of even 10 years ago, especially in terms of the **diversity** of students (and students' needs) that you will encounter. The answer to the question "Will my classroom be the like the ones I attended?" is more than likely a resounding no.

There are many reasons for the changing demographics in today's schools. For one thing, more students are coming to school than ever before. The National Center for Health Statistics reports that more babies were born in 2007 than in any other year in American history, even more than in the peak of the post–World War II baby-boom year of 1957. People are also moving to the United States from other parts of the world in record numbers. The New York City public school system has students who were born in 102 of the 104 countries represented at the most recent Olympics. Schools in some of the most prosperous suburbs, which have long served an all-White student body, now include students who are the children of South Asian or African American doctors, lawyers, and other highly educated professionals. Small farming towns have as many students who were born in Latin America as they do students who were born locally. Long-term residents of the United States are also moving around more and intermarrying more frequently. Traditional notions of **ethnicity** are fading.

Beyond population demographics, a number of social movements have led schools to include more students who do not come to school speaking English, or who have a physical or learning disability, in what were previously considered "regular education" classrooms. As a result of these changes, the nation will need a growing number of teachers in the coming years, and those teachers need to be well prepared to embrace a diverse group of learners.[2]

> **ethnicity**
> Real or presumed characteristics and customs that identify members as part of a racial or cultural group.
>
> **diversity**
> Refers to the wide range of differences between people, most often associated with racial and ethnic identities, but also including variations in gender, beliefs, customs, sexual orientation, income, and other intangible distinctions.

Who Attends School Today?

Race and Ethnicity

The changing demographics just described are part of an extraordinary change in the overall U.S. population. In 1995, all "minority groups" made up 26% of the nation's people. By 2050, that percentage is expected to rise to 47%, with the greatest changes among young people. The emergence of what is sometimes called a "majority minority" student enrollment has been a long time coming, and this growing racial and ethnic diversity is but one of several indicators of the changing nature of today's and tomorrow's students.

The percentage of non–European American students in the public schools has grown from 22% in 1972 to 31% in 1986 to 43% in 2006 to 50.3% in 2015. At the same time, the percentage of White students has declined from 78% to 49.7%. (Note that all of these numbers are percentages. The actual number of students—including White students—has grown through all of these years.)

The most dramatic change is the growing number of Hispanic students who today represent almost one out of four students. In 1972, Hispanic students made up only 6% of the nation's student body; that percentage had grown to 11% in 1986 and 23% in 2011. The percentage of African American students has remained static, at around 15%–17%. In 2006, Asian and Pacific Islander students constituted about 4% of the total, and this percentage is expected to grow, also quite dramatically, in the near future. Another group that is likely to grow comprises those who are of "more than one race" or "other," as the number of children of parents of many different racial and ethnic categories grows in the next generation. For a student who may have a father of mixed Chinese and English origins and a mother from Latin America, for example, the very idea of race makes little sense. Finally, American Indian/Alaska Natives make up about 1% of today's students.

The rapid growth in the racial and ethnic diversity of American students has come about for many reasons. More European Americans are not having children or are having smaller families, compared with other Americans, whereas many so-called minority families, especially Hispanic families, are much larger. In addition, in recent decades the United States has seen the largest number of immigrants in history. The two dominant features that characterize this most recent wave of immigration are (1) its intensity—the immigrant population grew by over 30% in the 1990s, and (2) the shift in the sources of new immigration. Prior to 1965, the majority of immigrants were Europeans or Canadians, whereas today more than 50% of immigrants are from Latin America and 25% are from Asia.

 DID YOU KNOW?

The earliest version of the Pledge of Allegiance was written in 1892 to commemorate the 400th anniversary of Columbus's landing in America. The original version did not include the phrase "of the United States," which was added in 1923 to reinforce the idea that the United States was now their homeland for the huge number of immigrants. Nor did it include the words "under God," which were added in 1954 to differentiate the United States from atheist communism during the Cold War.

Although this combination of immigration and differential birth rates has changed the racial and ethnic makeup of the school-aged population of the United States, no one school reflects exactly that diversity. There are many segregated, predominantly White schools, just as there are segregated, primarily Black or mostly Hispanic schools. Many schools come very close to having homogeneous student bodies. Schools are also, perhaps even more, segregated by the economic backgrounds of their students. Some schools with students from a wide range of ethnic groups have a student body that may be mostly upper-middle class or mostly poor depending on who lives near the school. Most poor students are concentrated in major cities or rural parts of the country, whereas in other areas of the nation's major cities, as well as in many suburbs, students come from much more prosperous families.

The racial and ethnic makeup of students has changed in different regions of the United States. Many African American families have relocated in the past 30 years, with an increase in the number of such families in the Northeast and Midwest. The percentage of Black students remained constant in the South, at one-quarter of the total, and dropped slightly in the West. (Again, percentages, not actual numbers, are reported here. The total numbers of Black and White students increased significantly across the country and in all regions over the past 30 years.) The percentage of Asian students has grown throughout the country but especially in the West. The percentage of Hispanic students has also grown, and this group now represents well over one-third of all public school students in the West. (Hispanics constitute a majority in New Mexico and are represented in significant numbers in California and Texas.)

Table 3.1 The Changing Faces of Public School Children

	1995	2008	2011	2018 Estimate
White	64.8%	54.9%	51.9%	47.4%
Black	16.8%	17.0%	15.8%	15.1%
Hispanic	13.5%	21.4%	23.7%	28.1%
Asian/Pacific Islander	3.7%	5.0%	5.1%	5.3%
American Indian/ Alaska Native	1.1%	1.2%	1.1%	1.0%
Two or more races	N/A	0.5%	2.6%	3.2%
Total K–12 enrollment	44.8 million	49.2 million	49.5 million	50.5 million

Source: National Center for Educational Statistics, 2013 Tables and Figures, Table 203.50. http://nces.ed.gov/programs/digest/d13/tables/dt13_203.50.asp

Accessed December 21, 2014.

Table 3.2 (a–d) **The Changing Face of Public School Children—by Region**

Northeast

	1995	2008	2011
White	69.6%	62.6%	59.7%
Black	15.2%	15.2%	14.7%
Hispanic	11.1%	15.7%	17.5%
Asian/Pacific Islander	3.7%	5.8%	6.4%
American Indian/ Alaska Native	0.3%	0.3%	0.3%
Two or more races	N/A	0.3%	1.4%
Total K–12 enrollment	7.9 million	8 million	7.95 million

Midwest

	1995	2008	2011
White	79.3%	72.0%	68.5%
Black	13.8%	15.2%	14.0%
Hispanic	4.2%	9.0%	10.7%
Asian/Pacific Islander	0.9%	2.9%	3.0%
American Indian/ Alaska Native	0.9%	0.9%	0.9%
Two or more races	N/A	N/A	2.9%
Total K–12 enrollment	10.5 million	10.7 million	10.5 million

South

	1995	2008	2011
White	59.3%	49.7%	46.6%
Black	26.3%	25.8%	23.9%
Hispanic	11.7%	20.5%	23.0%
Asian/Pacific Islander	1.7%	2.9%	3.0%
American Indian/ Alaska Native	0.9%	1.1%	1.0%
Two or more races	N/A	N/A	2.4%
Total K–12 enrollment	16.1 million	18.5 million	18.95 million

West

	1995	2008	2011
White	54.7%	42.5%	39.8%
Black	6.4%	6.1%	5.3%
Hispanic	27.8%	37.9%	40.6%
Asian/Pacific Islander	8.7%	9.5%	9.2%
American Indian/ Alaska Native	2.4%	2.2%	1.9%
Two or more races	N/A	1.9%	3.2%
Total K–12 enrollment	10.3 million	11.97 million	12 million

Source: National Center for Educational Statistics, 2013 Tables and Figures, Table 203.50. http://nces.ed.gov/programs/digest/d13/tables/dt13_203.50.asp

Accessed December 21, 2014.

Note: The Center did not give the option of "two or more races" until after 1995.

Black Americans Demographic charts can mask as many differences as they illustrate. For example, people of many different backgrounds are included in a single category of "Black Americans." Many Black Americans are African Americans who are the descendants of slaves brought to these shores between the 1500s and the 1800s. More Africans than Europeans came to North America prior to the American Revolution, and their descendants have been in this country longer than there has been a country, far longer than the ancestors of many European Americans. However, other Americans who are classified as Black are the descendants of more recent immigrants or are immigrants themselves. For the past century, there has been a steady movement of people back and forth between the United States and the now mostly independent islands of the Caribbean. These citizens, often called Afro-Caribbean, bring to their schooling their own quite different cultural experiences and expectations and, in many cases, differing languages, such as Haitian Creole or Jamaican Patois. Finally, among recent immigrants, many come to the United States directly from Africa. Their families have lived for generations in nations and cultures where Africans were the majority and where the experience with racism was with European colonialism—English or French or occasionally Italian, Dutch, or German—rather than American slavery and segregation. An urban teacher, Black or White, who has a number of students who have immigrated from Senegal, and whose families want to be sure that they maintain their native-born mastery of the French language, needs skills different from those of another teacher who may have many students whose African American grandparents migrated north from Alabama or Mississippi. The fact that both groups of students are classified as "Black" is not the only or perhaps even the most significant information these teachers need to know.

Hispanics The number of students classified as Hispanic is growing rapidly, both in total numbers and in the percentage of all students. People of many different backgrounds classify themselves, or are classified by others, as Hispanic or, as many prefer, Latino. Some Latino or Hispanic students, especially in the southwestern United States, come from families that have been here for generations, in some cases living in the same area since the current states of California, Arizona, New Mexico, and Texas were part of the Republic of Mexico before 1848. Other Hispanic children have parents and grandparents who came to the United States from Puerto Rico, which has been part of the United States since the Spanish-American War of 1898 and whose residents are U.S. citizens. Many others are from Cuban families, most of whom came to the United States after the Communist Revolution in Cuba in 1959. Still others are the children of immigrants from every country of Central and South America, who have come to the United States, as most immigrants have, to seek greater political freedom and economic opportunity—to make a better life for themselves and their descendants. Today, the majority of Hispanic students in Florida, especially in the Miami area, are of Cuban descent; the majority in New York and many other parts of the Northeast are from Puerto Rican families; and the majority in the West are of Mexican descent. But like all other residents of the United States, Hispanic families move around, and it is easy to find Mexican children in New England, Cuban children in the Northwest, or children from any other Hispanic community in any of the nation's fifty states.

Native Americans American Indians and Alaska Natives—descendants of people who have been in the United States the longest—comprise 1%–2% of all students (although their actual numbers are growing). For centuries, European diseases, to which they had no immunity, and European-style military operations, to which their arms were no match, reduced the original American Indian population to less than 10% of what it was when Columbus landed. In the late 19th century, federal policy began very slowly to change. Government boarding schools that were launched in the 1870s sought to transform American Indian youth into models of European American culture but failed miserably. Many American Indian adults today can tell stories of being beaten at the boarding school for speaking in their tribal language instead of English, and being forced to cut their hair and wear Western clothes, but proudly recall maintaining their language and culture in spite of the harsh rules.

Beginning in the 1930s, federal policy began to change and the boarding schools were phased out in favor of schools that kept young American Indians closer to their homes and families. In the 1960s, more and more Indian tribes were given control of their own schools, including the right to hire teachers and develop curricula that honored their culture and traditions. Schools like the Rough Rock Demonstration School of the Navajo Nation, in which the curriculum and policies of the school were under the direct control of Navajo people, became models of a new form of American Indian schooling. Today, tribes are building schools that reflect their culture and beliefs in everything from the architecture to the curriculum to the staff. Federal aid for education and the growing prosperity of many tribes, often due to the success

Teachable Moment
FUELING THE PIPELINE

By 2025, Hispanics (or Latinos) are expected to comprise about 20% of the U.S. workforce. However, currently only about half of Latino adults have high school diplomas. This number can be accounted for in part by the large number of recent immigrants in the Latino community, but the dropout rate among Hispanic students in U.S. schools is far too high. If the trend continues, many Latinos will be marginalized from active participation in civic life and from good jobs.

ENLACE (Engaging Latino Communities for Education) is a program primarily funded by the W. K. Kellogg Foundation that establishes partnerships among Hispanic-serving institutions. The resulting coalitions, which include colleges and universities, K–12 school districts, communities, and businesses, provide Hispanic students and their families with guidance and support from preschool through college graduation.

A critical academic juncture for Hispanic students is ninth grade, when many drop out of high school, primarily due to an unfamiliar environment, a decrease in community and family support, and schools that aren't prepared to meet their needs. Some ENLACE programs provide ninth graders with mentors, such as upperclassmen or college students, who help with the transition and act as role models.

In Santa Ana, California, where 80% of students are Hispanic, the ENLACE program is designed to link points along the "educational pipeline," from pre-K to graduate school. According to program director Lilia Tanakeyowma, "The concept is to prepare all students as if they are going to college." Their program is a collaboration of ENLACE staff members, teachers, and parents from the Santa Ana school district, along with Santa Ana College faculty. Through their combined efforts, the Santa Ana school system has upgraded its mathematics curriculum, requiring all eighth graders to take algebra and providing tutors when necessary. In addition, high school graduation requirements now mirror the requirements for admission to a California state university.

Programs have been established in thirteen school districts in seven states with the highest populations of Latino students: Arizona, California, Florida, Illinois, New Mexico, New York, and Texas. ENLACE, which also has its roots in the Spanish word *enlazar*, meaning "to link or weave together, to connect in such a way that the new entity is stronger than its parts" is providing one step toward building a more educated workforce and productive society.

Source: Ellen R. Delisio. "Program Links Hispanic Families to Education Resources." *Education World*, 2005, accessed September 1, 2009 from http://www.educationworld.com/a_issues/issues/issues201.shtml.

of their gambling industries, are supporting the construction of beautiful buildings that reflect American Indian values in a way that was unimaginable even a few years ago. In Wisconsin, the Indian Community School is built on a 124-acre site that maintains the wetlands, hills, prairies, and woodlands on which the Oneida, Menomonee, and Stockbridge-Munsee Indian tribes have long lived. In western New York, the Seneca Nation Education Department is managing a network of elementary and high schools that focus on its storytelling culture and ensure that stories are passed on in both English and tribal languages while at the same time addressing the Common Core standards that Seneca young people need for participation in the larger culture. American Indian communities are growing, and many remain closely connected to their tribes and their tribal cultures, religion, and traditions and are creating schools that foster this sense of community as well as the knowledge and skills needed in the larger American society.

Asians Asian Americans are by far the fastest-growing ethnic group and, in the near future, will more than likely comprise a much larger percentage of the nation's students, especially in the West. Some Asian students are from Chinese and Japanese families that have been in the United States for many generations. The historian Ronald Takaki tells the story of taking a taxi from an airport to a conference he was attending:

"How long have you been in this country?" he [the taxi driver] asked. "All my life," I replied, wincing. "I was born in the United States." With a strong southern drawl, he remarked: "I was wondering because your English is excellent!" Then as I had many times before, I explained, "My grandfather came here from Japan in the 1880s. My family has been here, in America, for over a hundred years." He glanced at me in the mirror. Somehow I did not look "American" to him; my eyes and complexion looked foreign.[3]

Although teachers will encounter young Ronald Takakis among their Asian students, other Asian children are immigrants or the children or grandchildren of immigrants, some from Vietnamese and Cambodian families whose lives were uprooted by the war in Vietnam in the 1960s and early 1970s or others, including many from southern Asia—India and Pakistan—but also from China and Korea who have come to the United States very recently.

Asian students often complain that they face a number of stereotypes based on the way issues of race are treated in schools and in the larger society. Some are seen as part of the "model minority," the students who are "always good at math" and generally take school seriously. However, these stereotypes make little sense, given that there are 30 Asian groups and 21 Pacific Islander groups. Generalizing about these many different groups of people, as if all Asians are alike, is terribly misleading.

Some Asian students also report a sense of being pulled in two different directions—by a family that wants them to maintain certain traditions yet also succeed in their new home and by a school that wants to "Americanize" them. The result can be a family that sees its children as conforming too much to the dominant culture and a school that still sees Asian students as "other." As one student reported, "It was very weird—on the weekend I was American to my people and during the week I was a foreigner [in school]."[4]

More Than One Race The charts in this chapter include a new category of "two or more races," which in 2011 comprised 2.6% of all students and is estimated to rise to 3% or 3.5% of all students before long. Today, more and more young people are resisting a single ethnic category, seeing ethnic labels as something that someone else, especially someone in authority, seeks to place on them. Looking at urban communities in the United States and how they have changed over the past 20 years, researchers Shirley Brice Heath and Milbrey W. McLaughlin write: "Marriages across different races, nationalities, and languages dramatically increased in number, and parents often did not want their children boxed under one ethnic label. Children with one African American parent and one Puerto Rican parent and several Portuguese or Dominican Republican friends saw only psychological hazard in proclaiming a single label for themselves." The old labels remain familiar to educators, sociologists, and politicians, but today's youth often revel in their diversity and, as youth of every generation, enjoy trying on different identities at different points in their own development. Thus Heath and McLaughlin report, "A large urban school district, for example, in the last decade passed a regulation that students could change their designated ethnicity only once every three years."

Even as it is important for teachers to understand, respect, and value the ethnic diversity of today's school students, and the individual students in a classroom, it is also equally, perhaps even more, important for teachers to understand that the meaning of ethnicity for individuals and communities is based on an ever-changing and often illusive set of categories. Based on their own studies of youth culture and their interviews with young people, Heath and McLaughlin have wisely warned all who seek to work with young people:

> Ethnicity seemed, from the youth perspective, to be more often a label assigned to them by outsiders than an indication for their real sense of self. Many young people told us repeatedly, "Ethnicity ain't what it's really all about."
> . . . Being the local tough kid's younger brother, the girlfriend of a prominent gang member, or a player on a winning local ball team counted more heavily in daily street life than one's label of ethnic membership. Many young people pointed out that at one time their communities may have been identified with a single ethnic group but that what they see today are different groups continually moving in and out of their housing projects and neighborhoods. They have learned to "hang with all kinds," "to be local," to get along, and to survive.[5]

All this makes understanding and engaging young people important and difficult business for any teacher. To ignore ethnicity, as to ignore any other attribute, is disrespectful and courts disaster. But to impose an ethnic name or a set of expectations, based on perceived ethnicity, on an individual student or a class is equally disrespectful and disastrous. Many things matter to our students. Having adults who take the time to know them as individuals and what they care about is high on the list.[6]

What About Me?

What Do You Want to Be Called?

White, Black, Hispanic, Asian, Native American, Pacific Islander. At some point in your life, you've probably had to check off your race or ethnicity on a form. But what if none of those labels truly reflects your own personal identity or accommodates the majority of us who have come from multiple backgrounds? For example, some people of Central and South American origin prefer to be called Hispanic; others prefer Latino. Many prefer to use a specific place of origin, such as Guatemalan, Mexican, Puerto Rican, Cuban, and so on. In the same way, some descendants of the first residents of this country prefer American Indian, others prefer First Peoples, and others, Native Americans. Many prefer specific tribal names, such as Sioux, Navajo, Apache, or Wampanoag. Today, many people from families of mixed racial and ethnic origins do not want to be called by the name of any one group. The term *Blasian* is now used by many of Black and Asian descent.

Most people agree that everyone has a right to be called what they want to be called and not to have a group name imposed on them by someone else. How would you "label" yourself in one (or many) words?

Learning the Language: What Are the Ongoing Debates Over Bilingual Education?

America: A Land of Many Languages

Bilingual programs have existed in schools in the United States far longer than most people realize. Beginning in the early 1500s, Europeans speaking Spanish, Portuguese, Dutch, French, and English, and bringing with them Africans speaking Ashanti, Yoruba, Kru, and other African languages, encountered American Indians speaking innumerable different languages of their own. As schools were founded in these lands, instruction also took place in many different languages. In 1664, when the English conquered New Amsterdam and renamed it New York, at least 18 languages were spoken on Manhattan Island, not counting the Indian languages. German language schools opened in Philadelphia as early as 1694, and by the mid-1800s, most major cities, including Baltimore, Cincinnati, Cleveland, Indianapolis, Milwaukee, and St. Louis, offered schooling in both German and English, while Louisiana supported schools that taught in both French and English.

After 1848, when most of the current states of California, Arizona, New Mexico, Texas, Utah, and Colorado were ceded to the United States by the Republic of Mexico at the end of the U.S.-Mexican War, most of the people who lived in those areas spoke only Spanish. In response, dual systems of Spanish and English schooling were developed, especially in New Mexico, which, in 1906, also set up a dual system of teacher preparation. As researcher Diego Castellanos said, "For much of the 19th century . . . American public education allowed immigrant groups to incorporate linguistic and cultural traditions into the schools . . . wherever immigrant groups possessed sufficient political power—be they Italian, Polish, Czech, French, Dutch, German—foreign languages were introduced into elementary and secondary schools, either as separate subjects or as languages of instruction."[7]

Japanese language schools were introduced in California early in the 20th century despite considerable opposition and hostility. The strong American tradition of local control of schools, and the strength of different linguistic groups in different localities, meant that what we now call *bilingual education* had a sufficiently strong constituency in many places (although in the 18th and 19th centuries, it was often monolingual instruction in a language other than English). This linguistic diversity was not without its critics. Throughout the 19th century, anti-immigrant groups demanded that people who were in America speak English, whether they had arrived via immigration or, as was the case for Mexicans of the Southwest or residents of Puerto Rico, through the conquest of previously Spanish-speaking lands. The opposition to non-English language schools was often liked with a general hostility to immigrants, known as **nativism**. Ironically, American Indians, whose languages had been spoken in the United States far longer than English, were often educated in schools that forced them to speak and learn only in English and that were consciously designed to wipe out every vestige of the Indians' language, customs, beliefs, and culture. Early in the 20th century, Theodore Roosevelt said, "We have room for but one language in this country and that is the English language, for we intend to see that the crucible turns our people out as Americans, of American nationality." When the United States entered World War I on the side of England and against Germany in 1917, anti-German feeling led to attacks on German-language schooling. By the 1920s and 1930s, bilingual schooling virtually disappeared in the United States; it was illegal in some places and declined due to lack of support in others. As late as the 1960s, schools in Texas had what they called "Spanish detention," where students were kept after school for speaking Spanish in the classrooms or hallways. Prior to 1973, it was a crime in Texas for a teacher to teach in any language except English.

> **nativism**
> Advocacy of policies favoring the practices and culture of native-born inhabitants of a region rather than recent immigrants—although European Americans were the only ones considered to be native-born inhabitants, rather than the American Indian population.

The civil rights movement of the 1950s and 1960s fueled changes and reform. In 1965–66, the National Education Association conducted a survey of the Tucson, Arizona, schools. The results, published as *The Invisible Minority, Pero No Vencibles*, portrayed the depth of the exclusion of Spanish-speaking children in Arizona's schools. Civil rights groups protested policies like Spanish detention. In 1970, the La Raza Unida Party organized school boycotts in Crystal City, Texas, demanding the development of new bilingual instruction. A Puerto Rican group, Aspira, sued the New York City public schools and obtained a consent decree guaranteeing the rights of Spanish-speaking students in New York. That same year, an advocacy group in San Francisco began the long process of demanding legal rights for Kinney Lau and 1,789 other Chinese immigrant students in that city.

Politicians soon followed. California governor Ronald Reagan signed legislation repealing the state's English-only school laws in 1967. In 1968, the U.S. Congress passed Title VII of the Elementary and Secondary Education Act, providing federal funds to support bilingual education programs, to prepare teachers able to work in them, and to develop appropriate new curriculum. In 1970, the U.S. Office for Civil Rights informed school districts that they had an obligation under the Civil Rights Act to develop programs for students in need of English-language instruction and that they "must take affirmative steps to rectify the language deficiency in order to open its instructional program to these students." In 1971, Massachusetts enacted legislation in favor of bilingual education.

Finally, in 1974 in *Lau, et al. v. Nichols, et al.* (Kinney Lau, one of the students impacted; Alan Nichols, president of the School Board) the U.S. Supreme Court ruled that San Francisco was wrong to claim that it did not discriminate against students who spoke only Chinese languages because it offered them the same instruction as other students (though the Chinese immigrant students could not understand the instruction). The high court upheld the views of Shirley Hufstedler of the 9th Circuit, who wrote, "These Chinese children are not separated from their English-speaking classmates by state-erected walls of brick and mortar but the language barrier, which the state helps to maintain, insulates the children from their classmates as effectively as any physical bulwarks."

With the *Lau* decision, the U.S. Supreme Court made it clear that, although school districts might use any one of several different approaches, students who came to school not speaking English could not simply be allowed to languish in English-only classrooms, as had too often been the norm. In 1975, when U.S. Commissioner of Education Terrell Bell announced federal guidelines for implementing the *Lau* decision, the so-called Lau Remedies, the full force of the federal government was put behind effective language instruction for all students.

It may have seemed that the issue of bilingual education was settled in the United States. The federal budget for bilingual education was $45 million, which supported programs offering bilingual education in English and 26 languages including Russian, French, Portuguese, Cantonese, Pomo, Cree, Yup'ik, and Chamorro. Congress voted not only to expand the funding but also to support stronger programs in bilingual education "to the extent necessary to allow a child to progress effectively through the educational system."

However, as rapid and impressive as the legal victories of the 1960s and 1970s were, opposition to these programs emerged quickly. Within the Latino community, some leaders worried about a new form of bilingual segregation. Diego Castellanos wrote of the fears of some that "bilingual tracks" might be the new form of **de facto segregation**. Another scholar, Alfredo Mathew, feared that bilingual education could "become so insular and ingrown that it fosters a type of apartheid." Longtime civil

> **de facto segregation**
> Segregation that is brought about for any number of reasons such as where people live or tracking in a school as opposed to a specific legal action.

rights scholar Gary Orfield wrote, "Without any serious national debate it seems that we have moved from a harsh assimilationist policy to a policy of linguistic and cultural separation." Even the programs designed to engage English-speaking and non-English-speaking students in two-way bilingual programs raised concerns, leading one Puerto Rican school administrator to lament, "The only ones that will emerge from the schools bilingual are the Anglo children. A natural language resource will be lost."

Lau v. Nichols

Under these state-imposed standards there is no equality of treatment merely by providing students with the same facilities, textbooks, teachers, and curriculum; for students who do not understand English are effectively foreclosed from any meaningful education.

Basic English skills are at the very core of what these public schools teach. Imposition of a requirement that before a child can effectively participate in the educational program he must already have acquired those basic skills is to make a mockery of public education. We know that those who do not understand English are certain to find their classroom experiences wholly incomprehensible and in no way meaningful.

. . . It seems obvious that the Chinese-speaking minority receives less benefit than the English-speaking majority from respondents' school system, which denies them a meaningful opportunity to participate in the educational program.
—U.S. Supreme Court ruling, *Lau v. Nichols*, 1974

At the same time, other critics with less initial sympathy to bilingual education were emerging. In 1974, Albert Shanker, the president of the American Federation of Teachers, wrote: "The American taxpayer, while recognizing the existence of cultural diversity, still wants the schools to be the basis of an American melting pot. . . . What these children need is intensive instruction in English so that they may, as soon as possible, function with other children in regular school programs."

In 1981, President Reagan said that he wanted teachers to be able to communicate with students who did not come to school speaking English: "But it is absolutely wrong and against American concepts to have a bilingual education program that is now openly admittedly dedicated to preserving their native language and never getting them adequate in English so they can go out into the job market and participate."[8]

Bilingual Instruction Versus an English-Only Curriculum

In the 1990s, more attacks on bilingual education emerged and several states passed laws demanding English immersion for all students. Bilingual programs became programs for "English language learners," and the goal of maintaining students' home languages receded as the focus became getting students to speak English as quickly as possible. As the **Readings** at the end of this chapter show, the debate between those who want schools to strengthen bilingual students' ability to speak and read in their native languages as well as in English and those who feel that schools must teach students English as thoroughly and quickly as possible is alive and well today. As discussed in the **Reading** by Bill Frey, whatever the outcome of the debates about the future of bilingual education, the United States is a nation—and especially a classroom—of immigrants. With or without bilingual classes, teachers must teach many children who arrive in school with little, if any, English. But how do you best respond to these students? Do you help them maintain their first language while they learn English, or do you leave the first language to the parents while the school focuses on intensive English instruction?

Perhaps nowhere has the fight over an appropriate kind of bilingual education been more intense than in California. Already split almost evenly between European Americans and people of color, California is one of the most diverse states in the nation. In addition to people of African descent, most of whom speak English (although some recent immigrants are from the Caribbean and speak Spanish or Haitian Creole), California includes large numbers of Spanish-speaking citizens—recent and not-so-recent immigrants from Latin America—as well as a rapidly growing Asian population, including people who speak Cantonese, Japanese, Vietnamese, Khmer, or one of a host of other languages.

 DID YOU KNOW?

California has the highest number of English language learners (ELLs) in the nation. One out of three students in that state is an ELL.

LEARNING THE LANGUAGE: BILINGUAL EDUCATION

- **Bilingual education:** Many reformers began to use this term in the 1970s and continue to use it today. As the term implies, **bi**-lingual education programs stress maintaining the students' home language, offering students school instruction in that language while ensuring that the students learn English. The goal is to encourage students who come to school not speaking English to become truly proficient in two languages before they graduate. In some schools, "two-way bilingual programs" help students maintain their home language and learn English while helping students whose first language is English learn a foreign language.
- **English language immersion:** Advocates of English language immersion programs believe that it is the family's job to maintain the home language and that school should teach students English as quickly as possible so that they can be fully integrated into school life.
- **English as a Second Language:** As programs have shifted from maintaining both languages for students (true bilingual education) to a focus on helping students learn English as fast as possible, many educators have begun to use the lessons of foreign language instruction to develop more sophisticated programs to teach the English language to students who first learned to speak and write in another language.
- **Programs for English language learners (ELL):** Since some states (most notably California) have mandated English language immersion over bilingual education, educators have begun using the term "English language learners" rather than "bilingual students." These school programs focus on helping students learn the English language (at a faster or slower pace depending on local policy) rather than on maintaining two languages.

Since the *Lau* decision of 1974, California, which educates more students learning English than any other state, has had a variety of bilingual education programs. However, in 1998, most of these programs were curtailed significantly when California voters passed Proposition 227, which mandated that students who came to school in California not speaking English be placed in structured English immersion classes for a maximum of 1 year and then be transferred to regular classrooms conducted "overwhelmingly in English." The debate around Proposition 227 was intense. Advocates of the new law claimed that bilingual education segregated non-English-speaking students and limited their life chances by denying them the full opportunities of schooling. Opponents of the new law saw it as a racist effort to return to the days when students who could not or did not learn English quickly enough were effectively forced out of school altogether.

Don Soifer, one of the supporters of Proposition 227, contended that "children in bilingual programs generally learn English slower, later, and less effectively than their peers. The bilingual approach delays for years the time when students can graduate to 'mainstream' classrooms."[9]

Other Californians held radically different views of Proposition 227. John Espinoza, a teacher in the Los Angeles Unified School District, believed that Los Angeles had developed an excellent program for English learners through its bilingual offerings until the new law effectively "ended bilingual education as we know it."[10]

Voters in other states have considered ballot initiatives requiring an end to bilingual instruction and a focus on English only, similar to the one in California. Initiatives passed in Arizona in 2000 and in Massachusetts in 2002 but were defeated in Colorado in 2002 and in Oregon in 2008. Nevertheless, proponents of more traditional approaches to bilingual education have found themselves on the defensive, and an increasing number of states refer to students in these programs as English language learners rather than as bilingual education students. This shift represents a clear change in the expectations for programs that serve students who come to school speaking a language other than English.[11]

A Growing Nation of ELL Students

Whatever one's own views on the debates about bilingual education, most of today's aspiring teachers are going to have students (sometimes many students) who do not speak English, or who still have not mastered the language and need substantial support to succeed in an English-speaking classroom. In April 2009, the journal *Educational Leadership* devoted an entire issue to the best ways of supporting English language learners. Although the articles in that issue did not generate the heat of the earlier California, Arizona, and Massachusetts debates, the educator-authors clearly had significantly different views on the best way to support these students. The **Readings** related to bilingual education in this chapter are taken from that issue. Orhan Agirdag, an educator in Belgium, cites the case of Europe—where many students cross borders and come to school speaking many different languages—in his discussion of the best ways to welcome all students in school while encouraging them to both maintain their home language and learn the language of their new home. Language, Agirdag insists, is part of many people's basic identity, and it is wrong to demean it in any way. He sees many advantages in encouraging students to both prize their native language and learn a second one. Such bilingualism allows students to maintain stronger ties with their family and community, and it fosters an adult society that is rich in linguistic ability. Although he does not disagree directly with Agirdag, Kevin Clark focuses on making English immersion work, a necessity in California, Arizona, and Massachusetts, where it is illegal *not* to do so. Clark also believes that "active, direct, and explicit" instruction in English will help students master their new language—and succeed in the schools of their new community—much faster than any alternative. He is less worried than Agirdag about maintaining a student's home language.

You can certainly learn from both articles, and from the many advocates of differing perspectives on the issue, but at some point you will need to decide where you stand as an individual teacher. At the same time, you must find a way to survive—with integrity—even in a system that may have official policies with which you disagree intensely. Knowing how to be an effective teacher of students who are English language learners, sometimes in the very early stages of learning English, is one of the key challenges facing anyone entering the teaching profession today.

Why Are Schools Still Racially Segregated?

In 1903, W.E.B. Du Bois, one of the nation's leading African American educators, wrote "the problem of the Twentieth Century is the problem of the color-line." When Du Bois wrote that, the United States was a nation marred by deep racial segregation and **discrimination**, and Americans spent most of the 20th century wrestling with the issue. They still are. Until 1954, schools in much of the country were racially segregated by law as well as custom, and in many states, Black children (and Latino children and Japanese children in the far West) were assigned to separate and far inferior school buildings, when there even were schools for them.

The U.S. Supreme Court's 1954 decision in *Brown v. Board of Education* ended the legal foundation, though not the reality, of racial segregation in schooling. It took more than a decade before the Court's ruling came to be enforced in many parts of the country. Throughout the late 1950s, 60s, and even 70s, politicians in the South and the North campaigned on a promise that racial integration would never come to their communities. Virginia Senator Harry F. Byrd, Sr., organized a resistance movement that led some Virginia communities simply to close all schools. Arkansas governor Orval Faubus tried to block Black students from entering Little Rock High School until President Dwight Eisenhower sent U.S. Army troops to escort the students to school. In 1963, Governor George Wallace of Alabama gained national prominence by "standing in the schoolhouse door" to block students. In the 1970s, schools in Boston, Massachusetts, found themselves in turmoil because the federal courts ruled that the school board's policies had intentionally maintained racial segregation in the city and had to be drastically changed in order to achieve racial integration. For some 20 years after *Brown*, slow and steady progress was made toward greater **racial integration** in the schools. Sadly, however, the movement to integrate public schools has not only stalled, but it has shifted backward.

In 2009, primarily to catch the attention of the new Obama administration, Gary Orfield, who has spent decades researching school integration, wrote: "Fifty-five years after the *Brown* decision, blacks and Latinos in American schools are more segregated than they have been in more than four decades. . . . Segregation is fast spreading into large sectors of suburbia and there is little or no assistance for communities wishing to resist the pressures of resegregation and ghetto creation in order to build successfully integrated schools and neighborhoods." Orfield has compiled a massive amount of evidence to make the case. The statistics are startling: 38.5% of Blacks and 40% of Latino students attend schools where more than 90% of the students are non-White. Only a small minority of students—seldom over 20% of the students of any race in any part of the country—attend schools that can truly be called multiracial.

For Orfield and other researchers, the practice of segregating students, especially poor students and those of color, not only into racially segregated schools but also into schools that lack many basic resources, "where everyone is poor, teachers transfer out as soon as they can, parents are powerless . . . is deeply harmful to students." As an aspiring teacher, you need to be well aware of this reality. Whether you pursue a career in a racially segregated school like the ones Orfield describes or in another kind of racially segregated school—one serving predominantly White students—you need to understand the larger legal and cultural structures into which you are entering. In the end, Orfield says, only leadership will change this situation, and teachers will need to be among these leaders.[12]

racial integration
The mixing, intentional or accidental, of members of different ethnic or racial groups in a single setting as opposed to racial segregation brought about by law or by informal powerful arrangements often linked to housing patterns.

discrimination
Unfair treatment that is based on differences in gender, race, or class or other differences rather than individual merit.

CONNECTIONS ➔⬅

In Chapter 4, we'll look at some of the issues related to teaching boys and girls differently, as well as the needs of special education students and some of the many hidden diversities a teacher needs to consider.

Teachable Moment
BROWN V. BOARD OF EDUCATION OF TOPEKA

On May 17, 1954, Chief Justice Earl Warren delivered the unanimous opinion of the United States Supreme Court:

We come then to the basic question presented: Does segregation of children in public schools solely on the basis of race, even though the physical facilities and other "tangible" factors may be equal, deprive the children of the minority group of equal educational opportunities? We believe that it does. . . . We conclude that in the field of public education, the doctrine of "separate but equal" has no place. Separate educational facilities are inherently unequal.

This far-reaching ruling in the case of *Brown v. Board of Education* effectively declared the laws of almost half the states—not only in the South but in places like Kansas and Washington, D.C.—to be illegal. At the time of the *Brown* decision, 17 states required their schools to be racially segregated and only 16 states prohibited racial segregation in the schools.

The *Brown* case was a merger of five different cases challenging school segregation in Delaware, Kansas, South Carolina, Virginia, and the District of Columbia. In Virginia, 16-year-old Barbara Johns had organized a student strike in 1951 to demand a new school building for the Black community in Prince Edward County. In the case that gave the decision its name, Linda Brown, a third-grade student in Topeka, Kansas, had to travel far past the nearest, all-White, school to attend the Black school to which she was assigned.

Brown was also far from the first challenge to racial segregation in the schools. In 1855, African Americans in Boston finally won a long battle to end legal segregation of the schools. Very soon after the Civil War, as Reconstruction-era state legislatures in the South began to create public school systems for Black and White students, they also created racially segregated systems that were challenged from the beginning. In the case of *Plessy v. Ferguson* in 1896, the U.S. Supreme Court ruled that state-mandated racial segregation in public facilities was legal ("separate but equal"). Beginning in the 1930s, the National Association for the Advancement of Colored People Legal Defense Fund, led by Charles H. Houston and Thurgood Marshall, began a meticulous campaign to overturn the school segregation that so many states mandated. They won their first victory in 1948 in a case against the University of Oklahoma; the ruling guaranteed all taxpayers the right to state-funded law schools. In 1946, the Court prohibited the segregation of Mexican American children in California. In 1950, in *Sweatt v. Painter*, the Court said that the segregated law schools of Texas deprived African American law students of a first-rate education. And finally, in the 1954 *Brown* decision, the Court said that all segregated schooling violated the U.S. Constitution's 14th Amendment guarantee that "No State shall abridge the privileges or immunities of citizens of the United States."

Questions

- Had you heard of the *Brown* decision before reading this book? Had you thought it was based on just one incident or that it was the culmination of many cases?
- If the Supreme Court said that school segregation was unconstitutional in 1954, why do many schools in the United States still seem to be segregated by race today?

How Can I Be Sure That I Am Reaching All My Students?

A recent survey of new teachers found that many of them were saying, "I wasn't prepared for the challenges of teaching in a diverse classroom." It is intriguing to note, however, that new teachers from urban areas reported that they were much better prepared to respond well to diversity than those who began teaching in the suburbs. People who planned on urban careers may have sought out more experiences with diversity or may have graduated from programs that emphasized

attention to diversity. The fact that less than a third of teachers in affluent schools said that they were prepared for the diversity they found in their schools says a great deal—about their preparation and also about the growing diversity of the nation's schools.[13] No matter where you plan to teach—in an urban, a suburban, or a rural school—a diversity of students will most likely be in the classroom with you.

Looking at Ourselves

To effectively embrace the diversity of your students, you must first look carefully at your own "place" in the diverse world of today. It is one thing for a new teacher to try to be respectful of, and to engage, all students. It is quite another thing for a teacher to examine where she or he falls personally. Tessie Liu, a professor at Northwestern University in Chicago, talks about the way in which the failure to examine one's own position in the world can be dangerous. She says that there is a special danger for students who are White and middle class to think that "they themselves embody the universal norm," even though they are sympathetic to the needs and concerns of others. Nevertheless, of these White and middle-class students, she says, "In their heart of hearts, they believe that white establishes not merely skin color but the norm from which blacks, browns, yellows, and reds deviate." Liu also sees that "many male students accept the reality of **sexism**, feel bad about it for women, but think that they are not touched by it. Even though they sympathize, for these students poverty, racism, and even sexism are still other people's problems." Distancing from problems—and people—in this way, Liu and many other educators would argue, is almost a sure way to guarantee that one will fail to connect with one's students.[14]

For White teachers—and teachers who are part of the majority in other ways, be it heterosexual teachers, teachers without disabilities, or teachers who have never struggled with the English language—it may be difficult to see oneself as in some ways quite privileged. In *Other People's Children*, a book that has come to be important to many educators, and a selection from which is included in the **Readings** for this chapter, Lisa Delpit argues that several aspects of such privilege are important to anyone thinking about the dynamics of contemporary education. Included in Delpit's list is her belief that "Those with power are frequently least aware of—or least willing to acknowledge—its existence. Those with less power are often most aware of its existence." This does not mean that students from more privileged backgrounds should avoid teaching. It does mean that they—and all teachers—need to be very aware of the power dynamics in a school and classroom, including the power of a dominant culture to define what life should be like for other students.

This is an issue that every teacher needs to think about, whether he or she is of the majority or the minority group on any specific form of diversity. As Delpit says, "For many who consider themselves members of liberal or radical camps, acknowledging personal power and admitting participation in the culture of power is distinctly uncomfortable." While Delpit is writing primarily about issues of race, the same things can often be said of straight teachers, able-bodied teachers, teachers for whom English is their first language, male teachers, and so on. None of us wants to see ourselves as privileged, but honesty is essential.

The issue here is not one of guilt. Indeed, guilt is quite unhelpful and the educator who keeps apologizing for his or her position—just as one who gets angry at the implication of guilt in any discussion of diversity—is unhelpful in the extreme. Simply worrying about one's guilt, or lack of it, is a diversion from the real issue, as Delpit notes, which is an ability to listen and "really hear." This means you must be willing to reconsider your power, educational philosophy, and relationship to others, whether they are students, parents, or other teachers. Really hearing means being ready to consider that you might be wrong about (for example) the best strategy to teach reading to a particular student or class, or your assumptions about what kind of classroom structure students need at a given time in their lives, or the background and strengths and weaknesses a student brings to class on a given day. It is not a matter of being a pushover; rather it is a matter of being willing to engage deeply in a sometimes-painful **dialogue** and to really speak and really listen.[15]

Several years ago, Peggy McIntosh, a White teacher, wrote a short piece, "Unpacking the Invisible Knapsack," that was designed to help teachers look at their often unexamined privileges as a means of seeing themselves as their students may see them. Reflecting on her own experience as a White feminist trying to get men to see their privileges, McIntosh came to realize that she, as a White woman, had never before examined her own race privilege and that many Whites—like many men—learn how to avoid recognizing their privileges. Thus, she sought to "unpack" the bag of privileges that Whites carry, whether they know it or not, or whether they want it or not. She posed questions such as whether one could go shopping and not be followed around the store or whether one can apply for a job or a credit card and not worry if race will be an issue. The point here again is not to feel guilty about what one has received in life. However, it is essential to be aware of what it means to some of our students who may be followed in a store or privately ridiculed for a lifestyle, or how people of a more dominant culture get uncomfortable in his or her presence. For students who have had these kinds of experiences and this knowledge of the world, a teacher who simply ignores issues of diversity and privilege can seem willfully ignorant even if that is not at all the intention.[16]

> **dialogue**
> Conversation or other form of discourse between two people or occasionally between groups.

Seeing Diversities

In her book, *Educating Teachers for Diversity: Seeing with a Cultural Eye*, Emory University professor Jacqueline Jordan Irvine addresses the statement she has heard often from aspiring teachers: "Race is not an issue until someone brings it up. What difference does it make anyway?" Irvine responds to this kind of statement, which she has heard so often:

> Many teachers erroneously believe that if they recognize the race of their students or discuss issues of ethnicity in their classroom, they might be labeled as insensitive or, worse, racist. However, when teachers ignore their students' ethnic identities and their unique cultural beliefs, perceptions, values, and worldviews, they fail as culturally responsive pedagogists. Colorblind teachers claim that they treat all students "the same," which usually means that all students are treated as if they are, or should be, both White and middle class.

Clearly for Irvine and for the future of our students, something much more sophisticated is needed. Not all students are White, and not all students want to be treated as if they are White or as if White is the norm. Our goal as educators must be to develop that more sophisticated approach to our students and the education that we offer them.[17]

In the **Readings**, Lisa Delpit says something very similar. If Irvine hears some teachers say, "Race is not an issue until someone brings it up," or claim to be "colorblind," Delpit hears, "I want the same thing for everyone else's children as I want for mine." This may be a noble sentiment, born of the best of intentions. Nevertheless, Delpit warns:

> To provide schooling for everyone's children that reflects liberal, middle-class values and aspirations is to ensure the maintenance of the status quo, to ensure that power, the culture of power, remains in the hands of those who already have it. Some children come to school with more accoutrements of the culture of power already in place—"cultural capital," as some critical theorists refer to it—some with less. . . . But parents who don't function within that culture often want . . . to ensure that the school provides their children with discourse patterns, interactional styles, and spoken and written language codes that will allow them success in the larger society.[18]

Notes from the Field

What are the benefits of a diverse classroom?

"I feel blessed to work in a school that has so much cultural diversity. It gives me the opportunity to learn about the cultures of my students as well as share my culture with them. It brings our community closer together to share food, songs, dances, and traditions with one another. It also allows the students to learn to embrace people who are different from themselves."

—*Valerie Geschwind, fourth-grade teacher*

Different students come to school with different needs. Those who, for whatever reason, come to school without certain "cultural capital" need the keys to that storehouse of information and skills as much as they need anything else out of schooling. To deny them that in the name of ignoring race or giving all students the same thing is to permanently tip the scales in favor of some children and against others.

Irvine calls for teachers to be both caring and competent, and it is probably important to add the word *curious*. A teacher who wants to learn about his or her students—who wants to learn *from* his or her students—will teach them a model of respect for diversity that will go a long way toward building an engaging classroom.

A final note is important to remember: It is all too easy to fall into the trap of viewing groups of people as neat and separate packages; to think of immigrants as one group, people of color as another, boys and girls as another, and students with disabilities or different beliefs as yet another. But human beings do not fall into such neat categories. In one classroom, a teacher may well have a wheelchair-bound African American lesbian; a Russian-speaking, nearsighted, Pentecostal boy; and a recent immigrant from India who is a very literate Hindu with a learning disability; along with students representing any of a hundred of other interesting and challenging mixes. Human beings come in all sizes and shapes and characteristics, all rolled into one beautiful, unique person.

So, who will my students be? A group of young people more diverse, more interesting, and more engaging than one can ever imagine, waiting for someone to build a classroom for them that respects them, engages them, and teaches them.

CHAPTER REVIEW

• Will my classroom be like the ones I attended?

The classrooms of today and tomorrow are more than likely going to be very different in many ways from those of even a few years ago, especially regarding the diversity of students (and students' needs). While the nation—especially the nation's school-age population—is becoming "majority minority," not every school reflects this growing diversity. While some communities embrace diversity, others are being resegregated at a rapid rate.

• Who attends school today?

In recent years, birth rates (especially in the Latino community) and immigration (including shifts in where immigrants are coming from) have increased significantly, and changing demographics indicate that the percentage of many "minority" groups (especially Hispanics and Asians) are growing rapidly. These changes are being reflected in the classroom. Thus, any future teacher must be prepared to enthusiastically embrace recent immigrant students along with students whose families have been in the United States for generations, students of all races, students who reject ethnic identifications, and students who do not come to school speaking English.

• Learning the Language: What are the ongoing debates over bilingual education?

Some people argue that in today's world of expansive immigration, schools need programs of bilingual education that strengthen attachments to the home cultures and languages of the nation's diverse students while also engaging those students in successful mastery of English as a second language. Others argue, with equal fervor, that the only way to ensure the integration of all students into a common culture and a successful educational experience is to ensure that students arriving in U.S. schools are immersed in English as rapidly as possible. Future teachers will need to function in schools that have adopted one policy or another or a combination of both while also remaining true to their own core values.

• How can I be sure that I am reaching all my students?

Simply saying, "I am colorblind" is not acceptable. Students need and want to be embraced in their uniqueness, and this means recognizing who they are in many different ways. To fail to respect a student's culture or language is to be disrespectful in ways that may disengage a student completely. However, no teacher can know everything there is to know about every culture that may be represented in a classroom. A teacher must be prepared to see students as individuals who define themselves by many different characteristics and are defined by the larger society by many more. And a teacher must think continually about how to mold a diverse classroom into a small society that models the kind of inclusive and welcoming behavior that we wish the larger society would adopt.

Readings

Who Attends School Today?

From "A PIVOTAL PERIOD FOR RACE IN AMERICA," IN *DIVERSITY EXPLOSION : HOW NEW RACIAL DEMOGRAPHICS ARE REMAKING AMERICA*

AUTHOR: WILLIAM H. FREY

William H. Frey, a senior researcher at the Brookings Institution in Washington, D.C., has been tracking the changes in the makeup of the American people for many years. As he writes in his book Diversity Explosion: How New Racial Demographics are Remaking America, *more babies of color have been born each year in the United States than White babies since 2011 and most of today's immigrants are not White. While the U.S. will be a "majority minority" country by the 2040s, Frey is clear that the school-age population is achieving this status much more rapidly and has already done so in many places.*

America reached an important milestone in 2011. That occurred when, for the first time in the history of the country, more minority babies than white babies were born in a year. Soon, most children will be racial minorities: Hispanics, blacks, Asians, and other nonwhite races. And, in about three decades, whites will constitute a minority of all Americans. This milestone signals the beginning of a transformation from the mostly white baby boom culture that dominated the nation during the last half of the twentieth century to the more globalized, multiracial country that the United States is becoming.

Certainly in the past, the specter of a "minority white" nation instilled fear among some Americans, and to some extent it continues to do so today—fear of change, fear of losing privileged status, or fear of unwanted groups in their communities. These fears were especially evident during the decades following World War II, when immigration was low and phrases such as "invasion," "blockbusting," and "white flight" were commonly used in the context of black-white segregation. Such fears are evident today in the public backlashes that sometimes occur against more permissive immigration and voter registration laws.

Table 3.3 U.S. White and Minority Populations, 1970–2050

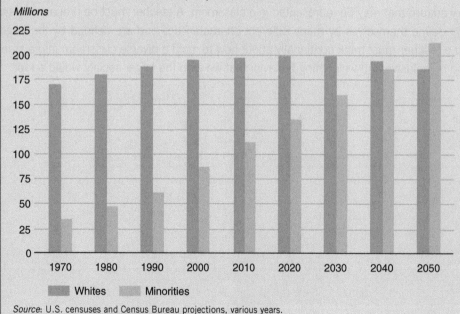

Source: U.S. censuses and Census Bureau projections, various years.

Yet if demography is truly destiny, then these fears of a more racially diverse nation will almost certainly dissipate. In many communities, a broad spectrum of racial groups already is accepted by all, particularly among the highly diverse youth population. Moreover, as this book illustrates, a growing diverse, globally connected minority population will be absolutely necessary to infuse the aging American labor force with vitality and to sustain populations in many parts of the country that are facing population declines. Rather than being feared, America's new diversity—poised to reinvigorate the country at a time when other developed nations are facing advanced aging and population loss—can be celebrated.

The sweep of diversity that has just begun to affect the nation is the theme of this book, which draws from my examination of the most recent U.S. census, census projections, and related sources. As a demographer who has followed U.S. population trends for decades, even I was surprised by the sheer scope of racial change that came to light with the 2010 census. The story that the data tell is not just more of the same. I am convinced that the United States is in the midst of a pivotal period ushering in extraordinary shifts in the nation's racial demographic makeup. If planned for properly, these demographic changes will allow the country to face the future with growth and vitality as it reinvents the classic American melting pot for a new era. In my experiences speaking publicly and answering press inquiries, I have seen the intensity of Americans' questions and thoughts about issues surrounding race. After having absorbed these startling census results and their implications, I wanted to interpret and expound on the dramatic shifts that they illustrate so that a general audience of readers can appreciate their force, promise, and challenges. Key among these changes are:

- *The rapid growth of "new minorities": Hispanics, Asians, and increasingly multiracial populations.* During the next 40 years, each of these groups is expected to more than double. New minorities have already become the major contributors to U.S. population gains. These new minorities—the products of recent immigration waves as well as the growing U.S.-born generations—contributed to more than three-quarters of the nation's population growth in the last decade. That trend will accelerate in the future.
- *The sharply diminished growth and rapid aging of America's white population.* Due to white low immigration, reduced fertility, and aging, the white population grew a tepid 1.2 percent in 2000–10. In roughly 10 years, the white population will begin a decline that will continue into the future. This decline will be most prominent among the younger populations. At the same time, the existing white population will age rapidly, as the large baby boom generation advances into seniorhood.
- *Black economic advances and migration reversals.* Now, more than a half-century after the civil rights movement began, a recognizable segment of blacks has entered the middle class while simultaneously reversing historic population shifts. The long-standing Great Migration of blacks out of the South has now turned into a wholesale evacuation from the North—to largely prosperous southern locales. Blacks are abandoning cities for the suburbs, and black neighborhood segregation continues to decline. Although many blacks still suffer the effects of inequality and segregation is far from gone, the economic and residential environments for blacks have improved well beyond the highly discriminatory, ghettoized life that most experienced for much of the twentieth century.
- *The shift toward a nation in which no racial group is the majority.* The shift toward "no majority" communities is already taking place as the constellation of racial minorities expands. In 2010, 22 of the nation's 100 largest metropolitan areas were minority white, up from just 14 in 2000 and 5 in 1990. Sometime after 2040, there will be no racial majority in the country. This is hardly the America that large numbers of today's older and middle-aged adults grew up with in their neighborhoods, workplaces, and civic lives. One implication of these shifts will be larger multiracial populations as multiracial marriages become far more commonplace.

The "diversity explosion" the country is now experiencing will bring significant changes in the attitudes of individuals, the practices of institutions, and the nature of American politics. Racial change has never been easy, and more often than not it has been fraught with fear and conflict.

Yet for most of the nation's history, nonwhite racial groups have been a small minority. Partly because of that, blacks and other racial minorities were historically subjected to blatant discrimination, whether through Jim Crow laws, the Asian Exclusion Act, or any of the many other measures that denied racial minorities access to jobs, education, housing, financial resources, and basic rights of civic participation.

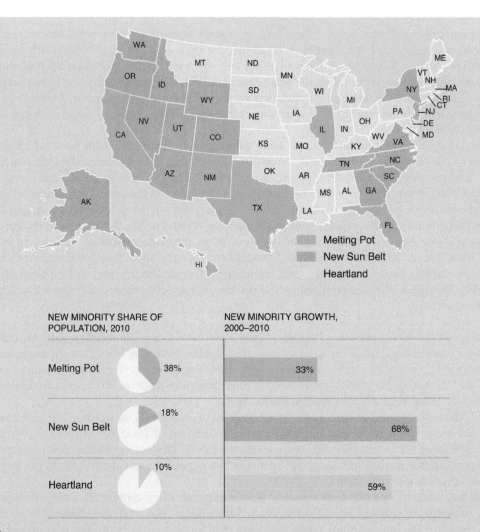

Figure 3.1
New Minorities in the Melting Pot, New Sun Belt, and Heartland Regions

What will be different going forward is the sheer size of the minority population in the United States. It is arriving "just in time" as the aging white population begins to decline, bringing with it needed manpower and brain power and taking up residence in otherwise stagnating city and suburban housing markets. Although whites are still considered the mainstream in the United States, that perception should eventually shift as more minority members assume positions of responsibility, exert more political clout, exercise their strength as consumers, and demonstrate their value in the labor force. As they become integral to the nation's success, their concerns will be taken seriously.

Questions

1. Were you surprised to learn that the nation is quickly moving toward a "majority minority" population?
2. What are some of the implications of this article for the classroom? In terms of who will be in school in the future? In terms of what schools should teach: Whose history? Whose literature?

Source: William H. Frey. "A Pivotal Period for Race in America." In *Diversity Explosion: How New Racial Demographics Are Remaking America*, 1–5. Washington, DC: Brookings Institution Press, 2014.

What are the Ongoing Debates Over Bilingual Education?

The following two articles appeared in the same issue of *Educational Leadership* in April 2009. They certainly do not represent either end of the spectrum of opinions held within the bilingual education debate, in which some people argue strongly for equal emphasis on maintaining a student's first language while helping that student learn English and others focus almost exclusively on helping a student learn English as quickly as possible. Nevertheless a careful reading of the two articles points to important differences—hinted at in the titles—between the two articles.

From "ALL LANGUAGES WELCOMED HERE"

AUTHOR: ORHAN AGIRDAG

This article by Orhan Agirdag (Ghent University in Belgium) reflects both his work among the many different linguistic groups of Europe and his analysis of the situation in the United States.

Indeed, not only in the United States, but also in various places around the world, educators are challenged by the difficulties of schooling language learners. One proposed solution has been bilingual instruction. Although a substantial body of research suggests that bilingual instruction is beneficial for language learners (Baker, 1996), other studies dispute these positive effects (Rossell, 2004). Even if we were certain about the purported benefits of this approach, schools often have difficulty implementing it.

For instance, it would not be feasible to provide bilingual instruction at a highly heterogeneous school in which students come from a great many linguistic backgrounds. With growing immigrant populations, this picture of linguistic diversity is becoming increasingly familiar to many educators. Schools can more easily implement bilingual instruction in relatively homogenous areas, such as the southwest region of the United States where large numbers of Spanish speakers live and where instruction in English and Spanish is feasible. It is less clear, however, how to provide bilingual instruction in places where students speak dozens of languages.

Legal constraints can also hinder the implementation of bilingual education. In some countries (such as Turkey), the law only permits instruction in the official language. Other countries (such as Belgium) only allow bilingual instruction for language learners as an educational experiment. In addition, more and more countries are reducing the amount of existing bilingual instruction (SkutnabbKangas, 2000). For example, in 2004, the Netherlands stopped subsidizing almost all forms of bilingual instruction, which reduced the existing bilingual education to a few, mostly privately funded, programs.

Language and Identity

Even in the absence of bilingual instruction, language learners should have the right to feel at home in school. Cultural discontinuity between students' home-based and school-based experiences can have a negative effect on their academic performance, well-being, and sense of belonging at school. The larger the gap between these two experiences, the greater the disadvantage of cultural discontinuity (Gay, 2000).

When students have to leave their primary language at the school gates, they also leave a part of their cultural identity behind. As Cummins (2001) noted, "To reject a child's language in the school is to reject the child" (p. 19). Therefore, educators must try to close the gap between language learners' identities, which are intricately tied to language, and the school culture.

Teachers and administrators often express willingness to create a supportive learning environment for all students. However, they do not always command the tools necessary to realize such an environment. The literature about multilingual school settings is often of little help because the subject is highly complex and the arguments are more politicized than practical (Gersten, 1999). For many educators, the question of what they can realistically do remains unanswered.

To move toward a supportive school setting for all students, educators can create a linguistically plural learning environment, even without bilingual instruction. Plurilingualism in school—that is, making all students' languages visible and valuable—is advantageous for various reasons. The presence of students' home languages in school not only affirms language learners' identities, but also reduces linguistic barriers, opening doors for educators to build improved relationships with the learners' families and communities.

The recommendations that follow are based on my research in Belgium, but they are meaningful for educators in other countries as well. For this reason, I use the term *language learners* instead of *English language learners*.

Practices to Avoid

Insisting on a Monolingual Classroom

First, educators should strive to avoid *ethnocentric monolingualism*, that is, expressions of the superiority of one group's language over another (see Sue & Sue, 2008). Ethnocentric monolingualism is harmful, not only because it stigmatizes language learners, but also because it fails to recognize the value of various linguistic backgrounds.

One obvious expression of ethnocentric monolingualism is forbidding students to use their native language in school. In many schools, teachers may even formally punish students when they "catch them" speaking their home language with peers. School staff members and teachers may tend to use punitive practices because they often believe that speaking the home language slows the process of language learning, assuming it is in *competition* with the language that students are supposed to learn.

However, sociolinguistic research has found quite the reverse. Repeatedly, studies have shown that proficiency in the first language is positively related to proficiency in the second language (Cummins, 2000), suggesting that students' proficiency in their native language accelerates language learning. By extension, excluding students' home languages from the classroom does not assist them; rather, it may actually hinder their learning process. . . .

Practices to Adopt

The key element to promoting plurilingualism is to acknowledge and value language learners' linguistic backgrounds in close cooperation with both students and their parents.

Welcome Languages in the Classroom

Teachers should create an instructional climate that makes room for all students' languages. They can do this in different ways, such as by hanging posters on the wall that list significant words (such as *welcome*) in different languages. Teachers can also reinforce plurilingualism in managing students' classroom behavior. For example, during my research I met a teacher who complained about the disruptive behavior of a Turkish-Belgian student in her class. Neither discipline nor praise seemed to improve his conduct. One day when I was observing in the classroom, I asked the boy, in Turkish, to be less noisy and to settle down and pay attention. This worked. Teachers can promote plurilingualism—and benefit, perhaps, from higher levels of student engagement—by learning a couple of key phrases, such as "Please quiet down" and "Nice job!" in languages that are commonly found in their classrooms. Teachers can also strengthen plurilingualism through comparisons with countries familiar to many of their immigrant students. For example, in geography, the teacher might compare the rather complicated linguistic situation of Belgium with that of Morocco, where Arabic and Berber are widely spoken.

Ask Students to Share Their Languages

Teachers should encourage students to bring their home languages into the classroom. For example, every day the teacher could ask a different student to share a significant word or sentence in his or her native language with the entire class. Both classmates and teacher could discuss this word or sentence: How does the student pronounce the word and what does he or she think about it? Afterwards, educators will notice that words like *friend* will have an effect on students' interactions beyond the classroom.

For example, at one of the schools in which I was doing research, I overheard Turkish-Belgian, Moroccan-Belgian, and Dutch pupils calling one another *kardas* on the school playground. *Kardas* is Turkish for *brother* or *friend*; it is often used to refer to friendly relationships with non-Turks. Now it has become a significant marker of interethnic friendship among pupils.

Have Students Help Their Peers

Teachers should encourage language learners from the same linguistic backgrounds to cooperate with one another to improve their progress. For instance, when a concept is unclear for a language learner, the teacher might call on another student from the same linguistic background to explain it. This is especially helpful when it comes to abstract concepts in math, such as *multiplication* or *mean*. After all, students often learn better from their peers than they do from their teacher.

Expand the School's Cultural Repertoire

School administrations should make the cultural repertoire of the school more plurilingual. Schools can easily do this by exposing students to subtitled movies, expanding the school's library of bilingual books and books written in different languages, providing materials in students' languages through the Internet, and helping students learn various songs in different languages.

One school in Antwerp reaches out to immigrant families by providing a welcoming message on the school Web site in 12 different languages. The message explains the school's system of communicating with parents using pictograms, which signal upcoming field trips, whether payment is required, and what their child should bring. The pictograms also indicate to parents when they are expected at school and for what reason.

Involve Parents

To realize an effective plurilingual learning environment, schools must involve students' parents. For example, teachers can call on parents to teach some aspects of their language to the whole class, including the teacher. In a French primary school, parents from more than eight different linguistic backgrounds taught students how to introduce themselves, count to 10, greet people, and say thank you in their languages (Helot & Young, 2002).

School-parent cooperation is crucial. Parental involvement in language learners' education often lags because of linguistic barriers. But when schools consider home languages not as obstacles but as assets, the "language wall" around the school breaks down.

Source: Ohran Agirdad. "All Languages Welcomed Here." *Educational Leadership* 66, no. 7 (2009), pp. 20–25.

From "THE CASE FOR STRUCTURED ENGLISH IMMERSION"

AUTHOR: KEVIN CLARK

Kevin Clark is president of Clark Consulting and Training, which is based in California. He has worked with school districts to design programs for English language learners (ELLs) for more than 20 years.

When Arizona voters passed a ballot initiative in 2000 that required all English language learners to be educated through structured English immersion (SEI), the idea seemed simple enough: Teach students the English language quickly so they can do better in school. But as other states, districts, and schools that have contemplated an SEI program have learned, the devil is in the details. As it turns out, the simple goal to "teach English quickly" frequently evokes legal wrangling, emotion, and plain old demagoguery.

Few people would disagree that English language proficiency is necessary for academic success in U.S. schools. Less clear, however, is the optimal pathway for helping language-minority students master English. Conflicting ideologies, competing academic theories, and multiple metrics for comparing different approaches have rendered many schools, districts, and educators paralyzed by confusion. Bill Holden, principal of a California elementary school in which ELLs are three-fourths of the student population, told me, "At a certain point there were just so many mixed messages and contradictory directives and policies that we didn't really know what to do."

Despite the controversy, however, many schools in Arizona and other states have implemented structured English immersion or are in the process of doing so. As I have worked with educators, school boards, and the Arizona English Language Learners Task Force to explore, design, and implement structured programs, a common theme emerges: These programs have the potential to accelerate ELLs' English language development and linguistic preparation for grade-level academic content.

Why Do Schools Implement Structured English Immersion?

Several factors usually account for school and district leaders' decisions to opt for structured English immersion. In three states (California, Arizona, and Massachusetts), the reason is straightforward: Laws passed through voter initiatives now require structured English immersion and restrict bilingual education.

Another factor is that most state student performance assessments are conducted in English, and schools or districts that miss targets face increased scrutiny and possible sanctions. This provides added incentive for schools to get students' English proficiency up to speed as soon as possible.

A third factor is the burgeoning subpopulation of ELL students who reach an intermediate level of English competence after a few years—and then stop making progress. These students (more than 60 percent of all ELLs in some districts, according to analyses I conducted for 15 districts) possess conversational English competence. But they lag in their ability to apply the rules, structures, and specialized vocabularies of English necessary for grade-level academic coursework; and their writing typically features an array of structural errors. My analyses showed that the typical intermediate-level ELL scores well below proficient on state-level tests in English language arts.

Some educators have acknowledged, in fact, that intermediate English competence is the logical outcome of their current practices and program designs. "Once we really analyzed our program for ELL students," one district superintendent told me, "we saw that we really didn't teach English to our students. We were teaching *in* English, but not really teaching English." . . .

Experience Fills in the Details

Notwithstanding the hodgepodge of definitions, mixed messages, and underlying emotions, educators have implemented structured English immersion programs at both the elementary and secondary levels. A framework for effective SEI is emerging that includes the following elements.

Significant amounts of the school day are dedicated to the explicit teaching of the English language, and students are grouped for this instruction according to their level of English proficiency.

The English language is the main content of SEI instruction. Academic content plays a supporting, but subordinate, role. English is the language of instruction; students and teachers are expected to speak, read, and write in English.

Teachers use instructional methods that treat English as a foreign language. Students learn discrete English grammar skills. Rigorous time lines are established for students to exit from the program.

Charting New Territory

Each of these program elements in some way runs counter to the assumptions and beliefs that have guided ELL program development throughout the last 30 years. In Arizona and elsewhere, advocates of structured English immersion face strong criticism from detractors who argue, among other things, that these programs are segregatory, experimental, not based on research, nonculturally affirming, damaging to students' self-esteem, and perhaps even illegal (Adams, 2005; Combs, Evans, Fletcher, Parra, & Jiménez, 2005; Krashen, Rolstad, & MacSwan, 2007).

Proponents of SEI maintain that students can learn English faster than many theories suggest, that grouping students by language ability level is necessary for successful lesson design, and that the research support for immersion language-teaching methods and program design principles is solid (Arizona English Language Learners Task Force, 2007; Baker, 1998; Judson & Garcia-Dugan, 2004). As for the question of self-esteem, SEI advocates point out that ELLs are motivated by measurable success in learning the fundamentals of English, as well as by the improved reading comprehension, enhanced writing skills, and higher levels of achievement in core subjects that come from these enhanced language skills.

On the legal front, ballot initiatives requiring SEI programs have been found to comport with federal law. Under the federal framework, as articulated in *Castañeda v. Pickard* (1981), immersion programs are viewed as "sequential," in that their goal is to provide foundational English skills before students participate in a full range of academic content courses.

SEI Programs in Action

George Washington Elementary School in Madera, California, enrolls more than 500 English language learners in grades K–6. Located in the middle of a Spanish-dominant portion of a town in central California, the school was a magnet bilingual education site for decades—and unfortunately one of the lowest-achieving schools in the district.

The school missed state and federal academic performance targets for years, and fewer than 3 percent of ELLs annually were reclassified as fully English proficient.

District data analyses showed that after the first full year of SEI program implementation, the school gained almost 30 points on state test metrics, and English language growth rates tripled in all grades, easily exceeding district and federal targets. The reclassification rate last year quadrupled to 12 percent. Perhaps most significant, almost 50 percent of the school's intermediate students advanced to the next level of proficiency or met the criteria for being fully English proficient. Before the SEI program, 70 percent of the school's ELL population regularly showed no English language growth—or even regressed—on the state's yearly English assessment.

Here's what an average day looks like for an ELL student at George Washington Elementary School:

- Pronunciation and listening skills, 20 minutes.
- Vocabulary, 30 minutes.
- Verb tense instruction, 20 minutes.
- Sentence structure, 20 minutes.
- Integrated grammar skills application, 20 minutes.
- English reading and writing, 60 minutes.
- Math (specially designed academic instruction in English), 40 minutes.
- Science, social science, P.E., 40 minutes.

At Yuba City High School in Northern California, almost half of the school's 450 ELLs test at intermediate or below on the state's language assessment. These students are enrolled in four periods of daily English language development courses: Conversational English and Content Area Vocabulary, English Grammar, English Reading, and English Writing. The school offers three levels for each course; students take an assessment every six weeks that could qualify them to move to the next level. Some students move so quickly that they exit the SEI program in less than a year. After the first year of Yuba City's SEI program, the proportion of students reclassified as fully English proficient tripled to 15 percent, nearly twice the state average.

Questions

1. If the authors of these two articles were advising a school on how to develop a program for students who arrive not speaking English (English language learners or ELLs, as they are called today), how do you think they would differ in the recommendations they would make? In what ways might they make the same recommendations?
2. What is each author's strongest argument in favor of his own recommendations?
3. If you were in charge of a school or district, which author would you listen to? Could you draw from both?

Source: Kevin Clark. "The Case for Structured English Immersion." *Educational Leadership* 66, no. 7 (April 2009): pp. 42–6.

How Can I Be Sure That I Am Reaching All My Students?

From "THE SILENCED DIALOGUE : POWER AND PEDAGOGY IN EDUCATING OTHER PEOPLE'S CHILDREN"

AUTHOR: LISA DELPIT

Lisa Delpit is the executive director of the Center for Urban Education and Innovation at Florida International University in Miami, Florida. Former recipient of the MacArthur Award and author of Other People's Children: Cultural Conflict in the Classroom *and* The Skin That We Speak: Thoughts on Language and Culture in the Classroom, *she asks the hard questions with which every aspiring teacher must wrestle in order to be a responsible teacher.*

A black woman teacher in a multicultural urban elementary school is talking about her experiences in discussions with her predominantly white fellow teachers about how they should organize reading instruction to best serve students of color:

> When you're talking to white people they still want it to be their way. You can try to talk to them and give them examples, but they're so headstrong, they think they know what's best for everybody, for everybody's children. They won't listen; white folks are going to do what they want to do anyway.
>
> It's really hard. They just don't listen well. No, they listen, but they don't hear—you know how your mama used to say you listen to the radio, but you hear your mother? Well they don't hear me.
>
> So I just try to shut them out so I can hold my temper. . . .

A soft-spoken Native Alaskan woman in her forties is a student in the Education Department of the University of Alaska. One day she storms into a black professor's office and very uncharacteristically slams the door. She plops down in a chair and, still fuming, says, "Please tell those people, just don't help us anymore! I give up. I won't talk to them again!" . . .

Thus was the first half of the title of this text born: "The Silenced Dialogue." One of the tragedies of this field of education is that scenarios such as these are enacted daily around the country. The saddest element is that the individuals that the black and Native Alaskan educators speak of in these statements are seldom aware that the dialogue *has* been silenced. Most likely the white educators believe that their colleagues of color did, in the end, agree with their logic. After all, they stopped disagreeing, didn't they? . . .

How can such complete communication blocks exist when both parties truly believe they have the same aims? How can the bitterness and resentment expressed by the educators of color be drained so that the sores can heal? What can be done?

I believe the answer to these questions lies in ethnographic analysis, that is, in identifying and giving voice to alternative worldviews. Thus, I will attempt to address the concerns raised by white and black respondents to my article "Skills and Other Dilemmas." My charge here is not to determine the best instructional methodology; I believe that the actual practice of good teachers of all colors typically incorporates a range of pedagogical orientations. Rather, I suggest that the differing perspectives on the debate over "skills" versus "process" approaches can lead to an understanding of the alienation and miscommunication, and thereby to an understanding of the "silenced dialogue."

In thinking through these issues, I have found what I believe to be a connecting and complex theme: what I have come to call "the culture of power." There are five aspects of power I would like to propose as given for this presentation:

1. *Issues of power are enacted in classrooms.*

These issues include: the power of the teacher over the students; the power of the publishers of textbooks and the developers of the curriculum to determine the view of the world presented; the power of the state in enforcing compulsory schooling; and the power of an individual or group to determine another's intelligence or "normalcy." Finally, if schooling prepares people for jobs, and the kind of job a person has determines her or his economic status and, therefore, power, then schooling is intimately related to that power.

2. *There are codes or rules for participating in power; that is, there is a "culture of power."*

The codes or rules I'm speaking of relate to linguistic forms, communicative strategies, and presentation of self; that is, ways of talking, ways of writing, ways of dressing, and ways of interacting.

3. *The rules of the culture of power are a reflection of the rules of the culture of those who have the power.*

This means that success in institutions—schools, workplaces, and so on—is predicated upon acquisition of the culture of those who are in power. Children from middle-class homes tend to do better in school than those from non-middle-class homes because the culture of the school is based on the culture of the upper and middle classes—of those in power. The upper and middle classes send their children to school with all the accoutrements of the culture of power; children from other kinds of families operate within perfectly wonderful and viable cultures but not cultures that carry the codes or rules of power.

4. *If you are not already a participant in the culture of power, being told explicitly the rules of that culture makes acquiring power easier.*

In my work within and between diverse cultures, I have come to conclude that members of any culture transmit information implicitly to co-members. However, when implicit codes are attempted across cultures, communication frequently breaks down. Each cultural group is left saying, "Why don't those people say what they mean?" As well as, "What's wrong with them, why don't they understand?"

Anyone who has had to enter new cultures, especially to accomplish a specific task, will know of what I speak. When I lived in several Papua, New Guinea villages for extended periods to collect data, and when I go to Alaskan villages for work with Native Alaskan communities, I have found it unquestionably easier, psychologically and pragmatically, when some kind soul has directly informed me about such matters as appropriate dress, interactional styles, embedded meanings, and taboo words or actions. I contend that it is much the same for anyone seeking to learn the rules of the culture of power. Unless one has the leisure of a lifetime of "immersion" to learn them, explicit presentation makes learning immeasurably easier.

And now, to the fifth and last premise:

5. *Those with power are frequently least aware of—or least willing to acknowledge—its existence. Those with less power are often most aware of its existence.*

For many who consider themselves members of liberal or radical camps, acknowledging personal power and admitting participation in the culture of power is distinctly uncomfortable. On the other hand, those who are less powerful in any situation are most likely to recognize the power variable most acutely. My guess is that the white colleagues and instructors of those previously quoted did not perceive themselves to have power over the nonwhite speakers. However, either by virtue of their position, their numbers, or their access to that particular code of power of calling upon research to validate one's position, the white educators had the authority to establish what was to be considered "truth" regardless of the opinions of the people of color, and the latter were well aware of that fact.

To explore those differences, I would like to present several statements typical of those made with the best of intentions by middle-class liberal educators. To the surprise of the speakers, it is not unusual for such content to be met by vocal opposition or stony silence from people of color. My attempt here is to examine the underlying assumptions of both camps.

"I want the same thing for everyone else's children as I want for mine."

To provide schooling for everyone's children that reflects liberal, middle-class values and aspirations is to ensure the maintenance of the status quo, to ensure that power, the culture of power, remains in the hands of those who already have it. Some children come to school with more accoutrements of the culture of power already in place—"cultural capital," as some critical theorists refer to it—some with less. Many liberal educators hold that the primary goal for education is for children to become autonomous, to develop fully who they are in the classroom setting without having arbitrary, outside standards forced upon them. This is a very reasonable goal for people whose children are already participants in the culture of power and who have already internalized its codes.

But parents who don't function within that culture often want something else. It's not that they disagree with the former aim, it's just that they want something more. They want to ensure that the school provides their children with discourse patterns, interactional styles, and spoken and written language codes that will allow them success in the larger society.

"Child-centered, whole language, and process approaches are needed in order to allow a democratic state of free, autonomous, empowered adults, and because research has shown that children learn best through these methods."

People of color are, in general, skeptical of research as a determiner of our fates. Academic research has, after all, found us genetically inferior, culturally deprived, and verbally deficient. But beyond that general caveat, and despite my or others' personal preferences, there is little research data supporting the major tenets of process approaches over other forms of literacy instruction, and virtually no evidence that such approaches are more efficacious for children of color.

Although the problem is not necessarily inherent in the method, in some instances adherents of process approaches to writing create situations in which students ultimately find themselves held accountable for knowing a set of rules about which no one has ever directly informed them. Teachers do students no service to suggest, even implicitly, that "product" is not important. In this country, students will be judged on their product regardless of the process they utilized to achieve it. And that product, based as it is on the specific codes of a particular culture, is more readily produced when the directives of how to produce it are made explicit.

"It's really a shame but she (that black teacher upstairs) seems to be so authoritarian, so focused on skills and so teacher directed. Those poor kids never seem to be allowed to really express their creativity. (And she even yells at them.)"

This statement directly concerns the display of power and authority in the classroom. One way to understand the difference in perspective between black teachers and their progressive colleagues on this issue is to explore culturally influenced oral interactions.

In *Ways with Words*, Shirley Brice Heath quotes the verbal directives given by the middle class "townspeople" teachers:

- "Is this where the scissors belong?"
- "You want to do your best work today."

By contrast, many black teachers are more likely to say:

- "Put those scissors on that shelf."
- "Put your name on the papers and make sure to get the right answers for each question."

Is one oral style more authoritarian than another?

But those veiled commands are commands nonetheless, representing true power, and with true consequences for disobedience. If veiled commands are ignored, the child will be labeled a behavior problem and possibly officially classified as behavior disordered. In other words, the attempt by the teacher to reduce an exhibition of power by expressing herself in indirect terms may remove the very explicitness that the child needs to understand the rules of the new classroom culture. . . .

To summarize, I suggest that students must be *taught* the codes needed to participate fully in the mainstream of American life, not by being forced to attend to hollow, inane, decontextualized subskills, but rather within the context of meaningful communicative endeavors; that they must be allowed the resource of the teacher's expert knowledge, while being helped to acknowledge their own "expertness" as well; and that even while students are assisted in learning the culture of power, they must also be helped to learn about the arbitrariness of those codes and about the power relationships they represent. . . .

In conclusion, I am proposing a resolution for the skills/process debate. In short, the debate is fallacious; the dichotomy is false. . . . The dilemma is not really in the debate over instructional methodology, but rather in communicating across cultures and in addressing the more fundamental issue of power, of whose voice gets to be heard in determining what is best for poor children and children of color. Will black teachers and parents continue to be silenced by the very forces that claim to "give voice" to our children? Such an outcome would be tragic, for both groups truly have something to say to one another. As a result of careful listening to alternative points of view, I have myself come to a viable synthesis of perspectives. But both sides do need to be able to listen, and I contend that it is those with the most power, those in the majority, who must take the greater responsibility for initiating the process.

Questions

1. If you are a student of color, have you ever experienced the kind of silencing that Delpit describes in this article? What was your reaction?
2. If you are a White student, have you experienced similar silencing for another reason, such as a time when you just knew something was right but somehow others would not listen to or hear you? What was your reaction?
3. Can you think of a time when you may have silenced someone else?
4. Do you agree with Delpit that students who are "not part of the culture of power" may need explicit instruction in the rules of the dominant culture? Can you imagine giving such instruction to a group of children or adolescents? What would that look like?
5. Is it true that those with power may be unaware of it while those without power are quite aware? What does that mean for teachers?

Source: Lisa D. Delpit. "The Silenced Dialogue: Power and Pedagogy in Educating Other People's Children." *Harvard Educational Review* 88, no. 3 (August 1988): 280–98.

Including Everyone
4

Who Sometimes Gets Overlooked in School?

QUESTIONS TO COME

In Chapter 3, we explored issues of diversity primarily in terms of race and ethnicity or status as a recent or not-so-recent immigrant, as well as home language of a student's family. In this chapter, we continue the discussion of diversity but with a different focus. We look at several groups of students who were often easily excluded from many schools or at least from many of the benefits of effective schooling until the 1960s and 1970s, including girls who experienced marginalization because of their gender, students with disabilities, and students who sometimes felt the need to hide their "difference," be it sexual orientation, religious belief, or family culture. We explore the legislation and programs designed to maximize the education and full inclusion of all students, including controversies regarding their effectiveness.

The **Readings** for this chapter introduce you to three key debates surrounding inclusion and exclusion in schools today. First, we examine a significant debate about what it means for schools to be gender fair. In spite of the advances made in the 1970s and 1980s by the women's movement, some researchers have been concerned that girls continue to receive a second-class education in far too many American classrooms. However, some argue that schools no longer discriminate against girls and, in fact, that the pressing issue is now the education of boys. In the first **Reading**, Sara Mead contends that although the needs of some boys, especially African American boys, are severe, other research overlooks significant barriers to academic success that female students continue to face while gender stereotypes can also significantly constrict the education of boys. She argues for removing the barriers that still hinder *some* boys and *some* girls while avoiding overgeneralizations in either case. In the next **Reading**, the California FAIR Act of 2011 describes new California policies that focus primarily on the full inclusion of gay and lesbian students. And the final **Reading** looks at issues of special

education: programs specifically directed at students with one or more of many disabilities or emotional or behavioral disorders. Barbara S. S. Hong and Kay A. Chick ask why learning comes so naturally for some and is so difficult for others. And what, they ask, is a learning disability? Only by answering these questions—and by understanding that there might, indeed, be multiple kinds of disabilities needing multiple kinds of responses—can teachers diagnose and support those students for whom learning does not come as easily as it might for others.

Historically Speaking: Who Was Left Out of American Schools?

Prior to the 1960s, many people, including teachers, assumed that the purpose of public schooling was to provide the best possible education to those students who were prepared to receive it. Half a century ago, although most Americans attended elementary school, more than half dropped out before finishing high school. If students did not stay in school because they did not feel welcome, or because a disability made school painful if not impossible, or because they felt school was "not for them," or because they were simply bored or disengaged, many people thought that was just fine.

Many people thought it was okay if girls did not receive an education equal to that of boys, even when they were in the same schools and classrooms. After all, career opportunities for women were limited by the social expectations of the day. Many middle-class European American girls were expected to settle happily into the role of stay-at-home wives and mothers while poor girls and girls of color were expected to work as domestics or in factories or in other menial jobs. It was also okay if students with various disabilities simply left school. Students in wheelchairs who could not climb the stairs, blind students or dyslexic students who could not read the texts, students who had deep-seated emotional problems that made conforming to the routines of school virtually impossible, and students who were, for whatever reason, slower to learn than their classmates, were often simply told to "go home": The education offered in the public schools was not for them. Teachers and administrators felt unequipped to handle the needs of students with disabilities and did not feel a responsibility to do so. Schooling, they said, "was not for everyone." As we see in the following sections, these were the realities faced by far too many young people not too long ago.

> **inclusion**
> Ensuring that all students, regardless of perceived ability, race, gender, or other differences, are offered the same education, usually in the same setting, and engaged and connected with the larger school community and given the same opportunities and education.
>
> **federal legislation**
> A law put into place by the federal government.

Primarily due to the intensive focus on the **inclusion** of all students (not just racial minorities) that grew out of the civil rights movement, and including the most recent **federal legislation**, a growing consensus has emerged that "no child should be left behind." This commitment to inclusion had a huge impact on the education offered to girls and to boys, to students with many different disabilities, as well as to students who did not speak English when they first came to school. Indeed, most people now view it as a serious problem when any student drops out without completing high school, no matter what the reason. As a result, many students who had previously been excluded from school—or at least were all too easily allowed, even encouraged, to exclude themselves—are now expected and encouraged to stay in school.

In 1870, only 2% of students graduated from high school. By 1970, that percentage had grown to more than 75% and it is now around 80% However, several important pieces of information are buried in these statistics. At the beginning of the 20th century, only about 6% of students completed high school. However, high schools were still not available in many parts of the country, outside of big cities. Even in the cities, most people saw a high-school diploma as a luxury for a privileged few. Completing eight years of school was plenty for most people, including, ironically, most teachers of the day. Only in the 1920s, as high schools became much more widespread—not just in big cities but in small towns and rural areas—did a quarter of the nation's 17-year-olds finish high school and more and more teachers began receiving a college education prior to entering their jobs. It took another 25 years for school districts across the country to require a college degree for all teachers and 50 years to get to the point where three-quarters of the students finished high school.

Table 4.1 100 Years of Graduates

Year	High School Graduation Rates (% of 17-Year-Olds)	Year	High School Graduation Rates (% of 17-Year-Olds)
1870	2.0%	1920	16.3%
1880	2.5%	1930	28.8%
1890	3.5%	1940	49.0%
1900	6.3%	1950	57.4%
1910	8.6%	1960	63.4%
		1970	75.6%

Source: Historical Statistics of the United States: Colonial Times to 1970, U.S. Department of Commerce, 1976, Washington, DC.

The fact that we now assume that every student should at the very least complete high school has fundamentally changed the job description of every classroom teacher. Schools, especially classroom teachers, have been expected to make significant adjustments to accommodate the needs and interests of a widely diverse group of students. Whereas teachers were previously expected to teach those who were willing and able to learn what was in the lessons and those who could also accommodate themselves to the physical surroundings and cultural assumptions of the schools, teachers are now expected to teach everyone—the better prepared and the underprepared, the able and the less able, the willing and the unwilling—and to do it to higher and higher standards so that many more students will graduate with the skills

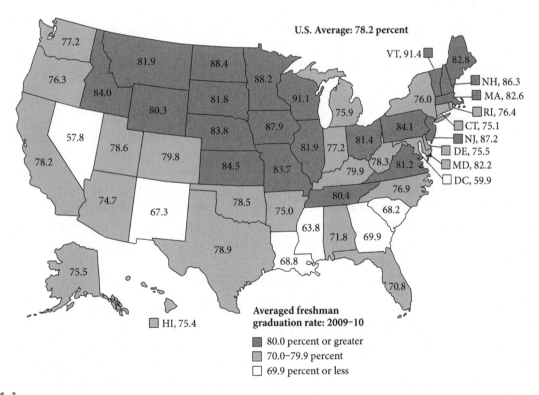

Figure 4.1
Averaged freshman graduation rate for public high school students, by state or jurisdiction (2009–10)

Source: U.S. Department of Education http://www.ed.gov/blog/2013/01/high-school-graduation-rate-at-highest-level-in-three-decades/

postindustrial society
A society in which information has replaced heavy industry as the lead engine of economic growth.

CONNECTIONS ➜⬅

In Chapter 10, we explore the issues surrounding drop-out rates today.

and knowledge needed to compete in a highly technical, **postindustrial society**. In spite of the widespread recognition of the importance of at least a high school education, the graduation rate remained stubbornly close to the 75% level for more than 40 years. In 2014, U.S. Secretary of Education Arne Duncan celebrated that the rate had increased slightly up to 78.2%, based on the latest statistics, including that the graduation rates for Latino (up 10 points from previous data) and African American students had risen more substantially—improvement definitely warranting celebration. Duncan has noted, however, that the dropout rate is still "unsustainably high for a knowledge-based economy and still unacceptably high in our African-American, Latino, and Native-American communities."

What Legal Actions Made School More Available for Many Young People?

In the 1960s and 1970s, a set of far-reaching changes in the economy, the cultural assumptions of society, and eventually the laws governing schools brought about a fundamentally new understanding of the answer to the question "Who should be in school?" By the end of the 1970s, the answer had become "everyone." A number of federal laws and U.S. Supreme Court decisions not only helped to create but also reflected the changes in expectations for schools that are at the heart of this chapter. Although many schools fail dramatically to live up to these expectations, and educators and members of the larger public continue to argue about the values behind these changes, no one can deny that the changes that took place between 1964 and 1975 fundamentally transformed schooling in the United States.

The Right to an Education

A series of court cases and legislation increased significantly the number of students attending school.

- 1964: Civil Rights Act of 1964 prohibits discrimination against students in school based on their race, color, sex, or national origin.
- 1968: Bilingual Education Act provides federal funds to encourage programs for students who do not speak English when they arrive in school.
- 1972: Title IX of the Education Amendments says that no one can be excluded from any school program on the basis of his or her sex.
- 1974: U.S. Supreme Court in *Lau v. Nichols* rules that schools must attend to the needs of students who do not speak English; programs for English language learners are no longer voluntary.
- 1975: U.S. Congress passes Public Law 94–142, which requires a "free appropriate public education" for every child in the United States no matter what his or her disability—physical, mental, or emotional. [Revised and expanded significantly by the Americans with Disabilities Act (ADA) of 1990 and further by the Individuals with Disabilities Education Improvement Act (IDEA) of 2004.]

The tone for this era was set when the landmark Civil Rights Act of 1964 prohibited discrimination against students based on race, color, sex, or national origin. Subsequently, Title IX of the Education Amendments of 1972 said that no one could be excluded, on the basis of his or her sex, from the benefits of any program in any school that received federal funds (and virtually every school in the United States receives federal money). Then, the U.S. Supreme Court's 1974 decision in *Lau v. Nichols*, combined with the 1968 Bilingual Education Act, said that school districts could not ignore the needs of students who did not speak English. And Section 503 of the Rehabilitation Act of 1973, followed by Public Law 94–142, the Education for All Handicapped Children Act (1975), said that every child, in spite of any handicapping condition, deserved a "free appropriate public education" designed specifically to meet his or her needs.

Looking back at the changes that took place in American education in the decade before 1975, Martha Ziegler, executive director of the Federation for Children with Special Needs in Boston and a longtime educational advocate, commented, "In November 1975, when the Education for All Handicapped Children Act was enacted into law, we had finally reached the ultimate objective for education in a democracy: Zero reject."[1] The nation's understanding of whom schools served and how they served them changed dramatically.

Boys and Girls Together: What Does It Mean for Schools to Be Gender Fair?

Most U.S. schools, unlike those in some countries, have long educated boys and girls in the same classrooms. So, if girls and boys sit next to each other in the same classroom with the same teacher, how can there be any problems regarding **educational equity**? The answer to that question is complex.

Debates about unfair gender differences in education are not new. In 1910, the Chicago reformer Jane Addams told the National Women's Trade Union League,

> There is an agricultural school in one of our Eastern cities, where the girls and boys are taught the possibilities of breadwinning as agricultural laborers, agriculturalists, gardeners, florists, or whatever you will. When it comes to the boy, he learns the chemistry of the soil, and gets down to the fundamental things in those particulars, but the girl is taught cooking and sewing. I am not saying that cooking and sewing are not necessary, but when we cheat a girl out of the training she ought to have for her breadwinning capacity, and substitute something that has nothing to do with the trade she is trying to learn, then we make a great and grave mistake.[2]

A half-century later, the 1964 Civil Rights Act included sex as well as race, color, and national origin when it outlawed discriminatory practices, especially in employment. It might have finally been a response to Jane Addams's complaint. However, in the early years, the Equal Employment Opportunities Commission, which was established to enforce the law, failed to give gender complaints serious attention and instead focused primarily on the still prevalent cases of racial discrimination.

With the founding of the National Organization of Women (NOW) in 1966, the women's movement had become a force to be reckoned with, growing dramatically in both the numbers of people involved and the political sophistication of the activists. By the 1970s, women had gained further political clout as more women were elected to Congress and as legislators of both genders began to pay more attention to women's votes. In the 1960s, Edith Green from Oregon, one of the senior women in the U.S. House of Representatives, heard a group of **school superintendents** say they were proud of special programs their schools ran to keep boys from dropping out of school. When Green specifically asked them about the girls, they responded that classes for girls were not nearly as important because the boys "are going to have to be the breadwinners." Several years later, Green got her opportunity to respond when she became the chief sponsor of what would be Title IX of the Education Amendments of 1972, passed by both houses of Congress and signed into law by President Richard Nixon.

> **educational equality**
> Students are regarded as equal in value and status and treated as thus.
>
> **school superintendent**
> Individual with executive and administrative responsibilities for a school district or a state, sometimes named commissioner of education or chief state school officer at the state level. Usually chosen by a board of education but in some cases chosen by the mayor of a city or—especially at the state level—sometimes through popular election.

The Impact of Title IX

When Title IX of the Education Amendments was passed, gender was added to the list of categories protected by federal law. From then on, schools and colleges receiving any federal funds were prohibited from discriminating against either employees or students on the basis of their sex. Despite resistance in many forms, Title IX has slowly transformed education in the United States.

When people hear the words *Title IX*, they usually think of athletics and sports facilities. Indeed, in 1972, only about 294,000 American high school girls took part in interscholastic sports; today, about 3 million girls play sports. But Title IX is much more far-reaching than sports.

With the passing of Title IX, traditional gender segregation in health, physical education, and vocational subjects became illegal, as did discriminatory guidance counseling or discrimination against pregnant and parenting teens. Although contact sports continued to be separate, athletic program clubs could not be, and schools needed to provide equal opportunities to girls and boys to participate in sports.

Prior to Title IX, girls who became pregnant were often forced to leave school or, at best, to attend segregated—and well-hidden—classes. Title IX prohibited that practice and in time school districts changed their practices to conform to the law's requirements. Although schools can still offer voluntary classes for pregnant and parenting teens, no girl can be kept out of any program, class, or extracurricular activity because of bearing a child. These were no small victories in schools where girls who became pregnant were routinely expelled.

Title IX

No person in the United States shall, on the basis of sex, be excluded from participation, be denied the benefits of, or be subject to discrimination under any education program or activity receiving federal financial assistance.

—Title IX, Education Amendments, 1972

---

vocational education
Training for a job or industry; comprises manual or practical activities.

Title IX also required schools to change the way **vocational education** was offered. Prior to the implementation of Title IX, vocational classes had usually been sex segregated and had reinforced stereotypes of appropriate sex role behavior. Boys took wood shop, girls took home economics, and that was that. In 1974 half of all female students in vocational education were in home economics courses while another 30% were in low-level clerical courses. The idea that there might be more options for all students or that both boys and girls might gain a lot by learning how to saw and how to cook was not considered in most places. Title IX opened up options for both boys and girls.

As Title IX was first being implemented, T.J. Wirtenberg studied the immediate impact of the change to sex-integrated classes mandated by Title IX. The effects were dramatic. Girls who took the newly integrated vocational education courses gained skills, described themselves as being more logical, and took a greater interest in nontraditional fields than girls in segregated home economics classes. Boys also expanded their interests and sense of competence. Amazingly, the differences became evident very early in the classes. Within the first 2 weeks, students in the integrated classes showed change in terms of skill, self-confidence, and interest. Clearly, something important happened for girls and boys when traditional sex role stereotypes were removed from course assignments, even before the content of the courses was changed.

Although the U.S. Office for Civil Rights was charged with implementing Title IX, it was mostly outside pressure, led by groups like NOW's Project on Equal Educational Rights, that led to real change. At the same time, federal grants to schools, colleges, and universities, but also to individuals and community organizations, funded through the Women's Educational Equity Act (WEEA), enabled schools to comply more fully with the new laws in thoughtful and well-researched ways.[3]

 DID YOU KNOW?

In 2002, Title IX was renamed the Patsy T. Mink Equal Opportunity in Education Act upon the death of the law's principal author, Representative Patsy T. Mink. A Japanese American, she cowrote the law partly in response to the racial and gender discrimination that she faced when pursuing her undergraduate degrees at two large universities.

Teachable Moment
TITLE IX SPORTS

Since the passage of Title IX in 1972, girls' participation in sports has soared. In that year, girls accounted for 7% of all participants in high school sports. By 2007, girls' share had grown to 41%, according to the National Federation of State High School Associations.

In the suburbs, roughly the same numbers of girls and boys play sports. A 2007 survey by Harris Interactive of more than 2,000 schoolchildren nationwide showed that 54% of boys and 50% of girls in the suburbs described themselves as "moderately involved" athletes.

However, much greater discrepancies were observed in urban areas. Only 36% of city girls in the survey described themselves as moderately involved athletes, compared to 56% of the boys. Girls in cities from Los Angeles to New York "are the left-behinds of the youth sport movement in the United States," said Don Sabo, a professor of health policy at D'Youville College in Buffalo, who conducted the study, which was commissioned by the Women's Sports Foundation.

In the suburbs, girls' participation in sports has become commonplace; so much so that few notice. In urban areas, girls' sports are still often seen as a luxury rather than an entitlement. Many urban schools lack free transportation and uniforms for their athletes, as well as full seasons of regularly scheduled games. Navigating these logistics is often the biggest hurdle, especially when frequent last-minute cancellations can occur because team members are stuck in traffic.

Coaches and organizers of youth sports in cities say that although many immigrant and lower-income parents see the benefit of sports for sons, they may expect daughters to fill needs at home, like tending to siblings or cleaning the house. Also, because parents are rarely able to attend games, they are especially concerned for their daughters' safety and thus often restrict their participation if they deem it dangerous.

According to the Women's Sports Foundation, girls who participate in sports receive a number of benefits. Research has shown that girls who play sports usually do better in school—with improved learning, memory, and concentration—and are more likely to graduate high school. Girls who play sports learn teamwork, goal-setting, and leadership skills that help them not only on the playing field but also in their future careers. In addition to the health benefits of regular physical activity, sports participation helps build a young woman's confidence through commitment, accomplishments, and social experiences.

Questions

- In what ways can you, as a teacher, link concepts learned through sports and physical activity to other areas of study, such as mathematics, business, and science? Can you link life skills—such as leadership, confidence, and commitment—to other areas of your students' lives?
- How can you help students and their parents advocate for more equitable support for girls' teams and to increase school and community support for girls' athletics?

As with other civil rights victories, changes in the treatment of girls in school have endured a sustained attack. In 1979 and again in 1981, Nevada senator Paul Laxalt proposed legislation to "withhold funds to any program that teaches children values that contradict demonstrated community beliefs, or to buy any textbooks that denigrate, diminish, or deny the historically understood role differences between the sexes." Had it passed, Laxalt's legislation would have allowed states and school districts "the right, with parental consultation, to limit or prohibit intermingling of the sexes in sports or other school related activities, free of Federal interference." President Ronald Reagan's administration tried multiple ways to undermine WEEA, and the program eventually ended under President George W. Bush.

Programs focused on **gender equity** in schools continue to be the subject of great controversy, but schools are without question different places, for girls and for boys, than they were prior to the passage of Title IX. Researcher Patricia Cayo Sexton is likely right when she says, "[D]espite some conspicuous problems, females are probably treated in a more **egalitarian** way in schools than in other institutions, including religious, familial, economic, and political institutions."[4]

Gender Equity

In their 1994 book *Failing at Fairness*, Myra and David Sadker did not mince words when they said, "Sitting in the same classroom, reading the same textbook, listening to the same teacher, boys and girls receive very different educations." They reported, "Girls are the majority of our nation's schoolchildren, yet they are second-class citizens." Their conclusion is based, among other things, on a careful look at the time teachers spend focused on boys, as opposed to girls, during a given day and the kinds of responses boys and girls elicit from their teachers, even when they are sitting in the same classroom.[5]

More recently, however, other scholars have begun to write about the "boy problem." Certainly gender discrimination hurts not just girls, but may impact girls and boys quite differently. A new postfeminist image of the macho male may well be leading some boys, perhaps relatively large numbers, to give up on schooling or to view academic success as a sign of being weak or feminized. Some versions of this new machismo can be found across all races and socioeconomic classes. New statistics may seem to say that boys are failing in school at faster rates than girls.

In fact, different scholars look at the same data and come to surprisingly different conclusions. While voicing some appreciation for the Sadkers' work, Michael Gurian and Kathy Stevens offer research and statistics in their article "With Boys and Girls in Mind" that lead them to conclude, "Our boys are now losing frightening ground in school, and we must come to terms with it—not in a way that robs girls, but in a way that sustains our civilization and is as powerful as the lobby we have created to help girls." If fairness in the 1980s and 1990s led educators to define gender equity as focusing especially on the educational achievement of girls, Gurian and Stevens seem to say that achieving equity requires a major focus on the learning needs and on the decline in achievement among boys.[6]

In the **Reading** for this chapter, however, Sara Mead directly challenges Gurian and Stevens's research and data. Mead concludes that "the truth is far different from what these accounts suggest. The real story is not bad news about boys doing worse; it's good news about girls doing better." According to Mead, both boys and girls are improving in their academic work, indeed for the most part improving fairly dramatically, but compared to boys, "girls have just improved their performance on some measures even faster." What one scholar sees as a crisis for boys another sees as a healthy closing of a once huge gap. Mead, however, is hardly satisfied when it comes to the education of boys—at least some boys. She notes real problems, especially in the educational achievement of African American and Latino boys, but she contends that crisis will best be addressed in the context of race rather than gender. If generalized statistics imply that all boys are making progress, Mead's more fine-grained research shows that some boys, like some girls, are doing just fine in school while others—especially boys of color and poor boys—are in need of significant new educational innovations.[7]

Myra Sadker died soon after the publication of *Failing at Fairness*, but David Sadker, working with Karen R. Zittleman, revisited the research and in 2009 published *Still Failing at Fairness: How Gender Bias Cheats Girls and Boys in School and What We Can Do About It*. In the new book, the authors conclude that "gender bias is alive and well, and in some ways growing." While some of the issues raised in the 1994 book have been addressed, other issues, including a lack of enforcement of Title IX and a backlash against gender equity, have created new problems. While the original Sadker and Sadker study focused specifically on issues impacting girls, Sadker and Zittleman looked at both genders and concluded, "Truth is, boys are gender stereotyped earlier and more harshly than girls, and their stereotype has tighter boundaries." The result is that too many boys are still afraid of studying in certain fields or of academic success because it can be seen as "acting like a girl." The barriers to academic and especially career success seem as serious as ever.[8]

Many current studies seem to indicate that girls are having greater success in school than boys. They drop out less often, they get in trouble less often, and they

> **gender equity**
> Provision of equal responsibilities, opportunities, and benefits to students regardless of gender.
>
> **egalitarian**
> The belief that all people are equal in value and merit.

Teachable Moment
THE LITERACY OF YOUNG BLACK MEN

In *A Search Past Silence: the Literacy of Young Black Men*, David E. Kirkland argues that most of the contemporary discussion of the educational needs of young Black men seriously misjudges the situation and, indeed, the potential of these students. Having spent time with six young Black men—Shawn, Derrick, Jose, Sheldon, Keith, and Tony—over a number of years, Kirkland writes:

Having followed the six young men for years, I find the debate over Black males and literacy interesting, if not absurd. At its most basic level, this debate is political, manufactured through base expressions of oppression that prop up legacies of privilege and deny the humanity of underprivileged in ways that make such questions as to whether Black men are literate promiscuously absorbing. . . . The dynamism of social tensions at work in the minds deliberating on Black males and literacy prevents even willing imaginations from achieving particular forms of understanding.

Based on his time with these six young men, and his own life as an African American scholar, Kirkland argues that the problem is not a lack of literacy at all, but rather that far too many educators and social commentators have looked for literacy in all the wrong places. "Perspectives on literacy of Black males that are validated only by 'achievement' tests also rests on a single story that fault Black males for not performing well in mainstream literacy settings." But what would happen if we look elsewhere? "Instead of deficit presumptions, how might we become open to the vaults of knowledge that bear the currency of these young men's lives to purchase nuanced perspectives on young Black men that suggest, first, that they are literate," Kirkland asks. Certainly in his research Kirkland has found some clear answers to his question, "For the young men featured in this book, print was also a tool to give those with limited power a bit more power to shape themselves and the worlds they inhabit."

Questions

1. How might the discussion of the education of African American men be different if educators took Kirkland's argument seriously? How do you think the authors cited in this chapter might respond to Kirkland's argument?
2. What might classroom teachers do differently to support students like Shawn, Derrick, Jose, Sheldon, Keith, and Tony?

Source: David E. Kirkland. *A Search Past Silence: The Literacy of Young Black Men*. New York: Teachers College Press, 2013, 135–7.

seem less dissatisfied. Some people today are calling for boys-only schools, or girls-only schools, as a way to attend to the needs of one gender at a time. Whatever the future brings, it will demand that teachers continue to attend to both the girls and the boys in their classes, and to find ways to be fair in the structure of their schools and in their individual interactions with students. Most of all, it will require constant attention to the difficult question of just what is fairness, after all.

Gender and Sexuality

Although the gender makeup of the nation's student body is not changing the way that racial and ethnic groupings are, when future teachers ask "*Who* will I teach?" it is also important to look at the changing *understanding* of gender and sexuality among today's young people. The fact that boys and girls go to school together, sit in the same classrooms, read the same books, and hear from the same teachers does not mean that boys and girls experience school in the same way. Girls and boys experience schooling differently because of differences in the way they experience life; the way they develop, especially in adolescence; and the way they respond to the world around them.

Contemporary views of sexuality are significantly different from those of the past. Whereas almost any mention of youth sexuality used to be taboo, many of today's young people are sexually active (and quite vocal about it). Not long ago, pregnant teens were excluded from school; today they can sit side by side with their peers. At least 35 states now allow single-sex couples to marry. Only a generation ago, virtually any mention of homosexuality in schools was unimaginable. Children with two mothers or two fathers now appear in more and more classrooms and images of gay and lesbian parents are in many textbooks, though in some places this still causes surprising controversy. In this ever-changing world, boys and girls experience schooling differently because an ever-changing youth culture views issues of gender and sexuality differently.

 DID YOU KNOW?

Of all the developed nations, the United States has the highest rate of teen pregnancy, twice that of England and Canada and eight times that of Japan and the Netherlands. Only one-third of teenage mothers finish high school.

In *Identity and Inner-City Youth*, Shirley Brice Heath and Milbrey W. McLaughlin write, "While ethnicity had come to be more and more a fluid academic concept after the 1960s, gender in both theory and practice escalated as a public issue and sociopolitical concern. . . . Lived experiences every day told the young that their gender mattered as much as if not more than their ethnicity to their patterns of survival and their identity."

Heath and McLaughlin, like many other scholars, make an important distinction between the biological differences between females and males and the changing social expectations of females and males at different points in history. As they say, "*masculine* and *feminine* are learned behaviors and are continuously variable."[9]

What Are Some of the Hidden Diversities Among Our Students? Sexual Orientation? Religion?

Many young people need special attention from teachers because they may be on the receiving end of exclusion or ridicule because of other kinds of diversities that are sometimes far harder for a teacher to identify. And many students may avoid ridicule, or the fear of ridicule, by keeping large parts of themselves secret. While some students wear their sexual orientation, their religion, or their culture as a badge of honor, too many other students feel the need to keep these and other very important parts of their core identities hidden in order to "fit in" in today's schools. Supporting all students without prying may be one of the most challenging issues facing today's teachers.

Lesbian, Gay, Bisexual, and Transgendered Students

There have always been gay and lesbian students, but for most of the nation's history, students whose sexual orientation was other than heterosexual quickly recognized the social forces stacked against them. Most pretended, with varying degrees of success, to pass for what was considered "normal," as abnormal as it might be for them.

Beginning in the 1970s, a movement of homosexual people "coming out of the closet" developed. Gay and lesbian students began demanding their rights in schools, sometimes with success and sometimes with disastrous results. A 2005 survey entitled "From Teasing to Torment" indicated just how hard it is to be a student in contemporary schools. The survey found that 65% of teens reported that they had been harassed during the past school year because of appearance, gender, sexual orientation, race, disability, religion, or a similar issue; one-third of teens reported that students in their school are frequently harassed because of their perceived or actual sexual orientation.[10] As the survey indicates, **harassment** in general and sexual harassment in particular takes many forms in school. The most common form of harassment reported in the study was for appearance: "the way they look or their body size." The next most common reason was for sexual orientation. The tragic results of this sort of harassment are the suicides of very young students who felt that they simply could not take the bullying in their school. Far more widespread is the quiet despair of too many students who keep such a low profile that teachers never notice and live young lives of silent desperation.

Much harassment happens out of the earshot of teachers, so that teachers do not hear students make negative remarks as frequently as the students report hearing them. Teachers, however, rate the problem of bullying and harassment as more serious than students do. Future teachers need to think carefully about how they will respond, not only to harassment but also to the manifold needs and strengths of students who do not fit the sexual "norms" of macho males and passive females, and who may be attracted as much or more to people of their own gender as to those of the opposite sex.

Educators and political leaders in many parts of the country are taking action to end the discrimination experienced by LGBTQ (lesbian, gay, bisexual, transgendered, and queer) students, ensuring that the curriculum is more balanced regarding the contributions of all people. The California FAIR Act, which is included in the **Readings** for this chapter, is a particularly significant law. The FAIR Act requires attention to the contribution of gay and lesbian people to the state's and the nation's history while banning any form of discrimination. The law is also controversial and other states have enacted virtually the opposite kind of legislation, making it illegal for teachers to portray LGBTQ people in a positive light or take any actions that might be seen as "promoting a homosexual lifestyle." Given the ways in which gay and lesbian relationships are embraced by some and frighten others, the discussion and heated debates are sure to continue. In the midst of it all, teachers will need to be sensitive to the needs of all their students—including those who are LGBTQ—by finding ways to teach a curriculum that is fair and accurate.

> **harassment**
> The act of persistently attacking, threatening, or annoying another person or group of people.

Religious Minorities

Another hidden group of students are those who do not fit cultural assumptions about what is "normal" religious practice. In the 19th century, many Roman Catholic students found the public schools to be bastions of Protestantism, including a curriculum that reflected a Protestant prejudice against "papist" religion. Most Jewish students who arrived later in the same century found more secular public schools, though many reported being required to sit through, even participate in, school prayers or the singing of Christmas carols.

 DID YOU KNOW?

There are an estimated 4,200 different religions in the world. Christianity has the most followers (2 billion people) followed by Islam (1.3 billion people).

Notes from the Field

How do you think education has changed since you first started teaching?

"Education in elementary schools has dramatically changed over the last 30 years. Educators are more aware of different learning styles and are more willing to address those differences in all the many areas of education. Also the children that we used to say 'fell between the cracks' are now being helped with research-based interventions. Committed leadership is the key to finding time, resources, and the energy that it takes to address these very real concerns of many of the students. Whereas in the past the classroom was mostly one culture, now many cultures are represented and the teacher must be able to relate to those cultures. Being able to educate students keeps evolving and teachers have to be willing to leave the comfort of their teaching style to address the needs of the student. New teachers—be flexible!"

—Lindy Stacy, first-grade teacher

In more recent times, especially since Supreme Court decisions in the early 1960s outlawed school-sponsored devotional exercises, schools have been more welcoming places for people of a range of religious persuasions (including those espousing no religious affiliation). Sometimes the cost of this openness has been a refusal to engage in discussions that are important or to recognize that, since the beginning of civilization, people have asked questions about gods, purpose, and the meaning of life (and afterlife). Schools continue to discriminate, however, and many teachers find themselves wishing they knew better how to proceed, such as when as a Sikh student is punished for wearing a ritual knife, or a Muslim girl is chastised for wearing a headscarf, or a conservative religious student (such as a Protestant fundamentalist or a Navajo traditionalist) finds the biology class discussion of evolution unresponsive to his or her concerns. In a nation changing as quickly as the United States, teachers need to know a great deal about the extraordinary variety of religious traditions, practices, beliefs, and nonbeliefs of the students they will teach and be thoughtful as to how to treat all students with respect.[11]

Special Needs: What Is the Best Education for Students With Disabilities?

In the last **Reading** in this chapter, Barbara S. S. Hong and Kay A. Chick ask us to ponder what it must be like for students for whom learning comes more slowly or is more difficult and then think of the kinds of educational programs that will address the needs of these students. They warn us not to seek the one perfect solution but to remember that different students need quite different kinds of interventions. Later in this chapter, Kelley S. Regan also asks teachers to improve the ways they think about students with emotional or behavioral disorders.

 DID YOU KNOW?

According to the National Education Association, public schools in the United States are now educating more than half a million more students with disabilities than they did a decade ago.

In a thoughtful work, "Confronting Ableism," Thomas Hehir asks, "What should the purpose of special education be?" He answers his own question by saying that "we can best frame the purpose of special education as minimizing the impact of disability and maximizing the opportunities for student with disabilities to participate in schooling and the community." He also makes it clear that this is easier said than done and lists many reasons why schools have a long way to go to reach the twin goals he outlines for special education: minimizing the impact of a disability and maximizing the opportunity for the student with the disability. Perhaps the most important reason, and certainly the most intriguing, is what he calls "ableism," society's pervasive negative attitude about disability.[12]

The Legal Foundation of Special Education

Many teachers find that educating students with special needs is their primary calling, but *every teacher* needs a strong foundation in special education. Classrooms are becoming increasingly inclusive, which means that students with learning disabilities or physical limitations are educated alongside other students and special accommodations are made for the instructional needs of all students. As a result, someone prepared as a "regular education" teacher of any grade can well expect to have students in class who need a wheelchair or a guide dog or an aide to get around, have attention deficit hyperactivity disorder (ADHD), are slower to learn certain concepts, or have a wide range of other mental or emotional challenges that make learning difficult for them and make including them in a well-integrated classroom a challenge for the unprepared teacher.

This didn't used to be the case. Throughout much of the nation's history, many students who had any of a number of different disabilities either were told to go home—that school was not for them—or were allowed to attend school but given no special services. Those who did attend school often fell further and further behind until dropping out seemed the only wise course. Massachusetts is today among the states offering the most services for students with special needs. One scholar has estimated, however, that in 1965 only 25% of the children potentially requiring special education in that state were enrolled in school. The majority of these students were simply excluded. As the civil rights movements of the 1950s and 1960s expanded to include not only African Americans and other people of color but also poor people of all races, women, people whose home language was other than English, and gays and lesbians, others came to demand their rights. These campaigns for full participation in American society were not separate movements. Disproportionate numbers of poor children, children of color, and non-English-speaking children had been classified as "handicapped" and were excluded from schools as having needs the schools could not meet. Parents and their advocates began to organize for change and for a legal mandate that every child deserved the best possible education.[13]

 DID YOU KNOW?

Approximately 17% of children have some type of developmental disability, including speech and language disorders, learning disabilities, or ADHD.

Public Law 94–142, Education for All Handicapped Children Act, 1975

The Congress finds that—

(1) there are more than eight million handicapped children in the United States today;

(2) the special educational needs of such children are not being fully met;

(3) more than half of the handicapped children in the United States do not receive appropriate educational services which would enable them to have full equality of opportunity;

(4) one million of the handicapped children in the United States are excluded entirely from the public school system and will not go through the educational process with their peers; there are many handicapped children throughout the United States participating in regular school programs whose handicaps prevent them from having a successful educational experience because their handicaps are undetected; . . .

It is the purpose of this Act to assure that all handicapped children have available to them, . . . a free appropriate public education which emphasizes special education and related services designed to meet their unique needs, to assure that the rights of handicapped children and their parents or guardians are protected, to assist States and localities to provide for the education of all handicapped children, and to assess and assure the effectiveness of efforts to educate handicapped children.[14]

Massachusetts was the first state to act when in 1972 the state legislature stipulated that the schools of the state had to offer a free and appropriate education to every child no matter what their disability. A little over 2 years later, in 1975, the U.S. Congress adopted a similar measure, which both recognized the breadth of the problem and mandated change.[15]

As a result of the passage of Public Law 94–142 in 1975, the core responsibility of U.S. schools and school districts changed. Every child had to be given an education, and that education had to be equal to the education offered to other students and in "the least restrictive environment" possible. No child or youth could be turned away because the school or district lacked the skill or resources to provide the needed services. The funds made available by Congress as well as the specific demands and prohibitions contained in the text of this and subsequent national laws governing special education are quite specific in six major areas:

- **Zero reject.** Every school district must provide a "free appropriate public education to every child in the district." No exceptions are allowed, no matter what the range or severity of the child's disabilities.
- **Nondiscriminatory assessment.** Since it had too often been the case that children of color and children who did not speak English were routinely misclassified, the law stipulates that special education decisions must be made by a multidisciplinary diagnostic team that includes the child's parents.

Teachable Moment
A NEW DAY FOR THE CIVIL RIGHTS OF STUDENTS WITH SPECIAL NEEDS

Robert K. Crabtree, a lawyer who advocates for the needs of students with disabilities, drafted much of the original Massachusetts special education law while working as a young intern with the state legislature. Recently he wrote:

A legal revolution began for children with disabilities and their parents in 1972, when the Massachusetts legislature enacted a special education reform act known as Chapter 766. A few years later, much of the model embodied in Chapter 766 was adopted in a 1975 federal statue called the Education for All Handicapped Children Act (EAHCA), later renamed the Individuals with Disabilities Education Act (IDEA).

These enactments spawned major changes in the basic structures, standards, and programs of public education for students with disabilities. The changes raised an enormous challenge to the bureaucracies that would be called upon to implement them—primarily public school districts, first of Massachusetts and then of the entire nation—and the prospect of those changes provoked significant resistance from those bureaucracies. It is unlikely that Chapter 766 and the later EAHCA could have been written into law without their advocates organizing a very deep and wide coalition of stakeholders to carry out the gritty work of convincing legislators to take the giant step those initiatives represented.

Two enormously important results of this process were the empowerment of a previously disenfranchised population and the creation of a new culture and community that united advocates and persons with disabilities across lines that had previously divided them.

Questions

1. Can you imagine what schools might have been like before the laws protecting the rights of students with special needs were enacted? For special education students? For everyone else?
2. Crabtree talks about the advocates for the laws "organizing a very deep and wide coalition of stakeholders to carry out the gritty work of convincing legislators." How many different kinds of advocates might be necessary to get such laws passed?

Source: Robert K. Crabtree. "Foreword." In *Parents Have the Power to Make Special Education Work,* by Judith Canty Graves and Carson Graves, 9–10. Philadelphia: Jessica Kingsley, 2014.

- **Least restrictive environment.** Certainly the most controversial aspect of the law, this provision says that, when possible, a child must be placed in a regular classroom in the nearest school and also that a continuum of other options should be available, from in-school specialists to special residential schools.
- **Individualized education program.** Every child placed in a special education category must have his or her own individual education plan (IEP) that will provide information to all educational personnel and safeguard the child's and the parents' rights to be sure that the original agreements about appropriate education are followed.
- **Parent participation.** Congress specifically mandated that parents be full partners in all stages of decision making, including curriculum and placements, thus giving special education parents a much greater say in their children's education than that held by parents of any other children.
- **Due process.** Every state and school district must have a review process that is seen as fair and impartial and that avoids the high cost of litigation in the courts.

With these provisions, Public Law 94–142 is seen by many—most of all by the parents of students with disabilities—as a bill of rights for students with disabilities (Congress in 1990 changed the language from *handicapped* to *disabilities*), even if there are those who, in the name of cost containment or concern with the education of "regular" education students, continue to resist.

Understanding the Wide Range of Disabilities

In *Exceptional Lives: Special Education in Today's Schools*, a team of authors led by Ann Turnbull describe the needs of many different kinds of students identified as special needs students in contemporary schools. Their list includes:

- Students who are gifted and talented
- Students with learning disabilities of many different kinds
- Students with communication disorders
- Students with emotional or behavioral disorders
- Students with attention deficit hyperactivity disorder
- Students with intellectual disabilities
- Students with severe and multiple disabilities
- Students with autism
- Students with physical disabilities and other health impairments
- Students with traumatic brain injury
- Students with hearing loss
- Students with visual impairments

While a teacher needs to know the characteristics of all of these quite different disabilities, that is only the beginning of what is needed. As the authors note, many students have more than one disability, and some can mask others. It is also important to note that some disabilities (especially autism) include a wide range of symptoms, skills, and levels of impairment that children can have. Some students on the autism spectrum can function quite well in regular classrooms while others with a much more severe kind of autism disorder cannot. Understanding the many kinds of disabilities is only the beginning. The real key for a teacher is not necessarily to be able to name the various disabilities or even diagnose them (something that should be done by a specialist), but rather to design the kinds of inclusive classrooms with carefully individualized instruction that allows students with disabilities to thrive along with their peers.[16]

 DID YOU KNOW?

Autism is the fastest growing developmental disability, with rates increasing by 10%–17% each year. One out of every 150 children is diagnosed with autism, and it is four times more prevalent in boys than in girls.

Responding to the Mandate

The same laws that provide for the needs of special education students have also stirred debates about the meaning of these rights. One set of debates has taken place primarily within the special education community itself. Understandably, parents want different kinds of educational placements and opportunities for their children. Some parents feel strongly that their special education children, even some with extensive and multiple disabilities, should remain in age-appropriate classrooms in a regular school. The call for inclusion is implied in the law itself, and many parents argue strongly against segregation of special needs youth in all but the most extreme cases. These parents often see separate schools as denying their disabled children essential social integration with their peers. They also worry that segregated classes will inevitably be seen as unequal.

Other parents argue almost exactly the opposite, that their special needs children either will not receive the necessary services in regular schools or will be made to feel far too uncomfortable by their less disabled peers and that they must be served in separate, often residential schools. Some parents argue that separate schools are "the least restrictive environment" for their children. Some deaf parents who contend that they and their deaf children are part of a distinct culture often join this category. Sometimes parents of gifted students agree. Still other groups of parents come to different conclusions about the most appropriate environment for their children. Since all parents wanting widely differing arrangements can claim that their choice for the schooling of their children is the least restrictive environment, and since federal law guarantees parents a significant say in the education of their children with disabilities, the issue can be exceedingly contentious.[17]

 DID YOU KNOW?

According to the National Institute of Mental Health, 2%–3% of children, or at least one child in a typical classroom, has ADHD. This represents about 2 million children in the United States; boys with ADHD outnumber girls with the diagnosis by three to one.

Another contentious area for special education has to do with the problem of inappropriate placements (the tendency in some places for special education to be a "dumping ground" for students whom the standard classrooms cannot easily accommodate), the cost of some placements, and the political clout that the laws give to special education parents. Parents have sometimes fought hard to have their children classified as in need of special education to get services for them, and some teachers have used the "special education" label to move disruptive students out of their classrooms.

Table 4.2 Challenges of 5- to 15-Year-Olds With Disabilities

Mental	79%
Sensory	17%
Physical	17%
Self-Care	16%

The total percent equals more than 100% because some students deal with multiple challenges.

Source: U.S. Census Bureau, Census 2000 Summary File 3.

The result has been a growing number of children classified as "special needs" and a growing cost for their education. As early as 1993 in Massachusetts, where many of the first special education legal rights were enacted and 17% of students are classified as special needs (one of the highest percentages in the nation), one report responded, "It simply is not fair to give absolute priority to the needs of 17 percent of the student body at the expense of the other 83 percent."[18]

Commentators from a wide spectrum have made similar arguments. Ellen Guiney, former executive director of the Boston Plan for Excellence, and a strong advocate for the public schools, offered a far-reaching critique of the special education programs in her city and, by implication, the state of Massachusetts and the nation. She wrote of the need to escape "the prevailing notion that special education is a place to put any student with learning or behavior problems; and secondly, the underlying premise that a heavy emphasis on implementing process measures, on meeting strict timelines, and on having teachers meet certification requirements will produce desired results." Guiney and many fellow educators and reformers across the nation have come to have grave doubts that the results are worth the cost, or are fair to the students involved or to the majority of students in the schools.

In Guiney's view, special education programs in Boston and throughout the nation need to address evidence showing that there are "too many students in special education, especially in substantially separate programs, and too many special education populations overrepresented by gender and race (Black and Hispanic students, especially males, are overrepresented in special education overall and are greatly overrepresented in substantially separate classes for certain disability areas.)" She also worries that not all difficulties should be classified as disabilities and that, in any case, the costs of special education are too high given the results.

Guiney found deep resentments among the special education students themselves. One told her, "Juvenile delinquency. That is what they treat us like. We're juveniles. And we're just a menace to society, so we have to be locked down here."[19]

Notes from the Field

What is one of the challenges you face as a teacher?

"When a parent is unwilling to get children the services they need or the assessment they need because they don't want their kids to be labeled. It makes my job hard."

—*Amy Mazza, pre-K teacher*

Inclusive Classrooms

Like many, including advocates for students with disabilities as well as critics of special education programs, Guiney argues that the solution is to "expand well-designed inclusion classrooms." Inclusive classrooms, they believe, offer the opportunity to bring children together rather than separate them, create integration rather than segregation, and end the sense of being "locked down" that too many special education students experience.

Inclusive classrooms require well-prepared teachers. Often they require a team in which one teacher focuses on the whole class while a partner is free to focus on the needs of students with special needs, often one at a time. Inclusive classrooms are not a panacea. If a teacher is not prepared, inclusion can be a disaster. If a teacher has more students than she or he can attend to, it is a recipe for failure. An inclusive classroom often works best with more than one teacher and a relatively small group of students; it should not be used simply to save money over the cost of other options. To thrive, some students need to be in classes with others who have the same disabilities. As with most ideas in American education, what works for some students may not work well for others. Nevertheless, inclusive classrooms that serve the needs of a wide range of students are the most popular approach to responding to the needs of special education students today, and most aspiring teachers should assume that they will teach in such a place.

In the middle of these sometimes-heated debates, teachers must find their way and serve all their students. It is one thing for parents, advocates, and public officials to debate policy. It is something quite different for a teacher to face a class filled with students with widely diverse needs. As special education researcher Robert Osgood says, during the past several decades, the ideal of inclusion has taken hold as a means to "break down distinctions between special and regular education in fundamental and dramatic ways." More recently, people worried about the burgeoning cost of special education have argued for inclusive classrooms, perhaps less on educational grounds than on the simple

CONNECTIONS ➜◀

In Chapter 10, we discuss the debates over sorting and tracking students by ability levels.

Notes from the Field

How is the "regular" classroom teacher affected by changes in special education?

"It's harder to include the students who have low IQ, severe learning disabilities, or behavioral issues. Many times the regular teacher has very limited support for included students. Most new teachers don't have a full understanding of the range of abilities they will see in a classroom. All of the students come to them with varying abilities, yet they are supposed to make sure all learn and do well on specific state tests. Today in special education, everything is data, data, data—but life is more than data."

—Deb Whitmore, special education teacher

mathematics of the money saved when a student is moved from a special placement—often in a small class or a specialized, even residential school—to a regular classroom.[20]

Some school districts and some teachers have responded to the need to develop more inclusive classrooms by having classes cotaught by a regular teacher and a special education teacher. When two teachers not only teach together but also take the time to get to know each other well, they can build on each other's strengths and can more than double the benefit to their students that either one alone might offer. Coteaching is not the only effective way to serve the needs of today's inclusive classrooms. But it is an important attempt to answer the question of what a teacher who has the right kind of support might be able to do in light of the diversity of today's students.[21]

Moving an increasing number of students with disabilities into regular, inclusive classrooms can save money, but some of the most effective means of developing these classrooms (such as coteaching) can be expensive to implement. For many students, the inclusive classroom provides a much better setting for their education, including their social development, than would a segregated setting. Inclusive classrooms can, indeed, be the least restrictive environment. With the right support in place—which often includes a special education expert, well-prepared teachers, and thoughtful accommodation to the students' needs—inclusive classrooms can be wonderfully engaging academic and social communities. But inclusive classrooms also make significant demands on teachers and on schools. When inclusion is done badly, or on the cheap, the result can be failure for students and teachers. This can happen if teachers are not prepared or if an effective team is replaced by one lone teacher who is expected to educate everyone and who may simply be overwhelmed by the range of demands.

LEARNING THE LANGUAGE: SPECIAL EDUCATION

- **ARD (admission, review, and dismissal) committee:** Committee responsible for making the educational decisions for a student. The parents, or adult students, are among the members of the ARD committee.
- **IEP:** Individual education plan written by the ARD committee; describes the specific, individualized services that a student will receive from special education.
- **Inclusion:** Classes with both regular education students and those with disabilities … with additional staff….
- **Residential school:** Separate schools that enroll special needs children.
- **Resource room:** In-school services for students with disabilities who are in a regular education class but need specific additional support.
- **Substantially separate:** Classes for students with disabilities who … are with other students only for noninstructional activities such as lunch.

Source: Ellen C. Guiney, Mary Ann Cohen, and Erika Moldow. "Escaping from Old Ideas: Educating Students with Disabilities in the Boston Public Schools." In *A Decade of Urban School Reform: Persistence and Progress in the Boston Public Schools,* edited by S. Paul Reville with Celine Coggins. Cambridge, MA: Harvard Education Press, 2007.

Teachable Moment
GIFTED STUDENTS

Although most of the discussion about students with special needs focuses on those with a physical, mental, or emotional disability that makes learning (or at least some forms of learning) difficult for them, gifted students (those who learn more quickly and who seem to surge ahead of their peers) may also require special attention.

Researcher Jennifer Stepanek makes the argument for special programs for gifted students, saying that although it is certainly true that all students can learn, "some students learn more quickly and are capable of higher level work than their age peers. Gifted students need different content and instruction in order to meet their needs." Many teachers are well aware that some of their students "get" a particular lesson much more quickly than others and that sometimes the students who learn most quickly end up being bored and disengaged in school as they wait for their classmates to catch up.

However, critics of gifted programs contend that the label "gifted" can too easily be applied to students who simply receive more home-based education and that the programs can often become another means of separating the haves and the have-nots. Critics note that many advocates of gifted education often count their own children among the gifted.

Although giftedness was once defined by a student's IQ (a single measure of intelligence), researchers now have doubts about IQ tests or any single measure. Howard Gardner's work on "multiple intelligences" leads us to believe that some students may well be gifted in some areas but average, or even below average, in others. Giftedness does not come in one shape or size, and few, if any, young people are gifted in all areas.

Stepanek offers alternatives to the standard debates about inclusion versus separate classes for gifted students. She argues that, for gifted students, there may be times (such as when students are working on open-ended problem-solving activities) when heterogeneous or mixed groups are best, while at other times (as when students are working on skill development or reviewing prior work) they do best in homogeneous groups with students of similar abilities.

Questions

- What do you think of Stepanek's assertion that "some students learn more quickly and are capable of higher level work than their age peers" and thus need special programs? What are the implications of this view for the development of inclusive classrooms and inclusive schools?
- Does it make sense to you, as Stepanek asserts, that heterogeneous groupings work well in some situations and that students should be separated by knowledge or ability into different groups, even different classes, at other times? Would you rather teach a diverse group of students or a mostly homogeneous group? Which is easier for the teacher? Which is better for the students?

Source: Jennifer Stepanek. "The Inclusive Classroom: Meeting the Needs of Gifted Students," ERIC document 444306, retrieved June 9, 2009 from http://www.eric.ed.gov.

 DID YOU KNOW?

In one survey of new teachers, 82% said they had learned about teaching children with special needs, but only 47% said that their preparation "helped a lot." Some 95% reported that they had students with special needs in their classes.

Anyone considering a career in teaching needs to develop expertise in the field of special education, regardless of the grade level or subject that person plans to teach. The inclusive classroom is the norm today, and while many teachers lead an inclusive classroom alone, an increasing number of teachers work as part of a team to provide the best educational services possible to a group of students. The students sitting in a classroom today reflect diversities of academic abilities, physical abilities, and mental and physical health that were previously excluded from schools and it is a teacher's job to teach all of them.

Writing for the journal *Teaching Exceptional Children*, Kelley S. Regan, a professor of special education at George Mason University, advocates four guiding considerations that she believes every teacher should follow to prepare to work effectively with students with Emotional and/or Behavioral Disorders (EBD). Her list of four "R's" applies well to all teachers seeking to be effective in today's diverse classrooms, especially with students with a wide range of disabilities. Regan recommends the following:

1. Reflection—"A mindset often preventing the progress of novice teachers is that of 'control' versus 'manage.' Consider that everything a teacher and a student does is behavior . . . Focusing on our own reaction is manageable and productive in effecting change in others."
2. Relationships—"A teacher of a child with EBD has the task of building trust with that student. Trust can be fostered by the teacher's sincerely demonstrating that she/he values the child, provides for their needs, and sets them up for success."
3. Roles—"The roles of the teacher and the student in a classroom need clarity. From one lesson to the next, the roles may vary . . . [but] clarity of expectations for everyone's role supports the success of student learning."
4. Resources—"A 'resource' is a broad term that certainly varies. However, one consistency is that any student identified with an EBD will have an IEP (Individualized Education Plan), and this documentation is the first step when identifying resources for the student to be successful in the classroom. . . . Such modifications may include adapting the length or type of paper-pencil tasks, using assistive technology, and/or permitting intermittent breaks while a student is working on a particular task."

Notes from the Field

What was it like growing up with a disability?

"I grew up very 'mainstream.' I was one of the few disabled students—at least one of the few with a visible disability—in most of the schools I attended. I went to a huge high school in New York, and while there probably were other disabled students, I didn't see them or connect with them. I was very eager to not acknowledge my disability because there was such a stigma associated with it. So I was caught in a way—on the one hand I knew I was different and that I was going to have a different life than others, but on the other hand I was not eager to acknowledge such a stigmatized identity."[23]

—Harilyn Rousso, president, Disabilities Unlimited Consulting Services

Regan's list provides a way for every teacher to begin to think about the best ways to serve every student. In a way, every student has special needs. Some of those needs may be disabilities. Others may be emotional or behavioral issues. Most students have unique ways in which they learn some things. (See for example Howard Gardner's list of multiple forms of intelligence in Chapter 5.) But an understanding of the need for continual self-reflection on the part of the teacher, for building trust with students, and for finding the resources that a student needs will serve every student—perhaps most of all those who do, indeed, have the wide variety of special needs that are found in today's classrooms.[22]

None of the debates presented in this chapter are going to be resolved soon. And no one entering the field of education should dare to ignore any of them. A teacher has a deep moral responsibility to teach, as effectively as is humanly possible, whatever group of young people ends up in front of her or him. A teacher also has a role to play in helping shape the policies by which students are assigned to individual classrooms and the expectations that every teacher and school will have for all children.

CHAPTER REVIEW

- Historically speaking: Who was left out of American schools?

Prior to the 1960s and 1970s, schooling was not considered a necessity for everyone, as it is today. Girls, students who did not fit a relatively rigid gender and cultural norm, and students with various disabilities were often excluded from the full range of educational opportunities.

- What legal actions made school more available for many young people?

Fueled by the civil rights movement of the 1950s and 1960s, a number of key court cases and legislation opened to everyone the doors of education. The landmark Civil Rights Act of 1964 prohibited discrimination against students based on race, color, sex, or national origin. Later, Title IX said that no one could be excluded, on the basis of his or her sex, from the benefits of any program in any school that received federal funds. Finally, Section 503 of the Rehabilitation Act of 1973, followed by Public Law 94–142, the Education for All Handicapped Children Act, required that every child, in spite of any disability, receive a "free appropriate public education" designed specifically to meet his or her needs.

- What does it mean for schools to be gender fair?

Some observers argue that, given the successes of the women's movement, education today should simply be blind to gender issues; others argue that gender-fair education means attending quite specifically to the different learning styles and the different attitudes toward schooling and school success for girls and also for boys.

- What are some of the hidden diversities among our students? Sexual orientation? Religion?

Not all differences among students can be easily seen. "Hidden" diversities may include sexual orientation and lifestyle preferences, as well as personal religious practices. Today's teacher must be able to equally embrace gay and straight students and students of many different religions (or none) by providing an environment of mutual understanding and respect, and by monitoring for and swiftly addressing instances of harassment and discrimination.

- What is the best education for students with disabilities?

Virtually no one would argue for a return to the "old days," when many students with physical, emotional, and mental "handicaps" (as they were then called) were simply excluded from schools. But many observers today argue passionately that special education programs have grown too extensive, too bureaucratic, and too expensive. Others argue that the extensive and bureaucratic nature of the programs, linked with the financial investment in them, is the only guarantee that advances in services for special needs students will be preserved. In the case of special education, many educators also debate what sort of classroom environment most effectively serves students with different special needs.

Readings

What Does It Mean for Schools to Be Gender Fair?

From "THE TRUTH ABOUT BOYS AND GIRLS"

AUTHOR: SARA MEAD

In "The Evidence Suggests Otherwise: The Truth About Boys and Girls," Sara Mead offers a biting critique of the work of other researchers of issues in gender education, especially Michael Gurian and Kathy Stevens. Mead argues that "with few exceptions, American boys are scoring higher and achieving more than they ever have before. But girls have just improved their performance on some measures even faster." She insists that most evidence points to a narrowing of the academic gap between boys and girls rather than to a growing failure on the part of boys. Mead cites Gurian and Stevens's work and critiques their methodology as part of her argument that we should come to conclusions different from those they advocate. Articles presented by these and other scholars have established an ongoing dialogue that subjects their own work, and that of their predecessors, to continued review and improvement.

If you've been paying attention to the education news lately, you know that American boys are in crisis. After decades spent worrying about how schools "shortchange girls," the eyes of the nation's education commentariat are now fixed on how they shortchange boys. In 2006 alone, a *Newsweek* cover story, a major *New Republic* article, a long article in *Esquire*, a "Today Show" segment, and numerous op-eds have informed the public that boys are falling behind girls in elementary and secondary school and are increasingly outnumbered on college campuses. A young man in Massachusetts filed a civil rights complaint with the U.S. Department of Education, arguing that his high school's homework and community service requirements discriminate against boys. A growth industry of experts is advising educators and policymakers how to make schools more "boy friendly" in an effort to reverse this slide.

It's a compelling story that seizes public attention with its "man bites dog" characteristics. It touches on Americans' deepest insecurities, ambivalences, and fears about changing gender roles and the "battle of the sexes." It troubles not only parents of boys, who fear their sons are falling behind, but also parents of girls, who fear boys' academic deficits will undermine their daughters' chances of finding suitable mates.

But the truth is far different from what these accounts suggest. The real story is not bad news about boys doing worse; it's good news about girls doing better.

In fact, with a few exceptions, American boys are scoring higher and achieving more than they ever have before. But girls have just improved their performance on some measures even faster. As a result, girls have narrowed or even closed some academic gaps that previously favored boys, while other long-standing gaps that favored girls have widened, leading to the belief that boys are falling behind.

There's no doubt that some groups of boys—particularly Hispanic and black boys and boys from low-income homes—are in real trouble. But the predominant issues for them are race and class, not gender. Closing racial and economic gaps would help poor and minority boys more than closing gender gaps, and focusing on gender gaps may distract attention from the bigger problems facing these youngsters.

The hysteria about boys is partly a matter of perspective. While most of society has finally embraced the idea of equality for women, the idea that women might actually surpass men in some areas (even as they remain behind in others) seems hard for many people to swallow. Thus, boys are routinely characterized as "falling behind" even as they improve in absolute terms.

In addition, a dizzying array of so-called experts have seized on the boy crisis as a way to draw attention to their pet educational, cultural, or ideological issues. Some say that contemporary classrooms are too structured, suppressing boys' energetic natures and tendency to physical expression; others contend that boys need more structure and discipline in school. Some blame "misguided feminism" for boys' difficulties, while others argue that "myths" of masculinity have a crippling impact on boys. Many of these theories have superficially plausible rationales that make them appealing to some parents, educators, and policymakers. But the evidence suggests that many of these ideas come up short.

Unfortunately, the current boy crisis hype and the debate around it are based more on hopes and fears than on evidence. This debate benefits neither boys nor girls, while distracting attention from more serious educational problems—such as large racial and economic achievement gaps—and practical ways to help both boys and girls succeed in school.

A New Crisis?

"The Boy Crisis. At every level of education, they're falling behind. What to do?"

—*Newsweek* cover headline, Jan. 30, 2006

Newsweek is not the only media outlet publishing stories that suggest boys' academic accomplishments and life opportunities are declining. But it's not true. Neither the facts reported in these articles nor data from other sources support the notion that boys' academic performance is falling. In fact, overall academic achievement and attainment for boys is higher than it has ever been. . . .

Reading

The most recent main NAEP assessment in reading, administered in 2005, does not support the notion that boys' academic achievement is falling. In fact, fourth-grade boys did better than they had done in both the previous NAEP reading assessment, administered in 2003, and the earliest comparable assessment, administered in 1992. Scores for both fourth- and eighth-grade boys have gone up and down over the past decade, but results suggest that the reading skills of fourth- and eighth-grade boys have improved since 1992.

The picture is less clear for older boys. The 2003 and 2005 NAEP assessments included only fourth- and eighth-graders, so the most recent main NAEP data for 12th graders dates back to 2002. On that assessment, 12th-grade boys did worse than they had in both the previous assessment, administered in 1998, and the first comparable assessment, administered in 1992. At the 12th-grade level, boys' achievement in reading does appear to have fallen during the 1990s and early 2000s. . . .

Math

The picture for boys in math is less complicated. Boys of all ages and races are scoring as high—or higher—in math than ever before. From 1990 through 2005, boys in grades four and eight improved their performance steadily on the main NAEP, and they scored significantly better on the 2005 NAEP than in any previous year. Twelfth graders have not taken the main NAEP in math since 2000. That year, 12th-grade boys did better than they had in 1990 and 1992, but worse than they had in 1996.

Both 9- and 13-year-old boys improved gradually on the long-term NAEP since the 1980s (9-year-old boys' math performance did not improve in the 1970s). Seventeen-year-old boys' performance declined through the 1970s, rose in the 1980s, and remained relatively steady during the late 1990s and early 2000s. As in reading, white boys score much better on the main NAEP in math than do black and Hispanic boys, but all three groups of boys are improving their math performance in the elementary and middle school grades. . . .

Overall Long-Term Trends

A consistent trend emerges across these subjects: There have been no dramatic changes in the performance of boys in recent years, no evidence to indicate a boy crisis. Elementary-school-aged boys are improving their performance; middle school boys are either improving their performance or showing little change, depending on the subject; and high school boys' achievement is declining in most subjects (although it may be improving in math). These trends seem to be consistent across all racial subgroups of boys, despite the fact that white boys perform much better on these tests than do black and Hispanic boys.

Evidence of a decline in the performance of older boys is undoubtedly troubling. But the question to address is whether this is a problem for older boys or for older students generally. That can be best answered by looking at the flip side of the gender equation: achievement for girls.

The Difference Between Boys and Girls

To the extent that tales of declining boy performance are grounded in real data, they're usually framed as a decline relative to girls. That's because, as described above, boy performance is generally staying the same or increasing in absolute terms.

But even relative to girls, the NAEP data for boys paints a complex picture. On the one hand, girls outperform boys in reading at all three grade levels assessed on the main NAEP. Gaps between girls and boys are smaller in fourth grade and get larger in eighth and 12th grades. Girls also outperform boys in writing at all grade levels.

In math, boys outperform girls at all grade levels, but only by a very small amount. Boys also outperform girls—again, very slightly—in science and by a slightly larger margin in geography. There are no significant gaps between male and female achievement on the NAEP in U.S. history. In general, girls outperform boys in reading and writing by greater margins than boys outperform girls in math, science, and geography.

But this is nothing new. Girls have scored better than boys in reading for as long as the long-term NAEP has been administered. And younger boys are actually catching up: The gap between boys and girls at age 9 has narrowed significantly since 1971—from 13 points—to five points even as both genders have significantly improved. Boy-girl gaps at age 13 haven't changed much since 1971—and neither has boys' or girls' achievement.

At age 17, gaps between boys and girls in reading are also not that much different from what they were in 1971, but they are significantly bigger than they were in the late 1980s, before achievement for both genders—and particularly boys—began to decline.

The picture in math is even murkier. On the first long-term NAEP assessment in 1973, 9- and 13-year-old girls actually scored better than boys in math, and they continued to do so throughout the 1970s. But as 9- and 13-year-olds of both genders improved their achievement in math during the 1980s and 1990s, boys *pulled ahead* of girls, opening up a small gender gap in math achievement that now favors boys. It's telling that even though younger boys are now doing better than girls on the long-term NAEP in math, when they once lagged behind, no one is talking about the emergence of a new "girl crisis" in elementary- and middle-school math.

Seventeen-year-old boys have always scored better than girls on the long-term NAEP in math, but boys' scores declined slightly more than girls' scores in the 1970s, and girls' scores have risen slightly more than those of boys since. As a result, older boys' advantage over girls in math has narrowed.

Overall, there has been no radical or recent decline in boys' performance relative to girls. Nor is there a clear overall trend—boys score higher in some areas, girls in others. . . .

The fact that achievement for older students is stagnant or declining for both boys and girls, to about the same degree, points to another important element of the boy crisis. The problem is most likely not that high schools need to be fixed to meet the needs of boys, but rather that they need to be fixed to meet the needs of *all* students, male and female. The need to accurately parse the influence of gender and other student categories is also acutely apparent when we examine the issues of race and income.

We Should Be Worried About Some Subgroups of Boys

There are groups of boys for whom "crisis" is not too strong a term. When racial and economic gaps combine with gender achievement gaps in reading, the result is disturbingly low achievement for poor, black, and Hispanic boys.

But the gaps between students of different races and classes are much larger than those for students of different genders—anywhere from two to five times as big, depending on the grade. The only exception is among 12th-grade boys, where the achievement gap between white girls and white boys in reading is the same size as the gap between white and black boys in reading and is larger than the gap between white and Hispanic boys. Overall, though, poor, black, and Hispanic boys would benefit far more from closing racial and economic achievement gaps than they would from closing gender gaps. While the gender gap picture is mixed, the racial gap picture is, unfortunately, clear across a wide range of academic subjects.

In addition to disadvantaged and minority boys, there are also reasons to be concerned about the substantial percentage of boys who have been diagnosed with disabilities. Boys make up two-thirds of students in special education—including 80 percent of those diagnosed with emotional disturbances or autism—and boys are two and a half times as likely as girls to be diagnosed with attention deficit hyperactivity disorder (ADHD). The number of boys diagnosed with disabilities or ADHD has exploded in the past 30 years, presenting a challenge for schools and causing concern for parents. But the reasons for this growth are complicated, a mix of educational, social, and biological factors. Evidence suggests that school and family factors—such as poor reading instruction, increased awareness of

Table 4.3 Four-Year High School Graduation

Rates by Race and Gender

	Male	Female
Asian	70%	73%
White	74%	79%
Hispanic	49%	58%
Black	48%	59%

Source: Jay P. Greene and Marcus Winters. *Leaving Boys Behind: Public High School Graduation Rates*, Manhattan Institute Civic Report No. 48, April 2006, http://www.manhattan-institute.org/html/cr_48.htm#05

and testing for disabilities, or overdiagnosis—may play a role in the increased rates of boys diagnosed with learning disabilities or emotional disturbance. But boys also have a higher incidence of organic disabilities, such as autism and orthopedic impairments, for which scientists don't currently have a completely satisfactory explanation. Further, while girls are less likely than boys to be diagnosed with most disabilities, the number of girls with disabilities has also grown rapidly in recent decades, meaning that this is not just a boy issue.

Moving Up and Moving On

Beyond achievement, there's the issue of attainment—student success in moving forward along the education pathway and ultimately earning credentials and degrees. There are undeniably some troubling numbers for boys in this area.

Boys are also more likely than girls to drop out of high school. Research by the Manhattan Institute found that only about 65 percent of boys who start high school graduate four years later, compared with 72 percent of girls. This gender gap cuts across all racial and ethnic groups, but it is the smallest for white and Asian students and much larger for black and Hispanic students. Still, the gaps between graduation rates for white and black or Hispanic students are much greater than gaps between rates for boys and girls of any race. These statistics, particularly those for black and Hispanic males, are deeply troubling. There is some good news, though, because both men and women are slightly more likely to graduate from high school today than they were 30 years ago.

The Source of the Boy Crisis: A Knowledge Deficit and a Surplus of Opportunism

It's clear that some gender differences in education are real, and there are some groups of disadvantaged boys in desperate need of help. But it's also clear that boys' overall educational achievement and attainment are not in decline—in fact, they have never been better. What accounts for the recent hysteria?

It's partly an issue of simple novelty. The contours of disadvantage in education and society at large have been clear for a long time—low-income, minority, and female people consistently fall short of their affluent, white, and male peers. The idea that historically privileged boys could be at risk, that boys could be shortchanged, has simply proved too deliciously counterintuitive and "newsworthy" for newspaper and magazine editors to resist.

The so-called boy crisis also feeds on a lack of solid information. Although there are a host of statistics about how boys and girls perform in school, we actually know very little about why these differences exist or how important they are. There are many things—including biological, developmental, cultural, and educational factors—that affect how boys and girls do in school. But untangling these different influences is incredibly difficult. Research on the causes of gender differences is hobbled by the twin demons of educational research: lack of data and the difficulty of drawing causal connections among multiple, complex influences. Nor do we know what these differences mean for boys' and girls' future economic and other opportunities.

Yet this hasn't stopped a plethora of so-called experts—from pediatricians and philosophers to researchers and op-ed columnists—from weighing in with their views on the causes and likely effects of educational gender gaps. In fact, the lack of solid research evidence confirming or debunking any particular hypothesis has created fertile ground for all sorts of people to seize on the boy crisis to draw attention to their pet educational, cultural or ideological issues.

The problem, we are told, is that the structured traditional classroom doesn't accommodate boys' energetic nature and need for free motion—or it's that today's schools don't provide enough structure or discipline. It's that feminists have demonized typical boy behavior and focused educational resources on girls—or it's the "box" boys are placed in by our patriarchal society. It's that our schools' focus on collaborative learning fails to stimulate boys' natural competitiveness—or it's that the competitive pressures of standardized testing are pushing out the kind of relevant, hands-on work on which boys thrive.

The boy crisis offers a perfect opportunity for those seeking an excuse to advance ideological and educational agendas. Americans' continued ambivalence about evolving gender roles guarantees that stories of "boys in crisis" will capture public attention. The research base is internally contradictory, making it easy to find superficial support for a wide variety of explanations but difficult for the media and the public to evaluate the quality of evidence cited. Yet there is not sufficient evidence—or the right kind of evidence—available to draw firm conclusions. As a result, there is a sort of free market for theories about why boys are underperforming girls in school, with parents, educators, media, and the public choosing to give credence to the explanations that are the best marketed and that most appeal to their preexisting preferences.

Unfortunately, this dynamic is not conducive to a thoughtful public debate about how boys and girls are doing in school or how to improve their performance. . . .

Dubious Theories and Old Agendas

Misapplying Brain Research to Education

Girls have, in general, stronger neural connectors in their temporal lobes than boys have. These connectors lead to more sensually detailed memory storage, better listening skills, and better discrimination among the various tones of voice. This leads, among other things, to greater use of detail in writing assignments.

—Michael Gurian and Kathy Stevens, *Educational Leadership*, November 2004

This paragraph offers a classic example of how some practitioners misapply brain research to education and gender. For starters, "neural connectors" is not a scientific term—by the time the research evidence behind this claim gets to readers of this article, it is dramatically watered down and redigested from what the initial studies said.

But the real problem here is that Gurian and Stevens attempt to string together a series of cause-and-effect relationships for which no evidence exists. Yes, there is some evidence of greater interconnection between different parts of women's brains. Yes, some studies have found that women remember an array of objects better than men do and that they are better at hearing certain tones than men are. (It's also worth noting that most of these studies were conducted not with children but with adults). And some teachers may say that boys do not use detail in writing assignments. But there is no evidence causally linking any one of these things to another. Gurian and Stevens simply pick up two factoids and claim they must be related. They also ignore many other potential explanations for the behavior they describe, such as the possibility that boys use less detail because they are in a greater hurry than girls, or that they tend to read books that have less detailed description and therefore use less in their own writing.

It would be unfair to imply that these authors write about boys for purely self-serving motives—most of these men and women seem to be sincerely concerned about the welfare of our nation's boys. But the work in this field leaves one skeptical of the quality of research, information, and analysis that are shaping educators' and parents' beliefs and practices as they educate boys and girls. Perhaps most tellingly, ideas about how to make schools more "boy friendly" align suspiciously well with educational and ideological beliefs the individuals promoting them had long before boys were making national headlines. And some of these prescriptions are diametrically opposed to one another.

In other words, few of these commentators have anything new to say—the boy crisis has just given them a new opportunity to promote their old messages.

Questions

1. How could different groups of scholars disagree so completely on the education of boys and girls when all claim that their work is based on solid research?

2. Think about schools where you have observed most recently. Can you find evidence that supports the arguments made in this or related articles?

Source: Sara Mead. "The Evidence Suggests Otherwise: The Truth About Boys and Girls." Washington, DC: Education Sector, 2006.

What Are Some of the Hidden Diversities Among Our Students?
From THE CALIFORNIA FAIR ACT OF 2011

In July 2011, the California legislature passed amendments to the Education Code that became known as the FAIR Act. The official Legislative Counsel's Digest provides the best overview of the law. While the major debate about the bill focused on its inclusion of sexual orientation in its provisions, the law also prohibited discrimination based on disability or religion, categories that had not previously been fully protected in civil rights laws. The law also cast a wide net, requiring the curriculum used in California to attend to the contribution of the diversity of its citizens while prohibiting practices or instructional materials that did not include the diversity of the state's residents. No other state has gone as far as California and some are actively resisting such definitions of diversity, but the FAIR Act illustrates the hopes and dreams of many.

An act to amend Sections 51204.5, 51500, 51501, 60040, and 60044 of the Education Code, relating to instruction. [Approved by Governor July 13, 2011. Filed with Secretary of State July 14, 2011.]

Legislative Counsel's Digest

Pupil instruction: prohibition of discriminatory content.

Existing law requires instruction in social sciences to include a study of the role and contributions of both men and women and specified categories of persons to the development of California and the United States. This bill would update references to certain categories of persons and additionally would require instruction in social sciences to include a study of the role and contributions of lesbian, gay, bisexual, and transgender Americans, persons with disabilities, and members of other cultural groups, to the development of California and the United States.

Existing law prohibits instruction or school sponsored activities that promote a discriminatory bias because of race, sex, color, creed, handicap, national origin, or ancestry. Existing law prohibits the State Board of Education and the governing board of any school district from adopting textbooks or other instructional materials that contain any matter that reflects adversely upon persons because of their race, sex, color, creed, handicap, national origin, or ancestry. This bill would revise the list of characteristics included in these provisions by referring to race or ethnicity, gender, religion, disability, nationality, and sexual orientation, or other characteristic listed as specified.

Existing law prohibits a governing board of a school district from adopting instructional materials that contain any matter reflecting adversely upon persons because of their race, color, creed, national origin, ancestry, sex, handicap, or occupation, or that contain any sectarian or denominational doctrine or propaganda contrary to law. This bill would revise the list of characteristics included in this provision to include race or ethnicity, gender, religion, disability, nationality, sexual orientation, and occupation, or other characteristic listed as specified.

Existing law requires that when adopting instructional materials for use in the schools, governing boards of school districts shall include materials that accurately portray the role and contributions of culturally and racially diverse groups including Native Americans, African Americans, Mexican Americans, Asian Americans, European Americans, and members of other ethnic and cultural groups to the total development of California and the United States. This bill would revise the list of culturally and racially diverse groups to also include Pacific Islanders, lesbian, gay, bisexual, and transgender Americans, and persons with disabilities.

Existing law provides that there shall be no discrimination on the basis of specified characteristics in any operation of alternative schools or charter schools. This bill would state the intent of the Legislature that alternative and charter schools take notice of the provisions of this bill in light of provisions of existing law that prohibit discrimination in any aspect of their operation.

This bill also would make other technical, nonsubstantive changes.

The People of the State of California Do Enact as Follows

SECTION 1. Section 51204.5 of the Education Code is amended to read: Instruction in social sciences shall include the early history of California and a study of the role and contributions of both men and women, Native Americans, African Americans, Mexican Americans, Asian Americans, Pacific Islanders, European Americans, lesbian, gay, bisexual, and transgender Americans, persons with disabilities, and members of other ethnic and cultural groups, to the economic, political, and social development of California and the United States of America, with particular emphasis on portraying the role of these groups in contemporary society.

SEC. 2. Section 51500 of the Education Code is amended to read: A teacher shall not give instruction and a school district shall not sponsor any activity that promotes a discriminatory bias on the basis of race or ethnicity, gender, religion, disability, nationality, sexual orientation, or because of a characteristic listed in Section 220.

SEC. 3. Section 51501 of the Education Code is amended to read: The state board and any governing board shall not adopt any textbooks or other instructional materials for use in the public schools that contain any matter reflecting adversely upon persons on the basis of race or ethnicity, gender, religion, disability, nationality, sexual orientation, or because of a characteristic listed in Section 220.

SEC. 4. Section 60040 of the Education Code is amended to read: When adopting instructional materials for use in the schools, governing boards shall include only instructional materials which, in their determination, accurately portray the cultural and racial diversity of our society, including:

(a) The contributions of both men and women in all types of roles, including professional, vocational, and executive roles.
(b) The role and contributions of Native Americans, African Americans, Mexican Americans, Asian Americans, Pacific Islanders, European Americans, lesbian, gay, bisexual, and transgender Americans, persons with disabilities, and members of other ethnic and cultural groups to the total development of California and the United States.
(c) The role and contributions of the entrepreneur and labor in the total development of California and the United States.

SEC. 5. Section 60044 of the Education Code is amended to read: A governing board shall not adopt any instructional materials for use in the schools that, in its determination, contain:

(a) Any matter reflecting adversely upon persons on the basis of race or ethnicity, gender, religion, disability, nationality, sexual orientation, occupation, or because of a characteristic listed in Section 220.
(b) Any sectarian or denominational doctrine or propaganda contrary to law.

SEC. 6. It is the intent of the Legislature that alternative and charter schools take notice of the provisions of this act in light of Section 235 of the Education Code, which prohibits discrimination on the basis of disability, gender, nationality, race or ethnicity, religion, sexual orientation, or other specified characteristics.

Questions

1. What political forces might have brought about the passage of the FAIR Act in California? Do those forces exist in other states?
2. Besides LGBTQ students, who else might benefit from the FAIR Act?

Source: Chapter 81 of the Statutes of 2011 (S.B. 48)

What Is the Best Education for Students With Disabilities?

From "UNDERSTANDING STUDENTS WITH LEARNING DIFFICULTIES : HOW DO THEY LEARN?"

AUTHOR: BARBARA S. S. HONG AND KAY A. CHICK

Barbara S. S. Hong and Kay A. Chick ask us to consider how students with various kinds of learning difficulties—many of whom are not labeled as students with special needs—experience school. Teachers, they argue, need to be mindful of how frustrating school can be for some students even as it appears easy for others. The goal, they insist, must be to connect with the desire most students have to learn and to encourage that impulse.

Why does learning come so naturally for some students and yet is so onerous for others?
Why do some students need constant reminders while others get on task right away?
Why is it that some students "just don't get it" even after countless repetitions and multitudes of practice?

Even though learning difficulties are common in classrooms, novice teachers are often unfamiliar with the specific challenges that students experience on a daily basis in the areas of reading, writing, computing, handwriting, spelling, reasoning, analyzing, and interacting. When students first begin to learn new concepts, such as fractions, contractions, punctuation, or telling time, they experience varying degrees of dissonance in finding a connection between prior knowledge and what they are currently learning (Piaget, 1926). Typical learning requires the simultaneous use of one's auditory, visual, and perceptual acuity to adequately process and translate information into comprehensible knowledge (Laasonen, Service, & Virsu, 2001). However, for some students, these processes can be time consuming, frustrating, and laborious. Learning can be an insipid process for students who have to second-guess what they are actually hearing and seeing. Inevitably, it is difficult for them to harness the motivation for learning particular skills, staying on task, or remembering the content.

Further complicating the process, some students with learning difficulties have limited and weak executive skills in two specific areas: (a) study habits (e.g., time management, organization, decision-making, self-regulatory behavior, problem solving, and logical reasoning); and (b) learning skills (e.g., staying focused, paying attention, developing long- and short-term memory strategies, and rehearsing test-taking skills). Students who experience any or all of these processing challenges could face a perpetual cycle of associating learning with anger, anxiety, frustration, and impassivity (Arthur, 2003; Huntington & Bender, 1993; Morris, Schraufnagel, Chudnow, & Weinberg, 2009). Over time, these feelings create a ripple effect that leads to emotional setbacks, breeding low self-esteem, poor self-image, and grim learned helplessness (Valas, 2001). Fortunately, with appropriate instruction, consistent practice, and meaningful feedback, students with learning difficulties can improve their perception and grasp new concepts with much more ease. This paper describes the characteristics of students with learning difficulties, identifies the types of challenges they face, and recommends strategies for remediating these difficulties through appropriate adaptations.

What Is a Learning Disability?

According to the Individuals with Disabilities Education Improvement Act ([IDEIA], 2004), a learning disability is a disorder in "one or more of the basic psychological processes involved in understanding or using language, spoken or written, that may manifest itself in an imperfect ability to listen, think, speak, read, write, spell, or do mathematical calculations. This term includes such conditions as perceptual disabilities, brain injury, minimal brain dysfunction, dyslexia, and developmental aphasia. The term does not include students who have learning problems that are primarily the result of visual, hearing, or motor disabilities; mental retardation; or environmental, cultural, or economic disadvantage" (IDEIA, 2004).

Throughout this article, "learning difficulty" is used instead of "learning disability" in order to generalize to students who experience challenges in learning due to weak processing skills, regardless of whether or not they meet the eligibility criteria of learning disabilities under the Individuals with Disabilities Education Act ([IDEA], 1997). This distinction is important for teachers to note because students who are not labeled as learning disabled can still encounter difficulties that significantly hinder their learning. It is, therefore, paramount for teachers to understand what these students are experiencing on a daily basis in order to effectively help them.

What Are Basic Psychological Processes?

When there is a disparity between what one sees (visual) and hears (auditory), disequilibrium or a zone of dissonance exists (Jerger, Martin, & Jerger, 1987). This disparity prevents students from completely processing the intended message, whether that information is in the form of words, numbers, pictures, or spatial orientation. This difficulty is the core of what students with learning difficulties experience. It is impossible to pinpoint a specific area of deficiency because basic processing requires the optimum functioning of what one sees and what one hears (Kavale & Forness, 2000). As a result, there is no one solution that can "fix" or "cure" a learning disability. What this means is that teachers need to learn how to use a combination of strategies to identify what works and does not work for each individual student. . . .

Final Words

Learning difficulties cannot be cured, but can certainly be improved through appropriate strategies and pertinent adjustments in instruction and assignments (Damon & Lerner, 2006; Terlecki, Newcombe, & Little, 2008). By and large, students are motivated to learn, regardless of their learning difficulties. Students want to find ways to compensate for their limitations, be on task, retain what they have learned, and, most of all, make their effort count. Limitations in any aspect of neurological processing can easily frustrate one's motivation to learn and be engaged. Accordingly, if teachers do not know what to look for, then it is almost impossible to know what students are seeing or not seeing, hearing or not hearing, in order to make any adaptations.

Teachers need to become more cognizant of how they teach and not just what they teach. Beyond teaching the curriculum, teachers should also try to integrate learning strategies and generalize contexts for students to retain information. Students' beliefs about themselves can be a powerful catalyst for their learning trajectories, impacting their sense of self-confidence and self-efficacy. Content only matters when the information learned can be processed, applied, retained, and generalized with some degrees of fluency (Willingham, 2009). Henceforth, when it comes to working with students with learning difficulties, the three rules of thumb are: (1) give students time to process; (2) expose students to effective learning and studying strategies; and (3) practice, practice, practice! As the saying goes, "Practice does not make perfect. . . . Practice makes permanent!"

Questions

1. What strategies advocated by Hong and Chick might be most useful to you as a teacher?
2. What might a general education teacher learn from this article about learning difficulties as they appear for many students?

Source: Barbara S. S. Hong & Kay A. Chick. "Understanding Students with Learning Difficulties: How Do They Learn?" *Kappa Delta Pi Record* 49, no. 1 (2013): 30–1, 36.

Philosophical and Psychological Theories
How Do Children Learn?

5

> To teach in a manner that respects and cares for the souls of our students is essential if we are to provide the necessary conditions where learning can most deeply and intimately begin.

BELL HOOKS

We teach so that others can learn. No one ever teaches just to teach or develops a curriculum for its own sake. Teaching is always (or always should be) done in the service of one goal: student learning.

Given this obvious truism, that learning is the purpose of all education, it is surprising how little we know about how human beings really learn. And most of what we do know about human learning is the result of very recent research. People have been teaching and learning for thousands of years, as long as there has been human life on this planet. Schools have been organized for hundreds of years to facilitate this process of teaching and learning for children and youth. Since the days of Socrates and Plato,

philosophers have debated the nature of human learning. Only in the past few decades, however, have psychologists been able to conduct basic research on the human brain so that we have the beginning—and still only the beginning—of a true science of human learning. This chapter focuses on the long history of philosophical debates and the much more recent work of psychologists in addressing the very human process of learning. Throughout the chapter, we focus on some key question for every teacher: "How will my students learn anything?" "What must I, as a teacher, do to facilitate the learning process?"

Psychologists differ substantially in their beliefs and ideas about how people learn. Nevertheless, to be a successful teacher, you must at least contemplate these ideas and come to some preliminary conclusions about your own stance. As researchers Morris L. Bigge and S. Samuel Shermis wisely note, "Everything teachers do is colored by the psychological theory they hold. Consequently, teachers who do not make use of a systematic body of theory in their day-by-day decisions are behaving blindly; little evidence of long-range rationale, purpose, or plan is observable in their teaching."[1] Of course, teachers may operate on the basis of unexamined theories or the folk wisdom of a school that often represents someone else's unexamined psychological theory. However, a true professional will grapple substantively with a range of theories of how children and adolescents learn and will come to his or her own informed conclusions, even if these conclusions are (as they should be) tentative and subject to change in light of new information and experience.

This chapter has three **Readings**. In *Teaching to Transgress,* the philosopher bell hooks describes what she sees as the key ethical as well as pedagogical responsibility of a teacher, though for her the two cannot be separated. She argues that education as the practice of freedom demands a level of freedom for the teacher as well as the student: the freedom to be authentic and to care not only for knowledge but also for the healing of souls. Then *How People Learn*, published by the prestigious National Academy of Sciences, represents the most cutting-edge research by psychologists and brain researchers on how human beings learn and what methods of teaching will be most effective with them. A teacher who wants to be a serious professional must attend to the new research that is represented here. In the final **Reading**, psychologist Howard Gardner lists his eight—or nine—categories of human intelligence and reflects on how he came to see human intelligence in these multiple forms rather than as a single hierarchy of intelligence.

What Have Philosophers Said About Human Learning?

Since humans have been able to think about more than the necessities of survival, philosophers have pondered the meaning of education and specifically the roles of the teacher and the learner in the educational process. In this section, we look briefly at what a few selected philosophers have said about education through the centuries and how this philosophical thinking can influence what you do as a teacher.[2]

Socrates, 470–399 BCE

Socrates is often considered the earliest of the ancient Greek philosophers. Since Socrates himself wrote nothing, all that we know of him is through the writings of others, especially his most famous student, Plato. Nevertheless, Socrates put an important stamp on education. What has become known as the Socratic dialogue emerged from this ancient philosopher's effort to lead his pupils to truth by continually asking them questions—questions that forced them to clarify their own views and deal with contradictions in their own thinking. In the end, Socrates also believed that there were significant limits to human wisdom but that the search for truth through continued questioning and clarification was always worth it. According to Plato, Socrates once said of another supposedly wise man, "Well, although I do not suppose that either of us knows anything really beautiful and good, I am better off than he is—for he knows nothing, and thinks that he knows. I neither know nor think that I know. In this latter particular, then, I seem to have slightly the advantage of him."[3] Socrates's continued questioning brought him into conflict with the authorities in Athens, who accused him of corrupting the youth. After being tried and found guilty of "promoting dangerous ideas," Socrates was forced to drink poison made from the hemlock plant, the method of capital punishment in ancient Athens.

Plato, 427–347 BCE

Although Plato studied with Socrates, he later came to different conclusions. If Socrates loved the questions, Plato wanted the answers. His goals for his students became much more specific—to help them move from a vague appreciation of the world to a clear understanding of objective realities that would help them understand what was good and how to lead ethical lives. In his most famous example, Plato asked his listeners to "picture men dwelling in a sort of subterranean cavern . . . fettered from childhood, so that they remain in the same spot, able to look forward only . . . [with] . . . light from a fire burning higher up and at a distance behind them." The result of living in this cave was that these men could only see shadows of themselves and of the world. They might argue all day long about the meaning of what they saw, but in the end, all the arguments were about shadows.

Human beings, Plato said, were a lot like these cave dwellers. We see what we call reality, but it may only be a shadow of reality. The educator's job was to drag the "occupants of the cave" into the light, which might be painful at first but which in time would allow them to see "things themselves, and from these he [sic] would go on to contemplate the appearance of the heavens and heaven itself." Having seen reality—and not the mere shadow of reality—students would never want to return to the cave, however painful the transition to light might be. The true educator facilitates just that transition, from the shadow of truth to real truth. Unlike many philosophers of education, ancient and modern, Plato also addressed the education of women, calling for the education of "female guardians" along with the male "philosopher kings" who would lead society.[4]

Aristotle, 384–322 BCE

A student of Plato, and perhaps the most famous Greek philosopher, Aristotle differed from Socrates and Plato in his focus not only on gaining a clear understanding of reality but also on using observation and data, not just argument, to gain that clarity. Aristotle also believed that every substance in the world had a nature (or potential) that it might or might not actualize. Just as an acorn could become a great oak (though most acorns would not), so could every human, if well educated, fulfill his potential as a reasonable and thoughtful person. As Aristotle wrote, "[F]or man, therefore, the life according to reason is best and pleasantest, since reason more than anything else *is* man." Further, he said, "Happiness extends, then, just so far as contemplation does, and those to whom contemplation more fully belongs are more truly happy." Such happiness, based on thoughtful contemplation, was the key to virtue in individual lives and in states, and it was the role of the educator to cultivate it in men. (Aristotle did mean *men*. He did not see such contemplation as the role of women.)[5]

Jean-Jacques Rousseau, 1712–78

One of the first modern philosophers, Jean-Jacques Rousseau was born in Switzerland, traveled widely in Europe, and lived much of his adult life in France. Although it may be hard to think of someone who was born 300 years ago as "modern," Rousseau continues to be important in educational thinking. His ideas about education were rooted in his belief that, in each country, most people had far too little freedom because a small elite held the political power. On a smaller scale, he saw most schools as structured in a way that robbed young people of their freedom to think, create, and explore. Thus, as he looked at the world around him, Rousseau said, "Man is born free and everywhere he is in chains." Rousseau also discussed the education of women, though his ideal woman was supposed to be dependent on males and not quite so free of her chains.

Recognizing that modern people cannot "return again to the forests to live among bears," Rousseau sought to develop a system of education that would foster human freedom. In his book *Emile*, he developed that system for an imaginary pupil, from birth to manhood. Emile's education started with "an incontestable principle that the first impulses of nature are always right. There is no original perversity in the human heart." And if this is true, then the teacher's role is simply to allow Emile's—and every student's—inner goodness to appear. School should not make students dull through instruction in the lessons that some adults thought children should receive. Rather, Rousseau advocated helping students spend less time learning their lessons and more time living freely in the world so that through a range of experiences they might become both wise and happy. Rousseau's goal for a student was to become someone who "knows nothing by heart, he knows a great deal by experience." Such a student would come to love what he knows and therefore love himself and his world of freedom.[6]

DID YOU KNOW?

One of the most-often quoted philosophers, Confucius (551–479 BCE) believed learning had nothing to do with intuition but resulted instead from long, careful study with a teacher (someone older and wiser) whose words and actions could be imitated. Confucius's succinct teaching style consisted of posing questions, citing passages from the classics, using analogies, and waiting for his students to arrive at the answers. According to Confucius, "He who learns but does not think is lost. He who thinks but does not learn is in great danger."

John Dewey, 1859–1952

John Dewey was one of the most influential philosophers of education in the United States as well as the world. Often called "the father of progressive education," Dewey was as many times a critic of **progressive education** as he was its defender. Although Dewey wrote a great deal in the course of his long life, his core beliefs focused on a few key elements. Moving far beyond Rousseau's individualistic approach, Dewey wrote in *The School and Society* (1899): "We are apt to look at the school from an individualistic standpoint. . . . Yet the range of the outlook needs to be enlarged. What the best and wisest parent wants for his own child, that must the community want for all of its children." Like Rousseau, however, Dewey was critical of the boring nature of much traditional education in which the "subject-matter of education consists of bodies of information and skills that have been worked out in the past." As he continued in *Experience and Education* (1938), that traditional approach is one of imposition from above and from outside. Progressive education, Dewey said, was different:

> To imposition from above is opposed expression and cultivation of individuality; to external discipline is opposed free activity; to learning from tests and teachers, learning through experience; to acquisition of isolated skills and techniques by drill, is opposed acquisition of them as means of attaining ends which make direct vital appeal; to preparation for a more or less remote future is opposed making the most of the opportunities of present life; to static aims and materials is opposed acquaintance with a changing world.

progressive education
An educational movement that began at the beginning of the 20th century. Many progressive educators believe that schools should begin with the life experience of the child rather than with a preset curriculum (child-centered educators) and that the "real world" of experience provides a better focus than starting with abstract ideas.

Finally, for Dewey, all this learning from experience—from the contemporary world of work and human activity—was also in the service of something larger. As Dewey said in *Democracy and Education* (1916), he was concerned with linking the "subject matter and method of education" with "the growth of democracy." For him, the two were always inextricably linked.[7]

Mortimer Adler, 1902–2001

Mortimer Adler agreed with Dewey about education's serving to broaden democracy, but he disagreed dramatically about the best kind of education to accomplish that goal. In *Paideia Proposal* (1982), he wrote, "'You propose,' the objectors may say, 'the same educational objectives for all the children.' Yes, that is precisely what we propose." Not only did he want the same objectives, he wanted the same course of study between kindergarten and the end of high school "with a satisfactory standard of accomplishment regardless of native ability, temperamental bent, or conscious preferences." To make exceptions by varying the curriculum according to individual student needs or interests was, Adler thought, to run a very grave risk of leaving some young people out of the democratic dialogue that was essential to a good society. Contrary to Dewey, Adler believed that great ideas had been developed over time, that a body of great works of literature embodied these ideas, and that this essential literature needed to be at the core of every young person's learning, if individuals were to have a good life and if free institutions were to be preserved in the larger society.[8]

Maxine Greene, 1917–2014

In an interview late in her long life, Maxine Greene said, "The only way to really awaken to life, awaken to the possibilities, is to be self-aware. I use the term *wide-awakeness*. . . . Without the ability to think about yourself, to reflect on your life, there's really no awareness, no consciousness." According to Greene, the purpose of education is to foster such an awareness or "awakeness," which is often done better through engagement with the arts than in a traditional classroom. Deeply concerned about the "prevailing cynicism" that characterizes "a world of fearful moral uncertainty," Greene calls on educators not to instruct in morals in any traditional way but rather to create significant encounters with works of art, with literature, and with life in ways that lead students to pose new questions, developing a new sense of moral urgency and passionate commitment to a better future for the human race.[9]

Paulo Freire, 1921–99

Brazilian educator Paulo Freire decried what he called "banking" in education, in which teachers simply make "deposits" in the blank minds of their students. He contended that the creation of "dialogue" must replace the banking model. Dialogue does not negate the role of the teacher who brings his or her unique expertise to the dialogue, including knowledge of the larger world, the academic disciplines, and the experiences of other people in other contexts. But the teacher must come to the dialogue always ready to learn from the students, as Freire said, "with humility."

Freire did not come to his educational ideas easily. After a brief career as a lawyer, he taught high school from 1941 to 1947. He then took on responsibility for adult literacy in poor communities in northeast Brazil. Freire quickly found that traditional methods of teaching literacy—starting with the alphabet and simple words—did not work with adults. They quickly became bored. Freire turned instead to asking people to think about the most pressing issues in their communities. In one famous example, a community needed a well. Freire focused the literacy campaign around writing a letter to the government demanding a new, deeper well. Freire's link of education and activism got him in trouble with the political authorities and, after the military coup in Brazil in 1964, he was briefly forced into exile, where he wrote his best-known book, *Pedagogy of the Oppressed,* in 1970.[10]

Jane Roland Martin, 1929–

Jane Roland Martin has focused on the fact that contemporary philosophers of education ignore the subject of women. In her book *Reclaiming a Conversation: The Ideal of the Educated Woman* (1985), Martin set out to change that situation. She insisted that "[i]n a society in which traits are genderized and socialization according to sex is commonplace, an educational philosophy that tries to ignore gender in the name of equality is self-defeating." Rather than ignoring gender, Martin seeks to raise the consciousness of women and men about the ways schooling has denigrated women and the work that is usually seen as "women's work," while building into the education expected for both women and men a greater respect for nurturing and an ethic of care. In attending to nurturing and caring as part of the core purpose of the curriculum, Martin argued, education could better serve "the full range of people's lives" and help all people address "the present perils to life on earth."[11]

CONNECTIONS →←

In Chapter 7, we discuss John Dewey and progressive education's goal of connecting curriculum with the current interests and experiences of young people.

bell hooks, 1952–

A feminist scholar committed to a multicultural approach to education, bell hooks believes that for teachers who care about "the practice of freedom . . . there is an aspect of our vocation that is sacred." As she describes in more detail in the first **Reading** for this chapter, she means that teachers must not only share information but also share in the intellectual and spiritual growth of their students and must come to see themselves as healers—of individual students and a broken world. To become such educators, hooks also insists that teachers must transgress the traditional boundaries that define teaching. They must take on the overlooked issues of gender, race, and class, but also the erotic and the political. Doing so will involve educational acts of "political resistance," she says. But, hooks warns, "Teachers who care, who serve their students, are usually at odds with the environments wherein we teach."[12]

 DID YOU KNOW?

bell hooks is the pen name of Gloria Jean Watkins. Although she originally chose to author under her great-grandmother's name to avoid confusion with another Gloria Watkins in her community, the spirit of her defiant ancestor—known as a woman who was not afraid to speak her mind—gave her a "writer-identity that would challenge and subdue all impulses leading me away from speech into silence."

Kwame Anthony Appiah, 1954–

According to Kwame Anthony Appiah, education should foster a kind of "rooted cosmopolitanism" in which students come to see themselves as citizens of the world (hence, becoming cosmopolitan) yet at the same time understand that they belong to a community and need to take responsibility for its destiny. Appiah worries about a kind of community identity that can separate men and women from other men and women and foster a cultural partiality that is dangerously divisive. He argues that a great respect for **individualism** that also focuses intensely on human rights—the individual rights of other free and independent humans—is both the key to building a better world and the best outcome of a truly liberal education.[13]

> **individualism**
> Stresses self-reliance and independence of the individual sometimes apart from the society or group.

The list of important philosophers of education, or philosophers whose work has important implications for education, could go on and on. The descriptions offered here only hint at these philosophers' core ideas regarding teaching and learning. A much deeper look at their work is needed to understand the value of what they have to say to those of us who teach. After this cursory review, though, we need to ask, "What does this philosophy have to do with me as a teacher?"

You can probably be a very effective classroom teacher without ever having read Plato or Greene or any of the philosophers discussed here. But a teacher will have a less rich personal and intellectual life if he or she does not think about some of the major questions these philosophers have raised. There are few better ways to engage these questions than to read the work of some of the wise people who have thought about these questions, over the decades and centuries.

> **existentialism**
> Stresses personal choice and responsibility while recognizing that human existence is wholly unexplainable and, perhaps, meaningless, in a chaotic universe.
>
> **essentialism**
> Viewpoint in which groups of people, classified by race or population, share the same inherent essences (made up of characteristics or properties) that define the group and distinguish it from other communities.

Some seek to put the different philosophers into different boxes: Maxine Greene represents **existentialism**, whereas Adler represents **essentialism**; Plato represents idealism, whereas Aristotle represents realism; and so on. The problem with these boxes is that they completely miss the rich complexity of these philosophers. Certainly, some fundamental disagreements exist among them. Greene is more than existentialism and Adler is more than essentialism, but Greene does worry about any effort to standardize education or to create a single set of standards, which for her are, by definition, far too confining of the human spirit. Adler, however, sees in standards and, indeed, in a single standardized curriculum for all students, the only key to a democratic education in which all people not only are created equal but also are allowed to be equal participants in a grand democratic dialogue that should be the outcome of effective schooling. Ironically, for all the philosophers' differences, that grand democratic dialogue is exactly the goal of their work, however different their proposed ways to get us there.

Teachable Moment
CULTURE . . . WHOSE CULTURE?

When Mortimer Adler spoke about passing on the great ideas—the culture—that had been developed over centuries, he had a pretty clear idea of what culture that was. For Adler, and for many contemporary educators, the purpose of schooling is to induct students into a particular culture that has been developing in Europe and North America since the time of the Greek philosophers, but especially in the past few hundred years. Knowing this culture includes knowing the work of philosophers such as Socrates and Rousseau; great writers such as Shakespeare, Walt Whitman, John Steinbeck, and Robert Frost; great music from Bach to Beethoven to contemporary classical work; and so on.

Other philosophers have questioned whether inducting students into this "grand tradition" was either wise or good. When Rousseau said that he wanted a student who "knows nothing by heart, he knows a great deal by experience" or when Dewey objected to education that is "imposition from above," they were objecting to an education that, as they saw it, too often simply told students to learn the traditional literature and ideas by heart rather than engage with the ideas as they were relevant to their the lives and experiences.

In today's increasingly diverse world, more and more people are challenging the ideas that there is "one great culture" or "one grand narrative" that all students should learn. Jane Roland Martin is far from alone in noting how often women and women's ideas and experiences have been left out of what was called "culture." Historians like E. P. Thompson have insisted that history is not simply kings, presidents, and military leaders, and that such history tends "to obscure the agency of working people, the degree to which they contributed, by conscious efforts, to the making of history." [*The Making of the English Working Class* (1963), pp. 12–13.]

With the increasing racial and ethnic diversity of American society, advocates of multicultural education have come to insist that there is not one culture that should be taught in schools but rather many cultures. The *multi* in multiculturalism is as important as the *culture*. Advocates of multiculturalism, though they differ greatly among themselves, insist that all students need to learn the literature and ideas of the African American experience—including the poems of Phillis Wheatley and Langston Hughes, the autobiographies of Frederick Douglass or Malcolm X, the novels of Zora Neale Hurston or Toni Morrison, and the music of Billie Holiday, Miles Davis, John Coltrane, Jimi Hendrix, or James Brown—as well as being exposed to works from the Latino (such as Carlos Fuentes or Gabriel Garcia Marquez), Asian (such as Amy Tan or Maxine Hong Kingston), and American Indian communities (Vine Deloria or the many collections of tribal legends now available)—every bit as much as they should be reading the works of European and European American writers.

Ironically, the growing emphasis on a diversity of cultures has led some White students to think that other people have "culture" and that European Americans "have no culture." Of course, all people have culture—many different cultures—and part of the joy of living in today's diverse world is that all of us can be informed by, shaped by, and influenced by cultural developments that have come from many different eras and all corners of the globe, including the many communities that make up contemporary U.S. culture.

Questions

• Thinking back on your own experiences as a student, would you say your school mostly taught the "grand tradition" of literature and history based primarily on the works of European and European American males, or were diverse cultures and both genders represented in the curriculum?

• If you are a student of color, did you first learn of your own cultural history in school or elsewhere? If you are a White student, what do you know about your own cultural (ethnic or religious) roots? Where did you learn about your roots? Whatever your race and culture, does having a cultural identity matter to you?

How Have Modern Psychologists Changed Our Way of Thinking About Learning?

Some of the names and ideas presented in this section may be familiar to you, especially if you have already taken a basic psychology course. If so, this brief review may link these ideas more directly to the classroom. Even if this is all new to you, you will likely revisit this material in more detail in future classes in child or adolescent development and, indeed, throughout your career as an educator. These scholars and the ideas they represent have helped shape the ways schools are organized and the ways in which teachers teach. Some familiarity with them is usually considered an essential part of teacher preparation. A teacher who is not familiar with research in educational psychology and who is not able to place his or her own classroom practice in a clear theoretical construct can still be a good teacher. He or she cannot, however, be the kind of "reflective practitioner" who knows not only how to get things done in a classroom but also *why* certain things make sense at certain times, with certain groups of students, but perhaps not at other times or with other students. Without some understanding of psychology, and indeed philosophy, it is almost impossible to move from being simply a skilled practitioner to a true educator—someone who can think deeply about the process of teaching and learning and help adjust instruction to fit different contexts.

Jean Piaget, 1896–1980

Swiss psychologist Jean Piaget focused on understanding the ways children think, reason, and learn. In the process, he wrote some of the most influential theories of child development. Piaget saw four basic stages through which every child must move. Each stage represents a significantly different way of thinking and viewing the world; teachers need to understand the stages and know where their students fall in the developmental process. Children must move through the stages in a steady and gradual way that can be predicted with relative accuracy (for most healthy children) based on their chronological age. Piaget's stages of development are as follows:

- sensorimotor stage (ages 0 to 2 years)
- preoperational stage (ages 2 to 7 years)
- concrete operational stage (ages 7 to 11 years)
- formal operational stage (age 11 to adult)

In *The Moral Judgment of the Child*, Piaget illustrates these four stages by discussing a child's emerging sense of the rules for a game of marbles. For an infant in the sensorimotor stage, there is no game of marbles as such, for a game involves a level of interaction that is beyond an infant. According to Piaget, if you "give a baby a marble, it will explore its surface and consistency, but will at the same time use it as something to grasp, to suck, to rub against the sides of its cradle, and so on." At this stage, it is fascinating to watch an infant interact with anything, inanimate or animate, but it would certainly make no sense to try to teach the infant the rules of any game. Such instruction would be absurdly beyond his or her stage of development.

The first stage does not last long, however. In the early years, certainly well before a child begins kindergarten or first grade, something Piaget calls "egocentrism" appears as the "state of cooperation," in which individual children, recognizing each other as equals, can understand the difference between themselves and an inanimate object (such as a marble) and can enjoy having other children around them engaging in similar play with the marbles. At this stage, however, it is still not reasonable to assume that the interaction will be governed by any external rules or that the children will focus on their interaction for long. Thus, in a game of marbles, a child who is 3 to 5 years old may do the things that one does when playing a game of marbles, but he or she is merely imitating what others do. The child may think he or she is playing the game, but the interaction with the other children is not really meaningful. So Piaget says, "He plays in an individualistic manner with material that is social. Such is egocentrism."

By the time the marble-playing child has reached the third stage, around age 7—in many schools in the United States, at the transition into second or third grade—the developmental stage changes significantly. The key change in moving to the third stage of development is a move from egocentric behavior to "the desire for mutual understanding." Up to this time, the child is happy with any success in the game of marbles no matter what success or failure other children may have. Now, with this transition, comes a desire to *win*, that is, to abide by the rules but at the same time acquire more marbles than the other children. As Piaget says, "The specific pleasure of the game thus ceases to be muscular and egocentric, and becomes social." At this stage, children insist on the adherence to common rules that lead to a conclusion that is accepted by all.

Finally, by age 10 or 11, the child has moved to what Piaget sees as the final stage of development, in which formal reasoning develops and, in the marbles game example, the child's interest moves to understanding the game and the rules that govern it. Piaget described observing a group of boys playing marbles who had reached this stage, "Not only do these children seek to cooperate . . . they seem to take a peculiar pleasure in anticipating all possible cases and in codifying them." Thus, throughout this fourth stage the dominating interest seems to be interest in the rules themselves. Children at this stage will make the game more complicated as a way to play with the rules as well as with the marbles. The management of the game has come to replace the sheer interest in winning and the earlier kinesthetic sense of pleasure in the act of touching or moving the marbles.[14]

Piaget's objective was simply to describe children's thinking, not to improve it.[15] Many other educators have spent the past half-century drawing out the details of what Piaget's stages of development mean for the classroom. If Piaget's stages analyze development correctly (which is certainly a subject of debate today), then it makes little sense to try to teach something before the child is ready to learn it, but it makes great sense to foster development and growth at the appropriate time. To return to the game of marbles, there would be little value in having kindergarten or first-grade students ponder the rules or possible changes in the rules of a game of marbles (or the rules of the classroom or the larger society), whereas the same discussion with a group of 10-year-olds in fifth or sixth grade might be extremely valuable. Knowing our students thus means knowing many aspects of their lives, including their developmental stages and what lessons they are or are not ready to learn and comprehend.

B. F. Skinner, 1904–90

The focus of B.F. Skinner's long and productive career as a psychologist was human behavior—how to understand it, predict it, and shape it. Because of his focus on behavior and actions, Skinner was much less interested in looking at brain activity or at emotions that were hard to measure. He wanted to know how to shape what people did, or, as he said, "We want to know why men behave as they do." With that knowledge, Skinner was sure that he could not only understand what people would do in similar circumstances but, by analyzing the causes of behavior, it would be possible to manipulate people so as to control their behavior in the future. Skinner was convinced that there were rules of behavior every bit as clear as the rules of navigation and, if these rules were understood, humans could be guided through their lives as surely as winds and tides could be used to guide a sailing ship.

For Skinner, the most efficient ways for teachers to teach and students to learn was through what he called **operant conditioning,** or positive reinforcement. In experiments with pigeons, Skinner provided the reinforcement with food; with children, he substituted praise for selecting the right answer or for engaging in the preferred action. Skinner did not have much patience with schooling that focused on students' learning through their own discovery or their own problem posing and problem solving. The purpose of schooling, he believed, was to transmit culture across the generations. Thus, although he noted that "[e]ducators have turned to discovery and creativity in an effort to interest their students," he believed it was much better to focus on "good contingencies of reinforcement [that] do that in a much more profitable way." Once a teacher had gotten a student to the right answer or the right action, the rest was fairly easy. The hard part involves getting people to behave in a certain way for the *first time* so that the behavior can be reinforced. Once the desired behavior has been exhibited, praise and other positive reinforcement should easily make it replicable.

If human learning is simply a matter of responding positively to operant conditioning or positive reinforcement, then the implications for teaching are fairly obvious. It is the teacher's role to decide what behavior and knowledge the student should have, present it clearly, and provide much positive reinforcement for the student who adopts the knowledge, ideas, or actions.[16]

> **operant conditioning**
> Use of positive or negative consequences to alter the responses and behavior of a student.

Teachable Moment
ARE YOU A SKINNERIAN?

No, it's not a term from the latest *Star Trek* movie. A "Skinnerian" is someone who practices the learning philosophy developed by B. F. Skinner. Skinner's operant conditioning was based on the premise that people would repeat positive behaviors if they received (and could look forward to) positive rewards.

Skinner believed there were five major obstacles to learning that called for five simple remedies:

Table 5.1

Obstacle	Remedy
People have a fear of failure.	Give the learner immediate feedback.
The task is not broken down into small enough steps.	Break down the task into small steps.
Directions are lacking.	Repeat the directions as many times as possible.
The directions are not clear.	Work from the simplest to the most complex tasks.
Positive reinforcement is lacking.	Give positive reinforcement.

Much research has confirmed Skinner's approach, especially regarding relatively straightforward tasks, such as learning how to ride a bike or how to sound out words as a first step toward reading. You may recall an instance when a teacher helped you learn something by breaking it down into smaller tasks and providing positive feedback.

Critics of Skinner, however, see his approach as too manipulative. All the decisions seem to rest with the teacher, and the student is treated as a relatively passive object to be led by immediate feedback and positive reinforcement to the end results that the teacher decides. Some observers feel this approach is better suited to helping rats learn how to run through a maze than to supporting young people in moving toward maturity.

Questions

- Following Skinner's philosophy, what kinds of lessons can best be delivered or broken down into a series of small steps? When might this approach get in the way of helping students cultivate a larger understanding of the issues?
- How important is positive reinforcement to you? When is the reward not as important as the process?

Lev Vygotsky, 1896–1934

Lev Vygotsky's key work was done in the Soviet Union in the 1920s and 1930s, but it was the translation of his work into English in the 1960s and 1970s that made his influence on education in the United States significant. The developmental theory most closely associated with Vygotsky is what he called the "zone of proximal development"—the stage just beyond the child's current one, which, with proper input and support, the child can be expected to reach. In Vygotsky's words, this is "the distance between the actual developmental level as determined by independent problem solving and the level of potential development as determined through problem solving under adult guidance or in collaboration with more capable peers."[17] In a sense, Vygotsky saw the teacher's role as speeding up the movement from one of Piaget's developmental stages to the next. Like Piaget, Vygotsky believed that certain developments needed to happen in order and the most that could be done was to move a child more quickly to the next level. A child certainly could not skip one stage and move on to the next, Vygotsky believed, but a well-taught student could move more effectively and confidently than a poorly taught one.

Vygotsky's plea that educators should focus on this zone of development has two significant implications. The first relates to what American educators have come to call *scaffolding*. Scaffolding was developed by educators using Vygotsky's ideas with very young children. Parents and teachers know that young children will at first walk more confidently if someone holds their hand but later will walk with equal confidence without an adult hand in place. In the same way, children will learn when there are supports for learning. In time, those supports need to be removed for the child to truly "own" the learning. They will not learn if the supports are not removed eventually, but they will not learn with confidence if they are removed too quickly or without thought.

The idea of scaffolding has increasingly come to mean that more advanced students also need models and immediate feedback in the beginning, but in time that same modeling and feedback only gets in the way. In the beginning, as a student moves gingerly into the next zone of development, the support is essential. In time it is not. Scaffolding also means that little is learned the first time something is taught. It is by revisiting a subject, while also fostering greater and greater degrees of independent thinking about the subject, that a student comes to understands it. Perhaps an obvious example of scaffolding is represented by this chapter and, indeed by this book, which introduces a number of key topics to the aspiring teacher but does so under the assumption that the important discussions of how students learn and how teachers teach will be revisited multiple times in future courses.

Vygotsky's approach to children's learning has a second, perhaps even more essential, element: For Vygotsky, learning takes place in social interactions. The focus of teaching and learning is not the individual child's development but rather the constant give and take of children with each other and with more knowledgeable adults who can prod and support a child in moving to the next zone and then support him or her once there. Thus, he placed a heavy emphasis on problem solving under adult guidance or in collaboration with more capable peers. According to Vygotsky, human learning is always attained in social contexts, never simply alone. These social contexts extend from generation to generation as people not only learn about but also change a given culture, even as they pass it on to the next generation. The child does not reinvent the whole of his or her culture but rather emerges into active participation in that culture one step at a time in collaboration with teachers. In this way, Vygotsky differed dramatically from Skinner. As Vygotsky saw it, children are not simply candidates for being shaped in certain ways by rewards and punishments, like pigeons. They are unique in their need for social interactions that will help them develop and in time will help them shape the development of others.

Jerome Bruner, 1915–

For decades, Jerome Bruner has been one of the most influential voices in educational psychology. Much more than Skinner, Bruner sees learning as an active process in which the learner has a key role, not merely responding to outside reinforcement but actively engaging in the process. Like Vygotsky, Bruner also sees learning as linking new information to what is previously known, not just previous information but also a previous "system of representation" that gives meaning and organization to ideas and information. Thus, according to Bruner, the interplay of the individual and the environment stimulates (or fails to simulate) learning. Learning is neither gradual nor inevitable, but as Bruner says, "appears to be much more like a staircase with rather sharp risers, more a matter of spurts and rests." These growth spurts seem to take place when certain new capacities begin to develop in a child, but it is not just a matter of individual development. Some things in the external environment can slow down the growth process, whereas others can speed it up dramatically. Given this tendency for learning and growth to take place in fits and starts, good teachers will structure their classrooms to create environments that will move learning along at a healthy pace.[18]

Given Bruner's view of how children and youth learn—and of the key roles of the larger culture, the development of language, and of motivation in encouraging the spurts in growth—he recommends making the student an active partner in the learning process and engaging him or her in problem solving that requires "the exploration of alternatives." Learning is not a lone enterprise, and "[man] is not a naked ape but a culture-clothed human being, hopelessly ineffective without the prosthesis provided by culture. The very nature of his characteristics as a species provides a guide to appropriate pedagogy." Thus, in Bruner's view, the effective teacher will design lessons that are taught and learned in the appropriate sequence. In these lessons, learning builds on prior knowledge and the social context in which it is happening. The context needs to include not just the school but also what society wants students to know. Teachers who understand this can provide optimal sequences of learning that will stimulate a series of intuitive leaps. This approach allows students to link new data with past experience and gives opportunities for confirmation checks before the new data are added to the learner's store of knowledge. According to Bruner, "[if] information is to be used effectively, it must be translated into the learner's way of attempting to solve a problem"; it is the teacher's role to help make that happen.[19]

Carol Gilligan 1936–

Carol Gilligan was an associate professor at the Graduate School of Education at Harvard in the 1970s, teaching and writing about young people's psychological and moral development, when she started to see a pattern that others had ignored: Looking at interviews she and her colleagues had conducted, she noticed that "the women's voices sounded distinct." Gilligan discovered that the recurrent problems in interpreting women's development were due to the repeated exclusion of women from the critical theory-building studies in psychological research. In her ground-breaking book, *In a Different Voice: Psychological Theory and Women's Development*, Gilligan noted that nearly all major psychologists up to her time, from Freud to Piaget, had studied White, middle-class men and boys and then generalized their findings into supposedly "universal" rules of child and adult human development.

For example, most psychologists, including Gilligan's mentor Lawrence Kohlberg, saw increasing individual separation from families and groups as an essential element in maturing. However, Gilligan found that for women, connections to family and community mattered much more, not because they were failing to mature but because maturity meant something different for them.

Following Gilligan's lead, more scholars began to ask similar questions about other groups of people who were excluded from the prime focus of most psychologists up to the 1980s, including poor people, African Americans, Latinos, and Asians and those who did not fit the scientific definition of "normal," which had too often meant European American middle-class males. At a moment in history when historians, sociologists, and educators were demanding a more multicultural approach to *what* was being taught in school—adding the voices and experiences of many different people to the school curriculum—Gilligan's research added the demand that educators pay much more careful attention to *who* was being taught. If different people learn and develop differently, at least in part because of their gender, race, ethnicity, and class backgrounds, then teachers have a responsibility to avoid seeking to fit all students into a single developmental mode. Rather, they need to respond to the needs of a very diverse group of learners who may gather in their classroom—a more difficult but ultimately a much more rewarding assignment.[20]

What Is the Link Between Brain Research and Day-to-Day Practice?

In 1996, the National Academies, including the National Academy of Sciences and the National Research Council (organizations traditionally known for leading the nation's research in physics, chemistry, biology, and engineering), called together scientists in the field of psychology to look at a new set of scientific questions. These national leaders in American science decided the time was right to focus on the schools and, specifically, to ask what the latest brain research tells us about how students learn. What began as a workshop on "The Science of Science Learning" quickly broadened to an effort to understand "the influence that cognitive science has on science and mathematics learning and teaching." The result was the publication of an influential book, *How People Learn: Brain, Mind, Experience, and School*, a selection from which provides a core **Reading** for this chapter.[21]

How People Learn and similar studies represent a substantial new development in the use of basic research in psychology and the activity of the human brain to understand how human beings, especially young humans in school, go about the process of learning.

Philosophers and psychologists, including those described earlier in this chapter, have been studying and speculating about these issues for a long time. Although much can be learned from their theories, current science gives teachers a significantly more rigorous look at the learning process. The reports of that research in publications like *How People Learn* enable us to reconsider effective teaching in new and exceedingly interesting ways. We are still very early in the process of learning all that scientific research can tell us about the human brain and the learning process. Yet, significant results of studies like those reported in *How People Learn* shed new light on the age-old question facing teachers regarding how children learn what they learn. We now know much more about how the brain works. As the authors of *How People Learn* say, research tells us that "both the developing and mature brain are structurally altered during learning. . . . Learning specific tasks appears to alter the specific regions of the brain appropriate to the task." Although teachers cannot observe the physical alterations in their students' brains that may take place while they are learning, they can see the results, especially if they know where to look.

Among the many conclusions of the many new studies in brain research are the following relevant findings about how early **cognitive abilities** relate to learning:

- Young children actively engage in making sense of their worlds. Research seems to say that Piaget was right about this. (Recall Piaget's game of marbles: At different stages, the children wanted to learn different aspects of the game as part of the process of making sense of their world.)

> **cognitive abilities**
> An individual's ability to process, comprehend, store, and analyze information.

- Young children may lack a lot of knowledge, but they do have abilities to reason with the knowledge they do have (if it makes sense to them).
- Children require assistance for learning. Adults play a critical role in promoting children's curiosity and persistence by directing children's attention, structuring their experience, supporting their learning attempts, and regulating the complexity and difficulty of levels of information for them. (Recall Vygotsky's zones of proximal development.)

At the same time, the current brain research also points to other significant conclusions about learning and about teaching, including the following:

- People must achieve a threshold of initial learning and then build on that. It takes time to learn complex subject matter, and students need that time before they can be expected to demonstrate their understanding.
- Students develop a flexible understanding of when, where, why, and how to use their knowledge to solve new problems, if they first learn how to extract underlying themes and principles from their learning. Understanding how and when to put knowledge to use in different contexts is an important characteristic of expertise that takes time to develop.

Brain research can (and will) tell us much more, but the findings described here provide an important window into what the latest scientific studies of learning tell us, as teachers, about the most effective ways of teaching.

DID YOU KNOW?

Human brains are as unique as faces. The basic structure is the same, although no two are identical. Babies are born with 100 billion brain cells; however, only a relatively small number of neurons are connected. By about age 10, a child's brain has formed trillions of connections. According to researchers, brain activity in this first decade of life is more than twice that of adults. Although new synapses continue to be formed throughout life, the brain is not able to master new skills as readily or to rebound from setbacks as easily as in those first crucial 10 years.

The results of the latest brain research tend to confirm the ideas of some earlier philosophers and contradict the ideas of others. As the authors of *How People Learn* conclude, "Traditional education has tended to emphasize memorization and mastery of text." But the latest research tells us that this approach does not work well for most students. When students begin to construct their own understanding of a topic—rather than memorizing someone else's views—and when students begin to be independent problem solvers, they learn not only the skills of problem solving but also the content of the ideas. For the first time, perhaps, the material seems relevant to the student and worth knowing—not because knowing the material will earn the student a good grade but because the information will help the student solve a problem he or she wants to solve.

How Can Teachers and Schools Serve a Range of Learning Styles?

Even in the seemingly most homogeneous classroom, many different learning styles will be represented. Too often, though, schools have been organized as if there was one right way to learn and those who did not learn in that way were somehow deficient. Today, many educators are acknowledging that people of different backgrounds—and different cultures, and genders—may learn differently and, according to researchers like Howard Gardner, that there is no one kind of intelligence—no overall measure by which people may be smarter or less smart—but rather multiple modes of intelligence. We need to explore these issues as we consider how we can adjust schools and teaching to serve a range of learning styles.

Race, Ethnicity, Class, Culture, Gender, and Learning

Looking carefully at issues faced by Hispanic students in schools in the United States, Eugene E. Garcia, the author of *Hispanic Education in the United States*, notes the challenge that some students face, given the cultural differences between their schools and their own communities:

> Schools attempt to assimilate minority students to mainstream values without considering the potential ramifications of doing so. When the values of the home and community are incongruent with the values of the school, minority children may experience confusion, stress, and adjustment problems that ultimately result in low self-esteem and poor academic performance. Hispanic students who do achieve may be viewed as assimilating and run the risk of being accused of "selling out" or "becoming a coconut" by their Hispanic peers. Peer rejection can be very damaging for racial and ethnic minority youth for whom the need for peer affiliation is very strong.[22]

Many other scholars have come to similar conclusions. Yet far too often schools are conducted as if such issues—confusion, stress, adjustment problems, and fear of success—were all individual problems to be addressed in counseling or through better motivation rather than being structural problems embedded in the very fabric of institutional education in the United States.

Victoria Purcell-Gates, a professor of literacy at Michigan State University, tells of a disturbing experience she had while visiting an elementary school in a midwestern city:

> A fourth-grade teacher grinned up at me knowingly as she condemned a young mother: "I knew she was ignorant just as soon as she opened her mouth!" This teacher was referring to the fact that Jenny, the mother of Donny, one of

her students, spoke in a southern mountain dialect, a dialect that is often used to characterize poor whites known variously as "hillbillies," "hicks," or "ridgerunners."

Purcell-Gates concludes that unless the school directly engages with Donny and his mother and the many students like him, school will not do anything to cross "the cavernous and uncrossable ravine that seems to lie between children of poverty . . . and their full potentials as literate beings." Engaging with Donny does not mean treating him just like every other fourth grader in the school; Donny may need some support that other students do not need. It also does not mean placing the blame on him or his mother or making the kind of snap judgments his teacher made. It does mean understanding that Donny needs very explicit instruction so that he will come to understand that he needs, in his own way, to be bilingual (even if in his case he needs to be bilingual between two different forms of English)—to honor and appreciate his home language and to have the skill to "code switch" and speak another language in school and larger public arenas including the world of work. To fail to give the Donnys of this world the clear explanations that they need, to pretend to treat them like every other student, is to fail to be their teacher.[23]

A generation of feminist scholars, of whom Carol Gilligan is the best known, also has found that traditional classrooms can be very unwelcoming places for girls and young women. Looking specifically at the study of mathematics, researcher Diana B. Erchick notes that, in math classes, women often find that they "fit the model of the silent learner who believes that authorities rarely tell you why something is as it is." Silencing students who not only need more explanation of why things are as they are, but who also desire to link their thoughts and feelings, is a recipe for failure. The research also shows that a mathematics program that is taught in a more student-centered way and in which the work is clearly connected to larger issues can be much more effective for women students.[24]

In all these cases—the Latino students and other students of color of both genders, poor and easily marginalized White students, and women of all races and ethnicities—the challenge to learning is cultural, not biological. Yet, in ignoring these powerful, socially constructed realities that have a dramatic impact on how different people learn and comprehend, schools do a substantial disservice to the majority of their students.

> **CONNECTIONS →←**
> Recall Lisa Delpit's discussion of the ways schools can fail "other people's children," in Chapter 3.

"Normal" Learning

Although it is essential to consider the impact of culture, gender, and other such variables on the ways students learn, such appreciation for social differences is only the beginning of our understanding of the wonderful diversity of learning styles represented in every classroom. In his insightful book *Schools That Learn*, Peter Senge reports:

Recently, a teacher commented to me that she had eighteen kids in her class and fifteen had different sorts of "learning problems." What is the real meaning of this comment? For the teacher, I believe it was an expression of frustration, a plaintive acknowledgment that she could not provide all that her kids required. But what does it mean when three-quarters of the kids in a class are "abnormal"? Does it not say something about how normal is defined?

Until we develop much more elastic and engaging understandings of the meaning of "normal," we are doomed to a cycle of failure, for ourselves and for our students. We will forever be plagued with the frustrations of the teacher who reported her problems to Senge. Although Senge has an appreciation for the ways a diversity of students can overwhelm a teacher, he also makes an important point: Something is profoundly wrong with the definition of what constitutes a "normal student" or normal success in today's schools.

In fact, Senge believes that one of the major reasons we are not able to think more creatively about how students learn, and how best to construct schools that will encourage learning, is that we are stuck in an industrial model of education in which the school is seen as a factory designed to

> **Notes from the Field**
>
> **What is a major challenge in teaching today?**
>
> "Number one is meeting the needs of all the different learners in the classroom and being able to differentiate instruction to help each child reach his or her individual benchmarks."
>
> —*Lori Talish, first-grade teacher*

turn out uniform parts. According to Senge, these industrial-age or factory-model assumptions about learning include the following:

1. Children are deficient and schools fix them.
2. Learning takes place in the head, not in the body as a whole.
3. Everyone learns—or should learn—in the same way.
4. Learning takes place in the classroom, not in the world.
5. There are smart kids and dumb kids.

Senge notes that these five assumptions are in some sense stereotypical and that most educators would disagree with them in principle. Nevertheless, he notes, "the system seems to embody these assumptions, and everyone acts as if they were correct—even if they would prefer to act differently."[25]

The challenge for a teacher is to create, as much as possible in the context of a system that is often beyond one's control, a very different kind of learning experience for the students in the classroom. Such efforts will never be perfect. However, partial success is far better, for the teacher and for her or his students, than accommodating a structure that is educationally wrong. Even worse is an approach to education that allows one's work to be shaped by unexamined assumptions that may be operating in a particular school but that are completely at odds with one's own beliefs and values.

Gardner's Multiple Intelligences

In Senge's discussion of these misleading industrial-age approaches to education, he also notes that substantial ground-breaking research undercuts these all-too-easy assumptions and, in fact, points to the reality that many different young people, and adults, have many different learning styles, different ways of knowing things, and different modes of intelligence and expertise. Indeed, the world would be a sad place if there was not this diversity of ways of knowing and looking at things. No one has explored the different forms of human intelligence and expertise more deeply than Harvard professor Howard Gardner.

Becoming disenchanted with what had been, at least for most of the 20th century, a general understanding of intelligence as a single, even measurable, amount, Gardner wrote: "Dating back a century to the time of the French psychologist Alfred Binet (1857–1911), psychologists believe that there is a single intelligence, often called 'g' for general intelligence; we are born with that intelligence; our intelligence comes from our biological parents and, as a result, intelligence is not significantly alterable; we psychologists can tell you how smart you are." But such a view, however widespread among psychologists in the scientific community, did not work when Gardner looked around at the world of real, live human beings. According to Gardner, individuals have different human faculties, and their strength (or weakness) in one intellectual area simply does not predict whether they will be strong or weak in some other area.

As described in the **Reading** in this chapter, Gardner's "multiple lenses on the mind" consists of eight forms of intelligence (now sometimes expanded to nine). All humans, Gardner says, have these eight or nine intelligences, and no two of us have them in exactly the same mix. That is what makes us both human and interesting. However, this newer, more complex understanding of intelligence has made intelligence much more difficult to measure. No longer could a single test or a single number (an intelligence quotient, or IQ) define a human as smart or not so smart. No one paper-and-pencil test could provide for the now much more complex analysis of intelligence needed to understand each human being. Instead, Gardner looked to other measures, including brain research (which shows us where in the brain different sorts of mental activity happen) and anthropology (which tells us what different societies have valued at different times in history).[26]

Gardner's multiple intelligences include:

1. linguistic intelligence
2. logical mathematical intelligence
3. musical intelligence

4.   spatial intelligence
5.   bodily-kinesthetic intelligence
6.   interpersonal intelligence (understanding of other persons)
7.   intrapersonal intelligence (understanding oneself)
8.   naturalist intelligence (the capacity to make distinctions in nature—"between one plant and another, among animals, clouds, mountains, and the like")

Gardner also describes what "may be a ninth or existential intelligence." According to Gardner, this is the "'intelligence of big questions.' When children ask about the size of the universe, when adults ponder death, love, conflict, the future of the planet, they are engaging in existential issues."

See, Listen, Move

As you think about the material in this chapter, you must be thinking about yourself as well as your future students. Are you a reader, a listener, or a doer? Everyone has his or her own preferred learning style, which may (or may not) correlate with different types of intelligence. Academic success comes with knowing not only your preference but also how to incorporate other styles to enhance learning (that is, how to think outside the box—or at least outside your comfort zone). The three primary learning styles are as follows:

- Visual learners: people who remember what they see better than they remember what they hear; who learn from charts and pictures; and who find reading very informative, often more so than listening to a lecture
- Auditory learners: people who remember what they hear better than what they see and who listen well to lectures and instructions, as well as to music and telephone conversations
- Kinesthetic learners: people who learn best from hands-on activities; who need to touch, build, and develop models in order to learn something; and for whom the physical act of writing something down or making a model or a collection is the best form of learning

---

Traditional schooling—in which teachers talk and students listen—has favored auditory learners over either visual or kinesthetic learners. Although schools are changing and finding better ways to include all learners, they are still essentially auditory places. Some have done well adding opportunities for those who learn best in visual forms but most have a long way to go to serve kinesthetic learners as well as they might. In much the same way that schools have favored linguistic and logical mathematical intelligence over other forms of intelligence, they have too often favored one learning style over others. But knowing more about multiple forms of intelligence and multiple learning styles can help make a teacher *much* more effective. Rather than labeling a student whose strength is in linguistic areas as smarter than a student whose strength may be in musical or interpersonal areas, and rather than labeling a student whose learning style is auditory as a better student than one who learns best kinesthetically, today's teachers have the challenge of learning more about their students and then tailoring their teaching to reach students with many different forms of intelligence and many different learning styles. It is no easy task, but it will dramatically improve the success and happiness of all students.

✔ CHAPTER REVIEW

- What have philosophers said about human learning?

  For hundreds of years, philosophers have debated how people learn as well as the best methods for facilitating the learning process. Rarely have philosophers agreed completely, although their approaches often have similar points or build upon each others' foundations, such as the early philosophers Socrates, Plato, and Aristotle, whose teacher-to-student-becomes-teacher relationships built on each predecessor's philosophy. "Modern" philosophers, such as Rousseau, Dewey, Adler, Greene, Martin, hooks, and Appiah, have each in his or her own way developed and influenced current thinking on teacher-student interactions that create optimal learning for all students.

- How have modern psychologists changed our way of thinking about learning?

  As with the philosophers, psychologists over the past 100 years have researched human learning and teaching with varying results. Piaget proposed the four levels of development through which a student must systematically progress before attempting subsequent learning. Skinner looked beyond the learning process itself at how to shape the process into desired results. According to Skinner's operant conditioning approach, immediate feedback and positive reinforcement produce the end results the teacher desires. A more student-driven approach, Vygotsky's "zone of proximal development," describes the stage just beyond the child's current one that the child can be expected to reach with proper input and support. Like Vygotsky, Bruner also sees learning as linking new information to what is previously known. Carol Gilligan reminds us that gender and other diversities will also impact the way people learn. The student must be an active partner in the learning process, engaging in problem solving and the exploration of alternatives.

- What is the link between brain research and day-to-day practice in schools?

  Although research on the brain and the learning process is still relatively new, reports such as *How People Learn* have provided significant information on how children learn and the ramifications of this information for teachers.

- How can teachers and schools serve a range of learning styles?

  Students learn in many different ways. Effective learning occurs when we look at how individuals learn best rather than when we follow a traditional, industrial model of education, in which teachers are dictators of information and students are receptacles for that information. Issues such as ethnicity and gender can play a role, as well as learning preferences for receiving and associating information. Howard Gardner's work supports the belief that we all possess a variety of intelligences, reflecting our strengths as individuals, which should be embraced in the learning process.

Readings

What Have Philosophers Said About Human Learning?

From *TEACHING TO TRANSGRESS : EDUCATION AS THE PRACTICE OF FREEDOM*

AUTHOR: BELL HOOKS

bell hooks has become a well-known philosopher of education because of her embrace of teaching as a moral responsibility—a responsibility to be open and honest with one's students while also encouraging them to be more open and honest with each other and with the teacher. In the process she encourages students and teachers to develop a critique of all of the hidden injustices in the larger society, including in the education process—to "transgress" and to practice a new-found personal and political freedom.

To educate as the practice of freedom is a way of teaching that anyone can learn. That learning process comes easiest to those of us who teach who also believe that there is an aspect of our vocation that is sacred; who believe that our work is not merely to share information but to share in the intellectual and spiritual growth of our students. To teach in a manner that respects and cares for the souls of our students is essential if we are to provide the necessary conditions where learning can most deeply and intimately begin.

Throughout my years as a student and professor, I have been most inspired by those teachers who have had the courage to transgress those boundaries that would confine each pupil to a rote, assembly-line approach to learning. Such teachers approach students with a will and desire to respond to our unique beings, even if the situation does not allow the full emergence of a relationship based on mutual recognition. Yet the possibility of such recognition is always present.

Paulo Freire and the Vietnamese Buddhist monk Thich Nhat Hanh are two of the "teachers" who have touched me deeply with their work. When I first began college, Freire's thought gave me the support I needed to challenge the "banking system" of education, that approach to learning that is rooted in the notion that all students need to do is consume information fed to them by a professor and be able to memorize and store it. Early on, it was Freire's insistence that education could be the practice of freedom that encouraged me to create strategies for what he called "conscientization" in the classroom. Translating that term to critical awareness and engagement, I entered the classroom with the conviction that it was crucial for me and every other student to be an active participant, not a passive consumer. Education as the practice of freedom was continually undermined by professors who were actively hostile to the notion of student participation. Freire's work affirmed that education can only be liberatory when everyone claims knowledge as a field in which we all labor. That notion of mutual labor was affirmed by Thich Nhat Hanh's philosophy of engaged Buddhism, the focus on practice in conjunction with contemplation. His philosophy was similar to Freire's emphasis on "praxis"—action and reflection upon the world in order to change it.

In his work, Thich Nhat Hanh always speaks of the teacher as a healer. Like Freire, his approach to knowledge calls on students to be active participants, to link awareness with practice. Whereas Freire was primarily concerned with the mind, Thich Nhat Hanh offered a way of thinking about pedagogy which emphasized wholeness, a union of mind, body, and spirit. His focus on a holistic approach to learning and spiritual practice enabled me to overcome years of socialization that had taught me to believe a classroom was diminished if students and professors regarded one another as "whole" human beings, striving not just for knowledge in books, but knowledge about how to live in the world. . . .

Progressive, holistic education, "engaged pedagogy" is more demanding than conventional critical or feminist pedagogy. For, unlike these two teaching practices, it emphasizes well-being. That means that teachers must be actively committed to a process of self-actualization that promotes their own well-being if they are to teach in a manner that empowers students. Thich Nhat Hanh emphasized that "the practice of a healer, therapist, teacher or any helping professional should be directed toward his or herself first, because if the helper is unhappy, he or she cannot help many people." In the United States it is rare that anyone talks about teachers in university settings as healers. And it is even more rare to hear anyone suggest that teachers have any responsibility to be self-actualized individuals. . . .

When education is the practice of freedom, students are not the only ones who are asked to share, to confess. Engaged pedagogy does not seek simply to empower students. Any classroom that employs a holistic model of learning will also be a place where teachers grow, and are empowered by the process. That empowerment cannot happen if we refuse to be vulnerable while encouraging students to take risks. Professors who expect students to share confessional narratives but who are themselves unwilling to share are exercising power in a manner that could be coercive. In my classrooms, I do not expect students to take any risks that I would not take, to share in any way that I would not share. When professors bring narratives of their experiences into classroom discussions it eliminates the possibility that we can function as all-knowing, silent interrogator. It is often productive if professors take the first risk, linking confessional narratives to academic discussions so as to show how experience can illuminate and enhance our understanding of academic material. But most professors must practice being vulnerable in the classroom, being wholly present in mind, body, and spirit.

Progressive professors working to transform the curriculum so that it does not reflect biases or reinforce systems of domination are most often the individuals willing to take the risks that engaged pedagogy requires and to make their teaching practices a site of resistance. . . . Professors who embrace the challenge of self-actualization will be better able to create pedagogical practices that engage students, providing them with ways of knowing that enhance their capacity to live fully and deeply.

Questions

1. hooks writes that, "it is rare that anyone talks about teachers in university settings as healers." Is it any more common to hear anyone talk of elementary or secondary teachers in this way?
2. What would it mean for a K-12 teacher to be vulnerable and take risks while encouraging students to do the same? How might that change a K-12 classroom?

Source: bell hooks. *Teaching to Transgress: Education as the Practice of Freedom*. New York: Routledge, 1994, 13–15, 21–22.

What Is the Link Between Brain Research and Day-to-Day Practice in Schools?

From *HOW PEOPLE LEARN : BRAIN, MIND, EXPERIENCE, AND SCHOOL*

AUTHORS: JOHN D. BRANSFORD, ANN L. BROWN, AND RODNEY R. COCKING

For as long as humans have tried to teach things to each other, from the most basic survival lessons to the most complex theories about how the universe works, people have speculated about how they themselves and other people learn. Only recently have scientists in psychology and related fields been able to do the kind of basic research that offers a new scientific understanding about how human beings actually do learn, and therefore about the most effective ways for other human beings—called teachers—to teach. In the past decade, the National Academy of Sciences, the nation's most prestigious organization of scholars, has commissioned important studies on the way the brain works and the ways people learn. The material presented here is an excerpt from the introduction to one of these studies. Anyone aspiring to be a teacher will gain a great deal by reading the entire How People Learn *text and other studies that are sure to follow. This research is still in its infancy, and corrections and new conclusions are bound to come out in the years ahead. Nevertheless, this reading gives an overview of the current state of our knowledge about the human brain and human learning.*

The essence of matter, the origins of the universe, the nature of the human mind—these are the profound questions that have engaged thinkers through the centuries. Until quite recently, understanding the mind—and the thinking and learning that the mind makes possible—has remained an elusive quest, in part because of a lack of powerful research tools. Today, the world is in the midst of an extraordinary outpouring of scientific work on the mind and brain, on the processes of thinking and learning, on the neural processes that occur during thought and learning, and on the development of competence.

The revolution in the study of the mind that has occurred in the last three or four decades has important implications for education. As we illustrate, a new theory of learning is coming into focus that leads to very different approaches to the design of curriculum, teaching, and assessment than those often found in schools today. Equally important, the growth of inter-disciplinary inquiries and new kinds of scientific collaborations have begun to make the path from basic research to educational practice somewhat more visible, if not yet easy to travel. Thirty years ago, educators paid little attention to the work of cognitive scientists, and researchers in the nascent field of cognitive science worked far removed from classrooms. Today, cognitive researchers are spending more time working with teachers, testing and refining their theories in real classrooms where they can see how different settings and classroom interactions influence applications of their theories.

What is perhaps currently most striking is the variety of research approaches and techniques that have been developed and ways in which evidence from many different branches of science are beginning to converge. The story we can now tell about learning is far richer than ever before, and it promises to evolve dramatically in the next generation. For example:

- Research from cognitive psychology has increased understanding of the nature of competent performance and the principles of knowledge organization that underlie people's abilities to solve problems in a wide variety of areas, including mathematics, science, literature, social studies, and history.
- Developmental researchers have shown that young children understand a great deal about basic principles of biology and physical causality, about number, narrative, and personal intent, and that these capabilities make it possible to create innovative curricula that introduce important concepts for advanced reasoning at early ages.
- Research on learning and transfer has uncovered important principles for structuring learning experiences that enable people to use what they have learned in new settings.
- Work in social psychology, cognitive psychology, and anthropology is making clear that all learning takes place in settings that have particular sets of cultural and social norms and expectations and that these settings influence learning and transfer in powerful ways.
- Neuroscience is beginning to provide evidence for many principles of learning that have emerged from laboratory research, and it is showing how learning changes the physical structure of the brain and, with it, the functional organization of the brain.
- Collaborative studies of the design and evaluation of learning environments, among cognitive and developmental psychologists and educators, are yielding new knowledge about the nature of learning and teaching as it takes place in a variety of settings. In addition, researchers are discovering ways to learn from the "wisdom of practice" that comes from successful teachers who can share their expertise.
- Emerging technologies are leading to the development of many new opportunities to guide and enhance learning that were unimagined even a few years ago.

All of these developments in the study of learning have led to an era of new relevance of science to practice. In short, investment in basic research is paying off in practical applications. These developments in understanding of how humans learn have particular significance in light of changes in what is expected of the nation's educational systems.

In the early part of the twentieth century, education focused on the acquisition of literacy skills: simple reading, writing, and calculating. It was not the general rule for educational systems to train people to think and read critically, to express themselves clearly and persuasively, to solve complex problems in science and mathematics. Now, at the end of the century, these aspects of high literacy are required of almost everyone in order to successfully negotiate the complexities of contemporary life. The skill demands for work have increased dramatically, as has the need for organizations and workers to change in response to competitive workplace pressures. Thoughtful participation in the democratic process has also become increasingly complicated as the locus of attention has shifted from local to national and global concerns.

Above all, information and knowledge are growing at a far more rapid rate than ever before in the history of humankind. As Nobel laureate Herbert Simon wisely stated, the meaning of "knowing" has shifted from being able to remember and repeat information to being able to find and use it (Simon, 1996). More than ever, the sheer magnitude of human knowledge renders its coverage by education an impossibility; rather, the goal of education is better conceived as helping students develop the intellectual tools and learning strategies needed to acquire the knowledge that allows people to think productively about history, science and technology, social phenomena, mathematics, and the arts. Fundamental understanding about subjects, including how to frame and ask meaningful questions about various subject areas, contributes to individuals' more basic understanding of principles of learning that can assist them in becoming self-sustaining, lifelong learners.

Learning With Understanding

One of the hallmarks of the new science of learning is its emphasis on learning with understanding. Intuitively, understanding is good, but it has been difficult to study from a scientific perspective. At the same time, students often have limited opportunities to understand or make sense of topics because many curricula have emphasized memory rather than understanding. Textbooks are filled with facts that students are expected to memorize, and most tests assess students' abilities to remember the facts. When studying about veins and arteries, for example, students may be expected to remember that arteries are thicker than veins, more elastic, and carry blood from the heart; veins carry blood back to the heart. A test item for this information may look like the following:

1. Arteries

   a. Are more elastic than veins
   b. Carry blood that is pumped from the heart
   c. Are less elastic than veins
   d. Both a and b
   e. Both b and c

The new science of learning does not deny that facts are important for thinking and problem solving. Research on expertise in areas such as chess, history, science, and mathematics demonstrate that experts' abilities to think and solve problems depend strongly on a rich body of knowledge about subject matter (e.g., Chase and Simon, 1973; Chi et al., 1981; deGroot, 1965). However, the research also shows clearly that "usable knowledge" is not the same as a mere list of disconnected facts. Experts' knowledge is connected and organized around important concepts (e.g., Newton's second law of motion); it is "conditionalized" to specify the contexts in which it is applicable; it supports understanding and transfer (to other contexts) rather than only the ability to remember.

For example, people who are knowledgeable about veins and arteries know more than the facts noted above: they also understand why veins and arteries have particular properties. They know that blood pumped from the heart exits in spurts and that the elasticity of the arteries helps accommodate pressure changes. They know that blood from the heart needs to move upward (to the brain) as well as downward and that the elasticity of an artery permits it to function as a one-way valve that closes at the end of each spurt and prevents the blood from flowing backward. Because they understand relationships between the structure and function of veins and arteries, knowledgeable individuals are more likely to be able to use what they have learned to solve novel problems—to show evidence of transfer. For example, imagine being asked to design an artificial artery—would it have to be elastic? Why or why not? An understanding of reasons for the properties of arteries suggests that elasticity may not be necessary—perhaps the problem can be solved by creating a conduit that is strong enough to handle the pressure of spurts from the heart and also function as a one-way valve. An understanding of veins and arteries does not guarantee an answer to this design question, but it does support thinking about alternatives that are not readily available if one only memorizes facts (Bransford and Stein, 1993).

Preexisting Knowledge

An emphasis on understanding leads to one of the primary characteristics of the new science of learning: its focus on the processes of knowing (e.g., Piaget, 1978; Vygotsky, 1978). Humans are viewed as goal-directed agents who actively seek information. They come to formal education with a range of prior knowledge, skills, beliefs, and concepts that significantly influence what they notice about the environment and how they organize and interpret it. This, in turn, affects their abilities to remember, reason, solve problems, and acquire new knowledge.

Even young infants are active learners who bring a point of view to the learning setting. The world they enter is not a "booming, buzzing confusion" (James, 1890), where every stimulus is equally salient. Instead, an infant's brain gives precedence to certain kinds of information: language, basic concepts of number, physical properties, and the movement of animate and inanimate objects. In the most general sense, the contemporary view of learning is that people construct new knowledge and understandings based on what they already know and believe (e.g., Cobb, 1994; Piaget,1952, 1973a, b, 1977, 1978; Vygotsky, 1962, 1978). A classic children's book illustrates this point.

Fish Is Fish

Fish Is Fish (Lionni, 1970) describes a fish who is keenly interested in learning about what happens on land, but the fish cannot explore land because it can only breathe in water. It befriends a tadpole who grows into a frog and eventually goes out onto the land. The frog returns to the pond a few weeks later and reports on what he has seen. The frog describes all kinds of things like birds, cows, and people. The book shows pictures of the fish's representations of each of these descriptions: each is a fish-like form that is slightly adapted to accommodate the frog's descriptions—people are imagined to be fish who walk on their tailfins, birds are fish with wings, cows are fish with udders. This tale illustrates both the creative opportunities and dangers inherent in the fact that people construct new knowledge based on their current knowledge.

A logical extension of the view that new knowledge must be constructed from existing knowledge is that teachers need to pay attention to the incomplete understandings, the false beliefs, and the naive renditions of concepts that learners bring with them to a given subject. Teachers then need to build on these ideas in ways that help each student achieve a more mature understanding. If students' initial ideas and beliefs are ignored, the understandings that they develop can be very different from what the teacher intends.

Consider the challenge of working with children who believe that the earth is flat and attempting to help them understand that it is spherical. When told it is round, children picture the earth as a pancake rather than as a sphere (Vosniadou and Brewer, 1989). If they are then told that it is round like a sphere, they interpret the new information about a spherical earth within their flat-earth view by picturing a pancake-like flat surface inside or on top of a sphere, with humans standing on top of the pancake.

The children's construction of their new understandings has been guided by a model of the earth that helped them explain how they could stand or walk upon its surface, and a spherical earth did not fit their mental model. Like *Fish Is Fish*, everything the children heard was incorporated into that preexisting view.

Fish Is Fish is relevant not only for young children, but for learners of all ages. For example, college students often have developed beliefs about physical and biological phenomena that fit their experiences but do not fit scientific accounts of these phenomena. These preconceptions must be addressed in order for them to change their beliefs (e.g., Confrey, 1990; Mestre, 1994; Minstrell, 1989; Redish, 1996).

A common misconception regarding "constructivist" theories of knowing (that existing knowledge is used to build new knowledge) is that teachers should never tell students anything directly but, instead, should always allow them to construct knowledge for themselves. This perspective confuses a theory of pedagogy (teaching) with a theory of knowing. Constructivists assume that all knowledge is constructed from previous knowledge, irrespective of how one is taught (e.g., Cobb, 1994)—even listening to a lecture involves active attempts to construct new knowledge. *Fish Is Fish* (Lionni, 1970) and attempts to teach children that the earth is round (Vosniadou and Brewer, 1989) show why simply providing lectures frequently does not work. Nevertheless, there are times, usually after people have first grappled with issues on their own, that "teaching by telling" can work extremely well (e.g., Schwartz and Bransford, 1998). However, teachers still need to pay attention to students' interpretations and provide guidance when necessary.

There is a good deal of evidence that learning is enhanced when teachers pay attention to the knowledge and beliefs that learners bring to a learning task, use this knowledge as a starting point for new instruction, and monitor students' changing conceptions as instruction proceeds. For example, sixth graders in a suburban school who were given inquiry-based physics instruction were shown to do better on conceptual physics problems than eleventh and twelfth grade physics students taught by conventional methods in the same school system. A second study comparing seventh–ninth grade urban students with the eleventh and twelfth grade suburban physics students again showed that the younger students, taught by the inquiry-based approach, had a better grasp of the fundamental principles of physics (White and Frederickson, 1997, 1998). New curricula for young children have also demonstrated results that are extremely promising: for example, a new approach to teaching geometry helped second-grade children learn to represent and visualize three-dimensional forms in ways that exceeded the skills of a comparison group of undergraduate students at a leading university (Lehrer and Chazan, 1998). Similarly, young children have been taught to demonstrate powerful forms of early geometry generalizations (Lehrer and Chazan, 1998) and generalizations about science (Schauble et al., 1995; Warren and Rosebery, 1996).

Active Learning

New developments in the science of learning also emphasize the importance of helping people take control of their own learning. Since understanding is viewed as important, people must learn to recognize when they understand and when they need more information. What strategies might they use to assess whether they understand someone else's meaning? What kinds of evidence do they need in order to believe particular claims? How can they build their own theories of phenomena and test them effectively?

Many important activities that support active learning have been studied under the heading of "metacognition," a topic discussed in more detail in Chapters 2 and 3. Meta-cognition refers to people's abilities to predict their performances on various tasks (e.g., how well they will be able to remember various stimuli) and to monitor their current levels of mastery and understanding (e.g., Brown, 1975; Flavell, 1973). Teaching practices congruent with a metacognitive approach to learning include those that focus on sensemaking, self-assessment, and reflection on what worked and what needs improving. These practices have been shown to increase the degree to which students transfer their learning to new settings and events (e.g., Palincsar and Brown, 1984; Scardamalia et al., 1984; Schoenfeld, 1983, 1985, 1991).

Imagine three teachers whose practices affect whether students learn to take control of their own learning (Scardamalia and Bereiter, 1991). Teacher A's goal is to get the students to produce work; this is accomplished by supervising and overseeing the quantity and quality of the work done by the students. The focus is on activities, which could be anything from old-style workbook activities to the trendiest of space-age projects. Teacher B assumes responsibility for what the students are learning as they carry out their activities. Teacher C does this as well, but with the added objective of continually turning more of the learning process over to the students. Walking into a classroom, you cannot immediately tell these three kinds of teachers apart. One of the things you might see is the students working in groups to produce videos or multimedia presentations. The teacher is likely to be found going from group to group, checking how things are going and responding to requests. Over the course of a few days, however, differences between Teacher A and Teacher B would become evident. Teacher A's focus is entirely on the production process and its products—whether the students are engaged, whether everyone is getting fair treatment, and whether they are turning out good pieces of work. Teacher B attends to all of this as well, but Teacher B is also attending to what the students are learning from the experience and is taking steps to ensure that the students are processing content and not just dealing with show. To see a difference between Teachers B and C, however, you might need to go back into the history of the media production project. What brought it about in the first place? Was it conceived from the start as a learning activity, or did it emerge from the students' own knowledge building efforts? In one striking example of a Teacher C classroom, the students had been studying cockroaches and had learned so much from their reading and observation that they wanted to share it with the rest of the school; the production of a video came about to achieve that purpose (Lamon et al., 1997).

The differences in what might seem to be the same learning activity are thus quite profound. In Teacher A's classroom, the students are learning something of media production, but the media production may very well be getting in the way of learning anything else. In Teacher B's classroom, the teacher is working to ensure that the original educational purposes of the activity are met, that it does not deteriorate into a mere media production exercise. In Teacher C's classroom, the media production is continuous with and a direct outgrowth of the learning that is embodied in the media production. The greater part of Teacher C's work has been done before the idea of a media production even comes up, and it remains only to help the students keep sight of their purposes as they carry out the project.

These hypothetical teachers—A, B, and C—are abstract models that of course fit real teachers only partly, and more on some days than others. Nevertheless, they provide important glimpses of connections between goals for learning and teaching practices that can affect students' abilities to accomplish these goals.

Key Findings

1. Students come to the classroom with preconceptions about how the world works. If their initial understanding is not engaged, they may fail to grasp the new concepts and information that are taught, or they may learn them for purposes of a test but revert to their preconceptions outside the classroom.
2. To develop competence in an area of inquiry, students must: (a) have a deep foundation of factual knowledge, (b) understand facts and ideas in the context of a conceptual framework, and (c) organize knowledge in ways that facilitate retrieval and application.
3. A "metacognitive" approach to instruction can help students learn to take control of their own learning by defining learning goals and monitoring their progress in achieving them.

Implications for Teaching

The three core learning principles described above, simple though they seem, have profound implications for the enterprise of teaching and teacher preparation.

1. *Teachers must draw out and work with the preexisting understandings that their students bring with them.* This requires that:

   - The model of the child as an empty vessel to be filled with knowledge provided by the teacher must be replaced. Instead, the teacher must actively inquire into students' thinking, creating classroom tasks and conditions under which student thinking can be revealed. Students' initial conceptions then provide the foundation on which the more formal understanding of the subject matter is built.
   - The roles for assessment must be expanded beyond the traditional concept of testing. The use of frequent formative assessment helps make students' thinking visible to themselves, their peers, and their teacher. This provides feedback that can guide modification and refinement in thinking. Given the goal of learning with understanding, assessments must tap understanding rather than merely the ability to repeat facts or perform isolated skills.
   - Schools of education must provide beginning teachers with opportunities to learn: (a) to recognize predictable preconceptions of students that make the mastery of particular subject matter challenging, (b) to draw out preconceptions that are not predictable, and (c) to work with preconceptions so that children build on them, challenge them and, when appropriate, replace them.

2. *Teachers must teach some subject matter in depth, providing many examples in which the same concept is at work and providing a firm foundation of factual knowledge.* This requires that:

   - Superficial coverage of all topics in a subject area must be replaced with in-depth coverage of fewer topics that allows key concepts in that discipline to be understood. The goal of coverage need not be abandoned entirely, of course. But there must be a sufficient number of cases of in-depth study to allow students to grasp the defining concepts in specific domains within a discipline. Moreover, in-depth study in a domain often requires that ideas be carried beyond a single school year before students can make the transition from informal to formal ideas. This will require active coordination of the curriculum across school years.
   - Teachers must come to teaching with the experience of in-depth study of the subject area themselves. Before a teacher can develop powerful pedagogical tools, he or she must be familiar with the progress of inquiry and the terms of discourse in the discipline, as well as understand the relationship between information and the concepts that help organize that information in the discipline. But equally important, the teacher must have a grasp of the growth and development of students' thinking about these concepts. The latter will be essential to developing teaching expertise, but not expertise in the discipline. It may therefore require courses, or course supplements, that are designed specifically for teachers.
   - Assessment for purposes of accountability (e.g., statewide assessments) must test deep understanding rather than surface knowledge. Assessment tools are often the standard by which teachers are held accountable. A teacher is put in a bind if she or he is asked to teach for deep conceptual understanding, but in doing so produces students who perform more poorly on standardized tests.

- Unless new assessment tools are aligned with new approaches to teaching, the latter are unlikely to muster support among the schools and their constituent parents. This goal is as important as it is difficult to achieve. The format of standardized tests can encourage measurement of factual knowledge rather than conceptual understanding, but it also facilitates objective scoring. Measuring depth of understanding can pose challenges for objectivity. Much work needs to be done to minimize the trade-off between assessing depth and assessing objectively.

3. *The teaching of metacognitive skills should be integrated into the curriculum in a variety of subject areas.* Because metacognition often takes the form of an internal dialogue, many students may be unaware of its importance unless the processes are explicitly emphasized by teachers. An emphasis on metacognition needs to accompany instruction in each of the disciplines, because the type of monitoring required will vary. In history, for example, the student might be asking himself, "who wrote this document, and how does that affect the interpretation of events," whereas in physics the student might be monitoring her understanding of the underlying physical principle at work.

   - Integration of metacognitive instruction with discipline-based learning can enhance student achievement and develop in students the ability to learn independently. It should be consciously incorporated into curricula across disciplines and age levels.
   - Developing strong metacognitive strategies and learning to teach those strategies in a classroom environment should be standard features of the curriculum in schools of education.

Evidence from research indicates that when these three principles are incorporated into teaching, student achievement improves. For example, the Thinker Tools Curriculum for teaching physics in an interactive computer environment focuses on fundamental physical concepts and properties, allowing students to test their preconceptions in model building and experimentation activities. The program includes an "inquiry cycle" that helps students monitor where they are in the inquiry process. The program asks for students' reflective assessments and allows them to review the assessments of their fellow students. In one study, sixth graders in a suburban school who were taught physics using Thinker Tools performed better at solving conceptual physics problems than did eleventh and twelfth grade physics students in the same school system taught by conventional methods. A second study comparing urban students in grades 7 to 9 with suburban students in grades 11 and 12 again showed that the younger students taught by the inquiry-based approach had a superior grasp of the fundamental principles of physics (White and Frederickson, 1997, 1998).

Bringing Order to Chaos

A benefit of focusing on how people learn is that it helps bring order to a seeming cacophony of choices. Consider the many possible teaching strategies that are debated in education circles and the media: lecture-based teaching, text-based teaching, inquiry-based teaching, technology-enhanced teaching, teaching organized around individuals versus cooperative groups, and so forth. Are some of these teaching techniques better than others? Is lecturing a poor way to teach, as many seem to claim? Is cooperative learning effective? Do attempts to use computers (technology-enhanced teaching) help achievement or hurt it?

This volume suggests that these are the wrong questions. Asking which teaching technique is best is analogous to asking which tool is best—a hammer, a screwdriver, a knife, or pliers. In teaching as in carpentry, the selection of tools depends on the task at hand and the materials one is working with. Books and lectures *can* be wonderfully efficient modes of transmitting new information for learning, exciting the imagination, and honing students' critical faculties—but one would choose other kinds of activities to elicit from students their preconceptions and level of understanding, or to help them see the power of using meta-cognitive strategies to monitor their learning. Hands-on experiments *can* be a powerful way to ground emergent knowledge, but they do not alone evoke the underlying conceptual understandings that aid generalization. There is no universal best teaching practice.

If, instead, the point of departure is a core set of learning principles, then the selection of teaching strategies (mediated, of course, by subject matter, grade level, and desired outcome) can be purposeful. The many possibilities then become a rich set of opportunities from which a teacher constructs an instructional program rather than a chaos of competing alternatives.

Focusing on how people learn also will help teachers move beyond either-or dichotomies that have plagued the field of education. One such issue is whether schools should emphasize "the basics" or teach thinking and problem-solving skills. This volume shows that both are necessary. Students' abilities to acquire organized sets of facts and skills are actually enhanced when they are connected to meaningful problem-solving activities, and when students are helped to understand why, when, and how those facts and skills are relevant. And attempts to teach thinking skills without a strong base of factual knowledge do not promote problem-solving ability or support transfer to new situations.

Designing Classroom Environments

Chapter 6 of this volume proposes a framework to help guide the design and evaluation of environments that can optimize learning. Drawing heavily on the three principles discussed above, it posits four interrelated attributes of learning environments that need cultivation.

1. *Schools and classrooms must be learner centered.*

    Teachers must pay close attention to the knowledge, skills, and attitudes that learners bring into the classroom. This incorporates the preconceptions regarding subject matter already discussed, but it also includes a broader understanding of the learner. For example:

    - Cultural differences can affect students' comfort level in working collaboratively versus individually, and they are reflected in the background knowledge students bring to a new learning situation (Moll et al., 1993).
    - Students' theories of what it means to be intelligent can affect their performance. Research shows that students who think that intelligence is a fixed entity are more likely to be performance oriented than learning oriented—they want to look good rather than risk making mistakes while learning. These students are especially likely to bail out when tasks become difficult. In contrast, students who think that intelligence is malleable are more willing to struggle with challenging tasks; they are more comfortable with risk (Dweck, 1989; Dweck and Legget, 1988).

    Teachers in learner-centered classrooms also pay close attention to the individual progress of each student and devise tasks that are appropriate. Learner-centered teachers present students with "just manageable difficulties"—that is, challenging enough to maintain engagement, but not so difficult as to lead to discouragement. They must therefore have an understanding of their students' knowledge, skill levels, and interests (Duckworth, 1987).

2. *To provide a knowledge-centered classroom environment, attention must be given to what is taught (information, subject matter), why it is taught (understanding), and what competence or mastery looks like.* As mentioned above, research discussed in the following chapters shows clearly that expertise involves well-organized knowledge that supports understanding, and that learning with understanding is important for the development of expertise because it makes new learning easier (i.e., supports transfer).

    Learning with understanding is often harder to accomplish than simply memorizing, and it takes more time. Many curricula fail to support learning with understanding because they present too many disconnected facts in too short a time—the "mile wide, inch deep" problem. Tests often reinforce memorizing rather than understanding. The knowledge-centered environment provides the necessary depth of study, assessing student understanding rather than factual memory. It incorporates the teaching of metacognitive strategies that further facilitate future learning.

    Knowledge-centered environments also look beyond engagement as the primary index of successful teaching (Prawaf et al., 1992). Students' interest or engagement in a task is clearly important. Nevertheless, it does not guarantee that students will acquire the kinds of knowledge that will support new learning. There are important differences between tasks and projects that encourage hands-on doing and those that encourage doing with understanding; the knowledge-centered environment emphasizes the latter (Greeno, 1991).

3. *Formative assessments—ongoing assessments designed to make students' thinking visible to both teachers and students— are essential. They permit the teacher to grasp the students' preconceptions, understand where the students are in the "developmental corridor" from informal to formal thinking, and design instruction accordingly. In the assessment-centered classroom environment, formative assessments help both teachers and students monitor progress.*

    An important feature of assessments in these classrooms is that they be learner-friendly: they are not the Friday quiz for which information is memorized the night before, and for which the student is given a grade that ranks him or her with respect to classmates. Rather, these assessments should provide students with opportunities to revise and improve their thinking (Vye et al., 1998b), help students see their own progress over the course of weeks or months, and help teachers identify problems that need to be remedied (problems that may not be visible without the assessments). For example, a high school class studying the principles of democracy might be given a scenario in which a colony of people have just settled on the moon and must establish a government. Proposals from students of the defining features of such a government, as well as discussion of the problems they foresee in its establishment, can reveal to both teachers and students areas in which student thinking is more and less advanced. The exercise is less a test than an indicator of where inquiry and instruction should focus.

4. *Learning is influenced in fundamental ways by the context in which it takes place. A community-centered approach requires the development of norms for the classroom and school, as well as connections to the outside world, that support core learning values.*

The norms established in the classroom have strong effects on students' achievement. In some schools, the norms could be expressed as "don't get caught not knowing something." Others encourage academic risk-taking and opportunities to make mistakes, obtain feedback, and revise. Clearly, if students are to reveal their preconceptions about a subject matter, their questions, and their progress toward understanding, the norms of the school must support their doing so.

Teachers must attend to designing classroom activities and helping students organize their work in ways that promote the kind of intellectual camaraderie and the attitudes toward learning that build a sense of community. In such a community, students might help one another solve problems by building on each other's knowledge, asking questions to clarify explanations, and suggesting avenues that would move the group toward its goal (Brown and Campione, 1994). Both cooperation in problem solving (Evans, 1989; Newstead and Evans, 1995) and argumentation (Goldman, 1994; Habermas, 1990; Kuhn, 1991; Moshman, 1995a, 1995b; Salmon and Zeitz, 1995; Youniss and Damon, 1992) among students in such an intellectual community enhance cognitive development.

Teachers must be enabled and encouraged to establish a community of learners among themselves (Lave and Wegner, 1991). These communities can build a sense of comfort with questioning rather than knowing the answer and can develop a model of creating new ideas that build on the contributions of individual members. They can engender a sense of the excitement of learning that is then transferred to the classroom, conferring a sense of ownership of new ideas as they apply to theory and practice. Not least, schools need to develop ways to link classroom learning to other aspects of students' lives. Engendering parent support for the core learning principles and parent involvement in the learning process is of utmost importance (Moll, 1990; 1986a, 1986b). Figure 5.1 shows the percentage of time, during a calendar year, that students in a large school district spent in school. If one-third of their time outside school (not counting sleeping) is spent watching television, then students apparently spend more hours per year watching television than attending school. A focus only on the hours that students currently spend in school overlooks the many opportunities for guided learning in other settings.

Applying the Design Framework to Adult Learning

The design framework summarized above assumes that the learners are children, but the principles apply to adult learning as well. This point is particularly important because incorporating the principles in this volume into educational practice will require a good deal of adult learning. Many approaches to teaching adults consistently violate principles for optimizing learning. Professional development programs for teachers, for example, frequently:

- *Are not learner centered.* Rather than ask teachers where they need help, they are simply expected to attend prearranged workshops.
- *Are not knowledge centered.* Teachers may simply be introduced to a new technique (like cooperative learning) without being given the

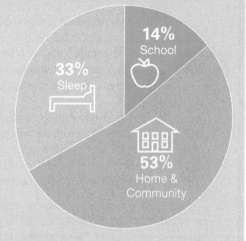

Figure 5.1

Students spend only 14 percent of their lives in school.

opportunity to understand why, when, where, and how it might be valuable to them. Especially important is the need to integrate the structure of activities with the content of the curriculum that is taught.

- *Are not assessment centered.* In order for teachers to change their practices, they need opportunities to try things out in their classrooms and then receive feedback. Most professional development opportunities do not provide such feedback. Moreover, they tend to focus on change in teaching practice as the goal, but they neglect to develop in teachers the capacity to judge successful transfer of the technique to the classroom or its effects on student achievement.
- *Are not community centered.* Many professional development opportunities are conducted in isolation. Opportunities for continued contact and support as teachers incorporate new ideas into their teaching are limited, yet the rapid spread of Internet access provides a ready means of maintaining such contact if appropriately designed tools and services are available. The principles of learning and their implications for designing learning environments apply equally to child and adult learning. They provide a lens through which current practice can be viewed with respect to K-12 teaching *and* with respect to preparation of teachers in the research and development agenda. The principles are relevant as well when we consider other groups, such as policy makers and the public, whose learning is also required for educational practice to change.

Questions

1. As you think about the schools you attended and those you have observed more recently, to what degree does the teaching reflect what these authors call the "latest scientific thinking" about how people learn? Did the teaching build on preexisting knowledge? Were the students encouraged to be active or passive learners?
2. As you read the *Fish Is a Fish* example, ask yourself if you have ever had an experience like the fish did, such as a time when you completely misunderstood something because you were hearing the story through an inappropriate filter? Try to think of specific examples.
3. Does this research mean a teacher should never give direct instruction to students? In light of the theories presented here, when might traditional "teaching by telling" be appropriate? When might it be inappropriate?
4. Late in the article, the authors say, "There is no universal best teaching practice." Why do you think they say that? Do you agree or disagree with their conclusion? Are there universally worst teaching practices?

Source: "Learning: From Speculation to Science," by John D. Bransford, Ann L. Brown, and Rodney R. Cocking, editors, 2000, *How People Learn: Brain, Mind, Experience, and School*, National Academies Press, pp. 3–27.

How Can Teachers and Schools Serve a Range of Learning Styles?

From "MULTIPLE LENSES ON THE MIND"

AUTHOR: HOWARD GARDNER

One of the nation's most respected educational psychologists, Howard Gardner is a professor at the Harvard Graduate School of Education. He has written dozens of books and articles, and his primary contribution to our thinking about education—the notion that there is not one but many forms of intelligence—has significant implications for every teacher. His work frees us from the traditional belief that some students are smarter than others on any single scale and calls on all teachers to cultivate the rich differences in learning styles and in basic intelligence that can be found in any classroom.

Let me provide a few contextual remarks. First of all, as a young person, the child of refugees from Nazi Germany, I had been a good student and a serious musician. When I began to study "real" psychology, I was intrigued by the fact that the arts were rarely mentioned in serious psychology circles. To have a mind was to be a scientist, or at least to think scientifically; many psychologists were ex-engineers or suffered from physics envy; the last thing that they wanted to do was to be seen as artistic "softies." Early on, I decided that I wanted to illuminate the nature of artistic thinking. Also, I was particularly interested in issues of creativity—how does a person conjure up something new, whether it is a sonnet, a symphony, a sketch, or a scientific theory?

My First Studies

For the first ten years of my professional career, I studied how the mind develops in children and how it breaks down under conditions of brain damage. As you may know, the single most important thing about a brain lesion is where the damage is. If one is right handed, and suffers injury in the middle areas of the left hemisphere, one is likely to become aphasic—to have a major disturbance of one's language facilities. But if you suffer injury to the right hemisphere, your language will be ostensibly fine, but, depending on the location and depth of the lesion, you are likely to be impaired in musical cognition, spatial cognition, and/or your understanding of other people.

With normal and gifted children and with brain damaged adults, I studied how human beings deal with various kinds of symbols. As I've already mentioned, I had a particular interest in the arts. And so I studied the development and breakdown of musical abilities, graphic abilities, metaphoric and narrative capacities, and other abilities crucial in the arts. Of course, when you look at these abilities, you necessarily encounter nonartistic capacities as well—mastery of ordinary language, calculation, understanding of other persons, and the like.

At the time that my studies began, I had been a convinced Piagetian—I believed that logical-mathematical thought was the center of all cognition. I believed that children passed through a series of qualitatively different stages, and that their mental world gets remade, whenever they enter the next stage. I believed that cognitive development is completed by the middle of adolescence, at the latest. And I never thought at all about intelligence tests.

I still think that Piaget is the greatest student of the development of the mind. Every student of cognitive development owes an incalculable debt to Piaget. And yet, with the benefit of hindsight, I can see that during that decade, I gradually lost my Piagetian religion. By 1980, I believed that there were a series of relatively independent cognitive capacities of which logical-mathematical thought was only one. I believed that stages were much looser than Piaget had envisioned, and, more importantly, that one's sophistication with one kind of mental representation did not predict one's sophistication with other mental representations. I believed that cognitive development continues well past adolescence, and that various cognitive capacities—like creativity, leadership, and the ability to change the minds of other persons—remain to be illuminated, despite Piaget's remarkable achievements. Finally, I had become deeply estranged from standard intelligence (IQ) testing.

The Organization of the Mind

In the West, a certain view of mind has held sway for a century. Dating back a century to the time of the French psychologist Alfred Binet, psychologists believe that there is a single intelligence, often called "g" for general intelligence; we are born with that intelligence; our intelligence comes from our biological parents and, as a result, intelligence is not significantly alterable; we psychologists can tell you how smart you are—traditionally, by giving you an IQ test, more recently, by examining the shape of your brain waves, perhaps ultimately, by looking at a chip on which your genes are encoded.

My research in cognitive development and cognitive breakdown convinced me that this traditional view of intellect is not tenable. Individuals have different human faculties and their strength (or weakness) in one intellectual sphere simply does not predict whether a particular individual will be strong or weak in some other intellectual component. I developed a definition of intelligence—a biopsychological information-processing capacity to solve problems or fashion products that are valued in at least one community and culture. I think of the intelligences as a set of relatively independent computers. One computer deals with language, a second with spatial information, a third with information about other people.

But how to figure out what is the right set of computers? I came up with a set of eight criteria of what counts as an intelligence. Unlike most approaches to intelligence, the criteria were not dependent on results of a paper and pencil test. Rather I looked at criteria from neurology: which brain regions mediate particular skills; anthropology—which abilities have been valued in different cultures across history and prehistory; special populations, such as prodigies, savants, and individuals with learning disabilities. All these individual have jagged intellectual profiles, ones not easily explained if one believes in a single "general intelligence."

Ultimately I came up with a list of eight, possibly nine, intelligences. I will mention each, and then give examples of individuals or roles that stand out in that particular intelligence:

1. Linguistic intelligence. The intelligence of a writer, orator, journalist.
2. Logical mathematical intelligence. The intelligence of a logician, mathematician, scientist—Piaget thought that he was studying all of intelligence, but he was really focusing on this particular intelligence.

Most tests of intelligence focus on logical and linguistic intelligence. They do a pretty good job at predicting success in school—but not nearly as good a job as last year's grades! My goal is not to denigrate these traditional *scholastic* intelligences, but rather to give equal attention to other intellectual faculties.

3. Musical intelligence. The capacity to create, perform, and appreciate music. Some people call this a talent. That is fine, so long as you recognize that being good with words or with numbers is also a talent. What I cannot accept is that linguistic facility is deemed intelligence, while skill with music or with other persons is *merely* a talent.
4. Spatial intelligence. The capacity to form mental imagery of the world—the large world of the aviator or navigator, or the more local world of the chess player or the surgeon—and to manipulate those mental images.
5. Bodily-kinesthetic intelligence. The capacity to solve problems or fashion products using your whole body, or parts of your body, like your hands or mouth. This intelligence is exhibited by athletes, dancers, actors, craftspersons, and, again, surgeons.

The next two intelligences have to do with the world of human beings.

6. Interpersonal intelligence involves the understanding of other persons—how to interact with them, how to motivate them, how to understand their personalities, etc. This skill is obviously important for people in business, teachers, clinicians, and those involved in politics or religion.
7. Intrapersonal intelligence is the capacity to understand oneself—one's strengths, weaknesses, desires, fears. Access to one's emotional life is important for intrapersonal intelligence.

Whether or not you have heard of multiple intelligence theory, you have certainly heard of emotional intelligence. What Daniel Goleman means by emotional intelligence is similar to what I mean by the personal intelligences.

8. Naturalist intelligence involves the capacity to make consequential distinctions in nature—between one plant and another, among animals, clouds, mountains, and the like. Scientist Charles Darwin had naturalist intelligence in abundance. Most of us no longer use our naturalist intelligence to survive in the jungle or the forest. But it is likely that our entire consumer culture is based on our naturalist capacity to differentiate one car make from another, one sneaker from another, and the like.
9. I have speculated that there may be a ninth or existential intelligence. I call this the "intelligence of big questions." When children ask about the size of the universe, when adults ponder death, love, conflict, the future of the planet, they are engaging in existential issues. My hesitation in declaring a full-blown existential intelligence stems from my uncertainty about whether certain regions of the brain are dedicated to the contemplation of issues that are too vast or too infinitesimal to be perceived. And so, recalling a famous Fellini movie, I speak of 8 1/2 intelligences.

So there you have it, my list of the multiple intelligences. Even if my approach is correct, I am sure that I have not identified all of the intelligences and that I have not described them perfectly. I am equally confident that each intelligence itself has separable components. But I am not interested in proving the existence of eight or nine intelligences, or 40–50 subintelligences, in particular. I am trying to make the case that we have a multiplicity of intelligences, each relatively independent of the others. From this claim—that we possess eight or nine relatively autonomous intellectual computers—three interesting claims follow.

a. All of us have these eight or nine intelligences; that is what makes us human beings, cognitively speaking. Rats might have more spatial intelligence, hummingbirds might have more musical intelligences, but we are the species that exhibits these particular intelligences. And that is important to know—whether you are a teacher, a businessman, or a parent.

b. No two individuals have exactly the same profile of intelligences, not even identical twins. And so whether you are a teacher, business person, or parent, you may assume that every person's profile differs from yours, and from every other person, even clones of one another.

c. Having an intelligence does not mean that you will behave morally or intelligently. Intelligences are simply computers that can be put to work. But you can use your interpersonal intelligence for moral purposes—like Nelson Mandela—or for immoral purposes, like Slobodan Milosevic. By the same token, you might have a computer that works very well, and yet use it very stupidly. A mathematically talented person might prove an important new theorem, but she might also waste her time multiplying ever bigger figures in her head.

The theory of multiple intelligences has aroused enormous interest among educators, and in many parts of the world. But that is a story for another occasion.

Questions

1. Think about yourself as you read Gardner's list of different kinds of intelligence. In what ways are you most intelligent? In what ways are you least intelligent?

2. If Gardner is correct that there are many different kinds of intelligence, why do so many people still categorize some people as "smart" or "gifted" and others as "stupid" or "slow?"

3. How different would schools be if they were designed to cultivate all forms of intelligence? What would happen to tests and grades?

Source: Howard Gardner. "Multiple Lenses on the Mind." Paper presented at the ExpoGestion Conference, Bogotá, Colombia, May 25, 2005. For a more complete explanation of Gardner's theories of multiple intelligences, see his *Intelligence Reframed*. New York: Basic Books, 1999.

Curriculum 6

What Will I Teach?

Debates over what is basic to the curriculum are also debates over identity.

WILLIAM PINAR

QUESTIONS TO COME

"What will I teach?" is a standard question asked by anyone considering a career in teaching, whether you will be teaching elementary, middle, or high school. How will you know what to teach your students? Who determines what they need to learn? How much freedom will you have, and how much will you have to follow a plan that has been developed elsewhere? All of these questions lead to a discussion of the *curriculum*—the content of what is taught in school.

As we explore the topic of curriculum, we will discover that there are many debates going on in the United States about *what should* be taught in school today and *who should decide* what is taught. At the moment, much of the national discourse about what should be taught in school surrounds the debate about the Common Core State Standards (CCSS), which began with discussions among state education leaders in 2007. After a two-year development process, the final standards were released in 2010. Initially, 48 states adopted the standards; by 2013, 45 states were still using the English Language and Mathematics standards. As implementation began, however, a wide-ranging backlash also developed, based in part on complaints about the testing that was planned to accompany the standards and also because of fears that the standards represented a federal takeover of what had previously been a state and district matter. The current battles over the Common Core, which we will explore in this chapter, are just the latest in many arguments about the appropriate curriculum for American teachers to teach and students to learn.

Since the 1980s, some educators and political leaders from across the parties have been pushing for new, clearer, and higher standards for the nation's curriculum—a movement greeted with applause in some quarters and harsh critique in others. Even before this, some educators began advocating multicultural education to ensure that the voices and life experiences of a greater range of people are included in the curriculum. Other educators were favoring a core of knowledge—not to be confused with the Common Core State Standards—that they believed every educated American needed to know, regardless of their own cultural background. We will explore the political battles surrounding these issues, especially the Common Core, in Chapter 11. In this chapter, we look at the significant impact the Common Core State Standards are having on the curriculum of most of the nation's schools.

The **Readings** for this chapter reflect the many areas of discussion about the curriculum—the question of *what should* be taught in today's schools. The first document focuses on the Common Core. The North Carolina–based

Hunt Institute played a key role in the development of the Common Core and produced a useful overview of what the standards include. Next, the **Readings** turn to the issue of multicultural education. Sonia Nieto, a widely respected leader in the multicultural education movement, lays out the case for multicultural education. In a final pair of **Readings,** two educators respond to the question, "How do different curricula reflect different views of the purpose of education?" Well-known author E. D. Hirsch, Jr., argues in favor of a common core of knowledge that must be presented in the curriculum of every school. Teacher and writer Bob Peterson counters that Hirsch's curriculum is deeply flawed because it reflects values that are not the right ones for a school to foster and, even if the values were better, it represents an imposition that stifles teacher and student creativity. (Remember that the core knowledge debate is not the same as the Common Core State Standards debate. Although there are overlaps, the core knowledge controversy began in the 1990s while the Common Core emerged only in 2007 and 2008.) Regarding what should be taught in schools today, there are few (if any) areas in which the authors of these pieces would agree—but they do encourage you to think critically and creatively about the matter.

What Is Curriculum? Why Teach *This* and Not *That?*

Defining Curriculum

"Debates over what is basic to the curriculum are also debates over identity," says William Pinar, one of the nation's leading curriculum theorists. In deciding what should be taught in school as well as what can be "skipped," educators make powerful decisions about how they want their students to experience and understand the world around them and their place in it. Schools cannot teach everything. Teachers; school leaders; local, state, and federal officials; and many others are always asking, "What knowledge is most important for our students at this moment in their lives?" They are continually picking and choosing, and making hard decisions. These decisions determine what gets taught in school—what the curriculum includes and what it excludes.[1]

On one level, the answer to the question "What is curriculum?" is a simple one. Curriculum is the "stuff" that is taught in school. Students have their textbooks, readers, and other supplemental literature, some published in hard copy and increasingly available on the Internet and in digital format. In addition, teachers have their guidebooks, supplemental materials, and directives from the school district and the state. All of this material is part of the formal curriculum. Students and teachers also receive informal messages about what they are supposed to be studying and learning, from school policies and from the culture in which they live. And of course the assessments, especially statewide standardized exams, help set the curriculum. Those things that will be tested will inevitably receive much more attention than those which are not included in such exams. For example, when the state says that students will be tested in language arts and mathematics but not in science and social studies, it has set the school curriculum every bit as much as when a publisher includes some material in a textbook and leaves out other information.

One cannot look at the materials of the curriculum apart from the human beings who use those materials. Science educator Meredith Houle, building on the work of J. T. Remillard, describes multiple forms of curriculum. First, she says, we must look at the *participatory relationship* between the written curriculum, which is often handed down from some higher authority, and the teacher who decides to, or is told to, use the curriculum. In the course of this relationship between curriculum and teacher, when the teacher designs a specific lesson plan to use the curriculum on a certain day in a certain classroom context, the *planned curriculum* comes into existence. Finally, the *enacted curriculum* represents what really happens in a classroom as a teacher seeks to put plans into practice. Remillard reminds educators that the curriculum will be modified as it is co-constructed by teachers and students in a particular context. These elements—the materials, the planning on how to use them by the teacher, and the reality of what takes place in the classroom—are equally part of what we mean when we use the word *curriculum*.[2]

The Goals of the Curriculum

One of the 20th century's most influential educators, Ralph Tyler, proposed in 1950 what came to be known as the "Tyler rationale"—four questions that should be asked before developing a curriculum:

1. What educational purposes should the school seek to attain?
2. What educational experiences can be provided that are likely to attain these purposes?
3. How can these educational experiences be effectively organized?
4. How can we determine whether these purposes are being attained?[3]

Tyler's questions have a fundamental logic. At their most basic, the questions ask the teacher to determine the goals of any given lesson, what steps should be taken to accomplish the goals, and finally, and most important, how the teacher knows the student learned what the teacher set out to teach him or her.

Many teachers shorten this list of questions to only two: (1) What sorts of experiences should I arrange for my class? and (2) How should I organize my students to move through these experiences? You may feel reasonably well prepared to face the classroom if you know what activities you are going to do with your students and how you are going to organize their day. However, this simplified version of Tyler's questions leaves out what may be the more important questions. As Tyler noted, it is essential to start at the beginning, "If we are to study an educational program systematically and intelligently we must first be sure as to the educational objectives aimed at."[4] If you, as a teacher, do not know what your long-term goal is and what you want to accomplish, not just in a given day but over the course of weeks and months with a group of students, and if you do not, to use more current language, have clear standards for what your students should learn, school can easily degenerate into busy work, into one thing after another, without long-term meaning or purpose. As Pinar noted, thinking about the curriculum is really asking questions about identity—national identity and individual identity—and not merely questions like "What do I do on Monday?" If such larger questions are not asked, you can come to the end of the term and realize that your students may or may not have learned a whole range of vaguely interesting facts and ideas, but they will not have had an education.

At the other end of the spectrum is the question of *evaluation*. Teachers can teach with great skill and enthusiasm and still find that some or all of their students fail to learn what their teachers thought they were teaching. Evaluation is, therefore, not merely a matter of giving the students grades. It is certainly not a matter of sorting the winners and the losers, though it can too easily degenerate into that. Indeed, the primary question of evaluation in curricular matters is not "Did the student succeed in learning?" but "Did the teacher succeed in teaching?" Sometimes it takes many different teaching methods and many different structured experiences before all the students in a class will "get" the content of a lesson. But the wise teacher is constantly evaluating his or her work. To separate evaluation from curriculum is to disregard the fundamental question of outcomes without which goals may never be met and experiences may never work.[5]

Although the so-called Tyler rationale has been used widely for more than 50 years, it has not been without its critics. Stanford professor Elliot Eisner was one of many to raise significant challenges. Eisner found Tyler's approach to be useful

> **CONNECTIONS →←**
> In Chapter 7, we further explore evaluation and assessment, and the teacher's role in the process.

Notes from the Field

How do you approach curriculum development?

"With empathy. I attempt to see every lesson through the lens of my students. As I write curriculum and lesson plans and present concepts, I'm perceiving the lessons through the eyes of a fourth grader. The question that goes through my mind is, 'How can I engage each student?' When I see the world fresh, I'm enthusiastic about learning and so are my students."

—Sarah Pennisi, fourth-grade student teacher

and rational, but he also found it seriously flawed, especially in fields like the arts, where student creativity is as important as student mastery of existing knowledge. Eisner said that clear objectives in curriculum design could easily mask the extent to which the same curriculum might lead to different outcomes in different contexts. (Recall Houle's emphasis on the interaction of curriculum materials, teachers, and students.) He also worried that overly rigid curriculum design could turn quickly into equally rigid systems of evaluation in which the entire purpose of education would be reduced to the most simplistic level, and thoughtful judgment by student and teacher would take a back seat to the quest for "right answers." These warnings are serious and as useful as a rational approach to curriculum development and implementation can be.[6]

Project-Based Learning

Project-based learning (PBL) is one of the latest curricular developments to be implemented in many schools around the United States. It is not a new concept. A century ago, John Dewey's colleague William Heard Kilpatrick advocated what he called the "Project Method," in which students learned by class projects. More recently, psychologists have argued that new research shows that most young people learn more by doing than just hearing. At the same time, society's shift from an industrial economy to one based on communications technology has meant that schools need more than ever to foster the social, interactive aspects of education.

These developments have pointed many educators in the direction of PBL. Of course, PBL means different things to different people, and the quality of implementation can vary widely. Overall, however, PBL calls on the teacher to develop a hands-on class project that will encourage students to learn a lesson that traditionally might have been taught through direct instruction and textbook reading. Examples of PBL might include the following:

- A social studies teacher asks students to design a student government association for a school. In the process, they study how governments, including the government of the United States, have been formed in the past and learn about the inevitable compromises of the legislative process—in a school or the U.S. Congress.
- A mathematics teacher has students develop a business plan for a venture they might launch in the school. They study the concepts of profit and loss, profit margin, and break-even point (which can be determined through either a spreadsheet or an algebraic equation).
- A science teacher asks students to design an energy-efficient house. They analyze different renewable energy sources, including how much energy wind turbines or solar panels generate in comparison with traditional sources of energy.

PBL requires teachers to be very clear about the learning outcomes they want to achieve, and they need to avoid "project-itis," in which the project itself takes over the students' time and energy and learning goals are marginalized.

When PBL is done successfully, teachers report that, among other things, it

- overcomes the divide between learning information and applying it
- helps students learn new things while also developing their ability to solve problems, communicate with others, and manage their own time
- connects learning to the real world and therefore helps students see learning as a something to do throughout their lives
- relates education to both future careers and responsible citizenship
- breaks down the divisions between different academic disciplines

The latest research on PBL shows that it is at least as effective as traditional instruction and sometimes is much more effective. PBL may appeal to many students who are not engaged in traditional academic pursuits, a significant issue among both disadvantaged and privileged students. This sort of disengagement is a significant contributor to the enormous dropout rate among high school students. Even many high-achieving students say that they are bored in school, and PBL engages them in ways that traditional classes do not. PBL helps students learn new material because they are motivated to solve a problem posed in their project. It also can help them be successful in traditional standardized forms of testing if the projects have been organized so that the ideas and concepts learned by doing the project relate to clear goals and learning outcome expectations.

Questions

- Were you assigned "projects" in school? Do you remember what you learned from them, or just the fact that you participated?
- Think about teaching in your area of interest. Can you design a project that would help students learn something that you think is especially important for them to know?

Source: This material was informed by Thom Markham, John Larmer, and Jason Ravitz. *Project Based Learning Handbook: A Guide to Standards Focused Project Based Learning for Middle and High School Teachers*. Novato, CA: Buck Institute of Education, 2003. Retrieved July 26, 2009, from http:// www.bie.org/index.php/site/PBL/pbl_handbook/.

Different Approaches to Curriculum

Herbert M. Kliebard, a leading historian of curriculum, describes four different schools of thought that have battled for control of the curriculum in U.S. schools:

- The *humanist* group believes that the traditional academic disciplines (history, English, mathematics, and the sciences, joined by other fields of study) represent the core of what should be taught to all students. Humanists believe that exercise of the mind in such study develops the ability to think rationally and could serve as a solid foundation for the future.
- A second group, *developmentalists*, believe that young people have widely disparate native abilities and that the curriculum should therefore be differentiated by developmental stage as well as by ability, sorting some for a college education and professional life and many more for much lower level careers.
- A third group, who came to be known as *social efficiency educators*, want to eliminate waste in education—waste of time and waste of money—by focusing schools on preparing students to fit with the needs of the national economy. They believe that scientific research and rigorous testing yield a scientifically based curriculum.
- Finally, a group of educators known as *social meliorists*, or *social constructionists*, believe that the school curriculum should prepare students who could build a more just and democratic social order. Though this group has often represented a minority view, at certain times (such as during the Great Depression of the 1930s and the civil rights movement of the 1950s and 1960s), the voices of social meliorists helped define the purpose of schooling in the United States.[7]

Kliebard notes that no one of these approaches has been dominant for long and that advocates of all four argue with each other as much today as they did a hundred years ago. Since the 1960s, some of the focus and some of the names have changed, but the battles have continued. E. D. Hirsch, Jr., whose views are included in one of the **Readings** and who argues for a return to what he sees as the "basics," shares a humanist trust in the traditional academic disciplines as a key to successful schooling. Bob Peterson, an elementary school teacher from Milwaukee, Wisconsin, challenges Hirsch's back-to-basics views in the **Readings** and could probably be classified most closely with the *social meliorists*. Although Peterson makes clear his appreciation that Hirsch "raises the issue of unequal access to knowledge and literature in our **stratified society**," he also sees Hirsch's proposals as making the inequity much worse. Hirsch and Peterson are not the first to argue about these issues—and they will certainly not be the last.

> **stratified society**
> Privileges and benefits are dispersed according to a socially constructed value system wherein some people and groups are considered subordinate to those that are more elite or entitled.

Although educators have fought and argued at national meetings, in local school boards, within faculty meetings of teacher education programs, and at the smallest gathering of teachers engaged in curriculum planning, no one school of thought has ever won. And no one perspective is likely to have a permanent victory. There are too many deep-seated debates about the nature and purpose of education in the United States for the question of the best curriculum to be resolved. Quite different approaches to the curriculum have had their moments of supremacy and of decline. Some have merged into indistinct coalitions, and some have been on the verge of disappearing, only to rise again as social conditions changed and schools were asked to respond to differing local or national conditions.

As Kliebard concludes, "in the end, what became the American curriculum was not the result of any decisive victory by any of the contending parties, but a loose, largely unarticulated, and not very tidy compromise."[8] Navigating that "not very tidy compromise" is the challenge facing every classroom teacher. Almost any curricular decision that can be made, by a state or federal agency or an individual teacher, is bound to elicit praise from some and hostility from others. In this situation, the more informed the teacher is, the more successful his or her voyage will be.

The Hidden Curriculum

Historian and longtime school leader Larry Cuban notes that when we talk about the curriculum of a school, we must always address at least two different but nevertheless linked curricula: "The *official* curriculum (what subject matter, skills, and values authorities expect teachers to teach) and the *taught* curriculum (what teachers believe about content and its presentation and what they actually do)."[9] In other words, what are teachers expected to teach *and* what do they actually teach—by their words, actions, procedures, and so on?

The official curriculum is usually stated in ways that reflect what citizens of a community—or at least those citizens with the most powerful voices—believe every child should know by the time they finish school. The official curriculum typically includes basic skills and values, such as democracy and fair play. It also includes content knowledge—such as the ability to read, write, and count; probably some knowledge of the community's and the nation's history and culture; and likely much more.

Yet communities, and those in authority in a given school or community, may also have a "hidden curriculum"—lessons that were taught very effectively though no one in the school acknowledged the fact. For example, half a century ago, schools in many parts of the United States were legally segregated by race. No one said that the purpose was to teach inferiority to some students and superiority to others, but that was as effectively a part of the curriculum as any other more overtly stated values. Racism was taught every day as students passed each other on the way to different schools, and it was repeated in classrooms as one group of students received new textbooks and another got the hand-me-downs.

Within individual classrooms, what teachers believe and what they do can differ radically. A teacher can deeply want to engage a class and make learning exciting, but he or she may succeed or may fail. Virtually all studies of teachers' interactions with male and female students come to the same conclusion—teachers call on boys much more often than they call on girls, and much more than they think they differentiate between them. A teacher who values and talks about gender equity may easily teach the opposite without realizing it. Both teachings are a real part of the curriculum—what gets taught and what gets learned. Teachers must always be on the lookout for the hidden curriculum they and other teachers and school leaders are teaching to the students at the same time they are thoughtfully and carefully teaching the subject matter and skills that are part of the school's formal curriculum.[10]

What Does the Common Core Mean for Today's Teachers?

As mentioned at the beginning of this chapter, the Common Core State Standards evolved from discussions among state education leaders in 2007 regarding the development of consistent national standards for what students should be learning. We will explore the lively controversy swirling around the Common Core State Standards in further detail in

Chapter 11 when we consider questions relating to the place of politics in education and the life of a teacher. As we will also discuss in that chapter, although a state's adherence to the CCSS is not required by federal law, federal funding certainly encourages a state to implement the standards. Currently, the standards are being implemented in 45 of the 50 states. Even in some of the states that are not using the Common Core State Standards, their new state curricular standards have a great deal in common with the heart of the Common Core enterprise.

CONNECTIONS →←
In Chapter 11, we discuss the politics surrounding the Common Core State Standards, No Child Left Behind, and earlier standards movements in American education.

Although the American Federation of Teachers, which represents over a million of the nation's school teachers, has called for a moratorium on implementing the testing related to the Common Core, the union strongly endorses the thrust of the standards, noting on its Web site that, "The Common Core State Standards have the potential to transform teaching and learning and provide all children with the problem-solving, critical-thinking, and teamwork skills they need to compete in today's changing world." Thus, no matter how the debates over the CCSS continue to play out, it's critical for aspiring teachers to be familiar with them and know how to effectively teach to Common Core expectations when they seek to enter the profession—from the job interview to planning their first lessons.

The Common Core's Impact on Curriculum

The overview of the Common Core that is included in the **Readings** for this chapter lists several goals for the common standards, including preparing all students for a 21st-century world (ensuring that high school graduates are ready for college or a career in the current economy) and allowing students to move from state to state without losing time or needlessly repeating material. (Now is a good time to tackle that **Reading** if you haven't already done so; it will help put this and further discussions of the Common Core into context.) The Hunt Institute material in this **Reading**, like other descriptions of the Common Core, highlights specific goals for literacy and mathematics for all students.

The English Language Arts/Literacy goals require teachers to use much more complex and rigorous material, starting in the earliest grades, than most students currently encounter. They also use more nonfiction readings, ensuring that students can read many different kinds of material, gain a familiarity with complex texts and academic vocabulary, write about it, and use evidence gained from the reading to make their own arguments. The focus on helping students seek and use evidence to make clear and coherent arguments runs through all of the education reform literature and lies at the heart of the Common Core.

In the Mathematics standards, which have been more controversial than the Language Arts ones, teachers and students are asked to follow the example of other countries that have been especially successful in teaching math—limiting the number of topics addressed and ensuring that there is time to explore some topics in greater depth than has been the norm in the United States. In addition to a solid foundation in whole numbers, addition, subtraction, multiplication, division, fractions, and decimals, students should transition to algebra by the middle grades. More controversial, however, is that students are also asked to make applications to the real world: By middle and high school they are expected to use mathematical models to answer real-world questions at a high level.

The new Mathematics standards have led to confusion and anger on the part of many parents, especially when parents try to help their children with math homework and find themselves utterly confused by it. *Education Week* quoted a parent from Toledo, Ohio, watching her third-grader do math problems: "I was like, wait a minute, I don't understand what you're doing." Many schools throughout the country have begun holding math nights, posting videos, and sending materials to parents explaining the kinds of math expected in the new standards. In some cases, including with the Toledo mother, the new material has worked and parents are convinced that their children are understanding mathematics better than they ever had. In other cases, parental frustration has simply fueled the backlash against the whole Common Core enterprise.

Testing the Common Core

The 45 states that are using the Common Core have each joined one of two multistate consortia that are developing the assessment exams for testing student success in meeting the Common Core standards. These two consortia—the Partnership for Assessment of Readiness for College and Careers (PARCC) and the Smarter Balanced Assessment

Teachable Moment
MALALA YOUSAFZAI AND THE COMMON CORE

When Malala Yousafzai was only 16 years old, this Pakistani schoolgirl insisted on her right to receive the same education as boys. As a result, she was the victim of a Taliban assassination attempt. She recovered, wrote the best-selling autobiography *I Am Malala: The Girl Who Stood Up for Education and Was Shot by the Taliban*, and has been honored by the United Nations.

In conjunction with the publication of Malala's book, the American Federation of Teachers (AFT) developed a lesson for grades 5–10, closely aligned with the Common Core standards, to teach students about human rights, while also having students engage in close reading of a nonfiction text, search for evidence, and develop a clear and coherent argument—all at the heart of the Common Core expectations.

The lesson, like hundreds of others, is available from Share My Lesson (http://www.sharemylesson.com), a Web site supported by the AFT. This pool of resources developed by teachers for teachers provides interesting and engaging Common Core–ready materials for classroom use at every level.

In other "Share My Lesson" downloads, teachers can find math lessons in which students use five pieces of evidence and perform various math problems in order to eliminate nine of ten suspects for a crime, or use real-world examples to learn about math ratios. Along with the Malala Yousafzai lesson, the various English language arts lessons include ones that use the history of World War II or the winter holidays to select and present information from a text in a relevant way, compare the perspective of different authors, and read closely for textual details.[11]

See Share My Lesson at http://www.sharemylesson.com.

Questions

- Have you heard the Common Core discussed at your school or at home? If so, would the discussions benefit from a look at the material in Share My Lesson?
- Are you surprised that a union would offer so much curriculum material? Did you know that the teacher unions were so deeply involved in Common Core implementation?

Consortium (SB) have published and tested much of their work. Referring to the two major testing consortia, Katherine Stahl, a literacy professor, and Jason Schweid, a researcher at the New York State Education Department, write that in the field of literacy, "Test items today go far beyond a regurgitation of literal information. Students will need to demonstrate new learning as a consequence of PARCC's and SB's performance tasks. To navigate these novel experiences with the variety of texts provided, students will need to generate inferences, monitor their own comprehension, and then adjust accordingly to produce high-level responses." After learning more about the Mathematics standards, another parent at the Toledo school mentioned previously said that while it was not the way he had learned math, the Common Core is expanding students' "overall thinking and showing there's more than one way to do it."

On the AFT Web site, there is a description of the impact of the Common Core by one New Mexico teacher who says, "It makes it very easy for teachers to look at the end goal and backward-plan to make sure that your children have critical-thinking skills. We're moving away from rote memorization, drilling children, and moving more toward getting deeper into the content and really being able to not only apply our knowledge but transfer it from one thing to another. Critical-thinking skills are back! Science and social studies are back!"

Clearly, there is widespread enthusiasm for the challenge that the Common Core offers on the part of many teachers and parents who have taken the time to understand the standards and their meaning in practice. As we will see in Chapter 11, others who have taken equal time to understand the standards and their implementation have come to quite different conclusions. The Common Core remains an area where wise and well-informed people deeply disagree. In the middle of all of those disagreements, teachers from New Mexico to Ohio to New York and in most other parts of the United States are continuing to teach to the new standards as best they can even as they advocate for what they believe is best for the teaching profession and for the students who are served by it.[12]

What Are Some of the Current Debates About Multicultural Education?

Few debates in the area of curriculum—besides the Common Core—have generated as much discussion as the topic of multicultural education. Multicultural education has had many supporters—some of whom advocate quite different things from each other. Multicultural education has also had powerful critics who also disagree among themselves. These debates among and between these advocates and critics of multicultural education reveal a great deal about not only what they want taught, or not taught, but also the widely differing beliefs about the purpose of schooling and the national identity that these diverse voices support. If Pinar is right that debates about curriculum are also debates about identity, then the battles over multicultural education represent significantly different versions of the national identity that different educators want the schools to teach.

James Banks, considered by many to be the "father of multicultural education," describes the origins of a movement that has transformed the curriculum of many, though certainly not all, schools in the United States in the past half century. "Multicultural education," Banks says, "grew out of the ferment of the civil rights movement of the 1960s. . . . The consequence of the civil rights movement had a significant influence on educational institutions as ethnic groups—first African Americans and then other groups—demanded that the schools and other educational institutions reform curricula to reflect their experiences, histories, cultures, and perspectives."[13]

An example of these roots of multicultural education can be found in the **Readings** for this chapter, as Sonia Nieto locates her commitment to the field in her own experience growing up in Brooklyn, New York, during the 1940s and speaking only Spanish when she entered the first grade. Like many of her peers, Nieto assumed that her sense of being different meant that there was something wrong with her. As an adult educator she wanted to ensure that the next generation of students would not have this sense that something was wrong with them. Nieto also defines multicultural education as affecting not just the curriculum but also all aspects of the life of a school. She sees multicultural education as being part of a larger school reform effort as well as being a movement that challenges racism and advocates for ethnic, linguistic, religious, economic, and gender pluralism. It affects the culture of the schools where it is adopted as well as the school's curriculum and the pedagogy (how the curriculum is taught).[14] In this view, multicultural education becomes the philosophy at the heart of the school—a philosophy with a clear sense of the kind of identity that schools should foster and a clear sense of mission based in a social meliorist approach to the curriculum.

Once launched, the movement for multicultural education led educators to look carefully at the content of the curriculum, to see whose stories were told and whose were excluded. Banks notes:

When feminists (people who work for the political, social, and economic equality of the sexes) looked at educational institutions, they noted problems similar to those identified by ethnic groups of color. Textbooks and curricula were dominated by men; women were largely invisible. Feminists pointed out that history textbooks were dominated by political and military history—areas in which men had been the main participants. Social and family history and the history of labor and ordinary people were largely ignored. Feminists pushed for the revision of textbooks to include more history about the important roles of women in the development of the nation and the world.[15]

The origins of the movement for a multicultural curriculum in the schools are important to understand. Multicultural education was not born because a group of curriculum experts were trying to come up with the next big idea for what should be taught. On the contrary, the pressure to change the curriculum of American schools came from outside the schools—from movements to include the nation's full diversity, especially people of color and women, in all aspects of national life. Once again, a curricular debate was also a debate about identity. To understand the importance of multicultural education, simply open a textbook that was used in schools in the 1950s and early 1960s. Virtually all Americans were White, and almost all important actions involved men. Women were included but, with few exceptions, were passive bystanders. African Americans, Latino Americans, and Asian Americans were virtually invisible, not only in history books, but also in literature and in the examples used in mathematics and the sciences. From learning to read by following the stories of Dick and Jane—two White children who lived in the suburbs with their dog Spot—to high school history books that told of America's "discovery" by Europeans as if the land had been uninhabited, to science texts that told of the exploits of European American males, the identity taught in these texts was of a White, mostly middle class, male-dominated nation. The much more inclusive story of the nation's history, literature, science, and culture that is told in most schools today is vastly different from that of decades not long gone.

 DID YOU KNOW?

Between the 1930s and the 1960s, the *Dick and Jane* series of readers was used in teaching 85 million children to read—approximately 80% of all first graders. The series was conceived in 1927 by Zerna Sharp, who believed that children would read better if they identified with the characters in the illustrations and read words that sounded familiar. The first African American main characters didn't appear until 1965 in *Now We Read*. The series was discontinued in 1970.

As it has developed over recent decades, the movement for a more multicultural curriculum has become increasingly sophisticated. Not surprisingly, the movement has also experienced resistance. Some people, including the prominent American historian Arthur M. Schlesinger, Jr., came to argue that there was a danger of multicultural education pushing out what they see as the main story line. Thus, Schlesinger saw the call for multicultural education as an "attack on the common American identity."

Schlesinger developed his critique of multicultural education in his 1991 book *The Disuniting of America* in which he bridled at the critique of European American culture that he saw within multiculturalism. He wrote:

Is Europe really the root of all evil? The crimes of Europe against lesser breeds without the law (not to mention even worse crimes—Hitlerism and Stalinism—against other Europeans) are famous. But these crimes do not alter other facts of history: that Europe was the birthplace of the United States of America, that European ideas and culture formed the republic, that the United States is an extension of European civilization, and that nearly 80 percent of Americans are of European descent.

Needless to say, such dramatic rhetoric raised new anger, not only among the advocates of multicultural education but among many of its critics. And to what would probably have been Schlesinger's amazement, within 25 years of the time he wrote this, European Americans constituted less than half of the school-age population of the country.[16]

Some teachers who might or might not agree with Schlesinger nevertheless argue that there is simply no time to cover all of the material that multicultural education demands or for teachers to learn so many different stories. Such critics see in multicultural education the perhaps-unintended result that history and other subjects become an unintelligible muddle in which so much information is presented that no story line makes any sense.

Even more troublesome to some critics is the concern that respect for multiple cultures can quickly become a kind of "value-free" education. In the article, "The Pitfalls of Multicultural Education," Albert Shanker, former president of the American Federation of Teachers, attacked the movement, asking with scorn:

Do we really want them to "respect and accept" the "values, beliefs, and attitudes" of other people, no matter what they are? Do we want them to respect and accept the beliefs that led Chinese leaders to massacre dissenting students in Tiananmen Square?[17]

Others, who may not be as hostile to the goals of multicultural education as Schlesinger or Shanker still saw multicultural education as perhaps important for classrooms in which there are many students of color but virtually irrelevant for segregated European American classrooms. Still others say that although multicultural education is fine for history teachers, it has nothing to do with those who teach science or mathematics.[18]

While the critics raised their challenges, advocates of multicultural education kept up their work, developing new curricular materials, providing professional development workshops for teachers struggling with implementation, and expanding the meaning of their enterprise. James Banks saw multicultural education as "a broad concept with several different and important dimensions" and in his long career he has explored many of them. In one work, Banks listed five areas that need to be given careful attention in any effective program of multicultural education:

1. **Content integration.** Teachers should include, for example, the stories of Native Americans, Africans, Asians, as well as European immigrants in the story of the United States and the lives of women as well as men. Stories from diverse cultures should be used in word problems in a math class or in science experiments.
2. **The knowledge construction process.** This is more difficult and requires teachers and eventually their students to look at the ways certain dominant cultural assumptions are included in the curriculum. It involves asking students, for example, "Why do you think so many of the famous scientists are male?" or "Why did it take more than 200 years for the country to elect anyone other than a white male as president?"
3. **Prejudice reduction.** It is not easy to grow up in the United States without inheriting a whole mix of racial and gender stereotypes. Banks would argue that directly challenging this sort of built-in prejudice is also part of a teacher's job.
4. **An equity pedagogy.** For example, many teachers find that students from upper-class families initially do better in school than students from poor families, that boys are more likely to talk in class, and that some students are easily marginalized if they belong to a racial group that is underrepresented in a class. Banks would argue that a teacher should pay special attention to ensure that the poor children get the academic support they need to do as well as their better-off peers, that classes need to be structured so that girls are led to speak as much as boys, and that every student is incorporated into the culture of the classroom.
5. **An empowering school culture.** Multicultural education does not stop at the classroom door. How teachers of different races interact in the lunchroom and in curriculum planning meetings, how the school sorts its students, and if the building feels welcoming are all part of building a multicultural school culture.

In outlining this wide range of goals for what multicultural education should accomplish in the transformation of schools and the larger society, Banks understands that different people understand multicultural education in different ways. There is no one-size-fits-all definition. Indeed, he notes, that different educators use the term *multicultural education* to describe many different programs:

In one school district, multicultural education may mean a curriculum that incorporates the experiences of ethnic groups of color; in another, a program may include the experiences of both ethnic groups and women. In a third school district, this term may be used . . . to mean a total school reform effort designed to increase educational equity for a range of cultural, ethnic, and economic groups.[19]

Given the elastic nature of the term, it is also important for everyone to develop his or her own clear definition.

Teachable Moment
A MISSION OF MULTICULTURALISM

Following is the mission statement from the Amherst Regional Public Schools in Massachusetts, along with their policy statement that outlines their commitment to becoming a multicultural school system:

The mission of our schools is to provide all students with a high quality education that enables them to be contributing members of a multiethnic, multicultural, pluralistic society. We seek to create an environment that achieves equity for all students and ensures that each student is a successful learner, is fully respected, and learns to respect others.

Diversity is a strength because it challenges every student, every teacher, and every person in the school system to understand, respect, and value the differences among us. In the four towns that comprise the school district, more than thirty languages are spoken in the homes of our students and nearly 30% of the entire student body belongs to the ALANA (African American, Latino, Asian, and Native American) population. In every elementary school classroom there is at least one student who is learning English as a new language—from the nearly 300 students who receive instruction in English as a Second Language, to those enrolled in Transitional Bilingual Educational programs, which teach academic subjects in the native language until the ability to learn English is acquired. Creating a diverse school community that reflects the community at large includes addressing racism and other forms of discrimination in the classroom to help students understand the nature and complexity of a multicultural society. But diversity isn't something that can be forgotten when the bell rings at the end of the school day. All of our schools are devoted to promoting equity in all aspects of education, inside the classroom and out. The commitment to equity is demonstrated by having set specific goals for Becoming a Multicultural School System (BAMSS). These explicit goals call for equity in hiring, establishment of a multicultural curriculum, and attention to the needs of each and every student.

Questions

- Ask yourself, "Would I want to teach in a district with as clear and explicit a commitment to diversity as Amherst, Massachusetts?" Would this make the district appealing to you? Unappealing? Or is it irrelevant?
- Can schools succeed if their mission is to "provide all students with a high quality education?" Is this standard too high?

Source: Amherst Regional Public Schools. "Mission Statement" and "A Commitment to Equity." Retrieved July 6, 2009, from http://www.arps.org.

How Do Different Curricula Reflect Different Views of the Purpose of Education?

The final set of **Readings** for this chapter gives graphic examples of the ways that two different educators with quite different philosophies of education approach the curriculum. E. D. Hirsch, Jr., one of the nation's best-known curriculum advocates, has developed something he calls the *core knowledge curriculum*. Hirsch answers the "What will I teach?" question very specifically. He says: "Teach this core knowledge." Hirsch understands that the debate can go on forever about what core knowledge is of most importance. He is clear "not to claim that the content we recommend is better than some other well-thought-out core. . . . But one must make a start." And having a core of knowledge avoids what Hirsch sees as the too-common situation in which there is no agreement at all about what knowledge is most important.

Bob Peterson, another highly regarded teacher, has serious problems with Hirsch's curriculum model. Peterson has multiple complaints about the core knowledge curriculum: it "misdiagnoses what ails American education," it defines knowledge in such a way that small bits of information or facts pass for understanding, and it "focuses almost exclusively on contributions and perspectives of mainstream European Americans." (Recall the debates you just read about multicultural education in this chapter.) In the end, Hirsch and Peterson have different goals for what students will learn in school, they seek to foster different senses of identity in their students, and thus they answer the question of what to teach quite differently.

The debates about what should be taught in school, be it over a common core of knowledge, multicultural education, or the Common Core Standards, open up many of the deepest divides in our society. One cannot begin to develop or think about teaching a multicultural curriculum without also thinking about race and about what constitutes the uniting elements in American society and culture. Heated debates about any national standards of what should be taught in schools should come as no surprise, even if the standards were not accompanied by tough testing measures. Historically, states and often local schools and districts have set the appropriate standards for their students. Thus, national efforts are relatively new. As education scholar Michael Apple reminds us, "In a society driven by social tensions and by increasingly larger inequalities, schools will not be immune from—and in fact may participate in recreating—these inequalities. If this is true of education in general, it is equally true of attempts to reform it."[20]

Education professor and advocate for multicultural education Christine Sleeter provides a helpful way of looking at some of the current, confusing debates about educational standards. Like a long line of advocates for multicultural education and educational equity, Sleeter insists that culturally relevant standards are essential to measuring meaningful progress in achieving equity. "But," she warns, "efforts to offer all children an intellectually rich curriculum have become conflated with standardizing what everyone should know, thereby reducing the diverse funds of knowledge with which next generations have awareness or familiarity. *High standards* and *standardization* are not the same thing, yet they have been treated as if they were." For Sleeter, standards refer to a clear public measure of quality: What do the students need to know? Standardization, however, is an unnecessary rigidity in defining the particular ways that teachers are supposed to meet the standards.[21]

Two professional development experts, Deborah E. Burns and Jeanne H. Purcell, who have spent many years working with teachers to help them survive in a changing and increasingly standards-based world, describe how important they believe it is to engage teachers in a discussion of the standards and in the multiple ways that the standards can be met. Reporting on their work with teachers in three Rhode Island school districts, Burns and Purcell had asked teachers to look at the standards from multiple perspectives. One teacher suddenly saw options that had not been apparent before and exclaimed, "Now I see how I can make my learning outcomes more challenging for my students. I need to incorporate all types of learning for students, not just facts." Another said, "I could teach this piece of knowledge from six different perspectives. It's just a matter of deciding what to pick for my particular group of students within the time frame." When teachers come to see their essential role in the standards movement—and the Common Core specifically—as being in the key position of moving from general goals to specific learning outcomes, then they will have the opportunity not only to discuss the standards but also "to own them, breathe life into them, and incorporate them into the curriculum."[22]

The standards, and the state tests that measure them, have had a huge impact on schools and specifically on teachers and principals. In too many places the standards and the tests have come to be viewed as an impossible barrier that drives everything else out of the school day and takes the life out of teaching. Critics of the Common Core fear the same thing happening again. However, the kind of data that the tests provide can help schools break through the tendency to have low expectations for all students and instead focus on just what it will take to help every student succeed. A lot depends on the nature of the standards and the tests, but a lot also depends on the approach individual educators take to using them.

Of course, no educator wants to be seen as opposing high standards. No one advocates for mediocrity. Nevertheless, the standards debate is a complex one for all of us. Who sets the standards? Who measures progress toward meeting the standards? How much freedom and flexibility should an individual classroom teacher have in deciding the standards to be met and the means of meeting them? These debates are alive and well in every classroom, school board, and legislative hall in the United States today, and it is here that today's and tomorrow's curriculum is being defined.

Vito Perrone, who spent a lifetime as a teacher and teacher of teachers, as well as an ardent critic of what he saw as misguided education reforms, summarized the current situation and its cost:

> In too many school systems teachers are not expected to make significant decisions about what to teach. And the decisions that are open to them often have fairly rigid boundaries. Elaborate curriculum guides with detailed objectives organized around subject fields and extending to the sequence of topics to be taught are not uncommon, leaving little room for the personal interest or invention of teachers or students.

Perrone made it clear that he thought that allowing this situation to continue was a mistake: "Learning in such schools invariably gets reduced to small pieces of knowledge ordered by a predetermined sequence with considerable stress placed on coverage." To move from mere coverage to creating the kinds of intellectually challenging communities—for students and for teachers—that schools ought to be, Perrone argued, is the challenge facing teachers today. Like others, Perrone also asserted a teacher's right—indeed, duty—to be active in helping to create intellectually challenging communities in schools.[23]

Advocates of higher and more specific standards will argue with Perrone that, although the standards set out the basic outline of what teachers are expected to teach, many teachers still have significant room to incorporate their personal interests or to be inventive. Indeed defenders of the Common Core insist that it gives them new freedom. As the New Mexico teacher argued regarding the Common Core: "How you achieve your goals, and how you meet your standards, is up to you." Even if others see such a view of the Common Core as romantic, they would agree that the key for effective teaching is to use the standards as a launching pad, not as a rigid formula. Schools and school districts have embraced the standards in different ways, from mandating approaches like direct instruction or even a scripted-curriculum approach (a model of implementing the reading standards that scripts virtually every word a teacher says) to encouraging much more open-ended arrangements that use the standards as only a starting point for teacher-led curricular planning.

Part of asserting one's right and duty to help shape the curriculum involves returning to the Tyler rationale discussed at the beginning of the chapter. Whatever the mandates of their schools, individual teachers—as well as curriculum leaders and school boards—must ask the same basic questions about the curriculum. Recall that Tyler asked teachers to focus on four questions: What is the purpose? What experiences attain the purposes? How can these experiences be organized? How can we determine whether the purposes are being attained?

To a much larger degree than at any time in history, the first of Tyler's questions is being determined at the national and state levels as people develop the Common Core or alternative standards and state bodies mandate them for all schools. Nevertheless, individual teachers can add their own sense of purpose to their classrooms, claiming great freedom in how they implement the standards. The next two questions regarding the development and organization of student experiences leave much room for teacher involvement in most situations. In extreme cases, such as with direct instruction, all questions of experience and organization are answered, but most teachers find themselves in situations closer to those described by Burns and Purcell. With the right time and planning, they can design and craft their own classes in response to their students' individual needs.

It is in the arena of Tyler's last point—determining if the standards have been met—that some of the greatest controversy arises today. Nearly every state now has state-level tests, many of which a student must pass in order to graduate from high school. With the Common Core, states will select one of two nationally developed tests. Teachers and principals, as well as students, are evaluated based on how well students do on these tests. The temptation to "teach to the test" is certainly significant today. Among the most pressing questions currently is whether such pressures will foster more creativity on the part of teachers to help their students achieve well, or whether the pressures will simply move most teachers toward a mindless conformity to preplanned "test prep" instruction. We will explore this issue in more depth in the next chapter.

Returning once again to Pinar's statement that "[d]ebates over what is basic to the curriculum are also debates over identity," we know that teachers will be able to ask not only "What will I teach?" but also "What sort of identity am I trying to foster in my students?" and questions like "What sense of themselves and what sense of place in a national identity am I developing when I select the stories to use to teach a first grader to read or a middle-school student to engage with algebra or a high school senior to think about advanced study in the sciences, world history, and the best way to prepare for college and life beyond?" The day-to-day questions of curriculum are best framed in the answer to these much larger questions.

✅ CHAPTER REVIEW

- What is curriculum? Why teach *this* and not *that*?

The total curriculum (that is, the "stuff" that gets taught in school) comprises both the official curriculum, which is planned course content, as well as the hidden curriculum, which involves all the messages that students receive about their education. Debates over the structure of curriculum and a teacher's ability to affect it have been ongoing for many years. The Tyler rationale is a model that outlines the overall objectives of curriculum development and looks beyond simply planning and executing lessons to the educational purposes and subsequent evaluation. Primarily four schools of thought (humanists, developmentalists, social efficiency educators, and social meliorists) have and continue to dominate the discussion of curriculum in the United States.

- What does the Common Core mean for today's teachers?

Although the emergence of the Common Core State Standards has been the subject of great controversy, teachers in 45 of the 50 states are currently expected to implement the standards in their classrooms. Even as some teachers oppose the standards, other teachers embrace them, finding in the Common Core a new level of freedom to design their own ways of implementing the day-to-day curriculum and agreeing with the underlying goals of higher levels of reading and writing, greater attention to the use of evidence in making an argument, and higher-order thinking skills in mathematics that lead students to a much deeper understanding of mathematical formulas used to solve real-world problems.

- What are some of the current debates about multicultural education?

Multicultural education has many advocates (who often disagree with each other) as well as many opponents (who likewise disagree). Often referred to as the "father of multicultural education," James Banks outlined critical areas that must be given attention in any effective program of multicultural education: (1) content integration, (2) the knowledge construction process, (3) prejudice reduction, (4) an equity pedagogy, and (5) an empowering school culture. Critics of multicultural education cite a variety of concerns, including loss of students' perceived national identity, issues with a "value-free" education, and unfair expectation on teachers to learn and address a plethora of cultural nuances.

- How do different curricula reflect different views of the purpose of education?

Pinar's assertion that the debates regarding curriculum are really debates about identity comes full circle when we review the various philosophies of curriculum, such as Hirsch's core knowledge curriculum, which contends that curriculum must start with a specific body of knowledge that all should be expected to learn. However, Hirsch's critics claim that such an approach limits the cultural perspectives and the range of ideas that might arise and be discussed in the classroom. These types of debates—about identity, perspectives, and knowledge—are central to the ongoing standards and curriculum discussion.

Readings

What Does the Common Core Mean for Today's Teachers?

From THE COMMON CORE STATE STANDARDS, 2012

AUTHOR: THE JAMES B. HUNT INSTITUTE FOR EDUCATIONAL LEADERSHIP AND POLICY

James B. Hunt was the Democratic governor of North Carolina from 1973 to 1977 and again from 1993 to 2001. During his tenure in office, he became known as the "education governor" and possibly the most respected leader in the field among both his Democratic and Republican peers. After leaving office, he established the Hunt Institute to help other governors and policy leaders understand the complex reality facing them as leaders. Beginning in 2006, the Hunt Institute played a key role in uniting the players who eventually developed and endorsed the development of a Common Core State Standards. Many governors and chief state school officers were concerned that state standards seemed to be developed in a haphazard way and that state achievement data had little meaning when compared with another state. In response, the Hunt Institute commissioned a study of state standards and the result was that both the National Governors Association and the Council of Chief State School Officers then created a process by which the new Common Core State Standards were developed in 2009.

Why Common Standards?

When the Council of Chief State School Officers and National Governors Association joined together to lead a voluntary effort by states to create common standards, they had the following goals:

- Prepare all students for a 21st century economy, with increasing global competition, that requires more skills and knowledge;
- Reduce the large numbers of high school graduates entering postsecondary education unable to handle the demands of credit-bearing courses, and improve the ability of high school graduates to meet basic entry-level job skills requirements;
- Address the impact of family mobility's effect on students, as they encounter highly varied academic expectations between states; and
- Promote economies of scale and efficiencies so states can make better use of limited resources to better direct them to improving student achievement.

Common Core State Standards in English Language Arts and Literacy in Science, History/Social Studies, and Technical Subjects, 2012

How Are Common Core State Standards Different?

The English Language Arts Common Core State Standards (ELA CCSS) are based on a **large body of evidence** *including the most current scholarly research, surveys on what skills are required of students entering college and workforce training programs, assessment data identifying college—and career—readiness, and comparisons to standards from high-performing states and nations. The ELA CCSS also build on the firm foundation of the NAEP [National Assessment of Educational Progress] frameworks in reading and writing, which similarly draw on an extensive body of scholarly research and evidence. By focusing on the most essential elements of readiness for college and career, teachers and students will spend their time and efforts on the skills required to prepare for postsecondary success.*

Highlights of the CCSS ELA and Literacy in Other Subjects

- Greater focus on text complexity. The texts students are reading today are not of sufficient complexity and rigor to prepare them for the literacy demands of college and the workforce. The ELA CCSS devote as much attention to the complexity of what students read as to how well students read them. As students advance through the grades, they must develop more sophisticated comprehension skills and apply them to increasingly complex texts.
- Shared responsibility for students' literacy development. Most college and career reading consists of sophisticated, informational text in a variety of content areas. The ELA CCSS include a significant focus on informational text in grades 6–12 and a special section designed for history/social studies and science teachers to address content literacy in their respective disciplines. This focus is in addition to, not in place of, literary texts.
- A focus on writing to argue or explain in the later grades. The ELA CCSS include developing writing skills in three areas: argument, information/explanation, and narrative. As students progress toward high school–level work, the emphasis shifts to increasingly greater focus on writing to argue, inform, and explain by using evidence from sources (corresponding to the shift in emphasis found in NAEP).
- Research and media skills integrated into the CCSS as a whole. In college and the workforce, students will need to research information and will also consume and produce media. Media is embedded throughout the ELA CCSS rather than being treated as a separate section—and students are expected to research and utilize media in all content areas.
- Recognition that both content and skills are important. The ELA CCSS require certain critical content for all students, including classic myths and stories from around the world, America's Founding Documents, foundational American literature, and Shakespeare. Appropriately, the remaining crucial decisions about what content should be taught are left to state and local determination. In addition to content coverage, the ELA CCSS require that students systematically acquire knowledge in literature and other disciplines through reading, writing, speaking, and listening.

Key Instructional Shifts in ELA and Literacy

English Language Arts instruction will have to change as the ELA CCSS are implemented to meet more rigorous expectations:

Building knowledge through content rich informational text—Nonfiction, informational texts often contain unfamiliar vocabulary and help students build background knowledge in the content areas. In elementary grades, there should be a 50/50 balance between literature and informational texts (far more than what children currently encounter in most classrooms). This shift allows elementary school teachers to develop students' literacy skills through other content areas including science, history, social studies, and the arts. As students move through middle school and into high school, the balance should change and become tilted towards nonfiction/informational texts as the ELA CCSS expect teachers in the content areas to develop students' content literacy skills by requiring reading and writing. English classes will remain primarily focused on literature and poetry, though students should also be exposed to nonfiction.

Reading and writing grounded in evidence—As students develop their literacy skills in English and other content areas, they should be asked to read closely and answer questions that are entirely dependent upon the text. Similarly, the majority of student writing assignments should require students to respond to prompts about the texts so that they can demonstrate their understanding using evidence from the text to support their writing. New assessments will also require students to answer text dependent questions and write to inform, explain, or persuade.

Regular practice with complex text and academic vocabulary—The reading level of many students today is too low and there is a huge gap between the complexity of what they are reading in high school and the expectations of college and the work place. The ELA CCSS require an increase in text complexity as students progress from K to 12. A detailed explanation of text complexity can be found in Appendix A of the ELA CCSS: http://www.corestandards.org/assets/Appendix_A.pdf.

Because there are significant changes in the expectations contained in the ELA CCSS, educators will need to revise curriculum and identify instructional materials aligned with the new standards. They will also need time to collaborate and opportunities for professional learning to support the transition required to help *all students* master the ELA CCSS and literacy in the other content areas. Common standards allow educators throughout the country to learn from and share best practices with one another.

Common Core State Standards in Mathematics

How Are Common Core State Standards Different?

The Common Core State Standards in Mathematics (CCSSM) are a breakthrough in focus and coherence and articulate a progression of learning that deepens a student's ability to understand and use mathematics. The CCSSM are informed by a large body of evidence—including the *latest scholarly research, surveys on what skills are required of students entering college and workforce training programs, assessment data identifying college—and career—readiness, and comparisons to standards from high-performing states and nations.* Notable in the research base are conclusions from the Trends in International Mathematics and Science Study (TIMSS), and from studies of high-performing countries, that the traditional U.S. mathematics curriculum must become substantially more coherent and focused. *The CCSSM addresses the problem of a "mile wide and an inch deep" curriculum that has plagued many states for years.* See the research of Dr. William Schmidt: http://www.edweek.org/ew/articles/2012/07/18/36schmidt.h31.html?qs=william+schmidt

Highlights of the CCSSM

- *Focus as seen in high performing countries.* In the past, many teachers rushed through material in an effort to cover a broad swath of topics at every grade. As a result, students learned enough to get by on the next test, but did not engage in deep learning or understanding. Teachers then spent significant time reviewing concepts again the following year. The CCSSM focus on critical elements for future learning and application, giving students enough time at each grade level to develop the procedural fluency and conceptual understanding that are needed to truly master mathematical concepts. *By limiting the topics addressed in each grade, teachers will have more time to teach for understanding.*

- *A solid foundation in whole numbers, addition, subtraction, multiplication, division, fractions, and decimals.* Taken together, these elements support a student's ability to learn and apply more demanding math concepts and procedures that follow in the upper grades. The CCSSM devote attention to these building blocks, aligning with practices of high-performing countries and the recommendations of our own National Research Council's Early Math Panel report. For example, kindergarten expectations are focused on the *number core*: learning how numbers correspond to quantities, and learning how to put numbers together and take them apart, which lays the foundation for the addition and subtraction skills found in the first-grade Math Standards. This logical progression of concepts and skills continues through 8th grade.

- *Middle school preparation for algebra.* The CCSSM for middle school are robust and provide a coherent and rich preparation for high school mathematics. By including the prerequisites for Algebra 1 in grades K–7, students who master the K–7 standards can move to Algebra 1 in 8th grade. At the same time, grade 8 standards are also included and provide students the opportunity to further develop pre-Algebra skills and prepare for rigorous Algebra in high school. Both paths are available and allow states and local districts to determine course projections and *what is best for individual students.*

- *Application to the real world.* In middle and high school, the CCSSM call on students to practice applying mathematical thinking to real world issues and challenges; they prepare students to think and reason mathematically. The CCSSM set a rigorous definition of college and career readiness, not by piling topic upon topic, but by demanding that students develop a depth of understanding and ability to apply mathematics to novel situations, as college students and employees regularly do.

- *Emphasis on mathematical modeling.* The CCSSM require middle and high school students to use mathematics and statistics to analyze problems, understand them better, and improve decision making. As students choose and use appropriate strategies to solve problems, they develop a better sense of quantities and their relationships in physical, economic, public policy, social, and everyday situations. Students are encouraged to use technology, allowing them to vary assumptions, explore consequences, and compare predictions with data.

Key Instructional Shifts in Mathematics

Mathematics instruction will have to change as the CCSSM are implemented to fulfill the requirements of greater focus, coherence and attention to rigor:

Focus—Teachers will focus on a limited number of topics at each grade level allowing students to develop deep content understanding rather than memorizing procedures and formulas, such as fewer topics each year in greater depth.

Coherence—Teachers connect math concepts *within* and *across* grades following the learning progressions defined in the standards and build new understanding onto previously built foundations, helping students to see that math makes sense.

Rigor—With equal intensity, teachers focus on helping students develop *deep conceptual understanding, procedural skill and fluency* (including accuracy in arithmetic computations) and the *application of math skills in complex problem solving*. Since the cognitive demand of some of the standards has changed and concepts previously taught may now appear in different grade levels, educators will need to revise curriculum and identify instructional materials that align with the CCSSM. They will also need time to collaborate and opportunities for professional learning to support the transition required to teach the CCSSM. Common standards allow educators from throughout the country to learn from and share best practices with one another.

Questions

1. How might a classroom organized around the Common Core State Standards differ from the one you attended? Would it?
2. At this point in your review of the standards, do you think they would improve classroom instruction? Hurt it? Make little difference?

Source: The James B. Hunt Institute for Educational Leadership and Policy. "The Common Core State Standards."

Does a Multicultural Education Improve the Curriculum?

From *AFFIRMING DIVERSITY : THE SOCIOPOLITICAL CONTEXT OF MULTICULTURAL EDUCATION*

AUTHOR: SONIA NIETO

In this selection, Sonia Nieto, from the University of Massachusetts at Amherst, provides a clear definition and a compelling case for the importance of multicultural education based on both her scholarly research and her personal autobiography.

Multicultural education cannot be understood in a vacuum but rather must be seen in its personal, social, historical, and political context. Assuming that multicultural education is "the answer" to school failure is simplistic at best, for it overlooks important social and educational issues that affect the daily lives of students. Educational failure is too complex and knotty an issue to be "fixed" by any single program or approach. However, if broadly conceptualized and implemented, multicultural education can have a substantive and positive impact on the educational experience of most students. That is the thesis of this book.

I have come to this understanding as a result of many experiences, including my childhood and my life as a student, teacher, researcher, and parent. As a young child growing up in Brooklyn, New York, during the 1940s, I was able to experience firsthand the influence that poverty, discrimination, and the perception of one's culture and language as inferior can have. Speaking only Spanish when I entered the first grade, I was immediately confronted with the arduous task of learning a second language while my already quite developed native language was all but ignored. Some forty years later, I still recall the frustration of groping for words I did not know to express thoughts I could very capably say in Spanish. Equally vivid are memories of some teachers' expectations that because of our language and cultural differences, my classmates and I would not do well in school. This explains my fourth-grade teacher's response when mine was the only hand to go up when she asked if anybody in the class wanted to go to college. "Well, that's O.K." she said, "because we always need people to clean toilets."

I also recall teachers' perceptions that there was something wrong with speaking a language other than English. "Is there anybody in this class who started school without speaking English?" my tenth-grade homeroom teacher asked loudly, filling out one of the endless forms that teachers are handed by the central office. By this time, my family had moved to what was at the time a working-class and primarily European American neighborhood. My classmates looked in hushed silence as I, the only Puerto Rican in the class, raised my hand timidly. "Are you in a special English class?" he asked in front of the entire class. "Yes," I said, "I'm in Honors English." Although there is nothing wrong with being in a special class for English as a second language (ESL), I felt fortunate that I was able to respond in this way. I had learned to feel somewhat ashamed of speaking Spanish and wanted to make it very clear that I was intelligent in spite of it. Many students in similar circumstances who are in bilingual and ESL classes feel guilty and inferior to their peers.

Those first experiences with society's responses to cultural differences did not, of course, convince me that something was wrong with the responses. Rather, I assumed, as many of my peers did, that there was something wrong with us. We learned to feel ashamed of who we were, how we spoke, what we ate, and everything else that was "different" about us. "Please," I would beg my mother, "make us hamburgers and hot dogs for dinner." Luckily, she never paid attention and kept right on cooking rice, beans, platanos, and all those other good foods that we grew up with. She and my father also continued speaking Spanish to us, in spite of our teachers' pleas to speak to us only in English. And so, alongside the messages at school and in the streets that being Puerto Rican was not something to be proud of, we learned to keep on being who we were. As the case studies point out, these conflicting messages are still being given to many young people.

Immigration is not a phenomenon of the past. In fact, the experience of immigration is still fresh in the minds of a great many people in our country. It is an experience that begins anew every day that planes land, ships reach our shores, and people make their way on foot to our borders. Many of the students in our schools, even if they themselves are not immigrants, have parents or grandparents who were. The United States is thus not only a nation of immigrants as seen in some idealized and romanticized past; it is also a living nation of immigrants even today.

The pain and alienation of the immigrant experience, however, have rarely been confronted in our schools. This experience includes the forced immigration of enslaved Africans and the colonization of American Indians and Mexicans from within. Because schools have traditionally perceived their role to be that of an assimilating agent, the isolation and rejection that come hand in hand with immigration and colonization have simply been left at the schoolhouse door. Curriculum and pedagogy, rather than using the lived experiences of students as a foundation, have been based on what can be described as an alien and imposed reality. The rich experiences of millions of our students, their parents, grandparents, and neighbors have been kept strangely quiet. Although we almost all have an immigrant past, very few of us know or even acknowledge it.

What the research reported in this book suggests to me is that we need to make this history visible by making it part of the curriculum, instruction, and educational experience in general. Whether through the words of Manuel, who claims that he cannot be an American because it would mean forsaking his Cape Verdean background, or those of Vanessa, who knows nothing about her European American past and even feels uncomfortable discussing it, it has become clear that the immigrant experience is an important point of departure for beginning our journey into multicultural education. This journey needs to begin with teachers, who themselves are frequently unaware of or uncomfortable with their own ethnicity. By going through a process of reeducation about their own backgrounds, their families' pain, and their rich legacy of stories, teachers can lay the groundwork for students to reclaim their own histories and voices.

As an adult, I have come to the conclusion that no child should have to go through the painful dilemma of choosing between family and school and of what inevitably becomes a choice between belonging and succeeding. The costs for going through such an experience are high indeed, from becoming a "cultural schizophrenic" to developing doubts about one's self-worth and dignity.

Some Assumptions

It is necessary to clarify a number of assumptions embedded in the text. The first concerns who is included in multicultural education. My perspective is that multicultural education is for everyone regardless of ethnicity, race, language, social class, religion, gender or sexual preference. My framework for multicultural education is thus a very broad and inclusive one. Nevertheless, although I refer in the text to many kinds of differences, I am particularly concerned with race, ethnicity, and language. These are the major issues that provide a lens through which I view multicultural education. This perspective is probably based on a number of reasons, not the least of which is my own experience. Another reason concerns the very history of multicultural education. A direct outgrowth of the civil rights movement, multicultural and bilingual education was developed as a response to inequality in education based on racism, ethnocentrism, and language discrimination. Although I believe it is imperative to include other differences, for me it is necessary to approach an understanding of multicultural education with a firm grounding in these three areas.

This brings up another dilemma related to inclusion. It is easier for some educators to embrace a very inclusive and comprehensive framework of multicultural education because they have a hard time facing racism. They may prefer to deal with issues of class, exceptionality, or religious diversity because, for them, these factors may be easier to confront. Racism is an excruciatingly difficult issue for most of us. Given our history of exclusion and discrimination, this is not surprising. Nevertheless, I believe it is only through a thorough investigation of discrimination based on race and other differences related to it that we can understand the genesis as well as the rationale for multicultural education. I will also refer to gender, social class, and exceptionality because these areas provide other important lenses with which to view inequality in education. However, because no one book can possibly give all of these issues the central importance they deserve, I have chosen to focus on race, ethnicity, and language.

Another assumption that guides this book is that teachers should not be singled out as the villains in the failure of so many students. Although some teachers do indeed bear the responsibility for having low expectations, being racist and elitist in their interactions with students and parents, and providing educational environments that discourage many students from learning, most do not do so consciously. Most teachers are sincerely concerned about their students and want very much to provide the best education they can. Nevertheless, they are often at the mercy of decisions made by others far removed from the classroom. In addition, they have little to do with developing the policies and practices in operation in their schools and frequently do not even question them.

Teachers are also the products of educational systems that have a history of racism, exclusion, and debilitating pedagogy. As such, they put into practice what they themselves have been subjected to and thus perpetuate structures that may be harmful to many of their students. Furthermore, the disempowerment felt by so many teachers is a palpable force in many schools. Finally, schools cannot be separated from communities or from our society in general. Oppressive forces that limit opportunities in the schools are a reflection of such forces in the society at large. Thus, the purpose of this book is not to point a finger but to provide a forum for reflection and discussion so that teachers take responsibility for their actions, challenge the actions of schools and society that affect their students' education, and help effect positive change.

Questions

1. Nieto clearly places her commitment to multicultural education in her own experience growing up as an immigrant child in New York City. To what degree can you identify with Nieto's experiences? To what degree are your views of multicultural education based on your own experience growing up?
2. Nieto answers the question "Who is included in multicultural education?" with a clear answer: "Everyone." Do you agree? Are European Americans multicultural? Why or why not?
3. Given his critique of multicultural education included in the chapter, what might Arthur M. Schlesinger, Jr., say in response to Nieto's essay?

Source: Sonia Nieto and Patty Bode. *Affirming Diversity: The Sociopolitical Context of Multicultural Education,* sixth edition. Upper Saddle River, NJ: Pearson, 2012.

How Do Different Curricula Reflect Different Views of the Purpose of Education?

The two authors whose work is presented here—E. D. Hirsh, Jr., and Bob Peterson—could not differ more radically in their answer to the question "What should schools teach?" and by extension "How should they teach it?" You must dig further, however, to find the differences and similarities in their answer to the question Pinar asks about the core identity (for individuals and a nation) embedded in their different approaches to the curriculum. It is important to read these two articles with reference to each other. Although Hirsch and Peterson hardly represent all of the many different perspectives on curriculum, viewing these two articles as a debate about two different philosophies of education is an invitation to join the debate yourself.

From "THE CORE KNOWLEDGE CURRICULUM : WHAT'S BEHIND ITS SUCCESS?"
AUTHOR: E. D. HIRSCH, JR.

E. D. Hirsch, Jr., is one of the most well-known curriculum reformers in the United States today. With the publication of his 1987 book Cultural Literacy: What Every American Needs to Know, *Hirsch in a dramatic way joined the battles about what schools should teach. In that and subsequent books, and in the work of the Core Knowledge Foundation, which Hirsch founded, he advocates forcefully that there is a core knowledge—a common set of information—that every American should know. Some people agree with Hirsch, some disagree, but few can ignore his ideas and their impact on schools.*

The Mohegan School, in the South Bronx, is surrounded by the evidence of urban blight: trash, abandoned cars, crack houses. The students, mostly Latino or African American, all qualify for free lunch. This public school is located in the innermost inner city.

Mohegan's talented principal, Jeffrey Litt, wrote to me that "the richness of the curriculum is of particular importance" to his students because their educational experience, like that of "most poverty-stricken and educationally underserved students, was limited to remedial activities." Since adopting the Core Knowledge curriculum, however, Mohegan's students are engaged in the integrated and coherent topics like: Ancient Egypt, Greece, and Rome; the Industrial Revolution; limericks, haiku, and poetry; Rembrandt, Monet, and Michelangelo; Beethoven and Mozart; the Underground Railroad; the Trail of Tears; *Brown v. Board of Education*; the Mexican Revolution; photosynthesis; medieval African empires; the Bill of Rights; eco-systems; women's suffrage; the Harlem Renaissance—and many more.

The Philosophy Behind Core Knowledge

In addition to offering compelling subject matter, the Core Knowledge guidelines for elementary schools are far more specific than those issued by most school districts. Instead of vague outcomes such as "First graders will be introduced to map skills," the geography section of the *Core Knowledge Sequence* specifies that first graders will learn the meaning of "east," "west," "north," and "south" and locate on a map the equator, the Atlantic and Pacific Oceans, the seven continents, the United States, Mexico, Canada, and Central America.

Our aim in providing specific grade-by-grade guidelines—developed after several years of research, consultation, consensus-building, and field-testing—is *not* to claim that the content we recommend is better than some other well-thought-out core. No specific guidelines could plausibly claim to be the Platonic ideal. But one must make a start. To get beyond the talking stage, we created the best specific guidelines we could.

Nor is it our aim to specify everything that American schoolchildren should learn (the Core Knowledge guidelines are meant to constitute about 50 percent of a school's curriculum, thus leaving the other half to be tailored to a district, school, or classroom). Rather, our point is that a core of shared knowledge, grade by grade, is needed to achieve excellence and fairness in elementary education.

International studies have shown that *any* school that puts into practice a similarly challenging and specific program will provide a more effective and fair education than one that lacks such commonality of content in each grade. High-performing systems such as those in France, Sweden, Japan, and West Germany bear out this principle. It was our intent to test whether in rural, urban, and suburban settings of the United States we would find what other nations have already discovered.

Certainly the finding that a school-wide core sequence greatly enhances achievement *for all* is supported at the Mohegan School. Disciplinary problems there are down; teacher and student attendance are up, as are scores on standardized tests. Some of the teachers have even transferred their own children to the school, and some parents have taken their children out of private schools to send them to Mohegan. Similar results are being reported at some 65 schools across the nation that are taking steps to integrate the Core Knowledge guidelines into their curriculums.

In the broadcast feature about the Mohegan School, I was especially interested to hear fifth grade teacher Evelyn Hernandez say that Core Knowledge "tremendously increased the students' ability to question." In other words, based on that teacher's classroom experience, *a coherent approach to specific content enhances students' critical thinking and higher-order thinking skills.*

I emphasize this point because a standard objection to teaching specific content is that critical thinking suffers when a teacher emphasizes "mere information." Yet Core Knowledge teachers across the nation report that a coherent focus on content leads to higher-order thinking skills more securely than any other approach they know, including attempts to inculcate such skills directly. As an added benefit, children acquire knowledge that they will find useful not just in next year's classroom but for the rest of their lives.

Why Core Knowledge Works

Here are some of the research findings that explain the correlation between a coherent, specific approach to knowledge and the development of higher-order skills.

Learning can be fun, but is nonetheless cumulative and sometimes arduous. The dream of inventing methods to streamline the time-consuming activity of learning is as old as the hills. In antiquity it was already an old story. Proclus records an anecdote about an encounter between Euclid the inventor of geometry, and King Ptolemy I of Egypt (276–196 B.C.), who was impatiently trying to follow Euclid's *Elements* step by laborious step. Exasperated, the king demanded a faster, easier way to learn geometry—to which Euclid gave the famous, and still true, reply: "There is no royal road to geometry." . . .

Because modern classrooms cannot effectively deliver completely individualized instruction, effective education requires grade-by-grade shared knowledge. When an individual child "gets" what is being taught in a classroom, it is like someone understands a joke. A click occurs. If you have the requisite background knowledge, you will get the joke, but if you don't, you will remain puzzled until somebody explains the knowledge that was taken for granted. Similarly, a classroom of 25 to 35 children can move forward as a group only when *all* the children have the knowledge that is necessary to "getting" the next step in learning. . . .

Just as learning is cumulative, so are learning deficits. As they begin first grade, American students are not far behind beginners in other developed nations. But as they progress, their achievement falls farther and farther behind. This widening gap is the subject of one of the most important recent books on American education, *The Learning Gap* by Stevenson and Stigler.

This progressively widening gap closely parallels what happens *within* American elementary schools between advantaged and disadvantaged children. As the two groups progress from grades 1–6, the achievement gap grows ever larger and is almost never overcome. The reasons for the parallels between the two kinds of gaps—the learning gap and the fairness gap—are similar.

In both cases, the widening gap represents the cumulative effective of learning deficits. Although a few talented and motivated children may overcome this ever-increasing handicap, most do not. The rift grows ever wider in adult life. The basic causes of this permanent deficit, apart from motivational ones, are cognitive. Learning builds upon learning in cumulative ways, and lack of learning in the early grades usually has, in comparative terms, a negatively cumulative effect. . . .

High academic skill is based upon broad general knowledge. Someone once asked Boris Goldovsky how he could play the piano so brilliantly with such small hands. His memorable reply was: "Where in the world did you get the idea that we play the piano with our hands?"

It's the same with reading: we don't read just with our eyes. By seventh grade, according to the epoch-making research of Thomas Sticht, most children, even those who read badly, have already attained the purely technical proficiency they need. Their reading and their listening show the same rate and level of comprehension; thus the mechanics of reading are not the limiting factor. What is mainly lacking in poor readers is a broad, ready vocabulary. But broad vocabulary means broad knowledge, because to know a lot of words you have to know a lot of things. Thus, broad general knowledge is an essential requisite to superior reading skill and indirectly related to the skills that accompany it.

Superior reading skill is known to be highly correlated with most other academic skills, including the ability to write well, learn rapidly, solve problems, and think critically. To concentrate on reading is therefore to focus implicitly on a whole range of educational issues.

It is sometimes claimed (but not backed up with research) that knowledge changes so rapidly in our fast-changing world that we need not get bogged down with "mere information." A corollary to the argument is that because information quickly becomes obsolete, it is more important to learn "accessing" skills (how to look things up or how to use a calculator) than to learn "mere facts." . . .

In fact, the opposite inference should be drawn from our fast-changing world. The fundamentals of science change very slowly; those of elementary math hardly at all. The famous names of geography and history (the "leaves" of that knowledge tree) change faster, but not root and branch from year to year. A wide range of this stable, fundamental knowledge is the key to rapid adaptation and the learning of new skills. It is precisely *because* the needs of a modern economy are so changeable that one needs broad general knowledge in order to flourish. Only high literacy (which implies broad general knowledge) provides the flexibility to learn new things fast. The only known route to broad general knowledge for all is for a nation's schools to provide all students with a substantial, solid core of knowledge.

Common content leads to higher school morale, as well as better teaching and learning. At every Core Knowledge school, a sense of community and common purpose have knit people together. Clear content guidelines have encouraged those who teach at the same grade level to collaborate in creating effective lesson plans and schoolwide activities. Similarly, a clear sense of purpose has encouraged cooperation among grades as well. Because the *Core Knowledge Sequence* makes no requirements about *how* the specified knowledge should be presented, individual schools and teachers have great scope for independence and creativity. Site-based governance is the order of the day at Core Knowledge schools—but with definite aims, and thus a clear sense of communal purpose.

The Myth of the Existing Curriculum

Much of the public currently assumes that each elementary school already follows a schoolwide curriculum. Yet frustrated parents continually write the Core Knowledge Foundation to complain that principals are not able to tell them with any explicitness what their child will be learning during the year. Memorably, a mother of identical twins wrote that because her children had been placed in different classrooms, they were learning completely different things.

Such curricular incoherence, typical of elementary education in the United States today, places enormous burdens on teachers. Because they must cope with such diversity of preparation at each subsequent grade level, teachers find it almost impossible to create learning communities in their classrooms. Stevenson and Stigler rightly conclude that the most significant diversity faced by our schools is *not* cultural diversity but, rather, diversity of academic preparation. To achieve excellence and fairness for all, an elementary school must follow a coherent sequence of solid, specific content.

Questions

1. What does E. D. Hirsch, Jr., believe to be the most basic things that every child in the United States needs to know? Do you agree?
2. Reflect on the schools you attended and any in which you have observed. Do you think they have a core curriculum, either that proposed by Hirsch or another? Or are they examples of places Hirsch describes as having only a "mythical curriculum?"
3. If the elementary school you attended became a Core Knowledge school, would it be better or worse than it was when you were there?

Source: E. D. Hirsch. "The Core Knowledge Curriculum: What's Behind Its Success?" *Educational Leadership* 50, no. 8 (1993): 22–30.

From "WHAT SHOULD CHILDREN LEARN? A TEACHER LOOKS AT E. D. HIRSCH"
AUTHOR: BOB PETERSON

Bob Peterson is a longtime elementary school teacher who teaches a bilingual fifth-grade class at La Escuela Fratney in Milwaukee, Wisconsin. He is also an editor of and regular contributor to the education journal Rethinking Schools, *in which this piece appeared originally.*

Hirsch's "cultural literacy" project is problematic on a number of levels. First, Hirsch misdiagnoses what ails American education, arguing that a lack of emphasis on "content" has left our children "culturally illiterate." Second, he defines knowledge in a way that equates learning with memorizing and teaching with the transmission of information. Third, his definition of "core knowledge" attempts to institutionalize a curriculum that focuses almost exclusively on contributions and perspectives of mainstream European Americans—albeit with a slight nod toward a more multicultural perspective. In this regard, he is smart enough to try to co-opt what he can't defeat.

Hirsch also makes some valuable points, however. He raises the issue of unequal access to knowledge and literature in our stratified society. And he argues that schools have a responsibility to ensure that all members of society have sufficient "intergenerational" knowledge so they can participate in the economic and political affairs of our nation. That his solution to these problems is off base does not negate the validity of this concern for equity.

Hirsch's Growing Popularity

E. D. Hirsch is a professor of English at the University of Virginia. His big splash on the educational scene came in 1987 with the publication of *Cultural Literacy: What Every American Needs to Know*. Combining theoretical analysis with entertaining anecdotes about illiteracy and a list of 5,000 things that "culturally literate" Americans need to know, Hirsch's book climbed to the top of the *New York Times* best-selling list. . . .

In critiquing Hirsch, it is essential to note that the debate over his views is part of a broader controversy in American society sparked by shifting demographics, the civil rights and feminist movements, increased immigration by people of color, and the changing global economy and rising prominence of Asia, Africa, and Latin America. As historian Ronald Takaki, author of *A Different Mirror*, has noted: "What is fueling this debate over our national identity and the content of our curriculum is America's intensifying racial crisis."

In response, Hirsch, [Allan] Bloom, [William] Bennett, and others have "attempted to create an ideological consensus around the return to traditional knowledge," according to Michael Apple, University of Wisconsin professor of education. They believe that the "'great books' and 'great ideas' of the 'Western tradition' will preserve democracy . . . increase student achievement and discipline, increase our international competitiveness, and ultimately reduce unemployment and poverty."

This "return to tradition" perspective contrasts sharply with those who in recent decades have pushed for a more inclusive definition of American culture and school curriculum. For instance, Theresa Perry and James W. Fraser point out in their book *Freedom's Plow: Teaching in the Multicultural Classroom*, "If there is to be democracy in the 21st century, it must be multiracial/multicultural democracy. . . . The debate is about the United States of America, and what its definitive values and identity will be in the next century."

The debate over Hirsch, then, is about far more than culture and education; it strikes at the core of our vision of this country's future. The irony is that Hirsch, in his attempt to define the twenty-first century American identity, relies on educational methods and content that dominated the nineteenth century.

Hirsch and Culture

My criticism of Hirsch's perspective fall into two categories: his definition of "national culture" and his definition of knowledge.

Hirsch writes about a "single national culture" that all literate people share. He argues that middle-class children acquire mainstream literate culture "by daily encounters with other literate persons" and that "disadvantaged" children don't. Schools, he argues, should provide an "antidote to [the] deprivation" of "disadvantaged" children by making "the essential information more readily available." As he writes in *Cultural Literacy*, "We will be able to achieve a just and prosperous society only when our schools ensure that everyone commands enough shared background knowledge to be able to communicate effectively with everyone else."

Hirsch admits that multicultural education is "valuable in itself" but then goes on to add an all-important caveat that it "should not be allowed to supplant or interfere with our schools' responsibility to ensure our children's mastery of American literate culture." Equal access to culture is an undeniably worthwhile concern and Hirsch's care for equity should be commended. But a deeper look at his assumptions and limitations reveals that implementation of his ideas would more likely marginalize instead of enfranchise those students Hirsch says he wishes to help.

There are several related issues here involving complex questions of culture in a changing society. One needs to look not just at Hirsch's rhetoric of concern, but also at his definition of "traditional culture," his neglect of "nonmainstream" cultural histories and traditions, and his dismissal of the need to teach children to think critically.

First of all, what is Hirsch asking children to learn? After reading eight books by Hirsch it is clear that his view of "American literate culture" is overwhelmingly European-American based. Moreover, while he talks about the "classless character of cultural literacy" he virtually ignores the history, tradition, and literature of and about the working class and other marginalized groups and their conflicts with dominant society. He knows better than to dismiss the contributions of women completely, but recognizes them in a way that doesn't question the status quo. . . .

Hirsch and Knowledge

The only conceivable way that a teacher could "cover" the amount of material prescribed by the Core Knowledge Foundation in the suggested time is if one defined learning as superficial acquaintance with "facts"—elevating word recognition to the status of knowledge. Although the *Core Knowledge Sequence* says it is "not a list of facts to be memorized," practical realities will push in that direction.

In analyzing Hirsch's books, it's clear that his definition of knowledge is synonymous with a superficial familiarity with facts and relies on rote memorization and the acquisition of disconnected bits of information. In fact, Hirsch himself admits that his lists will almost certainly lead to "the trivialization of cultural information." Moreover, it is likely that Hirsch's "core knowledge" curriculum might serve as fertile ground for a new crop of standardized tests that rely on "facts" rather than knowledge.

In an age where technological advances have led to what is uniformly acknowledged to be an "information glut," Hirsch stands firmly in a nineteenth century approach and boldly states that "only a few hundred pages of information stand between the literate and illiterate, between dependence and autonomy." And in many cases, Hirsch implies, it's not necessary to understand *why* something is important; one must just know that it *is* important.

When meeting with college-level English teachers from the National Council of Teachers of English and the Modern Language Association in 1987, Hirsch was criticized for the "narrowing of national culture" and the teaching of small bits of information. "A telling moment came when he [Hirsch] said it wasn't so important to read Shakespeare or see performances of the plays themselves—plot summaries or 'Lamb's Tales' would do fine," according to Peter Elbow, a professor of English at the University of Massachusetts at Amherst. Ultimately, Hirsch's emphasis on the transmissions of disconnected facts—what he calls "core knowledge"—directly contrasts with the need for students to think, analyze, critique, and understand their world.

Even if the facts that Hirsch promoted were completely multicultural, his approach would be flawed by his definition of knowledge. Students need more than facts. They need to understand the relationships between "facts" and whose interests certain "facts" serve. They need to question the validity of the "facts," to ask questions such as "why" and "how." They need to know how to find information, to solve problems, to express themselves in oral and written language so their opinions can be shared with, and have an influence on, broader society. It is only through such an approach that students can construct their own beliefs, their own knowledge.

In his sections on the American Revolution and the Constitution, for example, Hirsch essentially dismisses as irrelevant the pro-slavery, antiwoman assumptions of our Founding Fathers. No mention is made that about 40 percent of the delegates to the Constitutional Convention were slave owners, that Washington himself had slaves, and that in 1779 he ordered that U.S. troops launch an expedition against the Iroquois Confederacy and seek the "total destruction and devastation and the capture of as many persons of every age and sex as possible. . . . "

Hirsch and Teaching

Embedded in Hirsch's viewpoint on culture and knowledge is his approach to teaching. First, rather than calling upon students to study less but understand more, he advocates a more-the-merrier approach—regardless of whether children understand what is presented to them. Second, he distorts the relationship between content and skills, criticizing what he claims are current emphases on "mental skills," "learning-to-learn skills," and "critical thinking skills."

On the issue of more versus less, good teaching requires a precarious balance between exposing students to lots of information and studying a few topics in depth. While Hirsch alludes to this balance, ultimately he advocates pumping as much information as possible into students. This stands in sharp contrast to the fine work of many teachers— whether in groups such as the Coalition of Essential Schools or as part of national curriculum groups such as the National Council of Teachers of English—who hold that "less is more" and encourage in-depth projects by students.

The question of content versus skills is a bit more complicated. Hirsch emphasizes content over skills largely on the grounds that students will understand what they read only if they have sufficient "relevant prior knowledge." Likewise, he argues that broader thinking skills also depend on a wealth of "relevant knowledge."

Like any good teacher, Hirsch recognizes that there is an important relationship between content and skills. No good teacher would deny the importance of prior knowledge in the educational process or that adults have important information to share with children. Hirsch, however, distorts this relationship by overemphasizing content to the degree that the teaching of skills all but disappears from the curriculum.

Despite Hirsch's rhetoric of giving children what they need to seek meaning from reading, his prescriptions make it likely that reading will become a mechanical process dependent on calling up what one has memorized. . . . The problem is not that students don't get the "core knowledge" and facts that Hirsch holds dear. Rather, the problem is that they are being bombarded with thousands of bits of disconnected information and rarely write, discuss, or read things that are meaningful to their lives.

For kids in my class who briefly read Hirsch's article on high mountains, or for the hundreds of thousands of others who are daily bombarded with facts either through Hirsch's series or one of several basal programs, the issue is not whether they will be able to recall 50, 500, or even 5,000 core facts. The issue is whether they will be in classrooms where they are respected and challenged—not only to understand the world but to develop the cross-cultural perspectives, critical skills, and moral courage needed to deal with the very racial, gender, class, and ecological problems that their tomorrow will bring.

Questions

1. As you read Peterson's critique of Hirsch, which author's argument did you find most compelling?
2. Peterson criticizes Hirsch in several different ways. You may agree with Peterson on some of these issues and with Hirsch on others. What is your view on the debate about "national culture"? What is your view on the debate about core knowledge? What is your view on the debate about the nature of good teaching?
3. In this article, Peterson says that Hirsch's approach "directly contrasts with the need for students to think, analyze, critique, and understand their world," yet in Hirsch's own piece, he says that his approach is the best one for facilitating just such analysis, critique, and understanding. How do you account for this difference? Which author do you think offers the best way to help students to understand their world?
4. How do you think Hirsch and Peterson would respond to the Common Core, which lays out standards but not a specific curriculum as does Hirsch? Is the argument about the Common Core the same one as is found here or a different one?

Source: Bob Peterson. "What Should Children Learn? A Teacher Looks at E. D. Hirsch." In *Rethinking Schools: An Agenda for Change,* edited by David Levine, Robert Lowe, Bob Peterson, and Rita Tenorio, 74–88. New York: New Press, 1995.

Motivating, Managing, and Assessing
How Will I Teach?

I believe that education, therefore, is a process of living and not a preparation for future living.

JOHN DEWEY

Now that we've examined the diversity of today's students, the insights of learning theory, and the nature of the curriculum, we will focus on how to put it together: on pedagogy. It is one thing to gain a solid intellectual understanding of what social scientists can tell us about today's students, what psychologists can tell us about learning theory, and what curriculum theorists can tell us about curriculum development, but it is quite another thing to pull it all together as an effective teacher of *real* students in a *real* classroom. In this chapter, we discuss various viewpoints on motivating students, keeping a classroom under control, and providing fair and accurate assessment of a student's progress.

All teachers worry about whether their students will be interested in what they have to teach. The first **Reading** for this chapter, from John Dewey's "My Pedagogic Creed," sets the role of teaching in the context of a larger quest for community—in the classroom and ultimately in the larger society. If the teacher can create the kind of community that Dewey describes, issues of student motivation and, indeed, student discipline, simply disappear. While the **Reading** is certainly a romantic picture of what is possible, it reminds all of us in education of our ultimate goals. Most of us as educators would be well served by writing our own 21st century version of our creed.

Whether they call it "control" or "discipline" or "classroom management," new (and not-so-new) teachers are always concerned about keeping order in the classroom, the subject of the second part of this chapter. The second **Reading** comes from a recent article in which a California teacher describes one school's effort to develop a system of restorative justice: Students are given a leading role in setting the tone for appropriate behavior and, through the school's Student Justice Panel, the lead responsibility for developing a response to school problems that will help restore core values, strengthen the sense of community, and build mutual respect so that the number of incidents requiring intervention will decline radically. "Restorative justice" might or might not work for everyone, but many educators see it as a significantly more promising practice than earlier forms of student discipline, especially the zero-tolerance policies that made schools quieter but at the cost of excluding far too many students.

As we discuss the issue of classroom management, we need to face the reality that incidents can and do arise that threaten the community of a classroom and indeed the safety of those within. Whether it's breaking up a fight between students, following school lockdown procedures when a possible threat is anticipated, or recognizing warning signs of a student's potential to harm others, teachers must be prepared to be the first line of defense in ensuring that all students feel safe and secure. In response to the tragic school shooting at Sandy Hook Elementary School in 2013, the short **Reading** by attorney Robert Crabtree asks if more intervention and better special education services might be a factor in avoiding future violent incidents. Crabtree reminds us that large-scale violence, like the more common smaller incidents—from bullying to fist fights to the student who brings a gun to school—all represent parts of a larger social fabric and are not isolated developments. Until we address the social fabric, and build in better support systems, he argues, violent incidents will continue to be all too common.

Finally, the chapter addresses assessment—ways in which individual teachers and higher authorities evaluate students. Assessment has become a loaded topic among teachers in recent years as high-stakes tests have been used to evaluate not only students but also their teachers, often in ways that parents and teachers deem unfair. But high-stakes tests are far from the only means of assessment used in a classroom. Every teacher wonders every day if his or her students are learning what is being taught, whether the kind of understanding that the teacher has in mind is actually happening. Clear and concrete evaluation rubrics are one key to fair and effective evaluation of students, providing information that seems reasonable to students but that is also essential to their teachers. The last **Reading** for the chapter provides a detailed rubric used by one New York City high school. Such rubrics are becoming more common in schools across the country, and being familiar with them is important.

How Will I Motivate My Students?

One of the reasons teaching can be such hard work is that teachers get caught up in the pressure to "cover the curriculum," abandoning their responsibility to make learning interesting and relevant. They worry (often with justification) about how they will be judged, especially by how their students score on certain external tests. They are not always sure how to stay in charge of a classroom full of energetic young people. Teachers sometimes forget that one of their essential responsibilities is to make learning interesting and engaging for their students, to find ways to connect what students must learn to be successful in life with the students' own interests and life experiences *right now*. On one hand, if students are not engaged, there is little chance that much actual learning will take place. On the other, a teacher who feels the need to be a circus performer in order to keep a class interested risks losing the respect of the class and diverting attention from the curriculum to the teacher alone.

Who has not been bored in school? Who has not wondered what the point of a particular lesson might be? Who has not practically (or actually) fallen asleep as a teacher droned on and on about a topic that might have been of interest to the person who developed the curriculum in a faraway state office but that does not seem interesting to the teacher and is obviously of no interest to the students? Happily, this is far from the whole picture. There are magical moments in classrooms when the curriculum, teachers' and students' passion for knowing, and the life experiences on which most real learning builds all come together.

Kristin Conradi, who directs the North Carolina State University Reading Clinic, reminds us that, "The word 'motivation' derives from the Latin word *movere*, which means 'to move.'" As it relates to literacy, for example, we ask, "What moves someone to engage in (and with) literacy?" The same, of course, is true of every subject. What gets a student excited about—and wanting to engage deeply with—literacy, or science, or history, or mathematics? Conradi answers, "It depends. What motivates Karl might be different from what motivates Natasha. What motivates kindergartners will be different from what motivates fourth graders." Motivation varies with a student's prior interests, with their developmental stage, and with the material, from traditional books to the latest technology available.[1]

Teachable Moment
KEEPING IT FRESH

As a teacher, you will have some days when you feel more like an entertainer, tap dancing on your desk to keep your students' attention. If only you could find a way to rap the periodic table or phrase the scientific method like a cleaned-up version of a late-night television joke, then maybe your students would be more interested in what you have to tell them.

Educators Barry Perlman and Lee McCann contend that an effective presentation begins with the teacher's attitude about the material. If you're disinterested in the topic you are teaching, then your students will recognize that quickly and will more than likely adopt an equally unenthusiastic view. So, rather than finding ways to cleverly rhyme "fluorine" and "chlorine" in a sentence, Perlman and McCann recommend you try the following:

- Put yourself in your students' shoes (or desks) as if this is the first time you've heard the material you plan to deliver. What are your expectations of what you'll be hearing? What would "grab" you or confuse you?
- After you have taught for a while, pretend you are teaching today's class for the first time. Remember the excitement, anticipation, satisfaction, appreciation, and revelation you felt when you first taught it.
- Think of ways you can "mix it up" by talking from various areas in the classroom, using visuals including the chalkboard, Microsoft PowerPoint, or video clips, and finding creative ways to physically involve students in the discussion.
- If you were a colleague critiquing your performance in the classroom, what would you advise or think about today's class period? What would be its strengths and weaknesses?

Perlman and McCann also suggest that sometimes to get your "mojo" back, you have to take a quick break. Go outside, even if just to walk around your building for a few minutes. It is amazing how seeing things from a different physical perspective changes your mood. "If you have energy," they say, "you will bring it to your students."

Questions
- Are there certain topics you dread having to teach? Do you have this negative attitude because you don't feel comfortable with the content or how to relay it to students? Are there other reasons?
- Think of a class presentation you sat in this week. Was the instructor genuinely enthusiastic about the material, or did it seem like he or she was just "going through the motions"? Even if the presentation was good, how could the instructor "mix it up" the next time?

Source: Modified from Baron Perlman and Lee I. McCann. *Preparing for a Class Session*. Association for Psychological Science, April 2007.

The problem of making the curriculum interesting and relevant to students and their teachers is not a new one. Well over a century ago, the reform movement known as *progressive education* was born in large part to overcome the terrible boredom experienced in school. Although the movement had many facets, finding better ways to engage students in their school experience was an important goal for many progressives. No one advocated this focus on student interests more than the philosopher John Dewey.

 DID YOU KNOW?

In a National Governors Association survey, 38% of teens aged 16 to 18 said that high school is easy, whereas 6% responded that it is hard. In another survey, one in five high school students said they were not motivated or inspired to work hard. Nearly 70% said that high school expectations are moderate to low.

CONNECTIONS →←

Recall the discussions of progressive education and its impact on the teaching profession in Chapter 1 and of John Dewey's philosophy in Chapter 5.

Throughout a long life, Dewey advocated finding ways to connect what happened in school to the "real life" of students so that they would invest more in their learning and take more away from what happened during the school day. Dewey wanted to change school from being a world where only teachers were active and students were passive (and often bored) and create an educational place in which students and teachers engaged in a mutual effort to understand the world. In his book *Experience and Education*, written much later in his career than the **Reading** for this chapter, Dewey described the difference between what he called traditional education and the progressive education with which his name has long been associated. Traditional education, Dewey said, assumes that "[t]he subject-matter of education consists of bodies of information and of skills that have been worked out in the past; therefore the chief business of the school is to transmit them to the new generation." This basic assumption accounts for much of the structure of schooling, as Dewey observed it a century ago and as many of us observe it today. So, he says, in these traditional schools, "the subject-matter as well as standards of proper conduct are handed down from the past, the attitude of pupils must, upon the whole, be one of docility, receptivity, and obedience."

Progressive education for Dewey had a different starting point. According to Dewey, "The traditional scheme is, in essence, one of imposition from above and from outside. It imposes adult standards, subject matter, and methods upon those who are only growing slowly toward maturity. Consequently, they must be imposed; even though good teachers will use devices of art to cover up the imposition so as to relieve it of obviously brutal features." Such imposition not only leads many students to disengage from school, it also leads more than a few to rebel in ways that undermine the effective management of a class. According to Dewey, the only way for schools to avoid the disconnect and brutality of traditional education is to connect the curriculum with the current interests and experiences of young people.

Many observers have misinterpreted Dewey and other progressive educators to imply that they were opposed to content. In fact, Dewey himself was deeply critical of those who became so focused on the individual child and his or her experience that they forgot that the purpose of schooling was to *teach* that child something that was new and beyond the child's experience. However, Dewey did argue that the only way to teach the new was to connect it to what the student already knew (often based on out-of-school experiences) and on what the student *wanted* to know. Only in this way, he said, could the child come to "own" the knowledge and have it be interesting enough to remember or connected enough to be of use.[2]

A more recent advocate of a progressive approach to schooling, Vito Perrone (1933–2011), had his own list of ways of "teaching for understanding."[3] For Perrone and his colleagues who helped create the Teaching for Understanding approach, the goal is to link the curriculum (what the larger society believes students need to know to be effective in the adult world), with the interests of students as thoughtful individuals (not mere receptacles for knowledge). The word *connected* appears a great deal in the writing of these proponents of Teaching for Understanding. The curriculum needs to be *connected* to the interests of the students. And the assessment system needs to be *connected* to an ongoing feedback loop to students and teachers regarding the depth of their understanding of the issues under consideration. Thus, Perrone calls for schools in which

- the students help select the specific books and articles to read or plays to produce after the teacher has outlined some clear goals.
- the students also have time to think for themselves and decide what Perrone calls "a particular direction" and topic to which they can make a personal commitment based on their own previous interests (often interests from outside of the class).
- teachers believe that they also have something to learn from their students and respect the opinions and experiences of their students, but they also bring their own passions and experiences to the class.
- students gain "expertness" from presenting their work to an audience that will expect high standards and from participating in the world outside of school through letters, service learning, and other work with those beyond the school's walls.

In such classrooms there has to be a lot of flexibility. Teachers need a clear plan, but they also need to be open to where the energy of the class will lead. Perrone concludes, "If we were to act on such understandings, students' experiences in schools would be much different, far more productive." After all, he insists, "It may seem obvious that our teaching should be directed toward understanding, that being able to give back information on a Friday test, too often the typical fare, is not sufficient."[4]

The discussion about Teaching for Understanding or engaging student experience in school life is not an either-or divide. After all, no one advocates "teaching for confusion," and no educators believe the classroom should be a boring place cut off from the larger world or the interests of students. The debates are ones of degree. When does a focus on student interest get in the way of serious attention to things that students *need* to learn to be successful in later schooling or adult life? When does the student's role in defining content get in the way of the teacher's responsibility to bring expert knowledge—his or her own and that of the textbooks—to the class? The same approaches that can at one moment make a classroom come alive can, if used incorrectly, also make it deadly dull. The challenge for every teacher is to be sure that their students' experience is engaging and linked to understanding, the "real world," and academic success.

How Will I Manage My Classroom?

I recently accompanied a group of first-year graduate education students on a visit to a nearby high school. Like most aspiring teachers, they were especially concerned about discipline and classroom management. One of them asked a high school senior at the school we were visiting, "What should a teacher do when a classroom is out of control?" The senior, wise perhaps beyond his years, responded, "No classroom starts out out-of-control." As this clever student was inferring, the key is to create the kind of classroom atmosphere where the "out of control" moment happens rarely, if it is not avoided completely.

Of course, for an aspiring teacher, few issues are more terrifying than the vision of a classroom in which the teacher is no longer in charge. No wonder most aspiring teachers worry a great deal about the question of "How will I control my class?" even when their professors tell them not to. A classroom that is "out of control" is a miserable place for students and teachers. It is also a place where no learning, understanding, or engagement is going on. It is not likely to be a place where many assessments, internal or external, show much progress. Many teacher educators bristle at the question of "control," since the best classrooms are places where students and teachers are deeply engaged in a set of meaningful activities that are so significant in their own right that issues of "control" or "classroom management" disappear. For an aspiring or novice teacher, however, the steps between "out of control" and "deeply engaged" can be mysterious and the fear of not making it to the latter is ever present. The Brazilian educator Paulo Freire describes a scene that may be all too familiar:

> I remember myself as an adolescent, and how much it hurt me to see the disrespect that one of our teachers left himself open to, being the object of abuse by most of the students because he had no way of imposing order on the class. His class was the second of the morning, and already beaten down, he came into the room where the young people with a mean streak waited to punish and mistreat him. On finishing this travesty of the class, he could not turn his back to the students and walk to the door. The boisterous jeers would fall on him, heavy and arresting, and this must have petrified him. From the corner of the room where I sat I saw him, pale, belittled, shrinking toward the door. He would open it quickly and disappear, wrapped in his unsustaining weakness.[5]

Although this particular memory comes from a different generation and a different country, the scene plays itself out in classroom after classroom in every place and time. None of us wants to be the beaten-down teacher whom Freire describes. All of us have probably seen him or her at one time in our lives. Thus, although many progressive educators bristle at the term, a number of scholars have attempted to provide answers to our questions and fears about classroom management and what it means to create the kind of classroom where learning takes place and civility rules.

Zero Tolerance and the School-to-Prison Pipeline

One approach to student discipline that has been widely used in American schools has come to be known as the *zero-tolerance policy*. In response to the concerns of many teachers, parents, and community groups about what seem to be out-of-control classrooms, many school systems—too many, some have said—adopted tough discipline codes that said, essentially, "One strike and you're out." A student who breaks certain rules, who gets into an argument with a teacher, or who threatens a student or teacher is expelled on the spot. In spite of the emerging critique, many schools still follow a zero-tolerance policy.

One advocate of this tough form of classroom management is Lee Canter. Canter's book, *Back to School With Assertive Discipline*, and the Canter Approach have been the basis for many professional development programs and seminars for teachers. Canter starts with some basic assumptions about the central role of discipline, saying, "[Y]ou need to get all of your students on *your* behavior track. Students need to know exactly what is expected of them." Once students know the rules, they must also be taught the consequences of breaking the rules. Students need to be taught to be responsible for their actions and understand that the choice is theirs: to follow the rules of the classroom and enjoy the rewards or to disregard the rules and accept the consequences. It is important to note here that the rewards are at least as important as the punishments and consequences. Canter contends that the "positive reinforcement system is the single most important tool you have to help students shape appropriate behaviors."[6]

Canter's approach may seem similar to that of B. F. Skinner, whose view of how learning can be fostered was discussed in Chapter 5. Like Skinner, Canter believes that the behavior of children can be controlled through the right use of stimuli—the rewards and punishments that Canter discusses. Like Skinner, Canter strongly implies that once students are taught the rules, and especially the positive success that goes with following the rules, most of the rest will be easy. For aspiring teachers, indeed for many veteran teachers, this approach has its appeal, even though the consequences for too many students may be disastrous.

But as with Skinner, many educators are quite critical of Canter and others who seem to adopt a behaviorist approach to discipline. A 2013 press release from the American Civil Liberties Union described student Kyle Thompson as someone who "likes playing football, playing video games, and hanging out with his friends." He had also been under house arrest and barred from school for six months for refusing to let a teacher see a note he had written. As the ACLU reported:

> Kyle is part of a national trend where children are funneled out of public schools and into the juvenile and criminal justice systems. Many of those children have learning disabilities or histories of poverty, abuse or neglect, and would benefit from additional educational and counseling services. Instead, they are isolated, punished and

pushed out. "Zero tolerance" policies criminalize minor infractions of school rules, while cops in school lead to students being criminalized for behavior that should be handled inside the school.

Maintaining classroom order is one thing. Pushing a student out of school is quite another.

Many educators describe the results of the zero-tolerance policies as a school-to-prison pipeline in which failing schools with inadequate resources implement zero-tolerance policies to keep order in a disorderly world. The result is not just suspension or expulsion (which by itself severely disrupts the education of students who, like Kyle, need it the most) but also often leads to school based-arrests, court involvement, and students finding themselves in juvenile or adult detention facilities—a sure road to longer and more severe incarceration in the future.[7]

An exhaustive report sponsored by the Justice Center of the Council of State Governments in 2014 came to similar conclusions:

Research and data on school discipline practices are clear: millions of students are being removed from their class-rooms each year, mostly in middle and high schools, and overwhelmingly for minor misconduct. When suspended these students are at significantly higher risk of falling behind academically, dropping out of school, and coming into contact with the juvenile justice system. A disproportionately large percentage of disciplined students are youth of color, students with disabilities, and youth who identify as lesbian, gay, bisexual, or transgender (LGBT).

The authors of this report make it clear that "There is no question that when students commit serious offenses or pose a threat to school safety they may need to be removed." But they also note that in a thorough national study, the majority of students in the discipline system were there for very minor infractions.[8]

As longtime Oregon teacher Linda Christensen notes, "The school-to-prison pipeline does not just begin with cops in the hallways and zero-tolerance discipline policies. It begins when we fail to create a curriculum and a pedagogy that connects with students, that takes them seriously as intellectuals, that lets students know we care about them, that gives them the chance to channel their pain and defiance in productive ways." If the purpose of schooling is to prepare demo-cratic citizens, isn't it counterproductive to organize classrooms in which the ability to participate in a democratic give and take, and the ability to see teaching and learning as moral callings, are undermined by the structure of the relationships?

None of this is easy. Christensen herself described a moment when she was teaching high school in which what she thought was a good plan turned into a full-fledged student revolt and she "came dangerously close to becoming the teacher who pushes students out of class and into the halls, into the arms of the school dean, and out into the streets." For a novice teacher, the task is an ongoing challenge.[9]

Restorative Justice

As more and more educators worry about the impact of zero tolerance and similar disciplinary policies and the school-to-prison pipeline that can be the result, there has been an active search for alternative policies that maintain order and safety yet also build a more supportive culture within schools, especially schools serving students who may experience more than their share of violence in the world around them outside of school. In this context there are a growing number of advocates of what is known as *restorative justice* as a key to creating a classroom and school climate in which respect replaces fear and a true learning community can be achieved. Certainly the example offered by the Oakland, California, teacher, Trevor Gardner in the **Reading** with this chapter is an example of how restorative justice can make students the leaders in solving problems while creating an atmosphere of fairness and mutual responsibility for appropriate behavior in a school setting.

What is restorative justice? As Gardner describes, it begins with a careful look at a school's core values. If, as was the case at the school he describes, the core values include an ongoing commitment to building a school community in which mutual respect—student to student and student to teacher—and a sense of fairness and justice are at the core, then, and only then, restorative justice might work. There are variations in how the program works. At Gardner's school, a Student Justice Panel of 12 student leaders, nominated by their teachers, is responsible (along with an adult facilitator) for hearing cases brought by students or teachers when an infraction of the rules or a disruption of community life takes place. Their goal is not primarily to punish a student but to restore the community. Thus, in the example he gives of a

Teachable Moment
EQUAL EXPECTATIONS

Being culturally aware is critical to any teacher who wants to have a classroom management style that is fair, equitable, and antiracist. Gloria Ladson-Billings, one of the best-known researchers about effective education, tells the story of observing a classroom of kindergarten and first-grade students. Four children sitting at a table—three White students and one African American student—are working on an assignment to write a sentence that describes their weekend. When asked about what she did on the weekend, the African American girl responds, "Oh, nuttin'." Moments later, she walks away from the table and from the assignment altogether. When the teacher asks the now-wandering student, "Would you like to try writing your sentence today, Shannon?" the student simply shakes her head no. The teacher seems to shrug it off, saying, "That's okay. Maybe you'll feel like writing tomorrow." For Ladson-Billings, this is clearly not okay. The teacher has given the child "permission to fail," when what she desperately needs is a "demand to succeed." There are multiple ways to make the demand, but the demand must be made, for all students, no matter their race, gender, or excuse.

Researchers Pedro A. Noguera and Jean Yonemura Wing tell an equally disturbing story of a different sort. Talking with a recent African American graduate of Berkeley (California) High School, they heard him relay an incident of arriving at class with a friend just after the bell had rung and being told, "You guys gotta be here when the bell rings, you gotta go to OCS [on-campus suspension]. Go." However, as the two African American boys walked to their suspension, two White girls arrived at the same classroom, even later, to be greeted with "Hurry up, hurry up, you're about to miss the assignment." The racism of the encounter was not lost on the student. Noguera and Wing noted,

A closer look at the Berkeley High School discipline system reveals countless stories in which students—the majority of whom are African American—are removed from spaces of learning and placed into spaces of punishment. Their stories reveal an approach to discipline that focuses on separating "bad" kids from "good" kids, while ignoring the racial implications of the practice. Meanwhile, the need to find ways to reengage students with learning, especially those who are most frequently punished, is rarely considered.

In both instances, the racism of the situation was immediately apparent to the outside observer, but not to the teacher. It is difficult to observe one's own actions, especially in times of stress, and yet such self-critique is essential if a teacher is to be effective. Classroom management (or discipline) can easily and with the best of intentions fall into "separating the bad kids from the good kids" on racial or other ethnic or gender lines. Doing so fails to engage students in learning, which is an essential component not only of an effective system of education but also, indeed, of effective discipline itself. It requires a self-reflective educator to manage the process well.

Questions

- If you were Shannon's teacher, or if you were the teacher in the high school in Berkeley, how do you think you would have handled the situation? How would having read this case study affect the way you might handle a future Shannon or a group of high school boys?
- Both Ladson-Billings and Noguera and Wing believe that race had a lot to do with the way the teacher acted in each situation, even though one teacher was especially easy on a student and another was especially tough. What do you think?

Sources: Gloria J. Ladson-Billings. "I Ain't Writin' Nuttin': Permissions to Fail and Demands to Succeed in Urban Classrooms." In *The Skin That We Speak,* edited by Lisa Delpit and Joanne Kilgour Dowdy, 109–110. New York: The New Press, 2002; Pedro Noguera and Jean Yonemura Wing, editors. *Unfinished Business: Closing the Racial Achievement Gap in Our Schools,* 121–2. San Francisco: Jossey-Bass, 2006.

food fight, the outcome is not a suspension or expulsion but rather an assignment of those involved to clean up the mess they created and help the community develop new norms.

In his 2005 essay "'Life Comes From It': Navajo Justice Concepts," Robert Yazzie describes the roots of restorative justice in Navajo justice systems:

> Navajo justice is a sophisticated system of egalitarian relationships, where group solidarity takes the place of force and coercion. . . . There is no precise term for "guilty" in the Navajo language. The word "guilt" implies a moral fault that commands retribution. It is a nonsense word in Navajo law due to the focus on healing, integration with the group, and the end goal of nourishing ongoing relationship with the immediate and extended family, relatives, neighbors, and community.

Of course, importing such a system from a culture in which everyone has operated by such terms for generations to a modern American school is no easy task.[10]

In a recent editorial, the editors of *Rethinking Schools* welcomed restorative justice as a significant step forward from the zero-tolerance policies that resulted in so many school expulsions and simply fueled the school-to-prison pipeline. But they also noted: "Simply announcing a commitment to 'restorative justice' doesn't make it so. Restorative justice doesn't work as an add-on. It requires us to address the roots of student 'misbehavior' and a willingness to rethink and rework our classrooms, schools, and school districts. Meaningful alternatives to punitive approaches take time and trust." These editors concluded that "restorative justice won't work as a Band-Aid when schools are being torn to shreds" by budget cuts, continual reorganizations, and fear of new outside mandates that disrupt school communities. In the end, "there is a strong relationship among curriculum, pedagogy, and restorative practices." With those connections, restorative practices can go a long way toward creating the kind of educational community in which teachers want to teach and students want to learn.[11]

 ## DID YOU KNOW?

The 2014 School Discipline Consensus Report noted that Texas students who were suspended or expelled for a discretionary school violations were nearly three times more likely to have contact with the juvenile justice system in the next year, where they will join the approximately 61,000 youth who are in juvenile justice residential placement facilities on any given day.

Teacher Behaviors in the Classroom

Vito Perrone wrote, "I don't particularly like the terms *classroom management* and *discipline*. . . . *Developing and maintaining productive classrooms* seems more appropriate, more useful as a formulation. It creates a more positive discourse." Nevertheless, Perrone understood the importance of the topic—to the teacher's well-being as well as to the creation of a healthy atmosphere for student learning. Because of the topic's importance, Perrone also spent time discussing it with generations of aspiring teachers whom he has taught. Working with current and future teachers, Perrone and his many collaborators came up with their own list of principles for developing and maintaining productive classrooms:

- **Be well prepared for each day.** Being well prepared starts with having a very clear goal or purpose in mind for each lesson and then being sure that the materials are ready, the technology works, and the class time has been planned out.
- **Use challenging ideas and materials.** It is difficult to maintain students' interest if the ideas under examination (the questions being posed and the materials being used) don't cause students to wonder, or if they make little connection to students' interests and the world.
- **Be reasonably consistent.** While absolute consistency is a false goal, students need to have a reasonably clear sense that the rules of the classroom will not change, that their work will be assessed by the same rules that were used the day before, and that when teacher and student come to an agreement, it will "stick."

- **Be clear about what really matters.** It makes little sense to expend energy lamenting all the things we believe our students should have learned before they ended up with us. If high-quality work matters, then we have to make sure the students know what high-quality work looks like and turn all our efforts toward helping them reach that high-quality work.

- **Show respect for the students.** Students know when they are being respected and seen as persons capable of achieving and being responsible. When students are resistant to teachers and the content, the resistance typically has its base in feelings of disrespect, which leads, not surprisingly, to students' disrespect of teachers.

- **Know the students.** Obviously this means knowing more than the students' names (though that is terribly important). It means knowing their interests, what they care about, the ideas that motivate them, and how they will likely respond to different situations.

- **Be physically present.** Teachers need to be present when their students arrive, greeting them and acknowledging their presence.

Notes from the Field

What advice would you give a new teacher?

"Make sure you are prepared each day to do something. If you do not have a lesson, the students will run all over you. Basically, you need to be able to control a class of students so that their time with you is spent learning. And mean what you say—if you tell someone to sit down or you will write them up, then you better do it. They need to be able to trust your word in all areas."

—Jennifer Seal, high school advanced placement teacher

In the end, Perrone, like any good educator, knows that "[a]ll of us have some difficult days, when things don't go as well as we would like, when we feel discouraged, sometimes angry at the behavior of our students." Teaching is a career that demands we stay resilient, keep coming back to our core values, and keep reminding ourselves that our students do want to learn and that "they desire self-efficacy and respect, and that we must not ever quit on them."[12]

In his book *Lost at School: Why Our Kids With Behavioral Challenges Are Falling Through the Cracks and How We Can Help Them*, Harvard psychologist Ross W. Greene proposes an approach to classroom discipline that he calls *collaborative problem solving*. Greene's approach might be seen as a small-scale version of the restorative justice programs many schools are adopting. But instead of looking to a school-wide organization, Greene begins his approach to student discipline with the assumption that when a student acts out in class, it is for a very simple reason—the student has an unsolved problem and "acting out" (that is, creating a confrontation with the teacher) is a result of that problem. For example, the student may be embarrassed because he or she cannot do a particular assignment. The student may have difficulty getting along with other students. The student (and this is certainly true of many students) may simply find sitting for the required amount of time to be a challenge. Whatever the unsolved problem, Greene says the key to discipline is to develop a collaborative relationship with the young person to *solve* the problem. Threatening punishments or saying that the school has "zero tolerance" will not do anything to improve a situation with a student who just does not understand an assignment. The student won't gain understanding from the threats. Threatening punishment when a student is already angry with another student or the teacher will not reduce the anger. And threatening punishment when a student desperately needs to move around is not likely to work as a long-term solution, even if it buys a few uneasy moments of stoicism. Taking the time to find a win-win solution, to engage in collaborative problem solving with a student, will accomplish much more.[13]

Linda Darling-Hammond, a longtime teacher educator, describes a study in which she compared the overall effectiveness of teachers she considered well prepared with those she considered ill prepared. The results were eye-opening. On one hand, the ill-prepared teachers all said that while they had the motivation, they did not have the skill or as one said, "I wasn't equipped to deal with it, and I had no idea." On the other, the well-equipped teachers knew how to use what they had learned—about student diversity, about curriculum, about child development—and put it together in a way that allowed them to engage in careful planning and come to school each day fully prepared: "I'm miles ahead of other first-year teachers. There are five other first-year teachers here this year. I am more confident. I had a plan for where I was trying to go. The others spent more time filling days. I knew what I was doing and why—from the beginning."

Having a plan—which also means taking the time to develop that plan, and knowing what one wants to accomplish with a group of students—is key to effective classroom management and direction. It is also, as we will see, a key to dealing with the ever-expanding role of assessment in the lives of students and teachers.

School Violence

While the kinds of school and classroom management issues most teachers face most of the time (indeed what most teachers face throughout their careers) can be the kinds of discipline issues described earlier—from a cafeteria food fight to an actual physical fight between students that may even result in a punch at a teacher—there have been all too many stories in the last decade of much larger scale violence in schools. While exceedingly rare, such terrible violence is still very much in the minds of educators, parents, and school children.

When the horrific story started to emerge about the shootings at Sandy Hook Elementary School in Newtown, Connecticut, on the morning of December 14, 2012, many people thought, "Oh no, not again." Quickly we learned that a seriously disturbed and very-well-armed young man had killed 20 first grade students, four teachers, and the school principal and psychologist. Although it was one of the worst school shootings in history, sadly it is not the only tragic incident of school violence in the U.S. In April 1999, two isolated and angry students at Columbine High School in Littleton, Colorado, carefully planned a murder spree in which 12 students and a teacher were killed before the two killed themselves. And the list of other school shootings is long, including the following incidents since 2000:

October 24, 2014, Marysville Pilchuck High School, Washington: four students killed
February 27, 2012, Chandler, Ohio, High School: three students killed
October 2, 2006, Amish School in Nickle Mine, Pennsylvania: five students killed
March 21, 2005, Red Lake Senior High School in Minnesota: five students and a teacher and guard killed on the Red Lake Indian Reservation
March 5, 2001, Santee High School, California: two students killed

The list could go on and on in a seemingly never-ending litany.

How, many people ask, is it so easy for so many seriously disturbed young people to get the guns with which to commit so many murders? What is happening in our schools and our society that there are so many socially isolated individuals who lash out with such violence and hatred? What, if anything, can be done about the situation? And, of course, for teachers there are the additional questions: What would I do if such an incident happened in my school? How have these kinds of incidents changed contemporary schools?

In fact, the murder of students and teachers at school is not new in American history. During Reconstruction, in an effort to intimidate newly freed African Americans from attending school, and those who chose to teach them, the Ku Klux Klan conducted many raids on schools, murdering students and teachers and burning school buildings. In almost every year of subsequent American history someone, somewhere has taken a rifle to school to hurt or kill someone. But the current outbreak of violence is of a different order in terms of its frequency and the lethal level of the murders. New kinds of rifles allow someone like the Sandy Hook killer to kill almost 30 people in a matter of minutes. New forms of alienation and the glorification of violence in everything from computer games to the daily news encourage disaffected young people to dream of vengeance and even glory.

But what is a teacher to do? The nation rightly honored the four brave teachers at the Sandy Hook Elementary School who gave their lives trying to protect their students. Indeed some contrasted their courage to the failure of lawmakers to pass effective anti-gun legislation.

In the event of a shooting at a school, the U.S. Department of Homeland Security offers a simple formula of Run/Hide/Fight. If at all possible, escape from the scene of the shooting and have escape routes in mind in advance. If escape is not an option, the next best thing is to hide as well as possible and as far out of sight, making every effort to keep silent (including silencing all cell phones). Only as a last resort should one fight with a shooter—but if there is no other option, using every means at hand to disable someone intent on an act of violence is appropriate.

At the same time schools have instituted new safety procedures. It is much more difficult to get into most schools today than it was prior to the Sandy Hook and Columbine incidents. Many schools lock their doors and visitors are often checked through cameras, metal detectors, and other forms of screening. The same security features that may make students and teachers feel safer also make them feel more isolated, with mixed results.

While the Homeland Security procedures can be wise advice and the day-to-day security procedures are probably inevitable, some people ask about the deeper need for treatment of a society where such things could happen. What needs to change in our culture, our laws, and our school policies to reduce violence? In the third **Reading** for this chapter, attorney Robert Crabtree notes that in the subsequent investigation of the Sandy Hook tragedy it became known that a clinic at Yale University had recommended intense psychological intervention for the young man who became a killer. But while he was a student, school officials never followed up with the recommended treatment. We will never know if a meaningful intervention would have changed the course of history, but the fact that it was not attempted remains part of the challenge.

It is, of course, important for schools to have security measures and for teachers to know the protocol for responding when tragedy strikes. It may be even more important for educators and policy makers to address the underlying issues in a society that allows sickness and violence to fester and to seek ways to create a more deeply engaged community—in the school and in the society at large.

 ## DID YOU KNOW?

More than 90% of U.S. schools have violence prevention programs. Urban schools are more likely than rural schools to use student-to-student or adult-to-student methods of violence prevention, such as individual attention, mentoring, tutoring, or coaching of students, even though school violence is hardly limited to cities and often happens in prosperous and isolated suburbs. More than 2,100 students were expelled in the 2003–4 school year for possessing a firearm at school.

How Will I Assess My Students in a Fair and Meaningful Way?

Assessment takes place in many forms and at many levels. Every effective teacher is continually asking, "How are my students doing?" "Are they individually and as a class understanding the material I am presenting?" "How can I be more effective with them?" Beyond these day-to-day assessments, teachers are expected to give grades.

Whether they are the traditional A/B/C/D/F or Pass/Fail, or a new and more creative approach, students expect grades, parents expect grades, and school administrators expect teachers to give grades. Far beyond anything an individual teacher does, states and the federal government are increasingly mandating more and more tests. Most states now have high-stakes tests that students must pass in order to proceed to the next grade or to receive a diploma. When Congress passed the No Child Left Behind Act (NCLB) in 2001, the federal government set a new requirement that every state test its students every year and that not only students, but also teachers, schools, and school districts, be measured by the results. With the emergence of the Common Core assessments, new and different—and hopefully better—tests will replace many of the existing tests, but testing is certainly not going away. Finally, the National Assessment of Educational Progress (NAEP) and other national and international measures assess how much students are learning and how their mastery of material compares to that of students in other classrooms

> **assessment**
> Informal or formal documentation of the particular skills, knowledge, and academic progress of a student or group of students.

in other places near and far. Teachers today face more pressures around more kinds of assessment than any previous generation of educators. Knowing how to teach—fostering student learning and engagement and success in such an environment—is critical to being a successful educator.

Classroom-Level Assessment

Good teachers are continually scanning the room to see who is paying attention, who seems to understand the material, and who is having trouble. Teachers also learn to double-check their initial assessments. Sometimes a student who seems completely "tuned out" is in fact deeply engaged in a conversation or a lesson. Similarly, some students have learned how to "fake it" and may not really understand or may not even be listening despite the thoughtful look planted on their faces.

> **CONNECTIONS →←**
> In Chapter 11, we discuss in detail the latest ramifications of the Common Core and earlier demands for assessment such as the No Child Left Behind Act.

To test their initial impressions and to gather more substantive feedback, teachers use multiple forms of assessment: giving students quizzes and longer examinations and assignments, anywhere from the drawings of a first grader to the reports and term papers of high school students. Increasingly, many schools are also asking for student portfolios (summaries of a student's work over a grading period or a year) that can show progress and mastery of material, however slowly gained, and that allow students to demonstrate their best work for assessment. Good teachers are generally wary of too much focus on tests as the sole measure of student learning, yet most teachers and most school systems require tests as one type of assessment.

Once a teacher has asked for written work—such as a quiz, a paper, or any project—he or she has an immediate obligation to assess that work. Students need feedback in a timely way if they are to learn from their work. They also need detailed and timely responses. Getting work back weeks after it was submitted is simply not useful to a student. "Good work" or "needs revision" written in red across the top of a paper is not sufficient feedback to enable a student to make sense of the evaluation. Many teachers also allow students to revise work, to take comments and suggestions seriously, and to try to do better. No professional writer, whether a newspaper reporter writing for an immediate deadline or the author of a novel or a textbook with a long-term contract, ever assumes that the first draft will be the final draft. It is interesting that, although most adults expect their written work to be edited, revised, and edited again, we do not always give students the same opportunity, even if an extended deadline will produce better quality work.

The evaluation of student work needs to be fair and needs to be perceived as fair by all students. Students often ask each other, "What'd she [or he] give you?" but the question implies that grades, especially positive grades, are dispensed by some sort of all-knowing benevolent, or mean-spirited, authority figure. In an effort to make grading fairer and to make the system of grading more transparent, many schools and individual teachers are now developing their own detailed grading **rubrics**. (The rubric used at New Design High School in New York City is included in the **Readings** for this chapter.) Most rubrics follow a similar pattern, beginning with a clear set of standards and then asking, for each standard, how well the student is doing. For example, a rubric might allow a teacher to indicate whether a student is "exceeding the standard," "meeting the standard," "approaching the standard," "emerging," or if there is simply "no evidence." The categories may or may not

> **rubric**
> Chart with outlined criteria levels for a project or course, which allows students and teachers to know the expectations and makes grading easier, less subjective, and fairer.

correspond to the traditional A/B/C/D/F grading system. But whether the standards are translated into letters or numbers, students who are graded with a rubric know in much greater detail what the teacher thinks they have accomplished and where their work has fallen short or needs revision. The process of grading is much more transparent. It is perceived as fairer because it *is* fairer. And students have much more information about what needs to be done to improve.

The best rubrics, like those from New Design, assess student work in multiple areas, such as personal responsibility, social responsibility, critical and creative thinking, content knowledge and skills, clarity of communication, and the like. Some students easily do well in some areas and need much more effort in others. It is important to reward and recognize success while insisting that success in some areas may not be sufficient if students cannot do minimally acceptable work in other areas. A clear rubric allows a teacher to assess the work across multiple domains and do so in a way that is transparent to the students, parents, and other teachers.

The school in which you teach will probably have its own rubrics, but the more familiar you are with rubrics, the more effectively you can use them to make your own judgments about what is working and what is not working for students.

High-Stakes Assessments

Since passage of NCLB in 2001, the debate about high-stakes assessments has become intense among teachers. The stakes are high for individual students because they may not be promoted to the next grade or allowed to graduate if they do not pass the tests. The proposed tests, which will be used in every Common Core state to measure students' ability to meet the new standards, are currently a subject of great controversy. Critics see these tests as the greatest problem that the Common Core represents while defenders of the Common Core say that the standards are meaningless if they are not assessed. Of course, much of the debate is not new. There are many educators who have argued for some time that high-stakes tests have created a significant new divide in American education and a barrier to the kind of equality that schools have long sought to foster. There are also many who argue that the same new assessments have created a new level of educational quality as school districts are held accountable as never before for the successful education of every student no matter their race, gender, or special need.

Despite the critique, advocates of standardized tests and tougher forms of accountability such as high-stakes tests have been winning the political argument in recent years. There are many advocates for higher levels of accountability—for students, teachers, and school districts—than has been typical of American education in the past. It is far too simplistic to say that all educators fall into one of two camps—pro-test or anti-test or pro–high stakes or anti–high stakes. Many observers take many different reasoned positions along the spectrum. Some favor tough assessments of individuals and districts on a regular basis and over many subject areas, some favor a minimal level of test-demonstrated competence for graduation, and some favor using standardized tests only to evaluate schools but not individual students or teachers. Yet others oppose all such use of standardized testing because they see huge flaws in the tests, grave inequity in almost any system of implementation, or feel that alternative means of assessment provide a clearer and fairer picture of student, teacher, and school district achievement. Yet in the middle of all these debates, individual teachers need to develop their own clear views *and* find ways to survive and thrive even when their views are not the ones being implemented in their school, their district, or the nation.

Researchers Martin R. West and Paul E. Peterson describe what they see as a slowly emerging consensus among one group of political leaders and educators in favor of much tougher forms of accountability than have existed in the past:

> The accountability movement has its origins in long-standing efforts to measure cognitive aptitude and ability. It is premised on the notion that standardized tests can and do measure an important dimension of educational quality. Such a position is increasingly uncontroversial, as evidence mounts that student achievement as measured by standardized tests is strongly associated with both individual and aggregate economic success.[14]

Many others would say that no such consensus exists and that, indeed, any effort to measure student achievement by standardized tests is, at best, highly controversial. For all the controversy, however, standardized tests are a major part of the educational landscape for teachers today.

Debates about standards and accountability, and the testing that often accompanies these movements, are among the most intense in education today. But as West and Peterson point out, while educators may be debating these issues, an accountability movement based primarily on standardized test scores has gained many supporters, especially in many state legislatures, the U.S. Congress, and among the last three presidents. And state legislatures, Congress, and presidents do make state and national law. While the breadth of the opposition to the Common Core testing may possibly begin

Teachable Moment
BLOOM'S TAXONOMY

Many educators use Bloom's Taxonomy as a way to understand different levels of teaching strategies and of assessments used to evaluate student learning. In 1956, psychologist Benjamin Bloom led a group of educational psychologists who studied the kinds of questions elementary and secondary students were asked on tests and in class. They developed a six-level classification of test questions that quickly came to be known as *Bloom's Taxonomy*.

The lowest level of questions, knowledge, gets by far the most attention in school. Many exam questions are at the simpler (and perhaps more boring) level than the more advanced questions that require students to move from learning and memorizing information to using that information to think creatively for themselves. Bloom and his colleagues found that over 95% of test questions that students are asked are at the knowledge level. Sadly, little has changed since that time, although as a result of Bloom's work, teachers and test makers are certainly attempting to use class assignments, in-class tests, and state-mandated high-stakes tests to probe students at increasingly advanced levels.

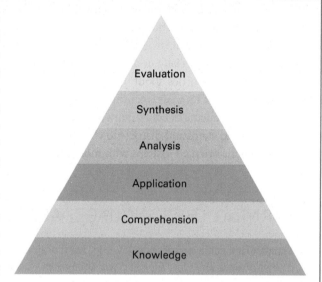

Figure 7.1
Bloom's Taxonomy

Examples of the kinds of questions that might be asked in the six categories include the following:

- **Knowledge.** When was the American Revolution fought? What is the name of the current model of the cell membrane?
- **Comprehension.** How did developments in the North American colonies in the 1760s and 1770s lead to the American Revolution? What is the purpose of the cell membrane?
- **Application.** How is the American Revolution related to the French Revolution and the Haitian Revolution? Demonstrate how the cell membrane regulates what comes in and leaves the cell.
- **Analysis.** What are some examples of the different motives of different people who participated in the American Revolution on the American and on the British sides? Differentiate between the functions of each part of the cell membrane.
- **Synthesis.** In addition to those listed in your textbook, can you think of other reasons that residents of British North America might have been ready for a revolution in the 1770s? If you had been advising the British Parliament, what might you have predicted when the Stamp Act passed? How would a rigid cell membrane structure affect how the cell itself functions?
- **Evaluation.** Different historians give different reasons for the causes of the American Revolution. Describe the reasoning of two differing historians and then give your own analysis. Do you agree more with one, or is there a third reason that you prefer? Based on your knowledge of the cell, defend or criticize the theory that the disease cystic fibrosis affects the endoplasmic reticulum.

Questions

- As you think about your own experience as a student, were you asked mostly knowledge-level questions on tests, or did the tests cover many different levels of Bloom's Taxonomy?
- Pick a content area other than the ones given in the examples here, and develop a set of six questions for the levels in Bloom's Taxonomy.

to tip the balance, advocates of assessment and accountability argue that without tests to measure student achievement and without accountability for failure to measure up, there is simply no seriousness about the quality of education in the United States.

Linda Darling-Hammond takes a different approach to the questions of accountability, standardized tests, and high-stakes tests. While hardly opposed to accountability (Darling-Hammond played a critical role in raising the standards and accountability measures for schools of education), she has grave reservations about the current accountability movement as institutionalized in federal law. Darling-Hammond sees much to admire in the federal goals of raising "the achievement levels of all students, especially underperforming groups, and to close the achievement gap that parallels race and class distinctions," but she worries about the gap between goals and reality. Indeed, she worries that the law's impact will be almost the opposite of its goals, that the new level of mandated testing "threatens to increase the growing dropout and pushout rates for students of color, ultimately reducing access to education for these students rather than enhancing it," and that it will lead states and districts to change their assessment and accountability systems, replacing "instructionally rich, improvement-oriented systems with more rote-oriented punishment-driven approaches."[15]

LEARNING THE LANGUAGE: ASSESSMENT

- **Standardized achievement tests:** A test is "standardized" when the same test is given to many students across a school district or state with clear right and wrong answers. A standardized test, as such, may or may not have anything to do with an individual student's academic success.
- **The accountability movement:** The current accountability movement is a combination of (1) clear standards; (2) tests that measure whether students meet the standards; and (3) specific penalties, for students, teachers, or schools, for failure to meet the standards. The penalties may include not allowing an individual student to graduate or closing or reorganizing a school in which large numbers of students fail a given test.
- **High-stakes testing:** This is one specific form of accountability in which a state or district requires students to pass a specific test in order to move on to the next grade or receive a diploma. The stakes are high for individual students in this case, as opposed to other forms of accountability that apply more to schools and districts. NCLB does not specifically require high-stakes tests, but some states have implemented them since the act passed (if not before).
- **Formal assessments:** The simplest definition of a formal assessment is a test designed by someone other than the teacher. Students in most schools are given many tests to assess how well they have mastered specific skills or bodies of knowledge (criterion-referenced tests) or how they compare with their peers in other schools, districts, states, and even other countries (norm-referenced tests). Formal assessments are used in many states to determine if students are ready to be promoted or to receive a high school diploma.
- **Informal assessments:** Teachers are continually assessing the progress of each of their students—scanning the class for who seems to be learning the material, paying attention to writing samples, reading and grading homework, and in the case of science classes, looking at students' success, or lack of success, in the lab. Increasingly many educators are paying careful attention to students' written work, using it not only to assess overall achievement but also to determine where students are demonstrating mastery, where students may be having difficulty, and what sorts of mistakes students may be making that can lead to future lessons being planned to address specific areas.
- **Common Core testing:** Two new testing consortia—PARCC (Partnership for Assessment of Readiness for College and Careers) and SB (Smarter Balanced Assessment Consortium)—have been set up by several states to prepare the tests that will be used to verify student achievement on the Common Core standards. These tests, and the fact that private companies are dominating the test prep industry and stand to make significant profit from the enterprise, represent a huge flaw in the Common Core movement in many minds.

A group of scholars is emerging today who take yet a different approach to the issue of high-stakes standardized tests. These scholars seek ways to support teachers, who must still work in schools that are increasingly dominated by the tests. In this context, Arthur Costigan begins the first chapter of *Teaching Language Arts in a Test Driven Era* by saying, "This book is about how to engage in best practices in Language Arts instruction in an educational era which is increasingly driven by high stakes tests and increased accountability." Costigan is no fan of many of the tests, but he also understands the reality of teachers' lives. He has come to believe that something close to what Vito Perrone and many of his Harvard colleagues call "Teaching for Understanding" will not only engage students more deeply in their own learning but also, in the end, give them a mastery of material that will serve them well on the tests themselves. Thus Costigan writes:

> I would like to point out, however, that the more involved students are with the real issues of contemporary society, the more their writing is likely to be rich, engaging, and, yes, even free from errors. I am not being naïve when I point out that doing real writing has a way of eliminating errors and making students pay attention to communicating the best way that they can, if only because they begin caring what they write, rather than adhering to imposed formulas.
>
> This is not naïveté, but serious accommodation to the reality of today's world.[16]

Another author, Judith McVarish, says much the same thing of the elementary mathematics curriculum. McVarish believes that teachers can find the right balance between test preparation and truly engaging instruction. McVarish makes it clear that she is opposed to "drill and kill" test prep, not only because it is a diversion from meaningful learning but also because it can be bad test prep. Instead, McVarish calls for a balance that focuses on the interests of children but also links those interests to material that they must know to succeed in today's schools. So she says, "[T]hough maintaining such a balance is not an easy task, I believe we can provide rich learning environments for students and still prepare them for taking standardized tests that have enormous, long-term implications." But, she insists, "The trick is to keep the power priority in proper alignment." This "trick" has been forgotten by far too many in today's world, but it is one that is essential to the successful teacher of the next generation.[17]

Finally, Deirdra Grode, a middle school social studies and language arts teacher and the 2008 ASCD Outstanding Young Educator award winner, writes, "When I first began administering state test preparation in my language arts classes, I found it incredibly boring. It felt so formulaic, and rarely did the stories or prompts engage my students or interest me. As a result, grading their work was as torturous as their completion of it. But, when I began embedding test preparation into the curriculum, the whole experience became much more positive." As Grode developed her own approach she came to believe that:

> Test prep can provide an opening for teaching a wide range of topics and integrating new activities into classroom lessons. . . . The amount of time spent on test prep has not decreased; however, it is hidden. As the test nears, I hear students ask, "Are we going to prepare for the test at all?" illustrating that the preparation material has fit organically into the coursework. And after the exams, I have yet to hear a student say they did not feel prepared.[18]

Teachers live in a world where test prep and the tests that follow are likely to be part of their lives for some time to come. There is little question that an overemphasis on testing cramps learning just as there is little argument that some form of assessment is essential to determining that student learning is taking the place. Finding the right balance, as a matter of state policy and individual classroom practice, remains a key challenge of the teaching profession.

 **CHAPTER REVIEW**

- How will I motivate my students?

No child comes to school as a blank slate. Some students arrive, as John Dewey and the progressive education movement suggest, with many experiences of life outside of the school building. Vito Perrone advocates "teaching for understanding," which links curriculum with the interests of students as thoughtful individuals. The wise teacher will find ways to address students' reasons for not learning and the experiences that students bring with them to make what happens in school more interesting and more productive for all concerned.

- How will I manage my classroom?

The management of a classroom requires more than making it an interesting and engaging place, although that is an essential starting point. A variety of philosophies exist regarding how to manage a classroom, including recent developments at restorative justice. All classroom management efforts require establishing clear expectations, and being prepared and consistent in your actions in the classroom. In all situations, planning is key, and classrooms need to be places where the structures and rules are clear and where the values of a democratic society are modeled. Since the events at Sandy Hook Elementary School in 2012 and Columbine High School in 1999, teachers and educators have been mindful of the possibility of massive school violence. While preparation and planning is important, so is early intervention that can, at least some of the time, stop a crisis before it becomes a killing.

- How will I assess my students in a fair and meaningful way?

Teachers have a responsibility to continually assess what learning is taking place in their classrooms. Assessment takes many forms, including informal assessments (such as scanning the classroom and asking questions to see if students are grasping the material) as well as formal assessments, such as high-stakes tests. Teachers have many options to ensure fair and accurate assessment, such as using a rubric that provides clear feedback to students and their parents regarding progress and areas for improvement. The accountability movement and the impact of standards and high-stakes tests generate heated discussion, especially regarding fairness for all groups of students.

Readings

How Will I Motivate My Students?

From "MY PEDAGOGIC CREED"

AUTHOR: JOHN DEWEY

John Dewey (1859–1952) has arguably been the most influential philosopher of education in the history of the United States. In the early years of the twentieth century, Dewey did more than anyone else to create what he called a new philosophy of education—*often known today as* progressive education. *At the beginning of the century, Dewey helped found and lead the "laboratory school" at the University of Chicago, where many so-called progressive ideas were developed and tested. Very early in his career, Dewey wrote a short piece that summarized what he believed about education and the teacher's responsibility. To address questions of how to motivate a class or control student discipline, Dewey answered simply, "Make the classroom a community." If teachers could live up to the demands of Dewey's creed—no easy or perhaps even possible task—questions of teacher and student classroom behavior would disappear.*

I believe that education, therefore, is a process of living and not a preparation for future living.

I believe that the school must represent present life—life as real and vital to the child as that which he carries on in the home, in the neighborhood, or on the playground.

I believe that much present education fails because it neglects this fundamental principle of the school as a form of community life. It conceives the school as a place where certain information is to be given, where certain lessons are to be learned, or where certain habits are to be formed. The value of these is conceived as lying largely in the remote future; the child must do these things for the sake of something else he is to do; they are mere preparation. As a result they do not become a part of the life experience of the child and so are not truly educative.

I believe that the discipline of the school should proceed from the life of the school as a whole and not directly from the teacher.

I believe that education is the fundamental method of social progress and reform.

I believe that all reforms which rest simply upon the enactment of law, or the threatening of certain penalties, or upon changes in mechanical or outward arrangements are transitory and futile.

I believe that the community's duty to education is, therefore, its paramount moral duty. By law and punishment, by social agitation and discussion, society can regulate and form itself in a more or less haphazard and chance way. But through education society can formulate its own purposes, can organize its own means and resources, and thus shape itself with definiteness and economy in the direction in which it wishes to move.

I believe, finally, that the teacher is engaged, not simply in the training of individuals, but in the formation of the proper social life.

I believe that every teacher should realize the dignity of his calling; that he is a social servant set apart for the maintenance of proper social order and the securing of the right social growth.

I believe that in this way the teacher always is the prophet of the true God and the usherer in of the true kingdom of God.

Questions

1. If you were to write your own "Pedagogic Creed" how similar or different would it be from Dewey's?
2. Does Dewey have ideas that help address motivation, management, and assessment in 21st century schools? Can you name a specific one?

Source: John Dewey. "My Pedagogic Creed." *School Journal* 54 (January 1897), 77–80.

How Will I Manage My Classroom?

From "MAKE STUDENTS PART OF THE SOLUTION, NOT THE PROBLEM"

AUTHOR: TREVOR GARDNER

The following article, written by a current teacher at Envision Academy of Arts and Technology in Oakland, California, describes in detail what the growing movement for restorative justice might mean in a school context. While the details and the challenges vary from context to context, the general principles remain the same.

Amid the chaos of lunchtime, a lone apple flies across the lunchroom, over tables, through conversations, and slams against the door on the other side of the room. Jose, the aspiring pitcher, begins to laugh, a satisfied moment of jubilation with two or three friends near him who were in on the scheme. Their laughter quickly fades as the boys realize Ms. Johnson, the principal, has caught them in the act. As she approaches, Jose turns his back in feigned ignorance. Even though Johnson literally watched as the shiny green apple was released from his hand, Jose denies throwing it. (The names of students, staff, and The City School are pseudonyms.)

Now 17, Jose has experienced enough encounters with authority in school and beyond to know that the first response to getting caught must be to deny culpability. Johnson quickly grows frustrated. The confrontation escalates. A few minutes later, Jose is leaving the principal's office to begin his five-day suspension.

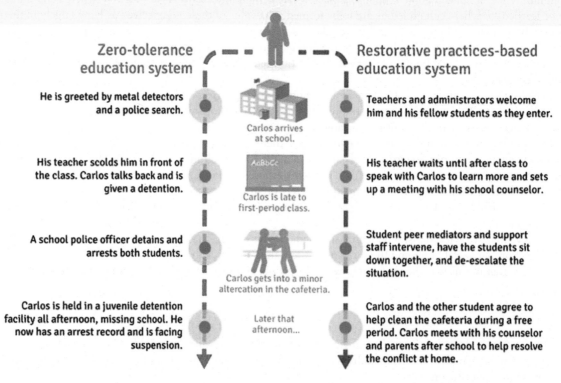

A Tale of Two Schools

Carlos had a heated argument with his parents before leaving for school, so he's running late. Let's see the difference that restorative policies and practices can make.

Zero-tolerance education system		Restorative practices-based education system
He is greeted by metal detectors and a police search.	*Carlos arrives at school.*	Teachers and administrators welcome him and his fellow students as they enter.
His teacher scolds him in front of the class. Carlos talks back and is given a detention.	*Carlos is late to first-period class.*	His teacher waits until after class to speak with Carlos to learn more and sets up a meeting with his school counselor.
A school police officer detains and arrests both students.	*Carlos gets into a minor altercation in the cafeteria.*	Student peer mediators and support staff intervene, have the students sit down together, and de-escalate the situation.
Carlos is held in a juvenile detention facility all afternoon, missing school. He now has an arrest record and is facing suspension.	*Later that afternoon...*	Carlos and the other student agree to help clean the cafeteria during a free period. Carlos meets with his counselor and parents after school to help resolve the conflict at home.

Learn more about restorative practices: www.otlcampaign.org/restorative-practices

Figure 7.2

A Tale of Two Schools

Graphic courtesy National Opportunity to Learn Campaign. Used with permission.

This scenario, repeated in some form thousands of times every day at schools and in classrooms across the country, was the first incident taken on by the newly formed Student Justice Panel (SJP) at The City School, a small charter school in San Francisco. The SJP was the product of teacher leadership and pressure to move toward a more restorative and responsive approach to student discipline. The initiative had considerable ideological support from several teachers but lacked a clear road map on how to apply this discipline philosophy in the day-to-day life of school.

Core Values

The City School (TCS) is a public charter high school serving about 400 students in San Francisco, one of a network of three schools established in 2002 with the mission of "transforming the lives of students, especially those who will be the first in their family to attend college, by preparing them for success in college, in careers, and in life." City School students reflect the diversity of San Francisco and come from every neighborhood in the city. There are about 20 educators teaching grades 9–12.

The Student Justice Panel (SJP) is a restorative justice model of school discipline, the purpose of which is to uphold the school's Core Values by working to restore damaged relationships between individuals and the community. The SJP is made up of about 12 student leaders nominated by their teachers and peers and is based on the beliefs that:

- TCS believes strongly in maintaining our Core Values of discipline, growth, community, justice, and respect;
- Each individual at TCS is responsible for the community as a whole; and
- TCS functions best when students take leadership and are given a strong voice.

SJP hearings consist of an adult facilitator, the community members involved in the violation of the Core Values, and at least four SJP representatives. Parents/family members may also be present, depending on need. Petitioners and respondents can also request to have additional student advocates present. Everyone at the hearing, including the respondent, will propose and discuss consequences aimed at restoration, and the SJP will decide on a course of action.

The shift toward restorative justice at TCS was largely a bottom-up movement. Although administrators were nominally supportive of the push, they were not the engine behind the change. The fuel for the changes came from a few teacher leaders, including myself, and eventually from students. This continues to be a challenging dynamic at the school, where there never seems to be enough time or resources to do work like restorative justice. Furthermore, the relationships and individualized attention needed to properly integrate a restorative discipline model often clash with the "sacrifice some for the good of the whole" doctrine that drives many school discipline policies. But this is a discussion for a different article.

The City School is by no means a place that relied heavily on punishment and removing "bad students" to maintain its school culture. Every adult in the building genuinely wants to do what is best for the young people they serve. However, like many schools with similar missions and goals related to equity, social justice, and college readiness, TCS faced a critical disconnect between what we wanted and what was actually happening as a result of school discipline policies and practices. We wanted to be true to our Core Values:

Community—We work hard and take responsibility for the success of all members of our community.
Respect—We seek to see the best in each other and treat one another with dignity.
Justice—We are empowered agents of change for social justice and equity.

We wanted to help students transform mistakes and bad choices into learning experiences. We wanted to create a school culture in which students learned to discipline themselves and each other so that referrals, suspensions, and expulsions would become the exception instead of the rule. But watching Jose walk out of the building reminded me that we were far from reaching these goals. We had so much work to do.

After the Apple Is Thrown

When members of the Student Justice Panel learn Jose has been suspended for five days for what students considered an innocuous act of playfulness, their justice meters go into "oh, hell, no" mode. After school that day, four SJP members rush into my classroom, filled with urgency and outrage.

"They can't suspend him for five days for throwing an apple!" one shouts.

After several minutes of questioning and analyzing the incident and the response to it, I agree that the SJP has a responsibility to raise its voice and respond to the apple incident.

I tell the SJP students that the first step in supporting Jose is communicating their perspective to Principal Johnson. She is reasonable, and I believe she also wants to do right by students. "Let's go down there right now," shouts Nicole. "I don't care if she is busy; she needs to do something about this."

I remind Nicole that Ms. Johnson is not our enemy and that if we approach her as though she is, we won't get anywhere. "Don't forget Ms. Johnson was actually very supportive of the SJP. We don't want to lose that support by coming at her disrespectfully," I offer my opinion to the group.

"I want to take her to the Student Justice Panel," Nicole exclaims. "Why does she think she can do this?"

"Requesting that Ms. Johnson come before the SJP is actually an option," I reply. "But for now let's focus on the situation with Jose and how we are going to get Ms. Johnson to listen to us."

Deondre steps in. Typically a quiet and reflective student who keeps his thoughts to himself, Deondre is a leader whom students trust to be honest and just. "We need a proposal that makes it clear why we think this is unfair. If we just rush into her office yelling at her, she will never hear us," he said. "And Jose did throw an apple across the cafeteria. Let's not front like he didn't do anything wrong."

Deondre's reasoning calms them and sends them into planning mode. They huddle around a desk and start to build their plan. I step back and listen, offering a few suggestions, but really just letting them work it out. After about 10 minutes, they're excited about their next step, but they still don't fully trust that the Student Justice Panel process is real or that Ms. Johnson will listen to them.

This is a common dynamic in schools: Adults have all the power, and students must be obedient and respectful—even when they are right (and righteous) in the face of injustice. This is the dynamic that leads to so many students blowing up over incidents that begin small. After many years of schooling, students have learned that the teacher's word is taken as truth, and their perspective won't matter. Being told to move seats or getting a detention for repeatedly talking can often lead to screaming at a teacher, storming out and slamming a door, or throwing a fit because that is their only source of power. They have seen models of struggle—from "The Maury Show" to the contentious political climate that values temper tantrums and threats of violence to win one's point. And they employ these competently when they find themselves powerless in classroom situations.

What makes the SJP so transformative is the shift in the dynamics of power it represents. Many schools have structures that are intended to encourage students to have a voice. But SJP actually has the authority to affect and even change school discipline decisions and policies. At The City School, any community member can bring another member of the community before the SJP for violating any of the school's Core Values; this includes students who have called teachers before the SJP. This can be extremely useful when a teacher is trying to reason with a student who is about to explode because of a perceived unfairness. The teacher can remind the student that she is not powerless in that situation but that her power does not lie in yelling and demonstrating anger. Her power lies in her peers, who will be the ultimate arbiters of justice in the Student Justice Panel.

The apple incident will be the test to see if the SJP is real. Is the school really willing to give students a voice in some discipline decisions? To be honest, as a teacher and lead organizer of the SJP, I'm not completely certain myself if the school leadership is willing to give up that kind of power. But we will give it a try.

The Meeting

Two of the SJP representatives, who were elected weeks before by peers in their advisory classes, go to Ms. Johnson's office to make an appointment to discuss the incident and their feelings about Jose's suspension. Ms. Johnson is game. The next day, Ms. Johnson meets with the four SJP members who initially raised the issue, myself, and the assistant principal of school culture.

Equally surprised, nervous, and excited, the four students gather in my room after school to discuss how to approach the meeting and what to ask for. They decide the fundamental issue is not that Jose is being punished for his actions but that the punishment does not fit his "crime." During the conversation, they realize that Jose has the main responsibility in restoring the situation. They agree that throwing the apple was wrong and that he needs to have consequences. But a five-day suspension won't accomplish anything except to push him further behind in his schoolwork and make him even angrier about coming to school. Furthermore, using Jose as an example is unreasonable.

The SJP group decides to ask Ms. Johnson to allow Jose to return to school the next day, having served one day of his suspension, on three conditions. Jose:

- Writes a letter of apology to the janitor (who would have had to clean up his apple mess if Jose had not been caught);
- Stays after lunch to clean up the cafeteria for a week; and
- Writes a reflection about which Core Values he violated and what it means to be responsible for his actions at school.

It takes less than a half hour to discuss the issue and come up with these consequences. The students walk away feeling good about their proposal.

The Meeting

At the meeting the next day, Deondre, Nicole, and two other Student Justice Panel students present the proposal to Ms. Johnson, making it clear why they believe their proposed actions are not only more just but actually hold Jose to higher expectations than simply suspending him. Ms. Johnson accepts the proposal. I can see the expressions on the faces of the four students change as they listen to Ms. Johnson's words. The Student Justice Panel is for real.

Jose agrees to the conditions and returns to school the next day—anything to avoid the five-day suspension. But, after a few days back, he fails to follow through on one of his commitments: staying after lunch to clean up the cafeteria.

This is a pivotal moment for the nascent SJP. Students had considered what would happen if a student didn't follow through with their restorative consequences and decided that this would trigger a return to their punitive consequences.

However, before the situation with Jose got to this point, students on the SJP—on their own with no adult prompting—spoke with Jose and convinced him that it was critical for him to keep his end of the agreement, both for his benefit and for the sake of the SJP process. In the following days, Jose followed through on the rest of his restorative consequences.

This demonstrates one of the powerful unforeseen benefits of the Student Justice Panel: Students take leadership and hold each other accountable for discipline. Sure, in this situation, Jose wanted to avoid more days of suspension. And schools must have discipline policies with punitive consequences to ensure accountability. Students could comply with school policies to avoid being punished for their actions, or students could comply with school policies because their peers hold them to high expectations. When the high expectations approach is at play, students are investing in building and maintaining a positive and respectful school community because they believe they have the voice and the authority to do so.

In Reflection

Several years and many "apple incidents" have passed since the Student Justice Panel began. In some ways, the panel has been incredibly successful. But the growth of the SJP and restorative discipline has met many challenges, and we are still struggling to implement these practices on an institutional level. Only a few of these challenges emerge from a lack of ideological support for the philosophy and practices. Often the challenges come in the form of resources. If we only consider time and school resources, sending Jose home for five days and forgetting about him until he returns is much easier than investing in the work required to transform his actions and his thinking, which is the goal of restorative discipline.

But given the connection between school discipline, dropouts, and the school-to-prison pipeline, the implications are critical. We owe it to Jose. We need to care deeply enough about his education and his humanity to invest in developing restorative discipline models that thrive in our schools and not simply operating systems that punish students when they make poor choices, like throwing apples when the principal is watching.

Trevor Gardner (trevor@envisionacademy.org) is lead humanities teacher at Envision Academy of Arts and Technology, Oakland, California.

Questions

1. Restorative justice has become very popular as a means of handling student discipline, especially as zero-tolerance policies have come under intense critique. In the example given in this article, can you imagine such a system working? For Jose? For a whole school?
2. How might students on a Student Justice Panel be viewed by other students? Could their status work for or against the success of the system described here?

Source: Trevor Gardner. "Make Students Part of the Solution, Not the Problem." *Phi Delta Kappan* 96, no. 2 (October 2014): 8–12.

From "TWO YEARS POST-NEWTOWN : WHAT'S CHANGED? WHAT NEEDS TO CHANGE?"
AUTHOR: ROBERT CRABTREE

Robert Crabtree, a lawyer in the Special Education & Disability Rights practice group at Kotin, Crabtree & Strong, LLP in Boston, Massachusetts, has long been an advocate for the rights of Special Education children and their parents. In this blog, posted just before the second anniversary of the Sandy Hook Elementary School shootings in Newtown, Connecticut, Crabtree links the murders with the failure to provide much needed services to highly troubled young people like the one who committed the Connecticut murders. While not every act of school violence can be anticipated, Crabtree reminds us that school violence and issues of proper support for students in need are not completely separate issues but need to be linked more effectively if the violence that we see in schools is to be addressed.

The Office of the Child Advocate for the State of Connecticut has issued a report outlining major factors contributing to the murder of children at the Sandy Hook Elementary School in Newtown, Connecticut two years ago. Although the Yale Child Study Center had evaluated the young man who committed that atrocity and recommended mental health services and special education services for him, the responses of both his mother and the special education staff at the school were found to be tragically inadequate to address the emotional issues that made him a pariah at school and resulted in his avoiding school completely.

The Council of Parent Attorneys and Advocates, Inc. ("COPAA"), a national organization with its eye on issues and initiatives that are important to our field, has issued a compelling statement using the findings in this report to advocate for additional funding for the federal mandate in IDEA. We join COPAA in urging that you let your federal legislators know how critical it is to increase funding for special education services, which include services for emotional disabilities and related services. We add to their plea a request that you let both local and national lawmakers know of your support for increased funding of *all* public education, as we attempt to understand and avoid the conditions that give rise to such desperate violence.

Along with full funding for services under IDEA [Individuals with Disabilities Education Improvement Act of 2004] should come much-expanded funding and meaningful options for children with serious mental health disorders. As many special education lawyers and advocates have also experienced, in recent years our caseloads have seen a major increase in the numbers of students afflicted with severely debilitating emotional challenges that prevent those students from being able to access an education. The Kafkaesque maze of bureaucratic blind alleys, inconsistent and often contradictory criteria of eligibility for services, and battles between school districts and state agencies over which agency, if any, must provide the key day and often residential services and supports necessary to address the student's needs is exhausting, incomprehensible and too often fruitless for parents who struggle, often literally, to save their children's lives. While underfunded government agencies battle over who, if anyone, should meet the needs of a student at risk, the student's risk all too often becomes a tragic reality. . . .

I would add . . . an additional plea: A society that makes the means of lethal violence so easy to acquire is making a tragic choice. As difficult as it may be to stand up to the knee-jerk absolutism and to ignore the carrots and sticks of national and local lobbyists for open access to weaponry, legislators need to find a way to stop the madness. To me it is obvious that the imposition of intelligent restrictions on access to the means of such violence should be part of any efforts to reduce the numbers and magnitude of events like those at Newtown and Columbine.

Educate fully and with open hearts and hands; support and treat those who are severely troubled; reduce access to the means of violence against oneself or others. Can we make this happen in this fractured political culture of ours? At this Thanksgiving time, can we at least imagine such a thing?

Questions

1. Do you think Crabtree is right to link the killings in Connecticut with the need for more special education services? Why or why not?
2. What would you propose if you were writing about a way to avoid future Sandy Hook-type tragedies?

Source: Posted on November 24, 2014 by KC&S Special Education Attorneys. Used by permission.

How Will I Assess My Students in a Fair and Meaningful Way?

From NEW DESIGN HIGH SCHOOL COMMUNITY HABITS RUBRIC

New Design High School is one of many new small high schools that have been created in the past decade as part of a national effort to break up large and seemingly impersonal comprehensive high schools into small learning communities in which faculty and students can get to know each other as they focus on a unique approach to a high-quality education. As New Design was being launched, the faculty created the following detailed rubric for evaluating student work. The rubric illustrates well another movement in contemporary education, one that allows students and teachers much more detailed discussion of both the fairness and rationale for any grading system while spelling out the criteria for assessment. As you read this document, you will see that it lays out clear criteria for exceeding, meeting, or failing to meet a long list of goals that the school has for its students. These lists allow teachers to recognize that a student may be exceeding expectations in one area and may be far from meeting them in another. It also allows a teacher to explain to a student or a parent exactly where the student stands and what steps need to be taken for a student to meet or exceed all of the many expectations that the school rightly holds for its students and graduates.

HABIT 1: PERSONAL RESPONSIBILITY

	Exceeding the Standard	*Meeting the Standard*	*Approaching the Standard*	*Emerging*	*No Evidence*
Be Punctual *Attendance*	Student is always present, on time and fully prepared to begin with his/her materials.	Student is usually present, on time, and fully prepared to begin with his/her materials.	Student is sometimes tardy and/or missing some materials, but is able to complete most required tasks.	Student frequently struggles to complete required tasks because of his/her attendance and/or lack of materials.	
Prepare and Produce *Student Work*	Student completes work that reflects a great deal of effort and goes beyond requirements in quality.	Student completes work that represents the student's potential and effort. All requirements of the task(s) are met.	Student completes work that approaches the student's potential and reflects some effort. Requirements of the task(s) are met, though at a basic level.	Student completes minimal work and shows little effort. Many requirements of the task(s) are unmet.	
Personal Growth	Student consistently and independently challenges her/himself as an independent thinker. Even without teacher prompting, student creates a plan of action, and follows through.	Student identifies challenges and takes risks to change her/his attitudes and habits to become an independent thinker. Student creates plan of action. Student follows through with plan to meet goals.	Student identifies challenges and is open to changing her/his attitudes and habits to become an independent thinker. Student creates plan of action, but sometimes struggles to follow through.	Student identifies challenges and is open to changing her/his attitudes and habits to become an independent thinker. Student creates plan of action, but rarely follows through.	

HABIT 2: SOCIAL RESPONSIBILITY

	Exceeding the Standard	Meeting the Standard	Approaching the Standard	Emerging	No Evidence
Professionalism *Behavior*	Student not only follows professionalism guidelines, but also consistently encourages others to act more professionally.	Student follows professionalism guidelines, helping to create a positive learning environment that helps both her/him and other students to excel.	Student mostly follows professionalism guidelines, but needs reminders every now and then in order to help her/him excel academically.	Student struggles and needs constant reminders of the professionalism guidelines. Lack of professionalism detracts from the learning environment.	

HABIT 3: CRITICAL AND CREATIVE THINKING

	Exceeding the Standard	Meeting the Standard	Approaching the Standard	Emerging	No Evidence
Define Problems *Asking questions*	Student is able to evaluate a situation and ask insightful questions that lead to defining his/her own problem.	Student defines the problem and poses questions that help clarify the problem.	Student defines some parts of the problem and poses questions that address the problem.	Student attempts but struggles to define the problem or pose questions that address the problem.	
Predict *Hypothesize Estimate Infer*	Student uses imagination, experiences and observations to make multiple logical predictions.	Student uses available experiences and observations to make a logical prediction.	Student uses limited experiences and observations to make a partial prediction.	Student uses limited experiences and observations to offer an illogical prediction.	
Talk to the Text	Student engages with the text: questions and comments are very detailed and reflect a deep understanding of the text.	Student "talks to the text" in order to further her/his understanding of the text.	Student somewhat "talks to the text," but more commentary in the margins is needed in order to further her/his understanding of the text.	Student minimally "talks to the text." Comments reflect little understanding of the text.	
Investigate *Gather Evidence*	Student gathers detailed, well-chosen evidence. Student's explanation reflects thorough thinking about the question.	Student gathers well-chosen evidence. Student's explanation reflects his/her thinking about the question.	Student gathers some evidence: attention is not paid to the quality of the evidence. It is difficult for student to explain how evidence addresses the question.	Student needs to gather more evidence in order to address the question.	
Analyze *Analyze Synthesize Justify Imagine Create*	Student creates a thorough and original analysis of the evidence to answer the question and prove her/his argument.	Student thoroughly analyzes evidence to answer the question and prove her/his argument.	Student analyzes evidence, but needs to be more thorough in order to more fully answer the question and prove her/his argument.	Student summarizes but fails to analyze evidence, therefore not proving her/his argument.	
Revise *Seek Other Perspectives Revise Work*	Student revisits the problem/question and reevaluates her/his answer. Detailed revisions are made to clarify and deepen original thinking.	Student clarifies thinking and alters ideas when necessary, to better explain his/her answer to the question/problem.	Student clarifies some thinking and addresses some concerns with the work. More revision is needed.	Student makes minimal revisions to work.	

HABIT 4: APPLICATION OF KNOWLEDGE IN SUBJECT AREA

To Be Created by Each Subject Area

Hold Content and Skills Constant

	Exceeding the Standard	Meeting the Standard	Approaching the Standard	Emerging	No Evidence
Understand Content *Curriculum Standards (What to Know)*	Student shows extensive knowledge of key concepts and content.	Student shows solid understanding of key concepts and content. Student applies content knowledge appropriately.	Student shows some understanding of key concepts and content.	Student shows limited understanding of key concepts and content.	
Demonstrate Content Area Skills *Skills Specific to the Discipline (What to Do)*	Student demonstrates sophisticated mastery of required skills, going beyond the requirements of the assignment.	Student demonstrates proficient mastery of required skills and is able to independently apply them when needed.	Student demonstrates beginning mastery of skills and attempts to apply them independently when needed.	Student demonstrates little mastery of skills and makes few attempts to apply them independently.	

HABIT 5: COMMUNICATION

	Exceeding the Standard	Meeting the Standard	Approaching the Standard	Emerging	No Evidence
Communicate Key Idea *Thesis Summary*	Student communicates main idea clearly. Main idea is thoughtful and detailed.	Student communicates main idea clearly. Main idea uses specific details.	Student communicates main idea. Main idea needs more detail.	Student needs to develop and clarify main idea.	
Organize Thoughts *Outline/Graphic Organizer Essay/Project Organization*	Student organizes thoughts clearly throughout work; details build upon each other in order to best support main idea.	Student organizes thoughts clearly and places details in appropriate sections in order to support main idea.	Student attempts to organize thoughts clearly, but details need to be reorganized in order to support main idea.	Student uses minimal organization in work.	
Writing Mechanics	Student work has no grammatical/ spelling errors.	Student work has few grammatical/ spelling errors.	Student work is understandable despite grammatical/ spelling errors.	Student work is difficult to understand due to grammatical/spelling errors.	
Present Ideas Orally	Student's eloquence and passion come across with his/her eye contact, body language, diction, voice volume, and tone.	Student uses appropriate eye contact, body language, diction, voice volume, and tone throughout presentation.	Student at times uses appropriate eye contact, body language, diction, voice volume and/ or tone.	Student minimally attempts to use appropriate eye contact, body language, diction, voice volume and/ or tone.	
Present Ideas Visually *Artwork Poster Graph/Table*	Student presents key ideas in vivid, clear, and unique manner.	Student presents key ideas in vivid, clear manner.	Student presents key ideas.	Student needs to clarify the key ideas to present and determine how best to present those ideas.	

Questions

1. As far as you know, has a teacher ever used a rubric like this to assess your work? If so, did the use of a rubric make the assessment seem more or less fair?

2. Can you imagine using a rubric like this in grading your students? Would it make your life easier, or is it too complicated?

3. If you were going to use a rubric like the New Design High School one, what changes would you want to make? What would you want to be sure remained unchanged?

Source: New Design High School Community Habits Rubric, distributed to all teachers at New Design High School, New York City.

Technology

How Is It Changing Our Schools?

With Noah Kippley-Ogman

> Across the world children have entered a passionate and enduring love affair with the computer . . . the love affair involves more than the desire to do things with computers. It also has an element of possessiveness and, most importantly of assertion of intellectual identity.

SEYMOUR PAPERT

QUESTIONS TO COME

If you were to compare the average classroom today—elementary, middle, or high school—with those of 20 or even 50 years ago, you would see surprisingly few physical changes. However, most classrooms of today do look different in one way—the almost omnipresent role of technology. From smart boards to e-books to classroom computers and tablets, students use technology like no previous generation. Indeed, today's students—including most of the students now preparing to be teachers and reading this book (in either hard copy or e-book format) grow up with a technological familiarity that is sometimes baffling to teachers who are just a few years older. Using language once applied to families who came to this country from abroad, today's students are "digital natives" while some of their parents and teachers are forever going to be "digital immigrants" for whom the world of technology is never going to come as naturally as it does to the current generation. The result is that schools that do not make full use of technology are going to seem out-of-date and boring places to their digital natives even as most teachers struggle to develop the appropriate technological innovations that will truly support active learning.

Computers were not available to any schools prior to 1975, when the first microcomputer was developed. In his 1996 State of the Union address, President Bill Clinton set what seemed like an impossible goal: a computer with

Internet access in every classroom. By 1999, 95% of schools and 63% of classrooms had not only a computer but also Internet access, a potentially powerful instructional and research tool. Far fewer teachers or school leaders knew what to do with the new resource and many distrusted it as an innovation that would undermine traditional ways of teaching and learning.

Today some schools provide laptops or tablets and the majority of students have computers at home as well as smartphones in their pockets, connecting them to both the knowledge and distractions of the outside world at a moment's notice. Some believe that technology has disrupted the routine of schools, but it has often been a very positive disruption, expanding the possibilities of education for many. In many classrooms, research is conducted online, often from a smartphone or Apple iPad, reading is done via an e-book, math problems are solved electronically, and the technological interests and expertise of students is at the heart of the learning process. We certainly have a generation of students wired to the world in ways that no former generation could have imagined.[1]

Although some teachers and schools have used the power of technology to fundamentally transform the way learning and teaching takes place in the modern classroom, many others simply tend to use technology in the same ways they use traditional materials. Thus, smart boards are used in place of old-fashioned chalk on blackboards, e-readers may replace some textbooks, and the Internet may speed some research, but the basic view of the classroom remains quite stable. In other classrooms, everything has changed dramatically. Courses have been "flipped," with initial instruction happening online after school hours while class time is spent discussing homework and solving problems together; student-led projects in which teachers serve as coaches have replaced traditional instruction in some schools; and the Internet and graphics programs have become central to the research and the production of highly illustrated student presentations, usually submitted and assessed electronically.

Today's students have grown up with technology. They have likely spent more time playing video and computer games than reading—often much more time. And they come to school with radically different expectations than their predecessors, assuming that, like the rest of their lives, education should be fast paced, well connected to the larger world, and experiential rather than plodding, isolated, or text-based. Such a situation, on the edge of what some observers see as a fundamental transformation of not only education but also the nature of knowledge, is fraught with both tremendous possibility and peril for all teachers. For those just entering teaching who, like their students but unlike their older teacher peers, have grown up with technology, the challenges to rethink the work of the teaching profession are significant.[2]

The **Readings** for this chapter will help us explore some of these questions. In a report from a Common Sense Media research study, *Zero to Eight: Children's Media Use in America 2013,* we learn just how fast children—including very young children—are taking to new technologies that were not even available only a few years ago. There has been a fivefold increase in ownership of tablets, such as iPads, and the number of children using smartphones has doubled from 38% in 2011 to 72% in 2013. To strategically use technology in the classroom, we need to begin our planning with a knowledge of what children know—and the technology that is a large part of their lives—before they ever arrive at the classroom door.

The next two **Readings** explore the use of specific technologies in classroom contexts. Carolyn Lorraine Webb, of the School of Education at Texas A&M University–San Antonio, explores the use of cell phones as learning tools and advocates a reduction in the general practice of banning cell phones when they can be an important learning tool. However, she also recommends paying careful attention to the potential for abuse that can occur with these devices. Following that article, Lotta Larson, who teaches at Kansas State University, explores the extraordinary potential of using e-books to facilitate instruction, meet the challenge of the Common Core, and engage students like "Joey" who dislike traditional reading assignments.

Historically Speaking: How Has Technology Been Used in Education?

We tend use the word *technology* to label computer or Internet-based tools that initially require some kind of connection, be it a plug into a wall socket or a wireless connection such as Wi-Fi. Whether or not that fulfills a true dictionary description, the reality is American education has been impacted again and again by new tools—new technologies.

Growth over time ↓

As students 100 years from now may have a hard time classifying a computer as "technology," today's students rarely consider the development of moveable type by Johannes Gutenberg in the 1430s, which allowed the widespread printing and distribution of books, as probably the most important technological innovation in education in human history. The key teaching tools used in primary schools in the 1400s included the hornbook—a handled wooden board with a lesson (usually an alphabet and a prayer) affixed and the slate (a personal chalkboard), which was still used until the beginning of the 20th century. The slate and the hornbook allowed a revolution in learning, helping make reading and writing accessible to a much larger swath of the population than previously imaginable. The printed book created the modern world.

The introduction of the textbook in the 18th century changed schools dramatically. Noah Webster's 1783 speller was a popular learning aid, breaking down the intricacies of spelling, grammar, and pronunciation into age-appropriate lessons. William McGuffey's readers, first published in 1836, offered another immensely popular age-graded series of texts that taught morals, vocabulary, and speaking. *McGuffey's Readers* were in common use in American classrooms through the beginning of the 20th century, selling perhaps 120 million copies. The standard textbook is a staple of today's classrooms, but was once new, like the other learning technologies discussed in this chapter.

Not all technologies caught on as completely the textbook. The history of 20th-century technological innovations for education is filled with big promises and disappointing results. The 1980s and 1990s came with a whole new genre of "edutainment"—electronic games that helped teach, although oftentimes did more "entertaining" than "educating." In Bill Ferster's *Teaching Machines*, he chronicles the promise and disappointment of educational technology from early teaching machines to 1990s programs like Oregon Trail and Math Blaster, and contemporary experiments using "big data" in education. Early teaching machines were complex mechanical devices that presented a chunk of material and a question to a student. When the student provided the correct answer, the machine advanced to the next chunk of material. The machines automated the teaching process, their inventors claimed, but were doomed for two reasons: their expense and because they upended the age-graded structure of schools. Teaching machines allowing students to learn at their individual pace meant that by year's end, some students would have mastered geometry while their peers in the same grade might have managed to learn only long division. Ferster argues that more than "effectiveness" matters in the success of technologies in the classroom. The new technologies must also fit with or at least be acceptable to the pattern of schooling and the lives of those who work in schools.[3]

→ *Garrett High School*

? DID YOU KNOW?

ALIWEB, considered the first true search engine for the Internet, appeared in 1993. Though its use was limited, it led to search engines that followed and changed how people access information. According to Google, 3.5 billion people use the Google search engine every day: 1.2 trillion per year.

In the last decade, we've seen a shift from computer to Internet-based resources, especially the use of instructional video clips (from a variety of sources, such as YouTube and TEDTalks), podcasts (which are downloadable audio or video broadcasts), and apps (a software application downloaded or utilized via the Internet). One of the early leaders in the field of instructional videos is Khan Academy. Founded in 2006 by Salman Khan to help his nephews with their homework, Khan Academy offers YouTube videos that have helped thousands master their lessons. Khan's educational videos are a significant improvement on educational radio and TV in a key way: they're available on-demand rather than broadcast to all pupils at the same time, and, thanks to smartphones, tablets, laptops, and desktop PCs, they're available everywhere. Some teachers are using Khan's videos and other like them to "flip" their classrooms. In a "flipped classroom," students watch instruction at home via online videos (oftentimes a narrated Microsoft PowerPoint presentation) that their teacher made or assigned and then do the traditional "homework" (such as problem sets and essays) in class, allowing teachers to work closely with individual students on the specific content and skills that he or she needs.

The flipped classroom experience does require the student to be responsible (and hopefully empowered) for reviewing and understanding the lesson at home and come to class prepared to ask clarifying questions (if necessary) and apply the instruction to real work.

How Is Technology Transforming Education?

Technology In and Out of the Physical Classroom

Technology has changed and will continue to change schools in both large and small ways. Many classrooms, for instance, have smart boards—whiteboards that connect to a classroom computer system to allow the digital capture and dissemination of whiteboard illustrations and the easy projection of a images on a computer's screen to the front of the class. Such technology can dramatically facilitate the recording of classroom discussion and debates. It also allows material to be saved and easily revisited by students studying at home.

Teachers in special education classes are finding adaptive technologies incredibly helpful. In December 2014, the well-known physicist Stephen Hawking, who uses a wheelchair and multiple forms of assistive technologies, wrote a commentary about the many ways these very new technologies have allowed him to do his work and live his life. A *Fortune* magazine article estimated that 15% of the world's people could have their lives improved by assistive technologies. In everything from new wheelchairs that follow voice commands to individual e-reading screens that allow students to adjust the size of the type or the speed in which questions are asked, to new testing technologies that adjust the difficulty of future questions to student success on past ones, technology is transforming the educational experience of many special education students.[4]

Technological tools are shaping the behind-the-scenes activity of schools. Learning management systems help teachers track grades, attendance, and behavior, and report the student's behavior and achievement data to parents and administrators. E-mail, text messages, and online postings allow teachers to keep parents informed of their school's activities and child's progress. However, some teachers complain that parents now expect immediate responses to e-mails and for grades to be posted instantaneously. Having these new methods of connecting also means that communication is actually taking up much more of a teacher's time and creates a new level of accountability.

Also, the amount of personal information and the ease of accessing it have raised privacy concerns by educators and parents. "How much information does the school have, or really need, on my child and my family?" some parents ask. How long will stories of misbehavior or learning difficulties be retained? These issues of "big data" certainly raise privacy concerns yet to be explored.[5]

Similarly, the growth of data collection and processing in schools through assessment tools, including standardized tests, has empowered other school stakeholders, such as state legislators, to take a more active role in evaluating teachers and their performance. (In Chapter 11, we'll further explore how politics play a role in education.)

The promise of technology in schools, at least for the enthusiasts, is more than improved classroom tools; it's a transformation of school itself. In their book *Rethinking Education in the Age of Technology*, Allan Collins and Richard Halverson describe several ways that technology has already allowed the reinvention of some parts of schools. These leading indications of radical change—which they call "seeds of a new education system"—include the tools used by homeschoolers, workplace educators, distance educators, and others.

Homeschoolers, Collins and Halverson report, are increasingly relying on online classes provided by organizations like Colorado Online Learning, which provides online coursework and teachers available via the Internet. Parents are also relying increasingly on tools like those on K12.com, a private online school cofounded by former U.S. Secretary of Education William Bennett. The results of online-only educations, however, are up for debate. A 2014 report from the University of Colorado's National Education Policy Center suggests that graduation rates and achievement rates on standardized tests in online-only schools lag far behind their brick-and-mortar peers.

Collins and Halverson point to distance education and learning centers like those run by Kaplan, the Princeton Review, Thompson, and Sylvan as models of technologically enhanced learning. These educational centers, whether physical or online, offer ways for parents, students, and schools to supplement the education they already offer. A school

[Handwritten margin notes: "Benefits"; "Better teacher, parent comm."]

without the resources to offer a remedial or advanced class can, thanks to distance-learning tools, send students online to get the education the school can't provide.[6]

Virtual high schools are already enrolling tens of thousands of students for just one course or for their whole school day. At Florida Virtual School (FLVS), for instance, students can supplement their school day with an online course, homeschoolers can take as many classes as they'd like, and students can also enroll in FLVS full-time and graduate with a diploma. Chartered as a public school through state legislation, FLVS is free to students in Florida. Students complete courses at their own pace, receive feedback from their teacher (a teacher is assigned to each course and is available from 8:00 a.m. to 8:00 p.m. seven days a week), and are required to have a monthly check-in phone call with the teacher.

Another trend in education that involves the extensive use of technology is **adaptive learning**, in which computer programs adapt the presentation of educational material according to individual student learning needs as indicated by her or his responses to questions and tasks. The original learning or reading has usually already taken place (although not always). The accuracy of the student's responses triggers feedback that pinpoints areas, specific topics, or ideas in which the student did not answer correctly and thus needs more instruction.

> **adaptive learning**
> Educational method that uses computer programs to adapt the presentation of educational materials to help individual students focus on content areas yet to be mastered.

The student isn't simply told that "B" was the wrong answer. Rather, the feedback may involve providing highlighted sections of an e-book, specific page numbers of a textbook that the student should review, and related content or suggestions for mastering the material. This individualization of the content helps the student specifically focus on areas of improvement. The teacher can also use the feedback to determine if there are certain consensus areas that a significant percentage of students are having difficulty with and thus either redesign the instruction or spend more time on the topic. Because of the complexity required with this extreme individualization, it can be difficult for a teacher to create such tailored feedback, especially for the higher grades. Recognizing this, educational companies have been rapidly developing platforms designed alongside their published content, initially focusing on courses in higher education. If proven successful—both educationally for students and teachers and financially for the developers—adaptive learning will be utilized at all levels of education.

 ## DID YOU KNOW?

Online learning, or distance learning, is gaining popularity at the high school level. In Alabama, students in all of the state's 371 high schools are able to take courses not offered at their schools through a **distance-learning program** that uses online and interactive video conferencing technology to link classrooms and offer coursework, including advanced placement and foreign languages, to students in schools where those courses may not be available. Alabama also introduced a requirement that, starting in 2009, all incoming freshmen must take at least one distance-learning class during their 4 years of high school.

Tom Vander Ark, a former school superintendent and a high-level Gates Foundation staff member, is now a venture capitalist investing in education technology companies. He believes these new digital tools will transform schools entirely and that many schools will soon look more like the Florida Virtual School than the traditional high school. In his book, *Getting Smart*, Vander Ark suggests that learning will take place outside of schools, mostly online, with students having their education tailored to their own needs and interests. This change would

> **distance-learning program**
> Courses or workshops in which the teacher and student are not physically together and instead interact through alternative methods; presently, these courses are conducted almost entirely on the Internet.

require "changing our job descriptions," Vander Ark notes. Parents will have to become educators, teachers will either become coaches or curriculum designers, and students will have to step up to manage their own learning. "The notion of 'educator' has come unmoored from its previous definitions and associations," Vander Ark suggests. And he predicts big

Notes from the Field

How has technology impacted teaching?

"Technology has become the foundation of most high school classrooms. Teachers utilize everything from Power Point to electronic grading systems to make teaching more efficient. In the end, those who benefit the most from the integration of technology in the classroom are the students and parents."

—*Joshua Ball, high school geography teacher*

changes, fast: "In five years, those learning at home through homeschooling and virtual charter schools will double to six million students, or about 10 percent of all students."[7]

Three Examples of Technology in Action

While scholars write about the technological revolution taking place in schools, hundreds of easily accessible programs and ideas like Scratch, the New Tech High Schools, and WebQuest are already making some of these changes real by bringing digital, online, educational tools to classrooms nationwide.

Scratch and ScratchJr

Initially designed by the Massachusetts Institute of Technology's Media Lab and later expanded by teams at Tufts University, the MIT Media Lab, and the Playful Invention Company (PICO), Scratch (http://scratch.mit.edu/) is used by millions of elementary school students. The new ScratchJr is expected to be used by equal numbers of younger elementary children ages 5 to 8.

Scratch and ScratchJr are software programs that teach children to do basic coding. Children can build their own games, make a film, and develop an animated presentation. At the same time, they are also learning how to do basic computer coding and how to solve problems, design projects, and communicate ideas electronically and without assistance.

As Mitchel Resnick, one of the original designers of Scratch, describes the application: "We saw that many young people wanted to create their own interactive stories, games, and animations, but traditional programming languages were not designed with kids in mind. There was clearly a need for a new type of programming language. At the same time, we knew that learning to program would be a rich learning experience. So we developed Scratch to meet a need—but also to provide new learning opportunities."

Resnick believes that engaging with Scratch helps children learn how to work in teams, build on each other's work, and stick to it even when the work is challenging. As Resnick says, "These skills are important for everyone, not just people who will grow up to become scientists, engineers, or computer scientists."

At the Cranford Burns Middle School in Mobile, Alabama, teacher Melissa Nordmann began using Scratch soon after its release in the fall of 2011. She did not always find it easy going. The first semester she found it hard to motivate the group using traditional questions. By spring, Nordmann had learned to set parameters that made her students more comfortable: only asking for information about them that their friends already knew—not "private" home life stories—and moving all journal entries from paper to online in a forum that could be shared not only with the rest of the school but also with other kids across the country.

During the second semester, students came alive using Scratch to design a learning game that could actually be used with students in a special education class. A special education teacher in the school helped the students and reminded them of the adjustments they would need to make in their new curriculum. As Nordmann described it,

The quality of the work went way up! One student redesigned a maze game so that the sprite could be moved with a finger instead of the arrows on the keyboard. Another student designed sprites in the shape of a four-way arrow and you tapped on the direction you wanted to move. A third student gave auditory directions instead of written directions. The player then tapped on the picture with a positive sound for a correct answer and a negative sound for a wrong answer.

Designing something "real" that would be used for other students, challenging their computer skills, and having fun while doing it helped to engage the students. As a result, their learning, their computer literacy, and their engagement with school all soared.

ScratchJr (http://scratchjr.org) was released in the summer of 2014 with the hopes of the same results being seen with even younger children. The Tufts University professor who helped launch ScratchJr, Marina Umaschi Bers, is convinced that, "As young children code with ScratchJr, they develop design and problem-solving skills that are foundational for later academic success. . . . And by using math and language in a meaningful context they develop early childhood numeracy and literacy."[8]

 ## DID YOU KNOW

Teen Tech Use

78% have a cell phone
47% have smartphones
23% have tablet computers
95% use the Internet
93% have a computer at home
74% use the Internet on their phones
81% use social networking sites
76% use Facebook
24% use Twitter

Source: "13 Things to Know About Teens and Technology," from Pew Research Center's Internet & American Life Project, 2014

Examples Within IN ↓

New Tech High Schools

New Tech High School in Rochester, Indiana, sits in a small rural town in north central Indiana amidst some of the richest farmland in the country. You would not necessarily expect to find there what some are calling the future of American schools. The New Tech high school movement began in Napa, California, in 1966 as an effort to connect student learning to the reality of the changing nature of the job market. It has now spread to many states, with especially enthusiastic participation by a consortium of high schools in Indiana. At the New Tech schools, students study world history by doing research and producing a video about a specific problem in the world today that can be addressed through a better understanding of history and geography. They learn biology by developing a video on genetics for their parents or on biodiversity and the water cycle for the community. The goal of New Tech is to use project-based group learning to generate discussion and problem-solving skills in the classroom. The project method, which was so much a part of progressive-era classroom reforms a century ago, seems to have emerged again at a time when many educators want to make sure that learning engages students in ways that fit the new kinds of jobs available in a global economy.

More than 156 schools in 26 states have adopted the New Tech model, and the state of Indiana has been especially active in promoting it. In Rochester, a new school district superintendent and a new principal were anxious to reinvent their schools. They determined that their high school dropout rate was too high and that their students, who came to school with a much more sophisticated sense of

> **CONNECTIONS →←**
> Recall the discussion of project-based learning in Chapter 6.

the world than their predecessors, needed a different kind of high school experience. If you visit a classroom at New Tech High School, you will notice there is very little "teacher talk"—but many students are deeply engaged in their projects, with teachers serving as coaches and advisors. However, the shift to the New Tech model is not always easy. One veteran, once a skeptic but now an enthusiastic supporter of the model, said, "Teachers have to come out of their comfort zones. In a traditional class, there's a lot of quiet and it's mostly the teacher talking." In the New Tech model, one sees clusters of young people working on projects, deeply engaged with each other and with the source of most of the information they seek—the Internet. In this setting, teachers become coaches rather than instructors, putting into action an approach that many discuss but few actually see.

Critics of the New Tech model wonder about the quality of the information that students are receiving. They fear that crucial aspects of what one should learn in high school are simply missed by the focus on depth over breadth. They may also worry that the almost-exclusive focus on group work disadvantages students who learn best alone and that there is a danger that a team's enthusiasm for the technology itself can run over the content that is the focus of the project. Although the debate is sure to continue, New Tech schools demonstrate one model of an entire school—and structure of schooling—transformed by technology.[9]

WebQuest

Bernie Dodge of San Diego State University has become something of an educational technology guru with his invention of WebQuest, a method for doing significant student-led research using the Internet. Dodge defines WebQuest as "an inquiry-oriented activity in which some or all of the information that learners interact with comes from resources on the Internet."

Dodge describes a time early in his development of the WebQuest method—in which students are given assignments that require them to use information found only on the Internet—when he was attempting to transform a classroom for aspiring teachers into one where technology played a larger role. Through "Treasure Hunts" and other activities, students were required to do online research in real time during classes as well as outside of class. Dodge described his own role after giving the students an assignment and letting them loose to do their own research. Instead of standing in front of the room talking at the students, he walked around the room "listening to the buzz of conversations" as students helped each other and were forced, by the assignment, to work as a group and to come to group decisions. He realized quickly that the life of the class was much richer than anything he had seen before in his own teaching. Students were asking more complex questions and thinking more seriously about their work. He loved what he saw and was determined to build on the experience. For Dodge, this was the beginning of a new way to teach teachers and to encourage them to teach their students.[10]

There are many parallels between classrooms that use WebQuest, what happens at New Tech High School, when teachers use Scratch or similar apps, and classrooms that have embraced technology not only as a tool for teaching but also as an organizational structure for schooling. In all these cases, the primary focus of learning moves from teacher talk to greater, direct activity on the part of the students. Advocates for this use of technology contend that it puts more responsibility on the learners themselves, with the ultimate goal of moving from collecting information to understanding the nature of knowledge. However, this is hardly a form of teaching that exempts the teacher. A good teacher who is using WebQuest or who is working at a New Tech school spends a lot of time defining specific research problems that will generate the kind of student research and learning needed for their curricular goals as well as developing the right list of resources and sites that will help students accomplish those goals. As Melissa Nordmann's reflection on using Scratch shows, sometimes this is a process of trial and error, learning from the students as well as from the program, while keeping in sight the learning outcomes that are the goals of the new technological usage.

Notes from the Field

How do I get started with using technology in the classroom?

One day, out of exasperation, I loaned my personal Kindle to a student who was a reluctant reader; he loved it. So I thought it might be a good idea to ask other people for their used digital reading devices and to see what would happen. For the first year, there were five to eight devices, and I loaned them out. I noticed that really skilled readers liked the devices and so did really struggling readers, particularly boys. In particular, struggling readers liked the coolness of the tech, that you can make the text bigger, that you can look up words, that you can have text-to-speech, and that you can hide what you're reading.

Mark Isero, Director of Instructional Development, San Francisco Bay Area

Cited in *edutopia*, December 16, 2014

At its best, technology can change the classroom from a place where teachers teach and students learn—mostly passively—to a place where students take the lead, organizing their learning, studying, and researching in ways that are meaningful to them, and producing meaningful work instead of absorbing the work of others. When teachers choose this approach to education, students take on a different identity as learners. They usually have much more confidence in their work—for it is *their* work—and they feel a sense of ownership of the outcomes that they cannot gain through listening, reading, and preparing to report the information back on a test. At its worst, however, the use of educational technology can be as humdrum as the worst traditional form of education and as distracting as the constant chatter of too many cell phone conversations. Many educators are not sure whether the introduction of technology into schools has been as good as its proponents argue, or as bad as its detractors fear. It is to these arguments that we now turn.

Are We on the Edge of a Wonderful New Era, or Is There a Downside to Technology?

Becoming an Information-Driven School

At the beginning of the 2012–13 school year, U.S. Education Secretary Arne Duncan gave a speech in which he said, "Over the next few years, textbooks should be obsolete . . . The world is changing." Besides e-books, Duncan wants to see a greater use of tablet devices, computers, and multiple forms of online learning. His goal is not only to replace physical books with electronic versions but also to create schools in which a student struggling with a math problem could turn to a video clip for help, get personalized feedback from a digital textbook, or interact with a student in another country who is studying the same topic.

Many claim that schools as we know them cannot survive, that they need to be completely transformed by the integration of technology and the changes in learning styles and worldwide connectivity that it brings. In his book *Teachers and Machines*, Larry Cuban reminds us, however, that this is not the first time such predictions have been made. More than a century ago, in 1913, the inventor Thomas Edison predicted, "[S]cholars will soon be instructed through the eye. It is possible to touch every branch of human knowledge with the motion picture." In 1922, Edison said, "I believe that the motion picture is destined to revolutionize our educational system and that in a few years it will supplant largely, if not entirely, the use of textbooks." Cuban wonders if those who predict unstoppable dramatic changes in schools today are wrong. Maybe they, like Edison a century before, are overestimating things. Perhaps, once again, the changes will not be as great as proponents or detractors expect.

Cuban is certainly cautious about making predictions of sweeping changes in schools. He describes what he sees as a standard response to proposals to introduce new technologies:

Not long after each innovation was introduced came academic studies to demonstrate the effectiveness of the particular teacher aid as compared to conventional instruction . . . [Then came] scattered complaints from teachers or classroom observers about the logistics of use, technical imperfections, incompatibility with current programs, or similar concerns. At a later point, surveys would document teacher use of the particular tool as disappointingly infrequent [and] stinging rebukes of narrow-minded, stubborn teachers reluctant to use learning tools that studies had shown to be academically

effective. . . . Few scholars, policy makers, or practitioners ever questioned the claims of boosters or even asked whether the technology should be introduced.[11]

For all the debates about the nature of today's transformation and the useful versus ineffective technologies that might be involved, all signs point to continued technological transformations in education, probably at an accelerating pace. As we move further from an industrial age into an information age, we find more and more examples of the use of technology in individual classrooms and huge transformations in entire schools. It should be no surprise that, as society rapidly changes from an industrial to an information-driven technological one, schools should be expected to keep up. If the industrial-era school too often taught students to be passive, information-age schools must help all students take charge of their own education and become problem solvers able to use the incredible resources available to even the most isolated schools.

The vision of the student as the driving force in his or her own education dates back at least to the progressive educators of the early 20th century. More recently, the late John Goodlad—who wrote a far-ranging critique of American education in the early 1980s—described the schools of the day as "a world of talky teachers and uninterested students, who work in a context of unclear goals and serious social and educational inequities." Technology has the potential to address all of these issues, putting an active and engaged student at the center of the educational process and making the best educational activities available to every student even in places marked by poverty. The fact that such schooling that uses technology can be *much* more interesting to students and often much more engaging to their teachers is a valuable byproduct that is transforming schooling and every aspect of the world in which schools are operating.[12]

Differing Views on Technology in Education

Seymour Papert: Advocate Extraordinaire

No one was an earlier or remains a stronger advocate for the use of technology in education than Seymour Papert. Since the 1970s, Papert, who teaches at the Massachusetts Institute of Technology, has embraced the use of computer-based technology in the schools and has urged others to do the same. Papert notes what many have observed, "Across the world children have entered a passionate and enduring love affair with the computer. What they do with computers is as varied as their activities. . . . [T]he love affair involves more than the desire to do things with computers. It also has an element of possessiveness and, most importantly of assertion of intellectual identity."

Given this "love affair," which extends to other digital media, it continues to frustrate Papert that schools are so slow to embrace the new technologies. Long before technology use became widespread in schools, Papert realized, students were spending hours playing computer games, tracking information, and keeping in touch with each other once they got home from school—not because they had been assigned to do so but because they wanted to. The creativity he saw, compared to the lack of creativity in many school assignments, was amazing.

Imagining a visit by teachers from the 19th century, Papert asks what the visitors would see when today's children leave school, arrive home, and turn on their computers: "While the technology itself might first catch the eye of our visitors, they would in time, being teachers, be struck by the level of intellectual effort that the children were putting into this activity and the level of learning that was taking place, a level that seemed far beyond that which had taken place just a few hours earlier in school."

Papert, like others before him, deeply dislikes the fact that traditional schooling "has an inherent tendency to infantilize children by placing them in a position of having to do as they are told, to occupy themselves with work dictated by someone else . . . because the designer of a curriculum decided that doing the work would shape the doer into a desirable form." He wants something radically different "because I am convinced that the best learning takes place when the learner takes charge." But he also believes that the new technologies make it possible to implement these changes to a degree previously unimagined. Today, children can truly start with their curiosity, seek to understand new ideas, and discover new knowledge as they seek to answer questions of their own asking.

Papert wrote in 1993, "Large numbers of children see the computer as 'theirs'—as something that belongs to them, to their generation." Many of the children he described are now adults, and some of those adults are becoming teachers. They bring with them a confidence in their own skill with what Papert calls the "Knowledge Machines" that are transforming schools, no matter what administrators, more senior teachers, professional developers, or policy makers do or fail to do.[13]

Neil Postman: Dissenter

In spite of the transformation taking place all around us, not everyone believes this "revolution" in education is a good thing. Neil Postman (1931–2003) urged educators to stop and ask where the introduction of computer-based technology is taking us as a society and specifically as teachers. In his book *Technopoly: The Surrender of Culture to Technology*, Postman made two basic points about the impact of computer-based technology on education: (1) The impact is far more profound than most people, including most proponents of computers in the classroom, have even dared think; and (2) this impact is undermining many values that we hold dear, including values about the importance of education.

Ironically, given their starkly different views of the positive or negative impact of computers, Postman sounded very much like Papert when he talked about the total impact of computers on schools and society. Postman insisted,

> A new technology does not add or subtract something. It changes everything. In the year 1500, fifty years after the printing press was invented, we did not have old Europe plus the printing press. We had a different Europe. After television the United States was not America plus television; television gave a new coloration to every political campaign, to every home, to every school, to every church, to every industry.

Postman believed that the very culture into which the new technology has been embedded becomes a different culture. People have access to different information, they think about things in different ways, and they value different ideas—all because of the impact of the new technology.

As a result of television and the Internet, many observers worry about a decline in reading (when these sources bring information so much more quickly and in such rich and colorful detail), in imagination (since they do the imaginative work for us), in face-to-face community (since they connect us to the world but tend to encourage us to stay at home rather than meet with our neighbors or participate in community activities), and in our view of our ability to shape the world (becoming passive consumers rather than active agents). The last thing Postman wants is more of that kind of technology in the schools of tomorrow.[14]

 ## DID YOU KNOW?

Surveys on sexting (sending nude or partially nude photos by smartphone) indicate that about one-third of kids in their upper teens have sexted. A recent study of seven public high schools in East Texas found that 28% of sophomores and juniors had sent a naked picture of themselves by text or e-mail and 31% had asked someone to send one.

Why do kids sext? One recent high school graduate told Hanna Rosin that "late at night, long after dinner and homework, her parents would watch TV and she would be in her room texting with her boyfriend. 'You have a beautiful body,' he'd write, 'Can I see it?' . . . 'I live literally in the middle of nowhere . . . Our way of being alone was to do it over the phone. It was a way of kind of dating without getting in trouble. A way of being sexual without being sexual, you know?'"

Source: From Hanna Rosin. "Why Kids Sext," *The Atlantic* (November 2014).

Virtual Bullying

As students use **social media sites**, such as Facebook and Instagram, and text at lightning speed, concerns about Internet safety have rapidly grown. An incident that raised the profile of this serious issue is the tragic story of Megan Meier, a 13-year-old student who committed suicide after she was cyberbullied.

In 2006, Meier befriended someone she thought was a boy who was interested in her on MySpace. According to Megan's mother, after about a month of friendly online interaction, Megan received a message from "Josh" saying, "I don't know if I want to be friends with you any longer because I hear you're not nice to your friends."

Around the same time, Megan told her mother that someone using Josh's account was posting cruel things about her online. Not long after these incidents, Megan, who had a history of depression, hanged herself.

The story gained national attention, largely because of the truth that was revealed several weeks after Megan's death: "Josh" never existed. A neighborhood mother had created Josh's MySpace profile and corresponded with Megan, allegedly to gain Megan's trust and learn what Megan was saying about her daughter.

This story may seem like an extreme case, but according to one report, nearly half of all teenagers report they have been the victim of cyberattacks. Everything from text messaging to e-mail can be used to bully victims. Some people create Web sites dedicated solely to harassment.

> **social media sites**
> Internet websites constructed through user-generated content, participation, and social interaction.

Nancy Willard, executive director of the Center for Safe and Responsible Internet Use, defines *cyberbullying* as "being cruel to others by sending or posting harmful material or engaging in other forms of social aggression using the Internet or other digital technologies." She identifies several forms that cyberbullying can take:

- **Flaming.** Online fights using electronic messages with angry and vulgar language.
- **Harassment.** Repeatedly sending nasty, mean, and insulting messages. (Harassment can also mean constant repetition of unwanted advances. Some girls report receiving 20 or 30 messages from a boy asking for a nude photo.)
- **Denigration.** "Dissing" someone online. Sending or posting gossip or rumors about a person to damage his or her reputation or friendships.
- **Impersonation.** Pretending to be someone else and sending or posting material to get that person in trouble or to endanger that person or to damage that person's reputation or friendships.
- **Outing.** Sharing someone's secrets or embarrassing information or images online.
- **Trickery.** Talking someone into revealing secrets or embarrassing information, and then sharing it online.
- **Exclusion.** Intentionally and cruelly excluding someone from an online group.
- **Cyberstalking.** Repeated, intense harassment and denigration that includes threats or creates significant fear. (Like more traditional in-person stalking, cyberstalking can make every moment on a computer—including at school research—a moment of fear.)

Bullying among school-age children is nothing new, of course. What's different about bullying online is that it's tougher for teachers to see, which makes it tougher for them to take action. However, teachers can now access many online resources to help them identify the signs, and they can talk with students and parents about how to prevent cyberbullying and address other online safety concerns.

Questions

- If you heard that one student was bullying another online, how would you handle it? Or, if you have been bullied online, how did you handle it?
- How might you talk with your students about Internet safety and cyberbullying in your classroom? Is it a teacher's responsibility to do so?

Sources: "Parents: Cyber Bullying Led to Teen's Suicide," ABC News, November 19, 2007, http://abcnews.go.com/GMA/ Story?id=3882520&page=1; "Educator's Guide to Cyberbullying and Cyberthreats," by Nancy Willard, April 2007, http://www.cyberbully.org/cyberbully/docs/cbcteducator.pdf.

Multitasking Technology

Other scholars have asked less philosophical and more practical questions about the effects and dangers of a technologically enhanced world and its impact on learning. Clifford Nass, for instance, studied multitasking in a world loaded with distracting devices, e-mail notifications, and updates from social media. Nass was impressed with his students' effortless ability to multitask and decided to study it in order to learn how to do it himself.

The results surprised him and the multitaskers he studied: The better people thought they were at multitasking, the worse they actually did on tests of cognitive performance. Multitasking, Nass and his colleagues showed, is a trick we play on ourselves. Instead of performing well at the many tasks we try to perform simultaneously, we perform worse on them than if we'd done them sequentially. Nass and colleagues' research suggests that teachers should not introduce multiple devices and activities that dilute student attention.

David Meyer, a psychology professor at the University of Michigan, makes essentially the same point. Young people think they can perform two challenging tasks at once, he says, but "they are deluded." Not only will all of the work be done less well, but also students will fatigue more easily and remember less of any of the tasks—and lessons learned from the tasks—if they are doing more than one thing at once.

Perhaps even more worrisome are eye-tracking studies done by Jakob Nielsen and his colleagues. When we read on screen, they learned, our eyes follow all of the first line, skip down the page, read a portion of a later line, and then even less of the rest of the material. This research should be a concern for advocates like Secretary of Education Arne Duncan who imagine middle-school students freed from their heavy textbooks by electronic texts. Will the switch to e-books negatively affect students' ability to read their assignments? This and many more questions related to technology lie ahead for us.[15]

What Is the Digital Divide, and How Does It Affect My Teaching?

In describing his own enthusiasm for the New Tech High School model, one of Indiana's business leaders says, "Our mission here is to bridge the digital divide." The term *digital divide* is often used in discussions of educational technology. According to a 2007 report, "Though an exact definition remains elusive, the term 'digital divide' generally refers to the disconnect that occurs between those with access to technology and those without, while recognizing the myriad factors that can have an impact on that inequity."

The digital divide has several aspects. First, significant differences exist in what technology is available to whom. A 2013 report from the Pew Research Center's Internet and American Life Project found that 93% of teens used a computer at home. However, if we disaggregate this number by race, a different picture emerges: 81% of European American students used computers at home, but only 64% of African American students did so. Three decades after computer use became widespread in schools and at home, students are still "digitally divided" in terms of what experiences they bring to school with them.

Another report expressed concern over the gender balance and gender roles represented in video games. Researchers analyzed 1,716 characters in video games and found that, of these, male human characters totaled 1,106 (64%), whereas female human characters numbered only 283 (17%). They also found that half of all female characters were "props or bystanders," meaning they did not engage in any action or provide useful resources, "while male characters were predominantly competitors."

Research on women pursuing computer science careers by Jane Margolis has shown that video games and other social forces, as well as the common idea that computers are appropriate gifts for young boys and not for young girls, shapes who ends up studying computer science.

While women were once a significant portion of college graduates with degrees in computer science, the number has been steadily declining since 1984. The gender gap in technology-related professions has grown even as it has shrunk in law, medicine, and physical sciences.

Many critics see schools in which European American students have many more interesting assignments on computers than are available to most students of color, even if all students have access to computers. They see wealthy schools

Teachable Moment
THE "APP GAP"

"Can I download this app?" is a frequent question parents hear, making this probably the fastest growing segment of commercial technology, thanks primarily to in-app purchases. However, there are still substantial gaps in access to the Internet itself. Although 69% of families with children age 8 or under report having some type of high-speed Internet access at home, the rates vary substantially by income, from 46% of lower-income families (under $30,000 a year) to 86% of higher-income families (over $75,000 a year). Access to mobile, Internet-enabled devices also varies significantly by income, from 61% of lower-income families to 91% of higher-income ones. The largest gap is in ownership of tablet devices, such as an iPad, Microsoft Surface, Kindle Fire, Galaxy Tab, or similar product: 20% of lower-income families have one of these compared to 63% of higher-income families (which own one or more).

Table 8.1 Internet and Mobile Media Access Among 0–8-year-olds, by Parents' Income

Percent who have each of the following in their households:	Total	Lower Income (<$30k)	Medium Income ($30–75K)	Higher Income (>$75K)
High-speed Internet access	69%	46%	71%	86%
Smartphone	63%	51%	62%	76%
Apple iPod Touch or similar device	27%	16%	25%	39%
Tablet	40%	20%	36%	63%
Any Internet-enabled mobile device (smartphone, iPod Touch, tablet, or similar device)	75%	61%	73%	91%
Percent whose parents have downloaded:				
Any apps for child to smartphone, iPod Touch, or tablet	58%	41%	54%	79%
Any *educational* apps for child to smartphone, iPod Touch, or tablet	53%	35%	49%	75%
Among those who own a mobile device, percent who have downloaded:				
Any educational apps for their child	69%	57%	64%	80%

Source: Common Sense Media. *Zero to Eight: Children's Media Use in America 2013*. San Francisco: Common Sense Media, 2013. Retrieved from https://www.commonsensemedia.org/research/zero-to-eight-childrens-media-use-in-america-2013.

Questions

- How should a teacher make appropriate assignments for the use of technologies by students in or out of the classroom, such as a math game for second graders, when some students have access to computers to practice at home while others don't?
- Should a teacher assign out-of-class activities that involve Internet access when some students do not have it available at home? Does this apply the same to students of various levels, such as elementary versus middle versus high school students?

having more computers and dramatically better computer instruction than schools that serve poor students. And they see a built-in bias in favor of boys over girls in the way that computers are used in schools and in the computer games students use at home. All these inequities are part of the digital divide.

Speaking at the 2007 conference of the International Society for Technology in Education, Sylvia G. Rousseau, of the University of Southern California, said, "As much as I admire technology . . . it has a mixed history in the way it has impacted our lives." Rousseau and many others believe that contemporary technology—television, video games, the Internet—all reinforce a cultural construct of race, class, and gender that undermines the achievement of some children while fostering the dominance of others. When low-income students use computers for drills while more privileged children use the same computers to construct new knowledge, or when the computers used in most classrooms open to a desktop screen that most middle-class children find familiar but children who have spent more time in rural fields or urban streets do not, then, as Rousseau says, "The issue isn't all technology, yet in this day, it has everything to do with technology."[16]

How Can I Use Technology to Improve My Teaching?

The supply of ideas for how to expand the use of technology in support of learning seems endless. Writing for the online publication *Mind/Shift,* Erin Scott offers some examples:

1. **Games and Group Work:** Ananth Pai's third-grade class in Parkview/Center Point Elementary School in Maplewood, Minnesota, uses a collection of seven laptops, two desktops, 11 Nintendo DS's, and a series of games and digital voice recorders to compete in games with other kids across the world, study fractions and decimals by riding a virtual ghost train, and to learn about constitutional rights with the Go to Court Game. In the process, student reading and math scores went from below average for third grade to mid-fourth grade levels.
2. **Learning Latin:** Kevin Ballestrini created an alternate reality in his Latin class at Connecticut's Norwich Free Academy. Students had to save the world by joining a shadowy organization that was part of Ancient Roman Society and, of course, learn Latin in the process.
3. **Reaching Students:** Ramsey Musallam, an Advanced Placement Chemistry teacher at Sacred Heart Cathedral Preparatory School in San Francisco, begins class with a test blast that utilizes students' smartphones, asking a challenge question for the day's lesson. "First person to tell me the units on K for a second order reaction gets chocolate," he texted on one day. Musallam knows it may be a gimmick but sees the phone blast as a fun way to stay connected and "think about what we're learning."
4. **Creative Play:** Santeri Kivisto and Joel Levin took the game Minecraft, which many already use to challenge students to build their own educational world, and developed MinecraftEdu (https://minecraftedu.com/)—a for-purchase program that allows teachers to tailor Minecraft to individualize the curriculum.

Harman Singh, founder of @WizIQ and a regular commentator on educational technology, has predicted that by 2018, global spending on edtech (education technology) for classrooms is projected to reach $19 billion. He challenges developers to make sure that all that money is producing the best possible technology to address real needs of real students. On Singh's long list are the following:

1. For successful flipped learning, it is essential to improve the basic technology for the online/at home portion of the experience. Passive video learning alone does not boost student achievement and better programs linked to new analytics to measure student responses are needed.
2. Far too many applications are exclusive to one device or operating system and leave teachers and their students trying to manage multiple applications on multiple systems. New applications must be flexible across multiple devices.
3. One of the greatest potentials for classroom technology is the kind of assistance it can provide for students with a wide range of disabilities.[17]

The introduction of technology into a school can take time. A recent article in *edutopia*, an online journal designed to encourage the creative use of technology, reminds teachers that, "There is no doubt that finding the time to integrate technology is an overwhelming task for anyone. . . . It begins with a focus followed by good instructional design—but ultimately, a healthy balance."[18]

This attention to balance may not be the complete rethinking of the nature of schooling that Vander Ark or the New Tech High School advocates want, but it is a blend that might work for many teachers. Many teachers have adopted a positive stance toward the new technologies and believe that they will only improve what goes on in their classrooms. The 156 New Tech schools across the country—and others like them that have made new technologies the core of the school structure—may be unique, but they are hardly alone. Many examples can be found of classrooms and curricula that have been fundamentally rethought because of the technology that is now so widely available and popular with so many students.

In their 2005 study of the use of digital resources by science and mathematics teachers, Katherine Hanson and Bethany Carlson (researchers from the Education Development Center in Newton, Massachusetts) found overwhelmingly positive responses to technology. Some of the most enthusiastic comments were about the impact of Internet resources on a teacher's curriculum planning. Hanson and Carlson heard things like, "some of the techniques discussed on the web and the motion videos on some of the topics help in giving me insights into handling a particular topic with greater depth," and "I don't have to reinvent the wheel. I can stay up-to-date easily. No zillion trips to the library. . . . [I] can collaborate with colleagues who aren't in my area. . . . I can learn new topics easily without taking a class or going to a conference."

Notes from the Field

How do you use the technological skills of your students to help them learn?

"The primary way I use technology is to fill in the more rote assignments that were typical in traditional classrooms. By using more interactive assignments, I can have confidence that most students can access basic information online. This allows the class to focus on synthesizing information from varying sources."

—*Darren Kawaii, seventh-grade social studies teacher*

Teachers in the study found that the new technologies gave them significant new ways to connect with their students and to help their students learn much more. They reflected that the Internet "allows my students to arrive at conclusions on their own as opposed to listening to me lecture," and "Web-based resources provide more universal access for multiple audiences. . . . [the Internet] also presents information that addresses audiences that do not learn from conventional classroom instructional strategies by presenting 'the picture' of an idea in a dynamic way. This facilitates abstraction for many learners (of all ages)."[19]

In this chapter we have seen examples of teachers and students "owning" their education when technology is used well in schools—not just as a skill to be mastered but as a tool to connect with the extraordinary resources of the modern world. However, most proponents of an expanded use of computer technology in schools will admit that, at times, something important can be lost. If intensive use of computers can widen the resources available to students and their teachers, they can also narrow the focus of activities and miss a sense of order and mastery that some older curricula afforded.

As with many of the topics discussed in this book, a new or aspiring teacher needs to consider the impact of technology on the classroom from multiple angles. Straightforward questions can be asked: How will I use the new technology that is available to me and how will it affect my classroom? What can I learn from others that

Teachable Moment
THAT'S NOT FAIR (USE)

Before the Internet, students who wanted to plagiarize a source at least had to type the material from the original source into their paper. Now, with copying and pasting, the Internet makes it ridiculously easy to claim others' work as one's own—and statistics suggest that students are not hesitating to plagiarize. According to a 2008 survey of teens by the Josephson Institute Center for Youth Ethics, more than one in three (36%) said they used the Internet to plagiarize an assignment.

Although more than a third of teens admitted to plagiarism using the Internet, even more are likely committing plagiarism without realizing it. George M. Bodner, who serves on the Ethics Committee of the American Chemical Society, suggests that "[c]onfusion about what constitutes plagiarism—not malicious intent—is the leading cause of plagiarism at the graduate school level." If graduate students conducting research are confused about what constitutes plagiarism and what is considered fair use, it is easy to see how not all middle or high school students would be clear on the matter.

To help set your students on the right path, it is important that you become educated about plagiarism and fair use. "Fair use" means that it can be legal and ethical to use a direct quote from the Internet or another source, including a book, in something you claim as your own work. According to the U.S. Copyright Office, fair use is limited to the following: "quotation of excerpts in a review or criticism for purposes of illustration or comment; quotation of short passages in a scholarly or technical work, for illustration or clarification of the author's observations; use in a parody of some of the content of the work parodied; summary of an address or article, with brief quotations," and similar use. Even when the quotation is within the fair use guidelines, it is essential to give a reference through a footnote or indication that these words were written by someone other than yourself.

Despite the laws in place, students may still not be clear on the concept of fair use—and it is certainly not safe to assume that they understand the rules and expectations regarding plagiarism. As a teacher, you have the opportunity not only to enforce the rules against plagiarism but also to use the discussion of plagiarism as way to challenge your students to consider issues of ethics and fairness. When a student's writing suddenly becomes "too good," there may be reason to suspect plagiarism has occurred. Although many college-level instructors use online services to check for plagiarism, this method is not as common for lower grades, which means that plagiarism is sometimes hard to catch, especially with so many sources of information available today. The key is to develop a sense of ethical responsibility within students so that they understand plagiarism is not acceptable.

The Internet offers numerous resources that you can use to become educated on this issue, and many conferences and lectures are dedicated to the topic as well. In addition, many schools are adopting honor codes and ethics policies to deal with these issues and to encourage ethical behavior; but these work only if students first understand them and then internalize them. By learning more and involving your students in the conversation, you can take a stand against plagiarism.

Questions

- Have you ever been uncertain about how or whether to cite a source, or if the way you paraphrased something was enough to avoid plagiarism? If so, how did you handle that situation? Would you handle it the same way now? Why or why not?
- Do you feel informed enough to discuss issues of plagiarism and fair use with your students? If not, what do you need to learn to be sufficiently informed and to feel comfortable talking about it?

Sources: Josephson Institute Center for Youth Ethics. *The Ethics of American Youth—2008 Summary,* http://charactercounts.org/programs/reportcard/; U.S. Copyright Office. "Fair Use," revised May 2009, http://www.copyright.gov/fls/fl102.html.

will help me be a better teacher? Will technology change schools and the work of teachers beyond recognition? Or is the truth somewhat closer to the arguments of Larry Cuban, who wonders if the current predictions about technology will suffer the same fate as Thomas Edison's 1922 prediction that the motion picture would supplant textbooks and teachers?

One of the most important things for a new teacher to remember, especially one who is her- or himself a technology native, is that there can be a big difference between technological literacy and skill at technologically based pedagogy. We may be expert at staying in touch with all our friends through Facebook and sending rapid text messages, getting all of our information via a smartphone or tablet, and teaching others how to use technology. Ensuring that students learn not only how to use technology but also to use that technology to explore and master the rich range of lessons that are expected in schools—the Common Core of learning if you will—requires not just mastery of technology but also mastery of the educational use of technology, which is a different and often more complex challenge.

 **CHAPTER REVIEW**

- Historically speaking: How has technology been used in education?

Although the presence of computers in classrooms is a product of the last two decades, earlier technologies also changed schools—sometimes with a huge impact and sometimes with virtually none. Certainly the development of the printing press in the 1400s created the widespread use of books which in turn became central to virtually all schooling. However, early ventures in "edutainment" software proved to be more entertaining than actually educating students. More recent trends have involved using Internet-based resources to both serve as and support instruction.

- How is technology transforming education?

The appearance of technology has caused teachers to rethink every aspect of what it means for teachers to teach, students to learn, and how to manage and communicate the effectiveness of that process. New tools are being used to support instruction, assist students with special needs, record and report grades and behavioral issues to parents and administration, and offer distance learning options for students. Many educators, such as those involved with Scratch, the New Tech schools, and WebQuest, are embracing technology and implementing it in ways that will allow students to take charge of their own learning, follow their own interests, and be connected to a wider world of research, information, and people.

- Are we on the edge of a wonderful new era, or is there a downside to technology?

The use of technology in education has both tremendous features and pitfalls. Some supporters want to see schools prolific with technology and believe we cannot develop highly educated students without it, while others think the fervor over advances in technology is overrated and unnecessary. Theorists like Seymour Papert and Neil Postman debate large-scale societal questions, such as "Should we introduce computers and other related technology into our schools at all?" and "What will be the benefits, and costs, if we do or do not do so?" Reports on the juggling of various technologies by students show that the multitasking that they claim to have mastered is actually producing worse results than if they were focusing on one thing at a time—something teachers need to keep in mind when determining when and how to use technology tools.

- What is the digital divide, and how does it affect my teaching?

Not everyone has the physical access to technology or opportunity to take full advantage of it, especially those in lower-income areas. Also, boys have traditionally been more involved than girls in activities such as gaming and thus have had more experiences with technology. That is changing as boys and girls spend more time using all aspects of technology on a daily basis, but the divide between better off and less well-off Americans is as strong as ever and has a significant impact on access to technology.

- How can I use technology to improve my teaching?

Connections to a larger world of research and to a global conversation are at the fingertips of teachers and their students. Teachers who use technology to create a place of inspired learning—rather than for old-fashioned drills—will be comfortable enough with the technology to test its limits. They will also be able to engage in an ongoing conversation with their students, who are rapidly developing their own technological expertise outside of the classroom.

Readings

How Is Technology Transforming Education?

From *ZERO TO EIGHT : CHILDREN'S MEDIA USE IN AMERICA 2013*

AUTHOR: COMMON SENSE MEDIA

Technology is inevitably transforming today's schools because it is transforming today's society and the lives of almost everyone in it, especially young people. The reality is that most schools are still playing catch up to kids' out-of-school technology use. This study from Common Sense Media shows how fast young people are moving in their embrace of technology in all forms.

Even a casual observer of children and families today knows big changes are afoot when it comes to children and new media technologies.

This report, based on the results of a large-scale, nationally representative survey, documents for the first time exactly how big those changes are. The survey is the second in a series of national surveys of children's media use; the first was conducted in 2011 (*Zero to Eight: Children's Media Use in America*, Common Sense Media, 2011). By replicating the methods used two years ago, we are able to document how children's media environments and behaviors have changed.

Teachers, parents, health providers, and child development experts all agree that the media children use can have a profound impact—both positive and negative—on learning, social development, and behavior. The only way to maximize the positive impact of media on children is to have an accurate understanding of the role it plays in their lives: which platforms they are using, the activities or content they are engaging on those platforms, and how their media use patterns vary by age, gender, or socioeconomic status. It is the purpose of this report to provide these data to all of those who are working to improve the quality of children's media, protect children from harmful content, and increase the supply of educational and pro-social content. This group includes policymakers, educators, public health advocates, content creators, and parents themselves. Because this study is based on a large, nationally representative sample of respondents who were recruited using probability-based methods of address-based sampling and random-digit-dialing, the results are a highly reliable method of documenting children's media use and how it has changed over the past two years.

We believe that public policy, parental decision-making, and the work of children's advocates will all be more effective if they are grounded in up-to-date, reliable data about children's media use. It is our goal to provide those data and thus to help shed light on the important role media play in the lives of infants, toddlers, and children everywhere.

Key Findings

Table 8.2

Ownership of Mobile Media Platforms, over Time

Among 0- to 8-year-olds, percent with each of the following in the home:

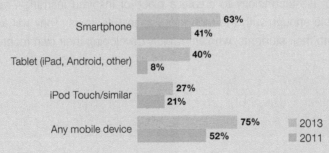

	2013	2011
Smartphone	63%	41%
Tablet (iPad, Android, other)	40%	8%
iPod Touch/similar	27%	21%
Any mobile device	75%	52%

Table 8.3

Screen Media Use, by Platform, over Time
Among children age 0-8, average time spent per day using:

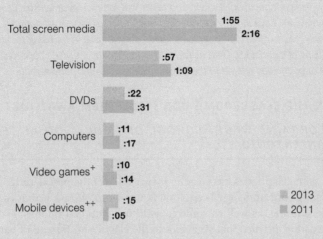

⁺Console and hand-held   ⁺⁺Such as smartphones and tablets

Use of Mobile Media, over Time
Among 0- to 8-year-olds, percent who have ever used mobile devices such as smartphones or tablets:

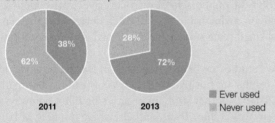

Figure 8.1

Time-Shifted vs. Live Television Viewing, 2013
Among children age 0-8, percent of viewing on a TV set that is:

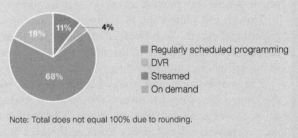

Note: Total does not equal 100% due to rounding.

Figure 8.2

Questions

1. If 72% of children under 8 use a mobile device at some point in their lives, compared to 38% in 2011, and many young children use these devices a great deal, what are the implications for a teacher who wants to teach with such devices? What sort of instruction is, or is not, necessary? What about the other 28% of kids?
2. If TV viewing is still the dominant way children spend media time, what is the future of educational television in classrooms? Is that a good thing?

Source: Common Sense Media. *Zero to Eight: Children's Media Use in America 2013*. San Francisco: Common Sense Media, 2013. Retrieved from https://www.commonsensemedia.org/research/zero-to-eight-childrens-media-use-in-america-2013.

How Can I Use Technology to Improve My Teaching?

The two articles that follow explore specific questions and ways that technology might be used in 21st century classrooms. Some readers of this book may well have already experienced such technology use as students in K-12 or college classrooms. These ideas may be relatively new to others. Both articles reflect an enthusiasm for using technology but also raise important questions about the limitations of technology. Even as we, and our students, embrace classroom technology with enthusiasm, the cautions as well as the opportunities offered in these two pieces are worthy consideration.

From "CELL PHONES IN THE CLASSROOM : DON'T PUT THEM AWAY JUST YET!"

AUTHOR: CAROLYN LORRAINE WEBB, SCHOOL OF EDUCATION AT TEXAS A&M UNIVERSITY–SAN ANTONIO

As the number of students with cell phones has steadily increased over the past decade, these technological advances have caused trepidation among educators over behavioral issues, from off-task activities to cheating (Prensky, 2005). On the other hand, mobile learning, as well as some tools to use with cell phones, are easy to set up, easy to use, and easy to integrate into existing instructional strategies in the classroom. Instead of banning devices, educators can counter the negative issues by embracing cell phones as a means to engage students in lessons. Although this article centers around the use of cell phones specifically, most of the suggestions are also applicable to other types of mobile devices, such as tablets.

Recent Studies

Research shows that students of all ages have access to cell phones. In a report published by Project Tomorrow in 2010, 98% of high school students possessed a cell phone, 31% of which included Internet access. Of students in grades 6 through 8, 83% had a cell phone—25% with Internet access. Forty-three percent of third through fifth graders possessed a cell phone, with 15% including Internet access; and 28% of early childhood students had a cell phone—12% with Internet access (Project Tomorrow, 2010).

Though cell phones are increasingly available to students, 88% of public school districts have written policies regarding them (Ed-Tech-Stats, 2010). Generally, these policies involve what *not* to do with such devices and the consequences for using them. In the last few years, however, several small-scale studies have emerged pertaining to how to use cell phones in the learning process.

The sample size in most studies has been limited. However, two studies are being conducted in North Carolina and the United Kingdom that involve thousands of students. Early results are positive in the areas of reading and math skills, as well as student motivation and collaboration (Manzo, 2010). Another study in progress by Elliot Soloway, a prominent researcher of mobile learning, involves districts in New York, Ohio, Texas, and elsewhere (Manzo, 2010). Unlike these, however, most studies have focused on the cell phone as a tool for communicating or capturing pictures and not on how the tool could be used for learning or justification for using it for learning. . . .

Learning Opportunities

"There is a 'digital disconnect' between how students use technology for their everyday communication and how they use technology in the classroom" (Kolb, 2008, p. 1). Outside of school, students may be texting, taking pictures, watching videos, and playing games. In school, Web 2.0 tools in conjunction with cell phones offer many opportunities to assist in learning before, during, and after class at all grade levels. Most of the opportunities are free, and implementation is easy.

Tables 8.4, 8.5, and 8.6 provide a sampling of Web 2.0 tools and applications common to most cell phones, and ways they can enhance learning for teachers and students. The listed resources specifically pertain to use with cell phones and are presented in three categories—collaboration and organization, curricular, and communication. Sites marked with an asterisk (*) are also accessible through a computer.

As has been the case since the inception of the Internet, websites do not always remain active and services do not always remain free. However, the growth of Web 2.0 tools continues; therefore, the types of services listed here

Table 8.4

Tool	General Features	Student Uses	Teacher Uses
FreeConferencePro.com*	Dedicated phone line for conference calls which can be recorded	• Communicate with one another for group projects and record conferences for the teacher or for future reference • Interview individuals for reports	• Conference with one or more students or parents while maintaining a transcript of the conversation • Discuss curricular ideas with other teachers from around the world
Nozbe.com*	Time and project management	• Organize assignments, tasks, homework	• Organize assignments, tasks, lesson plans
Camera	Video and still pictures	• Record group projects during rehearsal to review before presentation to class • Record video reminders for class assignments, events	• Take pictures of students to learn their names • Video record student presentations to review later while grading
Recorder	Voice recording app	• Record guest speakers to review later • Practice speeches before presenting in class	• Record oral speeches of students for later evaluation and to give to students with feedback • Record guest speakers for absent students
Notes	Notepad app	• Type notes directly into phone • Type questions for further research ideas	• Take notes in meetings • Jot down ideas for lessons

Table 8.5

Tool	General Features	Student Uses	Teacher Uses
Scvngr.com	Geo-gaming scavenger hunts (to participate in or to create yourself)	• Complete scavenger hunts as assigned by the teacher • Create a scavenger hunt as a group project to be completed by other groups in the class	• Create a scavenger hunt in the school for students to learn their way around • Hunt for pieces of a poem to introduce a unit on poetry • Hunt using directions to teach geography standards
Snapfish.com*	Video uploading, editing, and sharing	• Share pictures and videos pertaining to curricular topics • Document field trips • Create multimedia presentations for curricular topics	• Share pictures and videos pertaining to curricular topics • Document field trips • Create multimedia presentations for curricular topics
YouMail.com	Voice recorder	• Record oral histories • Practice a speech • Check in during field trips • Record a message to the teacher when absent	• Set up a prompt for students to reply to (get-to-know-you or curricular-based) • Set up oral quizzes • Use for speech practice
Hipcast.com*	Podcast creator	• Create podcast interviews for curricular reports • Create news broadcasts/radio shows	• Create podcasts of lectures for absent students • Create presentations/workshops for other educators
GoogleBlogger.com* (Edublogs.com has this capability for a minimal price)	Blog creator	• Blog about homework assignments • Write a daily/weekly journal for writing practice	• Post blog prompts on curricular topics for students to comment on • Write homework tips, help, ideas
ChaCha.com*	Quick Q&A on any topic	• Get quick answers to questions during research projects	• Research a student question during instruction

* Accessible through computers.

Table 8.6

Tool	General Features	Student Uses	Teacher Uses
Polleverywhere.com*	Live polls (free-form text or multiple choice)	• Create poll to use during a group presentation on a curriculum topic • Survey the class to collect data for a spreadsheet and chart	• Conduct polls at the beginning of a unit or topic of study to collect prior knowledge • Set up for students to use to text questions about the content during class
Qipit White app	Whiteboard or handouts converter to PDF files	• Take pictures of handouts or written notes and send to absent peers • Use pictures to study for exams or keep for future reference	• Take pictures for absent students of notes on the board, which can be uploaded to website or printed to handout • Use pictures for future reference in another class or for next year
Remind101.com	Reminder service (can be set up for future delivery)	• Create reminders of upcoming assignments, events	• Create reminders of upcoming assignments or events to be sent to students' phones • Create reminders of upcoming tasks or events to be sent to students' phones
Pulse.to	Group text messaging made easy	• Send texts about projects to everyone in a group without the need to enter everyone's information each time	• Send group texts to students or parents about upcoming assignments and events
Pinger.com	Group voice messages	• Send voice messages about projects to everyone in a group without the need to enter everyone's information each time	• Send group voice messages to parents or students about upcoming assignments or events • Send emergency messages for a call chain or list

* Accessible through computers.

that may be worth consideration should be available from more than one company. "Thousands of possible learning adventures are at one's fingertips. It's possible to access grammar lessons, language applications, Shakespearean plays of quotes, physics experiments, musical performances, and math review problems with a mobile phone" (Bonk, 2010, p. 63).

Accessibility

Two important limitations should be considered and addressed before making plans to use cell phones in a classroom setting. A discrepancy between the number of devices available for use as well as the capabilities of available devices may affect lesson ideas. In addition, school and district policies regarding the use of cell phones during school hours may deter efforts to implement some of the tools suggested.

The number of cell phones available for use within classrooms may vary and, as such, implementation of the use of these tools should be adjusted to accommodate for these variances. Teachers must determine how many devices are available and create instruction accordingly. In the classroom, students may share cell phones during cooperative and collaborative learning. At home or in school, students may be able to access certain tools through the use of a tablet or computer connected to the Internet.

Even with accommodations made for the number of available cell phones, capabilities of these phones may vary. Only a few of the tools mentioned earlier do not require Internet access; the majority do. As the Project Tomorrow (2010) study stated, approximately one-third to one-half of students' cell phones have Internet access. Other students may be able to access the Internet on their phones only by using an available wireless connection. The Institute of

Education Sciences (2007) found that virtually all public schools had Internet access by 2005, and 97% were broadband connections; in addition, 45% of public schools had wireless Internet access throughout the school by 2005.

Teachers wishing to implement cell phone access to the Internet should check the connections available by communicating with their principal or the information technology department. Teachers will need to explore the options listed here, as well as others, to accommodate for any accessibility issues.

Policies

Cell phone policies in educational settings vary from district to district and even school to school. Though educators and parents agree that cell phones in school can be significant distractions during instruction, parents feel their children are safer when carrying them (Obringer & Coffey, 2007). Beyond distractions, issues of harassment and privacy are of grave concern (Carroll, 2004). Yet, the same phone features that might be found harmful, such as a camera, also can be educational (Dyrli, 2004). Hartnell-Young and Heym (2008) suggested a gradual revision of policy "as attitudes and behaviours align with purposeful learning, until the school (and the community) reaches the tipping point, and mobile phone use is as natural as using any other technology in school" (p. 3). Technology has outpaced laws and regulations; therefore, policies should be viewed as in-progress rather than stagnate (Obringer & Coffey, 2007).

Issues of safety, privacy, and cyberbullying should be taken seriously and, therefore, addressed in school policy—just as schools have addressed other forms of bullying and Internet safety in computer labs. Teachers wishing to use cell phones in their classes should educate themselves on the current policies in their school and district. If prohibitions are in place, educators can make specific requests to use the devices, just as they have been able to request access to blocked Internet sites. If teachers have an educational plan, along with contingencies in place for any issues that may arise, administrators and technology departments are more likely to allow access. As issues arise, open dialogue about the pros and cons of educational uses of cell phones during class time can lead to policy revisions.

Conclusion

Research shows that mobile learning with cell phones is growing. The capabilities of cell phones as they apply in learning situations are documented. However, the impact of mobile learning on academic achievement has not been fully explored. More research is warranted to determine whether using cell phones increases learning.

Source: Carolyn Lorraine Webb. "Cell Phones In the Classroom: Don't Put Them Away Just Yet!" *Kappa Delta Pi Record* 49, no. 4 (October, 2013): 180–3.

From "FROM PRINT TEXTS TO E-BOOKS : THE CHANGING NATURE OF LITERACY"
AUTHOR: LOTTA LARSON

Joey, an energetic fifth grader, does not consider himself a "good" reader. Recently, he told his teacher, Mrs. Nelson, that reading is boring and he dislikes "thick books with lots of words." Unfortunately, Joey's response is not unique. There are countless reasons why some students struggle with reading: lack of motivation or interest, inappropriate or insufficient reading materials, poor reading skills, or even learning or print disabilities. The adoption of the Common Core State Standards has placed an increased emphasis on 21st century literacy skills and rigorous reading expectations, calling for students to be able to read and comprehend a wide range of complex texts independently and proficiently (National Governors Association [NGA] & Council of Chief State School Officers [CCSSO], 2010). At first glance, such an undertaking may seem unattainable for students like Joey. Fortunately, there are multiple ways teachers can support and motivate struggling or reluctant readers by making some relatively simple instructional changes through technology integration.

Over the past two decades, the use of technology has rapidly increased in schools and, as a result, many deeply rooted instructional beliefs and practices have been challenged. In particular, recent technology transformations have sparked a much-needed reassessment of effective literacy instruction. For learners to tap into the potential advantages of technologies, they need *new literacies*, or the "skills, strategies, and dispositions necessary to successfully use and adapt to the rapidly changing information and communication technologies and contexts that continuously emerge in our world." In short, as technologies change, contemporary literacy acquisition is most effective when learners have the ability to constantly adapt to an evolving society.

As the definition of literacy transforms, so does the idea of what constitutes text. In the past, texts involved printed recordings in magazines, books, or newspapers. Today, educators need to expand their understanding of traditional texts, which are often linear, static, and physically bounded, to include contemporary digital texts characterized as nonlinear, multimodal, and unbounded in time and space. Keep in mind that many students are already fervent technology users. This, of course, influences the way they play, learn, socialize, and, ultimately, transform the ever-expansive concept of literacy.

In many cases, however, schools are not meeting the demands of today's students because the biggest educational changes are, in fact, taking place outside the traditional school day. There is a clear discrepancy between the types of literacy activities students encounter at school (paper, pencil, print texts) and those they practice outside the class-room environment (digital reading and writing, Web 2.0). To make education more responsive to today's learners, teachers must recognize the plethora of technologies used outside the classroom to support literacy instruction. Tech-nology, when used effectively, extends the ability of teachers to meet unique needs of individual students. . . .

Digital Reading

The growing popularity of digital reading devices has rapidly enhanced the accessibility and affordability of e-books. A study by the Pew Internet & American Life Project revealed that one-fifth (21%) of American adults have read an e-book. This number appears even higher among children. The *2013 Kids and Family Reading Report* suggested that 46% of children have read an e-book and nearly 50% are interested in doing so (Scholastic, 2013).

In addition, today's youth encounter digital reading any time they go online, receive text messages, or engage in Facebook conversations. In other words, digital reading accounts for a large portion of students' daily literacy experiences. Consequently, literacy instruction must reflect this change. Across the country, more and more schools are incorporating digital reading experiences, including the use of e-books, to support this necessary shift.

Digital Reading Devices

Many e-books are retrieved from the Internet and stored on computers (laptops, desktops), tablets (e.g., iPad®), or portable devices (e.g., Nook® and Kindle™). The popularity and portability of these types of reading devices have helped generate an unprecedented e-book movement. In only two years, the number of e-book readers has quadrupled. With a click of a button, e-book readers have instant access to an infinite array of book titles and genres. This accessi-bility, of course, helps teachers satisfy individual students' needs and interests, while meeting the Common Core State Standards' call for integrating both literature and informational texts across the content areas (NGA & CCSSO, 2010).

Most e-books offer tools and features that invite readers to physically interact with the text by inserting notes; deleting or replacing texts; marking passages by highlighting, underlining, or striking through words; recording audio comments; attaching files and documents; and manipulating page layout, font size, and screen orientation. Teachers should examine the different tools and features afforded by their particular digital reading devices, because they vary by make and model. During whole-class instruction, the teacher may place the device on a visual presenter or connect a computer-based e-book to a projector so that students can visually follow along while learning how to access tools and navigate the digital text. Though not an exhaustive list, the following are some of the more common strategies used by teachers and students as they read e-book texts.

Customizing the digital page—To support individual reading comprehension and engagement, a first step is to encourage students to customize their e-books to suit individual learning needs. Visually impaired students, or struggling readers like Joey, may benefit from a larger font. Students also should personalize settings such as page orientation, margin size, background color, typeface, and line spacing to best accommodate their needs as readers. . . .

Responding to reading—Electronic books offer extended possibilities for personal interpretation of and engage-ment with texts, along with new options, scaffolds, and reading materials at all levels and for all purposes. In most e-books, readers can insert markups or notes anywhere in the text. As students insert notes directly onto the e-book pages, they engage in ongoing response to the unfolding plot. . . .

Looking up words—Many digital reading devices have a built-in dictionary, which makes the process of looking up words both quick and convenient. Recently, I visited Mrs. Nelson's fifth-grade classroom where Joey and his class-mates frequently accessed the dictionary while reading on Kindles. Immediately after looking up a word, the students inserted a digital note stating the definition or providing examples of the word's meaning. Particularly important for English Language Learners, the digital dictionary can be used to pronounce words; explain synonyms, antonyms, and word origins; and offer examples of word usage. . . .

Focusing on words and key passages—The highlighting tool allows readers to focus on particular words or passages within the text. As the fifth graders in Mrs. Nelson's room encountered words from their weekly vocabulary list, they habitually highlighted the words. Later, during whole-class discussion, the students accessed their highlights and digital notes and shared their findings with their peers. According to Mrs. Nelson, "This is a fun way for the students to pay attention to the assigned vocabulary and make it more meaningful. They act like word detectives." . . .

Listening to text—The Common Core ELA Standards also suggest that students in fifth-grade should be able to "summarize a written text read aloud or information presented in diverse media and formats" (Standard SL.5.2). Reading devices with text-to-speech capabilities can support this goal. . . .

Online e-Book Reading

When digital reading devices are not available, online e-book reading presents a viable option. To read online, students must have access to computers or tablets with high-speed Internet connection because these texts generally are not available for download. In classrooms with few computers, online e-books can be used during small-group reading centers or shared in a whole-class reading experience (using a projector and large screen). Features and contents of online e-book sites vary widely. For example, the *International Children's Digital Library* (http://en.childrenslibrary.org) is a free website that offers books in more than 60 languages—a priceless resource for culturally and linguistically diverse classrooms. This site's online books are comprised of authentic children's literature, each page carefully scanned and uploaded. A creative search feature allows students to locate books by language, reading level, subject, or dominant color of the book cover.

TumbleBook™ Library (http://www.tumblebooks.com) is a fee-based, online collection of animated, talking books. While the books' texts and illustrations are identical to those of their print counterparts, animations and audio bring movements and options for listening to, or reading along with, the narrator. The optional audio feature allows teachers to differentiate the reading experience to meet diverse needs and sustain reading fluency. Supporting English Language Learners, the TumbleBook collection includes books in both English and Spanish, ranging in reading levels from simple picture stories to more advanced chapter books.

StoryPlace (http://www.storyplace.org) is another example. This free website features multiple interactive stories in both English and Spanish. Students can customize the stories by selecting and naming characters or settings. Once created, some story parts are read aloud while students must independently read other passages. While not based on authentic literature, the stories are fun, animated, and range in difficulty from preschool to upper elementary. Using animated books can effectively help intermediate-level students learn to "analyze how visual and multimedia elements contribute to the meaning, tone, or beauty of a text" (Common Core Standard RL.5.7). In addition to hosting multimodal stories, this site features a resource section with suggestions for further readings and printable activities. . . .

By customizing the reading experience, students add to their already existing toolbox of reading strategies. For Joey, increasing the font size, accessing the dictionary, and highlighting passages he would like to revisit can support his reading comprehension. Moreover, digital reading can potentially help readers gain confidence in their reading abilities, especially if intimidated by thickness or number of pages of a printed book. For students like Joey, who often compares his thin, easy-to-read chapter book to his friend's volume of *Harry Potter*, this comes as a great relief.

The Teacher's Challenge

A rapidly changing, technology-rich world challenges teachers to differentiate instruction and integrate "new literacies into the curriculum to prepare students for successful civic participation in a global environment" (International Reading Association, 2009, n.p.). Digital reading is a big part of daily life, so it is important to teach related reading strategies. Simply placing digital reading devices in the hands of students, or accessing online e-books without appropriate and carefully designed instruction, will not magically increase reading scores and student motivation. King-Sars and Evenova cautioned that teachers should consider "the purpose of the technology and ensure that it complements the learning outcomes and that they are using it at an appropriate stage of learning."

While e-book tools support differentiated reading experiences, it is important to emphasize that using such tools should complement, not replace, students' existing inventory of traditional reading strategies. When reading a novel on a Kindle, for example, the text is, of course, digital. At the same time, the Kindle novel is still linear in nature because it contains few, if any, multimodal features (i.e., hyperlinks, audio, or video). Online e-books, however, may include a wide range of multimodal features, requiring students to navigate through multiple layers of text. In other words, just as traditional print texts demand a wide range of comprehension strategies, so do digital texts. When negotiating which comprehension strategies to use, educators should recognize that e-book texts come in many distinct forms.

It is no secret that integrating technology has the potential to engage and motivate students. This also appears to be true with e-book reading. Of course, digital reading should not aim to supplant print-based experiences, but rather work in tandem, because avid e-book users are also likely to read more traditional books. As teachers are challenged to implement the Common Core State Standards to elevate expectations that students read increasingly complex and diverse texts through the grades, technology can help spark a genuine passion and love for reading in all students. This notion extends far beyond the boundaries of both printed pages and digital screens.

References are available online at http://dx.doi.org/10.1080/00228958.2013.845505

Questions

1. How often do you use cell phones or e-books in your own personal life? How often have you used them as a student in a classroom setting? How might some classes you remember have been better—or worse—for the use of such technology?
2. What opportunities for using cell phones or e-books in the classroom would you add to Webb's and Larson's lists?

Source: Lotta Larson, "From Print Texts to e-Books: The Changing Nature of Literacy," *Kappa Delta Pi Record* 49, no. 4 (October, 2013): 168–73.

Professional Issues

9

Who Will Influence My Career?

> I hope to love my students so well that it doesn't even matter whether they like me. I want to love them in the way I love my own son—full of respect and awe for who they are, full of wanting their growth, full of wonder at what it means to lead and to follow the next generation.

MARGARET METZGER

QUESTIONS TO COME

Virtually every student in a teacher preparation program has spent at least 12 years in school—observing teachers closely. As Dan Lortie noted in his classic sociological study, *Schoolteacher*, "Teaching is unusual in that those who decide to enter it have had exceptional opportunity to observe members of the occupation at work; unlike most occupations today, the activities of teachers are not shielded from youngsters." In this way, teaching is quite different from almost any other profession where people may not feel that they know as much about what people actually *do* when they go to work. Almost everyone who has been a student believes they know what teachers do.

However, the true picture is much more complicated. Although some parts of a teacher's work are visible to students, other aspects—such as the rules and regulations that affect teachers; the salaries they are paid; and their interactions with colleagues, conversations with parents, meetings with supervisors, and participation in a teacher union or other organizations—can be hidden almost completely from students.[1] In this chapter, we seek to gain a better understanding of the daily life of teachers, especially those aspects that are not readily visible to their students.

The **Readings** for this chapter focus on two of the chapter's main topics—teacher unions and the people who impact a teacher's workday, for better and for worse. "Why

Teachers Should Organize" is from a speech given more than 100 years ago by Chicago teacher union leader Margaret Haley. In that speech, Haley laid out the rationale for having teacher unions and the importance of having organizations that give teachers a voice and protect their rights. In the second **Reading**, "The Desecration of Studs Terkel: Fighting Censorship and Self-Censorship," Portland, Oregon, teacher Bill Bigelow offers a humorous but ultimately very serious story of how he got into trouble with one school administrator, how other teachers and union leaders supported him, and ultimately how he found a different school with a different administrator to be a much more appealing place to work. Finally, in an exchange of letters entitled "Two Teachers of Letters," Clare Fox, who was about to become a teacher, wrote to her favorite teacher, Margaret Treece Metzger, asking advice about the rewards and pitfalls of teaching and received a long, thoughtful response outlining the good and the bad and most of all the incredible rewards of a long career as a classroom teacher.

Historically Speaking: How Has Teacher Work Changed—for Better or Worse?

In 1904, Margaret Haley, a Chicago teacher, stood in front of the National Education Association (NEA) to give one of the major speeches at their annual meeting. Haley was not an especially welcome speaker. At the beginning of the 20th century, the NEA was not the teacher-controlled organization that it is now. When Haley spoke, the NEA was dominated by the male elite of education—superintendents and college professors—who had little interest in hearing from an upstart woman from Chicago who had organized a union to challenge the policies and **prerogatives** of the male administrators and school board members who ran the Chicago schools.

> **prerogatives**
> Powers or privileges associated with a certain rank in a profession.

In her speech, Haley did not mince words about what she thought needed to happen to make schools better places for teachers and their students. Haley said that teachers needed to organize teacher unions to take charge of their own profession: "Nowhere in the United States today does the public school, as a branch of the public service, receive from the public either the moral or financial support needed to enable it properly to perform its important function in the social organism." These conditions, Haley told the NEA, meant that teaching could not be effective until changes were made, and the key to making the necessary changes was the creation of new organizations—unions of teachers modeled on the nation's growing labor unions—that would challenge the current unfair conditions in which teachers worked. Haley described these unhappy conditions very specifically:

1. *"Greatly increased cost of living."* Haley wanted a raise for all teachers everywhere.
2. *"Insecurity of tenure of office and lack of provision for old age."* Haley wanted tenure that would provide job security to protect teachers from getting fired if their political party lost the next election. She also wanted a retirement pension system for teachers.
3. *"Overwork in overcrowded schoolrooms."* Haley wanted smaller class sizes. The norm in many cities like Chicago was 50 or 60 students in a class. Teachers needed time to engage with individual students and time to think.
4. *"And, lastly, lack of recognition of the teacher as an educator in the school system, due to the increased tendency toward 'factoryizing education,' making the teacher an automaton, a mere factory hand, whose duty it is to carry out mechanically and unquestioningly the ideas and orders of those clothed with authority of position, and who may or may not know the needs of the children or how to minister to them."* She was tired of being a cog in a wheel and tired of an educational system in which school boards and high-level administrators, mostly men like the people in her audience, made all the decisions while the teachers, mostly women, were expected to carry out the decisions without ever thinking or using their own creativity or professional judgment in teaching.[2]

The problems Haley described were very real then, and many of these problems still exist today. Yet it is hard for today's teachers, for whom classes of 25 or 30 students can be a real handful, to imagine classes of 50 or 60 students.

When Haley spoke a century ago, teachers had no job security. In rural areas (which was still most of the country), they had to conform to the whims of the local school board, which often set the hour by which they had to be home in the evening and listed the things they could, and could not, do in their free time. In the nation's big cities, teaching was usually a patronage job, given to a voter (or the voter's daughter) in return for political favors and was forever revocable if the favors did not continue or if a different political faction or party came to power.

In 1896, Amelia Allison described in the *Atlantic Monthly* the political reality teachers faced, reporting the words of an anonymous teacher who described what happened when her father found himself at odds with one of the political parties in her city: "As our district was likely to have a close contest, it was suggested that my father be 'whipped into line.' The only lash that he could be made to feel, they thought, was a threat to remove me." The threat was made but also rebuffed. Happily for this teacher, the party that made the threats lost the election, and she continued in her position. It was hardly the kind of job security to inspire confidence or a long-term commitment to the profession.[3]

Rules for Teachers in 1915

1. You will not marry during the term of your contract.
2. You are not to keep company with men.
3. You must be home between the hours of 8 pm and 6 am unless at a school function.
4. You may not loiter downtown in any of the ice cream stores.
5. You may not travel beyond the city limits unless you have permission of the chairman of the school board.
6. You may not ride in carriages or automobiles with any man except your father or brother.
7. You may not smoke cigarettes.
8. You may not dress in bright colors.
9. You may under no circumstances dye your hair.
10. You must wear at least 2 petticoats.
11. Your dresses may not be any shorter than 2 inches above the ankles.
12. To keep the classroom neat and clean you must sweep the floor once a day, scrub the floor with hot soapy water once a week, clean the blackboards once a day, and start the fire at 7 am to have the school warm by 8 am when the scholars arrive.

Source: New Hampshire Historical Society

Slowly these things did change, although none have changed completely. Some of the points of Haley's speech sound all too familiar a century after it was given. Many teachers still complain about those who expect teachers to "carry out mechanically and unquestioningly the ideas and orders" of others "who may or may not know the needs of children." But significant victories have been achieved in the intervening decades: By almost any standard, teachers' work lives are better today. Classes are smaller, jobs are more secure, and salaries are better. Compared to many other professions, teachers still have a long way to go, but they have also come a long way in the past century.

How Much Do Teachers Get Paid?

An exhaustive study of teacher salaries conducted by the NEA, the nation's largest teacher union, indicated that the average teacher's salary in the United States for 2012–13 was $56,103. The average starting salary was $36,141. However, averages tell only part of the story. No one actually gets paid an "average" salary. Teacher salaries vary greatly depending on the state and district where one is employed. Part of the salary difference is due to cost-of-living differences around the nation. The median list price of a home in July 2014 was $141,100 in El Paso, Texas, and $902,800 in San Francisco, California. As a result, San Francisco teachers need a much higher salary than El Paso teachers just to have a decent place to live. In addition to living costs, however, part of the difference in teacher salaries in different cities and regions is due to the success of teacher unions and associations in bargaining for higher salaries for their members. In 2012–13, the highest average salaries were paid in New York ($75,279) and Massachusetts ($72,334), and the lowest in South Dakota ($39,018), Mississippi ($41,814), and Oklahoma ($44,373). Average salaries are, of course, significantly higher than starting salaries, and the highest-paid teachers—usually those with long seniority and advanced degrees—earn salaries that are well above average, just as novices earn much less. Some states are now experimenting with merit pay or pay for performance (with performance usually defined as the test scores of students), but these sorts of developments are in the early stages and, at least at this point, not widespread. For the most part, teachers' salaries are based on a complex formula in which years of service and advanced education are the two prime factors.[4]

 ## DID YOU KNOW?

Comparing teacher salaries by state is tricky business. In addition to the average salary, it is important to consider cost of living, benefits, and lifestyle when deciding where to live and teach. Teachers in New York and Massachusetts are among the highest paid, but those states are among the most expensive places in the country to live. The average salaries in South Dakota, Mississippi, and Oklahoma are the lowest, but those states rank significantly higher in affordability.

Table 9.1 Teachers' Salaries
2012–13 Average Starting Teacher Salaries by State
HIGHLIGHTS
2012–13 National Average Starting Teacher Salary: $36,141

State	Avg. Starting Salary	State	Avg. Starting Salary	State	Avg. Starting Salary
Alabama	$36,198	Indiana	$34,696	Nevada	$35,358
Alaska	$44,166	Kansas	$33,386	New York	$43,839
Arkansas	$32,691	Kentucky	$35,166	Ohio	$33,096
Arizona	$31,874	Louisiana	$38,655	Oklahoma	$31,606
California*	$41,259	Massachusetts	$40,600	Oregon	$33,549
Colorado	$32,126	Maryland	$43,235	Pennsylvania	$41,901
Connecticut	$42,924	Maine	$31,835	Rhode Island	$39,196
District of Columbia*	$51,539	Michigan	$35,901	South Carolina	$32,306
Delaware	$39,338	Minnesota	$34,505	South Dakota	$29,851
Federal Education Association (teachers in U.S. Department of Defense schools)	$45,751	Missouri	$30,064	Tennessee	$34,098
		Mississippi	$31,184	Texas	$38,091
		Montana	$27,274	Utah	$33,081
Florida	$35,166	North Carolina	$30,778	Virginia	$37,848
Georgia	$33,664	North Dakota	$32,019	Vermont	$35,541
Hawaii	$41,027	Nebraska	$30,844	Washington	$36,335
Iowa	$33,226	New Hampshire	$34,280	Wisconsin	$33,546
Idaho	$31,159	New Jersey	$48,631	West Virginia	$32,533
Illinois	$37,166	New Mexico	$31,960	Wyoming	$43,269

*2011–12

Source: NEA Collective Bargaining/Member Advocacy's Teacher Salary Database, based on affiliate reporting as of December 2013.

Table 9.2 Average Salaries of Public School Teachers, 2012–13 ($)

1. New York 75,279	27. Iowa 50,946
2. Massachusetts 72,334	28. Kentucky 50,203
3. District of Columbia 70,906	29. Indiana 50,065
4. Connecticut 69,397	30. Arizona 49,885
5. California 69,324	31. Colorado 49,844
6. New Jersey 68,797	32. Idaho 49,734
7. Alaska 65,468	33. Utah 49,393
8. Maryland 64,248	34. Nebraska 48,997
9. Rhode Island 63,474	35. Montana 48,855
10. Pennsylvania 62,994	36. Texas 48,819
11. Michigan 61,560	37. Virginia 48,670
12. Delaware 59,679	38. Maine 48,430
13. Illinois 59,113	39. South Carolina 48,375
14. Oregon 57,612	40. Alabama 47,949
15. Wyoming 56,775	41. Tennessee 47,563
16. Ohio 56,307	42. Missouri 47,517
17. Minnesota 56,268	43. Kansas 47,464
18. United States 56,103	44. North Dakota 47,344
19. Nevada 55,957	45. Arkansas 46,631
20. New Hampshire 55,599	46. Florida 46,598
21. Hawaii 54,300	47. North Carolina 45,737
22. Wisconsin 53,797	48. New Mexico 45,453
23. Georgia 52,880	49. West Virginia 45,453
24. Vermont 52,526	50. Oklahoma 44,373
25. Washington 52,234	51. Mississippi 41,814
26. Louisiana 51,381	52. South Dakota 39,018

Source: The U.S. average public school teacher salary for 2012–13 was $56,103. State average public school teacher salaries ranged from those in New York ($75,279) and Massachusetts ($72,334) at the high end to South Dakota ($39,018), Mississippi ($41,814), and Oklahoma ($44,373) at the low end.

NEA Research, Estimates Database (2013).

Another way to evaluate compensation is to compare salaries of teachers with those of other professionals. In 2012, accountants, for example, had a national average salary of $71,040, architects an average of $78,690, and computer software engineers in systems software an average of $93,280. None of these salaries had increased as much in the previous five years as did teacher salaries, and the average for all architects actually dropped slightly. Compared to many professions, teachers' salaries held relatively steady during the economic downturn of 2008 and 2009, even if school districts cut back on new hires during those years. Some occupations rank below the 2012–13 U.S. teacher average of $56,103, including community health workers ($37,490) and athletic trainers and exercise physiologists ($48,790). If salary is your major consideration, then teaching is clearly not the most desirable profession. However, teacher salaries are not the terrible national embarrassment that they were not all that long ago. The substantial benefits offered to teachers in terms of health care, pensions, and job security are often far better than those found in many other professions.

DID YOU KNOW?

President John F. Kennedy said, "Modern cynics and skeptics . . . see no harm in paying those to whom they entrust the minds of their children a smaller wage than is paid to those to whom they entrust the care of their plumbing."

Teachers, teacher unions, and many other people concerned about equity in education have spent the last century doing something about low and unfair teacher salaries. Soon after Haley spoke, women teachers in New York City began a campaign for "equal pay for equal work" for female and male teachers doing the same job. Up to this time, most school districts had two pay scales: one rate for women and a different, significantly higher rate for men holding the same positions. The female teachers rebelled, and by the 1920s in most major cities the old gender-based pay scales were abolished—though to this day men are more often promoted to the highest-paying administrative positions than women.

In addition to gender discrimination, teacher salaries were often unequal for teachers of different races. Well into the 1930s and 1940s, states and school districts that claimed to offer "separate *and equal*" schooling to White and Black students had two different pay scales for White and Black teachers. A White teacher with the same level of preparation and **seniority** could receive as much as 40% more than a Black teacher doing the same work. Among those who suffered from the two-tier salary schedule was Norma Marshall, a teacher in Baltimore, Maryland, and the mother of future U.S. Supreme Court Justice Thurgood Marshall. One of the younger Marshall's first cases as a civil rights lawyer for the NAACP, long before his elevation to the nation's highest court, was a successful 1937 challenge to Maryland's two-tier salary schedule that significantly improved Norma Marshall's salary. In a series of subsequent cases in the 1930s and 1940s, Marshall and the NAACP won a legal mandate for equal salaries for Black and White teachers a decade before their more direct assault on "separate and equal" that led to the *Brown v. Board of Education* decision in 1954.[5]

> **seniority**
> A ranking method that often grants employees promotions and other privileges (and protects employees from layoffs) based on the amount of time an employee has been at the company.

In addition to ending unequal salaries based on gender or race, teachers banded together to advocate for across-the-board raises for all teachers. In 1961, the federal government formally recognized the right of teachers to join unions. In the decade that followed, teacher unions gained ground, being recognized as the official bargaining agents for teachers in many school districts in the 1960s and 1970s. Once they were recognized officially, teacher unions immediately began their own negotiations with school boards, demanding contracts that stipulated significantly higher salaries than in the past, schedules for raises, improved benefits, and better working conditions. Recently, a number of state leaders have sought to undermine the bargaining power of teacher unions. Twenty-four states have enacted right-to-work laws that bar any requirement for an employee, including a teacher, to join a union as a condition of employment. Such laws significantly undermine the bargaining power of any union and, on average, both union and non-union employees in right-to-work states earn $1,500 less per year than those who work in states that allow full collective bargaining.[6]

Another area of compensation that many people don't consider as they start their careers is what kind of financial security they will have once they leave the profession (that is, with a pension or retirement fund). As many people learned all too painfully in the economic downturn that started in 2008, retirement planning is important for everyone, no matter what their age. Campaigns for retirement pensions for teachers began in the 1920s and expanded rapidly in the 1960s and 1970s. By now, teachers have better pension systems than do most professionals. Although the current economic climate is causing more people—teachers included—to work later in their careers that they had planned, teachers in most states (and each state's requirements are different) are typically eligible to receive full pension benefits after 30 or 35 years of service, regardless of age. Because these pension plans are funded through government retirement funds, unlike many private retirement plans (such as a company's 401k), they have historically been more stable as a guaranteed source of retirement income.

What Is Tenure?

Tenure is the right of a teacher to keep his or her job subject to good behavior. It is a significant right that nearly all teachers have today. Tenure is usually awarded after a relatively short probationary period, often 3 years. (College professors, by contrast, usually have to wait 7 years before being considered for tenure.) This is a far cry from the days when teaching jobs were awarded, and could be lost, based on political favoritism. Today, discussions of teacher tenure have shifted from concerns about protection from political interference—be it demands to join a certain party or challenges to freedom of speech—to an issue of ensuring continued excellence. Some observers worry that teachers have too much job security and that it is difficult if not impossible to get rid of a teacher who has become ineffective. Others argue that tenure continues to protect teachers, as professionals, from the whims of administrators or rapidly shifting political currents. Although there are heated debates about the advantages and disadvantages of the kind of job security that tenure offers teachers, virtually no one is proposing a return to the job insecurity that teachers faced a century ago. Today, however, many people, including many teachers, are advocating tougher standards for awarding tenure as well as streamlined procedures for removing ineffective teachers. An increasing number of teachers are saying that they cannot afford to have their own reputations undermined by others who cannot or will not pull their own weight.

Will I Join a Union?

Much has changed since Margaret Haley stood in front of the NEA in 1904 and called on teachers to get organized to fight for better salaries and improved working conditions. Schools are flexible institutions. They have changed over the years, sometimes for the better and sometimes for the worse. One of the most important forces for improving schools has been teachers. Sometimes working alone, sometimes in small informal groups, and sometimes in larger district and national associations and unions, teachers have changed schools dramatically. They will continue to do so as a new generation takes its place within the profession.

Decades of work by Haley and thousands of other teachers resulted in the creation of unions and associations of teachers across the United States, especially in large cities, during the early years of the 20th century. The NEA, which had greeted Haley with such limited enthusiasm in 1904, was transformed slowly from an organization led and controlled by administrators and college faculty into a teacher-led and teacher membership association that increasingly took on the identity of a union. At the same time, the American Federation of Teachers (AFT), which began with Haley's organizing efforts in Chicago, became a powerful union for teachers, especially teachers in some of the nation's largest cities that also had a strong history of labor union strength.

Today the NEA has over 3 million members, including teachers from the kindergarten to university levels, and it serves as the bargaining agent for teachers in 14,000 communities across the United States. The AFT has 1.6 million members, including K–12 teachers, **paraprofessionals**, and others working in schools and related fields who are part of more than 3,000 local unions. The two national unions no longer compete but instead work closely together toward what their leaders see as common goals. Today, most teachers in the United States are union members, and teacher unions are a large and powerful force in the lives of teachers, in schools, and in local, state, and federal policy.[7]

paraprofessionals
In the education system, workers—usually teacher aides or assistant teachers—who do not hold the state-required teacher certification but work alongside and assist primary teachers.

Adam Urbanski, the longtime president of the Rochester, New York, teacher union and a founder of the Teacher Union Reform Network (TURN) says there has been a danger that, as teacher unions become more and more like other industrial unions—focused on salaries, benefits, pensions, and work rules—they will lose sight of other professional concerns about the quality of schooling that also matter to their members. (See the Teachable Moment on TURN in this chapter.) There is no question that teachers' unions have done a great deal to improve the lives of teachers over the past half-century. As important as the hard-won gains in salaries, health care, and pensions, unions have also been the primary source of protection for teachers from unreasonable decisions by administrators and school boards. Nearly all teachers in the United States are protected today by tenure and union contracts, as none were a century ago. The protection offered

by tenure and union contracts is still far from absolute, but it is much greater than that experienced by past generations of teachers. The story of Bill Bigelow's experiences as a first-year teacher (in the **Readings**) offers one example of both the significance and the limits of this kind of protection.

 ## DID YOU KNOW?

In most school districts in the United States, teachers must join a teacher union when they accept a teaching job; thus, every teacher in the district is a union member by virtue of accepting a job there. These "closed shop" districts and states can have important advantages for teachers. On one hand, when every teacher in the district is a member of the union, it can draw on a broad base of union dues to grow in strength and present a united front when fighting for benefits, not only for salaries but also for health and retirement benefits and rules about working conditions. On the other hand, a teacher who disagrees with the union or does not like the idea of being a union member cannot quit the union without quitting his or her job. In "open shop" districts and states, union membership must be voluntary.

Source: "Right to Work States." National Right to Work Legal Defense Foundation, Inc., http://www.nrtw.org/rtws.htm

Today, there are more arguments about teacher unions than about most other topics in education. Some observers argue that, although unions may once have served an essential purpose, today they are only a barrier to further progress in education reform. Proponents of these views see unions as protecting mediocre teachers and making it far too hard to dismiss incompetent ones. They see the sometimes-rigid work rules required by teacher union contracts as stifling innovation and creative leadership. They argue that an employer-employee relationship built on the model of factory work is inappropriate to today's service-oriented professionals.

Nonetheless, many people want to protect teacher unions just as they are. After all, they argue, unions have forced teacher salaries to their current levels—yet those salaries are still too low and rising far too slowly. These union advocates say that much more needs to be done to bargain for quality pay for teachers. Although teachers have protections, they can still lose their jobs because of political views or philosophical differences with ever-changing administrative agendas. If the unions do not protect teachers, these advocates for traditional **unionism** argue, who will? And if teachers are not protected, who will want to enter the profession, and how many children will suffer because of the loss of good people?

> **unionism**
> Advocacy and support for unions.

A growing number of people seek a new way of viewing the place of teacher unions, including Adam Urbanski and other leaders of the TURN Network. Urbanski argues that teacher unions in America "must be reformed." He is certainly not making this argument as an opponent of unions. On the contrary, Urbanski has spent most of his life as a union member and many years as the president of the teacher union in Rochester, New York. But he is also a realist who knows that "unless it is voices from within the teacher union movement who are driving the call for reforms, there is a great risk that the voices from outside would be viewed as hostile 'bashing.'" Although Urbanski can bargain with as much toughness as any union leader to protect salaries and other benefits, he can also—perhaps with special effectiveness because of his background—call for fundamental change in the role of teacher unions today. He wants to work closely with parents. He wants to see continual improvement in the quality of teaching and the standards for teachers, and he wants unions to take the lead in promoting excellence rather than protecting mediocrity. He wants, above all, to see "better learning and higher achievement for America's children." He believes that unions must make this their top priority, even more important than their own appropriate self-interest in salaries and working conditions.

Teachable Moment
A CHANGING ROLE FOR TEACHER UNIONS

In 1995, Adam Urbanski, president of the Rochester New York Teachers' Association, and Helen Bernstein, president of the United Teachers of Los Angeles, California, convened a group of teacher union leaders from around the country to discuss what might come next for teacher unions. They realized that many people saw teacher unions as a barrier to education reform and that union representatives were rarely at the table when reform efforts were underway. The group decided they needed to do something to put teacher unions at the center rather than at the margins of reform efforts and to create a new organization—TURN—to find ways to restructure teacher unions at the local and national level so that they could and would play a leadership role in "building and sustaining effective schools for all students."

Today, TURN is a national organization with chapters in every part of the country that develops new ways to change national unions, rethinks the kinds of contracts that they negotiate with school districts, and keeps student learning at the heart of their efforts. TURN believes that because teachers are closest to students and to the learning process, and because of their link to parents and the larger communities, they are in a unique position to stimulate the necessary changes.

TURN's goals are clear:

- Continuously improving the quality of teaching.
- Promoting public education and in the union democratic dynamics, fairness, and due process for all.
- Seeking to expand the scope of collective bargaining to include instructional and professional issues.

In Rochester, New York, where Adam Urbanski remains the union president, he argues that "Teacher unions in America must be reformed. This can best happen if teacher unionists themselves recognize not only the need for change but also that it is in the enlightened self-interest of their unions to welcome the next logical stage in their unions' evolution." Among many initiatives it has accomplished, the Rochester union has:

- Negotiated a school-based planning process that involves teachers, parents, high school students, and school administrators in making decisions about each school's instructional program.
- Altered the traditional teacher evaluation process by developing the Performance Assessment Review for Teachers (PART)–a portfolio-based system that includes peer evaluations and parallels the principles and criteria of the National Board for Professional Teaching Standards.
- Negotiated a "professional day" provision that eliminates the teacher's dismissal time, so that the teacher's workday ends when the teacher's professional responsibilities (as determined by the teachers) are completed.

Urbanski contends that "We can succeed if we are passionate about change and commit for the long haul. But to do that, we first must instigate among our colleagues a revolution of rising expectations and create a vision that inspires others to aspire to more."

Questions

1. Urbanski says, "Including teacher unions as partners in transforming public education is essential to achieving the ultimate goal of improving student learning." Do you think this is a realistic or a desirable goal?
2. Do you think teacher unions have a responsibility to students and their families or should their responsibilities be limited to advocating for their members, the teachers? Do you think students and their families have a responsibility to teacher unions?

Sources: The TURN Web site (http://www.turnweb.org/about/), accessed December 31, 2014; Adam Urbanski. "TURNing Unions Around." *Contemporary Education* 69 (Summer, 1998).

Why Is Professional Development and New Teacher Mentoring Important?

Teachers, often working closely with administrators, parents, and community organizations as well as their own unions and in more informal gatherings, are addressing many of the problems that have long plagued the profession. In 2002, Dan Lortie looked at the changes in teachers' lives that had taken place since his book *Schoolteacher* was published in 1975. He saw two especially significant changes:

professional development
Lectures, group exercises, individual mentoring or other activities that provide skills and knowledge pertaining to the profession, for both career development and advancement.

reflective practice
A growing movement in many professions to encourage individuals to become "reflective practitioners" who continually ask *why* as they think about specific actions that they have taken in the course of a professional day.

- **Professional development**—activity focused on helping experienced as well as beginning teachers to strengthen their teaching capabilities—has had remarkable growth. Not long ago, school districts rejected plans to spend time and money on staff development, arguing that this was the responsibility of state agencies, and that it made little sense to invest in teachers who might move away. Today, we find an increasing focus on such undertakings at the local level.
- There is an increased emphasis on teachers analyzing their tasks and the choices they make in the course of their working day. *Reflective practice* describes the process in which teachers think longer and harder about what they do and work to guide their activities accordingly.

Teachers know they are never finished learning. However strong their initial preparation, there is always more to learn—about what to teach and how to teach.[8]

Teacher professional development has gotten much better in most places. Teachers once viewed nearly all professional development days as a time to listen to an "expert" selected by the district who might have no idea of the day-to-day realities of a specific group of teachers. Today, professional development often consists of much higher level activity, often conducted by and among a specific group of teachers with topics and leaders selected by teachers. Teachers today spend much more time talking to each other, comparing "what works," and looking carefully at specific examples of student work to see how they might more effectively help students improve while also treating students more equitably.

Teachers have sought increasingly to become what best-selling author Donald Schon calls a *reflective practitioner*: someone who continually thinks about one's professional work, discusses it with fellow professionals, and uses that thinking and those conversations to improve practice—one's own and that of one's colleagues. In other words, teaching today is a much more intellectually rigorous and engaging profession than it has ever been.

One of the most important kinds of teacher professional development, especially for teachers in the early years of their work, is one-on-one teacher mentoring. Ellen Moir, the founder and leader of the California-based New Teacher Center, works with school districts around the country to develop what she calls "competency-based, personalized professional development for both new and veteran teachers." Especially for teachers in the critical first three years of teaching, one-on-one support is essential to becoming the effective professionals they want to be. At the same time, the New Teacher Center has found that the experience of working as a mentor "fuels a veteran teacher's effectiveness." We all want to share what we have learned and, for a longtime teacher, the opportunity to teach novice teachers as well as children can make the difference in staying in or leaving the profession.

Another mentoring advocate, Audra Watson, director of Mentoring and Induction Strategies at the Woodrow Wilson National Fellowship Foundation in Princeton, New Jersey, insists on the following characteristics for a quality mentoring program:

- Mentors must visit at an appropriate frequency in order to understand the school context and provide a number of types of necessary interactions, including coteaching, modeling, observations, and personalized feedback sessions.
- Mentors must be carefully selected, trained, and compensated.
- Mentoring programs must align with school-based philosophies and structures.

While there are many considerations for a novice teacher, the depth and quality of the mentoring offered is one of the essential questions to ask of the leaders of the school and district when seeking a first job. Mentoring can make all the difference between success and failure in one's professional life.[9]

Who Are the People Who Impact a Teacher's Workday?

In 2004 and 2005, a survey asked 800 American teachers, "What are the biggest challenges you face in your work?" The researchers involved in the survey were careful to query a wide range of teachers and to talk with teachers in more prosperous schools as well as teachers from schools serving low-income children. The answers will probably not surprise those who are more familiar with what happens during a teacher's day. Almost a third of the teachers overall, and slightly more than that among the teachers in the low-income schools, listed "communicating with parents" as their most significant problem. Interestingly, "maintaining order and discipline" and "preparing students for testing" were seen as the biggest challenge by only one-fifth or less of the teachers. Given that school administrators and school system structures are in many ways responsible for issues of resources and also for "needed guidance and support," one can conclude that teachers' relationships with parents and with those in authority in school districts are challenges, perhaps greater challenges than their dealing with students and certainly greater than dealing with their peers (other teachers).

> **CONNECTIONS ➜⬅**
> The topics of maintaining order and discipline and preparing students for testing were explored in Chapter 7.

As a teacher, you must find ways to relate to the many people who will hold administrative authority over you, as well as the many other people—perhaps parents, most of all—who can be not only your allies but also your most critical opponents. How will you interact with the various people who have authority in your professional life? When should you stand your ground, and when should you compromise? When is it best to go it alone, and when should you reach out? When and how can you make a wide range of alliances and build the friendships you need? These are essential questions for you to consider as you strive to make connections with the people inside and outside of the classroom who will impact your teaching.

Fellow Teachers

Although the days of the one-room schoolhouse are long gone, many teachers still come to work, close their classroom doors, focus on their students, and then go home again. This isolation can give teachers a certain freedom. Indeed, some revel in the fact that "when you close your classroom door, no one really knows what you do." But the isolation can also be painful and ultimately self-defeating.

Notes from the Field

How does collaboration improve your curriculum?

"A teacher I worked with told me, 'One night at about 7 o'clock I was still working on a curriculum unit for *Sarah, Plain and Tall*, and I realized that all over the city other teachers were probably also developing lessons for the same book. It just didn't make sense.' And it doesn't. Establish a community of people who develop curriculum together. The work not only goes faster, but it's usually better because you have someone to talk through your ideas with."

—Linda Christensen, former language arts coordinator for the Portland (Oregon) Public Schools; editor of the journal Rethinking Schools; *and author of* Reading, Writing, and Rising Up: Teaching About Social Justice and the Power of the Written Word[11]

In her classic study of teacher work, Susan Moore Johnson found teachers split on the question of how isolated they were. Some teachers felt very isolated from colleagues, reporting that no one else in their school knew what or how they taught. One teacher commented, "I am isolated. I do what I want when I want to do it, and how I want to do it." A teacher of English language learners had given up on many aspects of the school, saying, "I tend to isolate myself. I was at a school that had a lot of problems with discipline. But I found that I could just have my own little world and control that." A high school social studies teacher generalized, "Teachers are isolated people. They don't know what others are doing. Things that work for them, they keep them year after year. You don't have time to sit down and discuss with each other from different areas. As small as this school basically is, I don't know all the people who are here."

Johnson reported that the majority of teachers she interviewed did not want such intense isolation. Many longed for more collaboration, including one who said, "I think that we could learn from each other. We really could." Another teacher was happy with the links with immediate colleagues in one department but noted that, "if there's isolation, it's from the rest of the building." Still, Johnson concluded that teachers agreed "virtually unanimously that the threat of isolation was ever present" but also that "the benefits of collegial interaction were many."[10]

Today, many schools are moving to reduce the level of isolation and create more collegial working conditions. One suburban elementary teacher Johnson interviewed painted a very different picture from other teachers:

We're just not individuals coming to work. We work together for the kids; we work together as colleagues, too. If I have an idea, I can go to people and say, "I think this might work with what you're doing." We communicate as far as what we do in our classrooms. I get a lot of support from the teachers here.

Table 9.3 The Biggest Challenges Faced by Teachers

	Elementary School	Secondary School	Schools With Less Than 50% Low-Income Students	Schools With 50% or More Low-Income Students
Base Number of Teachers:	501	270	362	422
Communicating with parents: 31%	31%	30%	24%	40%
Getting sufficient resources and materials: 22%	21%	24%	25%	19%
Maintaining order and discipline in the classroom: 20%	17%	23%	20%	20%
Preparing students for testing: 14%	16%	13%	17%	11%
Getting needed guidance and support: 9%	11%	7%	10%	8%
No answer: 3%	4%	3%	5%	2%

Source: Dana Markow and Suzanne Martin. *The MetLife Survey of the American Teacher*. Minneapolis, MN: Harris Interactive, 2005, p. 8.

Others reported similar arrangements from which they gained a great deal. Some found opportunities to team teach and one noted, "We really work together. All lesson plans are planned together so that we try to give all eighth graders the same education." Another junior high school teacher reported that the department was the place where teachers came together, noting, "We're in constant contact with each other. Everybody knows what everybody else is doing and gets ideas from each other." Another reported that her principal encouraged collaboration in which teachers not only shared lesson plans but "[w]e have a system where we can go into each other's classrooms—any classroom in the school up to grade four—and observe other teachers."

Although isolation can sometimes be appealing, as no one wants to have every move scrutinized, most educators conclude that it is a recipe for failure. As a teacher, especially a novice teacher, you need to have many mentors and to learn from, and also teach, other adults. One teacher Johnson interviewed remarked that "teaching's a lot more than just sitting in a classroom and teaching kids. . . . If you just do that you're going to be burned out real quick." Beyond survival, many of the teachers with whom she spoke made it clear that only through collaboration could teachers be a force for change in their schools:

> If we get our act together, and we want something to happen, we can make it happen for the most part, within the confines of what a school will allow. If we choose to pick an issue, that issue has to be addressed. If there is no universal feeling towards it, then it doesn't get addressed.[10]

Like other citizens, teachers are limited in what they can do alone. But no school or school leader can ignore a group of teachers who are clear, focused, and well organized. Not only will those teachers have a better sense of support, but they will be more able to make the school a better place for themselves and their students.[11]

Administrators

The acclaimed author Frank McCourt began his account of his years as a teacher in the New York City public schools with the words, "On the first day of my teaching career, I was almost fired for eating the sandwich of a high school boy." McCourt proceeds to tell the story of his very first class, which began with a small-scale fight in which one student threw his sandwich bag at another and a much larger fight was about to begin. He describes his first response:

> I came from behind my desk and made the first sound of my teaching career: "Hey." Four years of higher education at New York University and all I could think of was Hey.

But that was not enough to head off the incipient fight. Neither was McCourt's command to "[s]top throwing sandwiches," especially since the sandwich had already been thrown and laid there on the floor between the students. "Professors of education at New York University never lectured on how to handle flying-sandwich situations." But novice though he was, McCourt was also clear that "[t]hey had to recognize I was boss, that I was tough, that I'd take none of their shit." So McCourt decided to eat the sandwich and flipped the paper cover into the trash basket. The class cheered, and he had them. The dramatic move had succeeded. Except for one thing.

> My students smiled till they saw the principal's face framed in the door window. Busy black eyebrows halfway up his forehead shaped a question. He opened the door and beckoned me out. A word, Mr. McCourt?

The word, of course, was "I'm sure you understand, Mr. McCourt, it isn't seemly to have teachers eating their lunch at nine A.M. in their classrooms in the presence of these boys and girls." No asking about the situation. No hearing McCourt's early morning triumph of classroom management. Rules were rules and administrators were there to enforce them. McCourt's career began with both a success with students and a failure with administrators. As you read McCourt's book *Teacher Man,* you sense that both events marked his career for the next 30 years.[12]

School administration today is complex, with an extraordinary range of superintendents, deputy superintendents, principals, vice principals, and specialized teachers all interacting with classroom teachers on a regular basis. These positions were created for important reasons: to allow teachers to spend their time focused on students instead of on other matters and to represent the diverse needs and aspirations of democratic communities that expect many different things

Teachable Moment
TEACHER-TO-TEACHER PUBLICATIONS

Rethinking Schools is a quarterly magazine, an organization, a Web site (http://www.rethinkingschools. org), and one of the most valuable resources that any teacher, or aspiring teacher, can utilize. The curriculum resources it offers can be a gold mine of material for teachers—especially new teachers—who want to teach well. According to the organization's mission statement, *Rethinking Schools* is "committed to equity and to the vision that public education is central to the creation of a humane, caring, multiracial democracy." Examples of its newest publications include the following:

- *A People's Curriculum for the Earth: Teaching Climate Change and the Environmental Crisis*
- *Open Minds to Equality*
- *The New Teacher Book*
- *Rethinking Sexism, Gender, and Sexuality*
- *Teaching for Joy and Justice*
- *Rethinking Multicultural Education*
- *Unlearning "Indian" Stereotypes*
- *Rethinking Early Childhood Education*

Rethinking Schools began in 1986 when a group of Milwaukee, Wisconsin, area teachers began talking about not only how to improve what went on in their own classrooms but also how to help shape the education reform movements in the country. What began as a local community of teachers has become an important resource for educators across the country. When the group of educators who founded *Rethinking Schools* first gathered, they were concerned about the curriculum—including the hidden curriculum—in many of the textbooks they were asked to use, about the impact of testing on quality teaching, and more broadly about a kind of joylessness that they found in too many schools. These issues remain at the core of their work and, while they attempt to have an impact on national policy, they also seek to provide resources to classroom teachers who want to teach well.

Behind *Rethinking Schools* is a group of teachers who believe that schools need to do more than produce tomorrow's workers. Schools need to be places where students and teachers gather to talk, play, and work together in the present and begin to model a different society for the future. They help teachers who want to apply these same principles in what they teach and the way that they teach.

Questions

- What responsibility do teachers, especially beginning teachers, have to read journals like *Rethinking Schools* that will give them new ideas?
- What responsibility do teachers have to share their ideas with others and to try to shape the national dialogue about education reform as well as to succeed in their own classrooms? How will you participate in this dialogue and through what avenues? Information-sharing Web sites? Blogs? Professional journals? Conferences?

from schools. Teachers would say this happens with varying success and not always due to the support or involvement of their administrators (and sometimes in spite of it).

Another teacher, Bill Bigelow, tells a similar story in the **Readings** for this chapter. During Bigelow's first year of teaching in Portland, Oregon, a parent had complained about a student assignment, and when the vice principal of the school looked at the assignment, he too found the work "negative" and perhaps obscene, even though Bigelow had assigned a reading from an official text in use in the school. As you read Bigelow's article you will see that, like McCourt, he got off with a warning and a compromise.

Bigelow also discusses a range of ways in which teachers can find support as well as censure. For Bigelow, the first support came from Thurston Ohman, his union representative, who assured him, "You haven't done anything wrong," and "If they try to come after you in some way, the union will back you 100%." Bigelow also reflects on how rare the intrusions of people like his meddling vice principal really are. He notes that "in my experience, the intrusions of the Lloyd Dixons of the world are exceptions. . . . [W]e have an enormous amount of freedom." (Sometimes that isolation is not all a bad thing!) Even as Bigelow tells the story of his run-in with Lloyd Dixon, he reflects on other administrators who "were extraordinarily supportive and even enthusiastic about livelier, risk-taking teaching." He mentions Shirley Glick, who "offered nothing but encouragement" and notes that the reality of life as a teacher is that "[t]he Lloyd Dixons of the world exist, but so do the Shirley Glicks."

Finally, Bigelow reflects thoughtfully on what he might have done to reach out to the parent who first made the complaint and to other parents, whom he came—too slowly he admits—to see as allies rather than as censors. A great deal has been written about the characteristics of effective schools that seem to stand out for their success with students, including students from different racial and ethnic backgrounds, genders, and economic status. Nearly all of this literature, known logically as *effective school literature,* points to one variable above others in the recipe for success: strong, consistent, and inspired leadership. Thus, the principal who can sometimes be seen by teachers as the "evil administrator" may, in fact, be the key to the success of the whole school's approach to its students. Of course, this is not always the case. True tyrants are not strong and inspired and consistent leaders, and true leaders see a key part of their work as inspiring their team—the teachers and other educators who interact on a day-to-day basis with students. Teachers need to understand that teachers and administrators have different work lives, interact with different people, and may sometimes come into conflicts in which neither side should be seen automatically as right or wrong.[13]

In the 1980s, Harvard scholar Sara Lawrence Lightfoot conducted an extended series of case studies of the character and culture of effective high schools; she published the results in *The Good High School.* According to Lightfoot, "The tone and culture of schools is said to be defined by the vision and purposeful action of the principal. He is said to be the person who must inspire the commitment and energies of his faculty; the respect, if not the admiration of his students; and the trust of the parents." Lightfoot is also clear in using the word "his." The image of a school administrator in much of the effective school literature seems very male—a father figure or a general or a coach, an image of "steely objectivity, rationality, and erect posture." But Lightfoot wanted more of future school leaders, including a new definition of leadership that "includes softer images that are based on nurturance given and received by the leader."

This image is, perhaps, a model of leadership closer to Bigelow's Shirley Glick than to Lloyd Dixon. As a teacher, you'll definitely want to join a community led by someone closer to Glick than Dixon.[14] In my own career as a teacher—from fourth grade in New York City to various colleges and universities in Massachusetts and New York—I have also found my share of Lloyd Dixons as well as Shirley Glicks, though I am happy to report that the Glicks outnumbered the Dixons by a substantial margin.

Sonia Nieto tells of a teacher who responded to Nieto's question "What keeps you going?" by saying, "My principal. I have the most wonderful principal in the world. I wouldn't want her job for anything in the world, but I thank God (and her) every day that she does it. She creates a climate in our school that allows me to teach and grow the way I do."[15] A good principal can make all the difference in making teaching happy and productive work.

Parents and Community Members

Children and adolescents do not come to school as blank slates, and they do not view themselves only, or even primarily, as students. They are daughters, sons, siblings, and sometimes even aunts, uncles, and parents themselves—all living in many different family arrangements. They live in communities and walk and ride down urban sidewalks or suburban streets or country lanes and meet other children and adults. They may be active in a religious community or in youth or adult organizations. They may also be in a gang or in a host of other destructive **social networks**. Teachers' lives are going to be affected directly and indirectly by all these networks of relationships that children bring to school with them. The most successful teachers know this and do everything they can to connect with and indeed learn from other adults in their student's lives.

> **social networks**
> Groups of people who are linked for various reasons, such as beliefs, behaviors, or personal similarities.

Teachers need to tap into as many sources of support as possible, among parents and other community leaders. Bill Bigelow, who wished that he had reached out to parents earlier in his career, advises,

> Put down roots in the school community—go to students' games or performances; sit next to your kids' parents. Learn all you can about the community your school serves. Call parents; make them your allies. Especially call them to praise their kids and learn more about them.[16]

Ohio parent activist Lola Glover recommends reaching out and doing so quickly. She says that one of the biggest mistakes teachers make is not being in touch with parents until there's a problem:

And most parents don't want to hear the problem. If you start off that way with a parent, it will take some real doing to get on the right foot with them again.

It's not going to be easy to build an alliance with 30 parents, so start with one or two. Get those parents to be your liaisons. Let them know how much you care and what you are trying to accomplish in the classroom.

I am convinced that if students begin to see parents and people in their community and their schools working together, a lot of things would change. First of all, the kids' attitudes would change. Right now, kids' attitudes have not changed about school because they don't see any connection between home and school. They do not see any real efforts being made by either side to come together for the purpose of improving their schools or educational outcomes.

CONNECTIONS →←

Recall the discussion in Chapter 2 regarding the need for teachers to see their students as young people whose lives are lived in the midst of a web of important relationships.

While building these kinds of alliances is never easy, Glover also insists, "I know we'll never find the answer if we keep this division between us."[17] Welcoming family and the community into schools is not easy and there is no clear-cut way to do so. However, teachers and schools that cut themselves off from their students' families and communities risk a level of alienation that will defeat any other efforts they make.

Involving parents and community residents into the life of the school is more than building support for what teachers and administrators want to do. There is much to be learned from the knowledge of those who see children in different contexts than school-based educators are able to do. Reflecting on the preparation of teachers, Kenneth Zeichner, Katherina Payne, and Kate Brayko Gence argue that "teacher education needs to make a fundamental shift in whose knowledge and expertise counts and should count in the education of new teachers." They ask faculty at schools of education to "cross institutional boundaries to collaborate with communities and schools." These authors recognize that such boundary crossing is difficult and takes time. And they certainly do not ask professionals to give up their expertise; but they do ask them to listen to, learn from, and even at times defer to those who may know the educational context better than they. These wise words for teacher educators apply equally, if not more, to teachers and schools. A community-wide approach can provide support, expertise, and coherence in education, oftentimes sadly lacking when the conversation does not happen.[18]

At the same time, communities can be too intrusive. Some parents, especially in more prosperous communities, can become "helicopter parents," hovering over their children and their children's teachers at every moment. Some level of isolation from family and especially from less healthful community invasion is essential. Thus, Sara Lawrence Lightfoot observed another characteristic of good schools:

> I do believe that good schools balance the pulls of connection to community against the contrary forces of separation from it. Administrators at Kennedy [a public high school in the Bronx, one of New York City's poorest neighborhoods] vividly portray their roles as a "balancing act." They walk the treacherous "tightrope" between closed and open doors, between autonomy and **symbiosis**. Schools need to provide asylum for adolescents from the rugged demands of outside life at the same time that they must always be interactive with it.[19]

> **symbiosis**
> A sustained relationship between two people or two groups of people that is mutually beneficial.

The effective teacher lives her or his working life somewhere on that tightrope.

Don't Go It Alone

If there is a key theme to this chapter, it is very simple: Don't try to go it alone. Relationships with administrators, fellow teachers, unions and their leadership, parents, and community representatives are not always easy, but they are essential. This advice contradicts some popular images of the successful teacher as a kind of "lone ranger." Over several generations, numerous teacher autobiographies and other accounts tell of the lone teacher who stood up to the administration and the community in the name of the kids and succeeded against all odds. These can be inspiring stories, and they can remind us of just how important our work is. They can also be dangerous. Teaching is heroic work, but it is not generally the heroism of the lone individual as much as it is the heroism of the community of teachers.

A popular version of the lone-ranger hero teacher is Erin Gruwell. In her book *The Freedom Writers Diary* (which was made into a movie, *Freedom Writers*, starring Hilary Swank and Patrick Dempsey), Gruwell describes how she is able to turn things around in spite of all the odds. As a young, White teacher who initially has difficulty connecting to her deeply disengaged Asian, African American, and Latino students, Gruwell tells of how she finally made the connection and together with her "freedom writers" created new stories of overcoming oppression. It is an inspiring story. However, it is also one that has irritated many teachers.

In a review for *Rethinking Schools*, Chela Delgado named the problem that many teachers had with this and similar stories: "[I]t's a movie about a white savior." This is a dangerous role model for any teacher to follow. On one hand, Delgado appreciates the movie's major theme, saying, "There is something deeply worthwhile about Ms. G attempting to connect the oppression of her own people to the oppression experienced by her students." However, she says, the problem "isn't so much the kind of cookie-cutter stereotyping that we see in Hollywood's white-teacher-as-savior genre," but "it's the highly individualistic nature of these stereotypes." (Remember, Margaret Haley did not call on teachers to stand up to the system alone but to join with others.) Delgado is also deeply troubled by the depiction of race in *Freedom Writers* and similar stories. They are nearly all the story of the White teacher "saving" children of color. In this case, "[t]here is a marked absence of black and Latino adults." Thus, Delgado concludes, "Don't be fooled into thinking the short-lived triumph of one savior in one classroom is enough." Only larger alliances—across traditional dividing lines of race, class, and gender, but also among many teachers and many allies who are not teachers—will bring the kind of changes in teachers' work lives and in the structures of schooling that are needed if teaching is to be as rewarding a profession as it can be and if all the nation's children are to get the education they deserve.[20]

Students

Many classrooms remain overcrowded, but 50 students per class is no longer the norm. But smaller classes do allow a teacher to get to know, support, and learn from students in a way that larger classes do not. However, multiple studies and debates have long surrounded the effects of smaller class sizes for students. Research has been used to prove arguments from both camps—that smaller classes translate into higher-achieving students or that smaller classes don't make a difference or even, in some cases, negatively affect student achievement. Current research still stands divided on the issue, which makes class size a heated legislative and policy issue for administrators, educators, and parents—all of whom believe themselves to be correct in their opinions on the matter.

Proponents of smaller class size have cited the decreased workload on teachers, which reduces the risk of teacher burnout. Consider that a composition teacher, with a class of 25 students, will spend at least 8 hours reading, analyzing, and responding to each assigned paper if he or she spends 20 minutes on each one. If that same teacher has 125 students, which can be the case in secondary environments with multiple classes, the teacher will need almost 42 hours to respond to papers with the same level of consideration!

On the opposite side of the debate, researchers have found evidence that class size has little to no impact on student achievement, claiming that teacher quality is far more influential. A 2003 study in Louisiana found that as "the percentage of highly certified teachers in a district increased, so did the district's performance score," whereas class size seemed to have no effect on student performance, positive or negative. Often when states implement policies to create smaller classes, they must hire more teachers, many of whom are inexperienced and may be less qualified. As a 2002 study found, a 1996 law mandating smaller classes in California meant that 28,000 new teachers had to be hired, though many lacked experience or credentials. More experienced teachers went to new openings in wealthier areas of the state, leaving low-income schools with even more inexperienced teachers. In a follow up study that tracked California students over time, researchers found no differences in test scores for fifth-grade students who attended smaller classes while in third grade, so that any advantages were, at least, short lived.

With current budget cuts, many school districts are increasing class sizes. Having larger classes may be the only way these schools can avoid cutting arts funding or after-school activities. As school funding continues to be trimmed, schools will have to make difficult decisions for their students and—obviously—not everybody is going to be happy about it.[21]

Whatever the size of a class, building meaningful relationships with students is essential. Reflecting on her own long and successful career as a teacher in San Francisco, Judy Logan reminds us which relationships are the most important to any teacher: those with the students. Teachers spend far more work time with students than with all adults combined. More important, students are the point of all the work that goes on in schools (a reality that is sometimes forgotten by adults, who can be too busy and too overwhelmed by the many demands of the job). Thus, Logan writes,

Being student-centered doesn't mean that I am against parents or colleagues or administrators. It does mean I can sometimes treat the adolescent as the adult whom the parent does not yet see, the colleague may be still trying to control, the administrator may view as a threat ("What do you mean you don't want to salute the flag!"). . . . While I have many enriching and affectionate relationships with colleagues, parents, and administrators (my best friends are teachers), my deepest relationships are with my students.[22]

Being student-centered does not mean forgetting about the other adults in the school or in our lives, but it does mean keeping our "eyes on the prize" and not being diverted from the real point of teaching.

Notes from the Field

What is a lesson you've learned from your students?

"Never to let any of your students know that someone is your 'favorite' student. Treat all students as if they are your favorite."

—*Kristen Gallo, high school dean of faculty*

CHAPTER REVIEW

- Historically speaking: How has teacher work changed—for better or worse?

In 1904, Chicago educator Margaret Haley made the plea for teachers to be better paid and to have job security, a retirement plan, more manageable class sizes, and more say in the curriculum and decision-making process. Today, although teachers still face many hurdles, there have been great improvements in each of these areas.

- How much do teachers get paid?

The latest data from the AFT indicates that U.S. teachers make an average of just over $56,000. However, this value fluctuates widely based on geography, and cost of living must be taken into account. Although teachers' salaries were flat for many years, the average salary took an unexpected spike in 2006–7, outpacing many other comparable jobs and the inflation rate. Salaries remained relatively stable when other professions were losing ground in 2008 and 2009. In addition to salaries, teachers generally have pension plans that are more dependable than the average.

- What is tenure?

Tenure is the right of a teacher to keep his or her job subject to good behavior. It is usually awarded after a relatively short probationary period, often 3 years. Some argue that tenure is a problematic barrier to getting rid of low-quality teachers while others, especially teacher union representatives, argue that tenure is the only way to protect teachers' political and free-speech rights.

- Will I join a union?

Most teachers are required to join their local union once they accept a teaching position. During the past 100 years, teacher unions have fought hard to improve teachers' benefits and working conditions. There is debate today as to whether unions are still needed and, if so, what their role should be.

- Why is professional development and new teacher mentoring important?

Teachers must continually look for ways to improve their "craft," learning from experts in various areas of curriculum and class management as well as from each other. Individual teachers are encouraged not only to participate in professional development but also to find ways to support and encourage fellow teachers.

- Who are the people who impact a teacher's workday?

When a survey asked teachers to list their biggest challenges, a majority of the answers involved relationships, especially interactions with parents. Every teacher must find successful ways to communicate with fellow teachers, administrators, parents, and their students, taking advantage of any opportunity to collaborate and build supportive networks. Debates are ongoing regarding class size and what impact, if any, it has on student achievement. The most important relationships are with the students, who are the real reason for teaching.

Readings

Will I Join a Union?

From "WHY TEACHERS SHOULD ORGANIZE"

AUTHOR: MARGARET HALEY

Margaret Haley's 1904 speech to the NEA described the conditions faced by far too many teachers a century ago. It also reflects Haley's hopes and demands for change and her belief that a better type of schooling could be achieved through a public investment in teachers.

Nowhere in the United States today does the public school, as a branch of the public service, receive from the public either the moral or financial support needed to enable it properly to perform its important function in the social organism. The conditions which are militating most strongly against efficient teaching, and which existing organizations of the kind under discussion here are directing their energies toward changing briefly stated are the following:

- Greatly increased cost of living, together with constant demands for higher standards of scholarship and professional attainments and culture, to be met with practically stationary and wholly inadequate teachers' salaries.
- Insecurity of tenure of office and lack of provision for old age.
- Overwork in overcrowded schoolrooms, exhausting both in mind and body.
- And, lastly, lack of recognition of the teacher as an educator in the school system, due to the increased tendency toward "factoryizing education," making the teacher an automation, a mere factory hand, whose duty it is to carry out mechanically and unquestioningly the ideas and orders of those clothed with the authority of position, and who may or may not know the needs of the children or how to minister to them.

The individuality of the teacher and her power of initiative are thus destroyed, and the result is courses of study, regulations and equipment which the teachers have had no voice in selecting, which often have no relation to the children's needs, and which prove a hindrance instead of a help in teaching. . . .

Two ideals are struggling for supremacy in American life today: one the industrial ideal, dominating thru the supremacy of commercialism, which subordinates the worker to the products and the machine; the other, the ideal of democracy, the ideal of the educators, which places humanity above all machines, and demands that all activity shall be the expression of life. If this ideal of the educators cannot be carried over into the industrial field, then the ideal of industrialism will be carried over into the school. Those two ideals can no more continue to exist in American life than our nation could have continued half slave and half free. If the school cannot bring joy to the work of the world, the joy must go out of its own life, and work in the school as in the factory will become drudgery.

Questions

1. When you read Haley's complaint about how difficult it was to be a teacher 100 years ago, do you think you would have wanted to teach then? Why or why not? What other careers might have seemed preferable in 1904?
2. How much has *really* changed?
3. Where has the greatest improvement taken place? What is better now, and what still needs attention?
4. What do you think of Haley's proposed solution to the problems, that teachers needed unions, just as those in other fields of work needed them? Do they still need them?

Source: Margaret Haley. "Why Teachers Should Organize." *National Education Association Addresses and Proceedings*, 1904, 145–52.

Who Are the People Who Impact a Teacher's Workday?

From "THE DESECRATION OF STUDS TERKEL : FIGHTING CENSORSHIP AND SELF-CENSORSHIP"

AUTHOR: BILL BIGELOW

Bill Bigelow has had a long and successful career as a classroom teacher in Portland, Oregon, and as an editor of Rethinking Schools. *The following account of Bigelow's experience with difficult supervisors and parents during his first year of teaching is from an article he wrote for a Rethinking Schools publication.*

It began with a call that I was to report to the vice-principal's office as soon as possible. The voice at the other end indicated that it was urgent.

I was a first-year teacher at Grant High School in Portland, Oregon. The call gave me the creeps. From the moment we met I'd felt that Lloyd Dixon, the curriculum VP, could look deep into my soul—and that he didn't like what he saw. Whenever we passed in the hall he smiled at me thinly, but with a glance that said "I've got your number, Bigelow." He had a drawl that reminded me of the Oklahoma highway patrolman who gleefully arrested me in 1971 for not carrying my draft card.

It was my first year as a teacher. And I must confess, my classroom difficulties made me a tad paranoid.

Dixon's secretary ushered me into his office when I arrived. "It seems we have a problem, Bill," he said. He paused to look at me to make sure I was duly appreciative of the serious nature of the meeting. "The mother of a student of yours, Dorothy Jennings, called to say that you had given her smutty material, a book that discusses oral sex. What's the story?"

I explained to the vice-principal that the "smutty" material was Studs Terkel's *Working*, a book that includes interviews with dozens of people—auto workers, hotel clerks, washroom attendants, musicians—who describe what they do for a living and how they feel about it. I told him that it was a text the school had purchased and that I issued it to my ninth graders for some in-class reading during our career education study.

"Well, Bill, Dorothy apparently took the book home. And her mother's upset because of a section Dorothy read her about a prostitute, where she describes having oral sex."

I told him that I had not assigned that chapter and that students didn't have permission to take the books home, as I taught two sections of the class but had only 35 copies of the book. I didn't mention that indeed I had considered using the chapter, "Roberta Victor, Hooker," because it was filled with insights about sexism, law, and hypocrisy. (The alleged oral sex description was a brief reference in a long interview.)

Dixon ordered me to bring him a copy of *Working* so that he could read the passages I assigned, and to meet with him the next day. "You should be aware that I regard this as a serious situation," he said. And with that, New Teacher was waved out the door.

I went to see my friend Tom McKenna, a member of a support group I'd helped organize among teachers in the area. Tom suggested I talk with our union rep. My visit with Thurston Ohman, a big-hearted man with an easy from-the-belly laugh was a revelation. "You haven't done anything wrong," he assured me. "If they try to come after you in some way, the union will back you 100%."

Solidarity

It was a delicious moment, and I realized how utterly alone I'd felt up until that point. Ironically, in my history classes and my freshman social studies classes we'd recently studied the rise of labor unions, but until that instant I'd never personally been a beneficiary of the "injury to one is an injury to all" solidarity. Buoyed by my talk with Ohman, I returned to VP Dixon's office the next day. He wasn't worried about Mrs. Jennings anymore. But he was still upset. "Bill, I read over the pieces you assigned. Very interesting. Pretty negative stuff. My daughter is an airline stewardess.

"She doesn't feel like the gal in that book.

"Do you know that the reading on the auto worker uses the s-word five times and the f-word once?"

"The s-word?" I asked.

"Yes. On pages 258, 259, 261, and twice on page 262. The f-word is used on page 265."

I didn't want to laugh, but I didn't know what to say. His complaint was about an interview with Gary Bryner, president of the United Auto Workers local at the Lordstown, Ohio, General Motors plant. Given Mr. Dixon's comment about his daughter, I had a hunch that his ire was aimed more at Bryner's "negative" critique of the plant's deadening working conditions and his descriptions of workers' resistance than at his occasional use of s- and f-words. But this wasn't the time or place to argue politics. "I guess I didn't realize, Mr. Dixon."

"No. Well, Bill, here's what I'd like you to do. Get a black marker and every time this gentleman uses the s- and f-words, darken them so students won't be exposed to that kind of language. Will you do that for me, Bill?"

I know some people would have fought it. Had it not been my first year as a teacher—a temporary teacher, no less—I would have fought. Instead I made one of those compromises that we're not proud of, but that we make so we can live to fight another day. After school, marker in hand, I cleansed Gary Bryner of his foul language—in all 35 copies of *Working*.

Twenty-some years later, the censored books are still in circulation in Portland high schools.

I offer this instance of curricular interference as a way of acknowledging that administrative repression can be a factor in limiting the inventiveness of a new teacher. But in my experience, the intrusions of the Lloyd Dixons of the world are exceptions that prove the rule. And the rule is that we have an enormous amount of freedom.

Even as a first-year teacher the Jennings affair was my only brush with administrative censure. I frequently brought in controversial guest speakers, films, and additional readings. It was 1978–79, the year of Three Mile Island, the final months of the Sandinista revolution in Nicaragua, and a growing awareness of the injustices of South African apartheid. In class, we study all of these. No doubt, it's important for individuals early in their teaching careers, as well as those of us further along, to make an assessment of the political context in which we work. After all, if we lose our job, we don't do anyone any good. But generally, I believe that the most powerful agent of censorship lives in our own heads, and we almost always have more freedom than we use. The great Brazilian educator Paulo Freire once wrote that in schools we should attempt to fill up all the political space we're given. But we rarely do. That said, a few years ago a school district in an affluent Portland suburb terminated a good friend of mine at the completion of her third year of probation, spouting nonsense about her failure to teach critical thinking skills and the like. The obvious irony for those of us at her hearing was that she was fired precisely because she was successful at teaching her students to think critically. She had the misfortune of being one of the only non-tenured teachers in a progressive, pedagogically adventurous social studies department during the rise of the ferociously conservative Oregon Citizens Alliance. The political environment had shifted to the right; it was sacrificial lamb time.

It's worth mentioning that during my first years at Jefferson High School, following my year at Grant, I was gifted with supervising vice-principals who were extraordinarily supportive and even enthusiastic about livelier, risk-taking teaching. Shirley Glick was one of several VPs who offered nothing but encouragement as I felt my way toward a more critical and multicultural curriculum. The Lloyd Dixons of the world exist, but so do the Shirley Glicks.

Incidentally, I never met Mrs. Jennings. But she left her mark. For a long time I subconsciously imagined a Mrs. Jennings sitting at every student's home, hoping for a chance to chew me out for some teaching crime I'd committed: "You snake, why'd you use that book/film/article/poem with my innocent child?"

In my imagination, parents were potential opponents, not allies, and I avoided calling them to talk about their children or what I was trying to teach. This neglect was a bad habit to fall into. Even from a narrow classroom management standpoint, my failure to call moms, dads, or grandparents from time to time made my quest for classroom order a lonely campaign. Parents could have exerted a bit of pressure on the home front. But they also could have told me something about their son or daughter, offered a fuller portrait than what I saw in my daily slice of 47 minutes.

And that would likely have made me a more effective teacher.

Questions

1. What do you think of Bigelow's decision to make "one of those compromises that we're not proud of"? Would you have made the same compromise or handled things differently?
2. Bigelow says that for most teachers "the most powerful agent of censorship lives in our own heads." Do you agree? Can you think of examples, in your own life or among teachers you have known or observed, when such self-censorship was a reality?
3. Could Bigelow have found a better way to relate to Mr. Dixon? To Dorothy Jennings's mother? To Dorothy herself?
4. What do you think of Bigelow's self-criticism at the end of the article about the way he related to parents early in his own career? Do parents make for more effective teaching? How? How not?

Source: Bill Bigelow. "The Desecration of Studs Terkel: Fighting Censorship and Self-Censorship." In *The New Teacher Book: Finding Purpose, Balance, and Hope During Your First Years in the Classroom,* edited by Kelley Dawson Salas, Rita Tenorio, Stephanie Walters, and Dale Weiss, 123–26. Milwaukee: Rethinking Schools, 2004.

From "TWO TEACHERS OF LETTERS"

FROM MARGARET TREECE METZGER AND CLARE FOX

This chapter focused on the question "What will my life be like as a teacher?" In the exchange of letters that follows, two teachers reflect on their lives in the profession. One is a young teacher about to begin her first job. The response is from a senior teacher who, for all her reservations, has arrived at a clear answer to the question of whether teaching is right for her.

Spring 1984

Dear Mrs. Metzger,

I am writing to you as a former student who has just graduated from Brown University and who is considering teaching English next year. I remember you as a compelling and demanding teacher who seemed to enjoy her job. At the moment, you are the only person I know who would support my career choice. Almost everyone else is disparaging about teaching in public schools.

I am told that I did not have to go to Brown University to become a teacher. I am told that teaching is a "wonderful thing to do until you decide what you really want to do with your life." I am told that it is "nice" that I'm going to be a teacher. Why does it seem that the decision to teach in our society is analogous with the decision to stunt one's growth, to opt out intellectually in favor of long summers off?

But teaching matters. I know that. You mattered to me, and others teachers mattered to me. I enjoyed student teaching and I look forward to next year. I have imaginary dialogues with the students in my mind. I hear myself articulating my policy on borderline grades, explaining why I keep switching chairs from circles to rows as I flounder in my efforts to decide what's best, or laughing with the students as I struggle to overcome saying "okay" too often when I lecture. But I wonder how much teaching is actually an ego trip, a ploy to be liked, accepted, and respected by a group of people who have limited say in the matter. I also know the humiliation of a student's glare. I know there will be problems, yet I cannot deny the tremendous sense of worth I felt as a student teacher when students offered me their respect and when students worked hard and were proud of their effort.

I wonder where I would get this sense of worthiness if I were to work in a New York advertising firm or as an engineer at Bell Labs. And yet, going to work for a big corporation—whether in an advertising firm, a bank, or a publishing house—impresses me. It would seem "real," "grown up," as teaching never will. Nobody would tell me that being an engineer is "nice" or a wonderful way to figure out what I "really want to do".

For graduation, my mother and sister gave me a beautiful sleek attaché case. My reaction was twofold. First, I realized it would never be large enough to carry the load of an English teacher, and second, I realized that, should I ever decide to leave teaching, it would be perfect for the real world of professional writers and young executives.

My mother doesn't want me to go into teaching. She is afraid I will get "stuck," that my efforts will not be appreciated or rewarded, and that I will not meet men. When I called home from Minneapolis after a long, productive, and exhilarating day interviewing at schools, my mother congratulated me and suggested that I spend the evening putting together a second resume—a writing resume—before I forgot everything else I know how to do. She suggested I spend the following day visiting television studios scouting for writing jobs, "just in case."

And my mother has been in public education for almost 20 years! Granted, when she entered Boston College in 1952, she had to choose between teaching and nursing. I, however, have chosen to teach from among many options available to me as a Brown graduate with a strong liberal arts degree.

I write to you, Mrs. Metzger, because you were the first person to excite me about the processes of writing and because your integrity in the classroom has long been an influence on me—and on my decision to teach. You mattered. I am turning to you because you are a professional; and you continue to choose teaching after eighteen years. I welcome any advice, comments, or solace you could offer me.

Sincerely,

Clare Fox

Spring 1984

Dear Clare,

I admire your courage to consider teaching. Your friends and relatives are not alone in their negative opinions about teaching. I'm sure you read the claim in the President's Commission on Education that education is a national disgrace. *Newsweek*'s September 1984 cover showed a teacher in a dunce cap with the headline, "Why Teachers Fail—How to Make Them Better." NBC ran a three-hour special on education—an expose of inadequate schools. At least four blue ribbon studies have concluded that teacher education is inadequate, that the pay is the lowest of all professions, that schools have deplorable management, and that the job is full of meaningless paperwork.

I know that much of the criticism is valid. However, the reports sensationalize and do not tell the whole truth. I appreciate your letter because you are giving me a chance to defend a profession I love.

Clare, I look forward to teaching. By mid-August I start planning lessons and dreaming about classrooms. I also wonder whether I'll have the energy to start again with new classes. Yet after September gets underway, I wake up in the morning expecting to have fun at work. I know that teaching well is a worthwhile use of my life. I know my work is significant.

I am almost forty years old and I am happier in my job than anyone I know. That's saying a lot. My husband, who enjoys his work, has routine days when he comes home and says: "Nothing much happened today—just meetings." I never have routine days. When I am in the classroom, I usually am having a wonderful time.

I also hate this job. In March I wanted to quit because of the relentlessness of dealing with one hundred antsy adolescents day after day. I lose patience with adolescent issues: I think I'll screech if I have to listen to one more adolescent self obsession. I am physically exhausted every Friday. The filth in our school is an aesthetic insult. The unending petty politics drain me. Often I feel undermined on small issues by a school system that supports me well on academic freedom.

Like all jobs, teaching has inherent stresses. As you know from student teaching, you must know how to discipline a roomful of adolescents: you need to have a sense of purpose about what you are teaching; you need to cope with the exhaustion, and, as an English teacher you must get the paper grading under control. I am always saddened by the number of excellent teachers who leave teaching because they think these difficult problems are unsolvable.

A curious irony exists. I am never bored at work, yet my days are shockingly routine. I can tell you exactly what I have done every school day for the past eighteen years at 10:15 in the morning (homeroom attendance), and I suspect I will do the same for the next twenty years. The structure of the school day has changed little since education moved out of the one-room schoolhouse. All teachers get tired of the monotonous routine of bookkeeping, make-up assignments, twenty minute lunches, and study hall duties. I identify with J. Alfred Prufrock when he says, "I have measured out my life with coffee spoons." My own life has been measured out in student papers. At a conservative estimate I've graded over 30,000—a mind-boggling statistic which makes me feel like a very dull person indeed.

The monotony of my schedule is mirrored in the monotony of my paycheck. No matter how well or poorly I teach, I will be paid at the same amount. There is absolutely no monetary reward for good performance, or any recognition of professional growth or acquired expertise—my pay depends on how long I've taught and my level of education. I work in a school district in which I cannot afford to live. I am alternately sad and angry about my pay. To the outside world, it seems I am doing exactly the same job I did in 1966—same title, same working conditions, same pay scale (except that my buying power is 8% less than it was when I earned $5,400 on my first job). To most people I am "just a teacher."

But that is the outside reality. The interior world of the teacher is quite different. Although you have to come to some terms with the outward flatness of the career, I want to assure you that teachers grow and change. So little research has been done on stage development of teachers that the literature recognizes only three categories—intern, novice, and veteran. This is laughably over-simplified. There is life after student teaching; there is growth after the first year. You will some day solve many problems that seem insurmountable during your exhilarating student teaching and your debilitating first year.

Sometimes I am aware of my growth as a teacher, and I realize that finally, after all these years, I am confident in the classroom. On the very, very best days, when classes sing, I am able to operate on many levels during a single class; I integrate logistics, pedagogy, curriculum, group dynamics, individuals needs, and my own philosophy. I feel generous and good-natured toward my students, and I am challenged by classroom issues. But on bad days, I feel like a total failure. Students attack my most vulnerable points. I feel overwhelmed by paperwork. I ache from exhaustion. I dream about going to Aruba, but I go to the next class.

I keep going because I am intellectually stimulated. I enjoy literature, and I assign books I love and books I want to read. I expect class discussions and student papers to give me new insights into literature. As you may remember, I tell students that in exchange for my hard work, they should keep me interested and they should teach me. They do.

To me, teaching poses questions worthy of a lifetime of thoughts. I want to think about what the great writers are saying. I want to think about how people learn. I want to think about the values we are passing on to the next generation. I am particularly interested in teaching thinking. I love to teach writing. I am working now on teaching writing as a tool for thinking. Questions about teaching are like puzzles to me; I can spend hours theorizing and then use my classroom as a laboratory.

I am also intellectually challenged by pedagogical problems. I have learned to follow the bizarre questions or the "wrong questions." Some questions reveal chasms of ignorance. For example, "Where is Jesus' body?" or "Before movies were in color, wasn't the world dull just being in black and white?" Sometimes students make shocking statements which demand careful responses: "All athletic girls are lesbians" or "Sexually abused toddlers probably really enjoy sex." And every year, new students require new teaching skills—Cambodian boat children who have never been in school and are illiterate even in their own language, or handicapped children such as a deaf Israeli girl who is trying to learn English without being able to hear it.

And then there are all the difficult, "normal" situations: students and parents who are "entitled," hostile, emotionally needy, or indifferent; students who live in chaotic homes, who are academically pressured, who have serious drug and alcohol problems. The list goes on and on. No school of education prepared me for the "Hill Street Blues" intensity and chaos of public schools. I received my combat training from other teachers, from myself, and mostly from the students. You will too.

Sometimes I think I can't do it all. I don't want to be bitter or a martyr, so I am careful to take care of myself. I put flowers on my desk to offset the dreariness of an old school building. I leave school several times a week to run errands or to take a walk in order to feel less trapped. Other teachers take courses at local colleges, join committees of adults, talk in the teachers' lounge, or play with computers. In order to give to others, teachers must nurture themselves.

Ultimately, teaching is nurturing. The teacher enters a giving relationship with strangers, and then the teacher's needs must give way to students' needs. I want to work on my own writing; instead I work on students' writing. My days are spent encouraging young people's growth. I watch my students move beyond me, thinking and writing better than I have ever done. I send them to colleges I could never afford. And I must strive to be proud, not jealous, of them. I must learn generosity of heart.

I am a more compassionate person because I have known teachers and students. I think differently about handicaps because I worked with Guy, who is quadriplegic from a rugby accident. Refugee problems have a human face because I've heard Nazmul tell stories about refugee camps in Bangladesh, and I've heard Merhdad tell about escaping from Iran, hidden in a camel's baggage. I have seen the school social worker given suicidal students his home phone number, telling them to call anytime. I have seen administrators bend the rules to help individual students through personal crises. Every day I hear stories of courage and generosity. I admire other teachers.

Facing every new class is an act of courage and optimism. Years ago, the courage required was fairly primitive. I needed courage to discipline my classes, to get them into line, to motivate them to work. But now I need a deeper courage. I look at each new class and know that I must let each of these young people into my life in some significant way. The issue is one of heart. Can I open my heart to two hundred more adolescent strangers each year? Put bluntly, can I be that loving?

I hope to love my students so well that it doesn't even matter whether they like me. I want to love them in the way I love my own son—full of respect and awe for who they are, full of wanting their growth, full of wonder at what it means to lead and to follow the next generation.

Clare, when you consider a life's work, consider not just what you will take to the task, but what it will give to you. Which job will give self-respect and challenge? Which job will enlarge you and give you in abundance? Which job will teach you lessons of the heart?

With deep respect,
Margaret Metzger

Questions

1. Can you identify with the questions Clare Fox is asking at the beginning of this exchange of letters?
2. Do you know a teacher like Mrs. Metzger? Someone to whom you can ask similar questions? Someone who equally loves teaching?
3. Can you imagine yourself as a Mrs. Metzger some day? How do you think you would then answer Clare Fox's questions?

Source: Margaret Treece Metzger and Clare Fox. "Two Teachers of Letters." *Harvard Educational Review 56*, no. 4 (1986): 349–54.

10 Legal, Ethical, and Economic Responsibilities
How Can We Make Our Classrooms Fair?

> In my view, then, it is inequality—not some notion of gross inadequacy—of educational opportunity that raises a question of denial of equal protection of the laws. I find any other approach to the issue unintelligible and without directing principle.

JUSTICE THURGOOD MARSHALL, DISSENT, *SAN ANTONIO SCHOOL DISTRICT V. RODRIGUEZ*

Educators and political leaders talk about "leveling the playing field," or ensuring that "no child is left behind." The issue of fairness seems to be a high priority for just about everyone. Determining what is fair, however, is a much more difficult proposition. What seems fair to one person can seem very unfair to another. Actions that address an unfair situation for some can create unfairness—or be perceived to create unfairness—for others. And actions that can seem neutral or innocent to one person can be deeply troubling to another. As the Supreme Court case in the **Readings** for this chapter shows, the justices of the nation's highest court do not agree at all about what is fair in the realm of public education. Nevertheless

every teacher has a professional responsibility to seek to be fair—to every student, to colleagues, and in the school policies that they advocate—but doing so is neither simple nor free of pitfalls.

Fairness can be a difficult and often elusive concept in American education. Some failures of fairness are due to deep structural problems in the education system (perhaps most of all the financial arrangements for supporting public schools but also the pervasiveness of deep-seated racism, sexism, and other forms of **institutionalized inequity**). Some failures are due to our tendency to overlook inequities that are right in front of us. Yet other aspects of education that are seen as unfair to some represent the triumph of someone else's definition of educational justice. Some unfairness is due to the desires of those with privilege to maintain their privilege, some to simple oversight, and some to honest differences of opinion about what is best for children. Few failures are due to teachers' deliberate decisions to be unfair.

> **institutionalized inequity**
> Embedded practice of injustice and inequality that permeates a society and is often unseen; this is quite different from inequity that results from individual decisions.

In this chapter, we look carefully at some of the areas in which schools are failing at fairness, including why school funding isn't equal, how students are treated differently by perceived ability, why students drop out or their performance lags behind others, and what situations teachers will either face (or cause) that challenge their ethical commitments to their students, their peers, and their profession. In this chapter, we have two goals: (1) to understand the larger social issues that lead schools to operate as they do, and (2) to consider the ways in which teachers,

individually and in groups, can be fair, or as fair as possible, in the way they carry out their work.

As in other chapters, the **Readings** help us to engage these issues. The first **Reading** in this chapter explores an historic decision by the U.S. Supreme Court, *San Antonio Independent School District v. Rodriguez*, that was decided by the Court in 1973. Forty years since then, this case continues to define the terms of what is possible and impossible in equalizing school financing. Although several state legislatures and courts have improved the situation since the *Rodriguez* decision was handed down, it continues to represent the last word in federal policy. In the next two **Readings**, researchers Jeannie Oakes and Tom Loveless present radically different interpretations of one of the most debated issues of fairness in today's schools: tracking. Looking at what current research tells us about the impact of tracking and ability grouping on the long-term academic achievement of students, they come to very different conclusions about what works and what does not, and the fairness of decisions to track, or not to track, students.

Why Is School Funding Unequal?

It costs money to operate schools. Teachers need to be paid, buildings need to be maintained, and supplies need to be purchased. If some schools have significantly more money than other schools, many observers wonder how that situation could possibly be fair. School funding has traditionally been based primarily on the local property tax base, which means that wealthier communities that have a much higher tax base per pupil can have a huge advantage over poor districts that

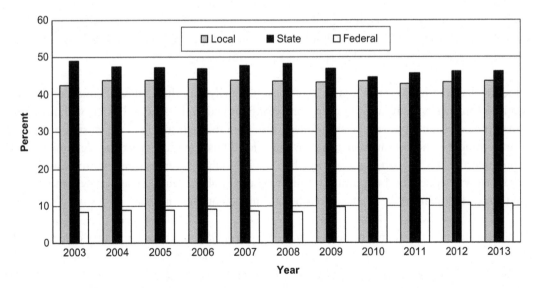

Figure 10.1
Annual School Revenue by Source, 2003–13

Source: National Education Association, "Rankings and Estimates," March 2014, p. 38

have far fewer funds available. In part to remedy inequities between districts, states have been financing more of the cost of running schools from state-generated revenues. In many states today, the state puts as much money into schools as local communities do, though this too varies significantly. In 1970, some states provided as little as 10% of school funds for their districts. By 2009, the lowest state contribution was closer to 30%. Many states more than matched local revenues, and some provided as much as 80% of the cost of local school operations. During these same years, the percentage of a local **school district**'s funds that come from the federal government has stayed at around 10%–12%.[1]

> **school district**
> A local area authority, often a single city or town, that administers primary and secondary schools in an established geographic boundary.

In 1971, the California Supreme Court ruled that a system of school finance "which invidiously discriminates among students on the basis of wealth violates the equal protection guaranty of the state constitution."[2] Many hoped that the result of California's *Serrano vs. Priest* decision could be meaningful change in the distribution of school funds in California and a national movement in the same direction. Neither development took place, however.

In California, a combination of legislative inaction and legal challenges as well as a 1978 statewide referendum—Proposition 13—that limited all property taxes, slowed the implementation of the *Serrano* decision to a crawl. The optimism generated by *Serrano* came to a halt in 1973 when the U.S. Supreme Court ruled 5–4 in a Texas case, *San Antonio Independent School District v. Rodriguez*, that unequal school financing based on differences in property tax receipts could not be challenged, at least not in the federal courts. Speaking for the Court's majority, Justice Lewis Powell wrote:

> The argument here is not that children in districts having relatively low assessable property values are receiving no public education; rather, it is that they are receiving a poorer quality education than that available to children in districts having more assessable wealth. Apart from the unsettled and disputed question whether the quality of education may be determined by the amount of money expended for it, a sufficient answer to appellees' argument is that, at least where wealth is involved, the Equal Protection clause does not require absolute equality or precisely equal advantages.

Where the Money Goes

In this opinion, Justice Powell offered two of the major arguments that have continued to be used in this debate: differences are not necessarily unfair as long as everyone gets a minimum education, and it is not clear that more money buys a higher quality education. Finally, Powell added a third argument that, coming from the Supreme Court, more or less closed the debate. He wrote: "Education, of course, is not among the rights afforded explicit protection under our Federal Constitution. Nor do we find any basis for saying it is implicitly so protected." Given that decision, further discussion of any federal role in fiscal equity in education seemed pointless.

Not everyone on the Court agreed with the majority; it was, after all, a 5–4 decision. As happened so often during the succeeding decades, Justice Thurgood Marshall spoke in a powerful dissent:

> The Court today decides, in effect, that a State may constitutionally vary the quality of education which it offers its children in accordance with the amount of taxable wealth located in the school districts within which they reside. The majority's decision represents an abrupt departure from the mainstream of recent state and federal court decisions concerning the unconstitutionality of state educational financing schemes dependent upon taxable local wealth. More unfortunately, though, the majority's holding can only be seen as a retreat from our historic commitment to equality of educational opportunity and as unsupportable acquiescence in a system which deprives children in their earliest years of the chance to reach their full potential as citizens.

Marshall, the lead attorney in winning the pivotal *Brown v. Board of Education* case, had a very different read of the U.S. Constitution than some of the other justices. For him, "[t]he fundamental importance of education is amply indicated by the prior decisions of this Court, by the unique status accorded to public education by our society, and by the close relationship between education and some of our most basic constitutional values."[3]

The result of the *Rodriguez* decision was that gross inequities continue to be the rule in terms of spending on pupils in different school districts around the nation, even in school districts that are geographically close to each other. Indeed,

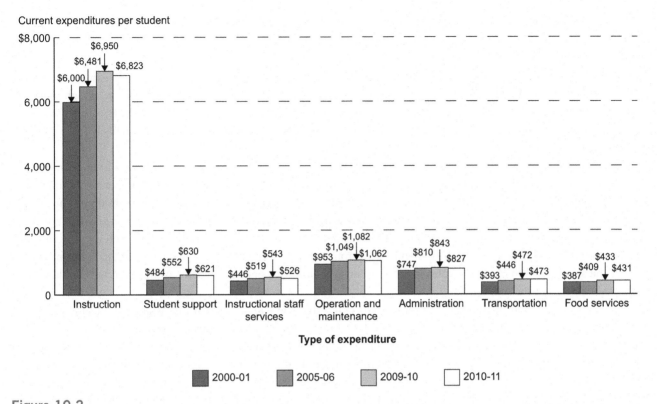

Figure 10.2
Current expenditures per student in fall enrollment in public elementary and secondary schools nationwide, in constant 2012–2013 dollars, by type of expenditure: 2000–1, 2005–6, 2009–10, and 2010–11

Note: "Instruction," "Student support," "Instructional staff services," "Operation and maintenance," "Administration," "Transportation," and "Food services" are subcategories of "Current expenditures." "Student support" includes expenditures for guidance, health, attendance, and speech pathology services. "Instructional staff services" include expenditures for curriculum development, staff training, libraries, and media and computer centers. "Administration" includes both general administration and school administration. "Transportation" refers to student transportation. Expenditures are reported in constant 2012–13 dollars, based on the Consumer Price Index.

Source: U.S. Department of Education, National Center for Education Statistics, Common Core of Data (CCD), "National Public Education Financial Survey," selected years 2000–1, 2005–6, 2009–10, and 2010–11. See Digest of Education Statistics 2013, Table 236.60.

for the past 30 years, some of the greatest inequities have been between cities and suburbs in the same metropolitan area. Although the Supreme Court's 1973 decision closed the door on federal appeals related to schools' dependence on property taxes, the story was far from over. Many state constitutions said much more about education and educational equity than the federal constitution. If Justice Powell was right, and education was not a right afforded by the federal constitution, it was certainly a right afforded in almost every state constitution.

Despite Justice Marshall's passionate dissent, the *Rodriguez* decision closed the door on federal appeals regarding school funding. Nevertheless, since then 40 out of the 50 state supreme courts have heard school finance cases. In about half the cases, the courts decided that, one way or another, overreliance on property taxes represented an unconstitutional (per the state's constitution) inequity in school finance. However, the reality is that winning a court case and bringing about change can be two different things. Legislatures and local agencies have ways of dragging their feet, sometimes for years, especially when money is involved. Equalizing the funding is of little help if the total funding for schools in the state is inadequate or shrinking.

Stan Karp, a longtime public school teacher in New Jersey who has studied issues of school finance, wrote that:

The property tax issue is both a root problem and, in some ways, a distraction from the core issues of adequacy and equity. Local property taxes still supply about 43 percent of all school funds. State support varies, but on average provides about 49 percent. The federal government's share of education spending, despite the huge impact of federal policies like NCLB, is still only 8 percent.

While federal spending is up to 12% and state funding is up also—significantly in some states—the core issues of adequacy and equity that Karp raises remains unaddressed in most places. Most schools do not have enough money to offer the education that children need. The differences in funding available to schools, which is huge across the nation, means that some children are getting a significant head start in life that is denied to others and not likely to be compensated for later on.

Although the nation's schoolchildren are becoming much more racially diverse, the majority of voters are largely European American. Thus, especially in many states and districts, a vote for more school funding is a vote to educate "other people's children," given that the majority of voters in many places do not have school-aged children. Thus, in the case of California, although the state did assume an increasing proportion of the cost of school funding, which equalized funding to some extent, the state also came up with less and less money overall. The result, as Karp notes, is that although in the 1960s California was fifth in the nation in per-pupil spending and a model for many educational reforms, by the 1990s the state was 30th of the 50 states in school spending, and teachers and students were suffering. Clearly, equalization alone was not the solution.

In New Jersey, however, the state supreme court ruled that the state constitution's requirement of a "thorough and efficient" education meant that even if the federal constitution was not relevant (see *Rodriguez*), the New Jersey Constitution was. The result in the case of *Abbot v. Burke* was that, frustrated by legislative foot dragging, the court ruled very specifically that the state had to raise money to ensure that the per-pupil spending in the state's 31 poorest districts matched the average level spent by the 130 richest districts. This was based on the assumption, as Karp said, that the richest districts "obviously knew what it took for kids to succeed educationally." The New Jersey court also required additional "supplemental funding" to offset the impact of poverty. The impact of these funds was such that by the late 1990s, the gap in math and language test scores for fourth graders in high poverty, so-called Abbot Districts, and for students in the best suburbs had been cut in half. New Jersey now had some of the highest high school graduation rates in the nation, including the highest rates for African American and Latino students.[4]

In rejecting the *Rodriguez* case, Justice Powell made it a point to say that there was still what he called the "unsettled and disputed question whether the quality of education may be determined by the amount of money expended for it." Many observers still debate that question. In his review of a number of recent books on school reform, *New Yorker* contributor James Traub captured one perspective:

And where many liberals, including [Jonathan] Kozol, go wrong is in overestimating the importance of school spending. Of course, schools should have a decent physical plant, books that aren't falling apart, computers, and so on, but per-pupil spending, [James] Coleman noted, has virtually no correlation with school success.[5]

Many people wonder why such an argument is made about schooling but not about other aspects of society. The late U.S. Senator Paul Wellstone made this point eloquently:

We need to rebuild our crumbling school buildings. I have asked senators during a floor debate how well they would do if we had no air conditioning during the hot Washington summers, if the heating was inadequate during the winters, if the toilets didn't work, if the copy and fax machines were broken, if there was no e-mail, if the roof leaked during rainstorms, if the building was decrepit, rather than majestic. "These are the conditions facing millions of schoolchildren," I shouted on the floor of the Senate. "What kind of message do we send these children? We are telling them that we don't value or care about them."

Wellstone was specific about what he suspected was at least one of the causes of much of the inequity. "Perhaps, certain children," he said, "are getting an especially strong dose of the 'we don't value or care about them' message."[6]

Teachable Moment
FROM: "EQUITY, ADEQUACY, AND THE EVOLVING STATE ROLE IN EDUCATION FINANCE"

Sean P. Corcoran and William N. Evans

All fifty state constitutions mandate a statewide system of public education, charging state governments with providing a "thorough and efficient system of free public schools" (or similar language). State legislatures fulfill this obligation by establishing compulsory schooling laws, curriculum standards, and institutions governing the formation and operation of school districts. Despite constitutional goals, states historically played only a minor role in the *financing* of public schools, leaving the funding and day-to-day management of schools in the hands of local governments.

This long-standing devolution of **fiscal responsibility** to local school districts all but dissolved over the past century. State aid in the form of flat grants and "minimum foundation" programs became common practice in the first half of the century; later, legal challenges to state school finance systems led to far-reaching reforms that further expanded the fiscal responsibilities of the states. . . . These challenges originated as "equity" suits that sought to break the link between local property wealth and school resources. A later wave of litigation instead sought "adequacy" in school expenditure, as defined by the level of spending necessary to reach some performance standard. Despite the disparate objectives of these challenges, the result was more often than not an increased state role in school funding. . . .

> **fiscal responsibility**
> Using available resources in a responsible and effective manner, balancing income and expenditures, and maintaining transparency in finances.

The national trend in state funding masks considerable variation across states in aid to local school districts. In 1970, for example, the fraction of school revenues from state sources varied across states from a low of 10–18 percent in New Hampshire, South Dakota, and Nebraska to a high of 60–70 percent in New Mexico, Alaska, and Delaware. . . . By 2001, the variation across states in the state share was much smaller, ranging from lows of 20–35 percent to a high of nearly 80 percent. Almost every state increased its share of public school revenues over this period, with Florida, Texas, and Pennsylvania being notable exceptions. Generally speaking, increases in the state share appear to reflect increases in state spending on education rather than declines in local revenues.

Explanations for this dramatic shift in fiscal responsibility for public schools from local to state can be found in part in a series of legislative and court-mandated reforms to state finance systems that originated in California's *Serrano I* ruling (1971) and continue to this day. These reforms arose initially in response to inequities generated by reliance on local property taxes for school funding, but in recent years have been driven by concerns over the adequacy of funding for public education, in particular the funding of education for students from disadvantaged backgrounds.

Pressure to reform state school funding originated in state legislatures and—more frequently—in the courts. At last count, litigants had challenged the constitutionality of state school finance systems in all but five states.

Questions

- Do you know how schools are financed in the state where you live or where you want to teach? Can you think of reasons why a teacher might want to know such information?
- Is it fair for states to step in when local communities traditionally raised the funds for their schools? By contrast, is it fair for children who live in a poor community to attend schools that are less well funded than the schools serving other children in a wealthier community?

Source: Reprinted from Sean P. Corcoran and William N. Evans. "Equity, Adequacy, and the Evolving State Role in Education Finance." In *Handbook of Research in Educational Finance and Policy,* edited by Helen F. Ladd and Edward B. Fiske. Routledge, 2007.

In some states, educators, parents, and their political allies have sought legislative support or have turned to the courts to ensure better funding for the schools. Believing that money makes a difference in the quality of education, they have sought to create a minimum base of funding that must be available to every school in their state. Increasingly, these advocates have started to campaign for what they call "adequacy" in school funding. It does not matter to them if all schools are funded equally if the amount of funding is not sufficient. Many observers today are less worried than those from a generation before about ensuring total equality in school funding. But they do want to be sure that, through political campaigns, legislative votes, or court decisions, every school has adequate funding to provide their students with a quality basic education.[7]

The nation's expectations for schools are changing. What might once have been an adequate level of school funding no longer serves today's expectations. Clear steps toward fairness in school spending have been made in some places and can be a model for others, if there is a will to do so. As Karp indicates, "Beneath the legal briefs, the legislative jargon . . . lie two central questions: Will we provide schools with the resources they need to make high-quality education possible, and will we provide those resources to all children, or only some children?"[8]

A recent report, *Funding Student Learning: How to Align Education Resources With Student Learning Goals,* notes that as important as the amount of money spent is the way it is spent. The authors describe "a finance system not capable of supporting high levels of student learning: not designed for it, not operated in order to accomplish it, not transparent enough to understand it, not accountable for it." The key is not only, or not even necessarily, more money but better ways to link the way school budgets are prepared and administered with the outcomes that educators seek in terms of effective programs for all students.[9]

Why Do Schools Sort and Track Students?

In the United States, the purpose of public education has never been completely clear. On one hand, throughout history many observers have said that the fundamental purpose of public education in a democratic society, as ours aspires to be, is to ensure that everyone has a solid basic education. According to 2001 federal legislation, the goal is "no child left behind." If education is really meant to be structured so that no one is left behind, then the standard of fairness—inclusion and equity to an increasingly high standard—seems pretty clear.

On the other hand, even a casual examination of the structure of schooling illuminates a second, and sometimes contradictory, purpose. According to educator Joel Spring, "schools are meant to be 'the sorting machine,'" selecting some students for high levels of academic achievement and social, political, and economic leadership; others to be the middle managers; and still others to be the failures who, because of the perceived **meritocratic** nature of schooling, say, "I have only myself to blame." If schools are inevitably the sorting machine, then the definition of fairness changes dramatically. Instead of ensuring success for all, schools must determine who succeeds and who fails without tipping the balance because of gender, race, wealth, or a hundred other ways by which the larger society privileges some and marginalizes others. If schools truly are sorting machines, then those who have power and position will use their status to ensure that their children are among the winners.[10]

> **meritocratic**
> Reward system based on person's ability or talent, rather than social status.
>
> **tracking**
> Educational practice of dividing students into different "tracks" based on perceived academic ability or achievement, with higher tracks given more challenging work.

Debates about fairness often come to a head around issues of **tracking** and ability grouping in schools. Many schools in the United States have traditionally encouraged various forms of tracking. Elementary school teachers have long divided students into different groups, such as the "Redbirds" and "Bluebirds" that Tom Loveless discusses in the **Readings** for this chapter. Of course, although teachers pretended that these were simply different groups, students nearly always knew which group was for the strong readers and which group was for "dummies." (Indeed, in my own experience as a fourth-grade teacher, the children were much better than the teachers at remembering which color was code for the "smarter" kids.)

DID YOU KNOW?

Colleges and universities are the most rigorous "trackers" of any educational institutions in this country, as some colleges are highly selective, some are moderately so, and others are open to virtually all in their admission policies. Students at a given college or university may be treated more or less equally once they get to campus, but higher education's selection process represents an extreme form of tracking.

Since their creation in the 19th century, American high schools have usually had different tracks for students based on both ability and perceived future plans. (Too often, those in authority made these decisions about ability and appropriate future plans based on students' race, class, or gender.) In 1892, when far less than 10% of all youth ages 14–17 even attended high school, the National Education Association appointed a prestigious group of educators known as the Committee of Ten, chaired by the president of Harvard University, Charles W. Eliot, to make recommendations about the best curriculum for the nation's emerging high schools. Under Eliot's leadership, the committee issued a report in 1893 that said that, although there might be different courses of study depending on students' interests, there could be no distinction between curriculum for the college bound and for those preparing for "life" (that is, those planning to work directly after high school). The Committee of Ten insisted that preparation for college, whether or not one attended, was preparation for life.

Although many praised the committee's report, others attacked it, including none more than G. Stanley Hall, perhaps the nation's most famous developmental psychologist at the time. For Hall, the Committee of Ten's report was filled with fallacies, especially the notion that all students should be taught in the same way and to the same extent regardless of "probable destination." To Hall, this recommendation flew in the face of the reality that students varied greatly in

> **CONNECTIONS →←**
> Recall the Chapter 1 discussion of how and why high schools were developed.

their abilities and included a "great army of incapables, shading down to those who should be in schools for the dullards or subnormal children."

At about the same time, W.E.B. Du Bois, the first African American to earn a Ph.D. at Harvard, famously attacked the system of vocational education for African Americans that had been developed after Reconstruction in the segregated South under the leadership of Booker T. Washington. In Du Bois's view, Washington and his White supporters had made a terrible bargain, creating a system of education for the newly freed slaves that condemned them to a permanent form of second-class citizenship, a kind of across-the-board tracking of all African Americans. Thus, in 1902, Du Bois wrote, "Industrial schools must beware of placing undue emphasis on the 'practical' character of their work. . . . The ideals of education, whether men are taught to teach or to plow, to weave or to write must not be allowed to sink to sordid utilitarianism. Education must keep broad ideals before it, and never forget that it is dealing with Souls and not with Dollars."

> **CONNECTIONS →←**
> In Chapter 4 we discussed how girls and women have and still are treated differently in education.

It was not only in the African American community that educators debated vocational education. Between 1910 and 1917, a growing chorus of educators argued for federal legislation (which eventually became the Smith-Hughes Act of 1917) that would create separate high school programs for job-skill training for a large subset of the adolescent population who were not to be college bound. The educational philosopher John Dewey vigorously attacked the plan for vocational education, insisting that "[t]he dominant vocation of all human beings at all times is living—intellectual and moral growth. . . . To predetermine some future occupation for which education is to be a strict preparation is to injure the possibility of present development." David Snedden, commissioner of education in Massachusetts and one of the architects of vocational education, found Dewey's attack "discouraging" and indeed "incredible" since arranging for "greater productive capacity" for these students headed for the world of work would only make their lives better, even if it also limited their future life choices.

In the end, Hall, Washington, Snedden, and their allies won and Eliot, Du Bois, and Dewey lost. High schools throughout most of the 20th century were highly tracked places where students were sorted early into quite separate vocational, general, and college prep tracks. As elementary schools became increasingly preparatory for high school (in contrast to the earlier common schools offering a rudimentary education to all) they too took on many aspects of a tracked system, preparing their students at earlier years to fit into one of the tracks that the high schools offered.

In the 1980s, researchers and advocates began to develop a significant body of literature that showed a negative impact of tracking on those students slotted for the lower tracks while showing that the most advanced students also benefitted from an untracked school. Suddenly, a new consensus seemed to have emerged. Throughout the 1980s and 1990s, few voices were raised in favor of tracking, yet the vast majority of schools remain tracked. Researchers had achieved something of a consensus, but many teachers simply did not believe research that contradicted the only way they had ever seen schools organized, and many parents worried that detracking would hurt their children who were in more advanced tracks.[11]

In her book *Crossing the Tracks: How "Untracking" Can Save America's Schools*, Anne Wheelock directly challenges the folk wisdom that tracking is essential for well-managed, effective schools. In her survey of schools from Massachusetts to California, Wheelock describes both the political context and the pedagogical methods of untracking. She found educators in many places who understood why parents and teachers believed that tracking was best for all students but who also worked to change both the perceptions and the reality within their schools. A principal from Kentucky whom Wheelock interviewed told her that the first essential move to untracking a school was to give parents the guarantee that their child is not going to be harmed. "Parents ask, 'Can you be sure my child is not going to be worse off?' I can say 'She won't be worse off, and we hope she will be better off.'"[12] This process, like all democratic processes, takes time. Parents need to know that they have a real voice and are not simply being consulted after the fact.

| heterogeneous groupings |
| Group of students mixed by ability or needs to discourage tracking. |

According to Wheelock, the schools that implemented **heterogeneous groupings** gained significant pedagogical opportunities. She insists that eliminating tracking only works when there is a "climate of high expectations and participatory learning for all," when there is support for "teachers' readiness for change and willingness to take risks," and when there is a "rich, high-level curriculum that reflects the goal of preparing students for a multiplicity of productive adult roles."[13] In a foreword to Wheelock's book, Jeannie Oakes elaborates on the themes she had explored earlier in *Keeping Track* (see the **Readings** for this chapter). The battle over tracking, according to Oakes, is really symbolic of a larger struggle over the purpose of education. Thus, she argues:

> Another norm that bolsters and legitimizes tracking is the American emphasis on competition and individualism over cooperation and the good of the community—a norm suggesting that "good" education is a scarce commodity available only to a few winners. Although the American system of public education was designed to promote the common good and to prepare children for participation in a democratic society, more recent emphasis has been placed on what a graduate can "get out" of schooling in terms of income, power, or status.[14]

As we noted at the beginning of this section, the American system of education has always been torn between promoting the common good and selecting and nurturing a few winners who will be the leaders—and prime beneficiaries—of society. Tracking is an ideal means of accomplishing the latter goal, for it identifies differences early and builds on them throughout schooling. A different model is needed, however, if the other goal—the democratic goal—is to be central.

Teachable Moment
TO TRACK OR NOT TO TRACK

While researchers debate the interpretation of their studies, and school boards, superintendents, and principals set district and school policy, teachers have to make day-to-day decisions about how students are tracked or not tracked. Oftentimes significant decisions about tracking and ability grouping are made by individual teachers. Jessie Singer describes her decision early in her first year as a teacher at Cleveland High School in Portland, Oregon, not to follow the well-meaning advice of a senior colleague to "just make it through the year" and wait until another day to ask larger questions. Instead, in addition to her teaching, Singer decided to look at her school "with the eyes of an anthropologist gathering data." What she found were disturbing questions. When she asked, "Who is represented and honored in the school?" she found that the answers led to other questions about how students were separated by social class, gender, or race.

When Singer started asking questions directly of students and teachers, she gathered significant new evidence. Heather, a sophomore in a "regular" class cried when she was asked about college preparation and wrote, "My counselor told me my freshmen year that I was not college material. She said I am a regular student and should just hope to get through the next four years. Why are you making me write a college essay when I am not headed there?" Deanna, a fellow teacher, said, "I feel like I am tracked in our department because I am not an honors teacher. I'm seen as just a regular teacher and my kids don't matter." If both teachers and students were feeling that many of them didn't matter because of the system of tracking, something needed to be done.

Singer also felt that her very "newness" allowed her to ask questions that others couldn't. Thus, in one department meeting, she asked her senior colleagues to consider, "Who is honored here?" She thought, "As a new teacher, I had an advantage. I felt I had a kind of permission to share my observations as a naïve and new agent." The conversations were still difficult. One teacher said, "My regular students are lazy and hard to deal with." But another asked, "What does it say about us as educators if we are only feeling successful with an already successful group of kids?"

In the end, Singer's questions, backed up by her research and the support that she had cultivated, led the department to untrack the ninth grade. She was pleased to report:

> We decided that all students should begin their time at Cleveland High School with an opportunity to be seen equally—without pre-assigned labels. As a result of this work, freshmen classes now represent the true population of our school with equal numbers of boys and girls, students from different neighborhoods, and diverse backgrounds. A colleague in my department who was initially resistant to the idea of untracking, walked into my classroom and said, "I love teaching my freshmen classes. In all my years of teaching this age group these classes are more engaged and more fun to teach than any I have taught before."

Quite an accomplishment for a first-year teacher who started out just asking questions! Of course, not every teacher is going to be as fortunate as Singer. She was in a place where questions were allowed if not always encouraged. She quickly found colleagues, in her school and beyond, so that her efforts were not isolated. As a result of her questions and her beliefs, she was able to develop a clear agenda and move quickly.

Questions

- How do you think you would respond if, as a new teacher, a senior colleague told you to stop asking so many questions and "just make it through the year"?
- Is this story of Jessie Singer's experience realistic? Can you imagine playing a similar role in your first year as a teacher?

Source: Jessie Singer. "Getting Students Off Track." In *The New Teacher Book*, edited by Bob Peterson and Kelley Dawson Salas, 210–16. Milwaukee, WI: Rethinking Schools, 2004.

Much more recently a new group of scholars (Tom Loveless, whose article is in the **Readings**, is an example), have begun to question the detracking agenda. Loveless would not argue for a return to the rigid tracking favored by G. Stanley Hall or David Snedden, and he decries the ways in which tracking has too often mirrored race and class divides in the past. Nevertheless, he and others do favor something like the system of tracking that exists in the majority of schools today. Loveless contends that tracking today is based on a combination of teacher recommendations, student grades, test scores, parental preference, and even students' own views. He sees important virtues in a system that for high-achieving students offers "tracked classes with an accelerated or enriched curriculum" that "are superior to heterogeneously grouped classes." He also believes that tracking or ability grouping allows teachers to provide more intensive remedial support to students who fall into the lower tracks, improving rather than harming their long-term educational prospects. Oakes sees major pitfalls in the same flexibility that Loveless advocates, which she believes can quickly shade into a vagueness that gives preference to a privileged few students. Teachers need to make their own decisions, even as they also often need to operate in schools and districts where higher authorities have already decided for or against tracking and ability-grouping arrangements.

Why Do Students Drop Out Before Completing High School?

Just over a century ago, Leonard Covello, a young high school student at Morris High School in New York City, decided to drop out. Unlike many dropouts, Covello eventually returned and went on to a career as one of New York City's most respected high school principals. But as an adolescent in 1905, he was bored with school and saw no connection between what he was studying and any future he envisioned for himself. He remembered the day well:

> What stands foremost in my mind concerning this decision was the indifference and the lack of guidance at the high school itself. I simply turned in my books at the school office and went away. That's all there was to it. No one spoke to me. No one asked me why I was leaving or discussed my problems with me.

As he celebrated that day with his friends, Covello wondered aloud if anyone at the school cared if he ever came back. A friend responded, "Come back? Does a jailbird wanna get back to prison?" Sadly, both the friend's response and the attitude of those long-ago school authorities at Morris High School have been repeated many times since then.[15]

Today, even though close to 80% of high school students graduate close to or on time, many students still get bored with school, and some still view school as a kind of prison. Students still slip between the cracks and school administrators may be as indifferent as those at Covello's high school. However, a century ago, more than 90% of high school students followed the road Covello took that day: They dropped out well before graduating. A century ago, few people—including teachers and administrators—worried about the drop-out rate. High school was for a minority, and plenty of jobs in the industrial economy did not require a diploma. Today, attitudes and opportunities have changed dramatically. Schools are held accountable for their drop-out rates, and most teachers and administrators will do all they can to keep students in school. School systems develop programs to encourage those who have left to return and complete their education. Today's postindustrial economy offers few opportunities for those who lack a high school diploma or proficiency in reading, writing, and mathematics.[16]

CONNECTIONS ➜🠔

In Chapter 4 we discussed the current movement toward an 80% high school graduation rate, which if achieved would be the highest in U.S. history.

 DID YOU KNOW?

Even though the national average for graduating from high school was 78.2% in 2009–2010, the state-by-state numbers ranged from a 57.8% graduation rate in Nevada to a 91.1% rate in Wisconsin and 91.4% in Vermont.

Source: National Center for Education Statistics. *Public School Graduates and Dropouts*, January 2013.

As we saw in Chapter 4, with passage of the Education for All Handicapped Children Act in 1975, most *legal* barriers to the full inclusion of all children in the nation's classrooms had finally fallen. However, cultural barriers can be more difficult to challenge than legal ones. Students who feel or are made to feel unwelcome will drop out or, perhaps more accurately, will be *pushed out* by failures—conscious and unconscious—on the part of schools to create the kinds of educational communities that truly leave no child behind.

Just as the Supreme Court's 1954 *Brown v. Board of Education* decision did not end racial segregation in schools, the federal legislation of the 1970s did not end other forms of exclusion. Well-known historians of education David Tyack and Elisabeth Hansot use the example of African Americans to explore the many forms of discrimination that continue in the schools:

> Beyond the bias built into law and clear policy, blacks also faced a more amorphous and less conscious kind of discrimination, which became labeled "institutional racism." Blacks found that civil rights laws did not dismantle many of the attitudinal, economic, and institutional hurdles they faced. In public education, civil rights groups targeted a number of forms of institutional racism: the omission of blacks and the use of negative stereotypes of African Americans in textbooks; biased behavior of teachers toward people of color, arguably all the more potent in its impact when unconscious; the use of racially unfair tests; bias in counseling; the failure to appoint and advance black employees; and the tracking of blacks into slow lanes or dead-end vocational programs that blocked them from further education or white-collar jobs.[17]

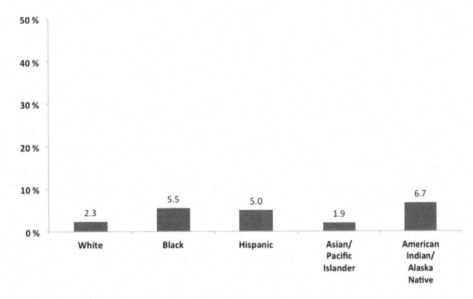

Figure 10.3

Public high school event dropout rate for grades 9–12, by race/ethnicity: School year 2009–10.

Source: U.S. Department of Education, National Center for Education Statistics, Common Core of Data (CCD), "NCES Common Core of Data State Dropout and Completion Data File," School Year 2009–10, Version 1a.

These more amorphous but often more powerful forms of discrimination continue in schools to this day, and they apply to African Americans, Latinos, and American Indians, girls of all races and ethnic groups, and also to many other young people never formally discriminated against or excluded, as well as to those whose exclusion or second-class status was officially ended in the 1950s, 1960s, and 1970s.

Researcher Michelle Fine spent the 1984–85 school year in another New York City high school asking herself—and the students, teachers, and administrators—why the majority of students still dropped out of that particular school prior to graduation. Fine listened carefully to their stories, including these:

Diana (a seventeen-year-old dropout): My mother has lupus. She's dying and those doctors are killing her. Nobody speaks English good in my family, and she wants me there. My brothers and sisters, they little and need me. . . .

Broderick (a sixteen-year-old dropout): Where else am I gonna make this money, even with a diploma? I know it's a risk. I just got out of Spofford [juvenile facility]. I worry about how my mother feels 'bout it. . . . Sometimes I feel it's immoral, when I sold Angel Dust to a pregnant girl. Won't do that again. But you can't have a heart up here. . . . If I don't give it to her, someone will.

Fine summarized the reasons for dropping out that she heard from Diana, Broderick, and too many others, saying that *drop out* really is not the right term—exclusion from the school would be a better one. At her school, Fine found that exclusion happens,

- "when my Momma comes and they show her no respect" . . .
- When national suspension and expulsion rates double for Black and Latino students compared with those for white (non-Latino) students . . .
- Inside the fifteen-year-old history book introduced by a white teacher to her African American student body with the following apology: "This book is not too good on Blacks."
- It existed in a literature class in which "good reading" signified the whiteness and usually the maleness of the authors, or a social studies class in which culture got defined as "what the Puritans and Pilgrims gave us," spoken to a group of African-American and Latino blank-looking faces . . .
- Exclusion was being held back in grade because you missed classes January through March, nursing your grandmother back to health after coronary surgery.
- It was feeling confused in class, but "embarrassed to ask for help."
- Exclusion was also being absent for five days and never being missed, or hearing that a diploma will bring you success, but knowing that your mother, uncle, and brothers, all graduates, can't find work.

Fine's list goes on. It includes students recruited to jobs or for-profit schools that turn out to be dead ends. It includes students who are continually silenced in school and demand the right to tell the truth about "racism; of an economy that declares itself prosperous while many live in poverty, sickness, and substandard (or no) housing; of an ideology of education as the Great Equalizer when there's little evidence; and of the secrets of sexism that claim the bodies and minds of their mothers, sisters, aunts, and themselves." The result of these realities is that in the school Fine studied—not that long ago—out of a student body of 3,200, only 200 students graduated in June 1985, and 70% of those who started ninth grade did not ever graduate. Across the United States, 25%–30% of all the nation's fifth graders never make it to a high school diploma.[18]

How much has changed in the 30 years since Fine completed her study? The answer is both a great deal and not very much. Many cities, including New York, have instituted multiple pathways to encourage students in danger of dropping out to obtain their high school diploma by a different route. In 2006, the City of New York offered a complex array of options, including afternoon and evening high schools for students who wanted to work full time, learning-to-work programs that blend high school classes with in-depth job readiness, transfer high schools that offer rigorous academic programs for overage students who want to try again, and GED (General Education Diploma) programs.

At the same time, increasingly rigorous standards and tests have discouraged some students, especially those who were already behind academically and who, with the new standards, come to feel that they will never make it. Students who never bothered to start high school are rarely counted as dropouts, and some who simply stop showing up are listed as having moved when in fact they have dropped out but never notified the school. In 2006, official New York Department of Education reports said that, overall, nearly 140,000 New York youths ages 16–21 were off-track for their age

Teachable Moment
WHAT CAN WE DO ABOUT THE DROPOUT PROBLEM?

If the United States is to be a truly democratic society, the drop-out rate needs to be addressed. A report from Jobs for the Future and the Everyone Graduates Center, *Graduating America: Meeting the Challenge of Low Graduation-Rate High Schools,* outlines the current situation and provides specific recommendations for change. The authors of this report wrote, "In his first major address to Congress, President Barack Obama envisioned a country where dropping out 'is no longer an option.' He linked improving high school graduation rates to restoring the nation's economic and political standing in the world."

They also insisted that:

Despite the temptation to quickly scale up interventions that have made an impact in a few places, it would be a waste of precious resources to do so without carefully analyzing the conditions that make success possible. Too often, good ideas are applied in the wrong places. And no single approach—or particular combination of federal, state, and local participation—will work for every low graduation-rate high school.

Nevertheless, the authors of this report made a number of specific recommendations to lower the drop-out rate, including:

Recommendation: No single strategy or approach will work for all states, districts, and schools. Capacity-building and technical-assistance efforts need to be flexible enough to allow those with the capacity to lead to do so, which will sometimes be the state and other times the district or school, often in concert with reform organizations. Federal and state leaders can use a variety of approaches to build capacity. For example, they can support community-led efforts to raise the graduation rate through a community investment fund, similar to a fund mandated in the 2009 Edward M. Kennedy Serve America Act.

Recommendation: Transforming or replacing all of the nation's low graduation-rate high schools will require investment in new school designs, as well as growing and spreading models that are effective for the low-income students who predominate in failing schools, including the substantial percentage of students who are not on track to graduate. More is known now than ever before about what works for this group of young people. Promising results are emerging from new small schools and programs that put them back on track to graduation. The federal government can provide incentives for states to reallocate resources and encourage innovators to expand the supply of such designs and models.

Recommendation: The whole nation suffers from the failure of high schools in Florida, California, and other large states. Like the financial services giant AIG, they are simply too big to fail. And many communities in states such as South Carolina and Michigan, where industry has left, may be too fragile to recover on their own. Graduation Bonds, similar to the Recovery Bonds mandated in the ARRA, could go a long way toward providing needed seed capital to enable districts to transform or replace low graduation-rate high schools and to develop new options for dropouts.

In Conclusion: In order to make progress, our nation's leaders and the public must get beyond the myth that "nothing works," that low graduation-rate schools cannot be transformed or replaced successfully. The growing knowledge base of promising strategies, combined with a more concerted effort to match reforms to the circumstances where they are most likely to succeed, can go a long way in helping the nation reach the president's goal of once again being the first in the world in the percentage of our young people who complete high school and earn a postsecondary credential as well.

Questions

- Can you imagine teaching in one of the high-drop-out-rate schools identified in this report? If you found yourself in such a school, are there things you, as a teacher, could do while waiting for state and federal action?
- The report recommends that federal and state leaders "support community-led efforts to raise the graduation rate through a community investment fund." If you were to receive such funds, can you imagine designing a new high school that would address the needs of students in danger of dropping out?

Source: Robert Balfanz, Cheryl Almeida, Adria Steinberg, Janet Santos, and Joanna Hornig Fox. *Graduating America: Meeting the Challenge of Low Graduation-Rate High Schools.* Oakland, CA, Boston, & Washington: Jobs for the Future, July 2009, http://www. jff.org/publications/graduating-america-meeting-challenge-low-graduation-rate-high-schools.

cohort or had already dropped out of school, and about half of all incoming high school freshmen become overage and behind schedule during high school.[19]

Why Is There an Achievement Gap?

achievement gap
Lower educational scores for populations of students based on gender, race/ethnicity, or socioeconomic status; most prevalent between students of color and White students.

In 2004, educator Jacqueline Jordan Irvine reflected on the current state of American education. The two factors that were her greatest disappointments after a career focused on improving the schools were the increase in segregation in schools, and the continuing decline in the school achievement of African American and Latino students. For Irvine, as disturbing as the stubborn continuity—even growth—of segregation might be, the more significant issue is the **achievement gap** between students of different races shown in test scores on most standardized examinations. Children of color are not being taught in ways that help them achieve at the same level as White students. Irvine continues:

This test-score gap is revealed in the fact that white students, on average, score 20 to 30 points higher than their black and Hispanic peers. But the importance of the discrepancy becomes even more apparent when considering what a 30-point difference means for the average black or Hispanic student. Seventeen-year old black and Hispanic students have skills in reading, mathematics, and science that are similar to those of a 13-year old white student.

CONNECTIONS ➔◄

Recall the Chapter 3 discussion of continued segregation in the schools.

These realities, with varying specificity, are true in the North and South, in urban and rural schools, and also in integrated suburban schools. While some of the achievement gap can be explained by gaps in income (as if that is in itself an acceptable explanation), it is also true that African American and Latino children perform less well in school even when compared with Whites of the same economic and social class.[20]

Beverly Daniel Tatum offers a partial explanation of the pervasiveness of racism that accounts for some of these differences. In her book *"Why Are All the Black Kids Sitting Together in the Cafeteria?" And Other Conversations About Race*, Tatum identifies a question that many teachers, especially many European American teachers, often ask each other: If integration is the goal, why do so many kids of color voluntarily segregate themselves in school, especially in high school? It is a very real and important question and deserves our attention. So, too, does the obvious reality that Tatum notes: "Conversely, it could be pointed out that there are many groups of White students sitting together as well, though people rarely comment about that."[21]

The question of self-segregation allows Tatum to look at not only some of the reasons for this choice on the part of many African American adolescents but also the social pain that leads to it. As her son David enters adolescence, Tatum asks, "Do the women hold their purses a little tighter, maybe even cross the street to avoid him? Does he hear the sound of automatic door locks on cars as he passes by? Is he being followed around by the security guards at the local mall?"[22] Given the likely answers to these questions, it is no wonder, Tatum concludes, that African American adolescents are likely to self-segregate. Finding others with whom they can share these experiences, with some degree of safety, becomes terribly important in adolescence.

Perhaps educator Asa Hilliard said it best. Surveying a wide range of efforts to make schools (especially urban schools serving poor students and students of color) more effective, he concluded: "There are literally hundreds of other examples that document excellent achievement in urban schools. Results like those would be typical *if we had the will to see it happen*."[23] Having the will to make change happen is essential to making schools fairer places for everyone.

In discussing the issues of fairness and unfairness in American education, it is important to note how rapidly things can change, sometimes for the better, sometimes for the worse, and sometimes just differently. In a particularly perceptive study of urban youth, *Identity & Inner-City Youth: Beyond Ethnicity and Gender*, Shirley Brice Heath and Milbrey W. McLaughlin noted that the experience of race and ethnicity at the beginning of the 21st century is different from what it was in the 1950s and 1960s, when many of the images related to these issues were created by the civil rights movement. Thus, they assert that policy makers (and teachers) can be thrown off balance if they retain "images from the 1960s of proud, protesting, largely homogeneous [African American] urban ghetto communities." The reality, these researchers assert, is that many of today's urban youth do not live in a community of one ethnic group, such as African American or Latino, but "what they see today are different groups continually moving in and out of their housing project and neighborhoods." The result is that "for today's youth, ethnicity comprises not the primary identity but an additional 'layer of identity.'"

Heath and McLaughlin found that gender roles have also changed and, if anything, mattered more than in previous decades among today's poor urban youth. Their interviews with inner-city youth led them to conclude that "lived experiences every day told the young that their gender mattered as much as if not more than their ethnicity." In many poor urban neighborhoods today, something that "amounted to a dual society" has developed. Young women and young men have taken on very specific—and very different—social roles. The young person that steps out of role is courting disaster. At the same time "many of the institutions that had lent social control for sustained family life in past generations, such as churches and gender-segregated religious clubs, no longer endured in inner cities."[24]

In the midst of the ever-changing reality faced by many of today's young people, teachers have a special responsibility to understand what is affecting their students' lives and then move from understanding to action. Teachers cannot fix all of the social, cultural, and economic forces that make life hard and discouraging for too many young people today. But teachers can—and must—be adults who offer young people hope. In the midst of an unfair and unjust world, teachers can help create classrooms and schools that, as Heath and McLaughlin say, give "visible and ongoing voice to a conception of youth as a resource to be developed and as persons of value to themselves and to society."[25] Students are not victims to be felt sorry for, but persons of value with unique strengths and needs.

Not only are students' lived experiences of ethnicity and gender changing constantly, but also the meaning of fairness is changing. Some forms of unfairness have been eliminated. State legislatures no longer pass laws mandating the legal segregation of schools by race. School districts no longer (for the most part) segregate girls and boys, requiring girls to focus on home economics while the boys learn industrial arts. High school drop-out rates for all students, and especially for African American students, are not what they were in 1950. Many forms of once-common racist and sexist language are not tolerated and are illegal in many schools. Victories have been won. In some ways, schools are manifestly fairer places than they were 20, 30, or 50 years ago. Some observers see this as a sign of inevitable progress and hope that the remaining forms of unfairness will also decline in due course. Others are not so sure and worry that as some forms of unfairness and discrimination disappear, new forms—sometimes more insidious forms because they come from unexpected quarters—may begin to emerge.

How Do Teachers Get Themselves Into Trouble?

Although the primary focus of this chapter is fairness toward students—in the classroom and in the nation—teachers are also expected to be fair and ethical in their relationships with each other and with their employer, the school district. In *Tough Choices for Teachers: Ethical Challenges in Today's Schools and Classrooms*, Robert Infantino and Rebecca Wilke explore a wide range of **ethical dilemmas** that teachers can encounter, including when it is permissible to use school

> **ethical dilemma**
> Problem for which no solution presents itself that is morally or ethically clear and acceptable in the circumstances.

supplies, what sort of stance to take toward grading and letters of reference, and the inevitable questions about a teacher's social life in and out of school.[26] Infantino and Wilke offer a series of snapshots of the kinds of ethical dilemmas that new as well as experienced teachers can easily find themselves facing:

- A newly minted social studies teacher has been asked by "Marcos" to write a letter of support for his college application. The problem is that Marcos is not working very hard and has been difficult in class. But he begs for the letter. A senior colleague says, "Just write a nice letter—you can skip some of the details." But while the new teacher certainly wants to support all of her students and does not want to keep one of them out of college, she also has grave reservations about sending off a vague letter which in the end fails to tell the truth about either the student's academic work or his behavior in class.

- A department chair is leading a search committee that includes one first-year teacher for a new hire in the department. In the midst of the committee's review of three strong candidates, one veteran teacher said, "You know, an African American male really would not fit in that well here. After all, we have so few students of color, and most don't even graduate." The committee then turns to the newest member. How should she respond?

- A first-year elementary teacher attends a faculty meeting where the group is told that things are disappearing from the school supply closet. Later she runs into one of the senior teachers walking down the hall with an armload of paper and other supplies. She looks shocked but the veteran says, "What's wrong?" and she continues "now you know when to sneak down here and get a few things when you need them. It's all for the good of the kids, right?" Is it, the novice wonders, for the good of the kids or is it old-fashioned theft?

- A new teacher is told by very influential parents that she needs to change a student's grade. The wealthy father is clear: "Matthew has always been a straight A student, and now he has a B+ in your class. This is simply unacceptable." The teacher stands her ground but wonders if the administration will back her up or even if she wants to stay in a profession with such pressures.

- A first-year teacher tells her close friend who is a teacher at a different school, "I really, really blew it! You know that cute boyfriend I was telling you about? Well, I didn't tell you everything. First of all, he's the assistant principal at the school here and, oh my gosh, I hate to even say it, but he's . . . he's also married!"[27]

These stories represent very real and immediate ethical dilemmas, and almost every teacher is going to face one if not multiple versions of these and others. Oftentimes, the "right" decision or action is far from clear. In a school where the supplies are kept from the students, is it wrong to grab supplies when the administration isn't looking and use them for the good of the kids? If a student is having a bad year, does a college admission office need to know that? If two consenting adults who happen to be on the same faculty are attracted to each other, is that anyone else's business?

Some ethical issues are crystal clear. One of my colleagues begins the orientation for new student teachers with the warning, "And don't date your students." Student teachers and recent college graduates may be close in age and attracted to their high school students, but crossing that student-teacher boundary is unacceptable in all circumstances (and more than likely illegal). However, many a teacher has engaged in what started as innocent behavior, from a mild flirtation with a colleague to a pat on a student's back, only to later find himself or herself in deep trouble, accused of improper behavior or even sexual harassment. Such accusations are not always fair, but it is important to be cautious in interactions with students and colleagues to avoid even the perception of improper behavior. (In the last example from Infantino and Wilke, the new teacher was fired. The tenured administrator she was dating was simply reprimanded.)

Notes from the Field

How can a teacher inadvertently get in trouble?

"As a male teacher, I think that there is always a slight paranoia in the back of my mind when dealing with female students in the classroom. I can look back and remember fifteen years ago when I was in school and it was not uncommon for male teachers to place a single hand on the back of a female student who was having issues in class to make her feel more comfortable. Now I am afraid of accidentally brushing against a female student because of what the consequences might be. I am not encouraged to cite a female on dress code violations because that insinuates that I was 'looking.'"

—*Eric Steele, high school history teacher*

Teachable Moment
SPELLING OUT DISCRIMINATION AND SEXUAL HARASSMENT

School districts have explicit guidelines regarding inappropriate or unlawful conduct on the part of employees and students. Following are excerpts from the St. Charles (Missouri) R-VI School District Board of Education's "Prohibition Against Illegal Discrimination and Harassment" policy that is distributed to employees and parents.

General Rule:

The St. Charles R-VI School District Board of Education is committed to maintaining a workplace and educational environment that is free from illegal discrimination or harassment in admission or access to, or treatment or employment in, its programs, activities, and facilities. Discrimination or harassment against employees, students or others on the basis of race, color, religion, sex, national origin, ancestry, disability, age, or any other characteristic protected by law is strictly prohibited in accordance with the law. The St. Charles R-VI School District is an equal opportunity employer. Students, employees, and others will not be disciplined for speech in circumstances where it is protected by law. The Board also prohibits:

1. Retaliatory actions based on making complaints of prohibited discrimination or harassment or based on participation in an investigation, formal proceeding or informal resolution concerning prohibited discrimination or harassment.
2. Aiding, abetting, inciting, compelling, or coercing discrimination or harassment.
3. Discrimination or harassment against any person because of such person's association with a person protected from discrimination or harassment due to one or more of the above-stated characteristics.

All employees, students, and visitors must immediately report to the district for investigation any incident or behavior that could constitute illegal discrimination or harassment.

Additional Prohibited Behavior

Behavior that is not unlawful or does not rise to the level of illegal discrimination of harassment might still be unacceptable for the workplace or the educational environment. Demeaning or otherwise harmful actions are prohibited, particularly if directed at personal characteristics including, but not limited to, socioeconomic level, sexual orientation, or perceived sexual orientation.

Additionally, the policy spells out behaviors that could constitute sexual harassment:

1. Sexual advances and requests or pressure of any kind for sexual favors, activities, or contact.
2. Conditioning grades, promotions, rewards or privileges on submission to sexual favors, activities or contact.
3. Punishing or reprimanding persons who refuse to comply with sexual requests, activities or contact.
4. Graffiti, name calling, slurs, jokes, gestures or communications of a sexual nature based on sex.
5. Physical contact or touching of a sexual nature, including touching of intimate parts and sexually motivated or inappropriate patting, pinching, or rubbing.

Questions

• Why do you think school districts issue statements like this? What might have happened that would lead a district to send such explicit rules to teachers and parents?
• If you were a teacher, would you find a policy like this to be reassuring (because you were protected) or a type of bureaucratic interference (because there are so many rules to follow)?

Source: St. Charles, Missouri R-VI School District Board of Education. "Prohibition Against Illegal Discrimination and Harassment," 2009.

Also, teachers hear racist, sexist, and homophobic comments and need to decide how to respond in the moment. Agreeing with a racist decision is just plain wrong, as one of the teachers in the earlier examples was asked to do (or appeared to be expected to do). The situation gets more difficult when a teacher overhears something and needs to decide when and if to respond.

Teachers will always need to balance many competing pressures—from administrators, parents, and students—within the confines of the economic environment in which they do their jobs and given the availability of resources. The reality is that schools are not always fair places, and some observers may ask, "Why rock the boat?" However, it is a teacher's responsibility to address injustices and create an environment that benefits all students equally. Kelley Dawson Salas, a fourth-grade teacher in Milwaukee, Wisconsin, describes ways that teachers can directly attack unfairness when they see it:

> Teachers can be agents of change. We shouldn't accept the idea that we don't have the power to do anything in the situation. Even if you don't see yourself as a political person or someone with control over what you're doing, in reality you're making thousands of political decisions every day. Not intervening when a student makes a racist comment is a political decision. Teaching from textbooks that emphasize only the European-American experience is another one. Those are political decisions that hurt students. You can also make choices that help students— choose to intervene when you hear a homophobic slur, choose to find books that represent the experiences of many different kinds of people, etc.[28]

Start small, perhaps—but in these and a hundred other ways, teachers are better situated than anyone else in this society to begin to slowly but specifically undo the great unfairness that has infected education, and so much else in our world, for far too long.

CHAPTER REVIEW

• Why is school funding unequal?

In many school districts, a significant amount of financial support comes from the local tax base. In wealthier areas, more education dollars are generated and thus the funding per student may be much higher, offering students more resources and attracting better teachers with better pay. To offset this difference, state funding has increased, although federal funds have historically remained around 10%–12%. There have been legal challenges to this system, but the Supreme Court ruled in *San Antonio Independent School District v. Rodriguez* that unequal school financing based on differences in property tax receipts could not be challenged in federal courts, though state courts have sometimes ruled that there must be greater equity between districts.

• Why do schools sort and track students?

In many schools, students are put on tracks based on ability and perceived future plans, which is too often decided by those in authority based on students' race, class, or gender. Over time, due to challenges to the process and its implications, tracking was refocused more on a student's ability (or lack thereof), as students with like abilities are grouped together. Supporters of both sides of the tracking debate believe their approach benefits students the most and provides them with the focus they need to succeed.

• Why do students drop out before completing high school?

Slightly more than 20% of U.S. students leave school before they complete high school, although in some states the number is much higher, even 40%. Students drop out for various reasons, including boredom, family issues, societal pressures, and a feeling of not belonging.

• Why is there an achievement gap?

Research shows that students of color lag behind others in test scores and academic achievement. Among the reasons that researchers offer for this gap is an underlying racism that continues to permeate society. This can lead to low expectations for students of color and can too often involve a mismatch between students' cultural assumptions and those of teachers and schools.

• How do teachers get themselves into trouble?

Teachers have an ethical, professional, and legal commitment not only to their students but also to their colleagues and employers. Teachers will often face complex situations and ethical dilemmas that will test their character and challenge their ability to "do the right thing," even if they believe they are being treated unfairly.

Readings

Why Is School Funding Unequal?
From *SAN ANTONIO INDEPENDENT SCHOOL DISTRICT V. RODRIGUEZ*, UNITED STATES SUPREME COURT, ARGUED OCTOBER 12, 1972, DECIDED MARCH 21, 1973

The financing of public elementary and secondary schools in Texas is a product of state and local participation. Almost half of the revenues are derived from a largely state-funded program designed to provide a basic minimum educational offering in every school. Each district supplements state aid through a . . . tax on property within its jurisdiction. Appellees brought this class action on behalf of schoolchildren said to be members of poor families who reside in school districts having a low property tax base, making the claim that the Texas system's reliance on local property taxation favors the more affluent and violates equal protection requirements because of substantial interdistrict disparities in per-pupil expenditures resulting primarily from differences in the value of assessable property among the districts. The District Court, finding that wealth is a "suspect" classification and that education is a "fundamental" right, concluded that the system could be upheld only upon a showing, which appellants failed to make, that there was a compelling state interest for the system. The court also concluded that appellants failed even to demonstrate a reasonable or rational basis for the State's system.

MR. JUSTICE POWELL delivered the opinion of the Court.

This suit attacking the Texas system of financing public education was initiated by Mexican-American parents whose children attend the elementary and secondary schools in the Edgewood Independent School District, an urban school district in San Antonio, Texas. They brought a class action on behalf of schoolchildren throughout the State who are members of minority groups or who are poor and reside in school districts having a low property tax base. Named as defendants were the State Board of Education, the Commissioner of Education, the State Attorney General, and the Bexar County (San Antonio) Board of Trustees. The complaint was filed in the summer of 1968 and a three-judge court was impaneled in January 1969. In December 1971 the panel rendered its judgment . . . holding the Texas school finance system unconstitutional under the Equal Protection Clause of the Fourteenth Amendment. The State appealed, and we noted probable jurisdiction to consider the far-reaching constitutional questions presented. (1972). For the reasons stated in this opinion, we reverse the decision of the District Court.

The first Texas State Constitution, promulgated upon Texas' entry into the Union in 1845, provided for the establishment of a system of free schools. Early in its history, Texas adopted a dual approach to the financing of its schools, relying on mutual participation by the local school districts and the State. As early as 1883, the state constitution was amended to provide for the creation of local school districts empowered to levy . . . taxes with the consent of local taxpayers for the "erection . . . of school buildings" and for the "further maintenance of public free schools." Such local funds as were raised were supplemented by funds distributed to each district from the State's Permanent and Available School Funds. . . .

Until recent times, Texas was a predominantly rural State and its population and property wealth were spread relatively evenly across the State. Sizable differences in the value of assessable property between local school districts became increasingly evident as the State became more industrialized and as rural-to-urban population shifts became more pronounced. . . . In due time it became apparent to those concerned with financing public education that contributions from the Available School Fund were not sufficient to ameliorate these disparities.

The wealth discrimination discovered by the District Court in this case, and by several other courts that have recently struck down school-financing laws in other States, is quite unlike any of the forms of wealth discrimination heretofore reviewed by this Court. . . . However described, it is clear that appellees' suit asks this Court to extend its most exacting scrutiny to review a system that allegedly discriminates against a large, diverse, and amorphous class, unified only by the common factor of residence in districts that happen to have less taxable wealth than other districts. The system of alleged discrimination and the class it defines have none of the traditional indicia of suspectness: the class is not saddled with such disabilities, or subjected to such a history of purposeful unequal treatment, or relegated to such a position of political powerlessness as to command extraordinary protection from the majoritarian political process.

We thus conclude that the Texas system does not operate to the peculiar disadvantage of any suspect class. . . .

Nothing this Court holds today in any way detracts from our historic dedication to public education. We are in complete agreement with the conclusion of the three-judge panel below that "the grave significance of education both to the individual and to our society" cannot be doubted. But the importance of a service performed by the State does not determine whether it must be regarded as fundamental for purposes of examination under the Equal Protection Clause. . . .

Education, of course, is not among the rights afforded explicit protection under our Federal Constitution. Nor do we find any basis for saying it is implicitly so protected. As we have said, the undisputed importance of education will not alone cause this Court to depart from the usual standard for reviewing a State's social and economic legislation. It is appellees' contention, however, that education is distinguishable from other services and benefits provided by the State because it bears a peculiarly close relationship to other rights and liberties accorded protection under the Constitution. Specifically, they insist that education is itself a fundamental personal right because it is essential to the effective exercise of First Amendment freedoms and to intelligent utilization of the right to vote. In asserting a nexus between speech and education, appellees urge that the right to speak is meaningless unless the speaker is capable of articulating his thoughts intelligently and persuasively. The "marketplace of ideas" is an empty forum for those lacking basic communicative tools. Likewise, they argue that the corollary right to receive information becomes little more than a hollow privilege when the recipient has not been taught to read, assimilate, and utilize available knowledge. . . .

We need not dispute any of these propositions. The Court has long afforded zealous protection against unjustifiable governmental interference with the individual's rights to speak and to vote. Yet we have never presumed to possess either the ability or the authority to guarantee to the citizenry the most effective speech or the most informed electoral choice. That these may be desirable goals of a system of freedom of expression and of a representative form of government is not to be doubted. These are indeed goals to be pursued by a people whose thoughts and beliefs are freed from governmental interference. But they are not values to be pursued by a implemented by judicial intrusion into otherwise legitimate state activities. . . .

We have carefully considered each of the arguments supportive of the District Court's finding that education is a fundamental right or liberty and have found those arguments unpersuasive. . . .

It should be clear, for the reasons stated above and in accord with the prior decisions of this Court, that this is not a case in which the challenged state action must be subjected to the searching judicial scrutiny reserved for laws that create suspect classifications or impinge upon constitutionally protected rights. . . .

The consideration and initiation of fundamental reforms with respect to state taxation and education are matters reserved for the legislative processes of the various States, and we do no violence to the values of federalism and separation of powers by staying our hand. We hardly need add that this Court's action today is not to be viewed as placing its judicial imprimatur on the status quo. The need is apparent for reform in tax systems which may well have relied too long and too heavily on the local property tax. And certainly innovative thinking as to public education, its methods, and its funding is necessary to assure both a higher level of quality and greater uniformity of opportunity. These matters merit the continued attention of the scholars who already have contributed much by their challenges. But the ultimate solutions must come from the lawmakers and from the democratic pressures of those who elect them.

Reversed.

MR. JUSTICE MARSHALL, with whom MR. JUSTICE DOUGLAS concurs, dissenting.

The Court today decides, in effect, that a State may constitutionally vary the quality of education which it offers its children in accordance with the amount of taxable wealth located in the school districts within which they reside. The majority's decision represents an abrupt departure from the mainstream of recent state and federal court decisions concerning the unconstitutionality of state educational financing schemes dependent upon taxable local wealth. More unfortunately, though, the majority's holding can only be seen as a retreat from our historic commitment to equality of educational opportunity and as unsupportable acquiescence in a system which deprives children in their earliest years of the chance to reach their full potential as citizens. The Court does this despite the absence of any substantial justification for a scheme which arbitrarily channels educational resources in accordance with the fortuity of the amount of taxable wealth within each district.

In my judgment, the right of every American to an equal start in life, so far as the provision of a state service as important as education is concerned, is far too vital to permit state discrimination on grounds as tenuous as those presented by this record. Nor can I accept the notion that it is sufficient to remit these appellees to the vagaries of the political process which, contrary to the majority's suggestion, has proved singularly unsuited to the task of providing a remedy for this discrimination. I, for one, am unsatisfied with the hope of an ultimate "political" solution sometime in the indefinite future while, in the meantime, countless children unjustifiably receive inferior educations that "may affect their hearts and minds in a way unlikely ever to be undone." Brown v. Board of Education (1954). I must therefore respectfully dissent.

The Court acknowledges that "substantial interdistrict disparities in school expenditures" exist in Texas . . . and that these disparities are "largely attributable to differences in the amounts of money collected through local property taxation," But instead of closely examining the seriousness of these disparities and the invidiousness of the Texas financing scheme, the Court undertakes an elaborate exploration of the efforts Texas has purportedly made to close the gaps between its districts in terms of levels of district wealth and resulting educational funding. Yet, however praiseworthy Texas' equalizing efforts, the issue in this case is not whether Texas is doing its best to ameliorate the worst features of a discriminatory scheme but, rather, whether the scheme itself is in fact unconstitutionally discriminatory in the face of the Fourteenth Amendment's guarantee of equal protection of the laws. When the Texas financing scheme is taken as a whole, I do not think it can be doubted that it produces a discriminatory impact on substantial numbers of the school-age children of the State of Texas. . . .

Under Texas law, the only mechanism provided the local school district for raising new, unencumbered revenues is the power to tax property located within its boundaries. At the same time, the Texas financing scheme effectively restricts the use of monies raised by local property taxation to the support of public education within the boundaries of the district in which they are raised, since any such taxes must be approved by a majority of the property-taxpaying voters of the district.

The significance of the local property tax element of the Texas financing scheme is apparent from the fact that it provides the funds to meet some 40% of the cost of public education for Texas as a whole. Yet the amount of revenue that any particular Texas district can raise is dependent on two factors—its tax rate and its amount of taxable property. The first factor is determined by the property-taxpaying voters of the district. But, regardless of the enthusiasm of the local voters for public education, the second factor—the taxable property wealth of the district—necessarily restricts the district's ability to raise funds to support public education. Thus, even though the voters of two Texas districts may be willing to make the same tax effort, the results for the districts will be substantially different if one is property rich while the other is property poor. The necessary effect of the Texas local property tax is, in short, to favor property-rich districts and to disfavor property-poor ones. . . .

The seriously disparate consequences of the Texas local property tax, when that tax is considered alone, are amply illustrated by data presented to the District Court by appellees. These data included a detailed study of a sample of 110 Texas school districts for the 1967–1968 school year conducted by Professor Joel S. Berke of Syracuse University's Educational Finance Policy Institute. Among other things, this study revealed that the 10 richest districts examined, each of which had more than $100,000 in taxable property per pupil, raised through local effort an average of $610 per pupil, whereas the four poorest districts studied, each of which had less than $10,000 in taxable property per pupil, were able to raise only an average of $63 per pupil. And, as the Court effectively recognizes, ante, at 27, this correlation between the amount of taxable property per pupil and the amount of local revenues per pupil holds true for the 96 districts in between the richest and poorest districts. . . .

The consequences, in terms of objective educational input, of the variations in district funding caused by the Texas financing scheme are apparent from the data introduced before the District Court. For example, in 1968–1969, 100% of the teachers in the property-rich Alamo Heights School District had college degrees. By contrast, during the same school year only 80.02% of the teachers had college degrees in the property poor Edgewood Independent School District. Also, in 1968–1969, approximately 47% of the teachers in the Edgewood District were on emergency teaching permits, whereas only 11% of the teachers in Alamo Heights were on such permits. This is undoubtedly a reflection of the fact that the top of Edgewood's teacher salary scale was approximately 80% of Alamo Heights'. And, not surprisingly, the teacher-student ratio varies significantly between the two districts. In other words, as might be expected, a difference in the funds available to districts results in a difference in educational inputs available for a child's public education in Texas. For constitutional purposes, I believe this situation, which is directly attributable to the Texas financing scheme, raises a grave question of state-created discrimination in the provision of public education. . . .

In my view, then, it is inequality—not some notion of gross inadequacy—of educational opportunity that raises a question of denial of equal protection of the laws. I find any other approach to the issue unintelligible and without directing principle. Here, appellees have made a substantial showing of wide variations in educational funding and the resulting educational opportunity afforded to the schoolchildren of Texas. This discrimination is, in large measure, attributable to significant disparities in the taxable wealth of local Texas school districts. This is a sufficient showing to raise a substantial question of discriminatory state action in violation of the Equal Protection Clause. . . .

The Court seeks solace for its action today in the possibility of legislative reform. The Court's suggestions of legislative redress and experimentation will doubtless be of great comfort to the schoolchildren of Texas' disadvantaged districts, but considering the vested interests of wealthy school districts in the preservation of the status quo, they are worth little more. The possibility of legislative action is, in all events, no answer to this Court's duty under the Constitution to eliminate unjustified state discrimination. In this case we have been presented with an instance of such discrimination, in a particularly invidious form, against an individual interest of large constitutional and practical importance. To support the demonstrated discrimination in the provision of educational opportunity the State has offered a justification which, on analysis, takes on at best an ephemeral character. Thus, I believe that the wide disparities in taxable district property wealth inherent in the local property tax element of the Texas financing scheme render that scheme violative of the Equal Protection Clause.

I would therefore affirm the judgment of the District Court.

Questions

1. Do you agree with the majority or the minority opinion in this case? Why?
2. Given what you have read in this chapter, what difference do you think it would have made in American education if the case had been decided in the opposite way?

Source: Supreme Court of the United States. *San Antonio Independent School District v. Rodriguez*, 411 U.S. 1 (1973) 411 U.S. 1, No. 71–1332. Decided March 21,1973.

Why Do Schools Sort and Track Students?

From "THE TRACKING WARS"

AUTHOR: JEANNIE S. OAKES

Jeannie S. Oakes is director of education and scholarship at the Ford Foundation in New York City. Prior to 2008, she was professor of education and director of the Institute for Democracy, Education, and Access at the University of California–Los Angeles. Since the publication of her book Keeping Track: How Schools Structure Inequality *in 1985, she has emerged as one of the nation's leading critics of tracking and ability grouping in public school classrooms, and her research has been cited by many who are successfully detracking schools. In "The Tracking Wars," she looks back on the many debates and the significant research of the past 20 years, much of it fostered by Oakes's 1985 book. Her conclusion is that, although much has changed, the pervasiveness of tracking, now sometimes called* ability grouping, *and its negative impact on students continue to be a reality in many schools.*

Much has changed over the past twenty years, but much remains the same. Academic standards and test-based accountability, ideas only germinating in 1985, now dominate American schooling. Market mechanisms for improving schools—choice and competition, relief from regulation, a focus on bottom-line outcomes, and straightforward privatization—that were pretty marginal in 1985 now sit at the center of the school reform stage. Equity remains a prominent value, but its framing has shifted dramatically. Desegregation has been supplanted for the most part by a high-stakes, "no excuses" agenda composed of reforms that push all schools, however segregate by race or social class, to have all students meet challenging academic standards, with "no child left behind."

These new directions in American schooling seem profoundly incompatible with practices that sort students into classrooms where they experience strikingly different and unequal resources, opportunities, and expectations. Nevertheless, tracking remains firmly entrenched in American schools. That tracking persists is not the result of inattention: neither is it for a lack of effective alternatives.

In the years since *Keeping Track* was published, tracking has reached educators', researchers', and the public's attention on several levels. More than ever before, Americans know that tracking exists; that students' assignments to various classes are not random, unstructured happenings; that this nearly ubiquitous schooling practice has been designed and implemented to achieve some purposeful end; and that tracking cannot be ignored in thoughtful examinations of schooling. Tracking is now more often understood as an active intervention in the lives of children—a willful practice chosen by policymakers and educators. Following close behind this increased awareness has been intense scrutiny to determine whether tracking actually accomplishes the educational purposes it purports to accomplish, and whether it is consistent with the democratic goals of schooling.

The answers to these questions have troubled many progressive policymakers, educators, and public commentators on educational quality and equity. Concerned that tracking violates a social justice standard that assures individuals and groups equitable access to educational resources and opportunities, many have argued that tracking is inconsistent with the American dream of schooling that provides every child an equal chance to succeed. Reformers around the nation moved to detrack schools. These progressives were joined by an unlikely set of allies: widely read conservative academics such as Diane Ravitch and Mortimer Adler, who argued that tracking's differentiated curriculum is antithetical to schooling's goal of ensuring that all students learn the traditional Western canon.

At the same time, however, tracking's defenders have charged that the research jury is still out, that any problem with tracking can be fixed without dismantling it, and that, if policymakers and schools move toward detracking too fast and unadvisedly, they place educational excellence at risk. Some claim that inequalities associated with tracking are gone, and that today's grouping is free of the problems of earlier times. The characterization of this debate as "the tracking wars" is not my own, but I can hardly disagree with it; it aptly describes the intensity of the responses and interactions among the critics and advocates of tracking and detracking. . . .

By the end of the 1980s, concerns about tracking had entered the popular discourse and influenced public policy goals. Harsh judgments about tracking's effects were reported in the popular media, including such articles as "Is Your Child Being Tracked for Failure?" (*Better Homes and Gardens*), "The Label That Sticks" (*U.S. News and World Report*), and "Tracked to Fail" (*Psychology Today*). Leading policy groups made recommendations for eliminating or at least curtailing tracking practices, and many school reformers took action.

The National Governors' Association, for example, proposed eliminating tracking as a strategy for meeting the ambitious national education goals they had set in 1989. The governors saw tracking as a major impediment to their goal of educating all students to demonstrate mastery of challenging subject matter, so that the United States would be first in the world in science and mathematics achievement on tests taken at the completion of grades four, eight, and twelve. The NAACP Legal Defense Fund, the ACLU, and the Children's Defense Fund all raised tracking as a second-generation segregation issue. And the U.S. Department of Education's Civil Rights Division targeted tracking as critical in determining racially mixed schools' compliance with Title VI regulations. Educator groups also adopted antitracking policy positions. At its national convention in 1990, the National Education Association recommended (albeit cautiously) that schools abandon conventional tracking practices. Several of the major subject matter organizations of teachers—the National Council for the Social Studies, the National Council of Teachers of English, the National Council of Mathematics Educators—all went on record as saying that tracking posed serious barriers to high-quality and equitable teaching and learning. Some state education agencies, including those in California and Massachusetts, declared that tracking should be eliminated, at least prior to senior high school. . . .

At the same time these policy initiatives were beginning, courts began to take a more intense look at tracking. In Rockford, Illinois; San Jose, California; New Castle County (Wilmington), Delaware; Woodland Hills, Pennsylvania; and Augusta, Arkansas, plaintiffs in school desegregation cases charged that the districts' tracking undermined desegregation because it resegregated minority and white students within schools. In 1994, the federal magistrate and judge in Rockford found, based in large part on analysis of its tracking practices, that the district engaged in racial discrimination. The same year, the federal judge in Arkansas ordered that the district cease its use of ability grouping by class. . . .

Other detracking efforts were very much homegrown. For example, an innovative San Diego high school English teacher, Mary Catherine Swanson, noticed that when her mostly white school became more diverse owing to an attendance boundary change, the school's tracking system relegated most of the newcomers to low-track classes. Outraged, Swanson created AVID (Advanced via Individual Determination), a scheme that placed supposed unqualified students into college-track classes and provided them with a support course in which they learned study skills and received academic tutoring. AVID has now expanded to schools across the nation. . . .

Objections to detracking were immediate and loud, often undermining the potential for reasoned dialogue about legitimate concerns that detracking would compromise the education received by the most academically able students. Such concerns could not be addressed in environments in which detracking was instantly assumed to be an assault on opportunities for high achievers. It wasn't so much that anybody questioned the findings of inequality (at least at first); rather the implications of heterogeneity were so totally unacceptable that thoughtful discussion was often derailed with caricatures and scenarios of doom. The loudest and most highly organized objections came from educators who specialized in "gifted and talented" education. Separate programs were the cornerstone of their practice and theory, and they feared, probably correctly, that calls for detracking placed those programs at risk. Supported by powerful parent advocacy groups, the gifted-education community soon came out swinging.

The arguments ran the gamut, asserting that gifted students were as far from the norm and as "needy" of separate learning environments as low-IQ students; ridiculing the idea of mixed-ability classrooms by comparing them to a varsity football team that accepts everyone who wants to play, regardless of skills; warning that detracking would place "our nation's most precious resource" (gifted students) at risk; and suggesting that average and below-average students feel better if they are not confronted each day by the intellectual superiority of their gifted peers. These arguments were bolstered by "research reviews" purporting to show that students, particularly gifted students, should be kept in separate homogeneous classes. Most shrewdly, opponents of detracking quickly defined tracking out of existence. As long as there was a theoretical possibility that a student's track might change, they contended, assignments to low or high classes was simply an educational determination more properly called "ability grouping." Conceding that the narrower, rigid tracking may well be bad, they distanced those critiques from "ability-grouped classes." High-ability groups, they concluded, are not discriminatory, even though minority students may be underrepresented in them. "Flexible groupings," particularly as applied to elementary classrooms, became the key definitional defense. . . .

The Research Battleground: Scientific Uncertainty or Solid Evidence?

Does Tracking Create Unequal Opportunity?

Working with a team of research colleagues at RAND and with the support of the National Science Foundation, I examined the relationship of race, social class, and tracking to students' opportunities to learn science and mathematics in a national sample of six thousand classrooms in twelve hundred schools. Survey data from school principals and from mathematics and science teachers allowed us to examine differences between schools and within schools. The results, which we ended up calling *Multiplying Inequalities*, were striking. Differences in opportunities to learn science and mathematics resulted from the combined effects of disparities between tracks within schools and differences among schools' tracking practices. Consistent with the data reported in *Keeping Track*, high-track classes consistently offered richer learning opportunities and more resources, including more highly qualified teachers, than low-track classes.

At the grossest level, we found that senior high school tracking shapes the number and type of academic courses students take. Low-track students are seldom required to take as many math and science classes as high-track students, and they rarely do. Additionally, those not preparing for college take advanced classes only rarely. In every aspect of what makes for a quality education, kids in lower-track classes typically get less than those in higher tracks and gifted programs.

At all levels of schooling, low-track math and science courses offered less demanding topics and skills, while high-track classes typically included more complex material and more thinking and problem-solving tasks. Teachers of low-ability classes also placed considerably less emphasis than teachers of high-track classes on more general learning goals, such as having students become interested in science and mathematics, acquire basic concepts and principles, and develop an inquiry approach to science and a problem-solving orientation to mathematics. The ability to meet such goals does not depend on students' prior academic achievement or skill levels. Researchers and educators increasingly see reaching these goals as possible for all but seriously impaired students, and policymakers increasingly describe them as essential for all students. Nevertheless, those teaching low-tracked classes typically reported these goals as less important for their students. Additional research is consistent with these findings of clear track-related differences in students' access to knowledge. . . .

Is Tracking Discriminatory?

Are the racial patterns fair? We certainly can argue that they are not fair, given that the differences in the quality of what students experience constrain rather than expand the opportunities of students in low-track classes and that African Americans and Latinos suffer these constraints more often than other students. . . .

My conclusion is that race itself does indeed influence track placements, Latinos and African Americans being more likely than whites and Asian students to be placed in low-track classes. Although the lower average of achievement of Latinos and African Americans certainly "explains" (in a statistical sense) much of the disproportionate assignment of these students to lower-track classes, we also find significant and disturbing evidence of racial bias. . . .

Certainly, these patterns reflected very real differences in minority and white students' previous learning opportunities and their effects on academic preparation. Yet these associations with students' prior achievement do not demonstrate that the schools in our study made fair and racially neutral assignments. In fact, students' race or ethnicity was often important in *determining* the probability of participating in college preparatory math and English, over and above their measured achievement. . . .

Does Tracking Affect Students' Schooling Outcomes?

The best new evidence from the past twenty years adds to *Keeping Track*'s claim that tracking fails to foster the outcomes schools value—academic excellence and educational equity. Tracking is particularly inconsistent with today's national goals of having all students meet high academic standards and leaving no child behind. There is little disagreement that grouping affects students' schooling outcomes with exactly the opposite effect. Nobody today makes evidence-based claims that students in low-track classes benefit from tracking. Incontrovertibly, tracking widens the inequality among students in what they learn in school: students in high-track classes learn more than students in low-track classes. In today's rhetoric, tracking systematically leaves children not in the high track behind. The widening gap is associated with obvious and measurable advantages that allow high-track students to reach their "potential" and disadvantages that depress the achievement of low-track students.

However, the research on the relationship between tracking and students' schooling outcomes is complicated. Researchers' answer to the question of whether tracking affects outcomes depends on their definition of tracking, the outcomes they are interested in, the specific formulation of their research questions, and their research methods. Since achievement test scores are the most frequently studied outcome, let's begin there: the research on tracking and ability grouping consistently finds that the achievement gap between students in high- and low-classes groups grows over time.

My colleagues and I found this differential effect of tracking on students' measured achievement in the Matchmaking studies of three comprehensive high schools as well as in our studies of tracking in San Jose [California], Rockford [Illinois], Wilmington [Delaware], and Woodland Hills [Pennsylvania]. In all of these schools, high-track placement led to achievement gains, and low-track placement had negative effects. Students in lower-level courses consistently demonstrated lesser gains in achievement than their comparably scoring peers in high-level courses. These results were consistent across achievement levels: whether students began with relatively high or relatively low achievement, those placed in lower-level courses showed smaller gains (or greater losses) over time than similarly situated students placed in higher-level courses.

Source: Jeannie Oakes. "The Tracking Wars." In *Keeping Track: How Schools Structure Inequality,* second edition. New Haven, CT: Yale University Press, 2004, pp. 214–21, 226–7, 229–31, 236–7.

From "THE TRACKING AND ABILITY GROUPING DEBATE"
AUTHOR: TOM LOVELESS

Tom Loveless is one of a small but growing group of researchers who have begun to challenge Oakes's research. Where Oakes sees a continuing problem, Loveless sees progress in eliminating the negative impact of old-style tracking and a new kind of tracking that fosters excellence in both high-level and low-level students. He is a senior fellow at the Brookings Institution, and the essay reprinted here was first published in The Fordham Report, *a regular publication of the conservative Fordham Foundation. As is clear from these two articles, Loveless and Oakes disagree strongly on the impact of tracking, especially in today's educational climate.*

What Is Tracking?

Thirty years ago, the terms "ability grouping" and "tracking" were used to identify two distinct approaches to grouping students.

> **Ability grouping** referred to the formation of small, homogeneous groups within elementary school classrooms, usually for reading instruction. Children of approximately the same level of reading proficiency would be grouped for reading instruction, perhaps into "redbirds" and "bluebirds."

Tracking referred to a practice in which high schools tested students, typically with both achievement and IQ tests, and used these scores to place their students into separate curricular tracks, or "streams," as they are called in Europe. . . .

Writers now use the terms "tracking" and "ability grouping" interchangeably. One hears, for example, that "tracking begins in kindergarten. . . ."

Tracking in High Schools

High school systems have changed significantly from the college-general-vocational tracks of yore. They are still distinguished by a hierarchy of coursework, especially in mathematics and English, but two and three track systems and mixed systems with both tracked and heterogeneous classes are prevalent. Typically, students are grouped independently from subject to subject. A student who is a poor reader but strong in mathematics and science, for example, can progress to advanced placement (AP) courses in calculus or physics. The independence of subjects is not pure, however. The vagaries of scheduling may still allow a student's placement in one subject to influence placement in another, and the mere existence of prerequisites can't help but link a student's present and past track levels. Nevertheless, it is more accurate to think of today's tracks as multiple pathways through different disciplines than as a single road winding through the full high school curriculum.

These tracks have diminished their preoccupation with students' destinations, most notably with deciding who will be prepared for college and who will be prepared for work. The honors track remains focused on college preparation to be sure, but, invariably, middle and low tracks also declare preparation for college as goals. With enrollment in vocational courses in steep decline, the focus of low tracks has shifted toward academic remediation. . . . Classroom studies indicate that low tracks continue to dwell on basic skills, featuring a dull curriculum and inordinate amounts of drill and practice. But such curricular banality may be caused by the lack of interesting materials or good instructional strategies for addressing stubborn learning problems, especially problems persisting into the high school years. Despite remedial students' academic deficiencies, counselors frequently point low track students toward community colleges. The bottom line is that all high school tracks may lead to colleges, albeit to dramatically different types of institutions.

Another change is that the high track has become more accessible. When principals are asked how they assign students to tracks, they report that completion of prerequisite courses, course grades, and teacher recommendations are the chief criteria, not scores on standardized tests. Parent and student requests are also factored into track placement. More than 80% of schools allow students to elect their course level provided prerequisites have been met, and many schools offer a waiver option for parents who insist, despite the school's recommendation, that their child enroll in a high track class. A degree of self-tracking exists today that was unheard of decades ago. . . .

The Research

In the last two decades, researchers have . . . analyzed large national surveys to evaluate tracking. High School and Beyond (HSB) is a study that began with tenth graders in 1980. The National Educational Longitudinal Study (NELS) started with eighth graders in 1988. These two studies followed tens of thousands of students through school, recording their academic achievement, courses taken, and attitudes toward school. The students' transcripts were analyzed, and their teachers and parents were interviewed. The two massive databases have sustained a steady stream of research on tracking.

Three findings stand out. High track students in HSB learn more than low track students, even with prior achievement and other pertinent influences on achievement statistically controlled. Not surprising, perhaps, but what's staggering is the magnitude of the difference. On average, the high track advantage outweighs even the achievement difference between the student who stays in school until the senior year and the student who drops out.

The second major finding is that race and tracking are only weakly related. Once test scores are taken into account in NELS, a student's race has no bearing on track assignments. In fact, African-American students enjoy a 10% advantage over white students in being assigned to the high track. This contradicts the charge that tracking is racist. Considered in tandem with the high track advantage just described, it also suggests that abolishing high tracks would disproportionately penalize African-American students, especially high achieving African-American students. Moreover, NELS shows that achievement differences between African-American and white students are fully formed by the end of eighth grade. The race gap reaches its widest point right after elementary and middle school, when students have experienced ability grouping in its mildest forms. The gap remains unchanged in high school, when tracking between classes is most pronounced.

Third, NELS identifies apparent risks in detracking. Low-achieving students seem to learn more in heterogeneous math classes, while high and average achieving students suffer achievement losses—and their combined losses outweigh the low achievers' gains. In terms of specific courses, eighth graders of all ability levels learn more when they take algebra in tracked classes rather than heterogeneously grouped classes. For survey courses in eighth grade math, heterogeneous classes are better for low achieving students than tracked classes.

These last findings are important because we don't know very much about academic achievement in heterogeneous classes. When the campaign against tracking picked up steam in the late 1980s, tracking was essentially universal. Untracked schools didn't exist in sufficient numbers to evaluate whether abandoning tracking for a full regimen of mixed ability classes actually works. The NELS studies that attempt to evaluate detracked classes, which thus far have been restricted to mathematics, point toward a possible gain for low achieving students and a possible loss for average and above average students, but these findings should be regarded as tentative.

To summarize what we know about ability grouping, tracking, and achievement: The elementary school practices of both within-class and cross-grade ability grouping are supported by research. The tracking research is more ambiguous but not without a few concrete findings. Assigning students to separate classes by ability and providing them with the same curriculum has no effect on achievement, positive or negative, and the neutral effect holds for high, middle, and low achievers. When the curriculum is altered, tracking appears to benefit high ability students. Heterogeneous classes appear to benefit low ability students but may depress the achievement of average and high achieving students.

Fosters Race and Class Segregation?

Critics charge that tracking perpetuates race and class segregation by disproportionately assigning minority and poor children to low tracks and white, wealthy children to high tracks. When it comes to race, the disparities are real, but, as just noted, they vanish when students' prior achievement is considered. A small class effect remains, however. Students from poor families are more likely to be assigned to low tracks than wealthier students with identical achievement scores. This could be due to class discrimination, different amounts of parental influence on track assignments, or other unmeasured factors.

The issue ultimately goes back to whether tracking is educationally sound. Those who complain of tracking's segregative impact do not usually attack bilingual or Title I programs for promoting ethnic and class segregation, no doubt because they see these programs as benefiting students. If low tracks remedied educational problems, the charge of segregation would probably dissipate. Does tracking harm black students? A telling study conducted by the Public Agenda Foundation found that "opposition to heterogeneous grouping is as strong among African-American parents as among white parents, and support for it is generally weak." If tracking harms African-American students, one would not expect these sentiments.

Questions

1. To what degree are Oakes and Loveless talking about the same thing and/or talking past each other?
2. Although they differ on many issues, Loveless and Oakes specifically contradict each other on at least one specific topic: Oakes found that African-American students with the exact same test score as Whites were placed in lower groups; Loveless said they were placed in a higher group. Do you think this difference is due simply to their looking at different districts, or something else? When these kinds of differences appear in the research, who is a teacher, an administrator, or a policy maker to believe? Can one still learn from such research?
3. Have you experienced tracking or ability grouping in school, such as different reading groups in elementary school, advanced placement in high school, or gifted and talented programs at any level? Did you benefit? Did you think it benefited or harmed other students?

Source: Tom Loveless. "The Tracking and Ability Grouping Debate," *Fordham Report* (August 1998), reprinted in Dennis L. Evans, ed., *Taking Sides: Clashing Views on Controversial Issues in Teaching and Educational Practice*. Dubuque, Iowa: McGraw-Hill-Dushkin, 2005, pp. 194–202.

Politics
What Is Its Place in Education?

11

It's no simple task to figure out what schools ought to teach and how best to teach it—how to link talented teachers with engaged students and a challenging curriculum. Turning around the great gray battleship of American public education is even harder.

DAVID KIRP, *NEW YORK TIMES*

QUESTIONS TO COME

280 What Are the Current Debates About the Standards and Why Are They So Intense?

289 What Is the Role of Federal Officials in Education?

292 What Is the Role of State and Local Governments in Education?

297 How Do Teachers Make Political Decisions in the Classroom?

300 Readings

Although many efforts have been made to "keep politics out of our schools," such a phrase is virtually meaningless. It is within the political process that decisions are made in a democratic society. To most educators, it certainly seems desirable to keep certain kinds of political influence out of the schools. Teachers have fought hard so that they cannot be fired if their political party loses the next school board election, and, in general, teachers are not hired because of their **political affiliations**, either. It is rare (though not as rare as some would hope) for a government official to intervene directly in a hiring decision for a teacher or in a promotion decision regarding a student, but most people also agree that this sort of political influence should be eliminated if professional educators are to do their jobs. Nevertheless, education is an intensely political activity, and it always will be.

> **political affiliation**
> Active association with a political group or entity; registration to vote in a specific political party.

The federal government—the federal courts, the president, and members of Congress—have long had a significant impact on education in the United States. State and local governments have an even larger role, given that education is primarily a state and local responsibility in this country. Elected leaders in state and local governments are the final authorities on a range of educational issues, including developing the curriculum and standards, hiring top school officials such as state commissioners and district superintendents (who do most of the hiring of the rest of the educational staff), making decisions about mandated testing, and determining the funds available for schools. Elected or politically appointed school boards set the salaries and working conditions negotiated for teachers, and they determine the resources available for building schools and for buying everything from computers to books and pencils. In this chapter, we seek to understand better the inevitable place of politics in the American system of public education.

This chapter has three **Readings**. In the *New York Times* article, education policy professor David L. Kirp looks at the good intentions and sometimes careless implementation that has created such a backlash against the Common Core State Standards, the most controversial issue in educational politics today. Following that article is a piece written by U.S. Secretary of Education Arne Duncan at the beginning of the 2014–15 school year in which he responded to some of the criticism of his policies, hoping to build a stronger base of support for future efforts. The final **Reading** is an interview conducted with Karen Lewis, president of the Chicago, Illinois, Teachers Union, in which she explains why teachers in Chicago went on strike in 2012 and what the pressing political issues in education are from the perspective of one local school district teacher leader.

. . . .

What Are the Current Debates About the Standards and Why Are They So Intense?

Ask most teachers, parents, or education policy leaders to name the most controversial issue in education today and the chances are very good they will say, "the Common Core State Standards." Some people, very liberal and very conservative ones, are passionately opposed to the Common Core. Others, liberal and conservative, defend the Common Core with equal intensity. When the Common Core State Standards were first emerging in 2007, no one involved in the process expected this sort of controversy. In the initial stages, there was near universal support for the Common Core. But the backers of the standards were probably naive to expect clear sailing. As we will read in this chapter, every earlier effort at the state and federal level to establish standards in certain subjects and for certain grade levels had run into intense debate, especially if there was to be an assessment system to determine if students were meeting the standards or not.[1]

The Birth of the Standards Movement

To understand the roots of the effort to create national standards, we must look back to the 1980s if not earlier. As a new school year began in September 1989, President George H. W. Bush and the National Governors Association, led by its co-chair Bill Clinton of Arkansas, met for an Education Summit and began the process of creating a set of National Education Goals that could guide both federal and local education efforts. In his January 1990 State of the Union address, President Bush presented these goals to a joint session of Congress. Four years later, Clinton, who by then had succeeded Bush as president, presented the same goals as legislation to Congress, resulting in the passage of the Goals 2000: Educate America Act that expanded the role of the federal panel designated to implement the goals.

In deference to the American tradition of **local autonomy** in education and the federal mandate to stay out of curriculum planning, both Bush (a Republican) and Clinton (a Democrat) insisted that not only implementation but also the design of specific policies and curricula would remain at the local level. Goals 2000 did not mean a national curriculum for the United States (although a national curriculum is the norm in many other countries). The role of the national movement was to build support, provide modest funds, and most of all outline the long-term goals themselves.

Unlike later legislation, Goals 2000 was hardly likely to stir significant debate. Who in 1990 could oppose the proposition that by the year 2000:

- All children in America will start school ready to learn.
- The high school graduation rate will increase to at least 90%.

- American students will . . . [have] demonstrated competency in challenging subject matter . . . so they may be prepared for responsible citizenship, further learning, and productive employment in our modern economy.
- American students will be the first in the world in science and mathematics achievement.
- Every adult American will be literate and will possess the knowledge and skills necessary to compete in a global economy and exercise the rights and responsibilities of citizenship.
- Every school in America will be free of drugs and violence and will offer a disciplined environment conducive to learning.[2]

Of course, we know now that the year 2000 came and went without most of the goals having been met. But the movement toward higher expectations and standards for the schools was not without substantial long-term impact on the curriculum of the nation's schools. And the national **standards movement** did not spring forth from the minds of presidents and governors. Many people trace the current standards movement further back to the surprise appearance of a major federal report, *A Nation at Risk*, in 1983. At about that same time, a number of reports appeared, all of which called for a much better school system, with much higher standards, for all American children. But among the reports, *A Nation at Risk* received by far the most attention with its ringing call to action that warned, "Our Nation is at risk. Our once unchallenged preeminence in commerce, industry, science, and technological innovation is being overtaken by competitors throughout the world."[3] Some observers viewed *A Nation at Risk* as a badly needed educational call to arms. Others saw it as a direct attack on the educational equity movements of the 1960s that had brought so many previously excluded students—disabled students, students who did not speak English, and students who were excluded from many aspects of schooling because of their race, ethnicity, or gender—into the mainstream of education by the 1980s. But no one ignored the report and its call for much higher standards for what should be expected of schools, teachers, and students.[4]

local autonomy
The ability of local school districts, state governments, or even individual schools and classroom teachers (rather than higher-level authorities in the state or federal government) to retain control over laws and policies affecting their citizens.

standards movement
A push to make educational institutions and sometimes individual teachers and students accountable for students' academic performance; often measured by means of standardized testing and evaluations.

 DID YOU KNOW?

China, India, and Singapore have national standards for the English language, as well as their native languages.

While some see the standards movement as originating in the conservative reform efforts of the 1980s, others insist that, in fact, the standards movement was born out of an earlier, substantial commitment to educational equity. For example, Edmund Gordon and Cynthia McCallister argue that *Brown v. Board of Education* ended racial segregation in the nation's schools in the name of equality—and one cannot guarantee equality without some standards against which to measure it. To those who hold this view, standards are the key to equity or, as McCallister says: "Determinations of equity are impossible absent a set of standards against which to evaluate a particular condition. . . . The standards provide a set of criteria against which educational justice is determined."[5]

Notes from the Field

How has your job changed since you began teaching?

"Starting at kindergarten, so much as changed. It used to be more about the basics—knowing their letters, counting, etc. What we teach kids now in kindergarten used to be taught in first grade. The expectations are for younger and younger kids to learn more and more."

—*Andrea Mackoff, first-grade teacher*

Throughout the 1980s, while debates about *A Nation at Risk* dominated the headlines, the National Council of Teachers of Mathematics (NCTM), a U.S. and Canadian organization of mathematics teachers, had been working to create the *Curriculum and Evaluation Standards for School Mathematics*. These standards were published in 1989 and have served as the model for a whole range of standards reports issued for the sciences, English, social studies, history, and other fields. The NCTM standards were the first discipline-specific standards for U.S. schools, developed by educators not political leaders, and they provided a solid foundation for the standards movement. NCTM added further detail to their standards with a 1991 publication that described effective mathematics teaching and a 1995 document on assessment in mathematics. Finally, in the late 1990s, NCTM appointed a new commission to revise and update all their recommendations, which resulted in a new *Principles and Standards for School Mathematics*, published in 2000. Unlike the vague Goals 2000, the NCTM standards were clear and specific on what U.S. and Canadian students should know about math. Leaders in other fields followed the model as they created their own standards.[6]

While NCTM and other organizations of teachers worked on standards in their areas, the National Education Goals Panel was created as a joint federal and state effort that took over the process of encouraging the development of national standards in virtually every field. Ultimately, the panel also took on an unexpected role of refereeing the fierce debates that some of the standards generated, most notably in history, between those who held radically different interpretations of the history of the peoples of the United States. As the battle over the history standards shows, this has always been a complicated business. Not only was there a debate about whether or not to have national standards, but even among those who wanted standards, just what those standards should be—and in the case of history whose stories should be included—the debate became intense. The standards debates, as with the earlier battles about multicultural education, once again came down to the fundamental question of identity: the national and personal identities that different groups of people thought the public schools should foster. As educational historian Jonathan Zimmerman has said of these "cultural wars," "at stake was nothing less than the nation's definition of itself." The debate about the history standards has been so fierce that none have ever been approved at the federal level and (to the chagrin of many textbook publishers) many states have different—and conflicting—standards for the way the nation's story should be taught.[7]

Goals 2000 and the standards movement always had its critics. The opposition has usually come from two perspectives. On one hand, experienced educators have asked the tough questions: Who is going to provide the resources to meet these goals? What kinds of policies are needed in terms of family leave, Head Start, and expanded kindergarten programs to ensure that "all children in America will start school ready to learn?" What kinds of resources—for retraining teachers, for providing curriculum, and for offering other incentives—will it take to increase the high school graduation rate to 90%? And what is the point of goals that have no meaningful resources behind them? On the other hand, any effort at national goals is seen as a step toward a national curriculum and national control of education, something to be opposed fiercely. Although a Republican president launched the national standards movement, the Republicans in Congress in the 1990s promised to "strengthen the rights of parents to protect their children against education programs that undermine the values taught in the home," and this included a deep distrust of what was by then a Democratic president's Goals 2000 agenda.[8]

No Child Left Behind

The largest—and probably the most controversial—level of federal involvement in public education came later and in a very different political context than the voluntary efforts for national standards and higher levels of school choice that characterized the 1980s and 1990s. After the 2000 presidential campaign, new Republican President George W. Bush moved quickly to develop legislation that would fulfill his campaign promises regarding education. Although initial planning was done within a relatively small circle, the new administration ultimately reached out to a wide range of liberal Democrats, especially Senator Edward M. Kennedy, a longtime leader in the field of education in the U.S. Senate.

The bill entitled "No Child Left Behind" (NCLB), which eventually became law, emerged from the inevitable compromises in the legislative process and contained a number of significant provisions:

- Each state was given the responsibility for setting its own specific subject matter standards and for developing a clear and specific definition of adequate yearly progress (AYP), which each school was expected to achieve. For the first time, each state was expected, by federal law, to have clear standards and to administer the federal National Assessment of Educational Progress exam.

- If schools fail to make AYP (as defined by their state) for 2 years in a row, parents must be notified of their right to send their children to a nonfailing public school in the same district.

- Federal sanctions apply to schools and districts. States are not required to establish accountability standards that have sanctions for individual students, although many states have also implemented high-stakes tests that require students to pass a specific exam or set of exams in order to be promoted or to graduate from high school and these often came to be seen as part of No Child Left Behind.

- Each state had to develop a specific definition of a "highly qualified teacher," and only such teachers could be employed in the future. The goal was to end the common practice of filling vacancies with teachers who are less than fully licensed, although the results have varied as districts found creative ways to define "highly qualified."

The federal government had never before asserted such a large role in public education in the United States.[9]

NCLB has generated extraordinary controversy. Some conservatives believed the law did too little, that the accountability standards were too low, and that there are too many loopholes. Others saw it as an inappropriate federal intrusion into local matters. Many liberals found several aspects of the legislation to be objectionable, especially the closing of schools that failed to meet AYP—an ever-expanding demand—and the testing that NCLB demands of schools.

Debates about NCLB are not simple, and they are not likely to be resolved anytime soon. While NCLB was supposed to be up for reauthorization in 2008, Congress after Congress—led by Democrats and Republicans—has simply let the law stand while they focused on other matters. The intense debate about the Common Core, which we will discuss next, has only added complexity to the issue. The leadership of the new Congress that convened in January 2015 promised to take up review and revision of the law. Supporters and opponents of the legislation cannot easily be divided into two camps. Some critics of NCLB believe the legislation does not go far enough, whereas some see it as a veiled effort to destroy all of public education. Many others like some aspects of the legislation but take strong exception to other elements. President Barack Obama has said that he supports the goals of NCLB—high standards and careful attention to the achievement of different groups of students—but he is critical of the lack of funding that has accompanied the law and is concerned that the tests used to measure progress have lacked attention to higher-order thinking skills.

Among authors traditionally viewed as educational conservatives, Frederick M. Hess and Chester E. Finn, Jr., are the most upbeat in their description of NCLB. However, they view the law as only a small first step in implementing a much larger accountability movement in education. Terry M. Moe, who is more conservative than Hess and Finn, has grave doubts about NCLB. Moe, who has championed charter schools and educational vouchers, doubts that any government intervention can by itself undercut the deeply established traditions in contemporary school structures. For him, only a much higher level of decentralization linked to more powerful parental choice will bring about effective changes.

Educational liberals also disagree with each other about many aspects of NCLB, even if many (though certainly not all) share other aspects of a common critique. Linda Darling-Hammond describes NCLB as basically a set of good intentions gone awry, whereas Alfie Kohn sees the same law as, from the start, a calculated attack on all aspects of public education as we have known it in the United States. Whereas both authors are highly critical of the ways in which the testing aspects of NCLB can narrow the curriculum and, in their views, force teachers to "teach to the test," Darling-Hammond believes there is still a significant opportunity to reform the law and, if such reforms are linked to adequate funding, make a positive contribution to American education. Kohn, however, sees little hope in rescuing any aspect of NCLB and urges educators to do everything possible to ensure the repeal of the act. Who, we must ask, are the players who will deal with, and hopefully untangle, this complex set of issues?[10]

The Common Core State Standards

While the roots of the Common Core State Standards stem from these earlier movements and legislation, the idea for something as specific as the Common Core first emerged from the chief state school officers (sometimes called the state Secretary of Education or the Commissioner of Education, who are both elected or appointed) and from the nation's governors, Republican and Democrat. The chief state school officers, themselves a very diverse group that include both political leaders and longtime professional educators representing all fifty states, met in Columbus, Ohio, in November 2007 and began the discussions from which the Common Core State Standards emerged. High on their agenda was a concern about what had come to be called the education standards movement and, indeed, the quality of education being offered to students in every part of the United States.

As mentioned, state standards had emerged in the 1990s as part of an initiative led by some professional societies, especially the NCTM, and pushed by the nation's governors and President George H. W. Bush. By the early 2000s, most states had specific standards for the core subjects. With the passage of NCLB in 2001, also with initial bipartisan support, states were also required to have some form of standardized assessment to see if students were learning what the standards said they were supposed to learn. As we saw in the discussion of school finance in Chapter 10, the U.S. Constitution does not mention education and the federal government has always been cautious about an extended role even though presidents from Lyndon Johnson to both George Bushes to Barack Obama have sought to shape and support public education. But while the federal role is limited, almost every state constitution makes it a specific role of the state legislature and governor to strengthen and extend public education. Since the beginning of widespread public schooling in the United States in the 1830s, state governments have been leaders in the push to make schools better.

By 2007, however, it was clear that the problem was that every state had its own standards—and even states with similar standards used different scores on the same tests to decide if a student had met the bar. Because of the variety of standards, a student who moved from one state to another might repeat exactly the same math or English lessons two years in a row and never cover other material that might be an important part of their education. Even more fundamentally, many education leaders worried that too many students were simply not learning what they needed for "college and career readiness," or even for full and effective participation in adult society. As a result, the state education leaders, backed by the National Governors Association, decided to develop a set of common standards that all states might follow. In 2008, they set up a series of advisory groups to do just that.

In the initial stages of its development in 2008 and 2009, the Common Core found a surprising unanimity of support, even across the normal partisan divides. The initiative for common standards emerged from the states in part because

> **CONNECTIONS →←**
>
> In Chapter 6, we looked at the impact of the Common Core on the day-to-day curriculum of schools.

state leaders are usually most keenly attuned to concerns about the quality of education in their respective states. But leadership in the effort also rested with the states due to the silence in the U.S. Constitution and because the 1965 Elementary and Secondary Education Act prohibits the federal government from engaging directly in curriculum development or even advocating for a specific curriculum.

When, after a period of public comment and widespread feedback, the Common Core was announced in 2009 there was very widespread support. At one point, 48 of the 50 states—all but Alaska and Texas—accepted the standards. But at the same time, opposition started to emerge. Part of the opposition focused specifically on the Obama administration's actions. As David Kirp says in the **Reading**, "Although the Obama administration didn't craft the standards, it weighed in heavily, using some of the $4.35 billion from the Race to the Top program to encourage states to adopt not only the Common Core (in itself, a good thing) but also frequent, high-stakes testing (which is deeply unpopular)." The federal government may not have created the Common Core but, after the muscle and money of the government came to be linked with state adoptions of the Common Core, many who had initially supported CCSS came to see them as a federal intrusion into state matters and rebelled. And it was not only the testing that was unpopular. President Obama, who had initially been elected with strong support, was in political trouble by this time and many who opposed the president came to oppose any policy he endorsed, including Common Core.

In addition to the partisan politics involved, the fact that the powerful Gates Foundation and a number of private companies were so deeply invested in the development of the curriculum and the testing that would inevitably be part of it made others suspicious. Just whose agenda was this, they asked, and who might benefit the most? The rapid implementation of the Common Core, resulting in some states giving tests to students even before they had very much time with the new curriculum or their teachers had been fully prepared to teach it, created a huge backlash. Students began to boycott the tests. In 2012, Seattle teachers led a district-wide boycott of the tests. Some governors who had endorsed the enterprise now sought to withdraw their states. And many parents—57% by the last public opinion poll—came to oppose the Common Core, often because of the testing requirements or, especially in the case of the math standards, they did not understand the direction that curricular implementation was taking. As we will see, similar opposition had developed to earlier standards movements, but seldom with the virulence that emerged after 2010.

At the national level, much of the opposition came from conservatives. In April 2013, the Republican National Committee passed a resolution that said, in part:

> Whereas, the Common Core State Standards (CCSS) are a set of academic standards, promoted and supported by two private membership organizations, the National Governor's Association (NGA) and the Council of Chief State School Officers (CCSSO), as a method for conforming American students to uniform ("one size fits all") achievement goals to make them more competitive in a global marketplace . . .
>
> Resolved, the Republican National Committee recognizes the CCSS for what it is—an inappropriate overreach to standardize and control the education of our children so they will conform to a preconceived "normal,". . . .

Longtime conservative groups like the Heritage Foundation, the Pioneer Institute, and the Koch Brothers joined in and funded the opposition to the Common Core.

The opposition to the Common Core did not only come from the political right, however. Writing in the *Huffington Post* in November 2014, Alan Singer noted that while some defenders of the Common Core have blamed an overemphasis on testing for creating the backlash, "when you look at the history of the push for national standards you realize Common Core is all about testing." In a subsequent article featured on its Web site by the New York Coalition of Radical Educators—a group hardly ever aligned with the Republican Party—Singer went on to link the involvement of the Gates Foundation, the Pearson publishing conglomerate, and similar companies to potentially huge profits from the Common Core. Thus he concluded, "From the start, Common Core has always been primarily about corporate profits and high-stakes testing." Writing for the left-leaning *Rethinking Schools*, education writer Stan Karp said, "Common Core has become part of the corporate reform project now stalking our schools."

The Common Core also has wide-ranging support. In spite of the national party's stance, Republican governors have often been at the forefront of defending the Common Core. When a movement developed in Arizona to withdraw from the Common Core, the state's usually conservative Republican Governor Jan Brewer simply renamed the standards the "Arizona College and Career Ready Standards" without changing them. Neighboring New Mexico Republican Governor Susana Martinez is a tough advocate for keeping the standards. And Louisiana Republican Governor Bobby Jindal, who originally supported the standards but changed his opinion (possibly as he developed national aspirations) and tried to withdraw was not able to convince the state legislature, the state board of education, or the state education chief, John White, to go along with him. Both national teacher unions, the National Education Association and the American Federation of Teachers, are strong CCSS supporters with statements of support and teacher-developed curricular plans featured on their Web sites.

In the midst of the debate, some have sought a middle ground. The American Federation of Teachers not only continues to support the Common Core but also reports that 75% of its members want to see the standards implemented. However, the union now calls for a moratorium on the testing and especially the use of the testing in student and teacher evaluations. While three states that once supported the Common Core have dropped out and others are considering doing so, 45 states plus the District of Columbia and several territories are still in the process of implementing the standards and repeal efforts have failed more often than they have succeeded.

If the American Federation of Teachers survey is accurate, and there is every reason to believe that it is, then most teachers do, in fact, support the Common Core and see it as a way to gain new freedom at the level of their own instruction while ensuring that their students are prepared to meet national expectations that will be the same from state to state and district to district. Nonetheless, there are teachers, like political leaders, who are passionately opposed to the Common Core, seeing it as a system that will hand education over to those who make the tests that will track student

Notes from the Field

"There is a lot of confusion about the Common Core standards. Some people think that they are only about standardized testing. That is not the case. The standards are a list of realistic expectations, for learning outcomes on each grade, that focus on critical thinking and depth of exploration. In my opinion, education desperately needed this shift to more in-depth problem solving. And, most importantly, the CCSS are not dictating exactly how we must teach. On the contrary, they are leaving the pedagogy to teachers. This is very exciting. Having creative freedom in the classroom is a gift to both students and teachers. It allows teachers to tailor curriculum to the interests and passions of the students, bringing joy into the process of teaching and learning."

—*Beth Koch, elementary teacher*

***

"I feel curriculum decisions should be made at the local level. It seems to me that decisions are made out of context. I think we are ignoring increasing diversity and seem to be trying to put too many 'square pegs into round holes.'"

—*Barbara Williams, seventh-grade speech arts and drama teacher*

success—a move that will consolidate control of public education in a few hands, mostly at testing companies and private foundations.

For the aspiring teacher, the controversy around the Common Core means several things. First, and perhaps most important, any prospective teacher interviewing for a job should be familiar with the Common Core. Responding "What's the Common Core?" in a job interview is a sure way to end the conversation. Familiarity does not have to mean support—but if you are applying for a job in one of the 45 states currently implementing the Common Core, you will need to have a working knowledge of how best to teach to the new standards, whatever your personal opinions. At the same time, as educational professionals, all teachers have a responsibility to be as informed as possible and develop their own opinions with evidence to support them, even as they find ways to survive and thrive whether the district and state where they teach is implementing policies with which they agree or not. While the future of the Common Core as a national effort to raise the standards for all students is very much a subject of debate today, the implementation of the Common Core in the majority of school districts around the country remains a reality with which every teacher and aspiring teacher must be prepared to contend.[11]

Teachable Moment
RACING TO THE TOP

In July 2009, just months after taking office, President Obama announced a new program, "a Race to the Top that will prepare every child, everywhere in America, for the challenges of the 21st century." Race to the Top funds became the dollars driving the education program of the Obama administration. The president was able to move quickly because Congress had already authorized a massive American Recovery and Reinvestment Act in early 2009 that provided billions of federal funds to stimulate the American economy and begin the process of pulling the nation out of the economic downturn of 2008. By investing $4.35 billion of those funds in education reform, the administration sought to accomplish two goals: (1) stimulate the economy in general with massive federal spending and (2) stimulate significant positive change in education by using the program to expand and also rework the previous administration's No Child Left Behind legislation and also build support for the newly emerging Common Core State Standards.

The Obama administration was very strategic about the rules for eligibility for Race to the Top funds. In order to even apply for a grant, a state had to:

- *Adopt standards and assessments that prepare students to succeed in college and the workplace and to compete in the global economy.* Although the administration did not say so, many read this to mean that states had to adopt the Common Core to be in the Race to the Top game.
- *Build data systems that measure student growth and success and inform teachers and principals about how they can improve instruction.* While by 2009 most states had tests to "measure student growth," many did not have

effective state-wide systems to use that data for larger evaluations and many states specifically prohibited the use of student test data for teacher evaluations. States that wanted the federal money had to change these rules, which lead to significant controversy.

- *Recruit, develop, reward, and retain effective teachers and principals, especially where they are needed most.* Though less controversial, this often meant support for alternative routes to teacher licensure.
- *Turn around our lowest-achieving schools.* Although a far less controversial demand, some worried this would result in an expansion of charter schools and school closings.

While the last two points were relatively uncontroversial, the first two caused significant concern, especially in states that were told they were not eligible to apply because of their existing policies. The ineligibility was most often linked to the requirement that states must have no "barriers to linking data on student achievement or student growth to teachers and principals for the purpose of teacher and principal evaluation." Following the often-made complaint during the George W. Bush administration that NCLB relied too heavily on standardized testing, many teachers protested the new rules as unfair, saying that it continued the excessive focus on such tests. Some also saw the requirement for standards and assessments as a thinly veiled attempt to put federal muscle behind the Common Core, even though it had initially been a state initiative.

After a tough national competition, Secretary of Education Arne Duncan announced the first two Race to the Top winners in July 2010: Delaware and Tennessee. Nine more states plus the District of Columbia met the requirements in 2011 and a third round of seven states in 2012.

Some of the educators who had been active supporters of Obama during his first election were unhappy when they heard the rules concerning the Race to the Top, worrying that future rules may worsen the "test frenzy" that some observers associate with NCLB and lead to a simplistic system for rewarding some teachers and punishing others. The two national teacher unions (the American Federation of Teachers and the National Education Association) took no formal position on Race to the Top, an unusual move for unions deeply concerned with federal education policy. Naturally, educators in states that did not win awards were not happy with the process, especially in states that had made significant changes in policy in order to meet the eligibility requirements.

While some states have challenged the rules for funding, more of them changed their own rules in order to be eligible for the funds. Certainly some of the growth of the Common Core and the current expansion of state data systems was a result of Race to the Top. By March 2014, as the funding wound down, the administration was proudly celebrating the success of Race to the Top. A 2014 U.S. Department of Education report gave examples of redesigned—and Common Core aligned—programs: the science and math curriculum in use in Ohio schools; a new College and Career Ready diploma and new High Tech High Schools in Hawaii; a significant increase in advanced placement classes and success on the exam in numerous states; new teacher induction programs; and the investment of $350 million of Race to the Top funds through two consortia of states in the development of the new Common Core assessments. For those within and outside of the administration who like the general direction of these reforms, Race to the Top has been a smashing success. For critics, it has moved education further in a direction they do not support.

Questions

- As a future teacher, how do you feel about the use of student test scores on your career evaluation? Do you think this approach has merit, or is it unfair to teachers?
- How do we hold schools accountable for student learning? Do you think student test scores are an appropriate way to track school achievement and progress? If not, what would be an appropriate measure?
- Should the federal government foster curriculum standards like the Common Core? Why or why not?

Source: See U.S. Department of Education, *Setting the Pace: Expanding Opportunity for America's Students Under Race to the Top,* March 2014.

❓ DID YOU KNOW?

A short-lived public uproar surrounded President Obama's televised speech to students on September 8, 2009, with some critics alleging that the president was trying to indoctrinate students with a "socialist" agenda and was overstepping his role. President Obama's speech focused on student accountability. He told students, "I'm working hard to fix up your classrooms and get you the books, equipment and computers you need to learn. But you've got to do your part too. So I expect you to get serious this year. I expect you to put your best effort into everything you do." Obama's speech is only one of many educational speeches that have ended up the subject of a political debate. In October 1991, Republican President George H.W. Bush delivered a televised speech to students, similarly stressing a good attitude and personal accountability. Some Democrats in Congress accused President Bush of "using children as political pawns."

LEARNING THE LANGUAGE: STATE AND FEDERAL POLITICS AND EDUCATION

A Nation at Risk report of 1982. A widely disseminated federal report developed during the administration of President Ronald Reagan that said the nation's schools faced "a rising tide of mediocrity." Many see this report as the beginning of the federal effort to set and enforce educational standards as part of an education reform agenda.

Goals 2000. President George H.W. Bush (the first president Bush) convened the nation's governors in 1989 to discuss ways to raise the standards and improve American education. In 1990 he proposed new education goals that under his predecessor President Bill Clinton became Goals 2000 in 1994. Some of the goals were:

- All children in America will start school ready to learn.
- The high school graduation rate will increase to at least 90%.
- All students will leave grades 4, 8, and 12 having demonstrated competency over challenging subject matter including English, mathematics, science, foreign languages, civics and government, economics, the arts, history, and geography.

The development of federal education goals in the 1990s also led many professional organizations, starting with the National Council of Teachers of Mathematics to set specific standards for student attainment in their field of study, thus the so-called *standards movement*.

No Child Left Behind Act of 2001. Officially the renewal of the Elementary and Secondary Education Act of 1965, this legislation was passed by the U.S. Congress in 2001. No Child Left Behind, unlike earlier versions of the act, required states to adopt state education standards of their own choosing and the development assessments including achievement tests that would measure student progress toward meeting the standards. Schools that did not make "adequate yearly progress" (AYP) in meeting the standards would receive a series of federal sanctions and eventually be closed. NCLB was up for renewal in 2008. To date no Congress has been able to tackle the issue of rethinking the NCLB expectations and instead has handled the issue through continuing resolutions. Thus NCLB remains the law of the land although Secretary of Education Arne Duncan has used his authority to enforce the act selectively, granting waivers to states on many occasions. The leadership of the new Congress that convened in January 2015 promised to finally revise NCLB but also has many other priorities.

Common Core State Standards were developed by the Chief State School Officers and the National Governors Association in 2007 and 2008 to create similar expectations for students in all parts of the country. These expectations were to be linked to evaluation systems that would document student success according to the same measure wherever the standards were in place. While the standards were developed at the state level and the federal government had no role, the facts that federal Race to the Top funds were directed to states that adopted the standards and these funds were used to help develop the Common Core assessments linked the Common Core to the Obama administration in the minds of many. After the Common Core State Standards were announced in 2010, 48 states initially adopted them—all but Alaska and Texas—but Virginia quickly went its own way and two others eventually dropped out, leaving 45 states, the District of Columbia, and a number of U.S. territories using the Common Core. Other states such as Virginia adopted separate state standards very similar to the Common Core while Oklahoma, Texas, and Alaska do not have such standards. (But just to confuse the situation, several large school districts in Alaska have adopted the Common Core, putting them in conflict with their state governments.)

Race to the Top Competition (RTT). Created by President Barack Obama in 2009, Race to the Top was a competition among the states funded by $4.35 billion from the American Recovery and Reinvestment Act of 2009, which had authorized a total of $787 billion in federal spending to stimulate the American economy. States had to apply in a competitive program for RTT funds and only applications that showed an embrace of high-level standards (usually meaning the Common Core), state accountability measures that linked student achievement data to teacher evaluations, and new efforts to recruit high-level teachers were considered. Eventually 18 states received some portion of the funds based on the quality of their application and their demonstrated need.

What Is the Role of Federal Officials in Education?

When educators from Asia, Europe, or Latin America visit the United States, they are struck by the limited role of the national government in U.S. schools, even if many Americans argue that the federal role is too large. Most other industrialized countries have a national department that is in charge of education and that sets the rules, a national curriculum, and national policies about teacher qualifications and expected outcomes for students. Yet, even with the extraordinary expansion of the federal government's role in school issues in recent years, most educational decisions are made at the state level. Nevertheless, the federal government is a serious player in education and has been for a century.

The Supreme Court and the Schools

In 2007, the U.S. Supreme Court, led by newly appointed Chief Justice John G. Roberts, Jr., declared that voluntary efforts to racially desegregate public schools in Seattle, Washington, and Jefferson County (Louisville), Kentucky, were unconstitutional. Announcing the 5–4 decision, Chief Justice Roberts said that "the way to achieve a system of determining admission to the public schools on a nonracial basis is to stop assigning students on a racial basis." Fifty-three years earlier, another newly appointed chief justice, Earl Warren, had announced the Supreme Court's decision that state-mandated segregation in the public schools of the United States was unconstitutional.

In the recent case, Seattle and Louisville had to move quickly to change their plans to foster racial integration, and leaders in many other school districts around the country realized that they too would have to either give up on the goal of racially inclusive schools or find new ways to accomplish the goal. The 1954 *Brown v. Board of Education of Topeka, Kansas* decision declared illegal the ways students were assigned to schools in every state in the South. Over the next decades, federal courts found that many northern districts had also illegally segregated their schools. After massive resistance in places as diverse as Little Rock, Arkansas, and Boston, Massachusetts, change came about slowly. For a period of time, more students than ever attended school with others of different races.

The decisions in *Brown v. Board of Education* (1954), *Parents Involved in Community Schools v. Seattle School District* (2007), and *Meredith v. Jefferson County Board of Education* (2007) reflect the ongoing dominance of race as an issue in U.S. education policy, but they also illustrate the extraordinarily large role of the federal government, along with state governments and local authorities, in schools in the United States. In a democratic society, local, state, and federal policy makers are elected or are appointed by elected officials; thus, it is inevitable that school policy will be highly political.

Throughout the 20th century, the federal courts have decided many issues affecting schools. The best-known and probably most far-reaching court decisions have involved issues of race and racial segregation. In the 1930s, the National Association for the Advancement of Colored People (NAACP) Legal Defense Fund began a concerted effort to challenge school segregation. The organization decided that the federal courts were the place to make their case. The NAACP legal team won test cases in the federal courts against university-level segregation and against lower pay scales for African American teachers. In the 1950s, these civil rights lawyers, led by future Supreme Court Justice Thurgood Marshall,

> **CONNECTIONS ➜◀**
>
> In Chapter 3, we looked at the *Brown v. Board of Education* ruling in the context of race in American education, and in Chapter 10 we looked at the impact of the *San Antonio v. Rodriguez* decision on school funding.

brought a case against a number of school districts that challenged segregation of elementary and high school students on the basis of their race. In 1954, the U.S. Supreme Court in *Brown v. Board of Education of Topeka, Kansas* ruled on these challenges, concluding that "'separate but equal' has no place" in public education. Many observers within the civil rights community had hoped that a unanimous decision by the justices of the nation's highest court would settle the issue, but many political leaders, initially in the South but in time around the nation, decided that the key to their own political futures was to promise "massive resistance" to the Court's order.

In September 1957, on the night before Central High School in Little Rock was to be integrated, Arkansas Governor Orval Faubus told the citizens of his state that "blood will run in the streets" if anyone attempted to integrate the school. He called out the state units of the national guard to block African American students, even though they had a federal court order demanding their admission. When Elizabeth Eckford, one of the new students, tried to walk to school on opening day, National Guard soldiers blocked her way and the White crowd jeered and taunted her. Due to the courage of children like Eckford and at the insistence of the federal courts, President Dwight Eisenhower sent regular U.S. Army troops to Little Rock to enforce the desegregation ruling. After some extraordinarily pain-filled months and years, Central High School and the schools of Arkansas were legally integrated. Some Whites created their own private academies, and some school districts found new ways to unofficially segregate the schools, but official policies of separate (and quite unequal) schools for European American and African American students were gone from the nation.

After the Seattle and Jefferson County decisions, the future of school integration seemed uncertain. Although Justice Clarence Thomas wrote in support of the majority decision that "It is far from apparent that coerced racial mixing has any educational benefits, much less that integration is necessary to black achievement," Justice Stephen G. Breyer wrote in dissent: "The last half-century has witnessed great strides toward racial equality, but we have not yet realized the promise of *Brown* . . . to invalidate the plans under review is to threaten the promise of *Brown*. This is a decision that the court and the nation will come to regret."[12]

Many other Supreme Court decisions have had direct impact on schools and teachers. In 1943, the Court in *West Virginia State Board of Education v. Barnette* ruled that public school students could not be compelled to recite the Pledge of Allegiance to the flag. In 1969, in *Tinker et al. v. Des Moines Independent Community School District*, the Court ruled

> **free speech**
> Ability to talk or exchange ideas without fear of censorship or limitation; guaranteed by the First Amendment.

that students at high schools in Des Moines, Iowa (and by implication the rest of the nation) could not be expelled for wearing black arm bands to school to protest the raging war in Vietnam. In that 7–2 decision, the Court ruled that "First Amendment rights, applied in light of the special characteristics of the school environment, are available to teachers and students." **Free speech**, the Court said, did not end at the schoolhouse door.

In another set of rulings, almost as controversial as those related to race, the U.S. Supreme Court ruled in *Engel v. Vitale* (1962) and *Abington v. Schempp* (1963) that schools could not offer officially sanctioned prayers or devotional readings from the Bible. In 1968, in *Epperson v. Arkansas*, the Court ruled that a state law disallowing the teaching of evolution was an unconstitutional infringement of the First Amendment separation of church and state. For some religious people, all three of these rulings meant that God had been kicked out of the public schools, although many deeply religious people also believed that the Court, following the First Amendment prohibition of "any laws respecting an establishment of religion," protected religious beliefs by keeping specific religious practices out of the public arena.

Supreme Court decisions affect many different elements of schooling in the United States. Battles about free speech, the place of religion in public schools, the costs of schooling, and a dozen other issues are far from over, especially as the membership of the Supreme Court changes, reflecting the differing politics of the presidents who appoint federal judges.[13]

Presidents and the U.S. Congress

Early in November 2008, within days of the election of Barack Obama as president of the United States, *Education Week* ran a special story on the president elect's views of the federal government's role in education. During his long presidential campaign, Obama had made several specific promises about the schools. Saying "the goals of this law were the right ones," he pledged to provide meaningful funding for a revised and improved No Child Left Behind Act. He had made a promise of federal funding "to recruit, prepare, retain, and reward" teachers. He had also proposed $18 billion for new K–12 programs plus $10 billion more for the development of new preschool programs. The first months of the new administration saw significant federal spending for educational programs (such as Teacher Quality Partnerships, which were specifically authorized by Congress, and the Race to the Top program that directed federal funds authorized for economic recovery after the economic downturn of 2008 to be used to improve education). The expanded federal spending encouraged school districts, universities, and states to take the quality of their programs very seriously.

As we have already seen, the Obama administration also became deeply involved in fostering change in many aspects of education. Although Congress has not revised NCLB, the administration has made its mark on education, most of all with the use of federal dollars to back the Common Core initiative.[14]

Presidents Bush, Clinton, Bush, and Obama were far from the first presidents to have a major impact on education. In 1917, Congress passed and President Woodrow Wilson signed the Smith-Hughes Act, starting a century-long policy of federal funding for vocational education. As part of his campaign for a Great Society, President Lyndon Johnson proposed much more broad-based federal funding for schools. The Elementary and Secondary Education Act (ESEA) of 1965 passed Congress by large margins in record time. Not one given to understatement, Johnson was clear about how much he valued the act:

> As a son of a tenant farmer, I know that education is the only valid passport from poverty.
>
> As a former teacher—and I hope, a future one—I have great expectations of what this law will mean for our young people.

In the 50 years since ESEA passed, federal funding has continued to be important to local school districts and teachers in a number of ways.[15]

 DID YOU KNOW?

The No Child Left Behind legislation that passed Congress in 2001 was actually a renewal of the Elementary and Secondary Education Act that was originally passed by Congress in 1965 and which was renewed, with far less controversy, every few years between 1965 and 2001.

A flurry of federal legislation during the administrations of Johnson and, later, Richard Nixon transformed education. Teachers' jobs changed dramatically as a result of legislation from the 1960s and 1970s, as well as from other court decisions that built on the *Brown v. Board of Education* decision and ruled that students could not be excluded from schools because of disabilities or an inability to speak English. These changes expanded teachers' responsibilities by requiring them to attend to a much more diverse group of students. None of these laws were passed without controversy, and, especially in the case of bilingual education, subsequent legislation at the federal and state levels has undermined many of the changes.

> **CONNECTIONS →←**
>
> Recall the Chapter 2 discussion of President Lyndon Johnson's war on poverty, how he used the ESEA to fund education, and subsequent debates about the ability of such funding to improve student achievement.

As we have already seen, in the 1980s the focus of federal policy shifted from a primary emphasis on equality of educational opportunity to the maintenance of high standards for students. In 1983, *A Nation at Risk* surprised many, as it had come from an administration that had promised to reduce if not eliminate the federal role in education. As we've discussed, *A Nation at Risk* was an important document in starting a new discussion of the meaning of educational excellence and the systems of standards and accountability that might produce a new level of educational attainment in the nation from which the standards movement, NCLB, and the Common Core all flowed.

What Is the Role of State and Local Governments in Education?

Former Speaker of the U.S. House of Representatives Tip O'Neill was famous for saying, "all politics is local." In no arena is that statement truer than in school politics. Decisions regarding education have generally been left to the states, and

> **CONNECTIONS →←**
>
> Chapters 3 and 4 detailed the succession of laws and court decisions that expanded educational rights to include all citizens.

many of the important decisions are left to the local communities. Elected or, occasionally, appointed local school boards set the curriculum, hire superintendents (who in turn hire the teachers), and generally decide what is taught by whom and on what schedule. Even when it comes to responding to the vastly expanded federal role in schools since NCLB became law and the Common Core State Standards emerged, many decisions about implementation happen at the local level.

Governors, State Legislatures, and Departments of Education

Governors, legislatures, and leaders in state departments of education have all responded to the change in national mood—perhaps even more than the specific changes mandated in NCLB and now expected in the Common Core. Florida, for example, was far ahead of NCLB in developing tough state-level accountability systems. Thirty years before NCLB, and even before much of the national pressure, Florida passed its 1971 Educational Accountability Act, which required statewide testing, the attainment of certain benchmarks to graduate from high school, and consequences for schools that did not perform well. Some states debated rejecting the federal money in order to avoid having to meet the NCLB requirements, although the federal dollars were a strong incentive to finding ways to function within the law's framework. While a few states—Virginia and Oklahoma for example—have withdrawn from the Common Core, many other state legislatures and state boards of education have considered doing the same but have not, partly due to federal funding but also in part because many teachers and other citizens lobbied hard to maintain what they saw as a significant improvement in education.[16]

State policy emanates from different power centers. Governors and legislatures control state spending on education and can also set basic legislative mandates for testing and standards. Most of the work of supervising education is left to state departments of education and to the chief state school officer (sometimes called the superintendent of public instruction or the commissioner of education). In some states, the commissioner or superintendent is an elected official. In other states, he or she is appointed by a state school board, whose members are often appointed by the governor. Appointed education leaders are more likely to work closely with other state agencies, while elected state leaders may be from the opposite party and engaged in almost constant political battles with their governors. Since governors and members of state legislatures are elected by the voters, state education policy is always political. However, being "political" is not always a bad thing. It means that elected officials need to be attuned to public sentiment and teachers, parents, and others can influence state policy when they are well organized.

Although the decisions that state governments have made about the Common Core and the ways they have chosen to implement NCLB have been the subject of

> **CONNECTIONS →←**
> Chapter 10 explained how most of a school's budget comes from state and local sources and how deeply politics impacts budget decisions.

great attention in recent years, state education officials are involved in all aspects of education. Most state education officials spend most of their time on matters far removed from reactions to federal policy. Each state determines the standards for becoming a teacher, and the state government licenses or certifies individuals to teach. The state approves certain university programs or alternative providers to prepare teachers. Special education regulations, policies for programs that teach English to non-English-speaking students, and a range of other regulations are set by state governments. State governments have the final authority to intervene in and even take over a local school district if they believe that the district is failing to serve the students as it should. In the end, states have the ultimate responsibility for public education in the United States.

Teachable Moment
CHARTER SCHOOLS

One of the major developments in education since the mid-1980s was led by a group of educators who were skeptical of what the federal government could do to improve schools. These critics sought to create "charter" schools and educational vouchers that would allow parents to take the funds a public school might receive for their child's education to any private school they selected. Whereas the federal government sought standards for every school, charter school advocates sought to remove as many mandates as possible from individual schools so that they could prosper in their own way.

Charter schools are publicly funded and maintain autonomy from selected state rules and regulations, in return for meeting accountability standards. They have grown rapidly as many supporters gained political influence. Many who at first opposed them came to embrace the flexibility that charter schools gave. The National Center for Education Statistics reports that from the 1999–2000 to 2011–12 school years, the number of students enrolled in public charter schools increased from 0.3 million to 2.1 million students. During this period, the percentage of public school students who attended charter schools increased from 0.7% to 4.2%.

Clearly this is a fast-growing movement. Of the 2.1 million students enrolled in charter schools, a higher percentage are racial or ethnic minorities, compared to students in traditional public schools. Nationally, 36% of charter school students are White, 29% are Black, 28% are Hispanic, and between 1% and 4% are of other races or two or more races. While there are many issues yet to be addressed about charter schools, the fear that they would encourage "White flight" from public schools has not turned out to be true.

A split sometimes occurs between advocates of charter schools (which are public schools that usually operate outside the purview of traditional school districts and are sometimes under the immediate direction of teachers, sometimes a nonprofit board, and sometimes a for-profit company) and advocates of vouchers (which give parents a voucher than can be used to pay tuition at a private school). Although the initial impetus for charter schools and vouchers came from conservative theorists, many liberal, community-based critics of schools have joined in support of the proposals.

Pedro Noguera, a liberal voice in American education, sees a split between educational progressives who focus on system-wide change, and who therefore oppose any efforts that undermine the strength of school systems (such as privatizing efforts including charter schools and school vouchers), and those who have given up on school systems and have already opened their own independent schools, but he sees this as a mistake. Thus he writes: "My personal

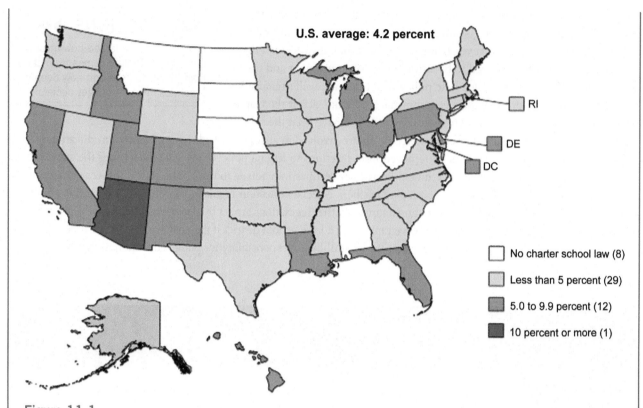

Figure 11.1
Percentage of all public school students enrolled in charter schools, by state or jurisdiction: school year 2011–12

Source: U.S. Department of Education, National Center for Education Statistics, Common Core of Data (CCD), *Public Elementary/Secondary School Universe Survey*, 2011–12. See *Digest of Education Statistics 2013*, Table 216.90.

> **privatization**
> Transition from government ownership to private-sector ownership. In education, refers to the use of vouchers and sometimes charter schools to encourage nonpublic ownership and control of schools.

commitment has been to put the needs of children first, and I have worked in a variety of ways to provide quality education to poor children of color. For this reason I have experienced no sense of contradiction in supporting independent private and charter schools, even while working to support public schools." However, Terry M. Moe, one of the original advocates for **privatization** and someone usually seen as an educational conservative, says that, although the movement has not gone as far as he hoped, "Parents have many more choices today than they did ten years ago, and both choice and competition are expanding (especially through the increasing numbers of charter schools)."

Questions

- Do you think it is more important to set clear national standards for all schools or to free educators from as many constraints as possible?
- What is the strongest argument in favor of charter schools? What is the strongest argument against them?

Sources: National Center for Education Statistics. "Charter School Enrollment," updated April 2014; Pedro Noguera, "What Will It Take to Improve America's Urban Public Schools?" In *City Schools and the American Dream*, 156–7. New York: Teachers College Press, 2003; Terry M. Moe. "Politics, Control, and the Future of School Accountability." In Paul E. Peterson and Martin R. West, editors, *No Child Left Behind? The Politics and Practice of School Accountability*. Washington, DC: The Brookings Institution Press, 2003.

Local School Districts and School Boards

Schools are nearly always governed by an elected (or occasionally appointed) school board that sets overall policy for a school district and hires a superintendent to be the full-time senior administrator of the district, responsible for all day-to-day decisions about the schools in that area. (In the case of charter schools, the school's board is usually considered the equivalent of a small school board and the president or principal is the superintendent.) There are 15,000 school boards governing regular districts as large as some of the nation's biggest cities and as small as districts that have only one elementary school. These boards have significant authority over the schools in their districts. As John Portz, a political scientist who studies school politics, writes:

> The term "governance" refers to the authority structure by which major decisions are made and resources are allocated within a school system. As defined in a report by the Education Commission of the States, "governance arrangements establish the rules of the game, that is . . . who is responsible and accountable for what within the system." A longtime observer of school politics noted that "governance is about control—who drives the education bus." Put differently, a recent study of school boards describes governing as "steering" the school district. Governing involves the establishment of educational goals and policies that follow a vision and set of core beliefs about how academic achievement can be realized.

The diverse authorities that Portz cites seem to be saying the same thing: school boards govern schools in the United States. Portz also notes that

> To be certain, school boards do not act alone or unfettered. They operate within numerous rules and regulations established by state governments and to a lesser extent, federal authorities. The superintendent also typically plays a role in school district governance and professional associations, particularly the teachers' union, might also have major governance responsibilities.

School boards have been criticized for being too actively involved in the details of school management, especially personnel decisions, that might better be left to professional educators, especially the superintendent that the board hires and should trust. They have been seen as too highly politicized and too anxious to cater to the immediate preoccupations of a portion of the electorate, such as activist teacher unions, anti-tax groups, activists concerned with one policy change or another, and so on. Some observers believe that school boards are merely an anachronistic leftover of a bygone era.

Others question how much power school boards really have. As education scholar Pedro Noguera reflects from his own experience as a member of the Berkeley, California, school board,

> I learned about the limitations of local government firsthand while working as assistant to the Mayor of Berkeley [California] during the 1980s and while serving as an elected member of the school board in the 1990s. Through direct experience, I learned that even with a relatively progressive local government in an affluent city, it was nearly impossible to solve problems such as chronic unemployment, drug trafficking, or homelessness.

Defenders of local control and local school boards see the democratic control of school through local school boards as an essential political instrument in a democratic society. For an educator like Deborah Meier, the only solution to the problems of democracy and democratic control of schools is more democracy. Meier is deeply offended by the increasing centralization and professionalization of schools—the tendency to create larger and thus more impersonal school districts that can make school decision-making more removed from individual citizens. In 1930, there were 200,000 school boards, compared with 15,000 today. The result is that each school board governs many more teachers and students, and thus it is much harder for the voice of a parent or other concerned citizens to be heard. This problem is exacerbated by the fact that there are also three times as many students in school today, state educational bureaucracies are much more powerful, and the federal government is much more involved in educational decision-making. Meier insists,

> We need to return schools to our fellow citizens yes, ordinary citizens, with all their warts. The solution to the messiness of democracy is more of it—and more time set aside to make it work. . . . That's what local school boards

CONNECTIONS ➔←

In Chapter 12, we discuss the role of schools in a democratic society.

are intended to be all about. If we can't trust ordinary citizens with matters of local K–12 schooling, whatever can we trust them with?

Others have a different opinion about the value of local school boards. Some of the nation's largest cities, including New York City, Chicago, Washington, D.C., Cleveland, Philadelphia, Baltimore, Los Angeles, and Boston, have abolished or drastically reduced the roles of elected boards, giving primary authority (and with it accountability) in school matters to the elected mayor. Mayoral control means that the city's political leader, who in most cities also controls the city budget, is responsible for the success of the schools. Having one point-person certainly avoids the finger pointing that can result when power is divided between an elected board (some of whose members may be interested in higher office) and a separate mayor.

Portz explains the appeal of these changes:

Mayoral involvement in governance is intended to align political and financial resources in the city in support of public education. In almost every instance, these are mayors in strong-mayor systems who exercise considerable authority over the allocations of resources within the city. Involvement in school policy brings the mayor into a system of "integrated governance" in which political and financial control is centralized to create a more rational and systematic allocation of educational resources.

The experiment of mayoral control versus the arguments in favor of control of schools at a much more community level seems destined to continue for the foreseeable future.[17]

For an aspiring or a new teacher, the politics of the school board, whether it is elected or abolished in favor of mayoral control, and what its powers are in relation to a professional superintendent or to state and federal officials, may all seem far beyond your immediate concerns. Nevertheless, all of us operate in political climates in which different people make decisions that affect our lives and the lives of our students. To ignore the politics of educational decision-making and to avoid the controversies about local control versus state versus national influence on educational decisions is to deal ourselves out of an important level of decision-making that affects many aspects of our work.

Hiring Decisions Teachers are hired at the local level. Neither the state nor the federal government hires teachers. School boards hire superintendents. In larger districts, superintendents hire human resource directors and principals, and they hire the teachers. After a person has met all the qualifications for a teaching position, one of these people in authority still needs to decide whether the individual is the right person for the job before he or she can gain a signed contract and step in front of a classroom. Even when there is a teacher shortage, as there often is in certain fields such as mathematics, the sciences, or special education, or in "hard-to-staff " districts (which usually means districts serving poor students in urban or in rural areas), you must connect with the right person in authority to get a teaching job.

CONNECTIONS ➔←

Chapter 13 offers more detail about getting a state license and finding employment in a school district.

highly qualified teacher
As defined by No Child Left Behind standards, a highly qualified teacher is one who holds a bachelor's degree, full state certification or licensure, and verifiable knowledge of the subject taught.

Licensure Whereas hiring decisions are local, holding a license to teach—the formal certification that one is qualified to enter a classroom—is a state decision. It used to be fairly easy for a person to become a teacher, but the requirements have risen steadily. Today, no state grants a teaching license to a person who does not hold a college degree and who has not completed some sort of program in education—usually a college or university-based undergraduate or graduate program that includes education courses and student teaching, or an "alternative route" offered by a school district or an organization such as Teach for America. Until quite recently, many districts could arrange waivers so that they could hire teachers, especially in high-needs shortage areas, who did not have the required state license. However, one requirement of NCLB is that every child be taught by a **highly qualified teacher**, which has generally come to mean a teacher who is fully licensed in the state in which he or she plans to teach.

How Do Teachers Make Political Decisions in the Classroom?

It is easy to think of politics as something distant and even sometimes unsavory, but all aspects of teaching, large and small, are political. Fifth-grade teacher Bob Peterson writes:

> All teaching is political whether we're conscious of it or not. We all make political decisions every day in the classroom. If we decide to put up a Halloween bulletin board instead of a bulletin board that indicts Christopher Columbus for being a war criminal, that's a political decision. If we decide to make Valentine's Day hearts with kids instead of celebrating Black History month, that's a political decision. And it's OK to do some of those things— I'm not against Halloween or hearts, although I oppose a holiday-driven curriculum—but we should do things self-consciously and recognize the political nature of our work.[18]

Valentine's Day hearts and Black History month may seem far removed from federal legislation and school board elections. And you might think of Halloween as "unpolitical" while an indictment of Columbus would certainly involve taking a "political" stance. Every decision a teacher makes about raising or not raising an issue or taking or not taking a stand is also a political decision.

Pedro Noguera describes a situation in his book *City Schools and the American Dream: Reclaiming the Promise of Public Education.* The last chapter of that book, "What It Will Take to Improve American's Urban Public Schools," reminds us that as important as state and federal policy is, there are also what Noguera calls "limit situations" in which, within certain limits, a teacher can make a very big difference. Limit situations can be important political opportunities for teachers to assert their limited but still very real power. In one example, Noguera describes a situation in which a committed math teacher, Paul Kurose, prodded his student Jamila about her unfinished work, rather than let it slide. After he had asked Jamila about her homework on several occasions, the frustrated student responded, "Do you think that you would be able to do your work if every night your mother was bringing a different man into your house to have sex and smoke crack?" Kurose suddenly realized the depth of what Jamila was facing at home and decided to not only give her extra time to do homework in his classroom after school, but also to help her get into an achievement program that would help her to gain college admissions. In deciding to intervene, Kurose made a political decision. There were, of course, risks involved. Jamila's mother might have objected or others might have thought he was exceeding his role. Another

teacher would have responded to Jamila's situation by reporting the family to child protection authorities. Kurose might have pursued any of these options. The one he did pursue involved political calculations—what was required by law, his own conscience, the limits of his position, and his time and energy. Clearly, Kurose's use of his power made an important difference.[19]

Another example of working within perhaps even more limited situations is offered by teacher and author Gregory Michie. In "Resisting the Pull of School-as-Usual," he writes, "It may be that you have to start with something small and seemingly insignificant—like bulletin boards." Michie says that though people rarely notice bulletin boards in schools, they can provide an opportunity, "the most visible one of all in many schools—to make a statement, to pose questions, to speak out on an issue, to bring kids' lives into classrooms or hallways." Michie describes seeing a bulletin board that said "They Were Here First," featuring American Indian tribes, another with information on the AIDS epidemic's impact in Africa, and another that invited students to share quotes they found challenging and inspiring. Of these very small-scale "limit situations," Michie writes:

> Those may not sound like such radical acts when placed alongside the more elaborate proposals of education's critical theorists. But once you're in a classroom of your own, you begin to realize that it's in the details, as much as in the big-picture theorizing, that critical conceptions of teaching find life. Kids can learn about equity and justice from the way community is formed in a classroom, how decisions are made, who is represented on the walls and bookshelves, and what sorts of interactions are encouraged and discouraged, whose thoughts and ideas are valued, and, yes, even what's on the bulletin boards.[20]

As students learn from all these observations, they—and their teachers—are entering into a political process that is a key element in American public education.

Education in the United States is highly political—from decisions made by the U.S. Supreme Court, Congress, or the president; to local school boards and superintendents and their human resource and budget offices; to teachers who help a student in trouble or who change a bulletin board; to taxpayer and legislative decisions on adequate school funding. The teacher who recognizes the political nature of education will have the best chance not only to survive what can at times be a difficult political minefield but also to make a positive *political* contribution toward improving education and the lives of children.

CHAPTER REVIEW

- What are the current debates about the Common Core State Standards and why are they so intense?

The Common Core State Standards are but the latest of a long line of efforts by state and federal officials to create something closer to a system of education in which students, no matter what district or state they are in, meet the same basic educational standards at about the same time, as other students in other places, even if they study different specific content in order to meet the standards. But many Americans—conservatives and liberals—object to what they see as unnecessary uniformity and centralized control in these standards. They especially object to the high level of testing that is required to ensure that students are, in fact, meeting the proposed standards. The debates over the Common Core, like the No Child Left Behind Act and the standards movement before it, are far from over.

- What is the role of federal officials in education?

For better or worse, politics at the federal, state, and local levels play a major role in education. At the federal level, the Supreme Court has handed down numerous rulings on issues that have affected how education is delivered and funded. Probably the most far-reaching court decisions have involved issues of race and racial segregation. The most notable of these cases, *Brown v. Board of Education of Topeka, Kansas*, legally ended segregation of the schools in 1954. Besides appointing Supreme Court justices, U.S. presidents, along with Congress, have had a significant impact on federal policies and funding for education; for example, the Elementary and Secondary Education Act of 1965 was passed during the Johnson administration. The ESEA became the No Child Left Behind Act of 2001 and is up for reauthorization today.

- What is the role of state and local governments in education?

Governors, state legislatures, and state departments of education play a significant role in deciding what is taught in a given state, how funds are used, and how teachers are licensed to work in their state. Local school boards select district superintendents, can govern local school districts that include anywhere from thousands of students to just a single school, and can have a tremendous impact on the education students receive, including hiring the classroom teachers.

- How do teachers make political decisions in the classroom?

Whether or not they are aware of it, teachers make political decisions every day in the classroom, including what messages are conveyed on bulletin boards, what topics they teach or ignore in class, what holidays they choose to recognize or celebrate, and how they respond to the needs and concerns of their students.

Readings

What Are the Current Debates About the Standards and Why Are They so Intense?

"RAGE AGAINST THE COMMON CORE"

AUTHOR: DAVID L. KIRP

> *In December 2014, David L. Kirp, who is a professor of public policy at the University of California, Berkeley, and the author of* Improbable Scholars: The Rebirth of a Great American School System and a Strategy for America's Schools *wrote the following piece for* The New York Times. *In it he looked at the strengths and weakness of the Common Core State Standards, but also at the issues of implementation that have created so much opposition. For someone who wants to understand the current politics of the Common Core, this short article is a good place to start.*

Starting in the mid-1990s, education advocates began making a simple argument: National education standards will level the playing field, assuring that all high school graduates are prepared for first-year college classes or rigorous career training.

While there are reasons to doubt that claim—it's hard to see how Utah, which spends less than one-third as much per student as New York, can offer a comparable education—the movement took off in 2008, when the nation's governors and education commissioners drove a huge effort to devise "world-class standards," now known as the Common Core.

Although the Obama administration didn't craft the standards, it weighed in heavily, using some of the $4.35 billion from the Race to the Top program to encourage states to adopt not only the Common Core (in itself, a good thing) but also frequent, high-stakes testing (which is deeply unpopular). The mishandled rollout turned a conversation about pedagogy into an ideological and partisan debate over high-stakes testing. The misconception that standards and testing are identical has become widespread.

At least four states that adopted the Common Core have opted out. Republican governors who initially backed the standards condemn them as "shameless government overreach."

Gov. Bobby Jindal of Louisiana, a Republican and a onetime supporter of the Common Core, sued his own state and the United States Department of Education to block the standards from taking effect. When Jeb Bush, the former Florida governor, recently announced his decision to "actively explore" a 2016 run for the White House, he ran into a buzz saw of opposition because of his embrace of the Common Core.

Rebellions have also sprouted in Democratic-leaning states. Last spring, between 55,000 and 65,000 New York State students opted out of taking tests linked to the Common Core. Criticizing these tests as "unproven," the Chicago schools chief, Barbara Byrd-Bennett, declared that she didn't want her students to take them.

In a Phi Delta Kappa/Gallup poll conducted last spring, 57 percent of public school parents opposed "having teachers in your community use the Common Core State Standards to guide what they teach," nearly double the proportion of those who supported the goals. With the standards, the sheer volume of high-stakes standardized testing has ballooned. "The numbers and consequences of these tests have driven public opinion over the edge," notes Robert A. Schaeffer of the National Center for Fair and Open Testing, known as Fair Test.

Students are terrified by these tests because the results can jeopardize their prospects for advancement and graduation. In New York, the number of students who scored "proficient" plummeted by about 30 percentage points in 2013, the first year of testing. Some 70 percent scored below the cutoff level in math and English; the 2014 results in math were modestly better, but the English language scores didn't budge.

Many teachers like the standards, because they invite creativity in the classroom—instead of memorization, the Common Core emphasizes critical thinking and problem-solving. But they complain that test prep and test-taking eat away weeks of class time that would be better focused on learning.

A Gallup poll found that while 76 percent of teachers favored nationwide academic standards for reading, writing and math, only 27 percent supported using tests to gauge students' performance, and 9 percent favored making test scores a basis for evaluating teachers. Such antagonism is well founded—researchers have shown that measurements of the "value" teachers add, as determined by comparing test scores at the beginning and end of the year, are unreliable and biased against those who teach both low- and high-achieving students.

The Obama administration has only itself to blame. Most Democrats expected that equity would be the top education priority, with more money going to the poorest states, better teacher recruitment, more useful training and closer attention to the needs of the surging population of immigrant kids. Instead, the administration has emphasized high-stakes "accountability" and market-driven reforms. The Education Department has invested more than $370 million to develop the new standards and exams in math, reading and writing.

Questioning those priorities can bring reprisals. During the search earlier this year for a New York City schools chancellor, Education Secretary Arne Duncan lobbied against Joshua P. Starr, the superintendent of schools in Montgomery County, Md., in part because he had proposed a three-year hiatus on high-stakes standardized testing.

Last year, Mr. Duncan said that opposition to the Common Core standards had come from "white suburban moms who realize—all of a sudden—their child isn't as brilliant as they thought they were, and their school isn't quite as good as they thought they were [sic]."

He has only recently changed his cavalier tune, acknowledging, "Too much testing can rob school buildings of joy and cause unnecessary stress."

It's no simple task to figure out what schools ought to teach and how best to teach it—how to link talented teachers with engaged students and a challenging curriculum. Turning around the great gray battleship of American public education is even harder. It requires creating new course materials, devising and field-testing new exams and, because these tests are designed to be taken online, closing the digital divide. It means retraining teachers, reorienting classrooms and explaining to anxious parents why these changes are worthwhile.

Had the public schools been given breathing room, with a moratorium on high-stakes testing that prominent educators urged, resistance to the Common Core would most likely have been less fierce. But in states where the opposition is passionate and powerful, it will take a herculean effort to get the standards back on track.

Questions

1. Given what you have read, do you believe that it is possible to separate the Common Core State Standards and the testing that has gone along with them? What would a test-free Common Core look like?
2. Given what Professor Kirp argues, how would you advise a state to implement, or not implement, the Common Core?

Source: David Kirp. "Rage Against the Common Core," Sunday Review, *New York Times*, December 27, 2014, http://www.nytimes.com/2014/12/28/opinion/sunday/rage-against-the-common-core.html.

A BACK-TO-SCHOOL CONVERSATION WITH TEACHERS AND SCHOOL LEADERS

AUTHOR: ARNE DUNCAN, U.S. SECRETARY OF EDUCATION

Well before David Kirp wrote the previous piece, opposition to the Common Core and related U.S. Department of Education policies was brewing. In his back-to-school message to teachers in the fall of 2014, U.S. Secretary of Education Arne Duncan tried to diffuse some of the criticism, voicing a new level of understanding and slowing the implementation of some of the more controversial policies. The politics of education are always a matter of give and take. In this speech, posted on his blog, Duncan showed he could give ground when he thought it necessary.

As teachers gear up for a new school year, I want to offer two thoughts. One is a message of celebration and thanks. The other is a response to a concern that has come up often in many conversations with teachers and families, and which deserves an answer.

First, the thanks. America's students have posted some unprecedented achievements in the last year—the highest high school graduation rate in the nation's history, and sharp cuts in dropout rates and increases in college enrollment, especially for groups that in the past have lagged significantly. For these achievements, we should celebrate America's teachers, principals, and students and their families. These achievements are also indications of deeper, more successful relationships with our students. All of us who've worked with young people know how much they yearn for adults to care about them and know them as individuals.

These achievements come at a time of nearly unprecedented change in American education—which entails enormously hard work by educators. Nearly every state has adopted new standards, new assessments, new approaches to incorporating data on student learning, and new efforts to support teachers.

This transition represents the biggest, fastest change in schools nationwide in our lifetime. And these efforts are essential to prepare kids to succeed in an age when the ability to think critically and creatively, communicate skillfully, and manipulate ideas fluently is vital. I have heard from many teachers that they have not received all the support they'd want during this transition. Yet America's teachers are making this change work—and I want to recognize and thank them for that and encourage their leadership in this time of change.

That's the easy part of this message. The harder part has to do with concerns that many teachers have brought to my door.

My team and I hold regular conversations with teachers, principals and other educators, often led by Teacher and Principal Ambassador Fellows, who take a year away from their schools to advise my agency. Increasingly, in those conversations, I hear concerns about standardized testing.

Assessment of student progress has a fundamental place in teaching and learning—few question that teachers, schools and parents need to know what progress students are making. And few question the particular importance of knowing how our most vulnerable students are progressing. Indeed, there's wide recognition that annual assessments—those required by federal law—have done much to shine a light on the places and groups of students most in need of help. Yet in too many places, it's clear that the yardstick has become the focus.

There are three main issues I've heard about repeatedly from educators:

1. It doesn't make sense to hold them accountable during this transition year for results on the new assessments—a test many of them have not seen before—and as many are coming up to speed with new standards.
2. The standardized tests they have today focus too much on basic skills, not enough on critical thinking and deeper learning.
3. Testing—and test preparation—takes up too much time.

I share these concerns. And I want our department to be part of the solution.

To those who are reading the last sentence with surprise, let me be clear: assessment is a vital part of teaching and learning, but it should be one part (and *only* one part) of how adults hold themselves responsible for students' progress. Schools, teachers and families need and deserve clear, useful information about how their students are progressing. As a parent of two children in public school, I know I want that. And in fact, most teachers and principals I talk with *want* to be held responsible for students' *progress*—through a sensible, smart combination of factors that reflect their work with students—not the level students came in at, or factors outside of their control.

But assessment needs to be done wisely. No school or teacher should look bad because they took on kids with greater challenges. Growth is what matters. No teacher or school should be judged on any one test, or tests alone—always on a mix of measures—which could range from classroom observations to family engagement indicators. In Nevada, educators include a teacher's contribution to the school community in their measures; in Hawaii, schools consider student feedback surveys and professional growth, such as leading workshops or taking university coursework. Educators in Delaware look at measures of planning and preparation such as lesson plans and descriptions of instructional strategies to be used for students with diverse needs. Federal policy rightly stays out of picking those individual measures, but ensures that in evaluating teachers, states and districts include student growth, and consider multiple measures.

But the larger issue is, testing should never be the main focus of our schools. Educators work all day to inspire, to intrigue, to know their students—not just in a few subjects, and not just in "academic" areas. There's a whole world of skills that tests can never touch that are vital to students' success. No test will ever measure what a student is, or can be. It's simply one measure of one kind of progress. Yet in too many places, testing itself has become a distraction from the work it is meant to support.

I believe testing issues today are sucking the oxygen out of the room in a lot of schools—oxygen that is needed for a healthy transition to higher standards, improved systems for data, better aligned assessments, teacher professional development, evaluation and support, and more. This is one of the biggest changes education in this country has ever seen, and teachers who've worked through it have told me it's allowed them to become the best teachers they've ever been. That change needs educators' full attention.

That's why—as I shared in a conversation with dozens of teachers at Jefferson Middle School in Washington, D.C., earlier today—we will be taking action in the coming weeks that give states more flexibility in key areas that teachers have said are causing worry.

States will have the opportunity to request a delay in when test results matter for teacher evaluation during this transition. As we always have, we'll work with them in a spirit of flexibility to develop a plan that works, but typically I'd expect this to mean that states that request this delay will push back by one year (to 2015–16) the time when student growth measures based on new state assessments become part of their evaluation systems—and we will work with states seeking other areas of flexibility as well. We want to make sure that they are still sharing growth data with their teachers, and still moving forward on the other critical pieces of evaluation systems that provide useful feedback to educators. We will be working in concert with other educators and leaders to get this right. These changes are incredibly important, and educators should not have to make them in an atmosphere of worry. Some states will choose to take advantage of that flexibility; others, especially those that are well along in this transition, will not need a delay. The bottom line is that educators deserve strong support as our schools make vital, and urgently needed, changes. As many educators have pointed out, getting this right rests also on high-quality assessments. Many educators, and parents, have made clear that they're supportive of assessment that measures what matters—but that a lot of tests today don't do that—they focus too much on basic skills rather than problem solving and critical thinking. That's why we've committed a third of a billion dollars to two consortia of states working to create new assessments that get beyond the bubble test, and do a better job of measuring critical thinking and writing.

I'm concerned, too, when I see places where adults are gaming tests, rather than using them to help students.

And we also need to recognize that in many places, the sheer quantity of testing—and test prep—has become an issue. In some schools and districts, over time tests have simply been layered on top of one another, without a clear sense of strategy or direction. Where tests are redundant, or not sufficiently helpful for instruction, they cost precious time that teachers and kids can't afford. Too much testing can rob school buildings of joy, and cause unnecessary stress. This issue is a priority for us, and we'll continue to work throughout the fall on efforts to cut back on over-testing.

There's plenty of responsibility to share on these challenges, and a fair chunk of that sits with me and my department. We encouraged states to move a whole lot of changes simultaneously, because of the enormous urgency to raise standards and improve systems of teacher support—not for another generation of students, but for today's students.

But in how this change happens, we need to listen carefully to the teachers, principals and other educators who are living it on a daily basis—and we need to be true to our promise to be tight on outcomes, but loose on how we get there.

From my first day on this job, the objective has been to work in a spirit of flexibility to help states and communities improve outcomes for kids. We need to make changes, but we are also making progress. I'm determined that, working in partnership, we'll continue to do both—be flexible and make progress for our kids.

Change is hard, and changes of significance rarely work exactly as planned. But in partnership, making course alterations as necessary, we will get there.

Questions

1. Do you think Secretary Duncan has answered the concerns of the critics described in the first Reading?
2. What else, if anything, should the Secretary do to improve support for his agenda?

Source: Arne Duncan is U.S. Secretary of Education. This post originally appeared on SmartBlog on Education, October 24, 2014.

What Is the Role of State and Local Governments in Education?

From "DEFENDING PUBLIC EDUCATION : AN INTERVIEW WITH KAREN LEWIS, PRESIDENT OF THE CHICAGO TEACHERS UNION"

AUTHOR: JOSH EIDELSON AND SARAH JAFFE FOR DISSENT *MAGAZINE*

In 2010, a slate led by Karen Lewis defeated the incumbent leadership of the Chicago Teachers Union (CTU). The new leaders promised deeper community engagement and a more aggressive defense of teachers and public education. They quickly developed a plan to oppose the projected closing of more than fifty Chicago schools. (The closing of ineffective schools had been part of the education plan of Arne Duncan when he was superintendent in Chicago prior to his elevation to U.S. Secretary of Education.) In 2012, with Lewis as president, the CTU mounted the city's first teachers' strike in a quarter-century, and the most dramatic recent challenge to the bipartisan education reform consensus. The two authors of this piece, representing the magazine Dissent, *met with Lewis to discuss teaching, school closings, gender discrimination, professionalism, union solidarity, and the union's long-standing support for the Democratic Party.*

Dissent: How does the current fight over school closures in Chicago fit into the larger aims of the union?

Karen Lewis: The school closures are one symptom of a really bad school policy that we as Chicagoans have been struggling with for over ten years. The leaders of No Child Left Behind came around and said, "Oh, if the school's bad, we're going to close it down because, you know, it's *bad*." As if the building makes something bad. And what's happened is, as schools close, they destabilize other schools that are close by. So there's this domino effect they never took into consideration.

   Children don't do better when schools close. They lose anywhere from three to six months on their learning or at least on their testing.

   I kept saying, "Why are they continuing to close schools, open up charter schools that don't do any better, and not even taking the kids that were in the schools that were closed?"

   But that was never good enough for the "reformers," so they started stepping it up. Instead of closing just one or two schools, they would close seven, eight, nine, ten. And they weren't keeping up with the children. So when schools would close, if kids didn't go to the school they were sent to, there was no way to find out where those kids went.

   Not all of them went to private school, not all of them went to charters, and not all of them left town. So where were these kids going?

   What inevitably happened was the increasing disruption of neighborhoods. Where I live, which is a kind of a gentrifying neighborhood, if I wanted to send my child to a traditional K–8 school, there would be none for my child to go to. And there didn't seem to be a "master plan" about why they were closing these schools. It wasn't like these were the worst performing schools. So it just seemed arbitrary and capricious.

D: How is the problem of violent crime in Chicago connected to problems with the schools?

KL: Chicago has a very different gang structure than most other cities. We've got a lot of Capulets and Montagues. There's no hierarchy. In Chicago, this block may be fighting against the next block. And they're not just defending drug territory. They're defending respect. Because our children have so little of it, if somebody disrespects them, it escalates outrageously.

Part of the problem is that we don't have counseling programs for children early enough. And we have almost gotten rid of play in preschool and kindergarten because we are so busy trying to get them to pass tests that we don't focus on the things that actually build their social and emotional learning along with their academics. Some of the conflict resolution that you should learn in play has disappeared.

In Chicago, we have issues of safety and a murder rate that is out of control. Think about Hadiya Pendleton, the young woman who was murdered after she'd performed at Obama's inauguration. She actually went to the school where I taught before I left the classroom, and I knew one of the kids that was involved in her killing. In Chicago, this stuff touches everybody.

When a school closes, our children have to walk from a neighborhood they know, where they know where the safe streets are, to one they don't know. It takes a while to do this process right. But the authorities want to rush it through, and this won't even save the money they claim it will.

D: I'm also interested in the role that gender plays in the fight over education. I know that Gloria Steinem wrote to you, saying that teacher-bashing was anti-feminist.

KL: Well, some 87 percent of K–12 teachers are women. There was a time when teachers were revered in the community, and now they're often demonized. Teachers have been an easy target, primarily because we're not used to fighting. We're not used to a lot of confrontation. We're used to saying, "Whatever you want me to do I'll do it because we all care about what's best for kids."

So, when people told us, "Go get masters degrees, because that will make you better," teachers rushed out and got masters degrees. Then it was: "Get endorsements in ESL [English as a second language], or special ed, or whatever," and we rushed out and did that. Then it was, "Become National Board–certified."

But it is never enough when the goal is really to destroy public education. That narrative that "teachers don't care about children" makes no sense. So I get up every morning to deal with children I don't like or I don't care about? It's just not the kind of thing you do.

We have to turn this discussion around and make sure people understand that we are now living in bizarro-world. We're supposed to think that the elite, who are very wealthy and very well educated and don't send their children to public schools, care more about black and brown children they don't know?

Part of the issue about gender is something that we don't ever bring up because it makes people very uncomfortable. There's still this paternalistic attitude of, "I'd like to protect women" combined with, on the other hand, "Let's cut them off at the knees. Let's put women out of work"—women who may be caring for their own children and families.

And it's also a kind of mythical thinking, as if children don't have their own parents who love them, that they don't live in communities with few appropriate places for the parents to work. So my question has always been, "If you love black and brown children so much, why do you hate their parents?"

D: I want to ask you about teachers and professionalism. To counter the attacks on teachers' benefits and bargaining rights, we hear some union leaders emphasizing the training that goes into being a teacher and the idea that they belong to unions of professional workers.

At the same time, you have some teacher unionists who specifically reject professionalism as an organizing principle and call themselves education workers. They argue that talking about professionalism obscures class dynamics and divides teachers from the person who watches the kids during lunch and the person who cooks the kids' food. What do you make of that?

KL: I think people need to find where they feel most comfortable. It's not an either/or.

My experience has been that the people who serve the food, the people who work as paraprofessionals, those are the people who actually have experience with children in those neighborhoods, because most work in the neighborhoods in which they live. And they are also the ones who can tell you exactly what's going on in a building. If you want to know something about a child, well, ask one of the lunchroom workers. They will tell you exactly what's going on in that child's family.

Still, professionalism is important on one level because the billionaires boys' club is saying, "We don't need professionals. We could just train somebody for five weeks and throw them in there and let them do it," like in the army.

But, in Chicago, there is a coming-together of the different unions. We're working right now with other unions that represent the janitors, the security workers, and the lunchroom workers, because school closings affect all of us. We have to defend professionalism, but we can't defend it as the only thing we're doing.

D: I wanted to ask you about the transformation that took place within the Chicago Teachers Union, with the CORE [Caucus of Rank and File Educators] caucus sweeping out the folks who had been running the union. I think observers on all sides recognize that your strike would have been hard to imagine before the transformation that took place within the union. Should locals in other cities follow your lead?

KL: I think every local has to decide what works for them. If you're teaching, you know that every kid isn't at the same place, so you have to vary how you teach them. Some people are ready to accept a different way of looking at a union. But other people don't agree with us and say, "I just want you to enforce a contract. I don't want to do this other stuff. I don't want to march. I just want to go in my room and teach."

The only problem is, you cannot wake up tomorrow and be in yesterday. So part of the issue is that what we wanted [when we challenged the union leadership] and what happened were two different things. We did not have an electoral strategy. We came together as a group of people that wanted to study the issue and wanted to move our union in a different direction.

When we ran, there were five caucuses running at the same time. Changing culture is absolutely the hardest thing you can ever do. To shift unions from the service model to an organizing model takes not just a few people that want to do it; it takes the will of rank-and-file members to become empowered in their schools and in their union.

I would think that any union wants its members to be more involved and to have fresh ideas. But right now we're in a resistance mode. It's funny how the opposition describes the unions as being very powerful, because we don't feel that way. If we're going to exert some power, we have to make that true.

D: You've talked and written about recognizing who your enemies are. Just because people are Democrats does not mean that they are not enemies. Does there need to be a break in the relationship between the teachers unions and Democrats?

KL: You know, this is the part that's the most difficult for me, because I hate politics, actually. For a long time I've felt we live in a one-party system. We just have two branches of it.

The key is to use the political system to hold our elected officials accountable through mass movements. I would like to see a whole new party that speaks for working people. But the way our system is set up, it's very difficult to have good conversations about third parties.

Let me give you an example of why that doesn't work well. In Illinois, in 2010, before we got elected, the teachers unions in Illinois decided *not* to give to the Democratic Party. So that's how we ended up with Senate Bill 7 [which includes restrictions on teachers' right to strike and revisions of tenure procedures]. We got punished for not giving them money. The reason we hadn't given them money was because the year before they came up with a really horrible pension bill.

In 2012, we had that same conversation. A lot of members asked, "Why are we giving the Democrats money?" Because when we didn't, we got smooshed. You cannot put all your eggs in a legislative basket. The problem with business unionists is that they rely on having good relationships with legislators. But if you don't have a mass movement behind you to move legislators, they don't take you seriously.

Then our members say, "Well, why aren't we suing [the Board of Education]?" OK, we have sued. But people watch too much TV. They don't understand that lawsuits aren't over in an hour or at the end of the show, when everybody walks away because they've been vindicated. Because the other side will keep fighting you.

So we started a case in 2010 after the school board illegally laid off our members, and we're still fighting that case! It's still in federal court three years later!

If you only go the legislative route and the legal route, you're playing by somebody else's rules. As [civil rights lawyer and Harvard law professor] Lani Guinier says, whoever makes the rules has an advantage. The legislative piece and the legal piece are out of our hands. But what we can control is our membership and having them active, having them involved, and having them push their legislators—but also having them take to the streets. And having the authorities understand that we will shut down your city. You will not be able to function without dealing with us fairly.

That's the way it is right now in Chicago. In the past, when school-closing hearings would happen, ten or twelve people would show up. We're now getting thousands of people to come to those hearings. And what they are saying with one voice is, "Keep your hands off my school."

Another question Lani Guinier asks is, "What are the stories the winners tell the losers to keep them playing the game?" A lot of people don't think about that. When you're playing on somebody else's turf, you don't have control. So the key is to change the rules of the game.

Questions

1. How do you think Karen Lewis would respond to the Common Core State Standards?
2. What does it mean for a union to challenge local or national education policies? Who should make the final decisions—the school board, the federal government, the teachers, or some other combination of representatives of these groups?

Source: The complete interview from which this edited excerpt is taken aired on April 22, 2013 on Dissent's Belabored podcast, featuring hosts Josh Eidelson and Sarah Jaffe. Belabored is available both on iTunes and dissentmagazine.org.

12 Public Education
What Is Its Purpose in a Democratic Society?

QUESTIONS TO COME

> We argue that schools are, and ought to be, political sites . . . . We are being political when we are democratically making decisions about questions that ask, "How should we live together?"

DIANA HESS AND PAULA MCAVOY

LIBERTY!
FREEDOM!
DEMOCRACY!
True anyhow no matter how many Liars use those words.
—Langston Hughes[1]

More than 50 years ago, poet Langston Hughes spoke to a worldwide movement of people he called "the folks with no titles in front of their names" who were rising up for rights in the United States and in Asia, Africa, and South America. His words also could have been applied to two centuries of debates about the purposes of public schooling in the United States.

Helping young people become active and engaged citizens, and giving them the tools needed to participate actively in democratic institutions—from voting to speaking and acting on what they believe to be right—is a core purpose of schooling if democratic institutions are to survive and thrive in future generations. More than preparing students for jobs or teaching basic skills, fostering democracy has been at the heart of public education in the United States for as long as Americans have cared about their school systems. However, in many ways this nation is deeply undemocratic, and schools have often been structured to perpetuate inequity and undemocratic social arrangements. Great strides have been made to make schools more inclusive, but many observers

marginalization
To demote populations of people based on economic or racial differences and push them to the lower edges of society or the sidelines in a policy debate.

democracy
Political system in which decisions and laws are put into place by the vote of the whole community and in which everyone's voice matters.

would say that our schools are organized to perpetuate the advantage of the few and the **marginalization** of too many young people.

In this chapter, we look at both the historic role that schools have been assigned in fostering a more democratic society and the ways that schooling, as an institution, has failed to live up to that assignment. In the midst of this discussion, we keep asking, "What is a teacher's role in making schools and the larger society more democratic?"

Three **Readings** look at what schools ought to do in a democratic society. Over a century ago, the philosopher John Dewey wrote *The School and Society*, a book in which he outlined some of his basic beliefs about the importance of schools to a **democracy** and arguing that a truly democratic classroom was the best guarantee of a larger society that was "which is worthy, lovely, and harmonious." Following that piece there is a short **Reading** written by the civil rights leader W.E.B. Du Bois entitled, "On Education," in which Du Bois calls on educators to move beyond technical issues to include moral character and the ability to envision and create a more just world in the goals of schooling. The final **Reading** is a chapter from David T. Hansen's book *Exploring the Moral Heart of Teaching* in which he explores the conception of teaching, and education, as a moral enterprise.

What Does a Democratic Society Expect of Its Schools?

Defining Democracy

At one level, *democracy* refers to a system of government "of the people, for the people, and by the people," as Abraham Lincoln said. Defined that way, democracy seems to mean, at minimum, a government based on the consent of the governed, as opposed to a **dictatorship** or an **oligarchy** based on birth, wealth, or power. Throughout the history of the United States, many observers have argued that to give (or withhold) informed consent, all citizens need a basic education that will enable them to be familiar with the issues and debates of the day.

dictatorship
Government rule by an individual who holds absolute power without hereditary lineage.

oligarchy
Political system in which power rests with a small group of elite, often wealthy, individuals.

However, to many others, democracy means much more than merely giving informed consent. It means the active involvement of all citizens in constantly re-creating the meaning of a good society for all—government *of* and *by* the people as well as *for* the people. Such an expanded definition of democracy goes far beyond voting, important as that is, and involves active engagement in our communities. It involves a certain way of living in the world, insisting on equality for ourselves and for all other citizens.[2]

The School's Role in a Democratic Society

Maintaining and expanding the notion of democracy is one of the oldest and most important roles that society has assigned to its schools throughout the more-than-200-year history of the United States. From the time the political leaders of the 13 British colonies on the mainland of North America declared their independence from King George, the language of democracy has been essential in shaping the nation's public schools. A democratic society needs to renew democracy continually through the education of its next generation of citizens. Since the time of the American Revolution, many of the nation's leaders have recognized that making democracy a reality requires educated citizens and voters, not only at election time but also in the daily lives of the people.

In our own time, when noted education professors James A. Beane and Michael W. Apple make the case for democratic schools, they naturally include issues like the democratic structure of social institutions, the open flow of ideas "regardless of their popularity," and concern for the welfare of others. They also argue that democratic schools should foster "faith in the individual and collective capacity of people to create possibilities for resolving problems." This is a much larger understanding

of the meaning of democracy and of the relationship between democracy and education. It is not sufficient to provide freedom to individuals and services to all, important as these are. A real democracy is more than this. A truly democratic society is structured around the beliefs that the solutions to contemporary social concerns reside with the people and that all of the people, if fully empowered—and well educated—will be wiser than any small minority or vanguard. Such a democracy cannot be taught through lectures and textbooks. Schools must create classrooms where the young will experience such a democracy, if they are to grow into adult citizens who can also practice it.[3] Thus, teachers have a key role in building democracy, but only if they are informed, reflective, thoughtful, and ultimately engaged themselves.

It is ironic that the question of what most Americans expect their schools to accomplish in terms of fostering a larger democracy is seldom at the center of public debates about 21st century education. Everyone seems to assume that the answer to that question is obvious and then they move on to other questions, such as how to raise standards and test scores, improve teacher preparation, and reduce drop-out rates. Or they ask the schools to address myriad other social problems—for example, by offering sex education and drivers' education, by tackling the current epidemic of obesity through the regulation of what food is available at schools and through education about good nutrition, or more generally by discouraging a range of adolescent behaviors that trouble adults. Schools appropriately have many roles, including ensuring basic literacy, developing students' higher-order knowledge and thinking skills, helping young people lead safe and productive lives, *and* inducting young people into full democratic citizenship. Nevertheless, the purpose of schooling in a democratic society needs to be central in our discussion of schooling and teaching.

Teaching Democracy

University of Wisconsin professor and Spencer Foundation executive Diana Hess has been at the forefront of those who argue that schools should teach democracy and, indeed, that such teaching always makes schools political places. In a 2015 book, written with Paula McAvoy, *The Political Classroom: Evidence and Ethics in Democratic Education*, Hess and McAvoy say:

> We argue that schools are, and ought to be, political sites. In this context, we use the term "political" as it applies to the role of citizens within a democracy: We are being political when we are democratically making decisions about questions that ask, "How should we live together?" By extension, the political classroom is one that helps students develop their ability to deliberate political questions. When teachers engage students in discussions about what rules ought to be adopted by a class, they are teaching them to think politically. Similarly, when teachers ask students to research and discuss a current public controversy, such as, "Should same-sex marriage be legally recognized?" they are engaging in politics.

Nothing less than this, Hess and McAvoy believe, will prepare students for democratic life or, as Hess wrote in 2009, the political discussions that are an essential part of learning to live in a democracy.

On one hand, Hess and McAvoy want to be clear that schools should not be "partisan institutions" or indoctrinate students in a particular political point of view—beyond a commitment to democratic dialogue. On the other, "Mastering their ability to talk across political and ideological differences helps create an informed citizenry—an essential component of a democratic society—by teaching students to weigh evidence, consider competing views, form an opinion, articulate that opinion, and respond to those who disagree." Offering anything less in the nation's public schools is a retreat from the kind of education that a democratic society needs.[4]

Others share Hess and McAvoy's concerns. According to the 2003 report *The Civic Mission of Schools*, sponsored by the Carnegie Corporation of New York, schools should continue to be the primary vehicle for encouraging civic duties because schools have the capacity to reach almost every young person in the country and because the country needs citizens who understand their civic responsibilities. Through class discussions and critical thinking exercises, teachers have the opportunity to lay the groundwork for future informed debate about key civic issues, one of the hallmarks of a democracy.

All teachers—not only social studies teachers—the report said, have a responsibility for providing their students with civic knowledge. *The Civic Mission of Schools* study suggests the following techniques and lessons to incorporate a civic mission—and education in democracy—in today's classrooms:

- Incorporate current news events and issues into everyday discussion.
- Implement mock trials and debates in the classroom.
- Design a service-learning program and encourage meaningful work.
- Offer extracurricular activities that take lessons beyond the classroom walls.
- Encourage participation in school government.

All of these ideas are ways to begin to fulfill the school's mission to teach democracy—and every teacher can build on them and propose yet more innovations.[5]

In a 2003 article, "Reconnecting Education to Democracy," Joel Westheimer of the University of Ottawa in Canada and Joseph Kahne of Mills College in Oakland, California, wrote, "For more than two centuries, democracy in the United States has been predicated on citizens' informed engagement in civic and political life. For much of that time, public schools have been seen as essential to support the development of such citizens."

But Westheimer and Kahne note that students—and their parents—are deeply divided on just what citizenship means. They asked different student focus groups in California to define what it means to be a good citizen. One answer they got was, "Someone who's active and stands up for what they believe in." But in another group they heard that in order to be a good citizen you need to "follow the rules, I guess, as hard as you can, even though you want to break them sometimes. Like cattle." Teaching citizenship, like teaching democratic debate, is difficult given this lack of consensus.

Nevertheless, Westheimer and Kahne propose some basic ground rules for teaching democracy in schools. While they value service learning programs as an opportunity for democratic engagement, they also note that, "Patriots in a democracy, for example, should be encouraged to challenge as well as support the government. Democracy requires more than community service; it requires citizen participation in the affairs of state." And finally they expand the lesson from their focus groups saying, "it is the basic conflicts of values in society that make democracy essential, and it is the ability to discuss these differences in an informed and productive manner that must be a priority for civic educators. Therefore, forms of patriotism that squelch debate and 'patriotic' curricula that obscure the need for debate are, in important ways, antidemocratic."[6]

The ideal of teaching democracy is on many minds in the 21st century. While Hess, McAvoy, the authors of *The Civic Mission of Schools* report, and Westheimer and Kahne may have their differences—and they do—they all agree that a democratic society cannot survive unless the next generation is taught to *value* and *practice* democracy, and school is the essential place to accomplish this goal.

Historically Speaking: What Is the Relationship Between a Universal Education and Democratic Citizenship?

The Educational Philosophy of Thomas Jefferson

Whereas it appeareth that however certain forms of government are better calculated than others to protect individuals in the free exercise of their natural rights, and are at the same time themselves better guarded against degeneracy, yet experience hath shewn, that even under the best forms, those entrusted with power have, in time, and by slow operations, perverted it into tyranny; and it is believed that the most effectual means of preventing this would be, to illuminate, as far as practicable, the minds of the people at large, and more especially to give them knowledge of those facts, which history exhibiteth, that, possessed thereby of the experience of other ages and countries, they may be enabled to know ambition under all its shapes, and prompt to exert their natural powers to defeat its purposes.

—*Thomas Jefferson*

At the time of the American Revolution, Thomas Jefferson proposed a new system of education for his home state of Virginia. He reminded his fellow legislators that even the best governments (including the new one they were in the middle of creating through their revolution) had a dangerous tendency to be "perverted into tyranny." The best protection against such a development would be "to illuminate, as far as practicable, the minds of the people at large." In addition, Jefferson proposed an educational system that he believed would promote public happiness by ensuring that "those persons, whom nature hath endowed with genius and virtue, should be rendered by liberal education worthy to receive, and able to guard the sacred deposit of the rights and liberties of their fellow citizens, and that they should be called to that charge without regard to wealth, birth or other accidental condition or circumstance."[7] The bill did not become law, but Jefferson's words nevertheless became famous as a call to his fellow American rebels about the importance of education for the kind of democracy they were attempting to create.

Jefferson believed education and democracy were inextricably linked. Unless all the people had a basic education so that they could participate in the democratic process and would know and recognize tyranny when it appeared, and unless leaders were developed from among all the people, not just those who could afford to pay for a college education, the experiment in democracy launched by the American Revolution would surely fail, Jefferson insisted. He never wavered in his belief that education was the key to preserving democracy. Over 40 years later, long after he had retired from his two terms as the nation's third president, Jefferson wrote, "I know no safe depository of the ultimate powers of the society but the people themselves; and if we think them not enlightened enough to exercise their control with a wholesome discretion, the remedy is not to take it from them, but to inform their discretion by education." Thus, from the beginning of the United States, education was given a central role in expanding and preserving the nation in the words if not in the actions of the founders.

In spite of Jefferson's noble words, the Constitution of the United States does not guarantee education for all, as the Supreme Court reminded the nation in 1973 in the *Rodriguez* decision. In fact, the words *education* and *school* do not appear anywhere in the nation's founding documents. Jefferson himself had a very narrow definition of "the people" who were supposed to benefit from the kind of education he proposed. He really meant free White males. Women were not included in the educational system that Jefferson proposed. Slaves, of whom Jefferson himself had many, the few African Americans who were free, and American Indians had no meaningful role in the society that Jefferson envisioned. In addition, neither Jefferson nor any of the founding fathers were successful in establishing schools that would deliver on their goals. Jefferson established the University of Virginia, but the lower-level schools he wanted did not materialize in his lifetime. For the most part, neither Jefferson nor the other founders expanded their vision of whom the schools should serve. Nevertheless, the generation that founded the United States as a nation described a vision of the role of education in a democratic society that would, in future hands, be expanded far beyond their wildest dreams.

Structuring a Democratic School System

The successive generations of men, taken collectively, constitute one great Commonwealth. . . . [E]mbezzlement and pillage from children and descendants are as criminal as the same offences when perpetrated against contemporaries.

Without undervaluing any other human agency, it may be safely affirmed that the Common School, improved and energized as it can easily be, may become the most effective and benignant of all the forces of civilization.

—*Horace Mann*

In the early 1800s, there were quite a few schools in many parts of the country, but they were often private and limited either to those who could pay or, in some instances, to the White male citizens of towns that taxed themselves for their support. A few cities also had charity schools to provide a limited education to the children of the poor. Almost from the nation's beginning, however, others argued for a wider definition of "schooling for all" and for the inclusion of women,

African Americans, American Indians, more recent immigrants, poor children, children living in isolated rural communities, and the like. Throughout the 19th century, women fought long and difficult battles for inclusion in schools as students and then as teachers. At the end of the Civil War, recently freed African Americans began a major drive to expand the educational opportunities available to them.

When Horace Mann became the first secretary to the newly created Massachusetts State Board of Education in 1837, he began almost immediately to institutionalize the Jeffersonian vision, while also expanding it. Mann consciously echoed Jefferson, writing in one of his annual reports that "the necessity of general intelligence, under a republican form of government, like most other very important truths, has become a very trite one." Yet trite or not, Mann believed that it was essential, indeed "that a republican form of government, without intelligence in the people, must be on a vast scale, what a madhouse, without superintendent or keepers, would be on a small one."

Mann also expanded the Jeffersonian argument about the link of schooling and democracy in two important ways. First, whereas Jefferson unsuccessfully called on his state legislature in Virginia to support schools, Mann argued with much greater success for public funding of education. He did not mince words. If the schools were essential to the future of the republic, and if every child had a right to an education (Mann included girls as well as boys, though he did not include the African American or American Indian residents of Massachusetts), then failure to adequately support the schools was a crime. Paying taxes for the schools was a fundamental part of citizenship, and failure to do so was theft from the next generation. More than 150 years later, school funding remains an issue, though few today are willing to call insufficient funding "embezzlement from children" as boldly as Mann did.

Mann also rejected the Jeffersonian plan for a modest basic education for all followed by an elite education for the future leaders. "The very terms, *Public School*, and *Common School*, bear upon their face, that they are schools which the children of the entire community may attend," he argued. The only way to make a democracy function, Mann believed, was for citizens to know each other, to mix with each other, and to be educated in common. Mann, a middle-class Whig politician and abolitionist, disliked **elitism** in any form. He was convinced that, in a democratic nation, leaders could not rise above the electorate. "By a natural law, like that which regulates the equilibrium of fluids, elector and elected, appointer and appointee, tend to the same level," he said. If that is true, he believed, then leaders and followers, legislators and voters needed the same education in the same institutions so that they could together create a unified democratic society.

> **elitism**
> Attitude that people of a higher intellect or ability are considered more worthy than others or should be given power and responsibility.

Mann has come to be known as the father of public education in the United States. That is certainly an overstatement, for schools existed long before his term of office in Massachusetts. He was, however, a powerful advocate for a state-supported system of common schools, available to all citizens, that was far broader than that advocated by any of his predecessors.[8]

Education, Slavery, and Freedom

Few people who were not right in the midst of the scenes can form any exact idea of the intense desire which the people of my race showed for education. It was a whole race trying to go to school. Few were too young, and none too old, to make the attempt to learn.

—*Booker T. Washington*

One reads in vain the words of Jefferson or Mann, or many of their contemporary education reformers, for any meaningful discussion of the education of African Americans. Although they and so many other Americans of their generation were deeply committed to expanding educational opportunity and to ensuring that the American democracy was founded on a literate and well-read **electorate**, and while Mann was also deeply committed to the abolition of slavery, both he and Jefferson and nearly all of their contemporaries were amazingly silent on the education of the 10%–20% of the nation's people who were not free. This is true despite the fact that both wrote a great deal about African Americans in other contexts: Jefferson, as the sometimes-ambivalent slaveholder, and Mann,

> **electorate**
> Population of voters in a country or geographic region.

as the courageous advocate for the abolition of slavery. It was as if to them, and the vast majority of their fellow European American citizens, African Americans existed in a completely different universe.[9]

However, the African American population did not passively accept the dominant culture's lack of interest in their education. Two decades before slavery ended in the United States, a group of free Blacks in Boston, Massachusetts, petitioned for an end to racially segregated schools in their city. The petitioners wrote "that the establishment of exclusive schools for our children is a great injury to us, and deprives us of those equal privileges and advantages in the public school to which we are entitled as citizens." In 1846, these African American citizens understood that

since all experience teaches that where a small and despised class are shut out from the common benefit of any public institution of learning and confined to separate schools . . . the teachers and the scholars are soon considered, and of course, become, an inferior class.[10]

It took another decade, but in 1855, the public schools of Boston were desegregated by state law, though the city would spend the next 150 years dealing with less formal but very real forms of school segregation.

During and after the Civil War, northern Whites in the union army and agents of the federal government's Freedmen's Bureau, created to respond to the needs of newly freed slaves, were continually amazed by newly freed Blacks' passion for education.[11] One northern teacher, who had gone to Florida to teach, told of a 60-year-old woman who, "just beginning to spell, seems as if she could not think of any thing but her books, says she spells her lesson all the evening, then she dreams about it, and wakes up thinking about it." A teacher in North Carolina said of a student, "[H]e thought a schoolhouse would be the first proof of their *independence*."[12]

That so many recently freed slaves saw the schoolhouse as "proof of their *independence*" surprised many White observers. However, this isn't surprising considering the nature of southern slavery during the previous half-century. According to James Anderson, the foremost historian of 19th-century African American education,

During the three decades before the Civil War slaves lived in a society in which for them literacy was forbidden by law and symbolized as a skill that contradicted the status of slaves. As former slave William Henry Heard recalled: "We did not learn to read nor write, as it was against the law for any person to teach any slave to read; and any slave caught writing suffered the penalty of having his forefinger cut from his right hand; yet there were some who could read and write."[13]

Even before the end of the Civil War, and with it the end of slavery, one of the most famous runaway slaves had explained the lessons he had learned early in life about the power of literacy. As he later told the story, a kindly woman had begun to teach the young Frederick Douglass how to read, but his White master quickly stopped the lessons. Douglass overheard him telling her that such lessons "would forever unfit him to be a slave."[14] Douglass remembered that "the argument which he so warmly urged, against my learning to read, only served to inspire me with a desire and determination to learn."[15] Douglass could not imagine anything better than being unfit to be a slave. Learn he did, so that in the years after he escaped from slavery, Douglass became one of the great writers and orators of his time.

John W. Alvord, the federal government's chief administrator for setting up schools for the formerly enslaved people during and after the Civil War, arrived in the South thinking he would have to start the very first schools. He found, however, that "throughout the entire South, an effort is being made by the colored people to educate themselves."[16] Soon the work of these schools was supplemented by the northern teachers like Charlotte Forten Grimké and so many others who were part of a vast crusade in the 1860s and 1870s to bring literacy to the newly freed slaves and to institutionalize a system of schools for them.[17] Sent by churches and the government, the best of these teachers became allies of the teachers who were already in the field.

Sometimes there were tensions between the White northern educators and their southern Black counterparts. One White teacher, William Channing Gannett, reported, "There is jealousy of the superintendence of the white man in this matter. What they desire is assistance without control."[18]

> **CONNECTIONS →←**
>
> Recall Charlotte Forten Grimké's teaching experiences during the Civil War as discussed in Chapter 1.

People who had recently been enslaved were not about to cede to anyone control over something as important as their education.

In time, the initial informal efforts were transformed into schools, school districts, and the development of teacher preparation colleges. After the Civil War, every southern state added to its constitution a provision for free public education. However, the creative energy of the first years did not last. Beginning not long after the end of the Civil War, there was an assault on the fundamental meaning of democracy as state after state effectively took away African American citizens' rights to vote, to participate in the larger society, or to receive a quality education. It is impossible to overstate the difficulties African American educators experienced in the years between the 1870s and the 1960s. As W.E.B. Du Bois wrote in 1934, "Public education for all at public expense was, in the South, a Negro idea."[19] It was not surprising that the civil rights movement of the 20th century would embrace equal educational opportunity with such commitment. For people who had known the absence of both schools and democracy, the link was indeed essential.[20]

Making Democracy "Come Alive" in School

We are apt to look at the school from an individualistic standpoint, as something between teacher and pupil, or between teacher and parent. . . . Yet the range of the outlook needs to be enlarged. What the best and wisest parent wants for his own child, that must the community want for all its children. Any other ideal for our schools is narrow and unlovely; acted upon, it destroys our democracy. . . . When the school introduces and trains each child of society into membership within such a little community, saturating him with the spirit of service, and providing him with the instruments of effective self-direction, we shall have the deepest and best guaranty of a larger society which is worthy, lovely, and harmonious.

—*John Dewey*, The School and Society, *1899*[21]

At the beginning of the 20th century, some progressive educators, such as John Dewey, were arguing that the link between education and democracy was more sophisticated and more complicated than earlier writers had suggested. Schools needed to be the model of the inclusive and **egalitarian** society that they were supposed to teach students to honor. At the beginning of the new 20th century,

> **egalitarian**
> The belief that all people are equal and should have the same political, economic, social, and civil liberties.

Dewey noted that only about 5% of the population finished high school and the majority dropped out by the end of fifth grade. Universal schooling had a long way to go. Progressive education, in the hands of Dewey and others, was a means of engaging more students in their schooling so that they would stay and participate for a longer period of time. It was even more fundamentally a philosophy that demanded a complete rethinking of the purposes and goals of schooling in a democratic nation. Preparing informed citizens was important, Dewey and his allies argued, but the goal was preparing citizens who would continually remake society in ways that were more democratic for all citizens.

Dewey wrote in "My Pedagogic Creed" (see the Reading in Chapter 7) that "I believe that education, therefore, is a process of living and not a preparation for future living." Democratic citizenship began when the child entered school, not when he or she graduated. He also wrote, "I believe, finally, that the teacher is engaged, not simply in the training of individuals, but in the formation of the proper social life." The progressive education movement, as defined by Dewey, was a means of preparing self-confident, active citizens who were ready to engage in the continuing process of social evolution and community building. Progressive teachers who understood this were the key players.[22]

Active learning, self-directed study, and participation in school governance were not merely new and more effective means of instruction; they were ways of creating in the school the small-scale model of the larger democratic society—a society that is not only well governed but also "worthy, lovely, and harmonious." In a sense, Dewey was the first American philosopher of education to take seriously Alexis de Tocqueville's observation in his 1835 *Democracy in America* that the American democracy always threatened to degenerate into anarchic individualism unless the forces of community were as central to democracy as those of individual liberty.[23]

> ## CONNECTIONS →←
>
> Progressive education is discussed in a number of contexts throughout this book, including Chapter 1 (history of the teaching profession), Chapter 5 (John Dewey and the philosophy of progressive education), and Chapter 7 (motivation as a key factor to student success).

Education Is a Civil Right

Our goal is First-Class Citizenship, and we will settle for nothing less.

—Ruth Batson[24]

Ruth Batson was chair of the education committee of the Boston branch of the National Association for the Advancement of Colored People (NAACP) when she testified before the Boston School Committee in 1963. Her demand for full equality in the treatment of African American students in the Boston public schools is a reminder that the civil rights movement had an impact on schools in every part of the United States. We've discussed the Supreme Court's *Brown* decision that ended legalized racial segregation in U.S. schools in 1954 in Chapter 3. However, the battle for *Brown*—the decades of litigation that preceded it and the ensuing decades of efforts to implement it—was part of a much larger national civil rights movement that included a deep commitment to a more democratic system of education.

For many civil rights leaders, ending racial segregation in the schools was but a first step—whether it was the "separate but equal" segregation of African Americans in the South, the effective segregation of Latino students (especially in the Southwest), the segregation of Asian students in California that lasted into the 1920s, or the informal racial segregation that was practiced in schools in every part of the United States. The larger goal was the creation of a society that allowed all its citizens full participation in democracy at all levels, in the "beloved community" as Martin Luther King, Jr., said. Education was considered the key to such participation. Whether it was the creation of Freedom Schools across the South, the quiet dignity with which young African Americans made *Brown* real by entering often hostile and dangerous White schools, or sometimes the creation of independent Black schools, civil rights organizers were also educational organizers.

Recent Visions of Democratic Schooling

The classroom, with all its limitations, remains a location of possibility. In that field of possibility we have the opportunity to labor for freedom, to demand of ourselves and our comrades an openness of mind and heart that allows us to face reality even as we collectively imagine ways to move beyond the boundaries, to transgress. This is education as the practice of freedom.

—bell hooks, Teaching to Transgress, *1994*[25]

bell hooks wrote those words more than 20 years ago. More recently, she has found herself often discouraged about the commitment to democracy that is found in American public schools and, more seriously to her, among American young people. Thus, in 2010 she wrote:

There is little public discourse among students today about the nature of democracy. Nowadays, most students simply assume that living in a democratic society is their birthright; they do not believe they must work to maintain democracy. They may not even associate democracy with the ideal of equality.

In the midst of such a serious situation, hooks's hope is that teachers will take on a stronger and clearer role as prophets of democracy. "The more I teach," she says, "the more I learn that teaching is a prophetic vocation. It demands of us allegiance to integrity of vision and belief in the face of those who would either seek to silence, censor, or discredit our words." Thus she calls on teachers to be agents of a new democracy, reminding their students of John Dewey's belief that "democracy has to be born anew in each generation, and education is its midwife."[26]

Over the last thirty years, others have also raised their own concerns about making schools more democratic institutions and more effective in the service of building a larger and more democratic society. Writing in response to the 1983 *A Nation at Risk* report that declared the nation to be at risk because of "a rising tide of mediocrity" in our schools, Ann Bastian and her colleagues challenged the assumptions behind the report as reinforcing "competitive structures of achievement modeled on and serving the economic marketplace." To these writers, such a focus "misconstrues the crisis in education." Bastian and her colleagues then named what they saw as the real crisis in education at the end of the 20th century:

There is a catastrophic failure to provide decent schools and adequate skills to low-income students; there is also a chronic failure to provide reasoning and citizenship skills among all students. . . . In establishing a framework for progressive alternatives, it is necessary to project a concept of education in which quality and equality are mutually inclusive standards.[27]

In their book, *Choosing Equality: The Case for Democratic Schools*, Bastian and her colleagues developed an argument that was grounded in the ideals of the civil rights movement and of Jefferson, Mann, Dewey, and many other philosophers of a democratic system of education. Like their predecessors, they demanded a system of education in which "quality and equality are mutually inclusive standards" because anything less was undemocratic and unfair. Anything less is also undemocratic because it fails to prepare citizens to take an active place in shaping the larger society into which they were moving.

Many educators have found ways to both embrace and expand the links between what happens in schools—or the potential for what could happen in schools—and the fostering of a larger democratic society. For example, Deborah Meier has worked tirelessly to create smaller schools that can be democratic learning communities within the large and bureaucratized school systems of New York City and Boston. For Meier, the key to building democracy is through face-to-face communities of students, parents, teachers, and others who can build trust among themselves, not just respond to outside pressures. Only in this way is it possible to build "a community-wide consensus about the essential purposes of schools and education—about what comes first." It is not important to do this just for purposes of governance, Meier insists, but because schools, which are supposed to teach democracy, can teach it effectively only if they model that same democracy. Thus,

> Schools need to be governed in ways that honor the same intellectual and social skills we expect our children to master and—ideally—in ways the young can see, hear, and respect. . . . Will it be neat and orderly? Probably not. But democracy is and ever was messy, problematic, and it is always a work in progress.

Meier would insist it is also the point of public education.[28]

Lisa Delpit created a significant controversy when in 1986 she asked,

> Why do the refrains of progressive educational movements seem lacking in the diverse harmonies, the variegated rhythms, and the shades of tone expected in a truly heterogeneous chorus? Why do we hear so little representation from the multicultural voices which comprise the present-day American educational scene?

Delpit was not turning her back on progressive pedagogy, although she certainly found some elements of that pedagogy highly questionable. However, in her continuing discussion of the education of *Other People's Children*, she insisted that a democratic education could not be governed by theories and research cut off from the voices and the lived experiences of the children and their parents in specific communities, shaped as they were by their own culture and tradition.

Delpit's work has led her to be critical of Dewey's call for an education for all that reflects what "the wisest and best parent" wants in *The School and Society*. She cautions, "To provide schooling for everyone's children that reflects liberal, middle-class values and aspirations is to ensure the maintenance of the status quo, to ensure that power, the culture of power, remains in the hands of those who already have it." The status quo, she reminds us, is profoundly undemocratic.[29]

More recently, Delpit has focused on the need for schools to respect the home language of their students, whether it is a "recognized" language or the speech patterns of the African American community, or another so-called dialect. Delpit has called for a much more respectful embrace of all students that not only demands high standards but also begins with respect and love. She says,

> We must treat all with love, care, and respect. We must make them feel welcomed and invited by allowing their interests, culture, and history into the classroom. We must reconnect them to their own brilliance and gain their trust so that they will learn from us. We must respect them, so that they feel connected to us. Then, and only then, might they be willing to adopt our language form as one to be added to their own.[30]

"Reconnecting students to their own brilliance" is also part of what it means for schools to be places where a democratic society is built.

The list could go on. There are as many disagreements as there are agreements among educators who seek to build more democracy in classrooms, schools, and society. Some seek only full integration into one culture, while others seek at least temporary separation in order to create the space to build a vibrant, if small-scale, culturally relevant democracy. However, viewing the schools as a foundation for an ever-expanding democratic culture has been one of the core purposes of public education in the United States for more than 200 years. There have been terrible failures, and the goal remains elusive, but it is one that every teacher needs to take seriously.

Teachable Moment
ORGANIZING A MOVEMENT

In *Teaching U.S. History: Dialogues Among Social Studies Teachers and Historians*, Diana Turk and her colleagues interviewed Adam Green, one of the foremost historians of the civil rights movement. Green says,

I think the single best way to look at the accelerated phase of black freedom—the era from the 1940s until at least the 1960s and possibly the 1970s—is to say that before you pay attention to leaders you have to pay attention to organizers. Of course, certainly it's important to think about the rank and file and the ways in which these were very much mass movements. But I think seeing the alternative to a leader-centric notion of history as being a mass-centric notion of history seems to me to be replacing one essentialism with another essentialism. So, for example, for many many years people thought about the Civil Rights Movement as a pantheon of great male leaders, like Martin Luther King and Malcolm X—and then there was Rosa Parks, who is often represented as a woman who stood up momentarily, and basically through her humble, quiet dignity created a certain kind of turn or spark or paradigm shift that gave rise to the kind of mass component of the movement.

But you know, one of the things that had to be understood in relation to making sense of Rosa Parks's role was that she had been an organizer. She had been someone who had worked within the NAACP as a very important member. And she had a deep understanding of the full operation that had been waiting for a case, basically, to kind of move the bus boycott campaign in Montgomery forward.

Reflecting on this interview, "Suzie," who teaches Advanced Placement U.S. History at a large urban high school, decided on a different approach than the standard lecture and discussion. After ensuring that her students had read about the Montgomery bus boycott and knew the stories of the major players, she proceeded with a new approach, described in the book:

"Imagine 99% of people in New York City decided to boycott public transportation," Suzie posed to her class. "In order to do so, what would we need to put in place to ensure our success?" Writing "bus boycott" in a center circle, she drew lines radiating out from the center, each line marking a different aspect that would need to be planned. "A team to lead," one student offered. "A charismatic leader," another followed. "People to join the group," a third proposed. "Funds for alternative transportation for publicity" another put forth. Each of these, along with "clearly outlined goals," "widespread publicity," and "communications network" Suzie wrote next to a single spoke emerging from the center circle. "Is this the job of one person?" she asked. A chorus of "no!" filled the room. "We need a lot of people!" "We need a leader!" "We need a hierarchy!" "We need technology!" "OK, now let's apply this to the whole Civil Rights Movement," Suzie proposed. "Were the masses as important as the leaders?" What about the organizers? What does it take to have a successful movement?" Discussion fairly flew from there.

Students began to think seriously about what it took to organize the Montgomery bus boycott and what democratic activism might look like and the range of people that would need to be involved for meaningful social change to take place. They moved from what Green calls a "leader-centric" view of history, which tends to breed passivity in students who learn that the only thing they can do is wait for the next great leader, to a far deeper understanding of the role of everyday people who have the courage to take on extraordinary roles, organizing, planning, and working together to make democracy a reality.

Because they were so deeply engaged, the students learned the material about this important moment in U.S. history far better than if Suzie had merely lectured or given a quiz based on the textbook (and subsequent test results showed that this was the case).

Questions

- Did you learn about the civil rights movement in your high school U.S. history class? Was it taught in a way that was similar to Suzie's or different? What would have happened if your teacher had used Suzie's methodology?
- Think about a lesson you want to teach someday at the elementary, middle, or high school level. In what ways could you teach it so that students would not only learn the material but also connect it to democratic activism in the way Suzie's lesson did?

Source: Diana Turk, Rachel Mattson, Terrie Epstein, and Robert Cohen. *Teaching U.S. History: Dialogues Among Social Studies Teachers and Historians*. New York: Routledge, 2009.

How Can We Make Our Schools More Democratic?

Schools Are Not All Equal

Most citizens believe in the principle that every child has the right to the best possible education, and this belief has fueled reform movements in every generation. Important progress has been made. For example, a century ago, only 5% of adolescents received a high school diploma, and half a century ago, only 50% of this age group did so. Today, more than 95% of young people receive either a high school diploma or a GED by the time they are in their mid-20s. (The 75%–80% graduation rate counts those who finish high school more or less on time. Another 15% or so of young people either finish eventually or learn a GED diploma, which is considered the equivalent of a high school diploma, by taking an exam.) Of course, a high school diploma alone is not the key to success that it was in 1900 or 1950. For most people, some higher education, if not a college degree, is a requirement for financial success in adult life. Not all high school diplomas offer equal access to higher education or a quality job.

CONNECTIONS →←

In Chapters 3 and 4, we discussed the many ways schools include or exclude students.

Unfortunately, the democratic ideal of a quality education for every child is far from being realized. Many students do not receive the kind of quality education that most people believe is their birthright because the community in which they live does not have sufficient resources to hire the best teachers or invest in buildings, technology, or laboratories. Students are still excluded from school or made to feel terribly uncomfortable because of their race, gender, or sexual orientation; because of a disability; or because their first language is not what is known as "standard English." Policies are invented that make schools less equal, and individuals in authority tolerate discrimination, often because they simply do not notice it or because confronting it would take a larger supply of courage than they have at the moment. The external things that make for a good education—safe streets, supportive families, a larger community of concerned adults—are not distributed evenly in this country, and schools are far from being able to make up for the inequities that exist in other parts of society, even if they were fully equal in the resources they provided for every child who attended them.

In 2004, on the 50th anniversary of the U.S. Supreme Court's *Brown* decision—considered at the time to be a landmark in democratizing schools by ending government-sanctioned racial segregation—Pedro A. Noguera and Robert Cohen wrote,

> Throughout the country, the more common experience for students is to attend schools that are separate and unequal—schools that are well-equipped and cater to the children of the affluent, and schools that barely function and serve the poor, white and nonwhite. Throughout America, a majority of poor children attend schools where learning has been reduced to preparation for a standardized test, where failure and dropping out are accepted as the norm, and where overcrowding and disorder are common.[31]

Noguera and Cohen have named a reality in American public education that is too often more accurate than the hopes of those who see schools as the nation's great equalizer.

According to the historian James Anderson, "Both schooling for democratic citizenship and schooling for second-class citizenship have been basic traditions in American education."[32] As a future teacher, you need to think about what is fair and unfair or democratic and undemocratic in the way that schools operate and ask how schools would be organized if they truly reflected our democratic commitments. What does the connection among school, democracy, and fairness mean in terms of what should be taught and how students should be treated? What policies should individual teachers and teacher-dominated organizations, such as unions and professional associations, advocate? Who is included in a democratic system of education? Perhaps most important, what can teachers—individually and collectively—do to help make our schools more democratic?

Few observers of public schools have probed as deeply as Jonathan Kozol. Kozol began his career as an elementary school teacher in Boston, was fired for encouraging his poor African American students to ask too many questions about the way they were treated in the Boston Public Schools of the 1960s, and has spent most of his life writing about children and the way adult society fails those young people. In *Savage Inequalities: Children in America's Schools*, published in 1991, he reported on the frightening state of education and the desperate unfairness that he saw in many schools that served the poorest of the nation's children.

To begin with, the majority of schools that serve poor children, despite some wonderful exceptions, are not happy places. Kozol summarized his own research, saying,

> My deepest impression, however, was . . . that these urban schools were, by and large, extraordinarily unhappy places. With few exceptions they reminded me of "garrisons" or "outposts" in a foreign nation. . . . [T]heir doors were guarded. Police sometimes patrolled the halls. . . . I often wondered why we would agree to let our children go to school in places where no politician, school board president, or business CEO would dream of working.

And the children, Kozol discovered, knew how unhappy these places were.

Fourteen years later, Kozol returned to some of the same schools and found that things were even worse in many places. In his 2005 book, *The Shame of the Nation*, Kozol describes two terrible failures of the democratic ideal that he sees in today's schools. First, he says,

One of the most disheartening experiences for those who grew up in the years when Martin Luther King and Thurgood Marshall were alive is to visit public schools today that bear their names . . . and to find how many of these schools are bastions of contemporary segregation.

Kozol relays stories that are nothing short of "apartheid schooling"—one set of schools for well-off, mostly White children and another set of very different schools for overwhelmingly poor students of color.

The second thing Kozol noticed in his recent visits to these segregated schools was how very different the education being offered to these students really was. It was not just a second-rate education—it was a profoundly distinct education. In observing one class, Kozol noticed, "No one laughed. No child made a funny face to somebody beside her." Every moment seemed tightly scripted. It is as if, Kozol says, "the differentness of children of minorities is seen as so extreme as to require an entire inventory of 'appropriate' approaches built around the proclamation of their absolute uniqueness from the other children of this nation."

Part of the power of Kozol's writing is his ability to listen carefully to the children who attend these schools and live in poor neighborhoods, then to record their wisdom. The students tell Kozol that they understand what is going on:

"It's like we're being hidden," said a 15-year-old girl named Isabel I met some years ago in Harlem, in attempting to explain to me the ways in which she and her classmates understood the racial segregation of their neighborhoods and schools. "It's as if you have been put in a garage where, if they don't have room for something but aren't sure if they should throw it out, they put it there where they don't need to think of it again."

How much farther could a society stray from building school communities that are microcosms of a larger society that is "worthy, lovely, and harmonious?"[33]

Teachers have been at the forefront of making schools more democratic for the past two centuries; however, much remains to be done. Whether one teaches in a school that serves poor youth or the more fortunate children of the middle class, every teacher has a responsibility to make schools fairer and more democratic for all.

Beyond the economic issues, a democratic society now, as 200 years ago, requires well-educated citizens who can understand public issues, make informed choices, and respond to the call to leadership in their communities. The challenge continues to be bringing practice closer to that belief while resisting more recent policies in many schools that seem to imply such diverse access is not, after all, such an appropriate goal. In a variety of ways, issues of access, inclusion, equality, and excellence are going to dominate the lives of the next generation of teachers just as they have most previous generations. Those entering the teaching profession need to be clear about their own beliefs and their expectations and the role they can play in a democratic system of education.

Notes from the Field

What Is a Major Challenge in Teaching Today?

"It is difficult to negotiate the tensions between what has status in our society and what you see important as a teacher."

—*Robin Hennessy, high school literacy coordinator*

 **CHAPTER REVIEW**

- What does a democratic society expect of its schools?

The full definition of democracy includes more than just educated voters. It involves an active citizenry that strives to create a government that is not only *for* the people but *of* and *by* the people as well. Schools have been considered an integral player in creating educated, responsible citizens to fulfill this ideal. To meet these expectations, teachers need to develop a curriculum, including in- and out-of-class experiences, in which students practice the kinds of democratic dialogues needed in the larger society.

- Historically speaking: What is the relationship between a universal education and democratic citizenship?

Since the founding of the United States, the concept of democracy has imposed great expectations on schools and teachers. Thomas Jefferson believed the country's new promise of democracy would fail if its citizens weren't active, educated participants. Horace Mann similarly believed that education was the key and should be funded for all citizens and inclusive regardless of class. However, African Americans typically were not covered under that "inclusive" expectation and were often denied the right to an education, whether formal or informal. Thus, upon the abolition of slavery, former slaves embraced education as the means to becoming active participants in shaping a democratic government and their future. John Dewey and progressive educators saw the role of schools as not only teaching the tenets of democracy but also engaging and motivating students for lifelong involvement in the democratic process. The civil rights movement challenged a system that supported equality for all but did not in fact provide it, especially in education. Today's vision for democracy seems to point to schools being models of ideal democratic societies—although this ideal has yet to be realized in many places.

- How can we make our schools more democratic?

National leaders from the American Revolution to the present day have argued that schooling for all of the nation's youth is essential to the success of a democratic society, but in every generation, young people have been excluded from schools or placed in second-class school situations where they do not have the opportunities of their more fortunate counterparts. The next generation of teachers will be challenged to play their part in ensuring that the schools of the United States truly leave no child behind.

Readings

What Does a Democratic Society Expect of Its Schools?

From *THE SCHOOL AND SOCIETY*

BY JOHN DEWEY

John Dewey wrote The School and Society *very early in his career, in 1899, and then published an expanded version in 1915. In this book, as clearly as in any of his writings, Dewey linked his commitment to a more liberating education for every child, a kind of child-centered education that encourages freedom not compliance, with his equally strong commitment to the creation of an educational system that fosters democracy—and equality—for all.*

We are apt to look at the school from an individualistic standpoint, as something between teacher and pupil, or between teacher and parent. That which interests us most is naturally the progress made by the individual child of our acquaintance, his normal physical development, his advance in ability to read, write, and figure, his growth in the knowledge of geography and history, improvement in manners, habits of promptness, order, and industry—it is from such standards as these that we judge the work of the school. And rightly so. Yet the range of the outlook needs to be enlarged. What the best and wisest parent wants for his own child, that must the community want for all of its children. Any other ideal for our schools is narrow and unlovely; acted upon, it destroys our democracy. All that society has accomplished for itself is put, through the agency of the school, at the disposal of its future members. All its better thoughts of itself it hopes to realize through the new possibilities thus opened to its future self. Here individualism and socialism are at one. Only by being true to the full growth of all the individuals who make it up, can society by any chance be true to itself. And in the self-direction thus given, nothing counts as much as the school, for, as Horace Mann said, "Where anything is growing, one former is worth a thousand re-formers."

Whenever we have in mind the discussion of a new movement in education, it is especially necessary to take the broader, or social, view. Otherwise, changes in the school institution and tradition will be looked at as the arbitrary inventions of particular teachers; at the worst transitory fads, and at the best merely improvements in certain details—and this is the plane upon which it is too customary to consider school changes. It is as rational to conceive of the locomotive or the telegraph as personal devices. The modification going on in the method and curriculum of education is as much a product of the changed social situation, and as much an effort to meet the needs of the new society that is forming, as are changes in modes of industry and commerce.

It is to this, then, that I especially ask your attention: the effort to conceive what roughly may be termed the "New Education" in the light of larger changes in society. Can we connect this "New Education" with the general march of events? If we can, it will lose its isolated character; it will cease to be an affair which proceeds only from the over-ingenious minds of pedagogues dealing with particular pupils. It will appear as part and parcel of the whole social evolution, and, in its more general features at least, as inevitable. . . .

The change that comes first to mind, the one that overshadows and even controls all others, is the industrial one—the application of science resulting in the great inventions that have utilized the forces of nature on a vast and inexpensive scale: the growth of a world-wide market as the object of production, of vast manufacturing centers to supply this market, of cheap and rapid means of communication and distribution between all its parts. Even as to its feebler beginnings, this change is not much more than a century old; in many of its most important aspects it falls within the short span of those now living. One can hardly believe there has been a revolution in all history so rapid, so extensive, so complete. Through it the face of the earth is making over, even as to its physical forms; political boundaries are wiped out and moved about, as if they were indeed only lines on a paper map; population is hurriedly gathered into cities from the ends of the earth; habits of living are altered with startling abruptness and thoroughness; the search for the truths of nature is infinitely stimulated and facilitated, and their application to life made not only practicable, but commercially necessary. Even our moral and religious ideas and interests, the most conservative because the deepest-lying things in our nature, are profoundly affected. That this revolution should not affect education in some other than a formal and superficial fashion is inconceivable. . . .

While our educational leaders are talking of culture, the development of personality, etc., as the end and aim of education, the great majority of those who pass under the tuition of the school regard it only as a narrowly practical tool with which to get bread and butter enough to eke out a restricted life. If we were to conceive our educational end and aim in a less exclusive way, if we were to introduce into educational processes the activities which appeal to those whose dominant interest is to do and to make, we should find the hold of the school upon its members to be more vital, more prolonged, containing more of culture.

But why should I make this labored presentation? The obvious fact is that our social life has undergone a thorough and radical change. If our education is to have any meaning for life, it must pass through an equally complete transformation. This transformation is not something to appear suddenly, to be executed in a day by conscious purpose. It is already in progress. Those modifications of our school system which often appear (even to those most actively concerned with them, to say nothing of their spectators) to be mere changes of detail, mere improvement within the school mechanism, are in reality signs and evidences of evolution. The introduction of active occupations, of nature-study, of elementary science, of art, of history; the relegation of the merely symbolic and formal to a secondary position; the change in the moral school atmosphere, in the relation of pupils and teachers—of discipline; the introduction of more active, expressive, and self-directing factors—all these are not mere accidents, they are necessities of the larger social evolution. It remains but to organize all these factors, to appreciate them in their fulness of meaning, and to put the ideas and ideals involved into complete, uncompromising possession of our school system. To do this means to make each one of our schools an embryonic community life, active with types of occupations that reflect the life of the larger society and permeated throughout with the spirit of art, history, and science. When the school introduces and trains each child of society into membership within such a little community, saturating him with the spirit of service, and providing him with the instruments of effective self-direction, we shall have the deepest and best guaranty of a larger society which is worthy, lovely, and harmonious.

Questions

- What do you think of Dewey's statement that "What the best and wisest parent wants for his own child, that must the community want for all of its children"? What do you think of Lisa Delpit's critique of that idea discussed earlier in this chapter?
- Do you find Dewey's ideas and his faith that schools can and indeed must ultimately create "a larger society which is worthy, lovely, and harmonious" to be romantic, realistic, or a little of both? What does it mean for you as a future teacher?

Source: John Dewey. *The School and Society.* Chicago: University of Chicago Press, Revised Edition, 1915; originally published 1899, pp. 3–28.

From "ON EDUCATION"

BY W.E.B. DU BOIS

W.E.B. Du Bois, one of the founders of the NAACP and a foremost advocate for African American rights during the first half of the 20th century, spoke to a group of educators at the end of World War II. The editor of the Du Bois papers found this speech among them without a note as to exactly when or where it was delivered, yet it remains a powerful statement of what a democratic society might expect of its schools.

You are of course aware that a new branch of learning has recently become popular which is called Semantics. Semantics has to do with the meaning of words and takes up the fact that very often we use the same word unconsciously with different meanings so that what is true of the word in one meaning is quite untrue in another meaning. I want to call your attention this morning to some differences of meaning in the word *education*. . . .

In order to make clearer what I mean I want to go over first the meaning of education in my life. From the age of five through my twenty-sixth birthday, over twenty years, were spent almost entirely in receiving an education according to the preconceptions of the late nineteenth century. . . . Now at the end of these twenty years of study and travel . . . I was not prepared to do any specific piece of work; I could not make a table or cook a meal or sew on a button. I could not carve nor paint; and the art of writing and revealing my thought had not been developed. On the other hand, I did have a rather firm grasp, and idea of what this world was, and how it had developed in the last thousand years. I knew something of the kind of human beings that were on earth, what they were thinking and what they were doing. I was able to reason rather accurately, and whatever there was that I had not been trained to do, the specific training that was necessary came rather easily because I had this general grasp.

Nevertheless, as I came into the twentieth century, I was aware of the widespread criticism of the sort of education which I had had, and the questioning in the minds of men as to how far that sort of education was really valuable and how far it could be applied to the youth of today. More especially during the present war [this speech was given late in World War II], this criticism has been sharpened and emphasized in the United States. We have seen young people who had training in mechanics easily get jobs that paid wages almost fabulous.

This has made the people say and doubtless you have had it emphasized here, that what education ought to do, is to prepare young people for doing work of this sort; and that it is a great waste of time to study what we used to call the humanities and art and literature, over periods which counted up into decades, rather than in a few years of intensive work made a man a capable workman in some trade or art where he could get an immediate and comfortable salary.

Now despite this, we look upon a curiously contradictory world. The technical advance of western European civilization in the last century has been the most marvelous thing which the world has seen. It can without exaggeration be called miraculous. Personally I never can get over the unreality of travel by airplane. When I was a boy we typified the impossible by comparing it to flying. Now we fly easily and with astonishing safety around the world. But not only that; we talk over immeasurable distances. We transport goods and ideas. We have a world whose technical perfection makes all things possible. And yet, on the other hand, this world is in chaos. It has been organized twice in the last quarter of a century for murder and destruction on a tremendous scale, not to mention continual minor wars. There is not only this physical disaster, there is the mental and moral tragedy which makes us at times despair of human culture.

Now when we compare the technical mastery which man has over the world, with the utter failure of that power to organize happiness, and peace in the world, then we know that something is wrong. Part of this wrong lies in our conception of education. There are two different things that we have in mind in education: One is training for mastery of technique; the other is training the man who is going to exercise the technique and for whom the technique exists. If, regardless of the man himself, we train his hands and his nervous system for accomplishing a certain technical job, after that work is done we still have the question as to why it is done, and for whom, and to what end. What is the work of the world for? Manifestly it is for the people who inhabit the world. But what kind of people are they? What they are depends upon the way in which they have been educated, that is, the way in which their possibilities have been developed and drawn out.

It is a misuse of the word *education* to think of it as technical training. Technical training is of immense importance. It characterizes civilization. But it is of secondary importance as compared with the people who are being civilized and who are enjoying civilization or who ought to enjoy it. Manifestly the civilized people of the world have got to be characterized by certain things; they must know this world, its history and the laws of its development. They must be able to reason carefully and accurately. Attention must be paid to human feelings and emotions which determine and guide this knowledge, and reason and action must follow a certain pattern of taste. These things: knowledge, reason, feeling and taste make up something which we designate as Character and this Character it is which makes the human being for which the world of technique is to be arranged and by whom it is to be guided.

Technique without character is chaos and war. Character without technique is labor and want. But when you have human beings who know the world and can grasp it; who have their feelings guided by ideals; then using technique at their hands they can get rid of the four great evils of human life. These four evils are ignorance, poverty, disease and crime. They flourish today in the midst of miraculous technique and in spite of our manifest ability to rid the world of them. They flourish because with all our technical training we do not have in sufficient quantity and for a long enough time the education of the human soul; the training of men to know and think and guide their feelings by science and art.

Questions

- Du Bois describes education for "technical mastery" and education of the people who are "going to exercise the technique" as two quite different things. Can schools do both? Does your own philosophy of education favor one goal over the other or seek to include both?
- Where do you think Du Bois and Dewey would agree? Disagree?

Source: W.E.B. Du Bois. "On Education." In *Against Racism: Unpublished Essays, Papers, Addresses, 1887–1961 by W.E.B. Du Bois,* edited by Herbert Aptheker, 249–52. Cambridge: University of Massachusetts Press, 1985.

How Can We Make Our Schools More Democratic?

From *EXPLORING THE MORAL HEART OF TEACHING*

AUTHOR: DAVID T. HANSEN

David T. Hansen is a contemporary educator who has written extensively about the moral and ethical aspects of teaching, as he does in this piece.

Conceptions of teaching have consequences. They influence how teachers think about and conduct their work. They shape what researchers investigate. They guide how teacher educators prepare new candidates. They play a role in what students come to expect from their teachers. And they underlie how administrators, policy makers, politicians, businesspersons, and parents perceive and judge teachers. In short, conceptions of what teaching is, and of what it is for, make a difference in educational thought and practice.

My aim in this book is to contribute to a conception of teaching that does justice to its time-honored importance in human life. I investigate why teaching is a moral and intellectual practice with a rich tradition. Those terms help capture why teaching has been such a long-standing priceless human activity. I mean "priceless" in the sense of having no substitute. No other practice, be it medicine, parenting, law, or social work, accomplishes what teaching does, even though there may be occasional overlap between them. This viewpoint turns attention to the importance of the person—the distinctive, irreproducible human being—who inhabits the role of teacher. It spotlights, in turn, why teaching entails paying attention to the persons who fill the role of student. These persons, whether they be children or adults, are themselves unique and noninterchangeable. They need teachers, at timely moments, to help them fulfill their promise.

In this introductory chapter, I outline this perspective on the practice by, first, examining the current conceptions of teaching. I raise the questions about them that center on the issue of whether teaching is an "empty cell" whose terms and meaning derive from outside the practice, in various political, economic, social, or other interests. I argue that teaching is an enduring practice whose moral and intellectual terms can be derived, to a vital degree, from *within*. Teaching has its own integrity, just as do the individual men and women who occupy the role in a serious-minded, thoughtful way. I discuss why the integrity of both the practice of teaching and of individual teachers threatens to fall out of sight whenever people cast teaching as merely a means to an end, with that end shaped from outside the practice. Public concerns and interests do merit a permanent place in talk about teaching. But such talk should be balanced by a grasp of why teaching is a moral and intellectual endeavor. . . .

Do ideals and idealism have a role to play in teaching? Two quick answers come to mind. The first is that they have no place, or at most a very limited place. According to this line of thinking, teaching is a well-defined occupation with well-defined goals. Our romantic impulses may tell us otherwise. They may lead us to envision teachers as artists and as transformers of the human spirit. However, a critic might argue, teaching is not an artistic endeavor because teachers are not artists, save from the point of view of method and even then only in a metaphorical sense. Unlike painters at their easels, teachers cannot create whatever they wish in the classroom. They are public servants beholden to the public to get a particular job done. Idealism is warranted as a source of motivation, but teachers' vision had better not take them away from the job itself. According to this point of view, the only ideal teachers should hold is, ideally, that of fulfilling their publicly defined obligations in a responsible and effective manner.

The second answer advances the opposite position. Teachers must have ideals, and their ideals must reach beyond mere social expectations. According to this argument, teachers are not bureaucratic hired hands whose only charge is to pass on to the young whatever knowledge and skills the powers that be have sanctioned. Teachers do play an important role in socializing students into expected custom and practice. However, as teachers, rather than as mere socializers, they also help equip students to think for themselves, to conceive their own ideals and hopes, and to prepare themselves for the task of making tomorrow's world into something other than a tired copy of today's.

Both answers contain truth. Teaching is not an empty cell to be filled in any fashion one wishes. The individual who occupies the role does not own teaching as if it were a possession that can be manipulated to suit personal taste. It is one thing to paint one's own canvases. It is another thing to paint, metaphorically speaking, with the hearts and minds of other people's children. Teachers have publicly defined tasks, ranging from teaching knowledge to treating students with respect. They must uphold these if they are to deserve the right to remain in the classroom.

However, teaching is also more complicated and more important than occupational language alone can capture. Teaching comprises more than a series of discrete tasks whose content and presentation can be prefabricated. Teaching is a moral and intellectual practice whose outcomes cannot just be punched in, at least if we associate teaching with education rather than with a narrow version of training. Moreover, to the extent that teachers exercise autonomy and initiative, their individuality comes to the fore. Issues addressed in previous chapters—person, conduct, and moral sensibility, crafting an environment for teaching and learning, developing a sense of tradition—all point to the ideals and attitudes teachers can bring to their work.

Neither of our initial answers to the question about ideals in teaching is sufficient. Moreover, both answers polarize functional and moral aspects of teaching that, in the final analysis, need to be brought into a working accord. . . .

Teachers will differ in the big ideals that guide their work, whether they be to help create a better society or to produce smart and caring people. Such ideals are warranted—for example, as sources of motivation—albeit within limits tailored by the terms of the practice. What teachers can agree on, it seems to me, is an ideal that will enable them to become the kind of person who can indeed have a beneficial rather than harmful or random, impact on students. Such an ideal will describe at one and the same time a disposition. Tenacious humility is a mane for this ideal. . . .

Tenacious humility does not tell teachers what materials or instructional methods to employ, all of which are discrete, specific decisions. Rather, in taking tenacious humility seriously as an ideal of personhood, teachers can build into their working lives continuity, or what some scholars call *narrative unity*. In reaching toward the ideal, teachers will be more likely to make specific educational choices that add up to a meaningful pattern rather than to a haphazard or random series. If they are tenacious about teaching well, and humble in their pretensions, they will be more rather than less likely to become a force for good in students' lives. Striving for this ideal will not prevent teachers from making mistakes and misjudgments. But it will enable them to learn and to keep working to improve. Tenacious humility constitutes a practical, humanizing ideal that can guide both big ideals and everyday practice, keeping them in the service of teaching and learning.

Questions

- Hansen begins his book by saying, "Conceptions of teaching have consequences." As you think about your conception of teaching—your philosophy of education—what consequences do you hope for? Will those consequences make your classroom, and the larger society, a fairer place in the future?
- In response to all of the Readings in this chapter, what do you think of the importance of ideas and idealism in education? How do ideas and idealism connect with the practical day-to-day duties of teaching?

Source: David T. Hansen. *Exploring the Moral Heart of Teaching: Toward a Teacher's Creed*. New York: Teachers College Press, 2001, pp. 1–2, 157–158, 173, 175.

Developing a Plan and a Personal Philosophy
Where Do I Go From Here?

> We need to support those teachers who love their students, who find creative ways to teach them, and who do so under difficult circumstances. We need to celebrate teachers who are as excited about their own learning as they are about the learning of their students. And we need to champion those teachers who value their students' families and find respectful ways to work with them.

SONIA NIETO

At the beginning of this book, we posed the simple question, "Why do I want to be a teacher?" That question most likely did not have a simple answer. Or maybe you hadn't even considered your reasons for pursuing a career in teaching. By now, however, you may have formulated a complex response, taking into account all the benefits, opportunities, challenges, issues, and obstacles related to teaching.

As you continue to explore the rewarding field of teaching, you need to find the best path to get the skills, experiences, and licenses that will help you land your first job. It is also critical for you to determine the kind of teacher you want to be and your own personal philosophy about education. You should consider how you will manage the challenges of the initial years on the job. Your goal will be to establish a successful routine that evolves continually and allows you to grow in both skills and personal satisfaction.

The **Readings** for this chapter are written by people who have spent many years teaching and finding ways to answer these same questions for themselves. In her book *What Keeps Teachers Going?*, the first **Reading**, Sonia Nieto reflects on how her own experiences and those of other teachers can help to answer the question, "How will I survive as a new teacher?" The second **Reading** focuses on the question "What kind of teacher do I want to be?"

Jacqueline Jordan Irvine discusses the characteristics of caring and competent teachers. Irvine finds that care and competence come in many different forms. What may look caring in one instance may not seem so caring in another.

Nevertheless, Irvine concludes that while each teacher needs to define care and competence in his or her own way, no one should enter teaching who does not want to be identified by these significant characteristics.

How Do I Get My First Teaching Job?

I once spoke with a newly appointed director of human resources in a large urban school district. Upon starting her new job, she discovered that the district's personnel office was not very friendly to new applicants. She heard the phone answered with "What do you want?" . . . hardly a way to encourage applicants. When she witnessed a young, enthusiastic applicant being turned away because "no one has time to conduct job interviews today," she intervened quickly. She took the applicant into her own office and conducted a job interview on the spot. The city gained a new and enthusiastic teacher that it otherwise might have lost. The policy for answering the telephone was also changed quickly; the new greeting: "How may I help you?"

In some years and in some school districts, there are lots of jobs for new teachers; in others, opportunities may be limited. It is hoped that when you begin the search for your first teaching job, you will be greeted with "How may I help you?" rather than "What do you want?" and that someone will want to interview you. But even if the door is not as open and welcoming as you wish, it is worth pushing through to your own classroom where the work really happens. Whatever initial greeting you receive, remember that it takes patience and perseverance to land the job you want.

Two different sets of authorities govern entrance into the teaching profession. The fifty states plus the District of Columbia grant licenses (or certification as it is called in some states) to be a teacher. The decision to grant a license is based on your having completed the required course of study, usually at a university-based teacher preparation program. But a license does not guarantee a job. It only makes getting one possible. Teachers are hired by the 15,000 different school districts or often by the principals of individual schools. Except in unusual circumstances, a school or district cannot hire anyone to teach who does not have the appropriate state license or certificate. However, only the individual district or school can offer a paid position as a classroom teacher.

CONNECTIONS ➜◄

In Chapter 11, we discussed how the issues of licensure and hiring are handled at the state and local levels, respectively, even though the federal government has become more involved in accountability issues and in defining a "highly qualified teacher."

State Licensure and Examinations

The majority of teachers gain their **state licensure** by completing a college- or university-based state-approved teacher preparation program. If you are reading this text for a college course, the odds are good that you are enrolled in such a program. In most states, the state department of education creates a set of standards for teacher licensure. The state then enters into agreements with colleges and universities offering teacher preparation programs in which the institution of higher education ensures that its curriculum for aspiring teachers meets the state requirements and the state reviews the school's curriculum (usually every 5 years). Many teacher preparation programs also have accreditation through the Council for the Accreditation of Educator Preparation (CAEP). CAEP was created in 2013 out of the merger of two earlier accreditation programs, but many teacher preparation programs have long been reviewed and approved by these agencies. If the college offers a state-approved program, then its graduates are essentially promised that the state will honor the institution's recommendation and they will be licensed as teachers if they complete all the requirements.

state licensure
(called *state certification* in some states) A formal document issued by the state that indicates the holder has met the teaching standards in a particular state—most often graduating from a state-approved teacher preparation program in a college or university—and has met any other requirements such as passing a state-approved exam.

If you are a college student studying to be a teacher, you should ask an advisor about the rules and regulations in your state and for your college just to be sure of your status. In addition to asking if you are enrolled in a state-approved program, you should also be clear about the specific license your curriculum will lead you to and carefully map out a program with your advisor to be sure you get there. Asking lots of questions early in your educational career hopefully ensures that you get the right answers early enough in your preparation program to make any necessary adjustments.

Many states offer a variety of teaching licenses, not just for elementary or high school teachers, but for early elementary grades versus later elementary grades or middle school, and specific licenses for high school teachers according to the subjects taught, such as chemistry, mathematics, history or social studies, English, biology, and the like. Other licenses are issued for special education teachers; for teachers of bilingual education or English as a second language; and for teachers of theater, art, dance, and so on. Knowing the kinds of licenses offered in your state and the specific license for which your curriculum is preparing you will help you to avoid serious disappointment in the future.

You may also find it useful to secure more than one license before beginning to look for a job. An elementary teacher who is also licensed in special education or bilingual education, a secondary chemistry teacher who can also teach physics, or a social studies teacher who has state approval to teach at both the middle and high school levels has a much better chance of finding a position than someone who can do only one thing. Many teachers add a second or third license after they have already begun teaching, but others use their undergraduate or graduate preparation programs to secure more than one license from the beginning. For a principal, knowing that a newly hired teacher can be flexible and possibly teach several different types of students has great appeal. Saying "I will only teach this one thing," is not a good way to get a job.

Although most teachers gain their initial license through a state-approved college or university program, there are "alternative routes" to teaching. Some alternative routes are through freestanding organizations such as Teach for America. Many school districts have their own in-district programs that recruit college graduates and offer an apprentice-style program that leads to teacher licensure. Finally, some states award licenses to individuals who can demonstrate experience in or advanced knowledge of a subject in which the demand for teachers is high (often mathematics, one of the sciences, or a foreign language). A major debate is ongoing between advocates of such alternative routes and those who believe that all prospective teachers should be required to complete a university-based program. Nevertheless, the majority of the nation's teachers still qualify for their jobs by completing a college- or university-based program, either as part of their undergraduate program or as a one- or two-year graduate program. The key for anyone aspiring to a career in teaching is to be sure that the specific path you are following will enable you to realize your goals.

> **specialization**
> Focused area of study and skill used in a specific teaching field; elementary teacher, high school chemistry teacher, special education teacher, or teacher of English as a second language are all recognized specializations.

During the past decade, most states have also added one more step in the process for earning a state license or certification: a state examination or other state-level review. If your state has such a review process—and most do—it will be important to start early in planning to fulfill the state requirements as well as those of your college so that you will not face any delay in seeking or qualifying for a job after graduation.

More and more states are now using a system called edTPA, formerly the Teacher Performance Assessment, which became fully operational in the fall of 2013 as part of their state licensure process. Not every state requires edTPA, but 35 states and the District of Columbia use at least some part of the edTPA program and more are starting to require the completion of a full edTPA review, including some of the nation's largest states like California and New York.

In a state or program that uses edTPA, a future teacher will be involved in a two-part review. First she or he will video an actual lesson that they are teaching as part of their student teaching experience. The video does not need to be sophisticated photography—a cell phone camera is fine—but it needs to clearly show the novice teacher and students interacting through the course of a specific lesson. Then the teaching candidate must write an analysis of the lesson, describing what worked, what did not work, and why, including the learning theories that support how the teacher approached the lesson. Once that is done, the future teacher submits both the video and the analysis to the Evaluation Systems operated by Pearson Education, which will evaluate the lesson and the description. A perfect lesson is not essential. More important is a good lesson accompanied by a clear description of not only what worked but also what did not work and what the teacher might do differently in the future. Being able to describe failures, and lessons learned from them, can be as important, as describing what worked and why one did those things.

The edTPA program was first developed at Stanford University for its own teacher preparation programs. Stanford then partnered with the American Association of Colleges for Teacher Education (AACTE) and expanded the program so it could be used across the country. Currently, edTPA is offered in 27 different versions for fields from Early Childhood to specific Secondary subject matter to Special Education to a wide variety of specialized fields linked to state licenses. As its organizers say, "edTPA is not about theory. It goes beyond classroom credits to ask teacher candidates to demonstrate what they can and will do on the job, translating into practice what research shows improves teaching." They view it as the equivalent of a medical licensing exam or the bar exam and want it to be as rigorous.[1]

Like almost everything in education today, edTPA is not without controversy. On one hand, for critics, edTPA's use of a for-profit company like Pearson Education simply means that it is one more step in the corporate takeover of education. Critics also worry about whether or not the scoring of edTPA will be culturally biased against candidates of color and whether there is sufficient evidence that a high edTPA score really means future classroom excellence.

On the other hand, defenders of edTPA argue that today's schools need a better guarantee than they have had in the past that a new teacher is fully prepared to teach effectively on the day that he or she first enters a classroom and that edTPA's focus on practice is a better measure than any previous one. Other defenders argue that edTPA focuses on outcome measures: what a future teacher can do, not just what she or he knows. And some also argue that edTPA forces a candidate to think carefully about teaching practice in a way that actually makes him or her a better teacher.[2]

Whatever the debates, edTPA is in wide use today and likely to be more so tomorrow. Aspiring teachers in many places need to meet its standards. In some states, edTPA replaced previous state exams while in others it is taken in addition to other, usually content-focused exams.

State teacher examinations were popular in the United States during much of the first half of the 20th century. After World War II, most states phased out these exams, replacing them with the program-approval agreements with colleges and universities that ensured much higher standards for new teachers than simply passing one examination. During the 1990s, however, as a new national debate emerged about the quality of the nation's teaching force and the programs that prepared them, many states began to create new examinations designed to ensure that the graduates of all programs met a single state standard for literacy, knowledge of subject matter, pedagogy, and often also an understanding of human development and other aspects of schooling.

The majority of states that instituted examinations used an already well-respected examination offered by the Educational Testing Service (home of the SAT tests) called PRAXIS. PRAXIS exams test an applicant's general knowledge, specific subject matter knowledge in the area in which one wants to teach, and understanding of pedagogy. Some states have created new examinations. The federal government currently provides a national "report card" listing the passing rate on the teacher examinations for each state and for each teacher preparation program, but the federal report card is now in the process of a major review and revision.

You need to know the rules in the state where you want to teach. Do you have to complete the edTPA process and/or take another examination? Does the program in which you are enrolled offer workshops or other means of preparing for these exams? When do you need to take an exam to avoid any delays in securing your initial teaching license? Others may engage in an extended debate about teacher examinations, but if you want to teach and your state requires such an examination, you still need to take *and pass* it.

Getting Hired

After completing a state-approved program and passing the required exams, you should be the proud holder of a state license to teach. However, a critical step remains before you can enter your first classroom as a paid teacher: You need to get hired. Making a good impression is essential and involves assembling the right **credentials**. No principal or district human resources office wants to hire someone who barely passed his or her courses or state exams. Given the organizational skills demanded for successful management of a classroom, no one wants to hire a teacher who does not demonstrate careful organizational skills in submitting an application for a job. In some high-needs areas (such as mathematics, special education, and foreign languages), many school districts will hire almost all applicants. In other areas

credentials
Certificates or awards that attest to the qualifications, skills, and knowledge learned through a course of study or some other measure.

Notes from the Field

What job hunting tip would you pass along to a recent graduate?

"Have several people look over your resume before you present it to a potential employer. If you know principals or English teachers who would be willing to review it, then by all means make sure that they do. I was recently on a committee of teachers selected to screen potential candidates for our new principal, and it was painfully obvious which ones had carefully edited their resumes and which ones had not. As a screening committee, our belief was that the unorganized resumes with glaring errors were written by people who did not pay much attention to detail nor cared to use professionalism within the one document that was supposed to make them stand out from all of the other candidates. A poorly constructed resume does not leave a good impression and is more likely to end up in the 'reject' pile. Remember that your resume is a reflection of who you are and may reveal more about you than you realize."

—Renee Notaro, sixth-grade English and visual/performing arts teacher

Teachable Moment
DEVELOPING A TEACHING PORTFOLIO

A teaching portfolio is a collection of materials and information that serves as a record of what you have taught, the impact of your teaching, and your development as a teacher. William Cerbin writes, "At its best a portfolio documents an instructor's approach to teaching, combining specific evidence of instructional strategies and effectiveness in a way that captures teaching's intellectual substance and complexity."

The Center for Instructional Development and Research at the University of Washington describes two types of teaching portfolios: a developmental teaching portfolio, which "is your own reflective record of your teaching [that] provides a place for you to document and reflect on various aspects of your teaching," and an evaluative teaching portfolio, which "you present to someone else to provide them with evidence for a decision about your teaching."

Whereas a resume captures where you have worked and what you have done there, a teaching portfolio provides greater details about your teaching experience, your success and your analysis of failures and how you plan to avoid them in the future. A teaching portfolio should also be a living document that "does more than simply list what you have done as a teacher. It is both a product and a process. The product is a set of papers that documents and reflects on your teaching effectiveness, your students' learning, and your teaching development over time. It is also a continuous process of editing, taking material out and adding new material, and, generally, reflecting on your progress as you grow as a teacher."

Thus, a teaching portfolio can be valuable not only when you are pursuing a teaching position but also when you are being evaluated in your current position and as a developmental tool that can support your progress as a teacher.

What should a teaching portfolio include? The contents of your teaching portfolio may be dictated by whether you are building a developmental, an evaluative, or an all-purpose portfolio, but in general, a teaching portfolio will include the following:

- **A reflective statement.** This outlines your teaching philosophy, gives examples of how you put this philosophy into practice, and explains your growth and evolution as a teacher.
- **Sample curriculum materials.** These could include class syllabi, lesson plans, or assignments. If you plan to teach in a state using the Common Core State Standards, the curriculum sample should certainly reflect familiarity with these standards and some level of success in meeting them.
- **Examples of teaching outcomes.** These might include samples of graded essays with your comments explaining the grading, or other student work that illustrates the impact of your teaching.

- **Evaluations of your teaching.** These could be formal evaluations from students or supervisors, or letters of evaluation from fellow teachers or administrators. Don't forget comments from your students; they can often be the best measure of effective teaching.
- **Additional supporting material.** This might include a video of you teaching, an explanation of ways you are involved in the school outside of the classroom, or illustrations of how you have used technology as a teaching tool. If you completed the edTPA review, include part of it here.

Throughout your teaching career, be sure to update your portfolio continually. According to the Second Language Teaching and Curriculum Center at the University of Hawaii at Manoa, "Increasingly, employers are asking for various portfolio elements before, during, and after the interview/hiring process. By putting together an organized, cohesive, reflective, and ever-growing portfolio, you better prepare yourself to show who you are as a teacher and what you offer to a potential employer."

Questions

- What materials do you already have that you could put in your teaching portfolio? What materials would you need to prepare or develop to put in your portfolio?
- What would you hope to communicate through your teaching portfolio? What should a future principal know about you regarding your educational philosophy, style of teaching, record of interaction with young people, etc.? What materials or documents will best express these aspects of your teaching?

Sources: Center for Instructional Development and Research, University of Washington. "Developing a Teaching Portfolio"; Graduate Student Instructor Teaching & Resource Center, University of California–Berkeley. "What Is a Teaching Portfolio?" and "What Should Be Included in a Teaching Portfolio?"; Teacher Portfolio & Preparation Series, Second Language Teaching & Curriculum Center, University of Hawaii at Manoa. "TiPPS for Teacher Portfolios."

(such as elementary education or social studies/history), although the jobs are just as important, those who are doing the hiring can be more selective. Some school districts can afford to be selective, whereas others have a hard time finding enough qualified teachers. No matter what, you need to be the strongest possible candidate for the job you want.

When asked what they look for in selecting a new teacher, principals and human resources officers usually say similar things. They want to know that the person will be a good "fit" for the position. Not all teachers and all schools are interchangeable parts. Different schools have different philosophies of education. Different districts, schools, and departments want teachers with different ways of teaching. Many school districts will ask you to submit a paper on your own philosophy of education as part of a portfolio of materials about you. Whether you submit it in writing or are asked the question in an interview, you need to be able to present yourself as a candidate who has a clear, well-thought-out, and specific philosophy of education when seeking a first job and establishing a successful career. Being vague or presenting yourself as someone who has not thought about these issues is not a strong starting point.

The question of "fit" is important, not just to those doing the hiring but also to the person seeking a position: you. Nothing could be worse than teaching in a place where you feel you simply do not belong because of differences in philosophy or approach to the education of young people. Research the district and school before you show up for an interview. Using the Internet, you can determine how a school and a district *want* to be perceived. Almost every school and school district has its own Web site, and these contain a great deal of information about where the schools are located, how well the students are performing, and what the school and the school district value the most. You will make a strong impression if you come to an interview having looked carefully at the available Web sites and any other information you can find. It will help you decide if this is a good place for you to work. When you get to your interview, ask a lot of questions. Principals and other administrators respect someone who comes to the interview well informed and curious. Few people mind answering questions about the place where they work.

Those who do the most hiring of teachers note that successful candidates have had some meaningful experience in teaching and can speak about that experience with a sense of personal authority and confidence. Nearly everyone applying for a teaching job has done some amount of **student teaching**. The person who has done more, or who has worked with young people in out-of-school circumstances and demonstrated that they like children and can be successful with them, is going to be the most appealing candidate. It also helps if you can describe moments of success with students as well as moments of failure, especially if you can also say what you would do to be sure that the failures are not repeated. Teachers have an extraordinary level of freedom from supervision once they are hired and in their own classroom. Those doing the hiring want to be sure that the person they are selecting will use that freedom correctly.

Finding a Supportive School

Questions to ask as you consider a first teaching job:

- Do the principal and other school leaders seem like people who will support me in continuing to learn this profession?
- Does the school have a clearly articulated philosophy of education? Is it one that I agree with or will find comfortable?
- Do I like my prospective teaching colleagues? Do other teachers in the school seem to be happy and like their jobs?
- Does the school have a system for mentoring new teachers?
- Am I going to teach what I want to teach, or does the school need someone in a different field than mine?
- How well is the school connected to the parents and surrounding community?

Teachable Moment
TEN TIPS FOR INTERVIEWING FOR YOUR FIRST TEACHING JOB

Getting an actual teaching position can be easy or difficult, involving both luck and your area of expertise. Landing your first job, however, depends a great deal on how well you sell yourself. Even an aspiring teacher with the best credentials won't get hired if they seem arrogant or incompetent to a hiring committee. Beth McDonald served as an elementary school principal in Massachusetts and New York for many years and hired many new teachers. Now teaching future teachers at New York University, she offers these ten tips to get a foot in the door and, beyond that, a real job.

1. In order to get the interview, your cover letter is the chance to sell yourself to the screening/**hiring committee** and set yourself apart from the many other applicants they may be considering. Address it directly to the school principal *by name* ("to whom it may concern" letters generally get tossed), make sure it is absolutely error free, and give the readers a sense of who you are and what you have to offer. A bland formulaic letter won't make the cut if the market is competitive. On the other hand, don't make it too long—no more than two pages in a font size that respects the readers' varying acuity.
2. Another thing to spend time on before interviewing is question and answer rehearsal. You may have a chance to do some mock interviews as part of your program or with a friend. If not, do it on your own by getting a good interviewing book or by finding a Web site that provides typical questions. Write responses out or use a voice-recording tool or a friend as a sounding board. The more you can anticipate and prepare, the more relaxed and confident you'll be. Have *concrete* examples or illustrations in mind to accompany your responses. If the school is in a Common Core state, let them know that you are familiar with the Common Core and how to teach to its standards, but don't get into a long analysis of the strengths or weaknesses of the Common Core. The committee is hiring a teacher, not a policy analyst.

3. Create a "leave behind" portfolio—whether or not you've also created a larger one-of-a-kind professional portfolio. Not all committees are interested in, or have time for, a thorough review of all applicants' portfolios. Bring along your full portfolio to pass around if asked to do so, or for you to make reference to a particular item in response to a question. Get attractive, professional copies made of just the essential items—cover letter, resume, letters of recommendation, one or two other items—and put them together in a nice folder that you can leave behind. Creating an electronic version will demonstrate your technology skills, which may count a lot. However, you can't count on people taking the time to look at it until you reach the finalist stage, so leave a hard copy.

4. Make sure you know where you're going! If possible, make a trial run before your interview. If you get lost or delayed on the day of your interview, you'll be late and stressed out—not a good way to start. Much better to arrive with time to sip the water you've remembered to bring and use a restroom.

5. Think professionally when you choose your clothing and your language. You may have heard or observed that a particular school is casual. There is plenty of time to further assess the school culture, rules, and administrative standards and adjust your style *after* you've been hired. Better a little too formal than a little too casual for the interview.

6. When you arrive, remember that you are creating a first impression for everyone you see: the security guard, parents in the hallway or office, the secretaries, students, a visiting school board member, PTA president, and other potential employers or coworkers—before you even meet with the hiring committee. All encounters should give people evidence of your professionalism, friendliness, confidence, and poise. Meanwhile, you are getting a sense of what is called the "school climate" by seeing how various interactions occur in the school and if you feel it is a place for you.

7. Do your best to relax and "be yourself." If you know that your hands shake when you're nervous, fold them in front of yourself and don't attempt to pick up the coffee or water you've been offered. Give people a sense of your personality as you warm up. The committee wants to get a sense of what you will be like as a colleague and you want them to know who you are—and choose you over others. You won't be happy for long in a place where you can't be yourself.

8. Just as the committee members are "sizing you up" as a potential colleague and teacher of their students, you should be alert to the social dynamics in the room. Do you feel comfortable or intimidated? Are people treating you and each other with respect? Does the principal or other leader seem to have positive relationships with the committee members? One effective way to convey your "people skills" while you assess body language and other indicators is to be generous with your eye contact. When responding to a question, share your eye contact with all in the room, rather than responding only to the individual who posed the question.

> **hiring committee**
> Designated group of people who hold authority in the school and decide which potential teacher applicant to place in an open position or make appropriate recommendations to a principal or other administrator who makes the final decision.

9. Provide evidence that you are positive, respectful, and nonjudgmental. You may have had difficult, even terrible, situations with cooperating teachers, students, parents, and professors along the way. In response to a question that asks about a challenge, convey your understanding of multiple perspectives and the complexities of dealing with conflict. That's a person they will want to work with—not someone who seems quick to judge or blame others. Save the venting for your journal or friends.

10. Finally, be prepared to figure out what to say when you don't know what to say. You're a beginner and can't possibly know everything about curriculum, special programs, or how to handle a particular situation. If you're really thrown a curve ball, it's generally better to talk about your eagerness to learn more from your mentor, colleagues, or professional development than it is to pretend you know more than you do and be "found out" later, or to give an opinion that you regret after the interview.

Source: Courtesy of Elizabeth McDonald, New York University

How Will I Survive as a New Teacher?

The Critical First Year

Kelley Dawson Salas teaches fourth grade in Milwaukee, Wisconsin. She recalls when she began teaching:

> My alarm had not yet gone off, but I was wide awake. My stomach was in knots and I knew I would not be able to eat breakfast. I longed to turn over, go back to sleep, wait for the alarm, hit snooze.
>
> But there was no way. It was September, a school day, a few weeks into my first year of teaching. . . .
>
> I dragged myself out of bed and called a friend. My worries poured forth: I'm no good at this. It's too hard for me to learn the things I need to learn. There are so many jobs that would be easier and pay better. Finally, I called the question: Should I just walk away from this whole thing?[3]

Few teachers cannot identify with these words—the wide-awake moments, the nausea, the self-doubt, the question "Should I just walk away?" They all seem to go with the territory of entering one of the most rewarding, and most challenging, professions.

The first year in any new field of endeavor is usually difficult, especially so in teaching where you will have 20 or 30 or more constant critics all day long in addition to fellow teachers and supervisors. All the colleagues and routines are new. Other people seem to have knowledge and expectations that are not shared immediately. Fair or not, the new person is always being watched to see if he or she measures up. All the issues of being new in any job can be exacerbated in the teaching profession. As educational researchers Betty Achinstein and Steven Z. Athanases note in their book *Mentors in the Making: Developing New Leaders for New Teachers*, "Most teachers still experience the 'sink-or-swim' career introduction, isolated in their classrooms, unsupported by colleagues, with little power over decision making and few opportunities for learning." Recall the discussion in Chapter 1 in which researchers noted that between 40% and 50% of new teachers leave within the first five years of teaching. The numbers can be even higher in high-poverty, urban, and rural districts where the need for first-rate teachers is the greatest. You don't want to be one of those statistics.

Notes from the Field

What do you wish someone had told you before you began teaching?

"I wish someone had told me it's not about how smart you are in your graduate school courses—it's how you execute in your own classroom when you teach."

—*Nekia Wise, first-grade teacher*

More school districts are taking seriously the problems facing new teachers. The "sink-or-swim" model that used to be the norm is fast disappearing in many places. However, not all **new teacher induction** and **mentoring** programs are equal. In many places, too little attention is paid to new teachers' needs to continue learning and the goals of the induction program are far from clear. Achinstein and Athanases see two quite different approaches to new teacher induction. Too many districts, they note, offer induction programs that focus on helping new teachers adjust to the status quo:

If one believes that the new teacher is a survivor in a challenging context, trying to impart basic knowledge to well-managed kids, then mentoring entails helping novices adjust to new environments, learn routines, keep management plans in place, and learn some tips and techniques of teaching. . . . These conceptions identify the purposes of induction as enculturating new teachers into the current system to help novices fit into their new environments, rather than critiquing or challenging existing schooling practices.

For most novices, there are certainly days on which this approach seems like it might be enough. Learning some tips and fitting in can seem appealing. In teaching, however, "survival" is never sufficient. Achinstein and Athanases ask for much more:

Recent reforms necessitate different norms than those identified in the survival models. These call for teachers to be change agents, reflective practitioners, collaborative colleagues, and lifelong learners—educators who are student-centered, equity-focused, and constructivist. These calls challenge the status quo of teaching and schooling and, therefore, of mentoring.

Idealistic as they may sometimes sound, only these kinds of norms for new teachers (or for any teachers) can move them from being cogs in a wheel to professional educators who take charge of their work and hold themselves accountable for the success of all their students. These norms are also absolutely essential if one is to resist some of the pressures to merely conform to the kind of deadening, highly scripted curriculum that is found in some schools today.[4]

One of the most effective means of addressing this problem has been the development of a robust system of teacher mentoring. In many school districts, every new teacher is assigned a senior colleague to act as a mentor. In some districts, the school or the school district selects the mentor. In other cases, the teacher union plays a major role. Some colleges and universities that prepare teachers have developed new programs to stay in touch with their graduates and to get them actively involved in the mentoring process. Recent research sponsored by the Carnegie Corporation of New York has demonstrated that multiple modes of mentoring—from the school in which the novice teacher is employed and from the university from which she or he graduated—may be the most effective. Some issues are so school specific that only someone intimately involved with the school can be an effective mentor; for other issues, especially in those moments of failure and frustration that every teacher experiences, a mentor who is a little more distant and not an employee of the school or district can be more helpful.[5]

> **mentoring**
> Act of serving as an advisor and trusted guide to a less experienced person; often part of a new teacher induction program.
>
> **new teacher induction**
> System of support and guidance offered to novice teachers in the beginning of their careers.

> **CONNECTIONS ➜←**
> In Chapter 9 we explored mentoring as a key component of the professional issues that every teacher needs to consider.

Staying, Surviving, Thriving, Contributing

Kelley Dawson Salas's friend gave her some important advice for the first year of teaching: "Don't add to your difficulties by beating up on yourself. Let up a little so you have the time and the space to become a good teacher." She fought the tendency to become isolated by taking advantage of professional development activities, collaborating with colleagues at her school, and joining with other education activists to engage in issues that were important to her. She also received plenty of less helpful advice of the "you need to be a drill sergeant" variety. Through it all, she created space and support

NEW TEACHER SURVIVAL GUIDE

Antonio Ramírez, a middle and high school teacher in Milwaukee, Wisconsin, developed a number of tips for how to survive as a new teacher—many things he learned the hard way or just needed to persevere through until he "found his groove." Although he wrote this piece for teachers of color, his advice can apply to all new teachers who are similarly learning to "find their groove":

1. **Communicate with students in nontraditional ways.** Your relationships with students are the best part about being a teacher. Every day, talk with students about things that have nothing to do with the classroom. Know what they like. Ask about and get to know their families. Attend a birthday party, quinceañera, or poetry reading after school.
2. **Don't fear discipline.** Don't think you can be a classroom teacher without learning how to discipline. Some new teachers command an interesting mix of respect and fear from the minute they step in a classroom. Some, including myself, don't. If you are like me, be aware of it and be aware that you can change it. Ask those teachers that discipline out of love and respect if you can sit in and watch them. The best way to learn how to teach well is sitting and watching an excellent teacher.
3. **Educate yourself.** Although it's difficult during the first hectic years as a teacher, don't leave all the theories you studied in teacher education courses back at school. Theories are tools that help reflect on the past and prepare for future experiences. Hours of sleep I lost by reading Paulo Freire, Gloria Ladson-Billings, Herbert Kohl, and bell hooks were more than made up for by a rejuvenated sense of purpose and energy.
4. **Have realistic expectations for yourself.** Throughout my first year, I'd feel like a master teacher one day and the next I'd be seriously considering what other career I should pursue after quitting. But a piece of advice that kept me sane through the first year of teaching came from a fellow teacher who said, "Your first year's goal is to survive. Nothing more." While this may seem a bit scary, it definitely helped to remember that simple goal on late Sunday nights when I had a mountain of papers and piles of unfinished lesson plans on my desk.

5. **Get to know your allies.** Meet other young teachers and like-minded teachers and staff as soon as possible. In my first year of teaching, I didn't have a support network of other teachers. Preoccupied with crafting the perfect lesson plan and keeping up with grading, I had lost contact with most of my university classmates. I didn't go out of my way to establish strong friendships with other teachers in my new school. As a result, I struggled in silence my first year.

6. **Don't be afraid to ask.** Some schools have a natural culture of "being in it together," where lesson plans, resources, and sympathy are spread around liberally. Most don't. Many new teachers in the latter situation fall into the trap of thinking they'll look incapable if they have to ask a question or for advice. In my experience, the reverse is true. The most successful teachers share, borrow, and steal colleagues' ideas and inspiration.

7. **Know your union.** Teachers' unions have also made consistent calls for increased support for new teachers and better recruitment of teachers of color. Teachers active in our union were committed, serious educators who fought for students and took time to mentor younger teachers.

8. **Take time to reflect.** Teaching has emotional, physical, and psychological aspects that are overwhelming, especially in your first years. Be sure to take time to truly reflect on successes and failures in the classroom and to congratulate yourself on your achievements. Think about your most difficult students and develop strategies on how to get through to them.

9. **Take time to not reflect.** The first years of teaching can easily take over your life. In my first year, I worked seven days a week, usually until nine or ten every night, and was miserable. Remember to continue to make time for parts of life that have nothing to do with school and that you truly enjoy. Stay connected with family and friends. Doing things to relax and take your mind off teaching will allow you to return to the classroom refreshed.

10. **Teach for at least two years.** I remember going to school just as the sun was coming up and being jealous of construction workers, bus drivers, and cashiers who didn't have to face classrooms full of students and desks full of papers every morning. I seriously considered quitting several times the first year. But by the end of my second year, I started to imagine myself as a truly good teacher. I was engaging more students in serious conversations about the meanings of race, history, and culture. I felt like I was really becoming a teacher.

 DID YOU KNOW?

Acknowledging how much support first-year teachers need, Texas A&M University–Corpus Christi developed a program called SOS: Strategies of Success, designed to support beginning teachers. The program has been working: The school conducted a study in 2005 to determine how likely program participants were to stay in teaching.[6] For the three cohort groups studied, SOS program participants had a 98% retention rate, compared to 88% for graduates of the teacher education program who did not participate in SOS, and 70% for new teachers across the state of Texas.

for herself that allowed her to do much more than survive. She knows her own doubts and shortcomings, but she is much better at coping. According to Salas,

Whenever I feel overwhelmed by the lack of support, I fight the urge to leave teaching. Instead, I try to speak up about what teachers need to succeed.

As I struggle toward my vision of good teaching, I remind myself of what I have accomplished so far. I am less isolated and have close ties with other progressive teachers. I am more confident about developing curriculum and a teaching style that reflects my politics. I still need time and guidance, but some of the conditions are in place for me to someday become the teacher I want to be.

I have a long way to go. But I'm on my way.[7]

This attitude, and not an attempt to be a "hero," is the key to success for nearly all teachers.

In the first **Reading** for this chapter, Sonia Nieto offers her own thoughts and those of other teachers she has interviewed in *What Keeps Teachers Going?* Nieto says that, although teaching is hard work, it is also possible to get good at it quite soon. As you face difficulties in teaching, especially in the beginning, it is important to remember Junia Yearwood's sense that the "light in [her students'] eyes" keeps her going after 20 years of city teaching and Mary Cowhey's report that a combination of parents, principals, students, colleagues, and the opportunity to continue her own life as a student help to keep her going. In reading these stories and many others, two conclusions quickly become clear. First, there is no magic bullet that sustains teachers year after year in the sometimes very difficult work of teaching. Second, a number of recurring themes—most of all, taking delight in your students, finding other teachers who can be a support network, and finding a school that is supportive of your approach to the profession—are absolutely essential if you are to survive and thrive in teaching over the long term.

Former principal and current teacher educator Elizabeth McDonald has some suggestions for surviving during that difficult first year and beyond. Among other things, she recommends:

- Maintain a life and interests outside of school. As important as it is to work hard and maintain a thoughtful commitment to your work, it is also important to your physical and mental well-being that you set boundaries, take breaks, and exercise.
- Maintain a sense of humor and perspective.
- Keep a journal as an outlet for your frustration and as grist for reflection.
- Network and find other teachers and all the resources available for teachers through the Internet.

Generations of teachers have found ways to survive and flourish in their careers while also maintaining a full life outside school. In the end, it is all a matter of balance and finding ways to maintain enthusiasm—for teaching and for life.

What Kind of Teacher Do I Want to Be?

During that challenging first year of teaching, merely surviving as a teacher and overcoming fears may seem like quite enough. In the end, however, every aspiring teacher wants to do more—to be not just an adequate teacher but an excellent one. As Robert Fried says in his book *The Passionate Teacher: A Practical Guide*, "good enough" is never really good enough. Any teacher truly worthy of his or her profession wants to be remembered as more than "a 'pretty good teacher' who made chemistry or algebra or tenth-grade English 'sort of interesting.'" We all want to be like the teachers Fried describes who "opened up the world of the mind to some students who had no one else to make them feel that they were capable of doing great things with test tubes, trumpets, trigonometry, or T. S. Eliot." Fried describes science teacher Maria Ortiz, a middle school teacher in Hartford, Connecticut, who told him: "I believe I make a difference not only by helping kids connect math and science to their lives, but also in understanding how to reach their goals in life—how to be somebody."[8]

The teacher who has helped us actually learn something *and* who also helped us develop and reach life goals is the teacher we all remember . . . and this is the teacher we also want to be.

In the final **Reading**, Jacqueline Jordan Irvine describes one of the key elements in teacher greatness. As Irvine reports, more and more policy makers are calling for the preparation of what are now called "caring and competent teachers." The trick, as she notes, is to be clear about what the words *caring* and *competent* mean and then prepare yourself to meet that standard.

In "Caring, Competent Teachers in Complex Classrooms," Irvine describes two very different teachers, both of whom in her judgment meet the high standard she would set for being a caring and competent teacher. There is Ms. Little, the White teacher who has a strong social consciousness that leads her to define being a caring teacher as well as a competent teacher as making sure that "her students pass the English Advanced Placement (AP) exam so that they can succeed in college and leave behind the desolation of the urban community in which they live." Little is clear that her caring and her competence drive her to focus on her students' academic success. As she says at one point, "I'm not their damn mama, I'm their English teacher."

The other teacher that Irvine describes, Ms. Moultrie, has a very different definition of both care and competence. As a caring, African American teacher working with mostly African American students, Ms. Moultrie, who is known as

Mama Moultrie, sees her role very much as a surrogate parent. She uses her classroom as "a pulpit from which she uses literature to teach values, racial pride and uplift, and hard work." The focus of all her work is on preparing her students for college *and* for life.

Irvine regards both Moultie and Little as models of caring, competent teachers; she believes there is no one definition of a caring, competent, or excellent teacher. She asks, "Is it possible to determine if one is more caring or more competent than the other?" The answer, it seems, is no. Both women are caring, effective teachers in spite of their different approaches to their work.

Part of being successfully caring *and* competent may be the third element that Robert Fried introduces into the equation: passion. Observing Maria Ortiz, and then other elementary, middle, and high school teachers, Fried notices that it is hard to name the unique essence of the best of them:

> Our inability to translate great stories into a useful pedagogy is due to our encountering something that people find hard to identify, talk about, or hold onto intellectually. I believe that what we are dealing with is passion.

Fried gives many examples of the kind of passionate teaching he is talking about. Irvine's Little and Moultrie certainly each have passion. Perhaps it is the combination of all three attributes—caring, competence, and passion—that makes for great teaching.

If both Irvine and Fried agree on anything, it is that the best teachers can be very different from each other. Neither author puts forth one model of great teaching. Moultrie and Little are very different teachers. Ortiz and the other teachers who appear in Fried's book are very different from each other. But all these teachers bring something special to their work. They know their subject, they know how to teach it, and they care deeply that their students will learn, succeed, and prosper—in school and beyond. Perhaps the right word for this is, indeed, passion.

Teachable Moment
TOP TEACHERS

What makes a top teacher? Is it dedication to students? Creativity in the classroom? Perseverance in engaging the community? It's all this and more. Since 1952, the National Teacher of the Year Program has honored exemplary teachers for their work. A committee of leaders in the field of education choose the National Teacher of the Year from the winners of State Teacher of the Year awards.

Sean McComb was selected as the 2014 National Teacher of the Year. McComb has spent the last eight years teaching English at Patapsco High School and Center for the Arts in Baltimore, Maryland. McComb reflects some of the same commitment to community reflected by John Dewey in Chapter 12's **Readings**. McComb writes: "My teaching is built on the belief that relationships and engagement can turn challenges into opportunities for excellence for all students. As we embrace that truth, we help awaken students to their full potential and the possibility to live out the American dream." McComb also takes his commitment to relationships and engagement to his faculty colleagues. He serves as a coach and trainer for new teachers as well as a curriculum writer for the school system.

Another English teacher, Rebecca Lynn Mieliwocki from Burbank, California, was Teacher of the Year for 2012. A middle school teacher, Mieliwocki reflected Robert Fried's sense of passionate teaching when she wrote: "Students learn best when they have the most enthusiastic, engaged teachers possible. I firmly believe that teachers must be held accountable for their students' success, from helping them meet personal or school-wide learning goals to achieving on district and state level assessments." For this teacher, teacher accountability, student learning, and passionate teaching are all part of the same mix.

Alex Kajitani was recognized as 2009's California Teacher of the Year and one of the top four finalists for the National Teacher of the Year award. Known as the Rappin' Mathematician, Kajitani's major focus is bridging the achievement gap that occurs in low-income schools. Realizing that his middle-school students could remember the words to their favorite rap songs, but not rules for improper fractions, Kajitani decided to craft raps for math fundamentals. The idea caught on and he began creating more raps, eventually putting together a "Routine Rap" that reminded students of the daily classroom routine and why it was important. Students are required to create their own math raps, as well, and often create and film their own music videos for the raps. As an excellent communicator and creative thinker, Kajitani reached out to students who otherwise might have given up on school. As a result, the math scores in his classrooms have shot up and are now above average for the district.

Washington state music educator Andrea Peterson received the 2007 National Teacher of the Year award, which was unusual because winners are not often art specialists. Peterson's teaching skills, however, far outweighed any doubts about her receiving the award. When Peterson began teaching in the Granite Falls School District in 1997, the music program had little funding and few resources—the secondary band owned only six percussion instruments, two of which were broken. To provide for her students, she lobbied the school board and administration for extra funds. After canvassing parents and the community, Peterson was able to revitalize the elementary and high school programs with more than $55,000 for new music equipment. Students now perform in state and national music competitions and can choose from a number of school programs, such as elementary choir, marching or jazz band, and high school chorus. Peterson believes in the ability of music to aid with other subject areas and, as such, has implemented cross-curriculum classes. In one of these classes, students are asked to create and perform an interpretive musical based on a book they have read in another class. Peterson knows that music can unlock a student's potential, whether by providing self-confidence and creativity, reinforcing mathematical concepts, or giving them discipline.

Finally, Kimberly Oliver received the National Teacher of the Year award in 2006. In her Maryland kindergarten classroom, Oliver holds the philosophy that every student learns in different ways and her teaching style must adapt to each. In a school where nine out of 10 students qualify for free or reduced-cost meals and three-fourths speak a language other than English at home, Oliver has had to adapt her teaching style to a variety of learning styles and challenges. She believes that for students to achieve they must have the support and compassion of an entire community. When she became a teacher, Oliver was faced with a school in danger of being restructured due to declining academic performance. She built up a professional learning community for staff that emphasized collaboration and began reaching out to parents with reading events, such as "Books and Supper Night," and regular phone calls. Through her creation of several programs that focused on consistency in curriculum, the school improved substantially and in 2001 had the greatest percentage increase in test scores in the school system. No Child Left Behind requirements were met, or exceeded, at the school from 2003 to 2005. Because of Oliver's persistence and determination, an entire community became involved with their children's education.

So, what do all of these educators have in common? What makes them top teachers? They all noticed problems and found unique solutions to them. They all used creative and persistent means to get their communities and administrations involved. In the end, however, despite differences in location, grade levels, and socioeconomic factors, these educators stayed focused entirely on one thing—their students.[9]

Questions

- As an aspiring teacher, what can you learn from reading about and following the careers of successful teachers such as those described above?
- Do you think these teachers established personal teaching philosophies early in their careers that helped them become "top teachers"? Or does a teaching philosophy develop over time? Or a combination of both?

Arriving in your first classroom, milestone though it is, is only the first of many steps. Much more will remain to be done to achieve the kind of professional mastery that makes a teacher feel comfortable in front of a class, confident in the management of the room, and sure that the students are learning what they need to be learning. Much more beyond that is needed to be the kind of teacher every teacher yearns to be—the caring, competent, and passionate teacher who is remembered for making a difference in the lives of many, many young people. Continuing to grow in that direction is part of the challenge, and the joy, of teaching.

We began this book by asking you, the aspiring teacher, to join in a conversation involving a series of questions that many people considering a career in teaching ask their instructors, their classmates, their families and peers, and themselves. As we've explored potential answers to these questions, we have read and reviewed a range of material from many different authors. Some of the authors agree with each other; others disagree sharply. In many instances, they agree with certain nuances but find other aspects that set their beliefs apart. Researchers and educators can look at the same data and often come up with different interpretations or solutions.

You were also asked to reflect carefully on your own education—all those years you spent in K–12 classrooms observing teachers and experiencing schools as institutions with their own unique customs and values. You also may have had the opportunity to observe classrooms more recently, examining what you remember, have read, or thought about what goes on in schools and what *should* go on in schools, and how schools are different from each other. You now have a more informed understanding of teaching and schooling and the role of professional educators. This experience of reading, observing, and pondering should leave you with a much clearer sense of your own educational philosophy and your own views about teaching. You should also be in a much stronger position to answer what are probably the most critical questions for you at the conclusion of this book:

- What kind of teacher do I want to be?
- How can I best prepare myself to be that kind of teacher?

Hopefully you have also engaged with other questions:

- Based on what you read, what surprised you the most about teaching?
- What events or statistics were the most eye-opening?
- What topics or issues had you not heard of prior to taking this course?
- Did your opinions change after reading different viewpoints? For which issues and why?
- Which authors or researchers inspired you the most? Whose philosophies resonated with you and seemed to mimic your own beliefs about teaching and education? Which ones did you disagree with the most?
- Most important, what questions do you have that weren't addressed in the text?

Keep the dialogue going and look for those answers in your next courses and your career. The answers to these questions are yours and yours alone and will continue to evolve in the years to come. It is hoped that you feel more prepared and empowered to embrace that process as you seek to find and develop your own answers and personal philosophies about teaching and your role and responsibilities as an educator.

✓ CHAPTER REVIEW

- How do I get my first teaching job?

  Each state grants teaching licenses (or certification) based on the completion of a required course of study, usually in a university-based teacher preparation program. Most states also require applicants to pass a state examination, the most widely used of which is the edTPA review. After receiving a teaching license, you will apply directly to a school district for a teaching position and may be interviewed by someone at the district as well as school level. Only by moving through that two-part process—getting your state license and then being selected by a school or district—will you reach your goal of a full-time teaching position in a specific school.

- How will I survive as a new teacher?

  As for anyone entering a new career, the initial year can be challenging, and teaching can be more challenging than many fields. Because of the high attrition rate, schools are providing more resources, such as mentoring, to support new teachers and help them transition into the profession. Although there is no one set of guidelines for how to survive and thrive as a teacher, every successful teacher has found his or her own way to balance the challenges of the profession with the goal of providing the most supportive environment and the most effective education possible for all students.

- What kind of teacher do I want to be?

  A number of adjectives could be used to describe a great teacher or great teaching. Just about everyone entering the profession aspires to become that kind of teacher or to deliver that kind of teaching. As described by Robert Fried and Jacqueline Jordan Irvine, it is most likely a combination of caring, competence, and passion that makes for great teaching.

Readings

How Will I Survive as a New Teacher?
From *WHAT KEEPS TEACHERS GOING?*

AUTHOR: SONIA NIETO

Sonia Nieto has spent her life in education, teaching, writing, talking with other teachers. She is among the leaders in the field of multicultural education, but she also cares deeply about the lives of teachers and values their voices much more than the opinions of those who want to tell teachers what they should be doing. In her book What Keeps Teachers Going? *she asks, "How do you stick with it, given that teaching is such hard work?" Her own answers and those of the many teachers with whom she spoke and corresponded provide encouraging answers to this basic question.*

From that day in 1965 when I first stepped into the fourth-grade classroom where I would start my student teaching, I have experienced the exhilaration, anguish, satisfaction, uncertainty, frustration, and sheer joy that typify teaching. Years later, when I began teaching teachers, I fell in love with the profession all over again. Working with teachers who would in turn prepare young people for the future seemed to me a life worth living. I am as certain today as I was then that this is true.

Yet I also am perplexed about why teachers remain in teaching, why they dedicate their lives to a profession ostensibly honored but generally disrespected by the public in a climate increasingly hostile to public education and fixated on rigid conceptions of "standards" and accountability. There is nothing wrong with standards; on the contrary, it is high time that this concept was used in reference to urban public schools. But unfortunately, the call for standards too often results in a climate that does little besides vilify teachers and their students. This is a punitive climate that may have ominous repercussions not only for many students but also for talented teachers, those who care most deeply about students.

Experience alone, as John Dewey reminds us, is hollow without reflection. My own evolution as a teacher might not have resulted in any particular insights were it not for the ongoing opportunities I've had to think about my experiences as part of the larger context in which education takes place. In what follows, I share my thinking as a teacher and teacher educator and the lessons I've learned along the way. . . .

Lessons Learned Along the Way

I became a teacher in 1966. But I am not now the same teacher I was in 1966, or in 1975, or 1990. As we all do, I have changed a great deal over the years, and so have my practices and ideas about teaching. These changes did not occur without warning; they have been responses to experiences that I have had as a teacher, teacher educator, mentor, mother, grandmother, scholar, and researcher. I have lately become more introspective about where I began, where I am now, and why and how I have changed along the way.

Teaching Is Hard Work. I studied elementary education in college knowing that I wanted to teach young children. But my first assignment was to Junior High School 278, a troubled school in Ocean Hill/Brownsville in Brooklyn. . . . I was one of 35 new teachers in a teaching staff totaling about 75. . . . I was young and naïve. As the only Puerto Rican staff member in the school, I thought I'd have a fairly easy time of it. I hadn't expected discipline to be so arduous; after all, I had been a student at similar schools. Yet the kids I faced every day seemed angrier and more oppositional than what I remembered. Most of all, I was not prepared for the hopelessness that permeated the school on the part of the students and staff. I often went home and cried.

Becoming a Good Teacher Takes Time. But I didn't give up. I vowed to improve my teaching and to create an affirming climate in my classroom. I worked hard to develop strong and positive relationships with my students and their families. . . . I also sought out teachers who believed in the young people, and I talked with them about my hopes and fears. . . . I knew I had a long way to go, but by that first winter, I began to notice a change: My students were listening and paying more attention, and they appeared to be more engaged in their learning.

Social Justice Is Part of Teaching. Two years after I began teaching in that junior high school in Brooklyn, I found out about an elementary school in the Bronx that was beginning an experimental program in bilingual education, only the second such school in the nation. . . . I was enthusiastic but wary. . . . For example, I had many questions about the feasibility of bilingual education (after all, I had never been in a bilingual program and I had done well, hadn't I?) and about the school's almost militant support for parental and family involvement. Within a short time, however, I saw with my own eyes the value of both, and I became one of the staunchest advocates for these innovations. I realized that although I had "made it," most others had not; I was one of the lucky ones. . . . After having come face to face with the effects of inequality at JHS 278, I began to think more seriously about what social justice meant for public education.

There Is No Level Playing Field. Given my own experiences growing up in a struggling, working-class Puerto Rican family in New York City in the 1940s and 1950s, I thought I knew firsthand about inequality. But my work as a teacher with my students whose lives were far more difficult than mine had ever been opened my eyes to the impact of daily, unrelenting injustice and hopelessness. I saw that successful student learning was not simply a matter of positive interactions between individual teachers and their students. I began to understand that conditions outside the control of most classroom teachers, including inequality in schools and outside them, prevented many students from learning.

Education Is Politics. "Education is always political" is a statement that the late Paulo Freire made famous in his landmark book, *Pedagogy of the Oppressed*. A few years after he wrote those words, he pointed out even more directly the relationship between education and politics. "This is a great discovery," he wrote, "education is politics!" And he added, "The teacher has to ask, What kind of politics am I doing in the classroom? That is, in favor of whom am I being a teacher?" These words became riveting to me as my own political awareness developed. . . . to work with future teachers, and to help them understand teaching as political and ethical work was exhilarating.

Teacher Autobiographies

A number of years ago, I began to experiment with what I called *teacher autobiographies*. In my work with teachers I asked them to write about how their backgrounds or experiences have influenced their decision to pursue a career in teaching. [Two of the responses to Nieto's request for autobiographies follow.]

My Journey—Junia Yearwood

I was born on the Caribbean Island of Trinidad and was raised and nurtured by my paternal grandmother and aunts on the island of Barbados. My environment instilled in me a strong identity as a woman and as a person of African descent. The value of education and the importance of being able to read and write became clear and urgent when I became fully aware of the history of my ancestors. The story of the enslavement of Africans and the horrors they were forced to endure repulsed and angered me, but the aspect of slavery that most intrigued me was the systematic denial of literacy to my ancestors. . . .

This revelation made my destiny clear. I had to be a teacher.

My resolve to someday become a teacher was strengthened by my experiences with teachers who had significant and lasting positive effects on my personal and academic growth. I gradually came to realize that the teachers whose classes I was eager to get to and in whose classes I excelled were the ones who treated and nurtured me as an individual, a special person. They pushed, challenged, and cajoled me to study and perform to my full ability. The believed in me; they identified not only my weaknesses but also my strengths and talents. They encouraged me to think, question, and enter into the "conversation" on an equal intellectual footing. They respected my thoughts and opinions and they showed me that they cared. In addition, and just as important, they looked like me. They shared my ancestry, my culture, and my history. They were my role models. . . .

The "light in their eyes," that moment when students are fully engaged and excited about learning, that Sonia Nieto has written about energizes, revitalizes, and keeps me focused. I share my students' successes, their challenges, their hopes, and their dreams. My commitment and passion for learning and teaching wax and wane, sparkle and flicker, but stubbornly keep burning like an eternal flame, a flame that I hope burns bright and helps guide my students on their academic and personal journey through life. In the words of Robert Frost, "I am not a teacher. I am an awakener."

A Way to Live in the World—Mary Cowhey

Teaching is a way to live in the world. I just can't see myself living in this world if I am not doing something positive. Size and effectiveness do not matter too much to me, if I nurture one plant or a large garden, if I help one person well, if I reach 20 children and their families in a year or thousands, what is important is that I do it and do it well, that I do it with heart. The process of teaching, of organizing, of caring, of nurturing—I believe it makes me a better person. . . .

I am thinking of your title/idea, what keeps teachers going in spite of everything. One thing that strikes me as I write this is the importance of the relationships with parents, with families. (By parents I mean all of their loving adults and caregivers). Children are such a mystery. . . . From the start of each school year, even before the school doors open, I work to build that relationship with families. Whether it is done by home visits or arranging some unhurried conversations with families early in the year, that foundation is vital. . . . I care about these families.

What else keeps me going in spite of everything? My principal. I have the most wonderful principal in the world. . . . She creates a climate in our school that allows me to teach and grow the way I do. . . .

Intellectual work—of course there is that. . . . New ideas, new questions to find answers to, new people to ask and find out, new problems to solve, new angles to see things from, motivation to do something that I might not have been passionate about before. . . .

Children. I teach my students like I want my children taught. I want them challenged and loved. . . . They need good teaching, the best. That drives me on.

Good teachers. I often think of teachers who really loved their subject or who really loved me or listened to me or encouraged me or took me seriously or pushed me to do my best work. . . .

[After many such conversations, Nieto concludes her book.]

It is by now a truism that the profession of teaching, although enormously significant in the lives of so many people, is terribly undervalued, undercompensated, and underrespected. We see signs for this everywhere: Teachers take second jobs as cashiers in convenience stores and clean houses during their summer vacations; they spend hundreds and sometimes thousands of dollars of their own money each year on classroom materials; and they spend even more on their continuing education, usually with no compensation from their school districts. Yet the current policy climate at both state and national levels is permeated by a profound disrespect for teachers, especially teachers in urban schools, and for the children they teach. Most politicians, for instance, although they speak often about education, rarely step foot in schools. They tend to stress only accountability, and the tone they use to speak about teachers is sometimes disparaging and unforgiving. But no first-year signing bonus, no teacher test, and no high-stakes test can take the place of a true, enduring respect for teachers. In fact, these things often get in the way of retaining good teachers because they question the intelligence, ability, and commitment of teachers.

One thing we learned from the inquiry group project that we are certain about is this: *No amount of decontextualized "best practices" will keep teachers engaged or committed.* The current discourse in education reform focuses on developing "best practices" as the antidote to both teacher burnout and student underachievement. Our work departs in an essential way from this stance. We have come to the conclusion that it is only when teachers are treated as professionals and intellectuals who care deeply about their students and their craft that they will be enticed to remain in the profession and that new teachers will be attracted to join. We hope that our work illustrates that, rather than a focus on dehumanized "best practices," we need to focus on students and those who best teach them. . . .

Teachers such as Junia need to be supported by teacher educators, administrators, school committees, politicians, and citizens who care about and support with words, deeds, and money the work of schools in our society. If we are really serious about expanding the opportunities for students in our urban public schools, rather than concentrating on high-stakes tests, we should be focusing our efforts on high standards, high expectations, and high finance.

This is the challenge that lies ahead. If we are as concerned about education as we say we are, then we need to do more to change the conditions faced by teachers, especially those who work in underfinanced and largely abandoned urban schools. We need to support those teachers who love their students, who find creative ways to teach them, and who do so under difficult circumstances. We need to celebrate teachers who are as excited about their own learning as they are about the learning of their students. And we need to champion those teachers who value their students' families and find respectful ways to work with them. Above all, we need to expect all teachers to do these things. The children in our public schools deserve no less.

Questions

1. Nieto says, "We need to celebrate teachers who are excited about their own learning." Think back to your own teachers—in school and in more informal settings—and think of one who was especially excited about learning. What difference did he or she make in your life?

2. Imagine that you have been teaching for three years. What kind of letter would you want to be able to write in answer to the question "What keeps teachers going?"

Source: Sonia Nieto. *What Keeps Teachers Going?* New York: Teachers College Press, 2003, pp. 9–15, 26–28, 101–105, 128–129.

What Kind of Teacher Do I Want to Be?

From "CARING, COMPETENT TEACHERS IN COMPLEX CLASSROOMS"

AUTHOR: JACQUELINE JORDAN IRVINE

Jacqueline Jordan Irvine is the Charles Howard Candler Professor of Urban Education Emerita at Emory University in Atlanta. Through her leadership of the CULTURES program at Emory, and in more than a dozen books and innumerable speeches and articles, she has become a national voice for insisting that excellence in teaching involves "seeing with a cultural eye" and respecting and engaging all students by understanding the full diversity of today's students.

Policymakers and teacher educators frequently refer to the National Commission on Teaching and America's Future (NCTAF) recommendation that every child deserves a competent teacher (Darling-Hammond, 1997a). Recently, the descriptor *caring* was added to the call for competent teachers, meaning that our students need, not just competent teachers, but *caring*, competent teachers. I believe, however, that the appeal for caring and competent teachers does not unearth the complexities of teaching, particularly in urban, culturally diverse classrooms. Educating educators is a daunting, persistent challenge. Unless we understand the complexity of the task and articulate a convincing mission in carefully crafted language, words such as *care* and *competence* easily will be reduced to being used in laudable yet shallow clichés and homilies.

No one would disagree that teacher education programs should produce caring, competent teachers, and we are challenged to train significant numbers of these teachers in a relatively short period of time. If we solely focus on the absolute number of teachers needed, we may note that demographers have informed us that school systems will have a demand for 2 million caring, competent teachers during the coming decade. Certainly, colleges of education will be unable to prepare enough teachers to fill these projected vacancies. There are only 1,300 teacher education programs in the nation, and one half of all graduates will not be teaching 4 years after they graduate (Olsen, 2000). Even if districts are successful in recruiting 2 million new teachers (which is questionable), more than 30% of beginning teachers will leave within their first 5 years. According to the National Center for Education Statistics (NCES) (1997), the situation is even more complex than these remarkable figures reveal:

- Forty-four percent of all schools do not have any teachers of color on their faculty.
- Teacher shortages do not exist in all subject matter fields. There are acute needs in science, mathematics, English for speakers of other languages (ESOL), and special education.
- Wealthy schools have more applicants than they need.
- Urban, culturally diverse, low-income schools, even those that offer so-called combat pay; magnet schools; and other innovative structural configurations have many vacancies and cannot attract and retain certified and experienced teachers.

Therefore, what seems to be a rather benign and commendable goal—preparing caring, competent teachers—is laden with issues of definition, interpretation, and assessment. As we know, the devil is in the details. First, I will address the complexity of the issue of care.

And Still We Rise: The Trials and Triumphs of Twelve Gifted Inner-City High School Students, written by a journalist (Corwin, 2000), illustrates the complexity of defining caring, competent teachers. There are two veteran caring, competent English teachers in the inner-city African American school of which Corwin writes. One is a White teacher, Ms. Little, who has a strong social consciousness and believes that her students' race and family income are irrelevant. The other equally caring, competent teacher is an African American woman, Ms. Moultrie, who is affectionately called "Mama Moultrie" by her students. Moultrie assumes the role of a surrogate parent and her classroom resembles a pulpit from which she uses literature to teach values, racial pride and uplift, and hard work. Little believes that her mission is to help her student pass the English Advanced Placement (AP) exam so that they can succeed in college and leave behind the desolation of the urban community in which they live. Little believes that Moultrie talks too much about race and social inequities and too little about essay structure and thesis development. She does not see herself in a parental role. "I'm not their damn mama," Little says, "I'm their English teacher" (p. 95). Moultrie responds to Little's criticism that she spends too little time teaching content and too much on preaching by proclaiming that she is preparing Black students not merely for college, but for life.

These two caring and competent teachers have different philosophies about their personal and professional roles as teachers, their mission, efficacy, practice, beliefs, students, and the communities in which they work. Is it possible to determine if one is more caring or more competent than the other? How will we decide? By what criteria will we measure degrees of competence and care? To answer these questions, an examination of the concepts of care and competence is required.

Complexity of the Issue of Care

I believe that teaching is synonymous with caring. Care as an essential quality of effective teachers was affirmed in a Gallup poll that developed an extensive personality profile of successful urban teachers (Van Horn, 1999). Responses in the poll revealed that of the 11 qualities presented, commitment and dedication were especially important. But what does it mean to say that a teacher cares? How do you identify a caring teacher? Who should define it? Can you teach it? Should we use care as an entrance or exit criteria in teacher education programs? And more important, how do you measure care?

Caring comes in many forms and manifests itself in different ways. In describing her favorite teacher, an African American student in my research (Irvine, 2002a) used the typical adjectives, *caring, sympathetic, dedicated, friendly*, and *funny*. But the student quickly added, "My teacher has all these wonderful qualities, but don't be fooled. She was in control."

The student proceeded to describe a particular incident in which everyone in the class failed a test. The student recalled:

The word passed quickly that Mrs. Washington was "P-Oed." When we walked into her class Mrs. Washington said, "Well, I guess that you heard that you have ticked me off." One student tried to explain and she told him to be quiet. Mrs. Washington ordered one student to open the windows because it was "getting ready to get hot in here." Then on the spot Mrs. Washington made up a rap about self-esteem, confidence, and hard work. We were clapping and laughing (and still scared) but Mrs. Washington had made her point.

Another African American student in my research (Irvine, 2002a) wrote the following excerpt about teachers:

I wish school had been more challenging for me. Some students don't like strict teachers. But I do. When I say strict I mean in the academics. They stress that you must complete all assignments. And when you do not complete the assignments, they aren't just nice to you and let you just slide by.

These students did not equate caring with being nice or friendly. None of them felt that they had been silenced or demonstrated any resentment toward their teachers. Caring for these students means firm, fair discipline, high standards and expectations, and an unwillingness on the part of teachers to let students "slide by." These "warm demanders" (Kleinfeld, 1975) are caring, competent educators whose public "take no prisoner" demeanor may lead some to conclude incorrectly that such teachers do not care about their students. It has been my experience that naïve classroom observers and evaluators often misinterpret the caring in what appears on the surface to be rather harsh disciplinary tactics.

My colleague and I provided the following example of warm-demander caring in an article that we wrote about why so few African American teachers are certified by the National Board for Professional Teaching Standards (NBPTS):

"That's enough of your nonsense, Darius. Your story does not make sense. I told you time and time again that you must stick to the theme I gave you. Now sit down." Darius, a first grader trying desperately to tell his story, proceeds slowly to his seat with his head hung low. The other children snicker as he looks embarrassed and hurt. What kind of teacher could say such words to a child? Most would agree that the teacher would not meet any local or national performance standards.

Ironically, Irene Washington, an African American teacher with 23 years of experience, is a recognized model teacher in her predominantly African American school and community. Similar to thousands of African American educators across the country, Washington teaches her African American students with a sense of passion and mission that is rooted in cultural traditions and a common history that she shares with her students. African American warm demanders, as well as other teachers of color, provide a tough-minded, no-nonsense, structured, disciplined classroom environment for young people whom society has psychologically and physically abandoned. Strongly identifying with their students and determined to give them a future, these teachers believe that culturally diverse children not only can learn but must learn. These previous descriptions are reminiscent of the acclaimed teaching style of Marva Collins, the African American teacher who started her own school in Chicago, and Jaime Escalante, the Hispanic teacher in Los Angeles who produced amazing results with his high school math students.

When asked about the teaching episode involving Darius, Irene Washington provided insight into the culturally responsive style that she uses:

"Oh that little Darius is something else. Now he knows that there are times I will allow them to shoot from the hip. But he knows that this time we're working on themes. You see, you've got to know these students and where they're coming from—you know, talk the talk. He knows what's expected during these activities, but he's trying to play the comedian. I know he knows how to develop a theme and I won't let him get away with ignoring my instructions."

She explained that her comments to Darius were motivated by a particular set of negative environmental circumstances and a sense of urgency not only to teach her children well but also to save and protect them from the perils of urban street life. She continued:

"Darius is street smart, street wise. You see he has older brothers who are out there on the streets, selling and using [drugs]. I know if I don't reach him, or if I retain him, I may lose him to the streets this early. That's what I'm here for—to give them opportunities—to get an education and the confidence. I certainly don't want them to meet closed doors."
She ended her interview on a pensive and reflective note, declaring that, "I know what it means to grow up Black."

(Irvine & Fraser, 1998, p. 56)

Research on Latino educators (Henz & Hauser 1999) documents another type of caring called *carino*. Examples of *carino* included instances in which teachers refer to their Latino students with kinship terms such as *mijo/mija* (son/daughter) or *mi amor* (my love). The Latino teachers thought that it was important to establish and foster a sense of *confianza*, which includes sharing cultural experiences with their students, listening to them, and relating to them as culturally connected relatives.

I am sure that many teachers who are demanding and who chastise and even punish students care about their pupils as much as do teachers who dialogue, co-construct, facilitate, negotiate, and celebrate voices. The task of teacher educators is to make sure that teacher education students and the people who evaluate and assess them understand the complexity of a term that seems so simple—*care*. We should continue to speak and write about our profession so that policy makers understand how teacher characteristics and traits, such as being caring, are influenced by the multiple layers and enigmatic nature of classroom practice.

Complexity of the Issue of Competence

The second term in our lexicon that needs further refinement and lucid thought is *competence*. Let's set the record straight. I believe that teachers should be competent and that their competence should be assessed with valid and multiple measures. Furthermore, I support high standards. Again, the issue is not whether teachers should be competent. Of course, they must be. No teacher should be allowed to enter a classroom without documented evidence of competence in literacy, numeracy, technology, and his or her subject matter field. However, similar to what occurs in the case of the term *care*, issues of measurement, validity, and reliability complicate the discussion of competence.

Unfortunately, such murky measurement issues have not discouraged or prevented the media's insatiable appetite for stories about teacher incompetence, particularly teachers' performance on state and national assessments. Although conventional wisdom insists that teacher education students are "idiots," as Massachusetts's Speaker of the House said (Laitsch, 1998, p. 1), recent data from the Educational Testing Service (ETS) (Gittomer, Latham & Ziomek, 1999) confirm that teacher education students are not less talented than their peers in other majors. Although teacher educators maintain varying positions on the merits of mandated competency, almost all agree with Berliner's (2000) contention that "raw intelligence is insufficient for accomplished teaching" (p. 358).

Complexities of Teaching

The complexities of teaching are revealed in the observation that teaching involves four essential elements:

1. some person
2. teaching something,
3. to some student,
4. somewhere.*

(*Many thanks to Judith Lanier, former president and chair of the Holmes Group, for our conversation on this subject.)

First, let's talk about "some person." It does matter who the teacher is. Indeed, we teach who we are. Teachers bring to their work values, opinions, and beliefs; their prior socialization and present experiences; and their race, gender, ethnicity, and social class. These attributes and characteristics influence teachers' perceptions of themselves as professionals. I am not purporting that there is a simplistic interpretation of this finding. People—including teachers—are not mere representatives of their ethnic group or passive recipients of their cultural experiences. However, we should understand that teachers are influenced by their past and present cultural encounters.

In addition to these cultural variables, teachers have preferences for the type of student whom they want to teach. They do not treat all students the same or have similar expectations for their success and achievement. In my research (Irvine, 1990a), I have found that when teachers were asked to describe their favorite students, they used descriptors such as *above average, friendly, cooperative, curious, affectionate*, and *outgoing*.

One of the teachers said, "I like working with Matt the best. He is well behaved and doesn't act up. He does what he is told and gives me no problems. He is very soft-spoken and tries hard to please me." Another admitted, "I found that I prefer to teach a more physically attractive kid who follows directions well. Most importantly, I like the ones that respond to me" (p. 52).

Second, it does matter what the "something" is that is being taught. Effective teachers love and care about the students whom they teach, and they also love and are excited about the subject that they teach. A thorough, deep understanding of the content contributes to teachers' ability to represent and deliver that content in various ways. Competent teachers know how to employ multiple representations of knowledge that use students' everyday lived experiences to motivate and assist them in connecting new knowledge to home, community, and global settings. Multiple representations of subject matter knowledge involve finding pertinent examples, comparing and contrasting, bridging the gap between the known (students' personal cultural knowledge) and the unknown (materials and concepts to be mastered).

My colleague and I edited a book in which we present culturally responsive, transformative lesson units in four subject areas that are aligned with content area standards (Irvine & Armento, 2001). Examples include the following:

- Teaching language arts by helping culturally diverse students to comprehend, interpret, evaluate, and appreciate text by drawing on the resources of their family and community.
- Teaching mathematics by identifying geometric shapes and patterns in African textiles and Navajo pottery.
- Teaching weather and other scientific concepts by first helping students to understand the connections between their culture and weather as portrayed in myths, folklore, and family sayings.
- Teaching social studies by arranging mock presidential elections in selected historical periods for which students assume various roles, such as women, slaves, Whites, and property owners; in addition, helping them to transform their own community by analyzing and reporting voting patterns in their neighborhood and executing a voter education project.

Effective teachers do not falsely dichotomize students as learners in school and nonlearners out of school (Moll, Amanti, Neff, & Gonzalez, 1992). Teachers' ability to demonstrate the connection between school and community knowledge is an essential element of subject matter competence. Students learn best when teachers' content knowledge is so deep and extensive that they help students to interpret knowledge, store and retrieve it, and make sense of the world in which they live. I believe that students fail in schools not because their teachers do not know their content, but because their teachers cannot make connections between subject-area content and their students' existing mental schemes, prior knowledge, and cultural perspectives.

Third, it does matter who is being taught—the student. The student's age, developmental level, race and ethnicity, physical and emotional states, prior experiences, interests, family and home life, learning preferences, attitudes about school, and a myriad of other variables influence the teaching and learning process. How many times do teacher educators remind students to "meet the needs of the learners in their classroom"? It's mind-boggling and humbling to contemplate the complexities of this much-heralded precept of effective teaching (Schulman, 1987).

Teachers are accountable for instructing students who are unmotivated, angry, violent, hungry, homeless, shy, and abused. Policymakers, and some school administrators, seem oblivious to the fact that students are not passive recipients of teaching. Students have preferences regarding the subject matter that they are taught and the people who teach them.

Fourth, it does matter where one is teaching. Urban, suburban, and rural schools differ from one another. Larger and small schools have different climates and teacher-student relationships. Private versus parochial, low-income versus privileged, elementary versus middle, charter versus non-charter, are not mere labels for schools. These distinctions matter. An all–African American school, for example, differs from a culturally diverse or all-White school. School policies, organizational structures, and personnel are relevant pieces of the context of teaching.

Ponder the powerlessness and ineffectiveness of caring, competent teachers (even those certified by the National Board for Professional Teaching Standards) working in overcrowded, underfunded schools with low-tracked curricula and insensitive, incompetent administrators. We have produced hundreds of caring, competent teachers in our programs who do not choose to stay in the profession for these very reasons. In a North Carolina study (Southeast Center for Teaching Quality, 2002), 14,000 teachers were surveyed to determine the type of incentives that would convince them to work in low-performing schools. Seventy percent of the teachers stated that they would not work in such schools, even with incentives such as increased compensation. What the teachers wanted were responsive, effective administrators, extra planning periods, and instructional support.

Hence, teaching is clearly a complex act involving some person teaching something to some student somewhere. *Context* is the operative word here. Caring, competent educators understand context and the complexity of teaching and do not use a set of rigid pedagogical principles in their classrooms. Instead, they modify what they have learned in teacher education, recognizing that mastery of pedagogical principles and subject matter content are necessary but not sufficient conditions for effective teaching. Caring, competent teachers recognize that they do not instruct culturally homogenized, standardized students in a nonspecified school setting. Teachers armed with such generic teaching skills often find themselves ineffective and ill prepared when faced with a classroom of diverse learners.

Questions

1. Which teacher, Ms. Little or Ms. Moultrie, best meets your own definition of a caring, competent teacher? Do you agree with Irvine that two such different teachers can both be caring and competent?
2. Do you think, as Irvine implies, that a teacher can be caring, sympathetic, friendly, and yet tough and "in charge"? Is this asking too much?
3. In the example Irvine gives, do you think Darius's teacher was fair to him?
4. Do you agree with Irvine that "context is the operative word" and that teachers need to teach quite differently in different cultural contexts, or do you ultimately think "good teaching is good teaching"?

Source: Jacqueline Jordan Irvine. "Caring, Competent Teachers in Complex Classrooms," in *Educating Teachers for Diversity: Seeing With a Cultural Eye*. New York: Teachers College Press, 2003.

Notes

Chapter 1

1. National Education Association, *Status of the American Public School Teacher,* pp. 67–68.
2. Ayla Gavins, "Being on a Moving Train." In *Why We Teach,* edited by Sonia Nieto, 101, 103–104. New York: Teachers College Press, 2005.
3. William Ayers, *To Teach: The Journey of a Teacher.* New York: Teachers College Press, 2001, p. 8.
4. Parker J. Palmer, *The Courage to Teach: Exploring the Inner Landscape of a Teacher's Life.* San Francisco: Jossey-Bass, 1998, p. 1.
5. Ayers, p. 8.
6. Jennifer Welborn, "The Accidental Teacher." In *Why We Teach,* edited by Sonia Nieto, 17. New York: Teachers College Press, 2005.
7. Herbert Kohl, *The Discipline of Hope: Learning from a Lifetime of Teaching.* New York: Simon & Schuster, 1998, pp. 331–333.
8. Jean Anyon, "Putting Education at the Center." In *City Kids City Schools,* edited by William Ayers, Gloria Ladson-Billings, Gregory Michie, and Pedro A. Noguera, 310–311. New York: New Press, 2008.
9. Welborn, p. 20.
10. Robert L. Fried, *The Passionate Teacher: A Practical Guide.* Boston: Beacon Press, 1995, pp. 11–23.
11. Judy Logan, *Teaching Stories.* San Francisco, CA: Create Space Publishers, 2013, p. xiv.
12. Welborn, p. 22.
13. Richard M. Ingersoll and Thomas M. Smith, "The Wrong Solution to the Teacher Shortage," *Educational Leadership* 60, no. 8 (May 2003): 30–33. For a more detailed discussion of these issues, see Richard M. Ingersoll, *Who Controls Teachers' Work? Power and Accountability in America's Schools.* Cambridge, MA: Harvard University Press, 2003.
14. Ellen Moir, "The Santa Cruz New Teacher Center Teacher Induction Model." Presented at New York University, March 1, 2006. For more information on the important work of the New Teacher Center, see http://www.newteachercenter.org.
15. Barbara McEwan in *Classroom Discipline in American Schools: Problems and Possibilities,* edited by Ronald E. Butchart and Barbara McEwan. Albany: State University of New York Press, 1998.
16. For more on the history of the teaching profession, see my *Preparing America's Teachers: A History.* New York: Teachers College Press, 2007. See also my *The School in the United States: A Documentary History,* 3rd ed. New York: Routledge, 2014. Donald Warren, editor, *American Teachers: Histories of a Profession at Work.* New York: American Educational Research Association/Macmillan & Company, 1989; and Dana Goldstein, *The Teacher Wars: A History of America's Most Embattled Profession.* New York: Doubleday, 2014.
17. Elaine P. Witty, "The Norfolk Conference on Diversity." In *Leading a Profession: Defining Moments in the AACTE Agenda, 1980–2005,* edited by Susan Cimburek, 18–20. Washington, DC: American Association of Colleges for Teacher Education, 2005.
18. Herbert Kohl, *The Discipline of Hope: Learning from a Lifetime of Teaching.* New York: Simon & Schuster, 1998, pp. 331–333.

Chapter 2

1. Sonia Nieto, *What Keeps Teachers Going?* New York: Teachers College Press, 2003, p. 21.
2. Horace Mann, *Fourth Annual Report* (1840), in Lawrence A. Cremin, *The Republic and the School: Horace Mann on the Education of Free Men.* New York: Teachers College Press, 1957, pp. 45–52.
3. Margaret Haley, "Why Teachers Should Organize," *Addresses and Proceedings.* St. Louis, MO: NEA, 1904, pp. 145–152.
4. See interviews with Glenn Seaborg and Alan Friedman, "Sputnik's Legacy," retrieved from http://whyfiles.org/047sputnik/main3.html. See also "Janet Whitla on the Evolution of EDC's Thinking," retrieved from http://main.edc.org/about/evolution.asp.
5. Lyndon B. Johnson, "Remarks in Johnson City, Texas, Upon Signing the Elementary and Secondary Education Bill, April 11, 1965," *Public Papers of the Presidents, Lyndon B. Johnson, 1965, Book 1.* Washington, DC: 1966, pp. 413–414.
6. Ellen Condliffe Lagemann, *The Politics of Knowledge: The Carnegie Corporation. Philanthropy, and Public Policy.* Chicago: University of Chicago Press, 1989, pp. 244–248.
7. Eric Hanushek, "The Economic Value of Higher Teacher Quality," *Working Paper 56.* Washington, DC: Center for Analysis of Longitudinal Data in Educational Research, December 2010, p. 3.
8. Kati Haycock, "Good Teaching Matters: How Well-Qualified Teachers Can Close the Gap," *Thinking K-16* 3, no. 2 (Summer 1998): 11–12.
9. Ibid.
10. Steve Farkas, Jean Johnson, and Tony Foleno, *A Sense of Calling: Who Teaches and Why.* New York: Public Agenda Foundation, 2000, p. 33.
11. Nieto, p. 19.
12. Ronald F. Ferguson, "Evidence That Schools Can Narrow the Black-White Test Score Gap," 1997, p. 32; Ronald F. Ferguson and Helen F. Ladd, "How and Why Money Matters: An Analysis of Alabama Schools." In *Holding Schools Accountable: Performance Based Reform in Education.* Washington, DC: The Brookings Institute Press, 1996; Dan D. Goldhaber and Dominic J. Brewer, "Evaluating the Effect of Teacher Degree Level on Educational Performance." In *Developments in School Finance,* 1996, p. 199; Eva L. Baker, *Report on the Content Area Performance Assessments (CAPA): A Collaboration Among Hawaii Department of Education, the Center for Research on Evaluation Standards and Student Testing, and the Teachers and Children of Hawaii,* 1996, p. 109; Jeff Archer, "Students' Fortune Rests With Assigned Teacher," *Education Week,* February 18, 1998.
13. Linda Darling-Hammond, "What Matters Most: A Competent Teacher for Every Child." In *The Right to Learn: A Blueprint for Creating Schools That Work.* San Francisco: Jossey-Bass, 1997, Chapter 3.
14. John D. Bransford, Ann L. Brown, and Rodney R. Cocking, eds., *How People Learn: Brain, Mind, Experience, and School.* Washington, DC: National Academy Press, 2000, pp. 5–6.
15. See Lee Shulman, *The Wisdom of Practice: Essays on Teaching, Learning, and Learning to Teach.* San Francisco: Jossey-Bass, 2004.

16. Robert L. Fried, *The Passionate Teacher*. Boston: Beacon Press, 1995, p. 16.

17. Jacqueline Jordan Irvine, *In Search of Wholeness: African American Teachers and Their Culturally Specific Classroom Practices*. New York: Palgrave-Macmillan, 2002, p. 142.

18. James P. Comer, "The Rewards of Parent Participation," *Educational Leadership* 60, no. 6 (March 2005): 38.

19. J. B. Diamond, L. Wang, and K. Gomez, "African-American and Chinese American Parent Involvement: The Importance of Race, Class and Culture." *FINE Network at Harvard Family Research Project*, 2004. Retrieved from http://www.gse.harvard.edu/hfrp/projects/fine/resources/digest/race.html; G. Valdez, "The World Outside and Inside Schools: Language and Immigrant Children," *Educational Researcher* 17, no. 6 (1998): pp. 4–18; Fabienne Doucet, "Divergent Realities: The Home and School Lives of Haitian Immigrant Youth," *Journal of Youth Ministry* 3, no. 2 (2005): 37–65. I am very grateful to my colleague Fabienne Doucet for pointing me to these articles and for opportunities to discuss these issues.

20. James P. Comer, "Parent Participation: Fad or Function?" *Schools*, p. 136.

21. Robert D. Putnam, *Bowling Alone: The Collapse and Revival of American Community*. New York: Simon & Schuster, 2000, p. 367.

Chapter 3

1. National Center for Education Statistics, Digest of Education Statistics (Table 203.50). Washington, DC. Retrieved from http://nces.ed.gov/programs/diogest/d13/tables/d13_203.50.asp.

2. National Commission on Teaching and America's Future, *Learning Teams: Creating What's Next*. NCTAF Report, April 2008, p. 12.

3. Ronald Takaki, *A Different Mirror: A History of Multicultural America*. Boston: Little Brown, 1993, p. 1.

4. Clara C. Park, A. Lin Goodwin, and Stacey J. Lee, *Asian American Identities, Families, and Schooling*. New York: Information Age Publishing, 2003, pp. vii, 16–21.

5. Shirley Brice Heath and Milbrey W. McLaughlin, eds., *Identity and Inner-City Youth: Beyond Ethnicity and Gender*. New York: Teachers College Press, 1993, pp. 18, 21.

6. National Center for Educational Statistics, 2013 Tables and Figures, Table 203.50.

7. Diego Castellanos, *The Best of Two Worlds: Bilingual-Bicultural Education in the U.S.* Trenton: New Jersey State Department of Education, 1983.

8. James Crawford, *Bilingual Education: History, Politics, Theory, and Practice*. Trenton, NJ: Crane Publishing, 1989, pp. 18–43.

9. Don Soifer, "Bilingual Education: Where Do We Go from Here?" Issue Brief, The Lexington Institute, June 19, 1998. Retrieved from http://lexingtoninstitute.org.

10. John Espinoza, "Speak the Truth About 227," October 17, 1998.

11. Jill Kerper Mora, "From the Ballot Box to the Classroom," *Educational Leadership* 66 (April 2009), pp 14–19.

12. Gary Orfield, *Reviving the Goal of an Integrated Society: A 21st Century Challenge*. Los Angeles: Civil Rights Project/Proyecto Derechos Civiles, UCLA, 2009.

13. Public Agenda, *New Teachers: "I wasn't prepared for the challenges of teaching in a diverse classroom."* Retrieved from http://www.publicagenda.org/LessonsLearned3.

14. Tessie Liu, "Teaching the Differences Among Women from a Historical Perspective: Rethinking Race and Gender as Social Categories." In Vicki L. Ruiz and Ellen Carol DuBois, eds., *Unequal Sisters; A Multicultural Reader in U.S. Women's History*. New York: Routledge, 2000, p. 628.

15. Lisa Delpit, *Other People's Children: Cultural Conflict in the Classroom*. New York: New Press, 1995, pp. 21–26.

16. Peggy McIntosh, *White Privilege and Male Privilege: A Personal Account of Coming to See Correspondences Through Work in Women's Studies*. Wellesley, MA: Wellesley College Center for Research on Women, 1988.

17. Jacqueline Jordan Irvine, *Educating Teachers for Diversity; Seeing With a Cultural Eye*. New York: Teachers College Press, 2003, pp. xv–xvii.

18. Delpit, pp. 28–29.

Chapter 4

1. Martha Ziegler, testimony to the National Coalition of Advocates for Students Board of Inquiry, cited in *Barriers to Excellence: Our Children at Risk*. Boston: National Coalition of Advocates for Students, 1985, p. 26.

2. Cited in Herbert M. Kliebard, *The Struggle for the American Curriculum, 1893–1958*. Boston: Routledge & Kegan Paul, 1986, p. 141.

3. William H. Chafe, "The Road to Equality, 1962–Today." In *No Small Courage: A History of Women in the United States,* edited by Nancy F. Cott, 547–549. New York: Oxford University Press, 2000; Marlyn E. Calabrese, "What Is Title IX?" In *Sex Equity in Education; Readings and Strategies,* edited by Anne O'Brien Carelli, 83–93. Springfield, IL: Charles C. Thomas, 1988; Barbara Bitters, "Sex Equity in Vocational Education." In Carelli, pp. 231–232. T. J. Wirtenberg, *Expanding Girls' Occupational Potential: A Case Study of the Implementation of Title IX's Anti-Sex-Segregation Provision in Seventh Grade Practical Arts.* Unpublished doctoral dissertation, University of California, Los Angeles, 1979. Cited and discussed in Helen S. Farmer and Joan Seliger Sidney, with Barbara A. Bitters and Martine G. Brizius, "Sex Equity in Career and Vocational Education." In *Handbook for Achieving Sex Equity through Education,* edited by Susan S. Klein, 348–349. Baltimore: Johns Hopkins University Press, 1985; Karen Blumenthal, *Let Me Play: The Story of Title IX.* New York: Atheneum Books, 2005, pp. 3, 23–40.

4. An excellent discussion of these issues can be found in D. B. Tyack and E. Hansot, *Learning Together: A History of Coeducation in American Public Schools*. New York: Russell Sage Foundation, 1992, pp. 242–292; Sexton is cited on p. 290.

5. Myra and David Sadker, *Failing at Fairness: How America's Schools Cheat Girls*. New York: Scribner's, 1994, p. 1.

6. Michael Gurian and Kathy Stevens, "With Boys and Girls in Mind," *Educational Leadership* 62 (November 2004): 21–26.

7. Sara Mead, "The Truth About Boys and Girls," Education Sector (June 2006). Retrieved from http://www.educationsector.org.

8. David Sadker and Karen Zittleman, *Still Failing at Fairness: How Gender Bias Cheats Girls and Boys in School and What We Can Do About It*. New York: Scribner, 2009.

9. Shirley Brice Heath and Milbrey W. McLaughlin, eds., *Identity and Inner-City Youth: Beyond Ethnicity and Gender*. New York: Teachers College Press, 1993, p. 23.

10. Harris Interactive and GLSEN, *From Teasing to Torment: School Climate in America: A Survey of Students and Teachers*. New York: GLSEN, 2005.

11. For a more detailed discussion of religion and religious and non-religious students, see my *Between Church and State: Religion and Public Education in a Multicultural America*. New York: St. Martins, 1999.

12. Thomas Hehir, *New Directions in Special Education: Eliminating Ableism in Policy and Practice*. Cambridge: Harvard Education Press, 2005, pp. 13–64.

13. For an excellent study of how the ideal of an inclusive classroom came to be the norm in U.S. schools, see Robert L. Osgood, *The History of Inclusion in the United States*. Washington, DC: Gallaudet University Press, 2005.

14. Public Law 94–142, Education of All Handicapped Children Act, 1975.

15. Edward Moscovitch, *Special Education: Good Intentions Gone Awry*. Boston: Pioneer Institute, 1993, pp. 1–6.

16. Ann Turnbull, Rud Turnbull, Michael L. Wehmeyer, and Karrie A. Shogren, *Exceptional Lives: Special Education in Today's Schools*, 7th ed. Upper Saddle River, NJ: Pearson, 2012.

17. Osgood, p. 166; Robert A. Henderson, "What Is This 'Least Restrictive Environment' in the United States?" In *Is There a Desk With My Name on It? The Politics of Integration*, edited by Roger Slee. London: The Falmer Press, 1993.

18. Moscovitch, p. 19.

19. Ellen C. Guiney, Mary Ann Cohen, and Erika Moldow, "Escaping from Old Ideas: Educating Students with Disabilities in the Boston Public Schools." In *A Decade of Urban School Reform: Persistence and Progress in the Boston Public Schools*, edited by S. Paul Reville with Celine Coggins. Cambridge, MA: Harvard Education Press, 2007.

20. Osgood, p. 197.

21. Marilyn Friend, "The Coteaching Partnership," *Educational Leadership* 64 (February 2007): 48–51.

22. Kelley S. Regan, "Improving the Way We Think About Students With Emotional and/or Behavioral Disorders," *TEACHING Exceptional Children* (May/June 2009): 60–65.

23. From Katherine Hanson, Vivian Guilfoy, and Sarita Pillai, *More Than Title IX: How Equity in Education Has Shaped the Nation*. Lanham, MD: Rowman & Littlefield, 2009, pp. 232–233.

Chapter 5

1. Morris L. Bigge and S. Samuel Shermis, *Learning Theories for Teachers*, 6th ed. New York: Longman, 1999, p. 5.

2. My discussion of the philosophy of education has been helped greatly by reading Tony W. Johnson and Ronald F. Reed, *Philosophical Documents in Education*. Boston: Allyn & Bacon, 2008. I recommend the book as an excellent place to start to learn more about the subject.

3. Plato, *Apology*, cited in Tony W. Johnson and Ronald F. Reed, *Philosophical Documents in Education*. Boston: Allyn and Bacon, 2008, p. 25.

4. Plato, *The Republic*, book 6, cited in Johnson and Reed, pp. 29–31; I am grateful to Jane Roland Martin (see note 11 below) for the reminder that Plato attended to the education of women as well as men.

5. Aristotle, *Nicomachean Ethics*, cited in Johnson and Reed, pp. 35–43.

6. Jean-Jacques Rousseau, *Emile*, cited in Johnson and Reed, pp. 76–81.

7. John Dewey, *The School and Society*. Chicago: University of Chicago Press, 1899; Dewey, *Democracy and Education*. New York: Macmillan, 1916; Dewey, *Experience and Education*. New York: Macmillan, 1938.

8. Mortimer J. Adler, *The Paideia Proposal: An Educational Manifesto*. New York: Macmillan, 1982.

9. Maxine Greene, *Releasing the Imagination: Essays on Education, the Arts, and Social Change*. San Francisco: Jossey-Bass, 1995; William Pinar, *The Passionate Mind of Maxine Greene*. London: Falmer Press, 1998; "Maxine Greene: The Importance of Personal Reflection," retrieved from http://www.edutopia.org/maxine-greene, accessed May 15, 2009.

10. Paulo Freire, *Pedagogy of the Oppressed*, 30th anniversary edition. New York: Bloomsbury Academics, 2000. (Originally published 1970.) See also Paulo Freire, *Letters to Christina: Reflections on My Life and Work*. New York: Routledge, 1996.

11. Jane Roland Martin, *Reclaiming a Conversation: The Ideal of the Educated Woman*. New Haven: Yale University Press, 1985.

12. bell hooks, *Teaching Community: A Pedagogy of Hope*. New York: Routledge, 2003, p. 91; see also hooks, *Teaching to Transgress: Education as the Practice of Freedom*. New York: Routledge, 1994; and her forthcoming *Plantation Culture*. New York: Routledge.

13. Kwame Anthony Appiah, *The Ethics of Identity*. Princeton: Princeton University Press, 2005, see especially pp. 212 and 268–269.

14. Jean Piaget, *The Moral Judgment of the Child*. New York: Free Press, 1997, pp. 31, 36–37, 42, 47–50.

15. Ruth M. Beard, *An Outline of Piaget's Developmental Psychology for Students and Teachers*. New York: Basic Books, 1969, p. 139.

16. B. F. Skinner, *Science and Human Behavior*. New York: Macmillan, 1953, p. 91, cited in Bigge and Shermis, p. 102. Bigge and Shermis provide a useful text for further study of all the people and theories presented in this chapter. B. F. Skinner, *Recent Issues in the Analysis of Behavior*. Columbus, OH: Merrill Publishing, 1989, pp. 99–103.

17. Lev Vygotsky, *Mind in Society: The Development of Higher Psychological Processes*. Edited and translated by M. Cole, V. John-Steiner, S. Scribner, and E. Souberman. Cambridge, MA: Harvard University Press, 1978, p. 86.

18. Jerome S. Bruner, *Toward a Theory of Instruction*. Cambridge, MA: Harvard University Press, 1966, pp. 5 and 27. See also Bruner's *Acts of Meaning*. Cambridge, MA: Harvard University Press, 1990, and the discussion of Bruner in Bigge and Shermis, pp. 133–153.

19. Bruner, *Toward a Theory of Instruction*, p. 126; Bruner, *The Relevance of Education*. New York: Norton, 1973, p. 131; Bruner, *Toward a Theory of Instruction*, p. 53.

20. Carol Gilligan, *In A Different Voice: Psychological Theory and Women's Development*. Cambridge, MA: Harvard University Press, 1982.

21. John D. Bransford, Ann L. Brown, and Rodney R. Cocking, editors, *How People Learn: Brain, Mind, Experience, and School*. Washington, DC: National Academy Presses, 2000, pp. vii and 358–359.

22. Eugene E. Garcia, *Hispanic Education in the United States: Raices y Alas*. Lanham, MD: Rowman & Littlefield, 2001, p. 146.

23. Victoria Purcell-Gates, "'… As Soon as She Opened Her Mouth!': Issues of Language, Literacy, and Power." In *The Skin That We Speak: Thoughts on Language and Culture in the Classroom*, revised ed., edited by Lisa Delpit and Joanne Kilgour Dowdy, 121–141. New York: New Press, 2008.

24. Diana B. Erchick, "Women's Voices and the Experiences of Mathematics," *Focus on Learning Problems in Mathematics* 18 (Winter-Summer 1996): 105–122; Joanne R. Becker, "Women's Way of Knowing in Mathematics Education." In *Equity in Mathematics Education: Influences of Feminism and Culture*, edited by Pat Rogers and Gabriele Kaiser. London: Falmer, 1995. Both are cited and discussed in Karen N. Bell and Elaine Kolitch, "Voices of Mathematical Distress and Resilience," *Women's Studies Quarterly* 28 (Fall/Winter 2000): 233–248.

25. Peter Senge, Nelda Cambron-McCabe, Timothy Lucas, Brayn Smith, Janis Dutton, and Art Kleiner, *Schools That Learn*. New York: Doubleday, 2000, pp. 35–42.

26. Howard Gardner, *Multiple Lenses on the Mind*. Paper presented at the ExpoGestion Conference, Bogotá, Colombia, May 25, 2005.

Chapter 6

1. See William F. Pinar, "'A Lingering Note' Comments on the Collected Works of Ted T. Aoki," *Educational Insights* 8, no. 2. See also William F. Pinar, *Understanding Curriculum*. New York: Peter Lang, 1995.

2. Meredith Houle, *Investigating the Role of Educative Curriculum Materials in Supporting Teacher Enactment of a Field-Based Urban Ecology Investigation*. Unpublished doctoral dissertation, Boston College, May 2008, pp. 8–14, citing p. 238 of J. T. Remillard, "Examining Key Concepts in Research on Teachers Use of Mathematics Curricula," *Review of Educational Research* 75, no. 2 (2005): 211–246.

3. Ralph W. Tyler, *Basic Principles of Curriculum and Instruction*. Chicago: University of Chicago Press, 1950, pp. 1–2, cited in Herbert M. Kliebard, *Forging the American Curriculum: Essays in Curriculum History and Theory*. New York: Routledge, 1992, p. 154.

4. Tyler, p. 3, cited in Kliebard, p. 154.

5. Tyler, p. 69, cited in Kliebard, pp. 162–163.

6. Elliot W. Eisner, "Educational Objectives—Help or Hindrance?" Reprinted in *The Curriculum Studies Reader*, edited by David J. Flinders and Stephen J. Thornton, 85–91. New York: Routledge Falmer, 2004.

7. Herbert M. Kliebard, *The Struggle for the American Curriculum*, 3rd ed. New York: Routledge Falmer, 2004, see especially pp. 1–25 (though this is, in fact, a summary of the book).

8. Kliebard, *Struggle for the American Curriculum*, p. 25, see also pp. 229–230.

9. Larry Cuban, *How Teachers Taught: Constancy and Change in American Classrooms, 1890–1990*, 2nd ed. New York: Teachers College Press, 1993, xix.

10. For a particularly thoughtful analysis of the hidden curriculum, see Michael W. Apple, "The Hidden Curriculum and the Nature of Conflict." In Michael W. Apple, *Ideology and Curriculum*, 3rd ed. New York: Routledge Falmer, 2004, pp. 77–97.

11. American Federation of Teachers, "Share My Lesson Posts Common Core-Aligned Lesson Plan Involving Malala Yousafzai's Campaign for Girls Education." Press Release, October 8, 2013. See also Malala Yousafzai, *I am Malala: The Girl Who Stood Up for Education and Was Shot by the Taliban*. Boston: Little Brown, 2013.

12. Material in the section on the Common Core from: American Federation of Teachers, "Frequently Asked Questions about the Common Core State Standards," and "Debunking Myths of the Common Core," Liana Heitin, "Schools Teach Common-Core Math to Two Generations," *Education Week*, December 3, 2014; Katherine A. Dougherty Stahl and Jason Schweid, "Beyond March Madness: Fruitful Practices to Prepare for High-Stakes ELA Tests," *The Reading Teacher* 67, no. 2: 121–125.

13. James A. Banks, "Multicultural Education: Characteristics and Goals." In James A. Banks and Cherry A. McGee Banks, eds., *Multicultural Education: Issues and Perspectives*, 6th ed. Hoboken, NJ: Wiley, 2007, pp. 6–7.

14. Sonia Nieto, *Affirming Diversity: The Sociopolitical Context of Multicultural Education*. Boston: Pearson, 2004, p. 346.

15. Banks.

16. Arthur M. Schlesinger, Jr., *The Disuniting of America: Reflections on a Multicultural Society*. Whittle Direct Books, 1991.

17. Albert Shanker, "The Pitfalls of Multicultural Education," *Education Digest* (December 1991).

18. For a thoughtful and even-handed discussion of these concerns, see David Tack, *Seeking Common Ground: Public Schools in a Diverse Society*. Cambridge, MA: Harvard University Press, 2003.

19. Banks, pp. 7, 20–25.

20. Michael W. Apple, "Do the Standards Go Far Enough? Power, Policy, and Practice in Mathematics Education," *Journal for Research in Mathematics Education* 23, no. 5 (1992): 412.

21. Carol Grant and Christie Sleeter, *Doing Multicultural Education for Achievement and Equity*, 2nd ed. New York: Routledge, 2011.

22. Deborah E. Burns and Jeanne H. Purcell, "Tools for Teachers," *Educational Leadership* 59 (September 2001): 50–52.

23. Vito Perrone, *A Letter to Teachers: Reflections on Schooling and the Art of Teaching*. San Francisco: Jossey-Bass, 1991, pp. 12–13.

Chapter 7

1. Kristin Conradi, "Tapping Technology's Potential to Motivate Readers," *Phi Delta Kappan* 96, no. 3 (November 2014): 54.

2. John Dewey, *Experience and Education*. New York: Touchstone, 1997. (Originally published 1938.)

3. There are many excellent studies of Leonard Covello's educational work. The best place to start is Leonard Covello with Guido D'Agostino, *The Heart Is the Teacher*. New York: McGraw-Hill, 1958. Also useful are Vito Perrone, *Teacher With a Heart: Reflections on Leonard Covello and Community*. New York: Teachers College Press, 1998; Paula S. Fass, *Outside In: Minorities and the Transformation of American Education*. New York: Oxford University Press, 1989; and especially Michael C. Johanek and John L. Puckett, *Leonard Covello and the Making of Benjamin Franklin High School*. Philadelphia: Temple University Press, 2007.

4. See Vito Perrone, *Lessons for New Teachers*. Boston: McGraw-Hill, 2000, pp. 104–119.

5. Paulo Freire, *Teachers as Cultural Workers: Letters to Those Who Dare Teach*. Boulder, CO: Westview Press, 1998, p. 56.

6. Lee Canter & Associates, *Back to School With Assertive Discipline*. Santa Monica, CA: Lee Canter & Associates, 1990, pp. 9 and 29.

7. Diana Scholl, "Why Is Kyle Thompson Under House-Arrest?" American Civil Liberties Union Press Release, September 24, 2013. Retrieved from http://www.acul.org/print/blog/racial-justice/why-kyle-thompson-under-house-arrest. American Academy of Pediatrics, Committee on School Health, "Out-of-School Suspension and Expulsion," *Pediatrics* 112, No. 5 (November, 2003).

8. Justice Center of the Council of State Governments, *The School Discipline Consensus Report: Strategies from the Field to Keep Students Engaged in School and Out of the Juvenile Justice System*. Boston: The Justice Center, 2014.

9. Linda Christensen, "The Classroom to Prison Pipeline." *Rethinking Schools* 26., no 2 (Winter, 2011–2012).

10. Robert Yazzie, "'Life Comes From It': Navajo Justice Concepts." In *Navajo Nation Peacemaking: Living Traditional Justice*, edited by Marianne Nielsen and James W. Zion. Tucson: University of Arizona Press, 2005.

11. The Editors of *Rethinking Schools*, "Restorative Justice: What It Is and Is Not," *Rethinking Schools* 29, no. 1 (Fall, 2014).

12. Vito Perrone, *Lessons for New Teachers*. Boston: McGraw-Hill, 2000, pp. 120–128.

13. Ross W. Greene, *Lost at School: Why Our Kids With Behavioral Challenges Are Falling Through the Cracks and How We Can Help Them*. New York: Scribners, 2008.

14. Martin R. West and Paul E. Peterson, "The Politics and Practice of Accountability." In *No Child Left Behind? The Politics and Practice of School Accountability,* edited by Paul E. Peterson and Martin R. West, 3. Washington, DC: The Brookings Institution Press, 2003.

15. Linda Darling-Hammond, "From 'Separate but Equal' to 'No Child Left Behind': The Collision of New Standards and Old Inequalities." In *Many Children Left Behind,* edited by Deborah Meier and George Woods, 3–4. Boston: Beacon Press, 2004.

16. Arthur Costigan, *Teaching Language Arts in a Test Driven Era.* New York: Routledge, 2008.

17. Judith McVarish, *Infusing Mathematics Reasoning Into Elementary School Classrooms.* New York: Routledge, 2008.

18. Deirdra Grode, "Taking a Creative Approach to Test Prep," *Education Update* 51, no. 7 (July 2009).

Chapter 8

1. U.S. Department of Education, "From Sesame Street to Transmediaville: the Future of Ready to Learn."

2. Larry Cuban, *Oversold and Underused: Computers in the Classroom.* Cambridge, MA: Harvard University Press, 2001; Diana G. Oblinger, "The Next Generation of Educational Engagement," *Journal of Interactive Media in Education* 8, Special Issue on the Educational Semantic Web, cited in Katherine Hanson and Bethany Carlson, *Effective Access: Teachers' Use of Digital Resources in STEM Teaching.* Newton, MA: Education Development Center, 2005, pp. 5–7.

3. Bill Ferster, *Teaching Machines.* Baltimore: Johns Hopkins University Press, 2014.

4. Harman Singh, "Education Is Being Flipped on Its Head by Technology. Teachers See the Promise—and the Pitfalls." Commentary, *Information Week,* December 29, 2014.

5. Anya Kamenetz, "What Parents Need to Know About Big Data and Student Privacy," National Public Radio. Retrieved from http://www.npr.org/blogs/alltechconsidered/2014/04/28/305715935/what-parents-need-to-know-about-big-data-and-student-privacy.

6. Alex Molinar, et al., "Virtual Schools in the U.S. 2014: Politics, Performance, Policy, and Research Evidence." National Education Policy Center, March 4, 2014. Retrieved from http://nepc.colorado.edu/publication/virtual-schools-annual-2014; Allan Collins and Richard Halverson, *Rethinking Education in the Age of Technology: The Digital Revolution and Schooling in America.* New York: Teachers College Press, 2009.

7. Tom Vander Ark, *Getting Smart: How Digital Learning is Changing the World.* San Francisco: Jossey-Bass, 2011.

8. John Shapiro, "Your Five Year Old Can Learn To Code With an IPad App," *Forbes* (August 6, 2014); ScratchEd Team, "Pilot Perspectives: Reflections on the Scratch Curriculum Guide by Melissa Nordmann of Cranford Burns Middle School," retrieved from http://scratched.gse.harvard.edu/stories/pilot-perspectives-reflections-scratch-curriculum-guide-melissa-nordmann-cranford-burns-midd; Alexandra Kahn, "ScratchJr: Coding for Kindergarten," *MIT News,* July 30, 2014.

9. Matt L. Ottinger, "New Tech High: Education Reform Comes to Indiana Classrooms." Indiana Chamber of Commerce, *Biz Voice* (November/December 2007): 72–76.

10. Linda Starr, "Meet Bernie Dodge—The Frank Lloyd Wright of Learning Environments!" (2007) www.educationworld.com

11. Larry Cuban, *Teachers and Machines: The Classroom Use of Technology Since 1920.* New York: Teachers College Press, 1986, pp. 4–11.

12. See for example, Tracy L. Steffes, *School, Society, & State: A New Education to Govern Modern America, 1890–1940.* Chicago: University of Chicago Press, 2012.
   See also, the obituary for John Goodlad, New York Times, January 2, 1015.

13. Seymour Papert, *The Children's Machine: Rethinking School in the Age of the Computer.* New York: Basic Books, 1993.

14. Neil Postman, *Technopoly: The Surrender of Culture to Technology.* New York: Vintage, 1993.

15. Eyal Ophir, Clifford Nass, and Anthony D. Wagner, "Cognitive Control in Media Multitaskers," *Proceedings of the National Academy of Sciences* 106, no. 37 (2009): 1583–1587. And for his life see Steve Chawkins, "Clifford Nass dies at 55; sociologist warned against multitasking," *Los Angeles Times,* November 6, 2013; Jakob Nielsen and Kara Pernice, *Eyetrackikng Web Usability.* Berkeley: New Riders, 2009; David Meyer is quoted in Annie Murphy Paul, "How Does Multitasking Change the Way Kids Learn?" *Mind/Shift* (May 3, 2013).

16. Pew Research Center, Internet and American Life Project, 2014; Andrew Trotter, "Technology Educators Decry New Digital Divide," *Education Week,* 26, published online, June 26, 2007.

17. Erin Scott, "Case Studies: How Teachers Use Tech to Support Learning," *Mind/Shift,* January 7, 2013; Harman Singh, "Education Is Being Flipped on Its Head by Technology. Teachers see the promise—and the pitfalls," Commentary, *Information Week,* December 29, 2014.

18. Andrew Marcinek, "Technology and Teaching: Finding a Balance," *edutopia,* March 11, 2014. Retrieved from http://www.edutopia.org/blog/technology-and-teaching-finding-balance-andrew-marcinek.

19. Katherine Hanson and Bethany Carlson, *Effective Access: Teachers' Use of Digital Resources in STEM Teaching.* Newton, MA: Education Development Center, 2005.

Chapter 9

1. Dan C. Lortie, *Schoolteacher.* Chicago: University of Chicago Press, 2002, p. 65. (Originally published 1965.)

2. Margaret A. Haley, "Why Teachers Should Organize." *National Education Association Addresses and Proceedings.* St. Louis, MO: National Educational Association, 1904, pp. 145–152.

3. Amelia Allison, "Confessions of Public School Teachers," *Atlantic Monthly* (July 1896): 107–108, cited in Nancy Hoffman, *Women's "True" Profession: Voices From the History of Teaching.* Old Westbury, NY: The Feminist Press, 1981, p. 271.

4. PayScale, "Salary Survey for All K–12 Teachers," http://www.payscale.com/research/US/All_K-12_Teachers/Salary/by_Degree and http://www.payscale.com/research/US/All_K-12_Teachers/Salary/by_Certification.

5. Juan Williams, *Thurgood Marshall: American Revolutionary.* New York: Three Rivers Press, 2000, pp. 89–91, 198.

6. Charles J. Russo and Daniel Raisch, "Teacher Unions, the Right to Work, and Fair Share Agreements," School of Business Affairs, University of Dayton, November 2012.

7. See the Web sites of the nation's two teacher unions, http://www.nea.org and http://www.aft.org. For more background on the history and growth of teacher unions in the United States, see Marjorie Murphy, *Blackboard Unions: The AFT and the NEA, 1900–1980.* Ithaca, NY: Cornell University Press, 1992.

8. Lortie, p. viii.

9. See the New Teacher Center (http://www.newteachercenter.org) and The Woodrow Wilson National Fellowship Foundation (http://www.woodrow.org).

10. Susan Moore Johnson, *Teachers at Work: Achieving Success in Our Schools*. New York: Basic Books, 1990, pp. 151–164.

11. Linda Christensen, "Voices From the Classroom." In *The New Teacher Book*, edited by Kelley Dawson Salas, Rita Tenorio, Stephanie Walters, and Dale Weiss. Milwaukee, WI: Rethinking Schools, 2004, p. 39.

12. Frank McCourt, *Teacher Man*. New York: Scribner, 2005, pp. 11–18.

13. See, for example, Ronald Edmonds, "Effective Schools for the Urban Poor," *Educational Leadership* 37 (October 1979): 15–24.

14. Sara Lawrence Lightfoot, *The Good High School: Portraits of Character and Culture*. New York: Basic Books, 1983, pp. 325–333.

15. Sonia Nieto, *What Keeps Teachers Going?* New York: Teachers College Press, 2003, p. 102.

16. Bill Bigelow, cited in Salas et al., p. 214.

17. Lola Glover, "We Must Act as If All the Children Are Ours." In Salas et al., pp. 218–219.

18. Kenneth Zeichner, Katherina Payne, and Kate Brayko Gence, "Democratizing Teacher Education," *Teachers College Record*, forthcoming.

19. Lightfoot, p. 322.

20. Chela Delgado, "White Teacher to the Rescue: A Review of Freedom Writers," *Rethinking Schools* 21:3 (Spring 2007).

21. Jennifer Medina, "Class Size in New York City Schools Rises, but the Impact Is Debated," *New York Times*, February 21, 2009, Health & Education Research Operative Services, "Project STAR: The Student/Teacher Achievement Ratio Study," n.d., Michelle Krupa, "Class Size Is Not So Important, Study Says," *Times-Picayune*, February 10, 2003.

22. Judy Logan, *Teaching Stories*. New York: Kodansha International, 1997, p. xxi.

Chapter 10

1. Sean P. Corcoran and William N. Evans, "Equity, Adequacy, and the Evolving State Role in Education Finance." In Helen F. Ladd and Edward B. Fiske, eds., *Handbook of Research in Educational Finance and Policy*. New York: Routledge, 2007.

2. *Serrano v. Priest*, 5 Cal, 3d 584, 96 Cal Rptr. 601, 487 p. 2d 1241 (1971) cited in David Fellman, ed., *The Supreme Court and Education*. New York: Teachers College Press, 1976, p. 283.

3. *San Antonio Independent School District v. Rodriguez*, 411 U.S. 1 (1973), Justice Powell delivered the opinion of the Court, Justice Marshall dissenting, cited in Fellman, pp. 284–296.

4. Stan Karp, "Money, Schools, and Justice," *Rethinking Schools* 21, no. 4 (Summer 2007): 27–30.

5. James Traub, "It's Elementary," *The New Yorker*, July 17, 1995, p. 77.

6. Paul Wellstone, "If We Are Not for Our Children, Who Are We For?" Epilogue in *Letters to the Next President: What We Can Do About the Real Crisis in Public Education*, edited by Carl Glickman. New York: Teachers College Press, 2004, pp. 257–259.

7. The Census of Governments. School Districts, 2005–2006.

8. Karp.

9. National Working Group on Funding Student Learning, *Funding Student Learning: How to Align Education Resources With Student Learning Goals*. Bothell, WA: University of Washington Center on Reinventing Public Education, 2008.

10. My own views on many of these issues of educational fairness are discussed in my book, *Reading, Writing, and Justice: School Reform as if Democracy Matters*. Albany: State University of New York Press, 1997. See especially Chapter 4, "Toward a New Kind of Child-Centered Curriculum: The Individual Child and a Democratic Society."

11. Two important voices in the research that has shown the negative impact of tracking have been John I. Goodlad and Jeannie Oakes. See especially John I. Goodlad, *A Place Called School: Prospects for the Future*. New York: McGraw-Hill, 1984; and Jeannie Oakes, *Keeping Track: How Schools Structure Inequality*. New Haven, CT: Yale University Press, 1985. For a useful look at parental resistance to ending tracking, see Amy Stuart Wells and Irene Serna, "The Politics of Culture: Understanding Local Political Resistance to Detracking in Racially Mixed Schools," *Harvard Educational Review* 66 (Spring 1996): 93–118.

12. Anne Wheelock, *Crossing the Tracks: How 'Untracking' Can Save America's Schools*. New York: The New Press, 1992, p. 71.

13. Wheelock, pp. 283–284.

14. Jeannie Oakes, "Foreword." In Wheelock, p. xiii.

15. Leonard Covello, *The Heart Is the Teacher*. New York: McGraw-Hill, 1958, pp. 52–53.

16. U.S. Department of Education, "Statement from Secretary Duncan on NCES Public School Graduates and Dropouts Report," January 22, 2013. See also National Center for Education Statistics, "Public School Graduates and Dropouts from the Common Core of Data: School Year 2009–2010," January 2013.

17. D. B. Tyack and E. Hansot, *Learning Together: A History of Coeducation in American Public Schools*. New York: Russell Sage Foundation, 1992, pp. 248–249.

18. Michelle Fine, *Framing Dropouts: Notes on the Politics of an Urban Public High School*. Albany: State University of New York Press, 1991, pp. 1–2, 21–25.

19. Office of Multiple Pathways to Graduation, "Developing and Strengthening Schools and Programs That Lead to High School Graduation and Post-Secondary Opportunities for Overage, Undercredited Youth," New York City Department of Education, June 22, 2006; Division of Assessment & Accountability, "An Examination of the Relationship Between Higher Standards and Students Dropping Out," New York City Department of Education, March 1, 2001.

20. Jacqueline Jordan Irvine, "Still Standing in the Schoolhouse Door"; Pedro Noguera and Robert Cohen, "The Legacy of 'All Deliberate Speed'"; and Richard Rothstein, "Social Class Leaves Its Imprint." In *Education Week* 23 (May 19, 2004): 38–40.

21. Beverly Daniel Tatum, *"Why Are All the Black Kids Sitting Together in the Cafeteria?" and Other Conversations About Race*. New York: Basic Books, 2003, p. 52.

22. Tatum, p. 54.

23. Asa G. Hilliard III, "If We Had the Will to See It Happen." In Glickman, p. 29.

24. Shirley Brice Heath and Milbrey W. McLaughlin, eds., *Identity & Inner-City Youth: Beyond Ethnicity and Gender*. New York: Teachers College Press, 1993, pp. 6, 25–30, and 222.

25. Heath and McLaughlin, p. 59.

26. Robert Infantino and Rebecca Wilke, *Tough Choices for Teachers: Ethical Challenges in Today's Schools and Classrooms*. Lanham, MD: Rowman & Littlefield, 2009.

27. Infantino and Wilke, pp. 22–23, 46–49, 59–60, 76–79, 104–105.

28. Salas, cited in *The New Teacher Book*. Milwaukee, WI: Rethinking Schools, 2004, p. 81.

Chapter 11

1. Common Core State Standards Initiative, *Development Process*, retrieved from http://www.corestandards.org/about-the-standards/development-process/; David L. Kirp, "Rage Against the Common Core," *New York Times*, December 27, 2014; Republican National Committee, *Resolution Concerning Common Core Education Standards*, April 12, 2013; Alan Singer, "Common Core: It Really Is All About the Tests (and Corporate Profits)," *Huffington Post*, November 17, 2014; Stan Karp, "The Problems with the Common Core," *Rethinking Schools*, 28: 2 (Winter 2013–14); American Federation of Teachers, *Frequently Asked Questions About the Common Core State Standards*.

2. The federal government issued a number of publications describing Goals 2000. See for example, *National Goals for Education*, July 1990; *Building the Best: Summary Guide, the National Education Goals Report, 1993*; and *Building a Nation of Learners: The National Education Goals Report, 1994*.

3. National Commission on Excellence in Education, *A Nation at Risk: The Imperative for Educational Reform.* Washington, DC: U.S. Government Printing Office, 1983.

4. One of the best critiques of *A Nation at Risk*, by a group of authors who saw it as undermining a national commitment to educational equity, is Ann Bastian, Norm Fruchter, Marilyn Gittell, Colin Greer, and Kenneth Haskins, *Choosing Equality: The Case for Democratic Schools.* New York: The New World Foundation, 1985.

5. Cynthia McCallister, *Toward "An Education on Equal Terms": Standards, Assessments and the Challenge of Educatonal Equity.* Unpublished paper, New York University, January 2007, p. 4; Edmund W. Gordon, *Education & Justice: A View From the Back of the Bus.* New York: Teachers College Press, 1999; Edmund W. Gordon and Associates, *Human Diversity and Pedagogy.* New Haven, CT: Yale University Center in Research on Education, Culture and Ethnicity, Institute for Social Policy Studies, 1988.

6. See National Council of Teachers of Mathematics, *Standards 2000 Project*, retrieved from http://standards.nctm.org/document/proposal/project.htm.

7. Jonathan Zimmerman, *Whose America? Culture Wars in Public Schools.* Cambridge, MA: Harvard University Press, 2002, p. 73.

8. John B. Bader, *Taking the Initiative: Leadership Agendas in Congress and the "Contract with America."* Washington, DC: Georgetown University Press, 1996). See the *Contract with America*, p. 79.

9. Patrick J. McGuinn, *No Child Left Behind and the Transformation of Federal Education Policy, 1965–2005.* Lawrence: University Press of Kansas, 2006.

10. I am grateful to former NYU graduate student Dana Grayson for insightful commentary on this material. Helpful background can be found in John Chubb's *Within Our Reach* and Deborah Meier's and George Wood's *Many Children Left Behind*. John E. Chubb, ed., *Within Our Reach: How America Can Educate Every Child*, Lanham, MD: Rowman & Littlefield, 2005. Alfie Kohn, "NCLB and the Effort to Privatize Public Education." In Deborah Meier and George Wood, eds., *Many Children Left Behind: How the No Child Left Behind Act Is Damaging Our Children and Our Schools.* Boston: Beacon Press, 2004, pp. 79–80. Linda Darling-Hammond, "From 'Separate but Equal' to 'No Child Left behind': The Collision of New Standards and Old Inequities." In Meier and Wood, eds., *Many Children Left Behind*, pp. 3–4. Frederick M. Hess and Chester E. Finn, Jr., "Introduction." In *Leaving No Child Behind? Options for Kids in Failing Schools.* New York: Palgrave Macmillan, 2004, pp. 2–4.

Terry M. Moe, "Politics, Control, and the Future of School Accountability." In *No Child Left Behind? The Politics and Practice of School Accountability*, edited by Paul E. Peterson and Martin R. West. Washington, DC: The Brookings Institution Press, 2003, pp. 80–86.

11. David L. Kirp, "Rage Against the Common Core," *The New York Times*, December 27, 2014.

12. Daisy Bates, *The Long Shadow at Little Rock* (Fayetteville: University of Arkansas Press, 1962); U.S. Supreme Court, *Parents Involved in Community Schools v. Seattle School District*, No. 5, Supreme Court of the United States 908 (2007); and *Meredith v. Jefferson County Board of Education*, No. 5, Supreme Court of the United States 915 (2007).

13. U.S. Supreme Court, *Tinker et al. v. Des Moines Independent Community School District et al.*, No. 21, Supreme Court of the United States 393 U.S. 503 (1969); *Engel et al. v. Vitale et al.*, No. 468, Supreme Court of the United States 370 U.S. 421: 82 S. Ct. 1261 (1962); *Abington School District v. Schempp*, Supreme Court of the United States 374 U.S. 203 (1963), *Epperson v. Arkansas*, Supreme Court of the United States 393 U.S. 97 (1968). For more discussion of these issues, see David Fellman, ed., *The Supreme Court and Education*, 3rd ed. New York: Teachers College Press, 1976. For a detailed discussion of the religion-related decision, see my *Between Church and State: Religion and Public Education in a Multicultural America*. New York: Palgrave-Macmillan, 1999.

14. See David L. Kirp, "Rage Against the Common Core," *New York Times*, December 27, 2014.

15. Herbert M. Kliebard, *The Struggle for the American Curriculum, 1893–1958*, 2nd ed. New York: Routledge, 1995, pp. 144–149. Lyndon B. Johnson, "Remarks in Johnson City, Texas, Upon Signing the Elementary and Secondary Education Bill, April 11, 1965," *Public Papers of the Presidents, Lyndon B. Johnson, 1965, Book 1*. Washington, DC, pp. 413–414.

16. National Commission on Excellence in Education, p. 5. For a thoughtful discussion of the impact of *A Nation at Risk* and the changing national dialogue about education, from a critical perspective, see Ann Bastian, Norm Fruchter, Marilyn Gittell, Colin Greer, and Kenneth Haskins, *Choosing Equality: The Case for Democratic Schools*. New York: New World Foundation, 1985. Jane Hannaway and Kendra Bischoff, "Florida: Confusions, Constraints, and Cascading Scenarios," and Alex Medler, "Colorado: Layered Reforms and Challenges for Seale," both in *Leaving No Child Behind? Options for Kids in Failing Schools*, edited by Frederick M. Hess and Chester E. Finn, Jr. New York: Palgrave Macmillan, 2004, pp. 89–111, 113–136.

17. John Portz, "Governing and the Boston Public Schools." In S. Paul Reville with Celine Coggins, eds., *A Decade of Urban School Reform*. Cambridge, MA: Harvard Education Press, 2007, pp. 63–64, citing Education Commission of the States, *Governing America's Schools: Changing the Rules*. Denver, CO: Education Commission of the States, 1999; Joseph Murphy, *Governing America's Schools: the Shifting Playing Field*. Paper presented at the annual meeting of the American Educational Research Association, Montreal, Canada, April 1999; Donald R. McAdams, *What School Boards Can Do: Reform Governance for Urban Schools*. New York: Teachers College Press, 2006; Deborah Meier, "NCLB and Democracy." In Meier and Wood, pp. 66–73.

18. Bob Peterson, cited in Salas et al., *The New Teacher Book* Milwaukee, WI: Rethinking Schools, 2004, p. 206.

19. Pedro Noguera, *City Schools and the American Dream: Reclaiming the Promise of Public Education*. New York: Teachers College Press, 2003, pp. 142–153.

20. Gregory Michie, "Teaching in the Undertow: Resisting the Pull of School-as-Usual." In Salas et al., *The New Teacher Book*, p. 194.

Chapter 12

1. Langston Hughes, "Freedom's Plow." In *Selected Poems of Langston Hughes*. New York: Vintage Classics, 1990, p. 291. (Originally published 1959.)

2. For an expanded discussion on the issue of the relationship between democracy and education, from which these paragraphs are partly drawn, see my *Reading, Writing, and Justice: School Reform as if Democracy Matters*. Albany: State University of New York Press, 1997.

3. Michael Apple and James A. Beane, *Democratic Schools*. Alexandria, VA: Association for Supervision and Curriculum Development, 1995.

4. Diana E. Hess and Paula McAvoy, *The Political Classroom: Evidence and Ethics in Democratic Education*. New York: Routledge, 2015, pp. 4–5.

5. Campaign for the Civic Missions of Schools, The Center for Information and Research on Civic Learning and Engagement and Carnegie Corporation of New York, 2003.

6. Joel Westheimer and Joseph Kahne, "Reconnecting Education to Democracy: Democratic Dialogues," *Phi Delta Kappan* (September 2003): 9–14.

7. Thomas Jefferson, "A Bill for the More General Diffusion of Knowledge." In *Crusade Against Ignorance: Thomas Jefferson on Education*, edited by Gordon C. Lee. New York: Teachers College Press, 1961, pp. 83–84. (Originally published 1779.)

8. Horace Mann, 10th and 12th Annual Reports (1846 and 1848) in James W. Fraser, *The School in the United States: A Documentary History*. New York: Routledge, 2009, p. 50.

9. James D. Anderson, *The Education of Blacks in the South, 1860–1935*. Chapel Hill: University of North Carolina Press, 1988, p. 5.

10. "Report to the Primary School Committee on the Petition of Sundry Colored Persons for the Abolition of schools for Colored Children," Boston, June 15, 1846, p. 2.

11. The best analysis of the 19th-century Black community's commitment to literacy and schooling is found in Anderson.

12. Eric Foner, *Reconstruction: America's Unfinished Revolution, 1863–1877*. New York: Harper Collins Perennial, 2002, pp. 96–97.

13. Anderson, pp. 15–16.

14. Frederick Douglass, *Narrative of the Life of Frederick Douglass: An American Slave*. Cambridge, MA: Harvard University Press, 1967, p. 58. (Originally published 1845.)

15. Douglass, p. 59.

16. John W. Alvord, *Inspector's Report of Schools and Finances, U.S. Bureau of Refugees, Freedmen and Abandoned Lands*. Washington, DC: U.S. Government Printing Office, 1866, pp. 9–10, cited in Anderson, p. 7.

17. W.E.B. DuBois, *The Souls of Black Folk*, 1903, reprinted New York: Crest, 1961, p. 31.

18. Anderson, p. 5.

19. W.E.B. DuBois, *Black Reconstruction in America, 1860–1880*. New York: Free Press, 1992, pp. 641–649. (Originally published 1935.)

20. Anderson, p. 278.

21. John Dewey, *The School and Society*, Chicago: University of Chicago Press, 1899, p. 7.

22. John Dewey, "My Pedagogic Creed," *The School Journal* 54 (January 1897): 77–80.

23. Alexis de Tocqueville, *Democracy in America*, edited and abridged by Richard D. Heffner. New York: New American Library, 1956.

24. Ruth Batson, "NAACP Boston Branch, Statement to Boston School Committee, June 11, 1963." In Fraser, p. 305.

25. bell hooks, *Teaching to Transgress: Education as the Practice of Freedom*. New York: Routledge, 1994, p. 18.

26. bell hooks, *Teaching Critical Thinking: Practical Wisdom*. New York: Routledge, 2010, pp. 14–15 and 181.

27. Ann Bastian, Norm Fruchter, Marilyn Gittell, Colin Greer, and Kenneth Haskins, *Choosing Equality: The Case for Democratic Schools*. Philadelphia: Temple University Press, 1985.

28. Deborah Meier, "NCLB and Democracy." In *Many Children Left Behind: How the No Child left Behind Act Is Damaging Our Children and Our Schools*, edited by Deborah Meier and George Wood. Boston: Beacon Press, 2004, pp. 76–78.

29. Lisa Delpit, *Other People's Children: Cultural Conflict in the Classroom*. New York: The New Press, 1995, pp. 11, 28.

30. Lisa Delpit, "No Kinda Sense." In *The Skin That We Speak*, edited by Lisa Delpit and Joanne Kilgour Dowdy. New York: The New Press, 2002, p. 48.

31. Pedro A. Noguera and Robert Cohen, "The Legacy of 'All Deliberate Speed,'" *Education Week* 22 (May 19, 2004): 39.

32. Anderson, p. 1.

33. Jonathan Kozol, *Savage Inequalities: Children in America's Schools*. New York: Broadway Books, 1991, second edition 2012, *The Shame of the Nation*, (1905).

Chapter 13

1. American Association of Colleges of Teacher Education, "About edTPA." Retrieved from http://edtpa.aact.org/about-edtpa

2. "Letters," *Rethinking Schools*, 28, no. 2 (Winter 2013–14).

3. Kelley Dawson Salas, "Time to Learn." In *The New Teacher Book*, edited by Kelley Dawson Salas, Rita Tenorio, Stephanie Walters, and Dale Weiss. Milwaukee, WI: Rethinking Schools, 2004, pp. 11–12.

4. Betty Achinstein and Steven Z. Athanases, *Mentors in the Making: Developing New Leaders for New Teachers*. New York: Teachers College Press, 2006, pp. 1–8.

5. Daniel Fallon and James W. Fraser, "Rethinking Teacher Education in the 21st Century: Putting Teaching Front and Center." In *21st Century Education: A Reference Handbook*, vol. 2, edited by Thomas L. Good. Thousand Oaks, CA: Sage Publications, 2008, pp. 58–67.

6. "Statistics and Rationale, SOS: Strategies of Success," Texas A&M University–Corpus Christi, College of Education.

7. Salas, p. 19.

8. Robert Fried, *The Passionate Teacher: A Practical Guide*. Boston: Beacon Press, 1995, pp. 11–23.

9. Council of Chief State School Officers, *National Teacher of the Year Program*.

Index